Walk This Way

Books authored or co-authored by Stephen Davis

Walk This Way
Hammer of the Gods
Bob Marley
Moonwalk
Fleetwood
This Wheel's on Fire
Reggae Bloodlines
Reggae International (editor)
Say Kids! What Time Is It?
Jajouka Rolling Stone
Old Gods Almost Dead

WALK THIS WAY

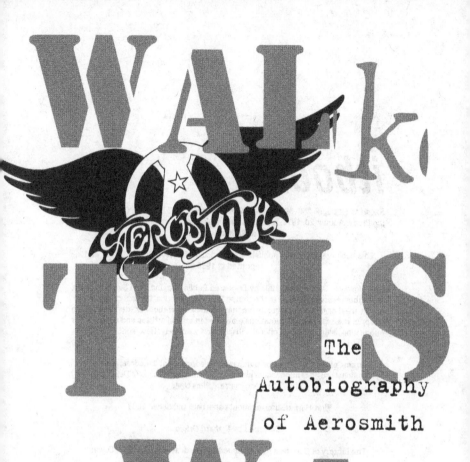

The
Autobiography
of Aerosmith

Aerosmith

with
Stephen Davis

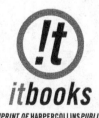

itbooks

AN IMPRINT OF HARPERCOLLINS PUBLISHERS

itbooks

Excerpts on pages 258–59 and 261–62 from "Aerosmith" by Ed McCormack, *Rolling Stone*, August 26, 1976, reprinted by permission of Straight Arrow Publishers, Inc. All Rights Reserved.

This book was originally published in hardcover by Avon Books in 1997 and reprinted in 1999.

HarperCollins books may be purchased for educational, business, or sales promotional use. For information, please e-mail the Special Markets Department at SPsales@harpercollins.com.

First HarperEntertainment paperback published 2003.

Designed by Richard Oriolo

The Library of Congress has cataloged the hardcover edition as follows:

Aerosmith (Musical group)
    Walk this way : the autobiography of Aerosmith / Aerosmith with Stephen Davis.
      p. cm.
    Includes bibliographical references.
    1. Aerosmith (Musical group) 2. Rock musicians—United States—Biography.
I. Davis, Stephen, 1947– . II. Title.
ML421.A32A3 1997   97-25598
782.42166'092—dc21   CIP

ISBN 0-06-051580-5

HB 10.09.2023

To our fans—
for years known as the Blue Army,
whose support has never wavered
and without whom this story
would never have been told.

Contents

Contents

Walk This Way

Prologue

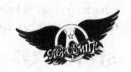

"**H**ey, man, you wanna know how I got sober after twenty-five years—gacked to the nines? You wanna hear how my band and my ex-manager intervened on me? Do you really wanna know what I went through on that day?

"Well, strap yourself in, 'cos here fuckin' goes."

Steven Tyler draws a deep breath into his slender frame, recently described by *The Times* of London as that of a "glamorous stick insect." He's sitting at his dressing table backstage at the Desert Sky Blockbuster Amphitheater in Phoenix, Arizona, 200 shows and eighteen months into an Aerosmith world tour. In two hours he'll face 17,000 Aeroheads and sum up a twenty-five-year career in a two-hour show whose songs are posted on a set list taped to the wall: EAT, TOYS, FEVER, RAG DOLL, SEASONS, MUSIC D.T. TALKIN', CRYIN', AMAZING, MA KIN, DEUCES, LAST CHILD, JANIE, STOP MESSIN', WALK ON DOWN, ELEVATOR, DUDE, SWEET E. A heavy black line separates the set from the three-song encore: DREAM ON, EDGE, WALK THIS WAY.

Steven checks his face in the brilliantly lit mirror. He's compared to Mick Jagger tediously often, but he actually more closely resembles that other icon of sixties culture, dancer Rudolf Nureyev, with whom Steven shares Russian blood and Tartar cheekbones. He sits before a carefully arranged tableau of personal totems that travel with him to every show: a talking skull; a hideous devil mask; seven bottles of aromatherapeutic scents for seven different days and seven different crowds; a Chinese statuette of Lord Buddha; two fresh packs of spearmint gum; a bone-handled nine-inch switchblade knife named 'Mongous; a scarf-draped altar for candles, incense, touchstones, arrowheads, crystals, pieces of jade, and a razor-sharp ninja star; three black leather roses; an electric shaver; two Smurfs; one bottle each of Tylenol and Bayer aspirin; and a CD player currently rotating discs by Howlin' Wolf, Snoop Doggy Dogg, and the Master Musicians of Jajouka.

"OK," Steven says with a sigh of resignation. "The intervention? The rebirthing of my old soul? That's what you want? Because no one's ever told the truth about this before . . ."

Steven Tyler: It happened like this. Five o'clock in the morning, sometime in 1986. I'm lying in bed with my girlfriend Teresa on Winchester Road in Brookline, Massachusetts. Alarm clock rings and I jump out of bed. Now, there's gotta be a good reason for someone to jump out of bed at 5 A.M. when they're still active in heavy drugdom, as I was and had been almost all my life.

Throw my clothes on, don't eat anything, run down the back stairway and jump onto the Beacon Street trolley. Yeah, there were a few autograph seekers even at that hour, but I had this secret little errand I wanted to take care of before I started my day.

So I kept my face covered, just a slit for my eyes, and buried myself in my copy of *Hammer of the Gods* until I got to Kenmore Square, where the methadone clinic was. A couple months before, me and Teresa checked ourselves in there, not to go into a treatment program or anything, but to try to wean ourselves off heroin and down to nothing, by ourselves. Two months later, I'm down to five milligrams, the lowest dose you can get. I'm trying to get sober on my own.

But I knew I was in trouble.

At the same time, my manager is giving me a gram of coke every day as a ration to keep me off the streets, and I had a doctor who was giving me pills, and I'm copping bags of dope on the side—'cos when you're a drug addict you don't play with your kids or go work on your art; you go and try to cop a bag of good Chinese heroin and everything else comes second. Your friends, the people you like, are drug addicts too. That's what you talk about. Call someone on the phone. "Where can we get some?" Rush over, go home, get high, call friends for more. That's it. My life was drugdom—caught up in the fuckin' drug world.

Tim Collins, our manager for the past three years at that point, had called me the night before, when I got home from one of these runs, to say there was an important band meeting at his office at six in the morning. That's why I'm on the street in Kenmore Square banging on the door of the methadone clinic—which is closed! A paranoid flash: Someone got wind that I was doing the methadone thing—but how? Were they watching me? Was I being followed?

So I get to the office feeling pretty weird. No methadone, so I'm jonesing, a little sick, vulnerable. And everyone's there. Aerosmith—the whole band—looking *real* somber, Tim Collins, our tour manager, and some guy I never saw before, who introduces himself as Dr. Lou Cox.

Right there I realized what was happening. The band had been rehearsing for our next album, which was absolutely positively make-or-totally-fuckin'-break. But I had been like nodding out at the piano, really out of it, and the guys were worried. But they were all doing drugs and Tim was snorting Peru, and now they were gonna single *me* out for something special.

Each of them had a pad of yellow paper in front of him, and they start in on me. "When you did this, I felt that."

And I'm like, "What's going on here? What's going *on*? What? *What?*" But the doctor tells me I can't talk, I just have to listen to all my friends—who I just got high with the day before—tell me what a schmuck I am and what a total fuck-up I've become! It's one thing to feel your guts wrenching from being called on drug addiction. It's another to hear your friends accuse you to make their point. But this guy Lou Cox said, "Steven, please be quiet and listen. Your friends wrote their feelings down because they love you."

In spite of everything, I'm resentful to this day.

So I started to get mad, really fuckin' pissed off. "FUCK YOU! I'LL KICK YOUR FUCKIN' . . ." I looked over at Joe Perry sitting there and screamed at the top of my lungs, "WHAT ABOUT YOU!!!!"

Before Joe could say anything, Lou Cox broke in to control the situation.

"Excuse me, Steven, but we don't want you to speak right now. We just want you to listen."

"WHAT THE FUCK IS GOING ON HERE???" I yelled. I was *howling*.

And Joe simply said, real quietly, "You know."

He was right.

I knew.

Tim Collins: By 1986, I had been managing Aerosmith for almost three years. I'd come up through the music scene in Boston and was as much of a coke slut as anyone in the business, until one day I woke in a Florida hotel suite with someone I didn't recognize and an almost fatal nosebleed. That was it for me. I was sick of cocaine anyway and needed to get myself clear to focus on the work I had to do with Aerosmith, which was to somehow help them fight their way back into the championship of rock 'n' roll. This was my mission.

So I quit. Did I tell the band I was doing this? No. It would have been considered treason.

That year—1986—was a big turning point for Aerosmith. They had recorded their first record for Geffen, a company that took the risk that Aerosmith was capable of coming back if given a chance. But the record was a commercial failure, only 300,000 sold, a disaster. David Geffen himself was disappointed in them, which isn't a place you want to be.

So they did a short tour that summer, short but profitable because few big acts were out that year. All over America, promoters wanted dates from Aerosmith, and my end alone came to $1 million. As the band started to think about making their next record, things were at least on a shaky equilibrium.

Except for Steven Tyler.

One night our tour manager called me at my hotel in Chicago and told me the band was messed up and fighting. This was a pretty tough guy, but there was fear in his voice. He thought he might be watching Aerosmith break up again, this time for good. So I flew out to the gig and found Steven completely wrecked on drugs. Needles in the dressing room. I went out to the front of the house and watched the band. As Steven lurched around the stage, forgetting lyrics, pissing off the rest of the band, ruining the show, I heard a voice in the middle of my own head.

Do something, the voice said, *or this guy's going to die.*

A few days later in New York, I called my friend Steve Mazarsky, who had managed the Allman Brothers Band. I told him my problem and he said, "You merely have to do what I didn't have the balls to do with the Allmans. You need to stand up to the band and put your job and your friendship with them on the line. What have you got to lose? If you don't, your band is gonna go down anyway, so what the fuck?"

"OK, but how do I do this?"

"You gotta have dinner with Jonnie Podell. You know him?"

Of course I did. He was a former big-time New York agent who became a drug addict and wound up homeless, on the street. But he had recovered to an inspirational degree, and now he was involved with Alcoholics Anonymous, counseling music people like us who desperately needed help. So I called Jonnie and we had dinner at a restaurant called Nirvana. I picked at my curry while he told me his harrowing story.

Jonnie Podell: I was an agent in New York, booking bands, so successful I only had four clients: George Harrison, the Allman Brothers, Alice Cooper, and Lou Reed. I was high all the time, much higher than my clients. Then I managed Lou, discovered Blondie, and found myself rich at twenty-five, married to a beautiful woman, great kids, everything you could want. At thirty-five, I found myself on a bench on a traffic island in the middle of Broadway—broke, divorced, nowhere to live, only caring about my next bag of dope. Then a drug addict friend of mine asked me to go to an Alcoholics Anonymous meeting with him and it changed everything. I went because I was frightened that my spirit was starting to go, and I knew I was near the end. At my first meeting, I had to take a dollar out of the basket they were passing so I could get home. But then I went from an empty life to a social life. Suddenly sober people knew my name and seemed glad to see me.

AA helped me to clean up and get back to the music business. Within a couple of years we'd signed the Beastie Boys and the Red Hot Chili Peppers and things were going good. One night I went to a club to cover a show by one of our baby bands and this guy comes up to me and says, "You're alive! I can't believe it." It was Tim Collins, who had come to my office in the old days and once had found me passed out on the phone, with Bill Graham shouting on the other end of the line.

A little later, Tim called me and asked for help with Aerosmith. "These guys are a mess," he said. "They've gotta stop taking drugs. Can you help?"

I told him that Tyler was going to be the most difficult because he has so many facets—the male, the female, the poet, the rock star, the sweet guy, the rock 'n' roll animal, the drug addict, the human being. I knew this guy was going to be like working with mercury, but they had no choice except to help him get sober for good.

Tim Collins: After dinner, we went for a walk in the park. It was a starry evening, and up near the zoo Jonnie stopped me and said, "Look, I know what you're up against. They call these guys the Toxic Twins, right? But you're going to waste a lot of valuable time trying to find an easier way to do this. A softer way. *There is none.* You either do this now or say good-bye to them because they're going to die."

Jonnie had also given me the number of a New York psychiatrist, Lou Cox, and I went to see him. I told him that I needed his help in staging an intervention for Steven Tyler. In my ignorance, I told him if we could intervene and get Steven into a serious rehabilitation program, it would be the solution to all our problems.

Lou explained that it doesn't really work like that. "Getting back to sobriety is a long, drawn-out, difficult process, not an *event*. Are you sure you're willing to go the distance with this process? Because that's what we're talking about here—an ongoing process that's never over."

But I was determined and arranged for Dr. Cox to come to Boston the following week to help us intervene on Steven.

Then I had to sell this to Aerosmith.

I went to the band's rehearsal hall in a warehouse in Watertown, Mass. One big wall was called "The Wall of Shame" because it was covered with frilly girls' underwear—bras, panties, garter belts, lingerie—that fans had thrown onstage during the summer shows. The band was there except for Steven, who was off somewhere getting high, and Joe Perry, Brad Whitford, Joey Kramer, and Tom Hamilton were upset and down on Steven as usual.

I took a deep breath and began the pitch of my life.

"Guys, I gotta tell you that Steven's not the problem. Steven has a disease. He's an alcoholic and a drug addict. The disease is the problem. We've been focusing in on Steven, but it's his disease we should be talking about.

"And it's not just Steven. Everybody needs help. *Everybody.* Things can't go on like this because it's not happening for us this way anymore.

You guys need to change your lives and get sober and I'll *promise* you this: We will turn this group around and make it the biggest band in the world by 1990."

I said a lot of other stuff too. It was a thirty-minute rah-rah speech straight from the depths of my soul. I finished, and there was dead silence. They glanced at each other uneasily. Joey Kramer looked at me like I'm completely nuts and said, "Hey, man, what the fuck are you doing? Some new kind of drug?"

I said, "Well, yeah, sorta. It is kinda like a new drug." But I just kept talking, and they were very quiet and looking at me. When I finished, there was a long, long pause. Finally Joe Perry said, very quietly, "What do we have to lose? I mean, Steven is just like, *broken*, man. Let's just do whatever it takes to get him fixed. 'Cause I agree with Tim. If it doesn't happen now, we're shit outta luck. That's for fuckin' sure."

God bless Joe, I thought to myself. Tom, Brad, and Joey were in as well, and suddenly, for the first time in months, there was hope in the room with us.

First we got everyone together at a pre-intervention meeting at the Sonesta Hotel, near my office in Cambridge. The band, their wives, a few of our people, and Lou Cox, who told us that this intervention wasn't going to be pure, because these other guys were taking drugs too—although, Joe Perry had agreed to enter a treatment program after his wife gave birth. It was the ultimate codependent experience, completely out of line with the traditional Twelve Steps of AA, but I had explained that we felt that Steven's life was literally on the line and we had to proceed. "Yes, you're right," I told Dr. Cox. "And eventually we're going to fix them all. Please, help us handle this crisis first."

Lou said, "Well, if this is going to work, we're going to have to approach Steven when he's not high."

Everyone smiled. "He's never not high," Joe Perry said.

"What about when he gets up in the morning?" the doctor asked.

Everyone laughed. I explained that Steven didn't get up in the morning, that he "came to" in the late afternoon. But I also promised I would have him at my office at six the next morning and everyone had to be there. Dr. Cox gave us all yellow legal pads and told everyone to write out their specific complaints about Steven's behavior.

Then I got on the phone and dialed Steven's number. This was when the rap version of "Walk This Way" was a huge hit record for Run-D.M.C.

and Aerosmith was getting some worldwide media attention for the first time in almost ten years.

"Steven, it's Tim. The BBC wants to interview you and Joe live tomorrow morning."

"No problem."

"And because of the time zone thing, it's gotta be at six. Is that gonna be OK?"

"Sure, man. No problem."

"OK, see you at the office. Be here at six sharp and you and Joe'll be interviewed by the BBC."

Steven arrived promptly at six the next morning. Sitting around the big redwood conference table in our office on First Street were the members of the band, our road manager, and Dr. Cox. Steven comes in:

"Oh! Hi—I didn't know *all* you guys . . . were gonna . . . do . . ." He looks at Dr. Cox. "And who the fuck are you?"

"I'm Dr. Lou Cox, Steven. Would you please have a seat?"

"What the *fuck* is this?"

And I said, "Steven, we have some things we need to talk to you about, and we'd like Dr. Cox to moderate. This means a lot to us and the band, so if you could just sit down with us and listen for a while, we'd really appreciate it."

We had all written lists on our yellow pads that detailed Steven's behavior while on drugs, and we'd even rehearsed this in advance. I went first.

"Steven—you came to the office last month and asked for money for dope. When I wouldn't give it to you, you punched a hole in the wall, signed it, and walked out."

"Steven—when we did all that blow at the Saratoga gig last summer, I saw you rage at your old lady in front of everyone."

"Steven—when you said your throat hurt in Chicago and we called the doctor, you rifled his bag and stole drugs when he wasn't looking."

And on like that, going around the table, each one taking a turn, everyone looking utterly miserable. This went on for *three hours*, with Steven arguing back all the while, furious, as enraged as I'd ever seen him be. This was mental martial arts, psychic jiujitsu. Watching Lou Cox battling with this disease and the mentality it brings on was like watching an old-time preacher wrestling with the devil. But I knew it wasn't Steven who was fighting us. It was his shadow, the dark side of his incredible talent and personality.

When it was over, Steven broke down. He put his head in his hands and cried. It was an incredible moment for all of us.

"You're right," he sobbed. "I need help. I'll go, but only if we're all in this together and you all get help too. I'll go."

Thank you, God, I murmured to myself.

"I'll go *tomorrow,*" Steven said.

And Lou said, very gently, "No, Steven. You have to go now. There's a bed waiting for you. We have a bag packed for you and everything is arranged."

Steven got a trapped look on his face, and what color was left in his cheeks completely drained away.

"Let me at least call my girlfriend and tell her what's happening," he pleaded. "I *have* to call her."

Lou said OK.

Steven Tyler: I sat at that fuckin' table for *hours,* and I fought and screamed at them and at last I said, "Let me at least call my girlfriend and tell her what's happening." I was freaking out, so they finally relented and said I could call her. I went into the other room and called Teresa and told her what was going on. And she was as upset as I was: "Don't let them *do* this. Don't let them *do* this to you. Can't you see that they're trying to break us up?" I saw her point, because we'd been through this twice before when they told me my girlfriend couldn't be in the same rehab as me.

Now my talons came out. I ran back in that room and did everything in my earthly power to get out of this. I'm screaming and kicking things and they're going, "No, no, no, we got your toothbrush and we want you to go right now."

But I fought them tooth and nail, those fuckers, because this whole thing was like, *off.* It wasn't pure. It wasn't "Let's get this *band* sober." What they did was they got a meeting together where they said, "Are you ready to tell Steven he's out of the band if he doesn't do this?" And these guys are all fucked up and stoned before they even got there! And they go, "Yeah! He's fuckin' *out!*" Somehow this dawns on me and I'm going, *Jesus, I'm being thrown out of my own band.* Once again—the story of my life—*I was the fuckin' scapegoat.* I was the guinea pig. I was the permanent Identified Patient!

I mean, I'm thankful—it's ironic—I'm grateful today because I got sober. But I'm resentful to this day over the way it happened. Dr. Cox never looked around and asked himself, why am I beating on *this* guy? It was always, "Steven is fucked up, let's get him better and all our problems will be solved." Because I'm the lead singer, the focus of attention, the fuckin' guy who gets paid to be crazy onstage. I'm the guy that has to climb the fuckin' trees! I'm the guy who's not afraid to say things and more often than not be sorry for it later, but that's how I am. I'm a tree climber, living out on a limb because how else are you supposed to pick the fruit? I'm the guy who everybody's old lady hated to death. And what the fuck did they think would happen to my talent, to my ability to be Steven Tyler, when my life and personality were smoothed out by rehab and therapy? Didn't they realize I was nothing without my drugs?

Tim Collins: When Steven came back into the room, my heart sank. He was stronger than ever! "You fuckers . . . FUCK YOU!! This band is fuckin' *nothing* without me! What're you gonna do, fuckin' *fire* me? I'm not a junkie and none of you guys is exactly sober. Are you? FUCKIN' ARE YOU?? *You're fucked up too!* Who are any of you to tell me what to do? I'm stopping on my own, I'm in a methadone program!"

We had to do the whole intervention all over again. It took us hours. When it was finally over, Steven was on his way to Chit Chat in Pennsylvania's rural Amish country. The rest of us were drained. I went home, turned off the phone and slept for hours.

Steven Tyler: And so I swallowed it. I remember saying to myself—and this is where my upbringing and my father and my family history come into it—I remember saying, *Just take it.* Something inside me said, *See this through.* Because when I was eight or nine years old, my favorite saying was "Now what'd I do?" Because everybody was always coming to me and saying, "You fucked up, you did this and got into that, and what's *wrong* with you, and like, how *could* you?" I was born guilty, and now here we go again. I tried to confront them, but . . .

Yeah, I swallowed it. I listened to them and they sent me away and it was the hardest thing I ever did because I hadn't told the rehab nurses I was also doing Xanax, an antianxiety drug. I was snorting two or three pills in the morning and at night. I'm taking the three worst drugs—Valium, methadone, and Xanax—all of them stay in the marrow of your bones. Man, I was in so much fuckin' pain I felt like a third-degree burn patient.

Did I withdraw? Terribly! I was left alone in the detox unit of that hospital. They put me on Clonidine, a drug that lowers your blood pressure. You have no buzz at all. Your body functions are slowed, but your brain is not, and you're so listless you can hardly move. My arms were all bruised because I was so out of it I couldn't walk through a simple door without banging into the wall. My brain is going, *What the fuck is wrong with me?* I felt like a half-empty balloon. You don't even have the willpower to cry. You just want to die. You don't even fuckin' wanna tie your shoes. I was wearing a blanket around my shoulders like a shawl, no shirt, long unwashed hair hanging around my face, my shoes untied and flapping, and I'm shuffling down the corridor and I hear people whispering, "Isn't that Steven Tyler from Aerosmith? Is he fucked up or *what?* Jeezus!"

That was my bottom, right there.

I was hallucinating like crazy. I'd close my eyes and flash back ten years: Aerosmith on tour in Europe for the first time, and I'm withdrawing from smack in a London hotel, real sick, shaking, throwing up, and I'm sobbing and carrying on while frantically pounding on Joe Perry's door.

"Joe! I know you got some heroin! I saw your eyes pinned, I *know* you're holding, please, I'm *begging* you, man, open up, will you just fuckin' give me . . ."

Door opens, just a crack. "Uh, sorry, Steven, I don't have any." SLAM. And I can hear him and his wife Elyssa in their suite, fuckin' whooping it up. I spent the rest of the night during and after the show vomiting and cursing them—hot heaping helpings of hate. I hated him and his fuckin' wife for that. I'd write song lyrics about her, like "Sweet Emotion":

You talk about things that nobody cares—who fuckin' cares what you say, Elyssa!—*You're wearing out things that nobody wears. You call my name but I gotta make clear, I can't say baby where I'll be in a year.* But it'll be at least a thousand miles away from you, baby! That was my angry side talking, the side that has to go down to the basement because I wanna get away from everyone and write a "Sweet Emotion" or "Janie's Got A Gun."

Somehow I got through this phase with a few tiny grains of sanity intact, but then I found out that the *real* ordeal was just beginning when I got clear again.

Tim Collins: Steven stayed in the hospital for forty-five days. When he was stabilized, Joe Perry and I went down for a family therapy session with him.

Steven's therapist was one tough, committed woman who put up with zero bullshit. She looked at me and said, "Well, what are you going to do when Steven relapses?"

I got offended. "What do you mean *when* he relapses?"

"Well, Steven's been to two other treatment centers," she said. "He's a chronic rehabber. We *know* he's going to relapse. Don't *you* know that? What are you, in denial?"

I said, "OK. When he relapses, I'll just bring him back here."

And she looks at me and says, "Why don't you just shoot him now?"

"Excuse me?"

"You're killing him. You provided him with drugs, you got him a doctor to give him drugs, you gave him money to get drugs, you brought his success back to him so he could get drugs. And now you want *us* to enable him. This is not a diet club, where you lose weight and then go back out and stuff yourself again. Steven is going to *die*, so you might as well take him out back and shoot him now because that's what you're doing anyway. You're killing him."

I got really pissed off, but I managed to stifle it and just asked her what she wanted us to do.

"I want you to tell Steven that when he relapses, you won't be his manager anymore. He has a good bond with you, and you're like a father figure to him now. If you don't stand up to him, he's going to keep up his self-destructive behavior. But if he knows you're going to leave him, it will have an impact. And, Joe, what about you? How are you going to handle this? What are you going to do?"

"I don't know," Joe answered. "I'll have to think about it."

"That's not good enough. You're Steven's *brother*. You have to say the same thing—that if he relapses you're not going to play with him in the band anymore, because that means more than anything to him."

Then she brought Steven in to see us.

He was very changed—cleaned up, looked different, without his Gypsy rock star regalia. Combed hair, normal clothes, *different*.

But he brightened up when he saw us. Joe *was* Steven's brother, and they had been through so much together. "Hey," Steven said. "How's it going?"

We chatted for a few minutes, and I think we let Steven know that Joe had also been through rehab and was also sober for the first time in maybe twenty years. Then the therapist said, really blunt, "So, Steven, I just asked your manager what he was going to do when you relapsed. Do you want to hear what he had to say?"

"Well, um, I'm not gonna relapse. I'm gonna get through this, join Alcoholics Anonymous, go to meetings, and get my life together." Steven sounded totally committed, really gung-ho.

I looked at him and heard myself saying, "Steven, if you relapse, I'm not going to manage you anymore."

He broke down. It was very heavy. And Joe piles on and says the same thing. Steven was visibly hurt and got really angry: "FUCK THE BOTH OF YOU! I'LL FUCKING SHOW YOU!!"

That's when I almost lost it. *Don't cry,* I wanted to say to him. *I didn't really mean it.* Because I thought we'd blown it. Now Aerosmith would break up and years of hard work would have gone for nothing but heart-break. But I also had a clear realization that we'd reached the turning point and the central issue. It was called codependency.

I sat there thinking, *Wow, I've been enabling this guy to kill him-self.*

Steven Tyler: A lot of other shit went down as well. You'll hear about it later. Eventually I came out of the hospital and got into AA and really got going on it. Gradually I found my way back to the land of the living, and Joe Perry and I took our places in Aerosmith once again. The rest is history, which is kind of the point here.

Over the years between then and now, we've spent a lot of time going over the whole Aerosmith saga, looking for clues that would show us where we went wrong and what we did right. Like they warned us, stay-ing sober became a process that involved continuous self-examination as a way of life. The story we're about to tell comes in part from this dynamic of change and redemption, and we hope it inspires anyone out there who needs some changes in their own lives, as well as a good read about a rock 'n' roll band.

Joe Perry always said that living the Aerosmith story was like living through the plot of a book—a long epic that pulls you in and doesn't let go until the final page is turned. That book would probably have to start up at Lake Sunapee, New Hampshire, where Aerosmith was born. It would have a cast of friends who had strange adventures of their own, beautiful girls who inspired us and in some cases became our wives, and

Walk This Way

many cool and uncool characters who drift through the past thirty years of our existence. Some are now dead, some are lost to us in other ways, and some survive as dear friends who share in the telling of this tale.

To them we say: Thanks for the ride. Hope you enjoy it too. And remember, the light at the end of the tunnel could be . . . you!

BOOK ONE

He who is a
legend in his
own time is
ruled by that
legend.

-Victor Hugo

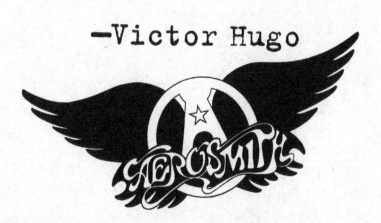

He who is a

legend in his

own time is

ruled by that

legend.

—Victor Hugo

Now What'd I Do? The True Adventures of Steven Tallarico

1

You could also call this
"Two Cellos and a Canoe."

—Steven Tyler

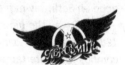

The Pennacook called the big lake, Soonippi, "Goose Water," for the millions of migrating birds that darkened the sky above the mountains twice a year. The Indians hunted and snared animals and fished along the lakeshore and the Sugar River until they started dying of smallpox around the time white settlers began arriving in New Hampshire along the old Military Trail from Rhode Island and Massachusetts in the 1760s. The legend goes that the last two Pennacooks were a pair of young lovers who took refuge from the spotted sickness inside the Indian Cave, the large rock-ledge formation overlooking Sunapee Harbor. Their bones were supposedly found many years later when hunters stumbled upon their hideaway.

The town of Sunapee was settled by families named Trow, George, Colby, Smith. For the next hundred years, it was a rural mountain backwater of farms and mills and occasional summer people attracted by the rugged mountains, Sunapee and Kearsarge, and steamboat rides on the 3,000-acre lake. Other towns sprung up: Georges Mills, New London, Newport, Claremont.

In the 1870s the first big hotels were built, and Lake Sunapee enjoyed a sixty-year run as a resort for wealthy New Yorkers. The Granliden Hotel, built in 1906, attracted important politicians and corporate executives, while the Ben Mere Inn and Indian Cave Lodge housed people from the Boston area who would later buy land and build summer cottages of their own. The hotels in turn attracted musicians for their house orchestras; later the big swing bands considered Sunapee an important and pleasant stop on their regular routes.

The Depression of the 1930s ended Sunapee's days as a fancy resort. Many of the mills closed after World War II, and the population began to drift away. All the old wood-frame hotels were torn down, and Lake Sunapee gradually became a typical quiet New England family resort, where young kids had their own motorboats and an ice cream cone tasted pretty good on Saturday night down at the harbor.

This was the genius of the place where, during the late 1950s and 1960s, rock 'n' roll bands gradually took over from the dance bands and combos that entertained Lake Sunapee on the weekends. After the Beatles hit, it was all over. Lake Sunapee was the address where the world first encountered Aerosmith as a rough beast, slouching toward Bethlehem to be born . . .

1: Animal
Crackers at
Trow-Rico Lodge

Steven Tyler: There's a life force that you get from your ancestors. My story starts with four brothers from Calabria, the arid mountainous southern toe on the boot of Italy. The family name was Tallarico, and for generations they lived in the town of Contronei, a place of olive groves and goats and a feudal economy that still exists today. The Calabrians are tough people, famous for the music and dancing that dominated raucous local festivals, so it was no accident my grandfather Giovanni Tallarico and his three brothers were all accomplished musicians.

Drought hit Calabria in the late 1800s, followed by huge earthquakes, which forced thousands of Calabrese to emigrate to America. Giovanni and his brothers arrived in New York and began working as professional musicians. By 1900 Giovanni was a professor at the Kimball School of Music in Waterbury, Connecticut. The Tallarico brothers played classical concerts—Mozart, Schubert, Mendelssohn—as a quartet: Giovanni and Francesco on mandolins, Michele on guitar, and Pasquale on piano. I have a tour brochure somewhere that advertises a 1918 appearance by the Tallarico Brothers at a fancy hotel in Akron, Ohio, "Rubber Capital of the World." They played chamber music all over the Eastern United States, and in the 1920s one of my grandfather's favorite places to play was the sumptuous Granliden Hotel on Lake Sunapee, a famous resort in the White Mountains of New Hampshire, a place that didn't take Prohibition that seriously.

My grandfather Giovanni married Constance Neidhart in 1912. She was a pianist who had studied at the Peabody Conservatory. They lived at 124th and Broadway in Manhattan and she gave piano lessons and rented out practice time on one of the two pianos in their big apartment. Over the years some of the people she worked with became famous. She taught and eventually gave a piano to a local Harlem kid named Seymour Kaufman, who became the Broadway composer Cy Coleman. In the 1950s two young piano students, Ferrante and Teicher, who later did "Exodus" and other hit movie themes, practiced in her living room. She was known as Mrs. T., and believe me, she was a big presence in my life.

In 1922, my grandfather was working in Lake Sunapee when someone told him about a property for sale, going for a song. Trow Hill Farm was a house and barn on 250 acres of fields and woods facing Route 11, which runs down the western side of the lake, and I think he got it for under $5,000 from Henry Trow, whose family ran the local sawmill. He brought up my grandmother and their two sons, Ernie and my father Victor, and they became pillars of Lake Sunapee's summertime musical community. In 1935, they built a few cabins on the property and started Trow-Rico, a children's music camp that lasted until 1940. After that, Trow-Rico Lodge became a musical resort, where people could rent cabins and enjoy the recitals my grandmother staged in the barn on Sunday afternoons.

My father, Victor Tallarico, began playing piano as a little boy. He trained at Juilliard in New York and has worked as a musician all his life. As a young man, he played in New York society bands—Ben Cutler, Lester Lanin, Mayer Davis, Joe Carroll—and later, while I was growing up, he worked as a high school music instructor and as a private piano teacher.

My parents met while my father was in the Army, at Fort Dix, New Jersey. My mother, Susan Blancha, was a secretary, and my father was actually dating her best friend. One night Victor came to pick this girl up. She wasn't home, so Victor asked Susan out instead when he heard her playing the piano. They got married after the war and moved in with my grandparents not far from the Apollo Theatre in Harlem, which is where they were living when I was born in 1948. We lived there until I was four years old.

I grew up under my father's piano. I'd sit under his big Steinway and play games and pretend things while listening to him practice for two hours every day. So I was literally immersed in Debussy, Chopin, and Liszt. That's where I got this emotional thing I have with music. My father was a schooled musician who was very much into technique. He'd play a Beethoven sonata in the living room and I'd almost stop breathing. So I got all my emotions and feelings through music, which gives off twice the emotions and feelings of any other art form. (The time I spent sitting under that piano still influences the way I write songs. It's easy for me to write at the piano. I'll play something in the key of C, F, F minor. If Joe or somebody plays some chords, I'll sing a melody over it. My gift has to do with all this listening to my father.)

The summer after I was born—and every summer after that—my parents took me up to New Hampshire, so that's where my childhood memories really come alive. We'd leave New York about seven in the morning and get there at night. On the way we'd see the giant stone dinosaur by the roadside near Hartford. My mom smoked in the car, we counted phone poles until I went crazy, and it was great to stop for a picnic of bread and hard-boiled eggs near Bellows Falls, Vermont, which was always called Fellows Balls in our family (hence my love for lyrical twists). I was usually asleep when we got to Sunapee, so my father would carry me in the house and when I woke up, we'd be there.

From the time I learned to walk, I was a total mountain boy, always barefoot and wild. I fished in our little pond, hunted birds with my sling-shot—twenty BBs shooting through the trees, *fffwwttt*—and I'd come back with sixteen blue jays hanging from my belt. Later I trapped animals and sold the pelts. From June to September up there, no one could even *find* me. I was always in the woods or hiding in the hayloft above the barn with my cousin Augie. I was off in my own world, the closest thing to heaven there was until I was old enough to push a lawn mower.

On weekends, the Tallaricos and our guests would gather for shows and parties in our barn. It had a concrete floor and a Ping-Pong table, a bar, a stove, and a Coke machine, which was my job to fill up. There was also a "stage," with a curtain pulled across the floor, and there my show business career began, putting on skits every Friday night. My Aunt Phyllis and Uncle Ernie would get all us kids together and we'd have rehearsals. The first thing Aunt Phyllis taught me was to pantomime this song called "Animal Crackers," which went "I'm just wild about animal crackers . . . firecrackers won't do!" This was my showstopper, a huge hit. From the time I was three years old, people would yell at me, "C'mon, Stevie! Do 'Animal Crackers'!" I also did "There's a hole in the bucket, dear Liza, dear Liza." Aunt Phyllis had me lip-synch to Nat "King" Cole records, and people thought this was really funny. When the kids were through, the adults would put on little plays, musicals, shadow acts, poetry, and dancing.

Some of this was hilarious, like when Uncle Ernie would dress up as a doctor and Aunt Phyllis as a nurse and they'd make one of the guests give birth to a huge doll. Aunt Phyllis was my second mother and Uncle Ernie my second father, because my father was always in the barn practicing on the Chickering piano for the Sunday night recitals. People would come out from town and my father and grandmother and some of their students would play. Aunt Phyllis was the one who taught me how to perform. She was the one.

We had another ritual at Trow-Rico: making hard cider in the fall. We'd get apples from the all-you-can-pick orchard, grind them through the cider press, and let the juice ferment. It got bubbly like champagne and tasted

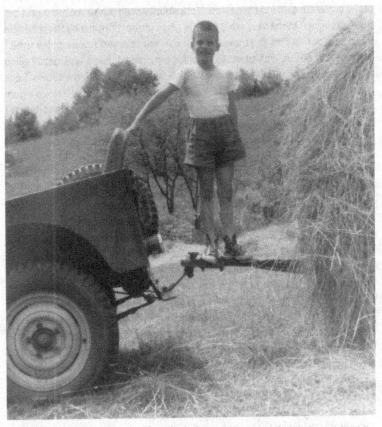

Steven Tallarico at Lake Sunapee, New Hampshire, on Uncle Ernie's jeep
(TYLER COLLECTION)

great. One night my cousin Augie and I drank a whole bottle with our Boy Scout mess kit tin cups in my cabin.

At first it was great. I went over to the barn and started working the room. Then it hit me and I started getting off, got scared, staggered out, and fell down in front of the double cabin. I found my way back to my room on my hands and knees, following the trail of apples that had fallen off the trees onto the path. It was my first time drunk, something I've never forgotten.

2: Nigger Lips

Steven Tyler: I started getting into trouble before I learned to walk. At nine months, I swallowed a penny. They pumped my stomach and my mom put the penny in my baby album. Then I ate an ant cup, which was another trip to the emergency room. Today you'd say I was hyperactive, but back in the 1950s I was a problem child. People were always yelling at me and my mantra was "Now what'd I do?"

My parents moved to an apartment in the Bronx when I was four—5610 Nederland Avenue—and I started school the next year at PS 81. I was this skinny little kid who got picked on. I got called Nigger Lips a lot at the bus stop, but things generally went OK until the fourth grade. Every morning we lined up with our classmates and marched into school. I found a broken lightbulb in the garbage—I was always getting into stuff—and I showed it to the girl next to me. She screamed—negative bonding, right?—and I chased her. She told her mother and they threw me out of school. I spent the next two grades at the Hoffman School with a lot of other brats and some retarded kids. Then we moved again.

My parents bought a house in Yonkers, north of the Bronx in suburban Westchester County. The grass was green, there were no fences, and there was a heavily wooded reservoir nearby in Sprain Brook Park where I could hunt and trap. I caught little animals, clubbed them on the head, took 'em home, skinned 'em, and sold the fur to make a little money. At school they said I smelled like a skunk and sent me home. There were deer and raccoon. One day I caught a baby coon and that was the end of my trapping career because he became my best friend. Me and Bandit would go down to the lake together and fish. Bandit finally got so big that my mom made me sell him to a guy that ran a gas station in the country. Later I heard that Bandit chewed through some wires in his owner's barn and the place burned down. I think we stopped going to that gas station.

Now I really started to get into stuff. I stuck a firecracker up a frog's ass and watched him explode. You've seen frog baseball on *Beavis and Butt-Head*? We *did* that shit! I snared herring gulls with wingspans of six feet, painted USAF under their wings, and let them go.

My father kept playing piano in our basement for two hours every day, and I went to sixth grade at PS 32 up on a hill about a mile from my house.

I went to Walt Whitman Junior High the following year, and on to Roosevelt High after that. The bad kids at the bus stop kept calling me Nigger Lips, and I'd get beat up. This made me hate that word more than anything else I can think of. I could cry right now, just thinking about it. You say "nigger" and I see the whole thing in my mind—people getting whipped, beaten. I would go home and cry about it and my mother would say, "Don't you worry about those lips of yours, Stevie. All the better to kiss the girls with those lips."

Then I started to grow my hair, and this was before the Beatles and everything. So the greasers started to make fun of me, and I began to pour a shot of Scotch whiskey into my orange juice in the morning, just to be able to face these people who were hassling me.

I used to cut school a lot and go to the reservoir and climb trees. There was this one big maple I really liked. It was my tree. One day in 1959 or '60, I'm up this tree and I see this kid pulling himself up along the vines.

"Who are you?" I said.

And this kid goes, "Ray-zan the Ape Man! You got a problem wit' dat?"

I yelled down, as tough as I could: "GET THE FUCK OUTTA MY TREE!!"

He got down and a day or two later—he didn't do it right away—Ray-zan the Ape Man beat the shit out of me. This is how I met Ray Tabano when I was about twelve.

Ray Tabano: I actually first saw Steven a couple weeks before this, just after my mother and I moved to Yonkers. I was cruising the neighborhood on my bike and some kid yelled at me and I stopped and this other kid—Steven—comes out of his house and eggs me on to kick this first kid's ass. I guess he'd been tormenting Steven or something. Then Steven kicked me out of his tree and I had to show him who was boss. But then we became friends.

There were two areas in Yonkers, Tanglewood and Lockwood, and both had gangs: hoody Italian greasers—very tough. The Roosevelt area where we lived was kinda in-between and didn't have a gang. So when we were in junior high, I broke away from the Little Tanglewood gang and formed my own gang, the Green Mountain Boys. Steven used to call us the Robin Hoods of Yonkers, stealing from the rich and giving to the poor, which was ourselves. Our main activities were hanging out at Tibbet's Brook swimming pool or at Adventurers' Inn, a pinball arcade on

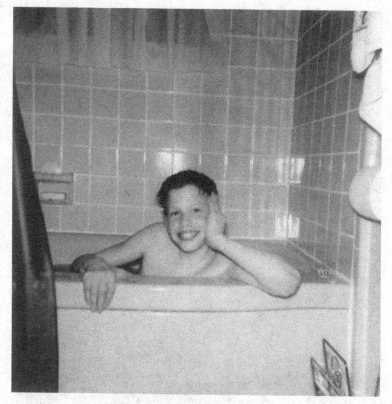

Steven at age thirteen in the bath, Yonkers, New York
(TYLER COLLECTION)

Central Avenue that later became a Nathan's hot dog joint. Our motto was "Green Mountain Boys don't mess."

Steven wanted to join my gang because it meant protection from other gangs, especially after we started high school. But he wasn't really one of the guys. Steven liked to keep to himself more, and he was into animals and other weird shit. If we all went to the store to buy hot dogs, he'd buy pickled lizard noses. If we all wore baggy pants, he'd go to the tailor and have his pants pegged so he'd look cool. So finally we said, "OK, you can be in the gang if you run across Central Avenue naked and buy us a lantern for the clubhouse." Also he had to steal some stuff as an initiation, but he messed up and got arrested for shoplifting.

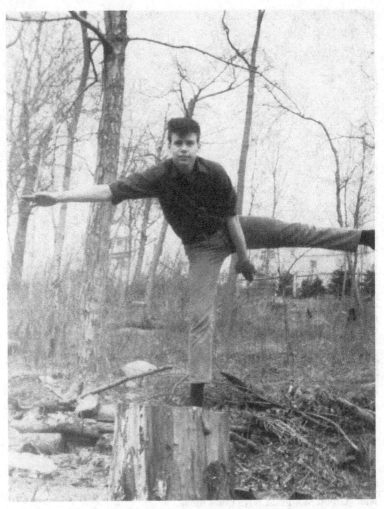

Steven, about fifteen years old, Lake Sunapee, New Hampshire
(TYLER COLLECTION)

So Steven got in, even though he wasn't tough. He was the opposite. He was a friend to the underdogs and the handicapped kids that we all fuckin' laughed at. He loved these people. I thought Steven was a fuckin' *saint.*

Steven Tyler: Yes, I ran naked across Central Avenue when I was thirteen years old. It was like my bar mitzvah! The Green Mountain Boys was really more like a club than a gang. If you weren't in something like that, you just weren't cool. Anyway, all we did was pick up girls and try to get in their pants under the aqueduct.

Eventually the "gang" turned into my first band.

I started really getting into music when I was twelve. My radio was tuned to all the Good Guys on WINS, WMGM, WMCA, WABC, twenty-four hours a day. I tried to pick hot singles by calling in the Vote Line telephone polls they had. I remember how proud I was when I picked Del Shannon's "Runaway" to be a big hit when none of the callers liked it.

When Raymond and I were both about fourteen, we used to go over to Raymond's father's bar on Morris Park Avenue in the Bronx. Ray's dad let us drink beer and jump onstage and do a couple songs when the band took a break. "OK, boys, show me what you can do." We did "I've Had It" by the Bell Notes (from Long Island) and "Cotton Fields" by the Highwaymen, a hit song in 1962. Ray played drums and I played guitar and sang. But this changed when I switched to drums so I could play in my father's band, Vic Tallarico's Orchestra, the following year.

My dad started giving me piano lessons when I was little, but I just couldn't quite get it. I'd yawn and he'd smack me. Then I got this drum box in maybe 1960; you pushed the buttons in time and you could mix all the styles together. Then I got these drum records by Sandy Nelson: *Let There Be Drums* and *Drums Are My Beat!* I heard him do some riffs on the snare drum and thought, *Wow, I've gotta learn this shit!* So I went over to WWDU—Westchester Workshop for Drummers Unlimited—which was like a clinic with kids in jackets and ties and their moms. I hated it, left after two weeks, and never came back.

I think my dad bought me my first set of drums, around the time I started playing in his band. I also had a paper route and some of the money came from that. We played mostly up in Sunapee in the summer, places like Indian Cave Lodge and Soo-ni-pi Lodge in New London. Uncle Ernie was on saxophone and we did stuff from the hit parade, Viennese waltzes, cha-chas, fox-trots, *The Tonight Show* theme, "Porgy and Bess." It was awful. They made me comb my long hair back and tuck it down my jacket. I'd sit there playing "Begin the Beguine," the social director would lead an old lady onto the dance floor, then people would waltz a little. The worst was when kids my age came in and went, "We're outta here!" I'd look at them, *girls my age*, and go, *Fuck!* I tried to play a little louder when kids came in, but it didn't work.

On the way home afterward, I'd sit staring out the car window, imagining myself doomed to this existence forever.

3: The Strangers

Steven Tyler: I didn't start out as a singer. I was the drummer in a band we had in junior high; one day we were working out "In My Room" by the Beach Boys and someone handed me a mike. So I sang it. These were the days, 1963–64, when you asked the kid who played snare drum in your school band to be in your group, but I was a little ahead of that. I'd already sat in with a group called the Maniacs in Sunapee, the first time I got to get on stage at The Barn and play "Wipe Out" and show what I could do.

There were two bands in Yonkers, and I was kind of in both of them. The Strangers were me on drums, Don Solomon on keyboards, Peter Stahl on guitar and Alan Strohmayer on bass. In early 1964 we were playing Friday afternoon mixers after school in Yonkers. I was the drummer and it was *so cool* because all the girls were there. Ray Tabano was in the other band, the Dantes, with Ricky Holtzman and Henry Schneiderman, who asked Ray to play bass because he had long hair, looked cool, and he protected them from the other gangs. If the Dantes had an important gig at Randy Goldstein's Sweet Sixteen party, they asked me to get up and sing with them. That's how come I was in both of these bands at the same time. The Strangers were "The Beatles," clean-cut and nice. The Dantes were "The Stones," scruffy, greasy, with longer hair.

Eventually my band, the Strangers, got really good. Don Solomon was the leader and the most talented musician. By Easter 1964, when my mother drove us up to Sunapee to play a weekend at The Barn, the local nightspot, we were pounding out rocking versions of the big hits of the day: "She's a Woman" by the Beatles, "Not Fade Away" by the Rolling Stones (their first big record), "Bits and Pieces" by the Dave Clark Five, "Little Children" by Billy J. Kramer and the Dakotas, and all the other shit we used to play. Our business cards read: THE STRANGERS—ENGLISH SOUNDS, AMERICAN R&B. Sometimes I'd do whole shows in an English accent.

School was a big problem for me. There were too many distractions and I couldn't pay attention. I got my education mostly on the streets of Greenwich Village.

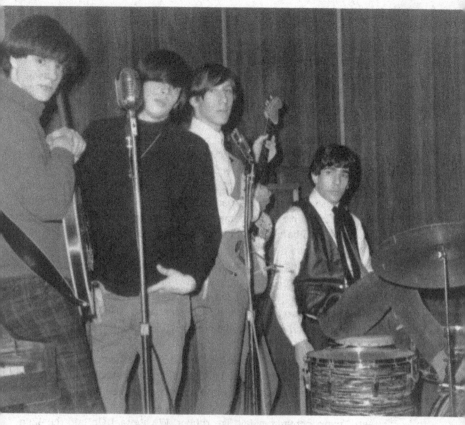

**The Dantes: Steven Tallarico second left, Ray Tabano left,
at Randy's Sweet Sixteen, 1964**
(COURTESY RAY TABANO)

We'd leave school at four o'clock on Friday afternoon and take the subway to the Village—me, Raymond, Ricky, his beautiful girlfriend Debby, and her girlfriend Dia. It was Bleecker and MacDougal, baby. We'd get a bottle of Seagram's 7, sit in the park, get 'faced, and walk the streets like everybody else, back and forth, back and forth. We'd check out the Kettle O'Fish, the Other Side, Ondine's, the Bitter End. You could eat at the Tin Angel upstairs. We'd go to the Café Wha? or the Night Owl, which had bands like the Lovin' Spoonful and the Fugs. One night, standing on the sidewalk, we heard a band playing inside, *really* good, and I got weirded out when I saw their name was the Strangers. They were a lot better than us, so we changed the spelling of our band to the Strangeurs.

There are a lot of Greenwich Village stories. One night when I was fifteen, five of us guys jumped into the car and headed down to Delancey Street. Raymond had some pot, we all got high, and we wanted to get laid. My first time! We hired the first lady we saw standing on the corner. She looked pretty old to us, fifty-five or sixty for all we knew, but she said she'd do us all.

We followed her down to this basement apartment, where six black guys were watching *Bonanza* on TV. She marched us through the kitchen—a chicken was boiling on the stove, black guys yelling, "Moth*afucka*!"—and into a back bedroom. She got $35 for doing all of us. I got to go fourth and it was disgusting, a terrible experience. I came out of the room with tears in my eyes and started to wash my dick in the kitchen sink. Black guy comes in and yells, "Moth*afucka*, you pissin' in my mothafuckin' sink?"

We thought we'd get the shit kicked out of us, but they let us go.

On the way home, we stopped at a red light and this beautiful chick comes up to the car. Raymond goes, "Now *this* is a bitch" and invited her into the car with us. He gets her into the backseat and started to fuck around with her until she started to like, moan, in a deep voice. "It's a *guy*," someone whispered, and we threw him out and drove back to Yonkers with our tails between our legs.

As we got older, we'd leave Yonkers on Friday after school and stay in the Village until Sunday night. I'd drop some acid at my house, get into the car, and be driven down to Times Square. Meanwhile, I'm getting off! Forty-five minutes later—peaking!—I'd get out of the fuckin' car and step into the street. *Vvvrroooommm*, it felt like *rubber*. *Wwhhooaa!* Go into the 42nd Street Florsheim shoe store because they sold Beatle boots with Cuban heels that were the only cool things to wear onstage. Then down to Paul Sargeant's on Eighth Street for hip clothes—collarless shirts, leather vests, checkered pants, *de rigueur* stuff. Then off to Washington Square to see this wonderful hooker we knew, Josie the She-Demon.

We went to a lot of rock shows, which made me crazy because I was completely starstruck. For me, this was everything. Obviously—look at me today—I wanted it so bad for myself, but then it was as much a thrill to meet somebody in the limelight as it was to put a worm on a hook or sleep all night next to a girl.

I wanted to meet stars.

I rushed the stage at the Brooklyn Fox to try to touch Mary Weiss, lead singer of the Shangri-Las, as she belted out "Leader of the Pack." The Shangri-Las (from Queens) were unreal. They did "Remember (Walking in

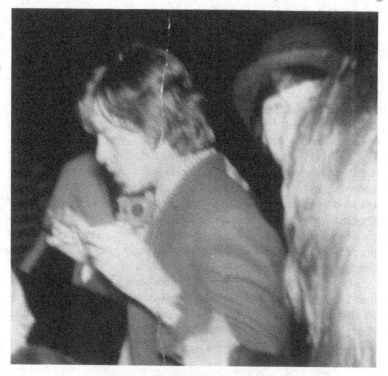

**Steven Tallarico mobbing Mick Jagger
outside New York's Gotham Hotel, May 1965**
(COURTESY DEBBY BENSON AND RAY TABANO)

the Sand)" and I flipped out. When the Animals came over from England the first time, it was phenomenal: they were playing "House of the Rising Sun" and I was so into it I ran down the aisle at the Academy of Music on 14th Street and shook Chas Chandler's hand.

The highlight of this whole era was when the Rolling Stones came to New York in May 1965.

To say I worshipped the Stones at this point would be a gross understatement. Everybody told me that I looked just like Mick Jagger with my big lips, and Keith Richards basically *was* the music I used to love more than anything. "Satisfaction" was the #1 record in the world and "The Last Time" and "Get Off of My Cloud" were constantly playing on the car radio and in my head.

We all bought tickets to the Stones' afternoon show at the Academy of Music. After the show, we were determined to get close to them somehow.

Debby and Dia rented a room at the Gotham Hotel on Fifth Avenue, where the Stones were staying, so they could get into the hotel, which left me and Raymond and the other guys standing outside on the sidewalk. Suddenly a gray Cadillac limo pulled up to the curb and Brian Jones got out, followed by Mick Jagger and Bill Wyman. I was trying to get next to Mick while Raymond's brother aimed his Polaroid at me. Ray was all over Brian Jones. Girls started screaming, my brown derby hat got knocked off and trampled, the Stones signed a few autographs and escaped into the hotel. We hung around for a while, buzzing like crazy just because we got to touch them!

Later that night, a funny thing happened. We got hooked up somehow with Monte Rock III and his campy friends. Monte was a hairdresser who dressed up in flashy pseudo-Mod clothes and went on *The Tonight Show* and sang a little, coming on as an outrageous hipster. We went up to his place, where he kept a chimp and a couple of mastiffs. So we're partying, popping amyl nitrate, and I think they gave us some Placidyls, a heavy downer. I came to about six hours later. My pants were off and our girlfriends were naked. Someone had their way with us!

Maybe it wasn't so funny, but it's a snapshot of a certain scene in New York, 1965. On the way back to Yonkers, the Good Guys were playing "Hang On Sloopy," "You've Lost That Lovin' Feelin'," and "Go Now!" by the Moody Blues.

4: Quest for Immortality

Steven Tyler: By the summer of 1965, the Strangeurs were playing four forty-five-minute sets a night at ridiculous clubs like Banana Fish Park out on Long Island. I was on drums and singing, which didn't work out the way I needed it to. Don Solomon and I talked about getting another drummer so I could be out front, but the other guys in the band didn't want to split the $75 we were getting for a night's work with another drummer. Understandable—if you didn't have to sing and play drums at the same time for three hours every night.

Think about it.

The truth was I *had* to get out front. I was after *total immortality*. I couldn't sleep nights, thinking about how famous I could be. I was terrified

I would die before I made my mark in the world. That summer in Sunapee, I went to an auction and bought a tool set—some chisels and a ball peen hammer so fuckin' heavy I could hardly carry it. I stole some goggles from Uncle Ernie's workbench and went out to this huge granite boulder behind Papa's Cabin, where my grandfather Giovanni used to live. This rock was the size of a tank, and I spent a couple days chiseling my initials into it so future generations would know Steven Tallarico was here.

Immortality. It's not much to ask for, is it? I wanted to sing on a record so after I died I'd still be singing. That way I could live forever.

This was also the summer I met Henry Smith, who became extremely important in all our lives.

Henry Smith: I met Steven and the Strangeurs in 1965 when they played at The Barn in Georges Mills on Lake Sunapee. My family lived in Westport, Connecticut, and we had a summer house in Danbury, New Hampshire. Steven was the local rock star and the kids packed any-place one of his bands would play. They covered "Everybody Needs Somebody to Love" by the Stones, the Beatles, the Beach Boys, "Mr. Tambourine Man" by the Byrds, "Money," "Louie Louie," the Kinks' "You Really Got Me," all the important songs of the day, and it sounded as good as the original records and sometimes better because Steven put so much energy into it. He could really get a roomful of kids going. It was incredible.

My brother Christopher and I got friendly with Steven, and the Strangeurs were such a good band that when the summer ended I started to book them into places where we lived in Connecticut. The first job I got them was the Christmas Cotillion of Fairfield County. My mother was in charge of this rather snooty debutante ball; usually they hired Peter Duchin's orchestra, but this year Duchin couldn't do it and my mother was crushed.

"Don't worry, Mom," I told her, "I know a band."

So I got the Strangeurs the job for $500, much less than Duchin charged, and everyone was happy until the Strangeurs showed up at the country club in long hair, dungarees, and a snotty attitude. Steven complained he didn't have anything cool to wear, so I cut the sleeves off my grandmother's mink coat and gave it to him to wear as a vest. They looked like the Rolling Stones but even more disreputable.

The chaperones were horrified. "How *could* you?" they hissed at my mother. But the band began to play some Yardbirds song and the kids just went nuts. By the end of the night, everyone said it was the best cotillion they'd ever had.

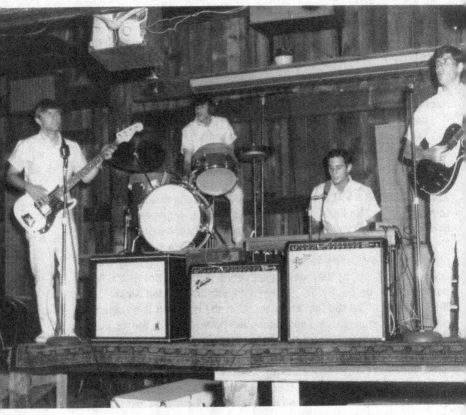

The Strangeurs at The Barn, 1965, Steven on drums
(TYLER COLLECTION)

The Strangeurs' resemblance to the Stones caused some funny scenes. Late in the year, the Rolling Stones came back to New York and we found out they were staying at the Lincoln Square Motor Inn on the West Side. So I borrowed my mother's little Dodge Dart and told her I was going to a band rehearsal in Yonkers. I picked up Steven and Alan Strohmayer, the bass player, who had a fringe of blond hair down over his eyes, which made him look like Brian Jones. An hour later we were pulling into the block the hotel is on, totally packed with kids, and Steven rolls down the window and starts talking to people in his English accent. They look at him and start screaming, "MICK!" And "Brian Jones" is in the backseat. Suddenly we were mobbed, then engulfed. "MICK! BRIAN! *EEEEEEEEEEE!!!!!!*" First the antenna breaks, then the wipers get bent, the windshield cracks, the car is totally scratched, and things look bad until the New York City cops battle their way to the car, throwing girls away right and left. They got really angry when they saw who we were— or weren't.

Steven ate it up. He loved it.

Later that night, my mom's waiting up for me.

"How was the rehearsal, Henry?"

"Great, Mom."

"That's very interesting, because I just saw you on the news, in my car, surrounded by a thousand crazy kids. You're *grounded!*"

Meanwhile, there was another band in Yonkers now, a slightly younger group of kids called the King Bees. We knew about them because Henry Schneiderman's little brother played in the King Bees and both bands rehearsed in their basement. The King Bees had a problem with their drummer. He was really good, but his father told him, "You can't play drums, I don't want you in this band," and took his drums away from him.

So one day this drummer—he was maybe thirteen years old—shows up at Steven's house and asks if he can borrow a set of drums so the King Bees could play that night. Steven said sure, the kid came down to the basement, and this was the first time I met Joey Kramer, which shows you how deep the roots of Aerosmith go.

5: High School
Confidential

Steven Tyler: I had a ritual in high school, at least before I got thrown out. I woke up at seven, went down to the basement, closed the door real quiet, and put my head under the sink in the laundry room. Then I'd connect the vacuum cleaner hose to the dryer and turn it on. I'd sneak upstairs into the kitchen, take a plastic juice cup and fill it to the top with Dewar's, and drink it. If there was no Dewar's, I'd drink vodka and orange juice. The sound of the dryer masked the noise of making my drink. Then back to the basement, where I'd blow-dry my hair with the hose so I wouldn't look like all the other idiots I knew at school with long hair. I hated the way they looked! I wore cowboy boots to school, tying the bottoms of my trousers to the boots with a self-invented system of buttons and dental floss so they'd stay down and look really cool.

Along with the ritual—getting drunk and doing my hair—I'd listen to my favorite songs on the big mono speaker I hooked up: "I Can't Explain" by the Who and "I Ain't Got You" by the Yardbirds. I paid close attention to the Yardbirds: They had a hard groove that nobody else was doing, keeping that beat just *going*. The Stones stuck to tight arrangements when they played live, while the Yardbirds would go into these improvisational rave-ups, especially after Jeff Beck replaced Eric Clapton in 1965. But I heard this as coming from Paul Samwell-Smith. To me, the Yardbirds' energy exploded from their bass player going up an octave and how he got up there. Later, after Jimmy Page joined, I bought their single "Goodnight Sweet Josephine." The other side was "Think About It." I'd listen to those songs over and over again: They were so cool and intense.

So every day I arrived at school looking like I'd just stepped off the set of *Shindig* or *Hullabaloo*. All the teachers hated me. They told me my hair was too long. They told me I was fucked up. They told me I was poison.

Maybe they were right.

Early in 1966, my band got an offer to go to Cleveland to do a teen dance party show on local TV called *Upbeat*. At high school the next day, I got called into the principal's office because of my hair. I went in wearing my usual turtleneck shirt with my hair tucked in. The principal says to me, "Tallarico, you look like a girl!"

I got all upset.

"Hey, man, I'm a professional musician. I'm *supposed* to look like this. Whaddaya want me to do? I'm doing a big TV show in Cleveland tomorrow. I *can't* cut my hair."

"Don't your parents *care* about your hair, the way you *look?*"

"Nah, my mother likes my hair and my father's a classical musician."

"Well, the other students can't concentrate if you're in class looking like a Mod beatnik or whatever you are."

So I told him I'd quit school right there and this shook him up because too many kids were dropping out, which made the school's statistics look bad. So it was a standoff.

The Strangeurs flew to Cleveland, the first time I'd ever been on a jet. We got a friend of ours from New Hampshire, David Conrad, to play the drums so I could just sing. We get there and find out that the Shangri-Las are on the show with us. *Dig it! Far out! Far fuckin' out!* There are no dressing rooms, so I go into the bathroom to change. I thought David Conrad was in the next stall taking a shit or something, so I climb over the wall. I looked down and saw . . . Mary Weiss! Lead singer of the Shangri-Las! And I can see her patch!! I'm like seventeen!!! This beautiful blonde with black leather pants down around her ankles, boner material, *major wood!*

Around this time I got fired from my job as a soda jerk in a drugstore on Central Avenue in Yonkers. I was stealing boxes of stuff and handing them out the back door to Ray Tabano. Then I got busted for stealing from the supermarket next door to the drugstore. That's how I met a guy named Pete Agosta, who became my manager.

Peter Agosta: I was the manager of the Shopwell super-market on Central Avenue and I kept catching Steven Tallarico shoplift-ing, so I made him a carriage boy so he wouldn't rob me blind. Later he told me he had a little band, and I went to see them play at a Sweet Sixteen party for [actor] Art Carney's daughter in Bronxville. They got the job because Steven's father was giving piano lessons to Art Carney's son. They were a good band. Don Solomon was the leader: He had a kingpin personality and a good voice, but Steve had all the Jagger appeal and the right moves. I knew they were going to go somewhere if he was out front.

So I started to manage them a little. First thing, Steve asked me to come to the high school and talk to the principal and explain about his long hair. They were making him slick his hair back and basically glue it behind his collar. "Steve's a *performer*," I told them. "He has to dress this way or he won't get work." But they didn't care, they just hated him.

The next thing I did was to put Steven up front. We hired a kid named Barry Shapiro to be the drummer. He was short like Ringo and could keep great time, and Steven helped him a lot. Steven was a musicians' musi-cian, with a very keen ear; the Strangeurs were a tight band, mainly be-cause Steven would freak if someone made a mistake.

In early March 1966, Steven heard that the Byrds were coming to play the Westchester County Center in nearby White Plains later that month. Steven *demanded* I get the Strangeurs the job of opening act. The Byrds had a hit record, "Eight Miles High," and were probably the hottest band in America. I badgered the promoter for a couple of weeks before I could even get my calls returned, but they didn't really want to know. Then I found out that ticket sales were slow, so I called them and said that the Strangeurs were the most popular band in the county and guaranteed them a sellout if they put us on the bill. They said OK, added us to the show, and all 3,000 seats sold out a few days after the posters went up.

The show was March 26, 1966. We got a few girls to sit down front and told them to start screaming when we went on. The Byrds' manager told us *ten times* that we couldn't play any of their songs, but Steven opened up with "Eight Miles High" anyway. Jim McGuinn and David Crosby were watching from the wings, totally shocked, as Steven did their song and girls began to scream. But they weren't our girls! Hundreds of girls began to scream spontaneously as the curtain opened and Steven jumped and pumped and did a hell of a show. The Strangeurs were only supposed to do two songs, but Steven just kept going and did six numbers because the kids wouldn't let them go.

Even the Byrds were impressed. As Steven came offstage, dripping wet, McGuinn says, "Great show, man." In fact, they liked us so much their manager hired the Strangeurs to open for the Byrds the following night in Asbury Park, New Jersey.

YONKERS HERALD STATESMAN
Two groups preceded the Byrds. First the Dillards [who were touring with the Byrds that year]: nice, nothing spectacular, modest applause. Then the Strangeurs, a Yonkers group, five Roosevelt High graduates. The tempo rose. Lead singer Steve Tallarico came on like Mick Jagger of the Stones: bottom lip hanging, tambourine slapping against thigh. This was more like it, and the audience responded. There were hand-waving shrieks and girls running down the aisles snapping pictures. The MC announced if the girls became too hysterical, the Byrds would cut short their concert. (March 27, 1966)

Steven Tyler: While the Byrds were doing their last number, "Roll Over Beethoven," a thirteen-year-old girl in green suede boots, matching umbrella cape, and tinted granny glasses almost started a riot when she vaulted over three rows of cops and made it onto the six-foot stage. A cop grabbed her around the waist and threw her off, but then twenty other girls made it up. The Byrds were laughing because it was more like a Beatle thing. The papers called it a "near riot."

Henry Smith: I remember the Byrds' show very well because Steven went out and played the whole show with his zipper open and his shirttail hanging out of his fly. I tried to get his attention, but once he starts a show, he's in another world. The kids probably thought it was part of the act. Steven acted like he was furious when he found out about it afterwards, but in a weird way I think he liked it.

Peter Agosta: Early in April 1966, I signed the Strangeurs to a management contract. All five musicians and their fathers signed because the band was underage. We signed the contract at Steven's house, and I visited Steven's bedroom up in the attic. There were framed photos of the Rolling Stones and the Walker Brothers [an Anglo-American group whose hair Steven really liked] on the walls, plus trophies of girls, animals he trapped, and stuff he'd stolen. *This is a strange kid*, I thought to myself. [The bookshelf contained *The True Story of the Beatles* by Billy Shepherd, *Raccoon Family Pets*, *3001 Questions and Answers*, a hollowed-out copy of *The Hardy Boys and the Disappearing Floor*, in which Steven hid his pot, *Trapping North American Furbearers*, *Steel Traps*, and *Deadfalls and Snares*.] After we signed the contracts, Steven's dad spruced him up and they left to play a Vic Tallarico date at the Westchester Country Club with Steven on drums.

Back then the most important music promotor in the New York area was a guy named Pete Bennett, who lived in Westchester. He was very well connected in the music business and did some work for President Lyndon Johnson and the Democratic Party. He was a very big wheel. The town of Yonkers even renamed the street he lived on Bennett Avenue. He'd seen us open for the Byrds, and he was very enthusiastic about Steven. He told other people in the business and his disc jockey pals, and we started to get better bookings at clubs and record hops hosted by various Good Guys from WABC. We worked every weekend after that for the next year. Henry Smith booked us into Staples High School in Westport, Connecticut, and we played places like the Northeast Jewish Center in Yonkers, the Club 42 in Tuckahoe, the Hampshire Country Club—wherever anyone wanted to pay us $150–$200 a night.

Then the record hops kicked in. Pete Bennett owned a Mod club in Yonkers called the House of Liverpool, and we opened there many times for acts like Jay and the Americans, the Animals with Eric Burdon, and Frank Sinatra, Jr., before the place was shut down. We opened for the legendary Kingsmen of "Louie Louie" fame at a dance hosted by deejay Gary Stephens. We played with Terry Knight and the Pack [later Grand Funk Railroad] at a club called the Jumping Jack in Yonkers, which paid us $375 for a three-night gig. That spring of 1966 was one of the busiest times of my life! Everything was going great until Steven got busted and it looked like he might go to jail.

6: The Nark in
Ceramics Class

Ray Tabano: Back then Steven and I wanted to get high without paying for it. We'd buy an ounce of pot for $20, break it up into six bags, sell four for $5 apiece, and have two left for ourselves. There was this detective in the Yonkers police named Bernie who knew what was happening. A big bust went down. Steven wasn't involved, but I was arrested with about twenty other kids. Everyone got off scot-free except me. I got on probation for resisting arrest, which was a big fuckin' drag at the time, but it kept me out of Vietnam later.

But this one detective was really out to bust someone now, so they planted a nark in Roosevelt High and deliberately targeted Steven. This guy weasled his way into our group via a friend of Debby's. He had good pot and Steven, being very naive about people, trusted him.

Steven Tyler: One day this new kid, Mike, shows up in ceramics class. He's sitting with a girl I know and they were tight and everything looked cool. Then he got to know all our girlfriends, started going out with them, and joined the family, so to speak. If we ran out, Mike would take us out to his car in the parking lot, reach up under the dashboard, pull out a nickel bag, and turn us on. He taught us new ways to smoke, little tricks with aluminum foil and chillums and shit. I never suspected anything. These were the days when we thought that if you crushed the seeds you could get high.

So one day [June 11, 1966] I bought a lid from Mike, rolled a few to take to that night's gig, and hid the rest in my stash at home in my hollowed-out book. That night the Strangeurs played a dance at the Ice Cream Parlor in Westport and the whole band got $100. There were some trampolines out back of this club and this kid comes out and tells me to stop jumping on them. It got my back up until I found out this kid was Scott Newman, a friend of Henry Smith's and actor Paul Newman's son. We went back to Scott's house after the show and ended up in the sauna with Paul Newman, drinking brandy all night.

Later the next day, I called up my mother to tell her I'd be late for dinner. She was in tears. She said the police had been to the house, searched my room, and found my stash. Sure enough, when I got home from Paul Newman's place, numb with fear, there was a black car in front of my house with three cops in it. I got out and they handcuffed me. I was indignant. "What is this?" I asked them. "Are you *proud* of this? Are you kidding?"

"Shut up, kid," they said. "This ain't no joke."

Meanwhile, my mother's at the front door in tears, my father just pulled up from work and he's in the driveway speechless. Humiliation, big time. The neighbors are watching. It made the papers the next day.

They took me down to the police station. A lot of my friends were busted too. All the girls are crying. Everybody's in one room with two-way mirrors all around, so we gave 'em the finger. And in comes this fuckin' guy, Michael, our friend, grinning, his hands on his belt with a badge that says DEPUTY SHERIFF—PUTNAM COUNTY. I'll never forget it as long as I live.

I said, "Mike, how can you *do* this? You are the lowest scum." He told me that his brother had died of a drug overdose and he had it in for anyone who used drugs.

"You fucker," I said. "*You're* the one who turned us on and showed us all those fuckin' tricks!"

They really tried to nail me. I was charged with twelve felony counts of dealing and possessing drugs, and I thought I was going to prison. I was really disillusioned. Before this, I didn't think I had an enemy in the world.

When I went to court, my lawyer suggested I plead guilty. I stood up before the judge and said, "Your Honor, I've been advised to plead guilty, but I would like to speak with you in your chamber, alone if possible." We went back there and I told him that I'd never smoked pot before I met this nark and that he'd turned me on and sold me my first ounce. I promised to be good and walk the true path of righteousness. I meant it at the time.

The judge—I think he was Italian—bought it, and I got off with a misdemeanor and a year's probation. I was branded Y.O.—Youthful Offender—which later kept me out of the Army. Which goes to show that it's all for a reason. Everything bad that happened to me, in the long run I'm better off for it. Every hardship, I've come out stronger.

Roosevelt High kicked me out. They told me not to come back in September. So I stole the bass drum I'd played in the marching band, carried it right out of school after the Strangeurs played the senior prom late that

June. I still have it. If you listen to the three big drum notes at the end of "Livin' on the Edge," there it is.

Peter Agosta: We played a lot of proms: New Rochelle, Eastchester, West Point, Nutley High in New Jersey on June 17, the week after Steven got arrested, and he's still very upset. Nutley is a wealthy, conservative town and their prom was very formal, uptight. We walked in, they took one look at us, and I knew we were in trouble. Steven was high. One song into the first set, Steven collapses. I didn't know what he'd taken or whether he was just drunk. We got him up and he seemed OK. I said we'd go back on and the girl from the prom committee said, "No, you're not! You *ruined* our prom!" They paid us our $200 and called the state police. We got a motorcycle escort to the George Washington Bridge. The police watched us cross the river to make sure the Strangeurs actually left New Jersey.

7: The Chain Reaction

Steven Tyler: My band was booked into The Barn, up in Sunapee, on the Fourth of July weekend in 1966. We drove to New Hampshire in Pete Agosta's Chevy and stayed at Trow-Rico like we always did.

The Barn was a legendary, notorious scene; the ground zero of the whole Aerosmith story, because this is where I eventually hooked up with Joe Perry and Tom Hamilton. But I digress . . .

The Barn was a B.Y.O.B. nightclub in an old barn owned by John Conrad, a gay queen with a golden heart. His brother Dick ran the place for him, at least for a while, and if he liked you well enough, he'd sell you a little pot in a matchbox. David Conrad, who played drums with us in Cleveland, was his nephew or whatever. John was wonderfully weird for Lake Sunapee. He always had a glass of wine in his hand, and he'd sit with his legs twined in a bar stool, going, "Nooowww, David . . ."

Anyway, this was the first time I remember encountering Joe Perry, and I was also starting to get friendly with Zunk Buker, the local badass, who literally knew us from day one.

Harold Wilder "Zunk" Buker III: I grew up in New London, New Hampshire, where my father was a pilot and an airline operator. I knew Steven almost from childhood because my cousin took piano lessons from his grandmother and I used to go to the recitals at Trow-Rico. Later I used to see him playing with his father's band at Indian Cave Lodge.

Steven wasn't your typical summer person, to say the least. He hung out with the local outcasts and always made sure he was the most outrageous person around. In my own way, I tried to be as outrageous as he was. I had my own plane, a fast car, some money, and we got high together a lot because that's what you did then. We even had the same girlfriend, at least until I got her pregnant and became a father at sixteen.

Steven was incredibly special. The local people didn't "get" him until the Beatles came out, but the kids thought he was a total hero and whenever his bands played The Barn, it was almost a riot.

The Barn was an old dairy farm, built around 1860, on Prospect Hill Road in the village of Georges Mills. It was part of Conrad Manor Lodge, owned by the Conrad brothers, a couple of sweet con men who kept it open all year, unlike most places that closed at the end of the summer. In an earlier era you could hear swing bands and it was like a dance hall. In the sixties, they brought in rock 'n' roll bands, and The Barn was *the* place to hang out on the weekend. The cops put up roadblocks just above the turnoff from Route 11 so they could shake down likely suspects like ourselves.

The Barn was also a place where it was easy to get into a fight. There was a lot of conflict in the area between locals and summer people, between downmarket Sunapee and upscale New London, between locals and Dartmouth students who came to date girls from Colby Sawyer College for Women in New London. The most legendary fight at The Barn happened one night in 1963 when the Dartmouth backfield skipped curfew the night before the Ivy League championship game and arrived at The Barn to party. The quarterback decided he wanted to dance with the girlfriend of a local guy named Larry Lara, who was the best bar-fighter I ever saw. If you were being chased by this guy in a car, it would be better if you crashed the car and died than for him to catch you. Larry knocked this Dartmouth football hero out with one punch. The band kept playing, the kid's teammates piled on and Larry knocked them cold too. Larry cleaned house. I think one of the Dartmouth players had to go to the hospital. Next day, Dartmouth lost the Ivy League crown, and the week after that the whole team, including some of the coaches, showed up at The Barn to kill this guy, who of course was nowhere to be found.

Anyway, when the Strangeurs played The Barn in the summer of '66, the place was jammed as usual. A lot of people were turned away, and among the kids milling around outside, trying to hear the band, were two local teenagers, fifteen-year-old Tom Hamilton from New London, and a sixteen-year-old guitarist named Joe Perry, whose parents owned a summer house on the lake. They came to see the Strangeurs, but they couldn't get in. I couldn't either because it was just mobbed.

Steven Tyler: The next night my band is eating at a place called the Anchorage, down at Sunapee Harbor. It's a combination restaurant and pinball arcade and a major hangout where people could dock their boats and get a burger and a Coke. So I'm sitting there eating some french fries and I realize that these are the best french fries I've ever had in my life—light, crispy, thick, perfect. I'd been eating french fries at the Anchorage for fifteen years and never had anything like these, so being me I had to go see who made 'em.

Back in the kitchen, this kid that made the french fries is flipping cheeseburgers. He has long hair over his eyes and thick black horn-rim glasses. I complimented him on the excellent french fries, but he was kind of sullen and didn't say much.

It was Joe Perry. It later turned out he was mad because we always threw food when we ate at the Anchorage and he always had to clean up after us.

After that, we went down to Connecticut, where Henry Smith had booked us into gigs around Westport for the rest of the month.

Peter Agosta: The Beach Boys were booked into Iona College in New Rochelle on July 24, and the promoters decided to hold a Battle of the Bands to decide who would open the show. There was an audition for this on July 13, which almost didn't happen because Steven *hated* to audition—he thought it was beneath him—and the other guys had to talk him into it. The actual battle was three days later and drew every group in Westchester, but the Strangeurs did "Paint It, Black" and won.

Pete Bennett was there, which was a big deal. He had all these connections, including LBJ's White House. He liked the guys, but he thought Steven was going to be the biggest star in America someday and he kept telling me he wanted to buy me out and work with Steven himself.

A few days later, the Strangeurs opened for the Beach Boys and Steven killed 'em. He did Beach Boys songs, Beatles stuff, "Walkin' the Dog," "Paint It, Black." After the show, the Beach Boys invited him downtown to hang out with them at their hotel, which Steven loved because he was so starstruck.

Then Pete Bennett told us he could get us a record deal, but we'd have to go down and audition for Date Records, which was part of CBS.

Steven Tyler: We drove down to CBS and took our gear up the freight elevators because security wouldn't let us in the front door. We got into some guy's office and he says, "OK, boys, you can set up in the corner." So we set up the drums and I sat down and this guy's sitting at his desk, taking calls. He finally looked up and said, "All right, play."

So we played him this song we'd written up in Sunapee called "The Sun." It was a psychedelic waltz about staying up all night and watching the sun come up in the morning. While we're playing, straight-looking guys came in wearing jackets and ties and sat down right in front of us. He stopped us halfway through and said, "I'll sign you up for six grand. How about it?" Me, I'm just this stupid, defective kid from Yonkers. I go, "All right, uh-huh," and we had a record deal just like that. I could hardly believe it.

Peter Agosta: We began to record "The Sun" at CBS Studios on August 25. The producer was Richie Gottehrer, whose hits included "My Boyfriend's Back" by the Angels, "Hang On Sloopy" by the McCoys, "Night Time" by the Strangeloves, and lots of others. "The Sun" took three weeks to record because Steven was a perfectionist and drove everybody crazy. He demanded his own mike, which no one had heard of before.

After that, the band went back to The Barn for Labor Day. They made $600 for the weekend. On September 9, we went back to CBS and finished "The Sun" and recorded "When I Needed You," an acid rock song that took about fifteen minutes to do. On September 29, the band recorded "You Should Have Been Here Yesterday" and "Ever Loving Man." Now they had enough to release two singles.

Then Date Records told us to change the band's name because we couldn't release a single as the Strangeurs since that name was already taken for legal purposes by the Strangers. So Steven and Don Solomon came up with Chain Reaction. Steven told me that Chain Reaction meant a continuous flow of high energy, and that's what they were all about. The guys also took stage names: Steve Tally, Don Sloan, Barry Shore.

The Chain Reaction's first single, "The Sun," shipped in late September 1966. It got a little play on WMCA and WABC, and I think Scott Muni played it a few times on WNEW-FM. We heard rumors that the record did well in Europe and that the flip side, "When I Needed You," was a minor

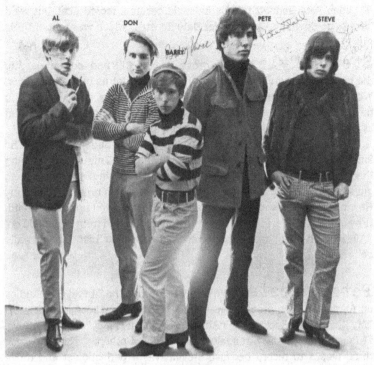

AL   DON   PETE   STEVE

The Chain Reaction
(TYLER COLLECTION)

hit in the South. Other than that, we played a lot of colleges that fall and winter as well as our usual circuit in Connecticut and New Jersey, and our record was never heard from again. ["You Should Have Been Here Yesterday" eventually came out as a single on Verve.]

8: The Yardbirds in Connecticut

Steven Tyler: After I got thrown out of high school, my parents sent me to Quintano's Professional Children's School on West 56th Street in New York. Some mornings I'd steal their car and feel so liberated and fuckin' cool riding into town, where I accumulated hundreds of parking tickets. You only had to show up a couple days a week to get a diploma at Quintano's, and I spent most of my time hanging out on the big rocks in Central Park, toking with my friends. There was a girl named Liz Agriss, who went out with Rick Zehringer, who played in the McCoys with his brother. I knew Rick because my bands had been opening for the McCoys in various places since I was maybe fourteen, and Liz and Rick and I got to be very good friends. (He changed his name to Rick Derringer when he started playing guitar with the Winter brothers a little later.)

Liz Derringer: Quintano's was a school for young actors, musicians, kids who worked and traveled. You went there if your parents were in the circus or something like that. There were no grades. You just went and tried to pay attention. Soupy Sales's sons went there and a lot of other famous people's children. The school occupied floors in two separate buildings, so the students were always on the streets or in the park. Rick would come to school and get me after visiting the nearby motorcycle dealer and we'd hang in the park with Steven.

Back then Steven was a slightly chubby, funny-looking kid with giant, very chapped lips. He dated my friend Michelle Overman and had a band that played the Café Wha? in the Village. We went to see them play with the Fugs and they were great, doing their own songs and a lot of covers.

In school Steven spent his time splattering spitballs on the blackboard: He liked to make them stick. In a school of generally offbeat kids, he really stood out. He was cynical, sarcastic, strange, and his wit was almost scary because he could really hurt you with it. He was also dynamic and would talk to anyone who interested him, unlike most of the kids, who were stuck in cliques.

Steven only wore blue. That was his trademark, his thing. I can't remember him in any other color. Once I asked him why and he said, "Liz, blue is the closest color to truth."

Steven Tyler: The Chain Reaction worked really hard that fall. We opened for the Lovin' Spoonful at the County Center and played the Cheetah on Broadway, which was a glitzy rock club in Times Square. Me and my friend Lee Ritter would drive down to 42nd Street and buy the new British imports by the Kinks, the Pretty Things, Travis Wammack, all these English groups who never got credit. If there was something new by the Yardbirds—"Shapes of Things, "Over Under Sideways Down," "Happenings Ten Years Time Ago"—we bought that first.

Then Henry Smith got us a gig opening for the Yardbirds at Staples

High in Westport [on October 22, 1966]. We drove up in my mother's station wagon and arrived at the same time as the Yardbirds arrived in their van. I got out and and carried an amp into the gym. I don't even know whose it was. Then I go out again and see Jimmy Page carrying my mike stand. That's how it was in those days.

I had seen the Yardbirds play somewhere the previous summer with both Jeff Beck and Jimmy Page in the band. In fact, I got them to autograph a piece of cardboard. In Westport we found out that Jeff had left the band and Jimmy was playing lead guitar by himself. I watched him from the edge of the stage and all I can say is that he knocked my tits off. They did "Train Kept A-Rollin' " and it was just so heavy. They were just an un-fuckin'-believable band.

We did record hops that winter [1966–67] with lots of different WMCA Good Guys: Jack Spector, Gary Stephens, Dandy Dan Daniels, all famous disc jockeys. We played Catholic high schools in Brooklyn and the Bronx. We did shows with the Left Banke, the Soul Survivors of "Expressway to Your Heart" fame, Leslie West and the Vagrants, the Shangri-Las, Jay and the Americans, Billy Joel's band the Hassles, Peaches and Herb (who were also on the Date label), and the Animals. Then, around March 1967, the band stopped happening. It was over.

Henry Smith: One night in Manhattan, I bumped into Brian Conliffe, the Yardbirds' English roadie, who was working as a doorman at Salvation, a club in Sheridan Square that Steven and I hung out at a lot. Brian didn't want to go back on the road with the Yardbirds and got me the job. My first trip with them was the Dick Clark Caravan of Stars, which featured the Yardbirds, the Shangri-Las, and the Mothers of Invention. Over the next two years the Yardbirds called me when they came to New York, and then I went to England and lived in Jimmy Page's gatehouse until the Yardbirds disbanded in 1968 and Jimmy Page formed Led Zeppelin, originally called the New Yardbirds.

Peter Agosta: That spring Pete Bennett wanted to buy out my contract with Steven. He told me he was going to put some money behind Steven and make him very big. But he didn't want the other guys in the Chain Reaction. He said they were second-rate and besides, it was Steven who made everything happen.

That night we were playing Trenchi's in Yonkers, a real dump, but Steven loved to play local places. He told me to book them anyplace, regardless of the money, because he wanted to stay busy and out of trouble.

Steven had to play—all the time. I told Steven about Bennett, and he got very upset because of his loyalty to the band. He told Don Solomon, who'd just gotten married, and Don freaked out. So Steven told me to say no to Pete Bennett. This was a real sacrifice for Steven, who was literally dying to make it big, and he had tears in his eyes, but he didn't hesitate for a minute. Steven Tallarico had a heart of gold. Later Pete Bennett talked to Steven, but he couldn't convince him. So Pete Bennett signed someone else.

Then some of the parents accused me of profiteering, which was ridiculous because I was going broke. My career was suffering because I was spending too much time with the band, and I was worried that my son was trying to emulate Steven, who wasn't really the role model I had in mind.

So we broke up. Chain Reaction's last gig was at the Brooklawn Country Club in Connecticut on June 18, 1967. We got $500 and that was it. A couple of months later, I heard that Steven was doing something with the Left Banke.

Steven Tyler: At Quintano's one day, this good-looking kind of Italian or Spanish guy was there and he said he was the lead singer in a band. "Oh, yeah? What band you with?" "The Left Banke." "You mean like, 'Walk Away Renee'?"

"Yeah, you wanna meet the band? Come over my house."

So I go over and I'm impressed that I'm hanging out with the guys in the Left Banke, which was the only other New York band besides the Young Rascals to break out of the local scene. They had a nationwide million-selling record under their belt, but they were the laziest motherfuckers that I ever saw. Then they said they were recording that night at Apostolic Studio. I said, "What are you playing?" And they go, "We don't know." I go, "*What?* How can you *not know* what you're doing?" That's how naive I was. I had no clue that other people wrote the songs. So I went to the studio with them and sang backup and played tambourine on a track called "Dark Is the Bark." I wound up on three tracks of the second Left Banke album. I may even have played a couple shows with them, but then they basically flushed themselves down the toilet and I had to find something else to do.

9: The Chain

Steven Tyler: In the fall of 1967, right after the Summer of Love, which I spent mostly bandless in Sunapee, I was just hanging around clubs in New York. I went back to playing drums with Don Solomon and our friend Frankie Ray from Yonkers in a three-piece band called the Chain. Ray Tabano wanted to play bass, but Don wouldn't let him join because Don could play a Rhodes bass box with his left hand, like Ray Manzarek of the Doors. We were doing "Love Me Two Times" at Ondine's and at the Cheetah, five sets a night for $500. Then into the car to make a frat party in Connecticut and some club in Vermont that same night. We lived like Gypsies, always on the prowl, living off the raw energy of rock 'n' roll.

It was a hard life, harder than most people think. You're onstage and you think you're going to fall over and die, but somehow you dip into the well and find your reserve that gets you through the song, then through the next one and the one after that. You learn to conjure up this energy and it becomes your life force. Eating and sleeping fall by the wayside, and music and fucking take the lead. That's what you become, and it prepares you for the long run.

It's dangerous. Don't try it at home.

One night in early 1968, we played Steve Paul's Scene on West 46th Street with Tiny Tim. He did "Tip-toe Thru' the Tulips with Me" and we fell over. The Scene was where English rock stars hung out in royal style. One night Paul McCartney's in there, Jimi Hendrix the next. I'd look over my rum and Coke and Mick Jagger is sitting there.

Zunk Buker: It took the Summer of Love a year to hit Lake Sunapee, but it hit with a vengeance in 1968, a wild summer when all the prep school and college kids arrived with suitcases bulging with LSD and pot. People were tripping in the trees and generally expanding their consciousnesses. The Chain was in town all summer, living at Trow-Rico.

The Barn was at its zenith. John Conrad was like a father to the local freak population, taking us in when things got bad at home, keeping us entertained with the bands he booked from Greenwich Village and Connecticut. The Chain had the best singer, but there was also Dario's Trip, the Third Grade, the Avanties, and the Deadbeats, this incredible rockabilly harmony band—six guys would arrive in their own hearse. There was also a band called Plastic Glass, but I don't think I ever heard them play. I only knew about it because the drummer, Pudge Scott, borrowed a drum kit that I owned. I asked him who else was in the band and he said, "Joe Perry and Tom Hamilton."

Steven Tallarico was living with his cousin Augie in a little cabin at Trow-Rico, but I usually found him in his parents' house. His mom would open the door and Steven would be behind her, twirling a big unlit joint behind her back, deftly palming it when she turned around. He'd borrow Uncle Ernie's jeep and drive us way up the power line to smoke hash in the woods, and if you knew him well you'd walk back down to the cabins afterward, because Steven stoned in a jeep in the woods was not a situation you had any great confidence in.

One night that August, I told Steven that I was leaving town to seek my fortune as a young outlaw pot dealer in California where good marijuana was (falsely) said to cost $25 a pound. It was a time when dealers were more glamorous than rock stars and more important to the community. I wanted more than anything to be part of this underground world.

And Steven says something like, "Zunky, what do you want out of this?"

And I said, "I want to be Jesse James."

He thought about this for a while, then he said, "I want to be Jim Morrison."

And so we parted ways and chased after our own separate myths.

Henry Smith: The Chain moved to Boston in September 1968. Peter Stahl from Chain Reaction was going to college there and the band realized that the odds against them making it in New York were very rough. It was hard to get work in New York unless you were Somebody; it was more a place to play after you'd made it elsewhere. This was the beginning of a long exile for Steven. I don't think he played again in New York for three years.

Meanwhile, Boston had half a million students and no big rock and roll scene. It was more of a folk and blues town back then. So Steven and Don Solomon decided to move up. They already had a small following because of New Hampshire. I was between Yardbirds tours, so my brother and I rented Apartment Zero at 39 Kent Street in Brookline, near Boston University, along with our friend Jim Currier. It was really just a basement, but we renovated it and made it livable. Steven lived there a little as well, moving back and forth between Boston and New York.

Late in the year I got a call from England saying that Jimmy Page had mutated the New Yardbirds into a new band called Led Zeppelin, and I started working with them just after they arrived at the end of the year to begin their first American tour.

Steven Tyler: I think Henry Smith told us he was leaving to go with Led Zeppelin around this time. I was devastated. Who was going to set up my drums at Murray's Clam Shack in Brattleboro, Vermont, that weekend? Then I realized that it was great for Henry to do this. Better than going to the moon with Neil Armstrong in an *Apollo* capsule full of babes!

Besides, at least I knew I'd have enough cymbals and drumsticks for the next two years, because Henry would give me what John Bonham threw out.

I was living on 21st Street in New York with a beautiful party girl named Lynn Collins in early 1969, at the same time I was working with my band in Boston. Late in January, Led Zeppelin played at the Boston Tea Party and I went to see them with Henry Smith. I sat cross-legged in the back of the room, smoking a joint, waiting to see whether Jimmy Page could live up to the hype of the huge advance Led Zeppelin had gotten. A couple of hours later, Led Zeppelin ran out of songs after they'd played their whole first album, so they had to do a bunch of Elvis Presley tunes because we wouldn't let them get offstage. They literally brought me to tears with the middle section of "Dazed and Confused." The dynamics and power were unbelievable! It was foreplay, fucking, and climaxing. Led Zeppelin was like great sex, and it was so heavy that it made me cry.

The only other time I ever cried over Led Zeppelin was an hour after the show, when Jimmy Page emerged from the dressing room with a beautiful girl on his arm. I would have been very impressed, except it was Lynn Collins, the girl I'd been living with up to that moment, and I was getting an incredible visual of my clothes being thrown out into the alley on 21st Street.

But Jimmy Page was such a motherfucker onstage that I couldn't hold it against him.

A few weeks later in New York, I met up with "Henry the Horse," as Zeppelin called him, and he took me over to Jimi Hendrix's studio, Electric Ladyland, where the band was recording its second album. Henry was John Bonham's drum tech, the place was empty, and I just sat down at Bonzo's drum set. Holy shit! I was a drummer at the time, and I could feel his power just sitting there at his drums. A little later I met Jimmy again and bought some red hash from a guy who had dropped by.

I think it was later that night we went over to the sound check at Madison Square Garden, where Led Zeppelin would play that night. When I got there, the road crew and the union people were all eating and the band hadn't arrived. The stage was empty and so were the 19,000 seats. The silence was deafening. I walked out to the stage and lay down, with my head hanging backward off the edge. I was overwhelmed by instant delusions of rock 'n' roll grandeur, imagining that I was roaming the land, raping and pillaging, disguised as an ambassador of rock. And I said to myself, *Someday a band of mine is gonna fill this fuckin' place.*

10: Groovy Way

Steven Tyler: That summer there was going to be a big rock festival up in Woodstock. Don Solomon, Ray Tabano, and I drove up in the station wagon and arrived at the site about fifty miles from actual Woodstock, New York, a day early, August 12 or something, before anyone was there. So I put on my English accent and told the guards we were Ten Years After and they let us drive into the main compound. We parked and set up our tent on a hill above where the Hog Farm had its kitchens.

Woodstock. We were ripped. Everyone was ripped. It was a disaster area from day one. Army helicopters dropped nets full of surplus hot dogs down to the Hog Farm, which was only cooking brown rice. Since there was no refrigeration, these huge piles of hot dogs soon began to rot, which isn't too cool if you're tripping your ass off, like I was. They had a truck full of cooking utensils they weren't using, so one morning I started to bang out rhythms on pots and pans. Ten minutes later I had thirty-five people banging along with me. An hour later there'd be two hundred people. It became a thing to do in the morning, like a tribal ritual or one of Robert Bly's men's clubs. It got pretty noisy.

There was a shortcut called Groovy Way between our camp and the stage. At night it had sparkling Christmas lights strung through the trees so you could see. It felt very mystical. There were lots of people selling pipes, sandals, and mescaline in these little booths. One guy was selling Tuinals and polished stones. He had a big homemade banner of a demon smoking a pipe, which I thought was so incredibly cool that I stole it while this guy was watching the Band or the Who one night.

The next day we ran out of money, and this guy had a big bag of Tuinals, so we went to his booth and Ray Tabano punched this guy out, grabbed his Tuinals, and we ran back up Groovy Way. Then someone stole our gas cap, and of course it rained and water got in the gas, so we were stranded. We couldn't leave if we wanted to. That's how come we had five days of peace and love instead of three. We were a day early and a day late at Woodstock.

Anyway, when it was all over, I went up to Lake Sunapee to hang out. The following week something happened that would change everything.

Zunk Buker: I had been in California for a while by then, out of touch with Steven and the scene in Sunapee. My partner and I had starved for our first few months in Southern California until we accidentally met the godfather of Mexican marijuana after we innocently returned a couple of extra kilos of pot that had been given to us by mistake. At three in the morning, this heavy Cuban cat and his bodyguard showed up at our house in the slums; instead of wanting to kill us, he told us that he'd heard a rumor that there were two crazy gringos in East San Diego who were honest. "What do you boys want? What can you handle? Hundred fifty keys a week? From now on, you guys are my lieutenants."

Six months later, we were rich.

In August 1969, we got 10,000 hits of Dealer's Choice LSD-25 from the legendary Brotherhood of Eternal Love in Laguna Beach. We headed for Woodstock to sell the acid. We only got as far as New Jersey, where we met some girls and missed the festival. A week later, I arrived in Sunapee and on Saturday night I stopped at The Barn to check out who was playing. It was a group called the Jam Band: Pudge Scott on drums, Tom Hamilton on bass, and Joe Perry on guitar. They were younger than me—the oldest, Joe, was only eighteen—but John Conrad said they were really good, so I decided to stick around.

There was this absolutely gorgeous young girl hanging around too. Her name was Elyssa Jerret, she was sixteen years old, and she said she was a friend of Joe Perry. I gave her a couple of hits of acid and later, just as the band was about to go on, I cleared a place for her on the bench next to me in front of the stage. Just then I felt someone squeezing in on my other side. Steven Tallarico! We hugged and the lights went down and the Jam Band started its set.

Two minutes into it, and these guys are *cooking*. "Red House," Jeff Beck, the MC5's "Ramblin' Rose." Here's Joe Perry: long hair in his eyes, black thick horn-rim glasses—*very strange* but with incredible charisma when he sang. Then they went into "Rattlesnake Shake" and the whole house began to rock. Joe literally couldn't tune his guitar at that point, but the band hit that slow-dragging Fleetwood Mac riff and I saw Steven's mouth open. He went pale. He couldn't take his eyes off Joe. The Jam Band was a little talent and a lotta magic and Steven felt it the minute he saw it.

The Jam Band finished "Rattlesnake Shake" with a crash and the crowd was cheering. Steven, Elyssa, and I were on our feet and dancing with everyone else. Tom Hamilton and Pudge were covered in sweat, but Joe seemed cool, calm, and collected, ignoring everyone except Elyssa, so beautiful you couldn't ignore her. I looked at Steven and he looked back at me. There was this moment. Something clicked. This little thing happened in an old barn in a remote corner of the United States on a summer night between Woodstock and Altamont in 1969 when the Great American Band got together. That's what was happening. As they started their next song, Steven leaned over and said, "Zunky, that's gonna be my next band."

So it was a historic night. Eventually Joe Perry took Elyssa home, still tripping. Next day she shows up at Joe's dock in her boat with a giant stuffed moosehead that she's touring around the lake. When I went over to the Jam Band's house behind The Barn later that night, Joe gives me one of his withering scowls and says,

"Hey man, what did you do to Elyssa?"

I stopped breathing for a second and said, "I gave her a couple hits of this acid."

"Pretty fuckin' funny . . . So, uh, whaddaya think of *Sweethearts of the Rodeo*?"

Flash! *or,* Joe Perry and Tom Hamilton in "America's Hometown Band"

2

I consider myself a hard rocker, traditionalist.

—Joe Perry

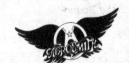

Hopedale, Massachusetts, lies in the Blackstone River valley about thirty miles southwest of Boston. It's a small town with a church on a village green, looking like it was painted by Norman Rockwell for the cover of The Saturday Evening Post, circa 1950s.

Hopedale was founded as a utopian society in the 1840s, during a *nationwide spiritual revival called the Great Awakening; its inspiration was the back-to-the-land commune movement based on philosophical transcendentalism preached by Ralph Waldo Emerson and his friend Henry David Thoreau over in Concord. Twenty-eight Hopedale founders settled five square miles of the "Dale" section of Milford, Massachusetts, as a farming and light industrial commune.*

Two brothers, Ebenezer and George Draper, started a business manufacturing automatic looms for the textile industries in Lowell and Lawrence that made cloth for the rest of the country. By 1856, the commune had failed and the Drapers owned the farm. In the 1880s the Draper Corporation had 3,000 employees and the political clout to secede from the town of Milford. The Drapers called their new town Hopedale because for decades it had been known as the "Dale of Hope" for new immigrants to America, who were able to find work and start new lives there.

Today Hopedale is a beautiful suburban town with public band concerts, a Little League parade, and kids riding bicycles on quiet streets. It's no longer a company town but a commuter community near Boston, very quiet and removed. It's the town where time stood still. Residents use words like "private" and "haven" to describe the atmosphere. Hopedale is basically what you want if you happen to be looking for the perfect American hometown. It's where Joe Perry grew up before he founded Aerosmith, America's hometown band, in September 1970.

1: Flash

Joe Perry: My father's family, the Pereiras, were fishing people from the Portuguese island of Madeira, simple folk who lived in dirt floor cottages until they migrated to Massachusetts, where there was plenty of work in the fishing and textile industries. My grandfather, Joseph Pereira, ended up in Lowell, Massachusetts, the textile mill town north of Boston, where my father, Anthony Perry, was born. He had thirteen brothers and sisters, most of whom died young, which is the way things were back then.

My father was in the Army Air Force in World War II, then afterward he trained as an accountant and met my mother, Mary Ursillo, whose family came from the area around Naples in southern Italy. I think it was my father who changed the family name to Perry. He wanted to mix in with postwar

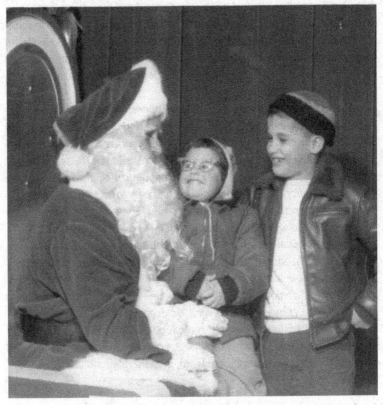

Joe Perry and sister Anne with Santa
(COURTESY ANNE PERRY)

American society. There was no Portuguese or Italian spoken in my house because both my father and mother wanted my sister Anne and me to grow up as Americans. So in a way, I was denied some of my heritage, the real ethnic part of their lives that some of my Italian cousins have.

My father went to work for the Draper Corporation in the early fifties, and we moved to the company town, Hopedale, Massachusetts, where my sister and I were brought up. We lived in a house the company built for its workers, most of them immigrants from Italy, Ireland, and Portugal. My parents were prominent in the community. My mom taught physical education in the public schools and my dad was elected several times as town treasurer. Although Hopedale was mostly Protestant, my mother raised us Catholic. I went to catechism class and did holy communion and confirmation and all that stuff, although I certainly wasn't pushed toward the priesthood the way some of my relatives were.

I would've made a lousy priest anyway.

We had a typical family. We'd load up in the car and go motoring, family trips to places in New England and Canada. On Veterans Day, my father would take us over to nearby Fort Devens to inspect the military hardware they had on display: tanks, machine artillery, machine guns, bazookas. So my love for guns goes way back to my childhood. People forget that our generation was raised with guns. Every kid in America was taught to shoot a .22 rifle by the time he was ten.

Later on, I wasn't real close to my father. He had cancer when he was young and had survived a serious operation, and no doubt he carried his own load of pain around with him. When I went off to school and didn't do very well, the gap between us widened. I have nice memories of him playing "Turkey in the Straw" on his harmonica once in awhile, but that's about it. So I kind of withdrew into my own world.

I had a radio in my room, a Heathkit radio that my dad gave me. It was a shortwave and AM set that got what it needed, WBZ and WMEX from Boston, the stations playing rock 'n' roll. I still have that old radio that brought Roy Orbison and Tina Turner into my life.

When I was little, we went to Lowell to visit with the Portuguese side of my family at Thanksgiving and Christmas. There was this "uncle"—a close friend of the family—who would pull his homemade ukelele out from behind the couch and play. I always got him to play this little guitar and I'd stare at his hands. I thought what he was doing was fascinating and really cool. Then, when I was six years old, the young guy next door and his friends would get together and play early rock 'n' roll—"Don't Be Cruel," "Rock Around the Clock," "Tutti Frutti," whatever was big in 1956. One guy played electric guitar, another guy played accordion, and they set up trap drums in the kitchen and just played. I thought it was so cool and still do, because it was folk music, just people sitting by the stove and playing, no different from a tribe of Aborigines sitting by the campfire banging sticks together.

I was really impressed. It was the first time I ever heard a live rock 'n' roll band.

A little before this, my parents bought some land on a lake in New Hampshire. We'd live there in the summer and my dad would commute. Sunapee was pretty dead by the time we started going there, no longer jumping like the twenties to the forties. Water-skiing was a big activity, and I remember going to a water-ski show when I was eight years old. The announcer came on the loudspeaker and said there was a medical emer-

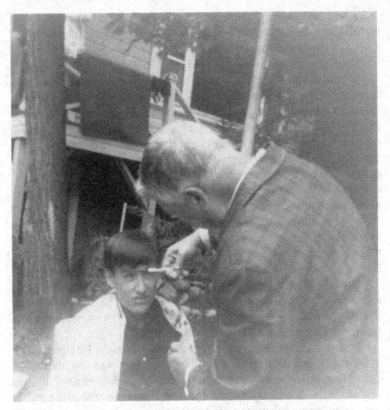

Joe Perry getting a haircut from his grandfather at Lake Sunapee
(PERRY COLLECTION)

gency and asked if there was a doctor present. When I got home a few hours later, all the adults were very somber, and my father took me aside and told me that my grandfather had drowned in the lake that afternoon. He'd had a couple drinks, went fishing, and fell out of our canoe.

As far back as I can remember, it was a struggle being in school. In fifth grade it was: "Joe, your grades are bad, you can do better than this, blah blah blah." I just wasn't a good fit. It used to make me feel bad, but now I know it's a pretty common syndrome. And I was way into music, taking lessons and everything, but the guitar was the first instrument I really liked.

When I was nine, I told my parents I wanted a guitar and they ended up buying me a Silvertone from Sears Roebuck for $14.95. It had a 45-rpm record that told you how to tune it. I'm left-handed and at first I tried to play that way; then I realized I was playing it upside down. So I learned to play right-handed because the guitar book said to hold it that way. Then I was running around the house and fell down and the neck of the Silvertone broke! My father fixed it, but it wasn't the same.

A year went by, the Beatles came to America, and now I wanted a guitar again. I played the broken Silvertone until I got a better acoustic guitar for my birthday. All this time my mother was trying to get me to play the piano because they didn't want me to play guitar, which meant the same thing to them as a tattoo and a hot rod. The assumption was I'd come to no good if I played that guitar. Then they gave in and said, "Well, if you want to play it so bad, you're going to take lessons." They sent me to this old Italian guy down the street. He was showing me classical flamenco-type stuff on an acoustic guitar, while I was thinking Chuck Berry. But they weren't going to get me an electric guitar, so I took a lesson from this guy. The next week my school bus drove by his house and I saw a hearse parked in his driveway. He'd had a heart attack. So my guitar teacher died.

Then I found this guy in town who gave lessons and had a band, Steve Rose, the local hot guitar player, very schooled, and I took some lessons from him. This was like the early prime of the Beatles, 1964 or '65, and I was really getting interested in the guitar, and not like a toy. I traded records with my friends and really learned by playing along with the records. I started to have a goal in my mind.

I wanted an electric guitar. I even mowed lawns, which I hated more than anything in the world, to try to save money to buy this Gibson I had in mind. I remember one Christmas I didn't get the electric guitar that I was so sure, so *positive* was going to be under the tree. I was even looking under the *beds*. It was like, *They knew what I wanted. Why didn't I get it?* But my parents felt strongly that it wasn't cool. One year they gave me a tape recorder instead and it was like, *What am I gonna do with this?* So I went around recording other bands, making tapes for them and stuff.

My first band was in Hopedale when I had my acoustic guitar. I think we called it Chimes of Freedom. This is the first year of the Beatles, 1964. We played together for a few years in Hopedale with John Alden and Tony Niro, playing guitars and pretending we were the Beatles. We'd sing Dylan songs and Byrds songs and one time we actually played at a party and sang in the corner, which was pretty amazing the first time, very nerve-wracking to play in public, and it wasn't very good. John Alden was a big Dave Clark Five fan because he played drums; he got us tickets to see Dave Clark at the Boston Arena. It was one of those Caravan of Stars shows with Gene Pitney and other people I forget. Everyone got twenty minutes, the first big concert I ever went to.

Eventually I got my electric guitar. I had an uncle on my mother's side who owned a music store in Lawrence, Massachusetts, Constantino's Music. Anyway, my mother took me there. She wouldn't get me a Gibson, but she got me a Guild Starfire 5. Then I met Dave Meade, who was a bass player, and he turned me on to *Chuck Berry on Top*, turned me on to *Having a Rave Up with the Yardbirds*, turned me on to John Mayall's *Bluesbreakers* album. I was off and running and never once looked back.

I didn't care about school. If I wasn't holed up in my room with my guitar, I'd read scuba diving magazines because my other ambition was marine biology. In the tenth grade my grades were so bad they thought a private school was my only hope of ever getting into college. So I took my sophomore year over again at Vermont Academy.

Looking back, I was probably unteachable. So I ended up latching on to the other ne'er-do-wells and weirdos like myself and I got a little band called Just Us together after they let me rehearse down in the basement of the dorm. Then I got into fights with the floor master, who would come down and literally take the guitar out of my hands and tell me I couldn't play anymore. It's the same old story about a kid who was obsessed with something. Anyway, I lasted there until it was almost time to graduate.

In the summers, I needed money like every kid. I hated mowing lawns, so I got a job operating the big Hobart steam dishwasher at the Anchorage, an ice cream parlor in Sunapee Harbor. I remember looking out the screened window one day and thinking, *Oh, that's Steven Tallarico*. I had seen his band play at The Barn and he had that song "The Sun" on our jukebox. I never talked to him or anything like that, but I knew who he was. Everybody in Sunapee did, with his Mod clothes from Greenwich Village and all that shit. Steven would come in with his bands and they'd act like they figured rock stars are supposed to, throwing food, real loud and obnoxious, wearing Carnaby Street outfits, the whole trip in this little town that looked up to them as the local rock stars. Then they'd leave and I had to go out to the booth and clean up after them.

All this time I was in little bands. I had a band in prep school, where we played some of the dances, a band at home in Hopedale with Dave Meade, and a band in New Hampshire with Tom Hamilton.

The first time we made any money was at Dave's brother's frat in Amherst, Mass. Dave calls up and says, "If we play at this fraternity house, they'll give us all the beer we want and five bucks each!"

I said, and I can remember these words coming out of my mouth: "Oh. You mean we get paid for this too?"

"Yeah! Come up right now."

So we lugged our stuff a hundred miles to Amherst in the family station

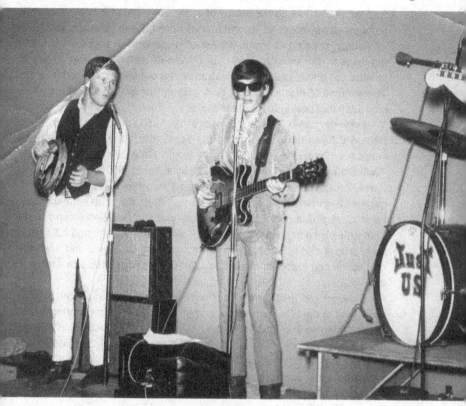

Joe Perry's prep school band, Just Us
(COURTESY ANNE PERRY)

wagon and played a whole bunch of blues. Dave Carchio was the drummer. That was where we got paid for the first time and could consider ourselves a band. We called it Flash, and Dave Meade started booking us. He'd go, "I know who we can talk to so we can rent the town hall for fifty bucks; they'll provide the police, we'll get somebody to take tickets. We'll run our own dances and split the money up." This arrangement lasted for years. In fact, when Aerosmith first started, Dave would book us in my hometown places, while Steven had his agent up in New Hampshire booking us up there.

"Flash" was a whole concept, an artistic submovement of the sixties that began in London in 1964 when the leaper energy of Cockney East London met the Art College Dandy style of the King's Road in Chelsea. Music fans know Flash as a style mostly of guitar playing, but it had its counterparts in fashion, haircuts, art, and movies as well. Flash was explosive built-up energy, popping at you in a blast of white light. It was feedback and psychedelic drones with more than a taste of R&B. Flash was a way of holding the guitar and moving with it, acting out the power of the music. The epitome of Flash was Jeff Beck playing his guitar behind his head, crouching and posing like a great dancer.

I saw the movie *Blowup* in Boston in 1967 and I got goose bumps when I heard the feedback that started the Yardbirds' "Stroll On," the retitled version of "Train Kept A-Rollin' " in the movie. *Blowup* itself is an extremely Flash artifact, the story of a fashion photographer in 1965 Swinging London [based on David Bailey] who may (or may not) have accidentally photographed a murder. Michelangelo Antonioni's film follows his surreal adventures through London's hippest scenes, and the Jeff Beck/Jimmy Page Yardbirds play a band in the film, which also had one of the first full frontal nude scenes and a Herbie Hancock jazz soundtrack. It was and is a very cool movie and it had an incredible influence on everything when it came out.

Flash was a rite of autodestruction: Pete Townshend smashing his guitar in front of the Who's Op Art backdrops, and Jimi Hendrix lighting up his at the Monterey Pop Festival that summer. Flash was Keith Moon's bass drum explosions and single-roll fusillades, Kenny Jones of the Small Faces, "puddin' basin" haircuts, and, later, rooster-style shag hairdos after Rod Stewart got one. It was a new kind of music, wild and kinetic, *not pop.* It was the coolest music of the sixties and sparked a whole fascination with the new English scene.

Up till then, I had been a confirmed Beatles fan, spending countless hours in the backseat of my parents' car on the way to Sunapee, driving them nuts playing Beatles songs, trying to figure them out. I had this image of the Beatles as four happy-go-lucky guys, with the Rolling Stones as their shadow side, more of a gang, "Paint It, Black," gloom and doom. The poor man's Beatles. The Yardbirds were like a way out of this, and Jeff Beck was incredibly influential to my development as a player. I spent years studying the Yardbirds, *Fresh Cream, Are You Experienced?*, John Mayall's *A Hard Road*, and, later, Jeff Beck's *Truth* and Ten Years After.

Aerosmith still plays "Train Kept A-Rollin' " today. It's hard stuff to get out of your blood. It's been in mine since 1967, the days of my bands Flash and Plastic Glass, a band I was in at Lake Sunapee that summer with my friend from nearby New London, Mr. Tom Hamilton . . .

2: Live Free or Die

Tom Hamilton: "Don't make a constant noise."

This is my father talking. My brother Scott and I are up to our usual war in the backseat, and my father, a somewhat taciturn Air Force colonel, is telling us to pipe down.

"Don't make a constant noise." He wasn't mean about it. We were just too loud, whether it was wrecking the house or playing Ventures albums at top volume.

I was born in Colorado Springs, Colorado, where my father was stationed at the time, 1951. He was born in Chicago and was a real child of the Depression in the 1930s. A lot of his attitudes about survival come from those days, and I think some of them got handed down to me, because to this day I'm a compulsive worrier and real conservative. Hey, I was raised in New Hampshire.

During World War II, my dad was a fighter pilot in the Army Air Force, a squadron leader in Burma. To me, he was a war hero and I grew up totally fascinated with the whole Eighth Air Force thing. I'd fall asleep as a kid pretending I was the waist gunner on a B-17 Flying Fortress. What made the teenage version of me tick: World War II, the Beatles, and the Three Stooges—the three basic elements of life when I was a kid.

At some point my dad left the Air Force and got into commercial aviation, flying Constellations for a while. This was a little after I was born. But then he quit and went back into the Air Force, so we moved around quite a bit. I never heard him talk about it—my dad is the definition of the word "stoic"—but I think he had one of those love/hate relationships with the Air Force that reminds me of the one I have with Aerosmith. I think we all feel that way—a whole lotta love and a little bit of hate. (Maybe "hate" is too strong a word.)

Anyway, we went from Colorado Springs to Virginia because my father was working at the Pentagon. I started kindergarten on Cape Cod, but after a year we moved to Wayland, Massachusetts, in the western suburbs of Boston. We lived there for maybe three years, the highlight of my childhood. We had a great neighborhood, I could ride my bike all over the place, I had tons of friends, and I stayed there until the third grade. It was classic fifties suburbia with the grill on the backyard patio and *South Pacific, My Fair Lady*, and Harry Belafonte on the big hi-fi speaker in the living room. My parents had tons of friends and would party their brains out and I just recall it as a fun time.

Then my dad left the Air Force, and we moved to Weston, the next town over. I wasn't thrilled because I had to leave my friends in Wayland. It was hard. I was there through sixth grade and it was a weird period. First I came down with scarlet fever and almost died in the Chelsea Naval Hospital. I still remember the dreams and delirium and the excruciating pain when the doctors did an emergency cut-down on my ankle in the middle of the night. I guess they figured I didn't need anesthesia. It felt like a blowtorch and I still have the scar. Then I broke my arm playing bombardment in the school gym and had to sleep sitting up in a heavy cast for seven or eight weeks.

I must have been about thirteen or fourteen. I remember having the cast when the Beatles first appeared on *The Ed Sullivan Show* in 1964.

My brother Scott played guitar and listened to the Ventures all the time on the hi-fi. This was a speaker cabinet shaped like a giant bowl, which my dad built into a kind of coffee table, really cool. My father was way into music: Frank Sinatra and Broadway musicals, all kinds of things. A lot of times I'll be reading about musicians I respect—Paul McCartney or Pete Townshend—and they talk about how their parents were very musical and I'll think, *What a spectacular advantage these guys had over me.* Steven Tyler, for instance, growing up under his father's piano.

What my parents gave me was just the love of music. If my parents weren't playing their records, it was my brother playing the Ventures, who were incredible. Then the Beatles came along. I started to buy their singles, invite my friends over, and we'd try to figure out the songs. I had two little Motorola transistor radios, not much bigger than a cigarette pack, that I'd arrange on my nightstand so that the waves would cross and the sound would get really big.

Anyway, Boston was an "English" town, very receptive to any new band coming from Britain. I never had the background in Motown or soul music—James Brown—that a lot of my contemporaries did. I just went from the Liverpool-type bands and the Rolling Stones to the Yardbirds and the next wave of loud English bands like Cream and Jeff Beck.

I went to New London High School in New Hampshire. My father finally left the Air Force and took a job helping my uncle start a factory up there, Pine Tree Castings, to make parts for the gun manufacturer Sturm-Ruger, which was owned by my mother's family. So we moved into an old yellow farmhouse on the corner of County Road and Little Sunapee Road in New London, with a spectacular view of nearby Mount Kearsarge. It was a postcard New England scene, but I was in shock. Until then I'd had the Beatles and I'd had Boston.

So when I was a teenager, I had to hitchhike—or I'd have to ask my mother to let me take the car down to Boston. I used to *sneak* the car to Boston when my parents were away. If some band I really liked was playing at the Psychedelic Supermarket, this ex-garage rock joint on Commonwealth Avenue near Kenmore Square, I would go down for the day and visit the head shops, and this was before I ever smoked any pot. I just wanted to know what was going on. It was strawberry incense, black light rooms, and underground comic books like Zap Comix and Gilbert Shelton's Fabulous Furry Freak Brothers from San Francisco. There was this whole new culture that was happening, but nowhere near New Hampshire at that point.

I was this innocent kid. I still thought it was just sleazy people who did drugs, but I was getting fascinated by the whole mind thing—altered states of consciousness—because it was already so tied into music. It also tied into my interest in science fiction, surrealism, fantasy, alternate universes—anything strange or paranormal.

Are You Experienced? No, but I wanted to be. Timothy Leary was saying, "Turn on, tune in, drop out," so eventually I wanted some pot to see what it was like. It was just something you had to experiment with. I never went for the dropout part. I thought that was for losers. I didn't think you had to give the finger to everything in life.

The ironic thing was I *was* pretty much of a dropout.

At first I really enjoyed high school, at least up to a point. I was on the tennis team, in the drama club, the student council. I got elected to stuff. I was all set up to be part of the Establishment, if I wanted it. Instead I started to grow my hair, which got me in trouble, so I just skated through the rest of it. I was like a smart kid who should have gotten good grades, but I thought studying was for boring people destined to live boring lives.

Then I did some acid with these five girls and really got in trouble. These girls and I dropped some acid in New London and I guess we weren't too discreet about it. I forget what happened, but I think one of the girls—did you ever see the Richard Pryor routine where he's on acid and has forgotten how to breathe?—told her mother. The mother dropped a note to the police chief and it got really weird. We weren't exactly arrested. Some kid came up to me in school a few days later and says, "Hey, you're in big trouble, man. You better call your mom."

I went home at four o'clock in the afternoon. My mother's in tears. The police had just been to the house, and when they came back, they told me they were going to prosecute me as a juvenile for dealing acid to these five girls. They told my terrified parents not to hire a lawyer because we wouldn't need one, it was an open-and-shut case. In my hindsight fantasies,

I hear myself yelling, "YOU BETTER GET ME A FUCKIN' LAWYER BE-CAUSE WE'RE GONNA BEAT THIS!"

But they didn't, because we were all scared, and I was like mortified that I was bringing this big load of shame onto my family and frightening them so badly. It was probably the first "acid bust" in that part of New Hampshire.

Here's what happened. As the "dealer," I got a $300 fine. The girls got $100 each. They also gave me a curfew that lasted six months. I got kicked off the tennis team, the drama club, the student council. They almost threw me out of school, but cooler heads prevailed.

I had to prove to the town authorities that I worked off my fine. I started mowing my father's lawn and then this great guy who had a nursery in my neighborhood hired me. The whole town was shitting on me, but he hired me right away and I worked it off, which took forever because $300 in those days was like $1,500 now. After that it was Tom versus the town in everyone's mind, including mine. I was the local outlaw. If there was a robbery over at Kingridge—the local ski area—people thought I'd assembled my gang of five zombie women. It was us on acid busting into the lodge on ski mobiles and blowing the safe.

All this happened near the end of my junior year, the spring of 1969. Then summertime came and Joe Perry returned to Sunapee from Boston. Every summer Joe and I would put a band together and that's how I worked off the rest of the fine: playing gigs with Joe and Pudge Scott.

When I was a little kid and we lived in Wayland, my brother had a Strat, a Fender Stratocaster, and this must have been the first electric guitar I ever played. He had a twin reverb amp, and when he wasn't home, I used to sneak into his room and turn the amp up. It was so loud it would scare the living shit out of me, but I learned to play around with it. Then my brother taught me my first guitar chords and kind of got me started. After that I taught myself. I think I had a guitar, but I can't remember what kind it was. I do remember that we had this great instructional album, *Play Guitar with the Ventures*, that had its own tablature that taught you how to play "Pipeline" and "Walk—Don't Run."

The first guitar I remember owning was a Fender Precision bass. In a way, Bill Wyman of the Rolling Stones was my bass teacher. I'd play along to "Under My Thumb" and "It's All Over Now" and that's how I developed a feel for it. My uncle gave us this Wollensack tape recorder and my brother and I figured out how to do all kinds of cool stuff with it—overdubbing with "sound-on-sound," a primitive multitracking system. It would also produce a lot of static: We'd just smash it on the side and continue. So I used to tape myself and play along with it. One day my friend Guy Williams, who played guitar, and I recorded ourselves on this Wollensack playing "It's All Over Now," and when I listened to the playback I just freaked. I thought it sounded so fucking cool that I bonded with the whole idea of playing the bass.

Most people learn how to play bass by copying their favorite bands and learning their parts, but I never really did that. I'd just learn the chords and stop there because I was lazy. I'd make up my own bass parts that would somehow sound like I knew what I was doing, but in retrospect I was probably playing a lot of fucked-up notes and sounding out of key. But the bands I was in always went for *feel* rather than precision. The main thing was that I was always interested in percussion, and I saw the bass guitar as the link between the drums and the rest of the band.

Before I met Joe Perry, I joined a band called Sam Citrus and the Merciless Tangerine in New London. Everybody wanted to play guitar in this band, but they already had two guitar players and they needed a bass. I wanted to be in a band, and as far as I knew that was the only one in our part of New Hampshire, so I borrowed the band's bass guitar and my brother gave me a few pointers.

There was no Sam Citrus, but we did dress up like tangerines. Our gimmick was to wear orange clothes. We'd get white clothes, dye 'em orange like Hare Krishna stuff, and wear this onstage. My French teacher was our keyboard player, and the first gig we ever did was at his frat house. I'm like fifteen years old, we're wading through beer cans, and all of a sudden my French teacher becomes this total *lunatic*, dancing on top of his keyboard. I thought, *Whoa, this is cool. I must be a man now.*

Anyway, that's how I learned. It must have been the following summer that I met Dave Scott, who was a twelve-year-old drummer whose family had a summer house on the lake. He and I started playing, and through him I met Joe Perry, and for the next four years we had bands together in the summertime.

3: The Jam Band

David "Pudge" Scott: I was four or five years younger than Tom Hamilton and Joe Perry, but I might have been playing drums at that point longer than they'd been playing guitar. My older brother was a drummer—he later played with the bands Earth Opera and Seatrain around Boston—and he probably set me down in front of the drums when I was three years old.

I was old for my age, but I was still only twelve when I teamed up with Joe and Tom for the first time.

We had a summer house next to the Sunapee Yacht Club, and Tom lived in New London. I know the first time I met him was at a spin-the-bottle party on Soonippi Beach, and we talked about music and got to be friends and talked about playing music together sometime. This was in maybe 1966.

The following summer I met Joe. I had heard about him through a friend of my brother's who went to Vermont Academy and said Joe was this really good guitarist. So one day I went up to him at the Anchorage and asked him if he was Joe Perry and he said he was. I told him about wanting to get into a band and he said, "Great, why don't you come up to my house and we'll listen to this new Jimi Hendrix record I just got, *Are You Experienced?*"

So that's what we did: sat in his room, played guitar, in awe of the Hendrix and Cream and Doors records we were listening to. Joe was a soft-spoken, down-to-earth kid, a typical guy, just a little more rebellious than the others. For one thing, he had longer hair—unusually long—and so he looked like more of a rebel. He looked tough, but he wasn't. He was just a nice guy and if you played music you just really wanted to be in a band with him.

That's how we put together Pipe Dream in the summer of 1967 in the basement of my parents' house. It was me, Joe, Tom, and a friend of Tom's from New London named Kathy Lowe. She sang the two Jefferson Airplane songs ["White Rabbit" and "Somebody to Love"] that every American band had to do that summer.

Tom Hamilton: Pudge's parents were real liberal and they used to let us rehearse down in the basement. That's the first time I ever heard Joe Perry play the guitar. He played on the same level as me and Pudge—crudely—but we had fun because we could play Stones songs, Beatles songs. We smiled when we realized we could play them all the way through because everybody knew the chords. Pudge wasn't a fancy drummer, but he had *great* time and was so steady, way ahead of where he might have been at his age. So we had a lot of fun and it was exciting because we were gonna put a band together and become part of this whole fun scene. We needed somebody to sing, so we got this girl Kathy Lowe, who was really good. She used to sing folk songs with her sister over at the local college.

This was Pipe Dream. Summer of '67. We didn't do that many gigs, but we got a couple of jobs on a boat that used to tour around the lake. I had an incredible time, but then in late August the nights got cooler and

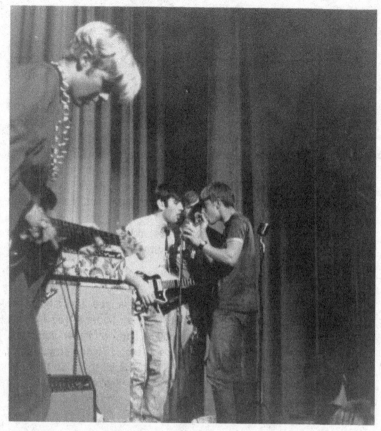

**Tom Hamilton, left, jamming with friends, New London, New Hampshire, 1967.
This band became Plastic Glass when Joe Perry joined.**
(HAMILTON COLLECTION)

the first leaves started to turn and the summer kids had to go back to Boston and we had to break up.

That winter I got together with a kid from my high school named John McGuire. He played harmonica, and we had a one-time-only band called Plastic Glass that played in the school auditorium. I wore a long flowing graduation robe I'd found in a closet and a chain around my neck crafted out of curtain rings. John McGuire was a grade or two older than me. He turned me on to blues and R&B, filtered through the Bluesbreakers, Jimi, Cream. He was more in contact with this outrageous music than I was because there was no outlet for it in New Hampshire, no radio stations, no *Rolling Stone*.

When Joe Perry returned for the summer of 1968, we got together again and formed Plastic Glass with me, Pudge, Joe, and John McGuire, who became the lead singer. He was an intense kid who really wanted to stick to the roots of the blues. We got little gigs at Slope 'N' Shore on Pleasant Lake in New London, at King's Ridge ski area, and even at The Barn. We played "Peter Gunn," Fleetwood Mac stuff, Yardbirds, Hendrix, "Train Kept A-Rollin' " because Joe Perry was way into *Blowup*. It was the Summer of Romilar, because all the kids were drinking this cough syrup. Whatever they replaced the codeine that used to be in it with was very psychedelic. You drank the stuff and you were a zombie. The greatest thing was that you'd wake up next morning and feel great, and you *definitely* wouldn't be coughing.

Anyway, Plastic Glass broke up at the end of the summer, but we would have anyway because John McGuire was a purist who looked down on our more Flash aspirations.

Joe Perry: John McGuire was a blues fanatic, a purist, and we were totally into the rock star side of it. We'd sit under a tree and talk about Boston and getting really big amplifiers and, you know, *doing it*.

And John would go, dripping with contempt, "You mean you guys wanna wear those funny white shoes?" Because all these Englishmen we liked wore white Capezios, which were basically ballet shoes.

And we said, "Yeah! That's *exactly* what we want to do." And John would just shake his head and moan, "No, no."

Tom Hamilton: An interesting thing happened the following summer, 1969, when it was time to put the band back together. John McGuire was there, but Pudge and I decided Joe's playing was too harsh for us. In the winter I'd been playing guitars with my friend Guy Williams and really had a blast, so that summer Pudge and I said, "Joe, we don't think we're gonna play with you this summer because we're going to play with Guy."

Joe looks at us and says, "Oh, yeah? Really?"

One day we're down at Guy's house, practicing. Joe comes over, plugs in, and proceeds to put on the most outrageous display of fucking guitar incredibleness that I'd ever seen in my life! He had practiced his ass off all winter and had all these moves with the whammy bar and he was playing all these outrageous sounds. The rest of us stopped playing. We just stood there watching this solo performance with our mouths open, and I understood that Joe had taken a huge leap. I don't know if it was motivation or just timing, but it only took ten seconds for Pudge and I to realize that it was back to Joe.

It shows a lot about Joe Perry. When he's determined about something, you better keep away from the traps because you're totally gonna get your feet cut off. So we put the group back together and called it the Jam Band. We played at Slope 'N' Shore and various boathouses around the lake, at camps, the Yacht Club, a few parties, and later became the house band at The Barn for $30 a night. John McGuire was in and out of it, and we lived for awhile at a summer house his parents used to rent out, with Robert Grasmere and John Andrews, who lugged our gear and were our buddies.

If you were a kid in Sunapee back in those days, there were two places your parents didn't want you to go: The Barn and the Tallarico place. Steven Tallarico was older than us and one of those kids who was a local legend every summer. I remember we couldn't get into The Barn for Chain Reaction, either because we were too young—it was a B.Y.O.B. place—or because it was too jammed. So we listened out in the parking lot. The band had a van and we'd watch the guy mix the sound from the inside of the van, out in the parking lot. To us, this was the Big Leagues. We'd stand outside and listen to them and just go, "Fuckin' A," because Steven was a total professional and anyone with eyes in their heads could see this guy was going to be a major star someday.

That first summer of the Jam Band I was more or less on my own because I'd left home after too many battles with my dad. My mother was planning to take a trip to Russia. All winter I'd been talking to her:

"Mom, when the summertime comes, I want to grow my hair long." And she said, "Fine." My father would be in the room but tuned out, and he didn't really understand that we had this agreement that Tom was going to grow his hair long because he was making money in a band and it was like his summer job. The minute my mother left, he put two dollars on the table and said, "Go get your hair cut. Today."

"Dad, wait a minute, there's an agreement, I don't have to cut . . ."

"This is my house. Are you defying me in my house?"

"I don't want to defy you, I just don't want to get a haircut."

"Son, you either get a haircut or you leave."

And I said, as calmly as I could, "Fine, I'll leave." So I lived on my own that whole summer. I stayed at people's houses, at Joe's house for instance when I could. Not that his mother was into harboring another long-haired rock 'n' roll-obsessed teenager. Some nights I was basically homeless.

There was this rundown flophouse nearby called the Harbor Hotel, and I got a job there as a chambermaid for two dollars an hour plus room and board. So I lived there for the rest of the summer, cleaned rooms during the day and had my band with Joe and Pudge at night. Sometimes we'd hitch into Boston to see a band. I remember getting off Route 93 on the elevated part of Storrow Drive that went right by Boston Garden and Joe saying, "Tom, can you *imagine* actually *playing* there someday?" That was our pipe dream.

It was near the end of that summer, sometime in August, that we were playing at The Barn and Steven Tallarico came to see us.

4: Gold-Top Les Paul

Joe Perry: My academic career ended in 1968 over the hair thing. People today take long hair for granted, but in 1968 there was almost a civil war in the country and having long hair was considered disrespectful to authority and an act of rebellion. If you were a kid, it was serious fuckin' business. So you learn all the tricks. You don't wash it for three weeks, plaster it down with Brylcreem, and stick it under your collar. I'd wash it when I went home on the weekend.

I never pushed my parents as far as hair was concerned, but it was the final straw at prep school, a big deal after they'd almost thrown me out for drugs. Anyway, I got really sick during senior year and I ended up in the infirmary. My hair had gotten real long, the longest in the school, maybe the longest in that part of Vermont. When I was about to get out of the infirmary, someone told me they were gonna make me cut my hair before history, which was my first class. I said I wasn't gonna cut my hair and it became a showdown, High Noon at first period. I made all the motions of going to class and the headmaster stands there and says, "Joe, you can't come in here if your hair is that long." I said, "OK, see you later," and walked out.

I just went back to my room and thought about all the stuff in the back of my mind that I really wanted to do. I called up my mother and just freaked out. I said, "Mom, you gotta come right away. I'm through here. Please come up and get me *today.*"

So she came and got me. I had quit school about three months short of graduation. I took a couple of weeks off at home to just cool out, then I figured I'd finish out my senior year at Hopedale High. I went in, shook hands with the principal, and he said, "There shouldn't be any problem. If you keep up your grades, you'll graduate in June." I was really relieved. As I was leaving, he said, "Oh, by the way, before you come in, do something about your hair."

I never went back. That afternoon I went to the personnel office of what was now called the Draper Division. (My father still worked there, but he would soon move on to the Bell & Howell Company.) I applied for a job in the factory. A week later I was working in the foundry. This is in the early spring of 1969.

A big company, the Rockwell Corporation, had bought the Draper Corporation in 1967 and the million-square-foot redbrick mill building still employed almost the whole town. They put me to work helping to pour molten steel in the foundry part of the factory for $2.38 an hour, the minimum wage.

I didn't see any daylight for eight hours a day, but I liked it because I was working to get money for equipment for my band. My fellow workers were immigrants from Portugal and Italy and most of them didn't speak English. The ones who did called me a hippie and made fun of my long hair. So I had to deal with all these redneck greasers all the time, people who *had* to work there because they couldn't find any other job. These guys were so rotten they used to throw things at me.

With no skills or high school diploma, they just gave me the lowest fuckin' job in this jungle of white-hot steel and sand, cleaning up shit, and I'd get burned and cut all the time, and at the end of the day I smelled pretty bad. I'd blow my nose when I got home and all the dirt and dust I'd been breathing all day came pouring out. My hair was full of gritty sand from the blast furnace. I learned a lot in that factory about patience. Sometimes you just have to live day to day. After three months, I pestered the foreman about a better job. He asked me if I could read and write.

This made me think about what I was doing. But I couldn't go back to school. I had this vision of supporting myself and getting a band together. So I worked five days a week. I painted my bedroom red and installed red lightbulbs. I started making enough money to get a car, a little MG. On Friday I went home, took a long shower, jumped in my car, and headed for Boston.

The place to go back then was the Boston Tea Party on Berkeley Street in the South End. It opened in late 1967 and was Boston's local version of the Fillmore East or the Avalon Ballroom in San Francisco. It was an old synagogue. It had a psychedelic light show behind the bands and a pretty good sound system.

All the big bands came through—Jeff Beck, the Doors, Big Brother, Spirit, Led Zeppelin, the MC5, the Who, and especially Fleetwood Mac, the English blues group that was almost the Tea Party's house band in 1968 and 1969. Their founder and guitarist Peter Green was an incredible player, the equal of Eric Clapton and Jimmy Page. I stood at the edge of the Tea Party's stage on many a night, staring at Peter Green doing "Stop Messin' 'Round," "I Loved Another Woman," "Oh Well," "Searching for Madge," and "Rattlesnake Shake."

On one of these weekends, I saw the Jeff Beck Group. This must have been late in 1968. It was Jeff Beck, Rod Stewart, Ronnie Wood, and the drummer, Mickey Waller. I'm down in front, watching Jeff in total awe. No one who was there ever forgot those early Jeff Beck shows. Rod Stewart, on his first trip to America, was so shy he sang from behind the amps. Next day I'm sitting in the foundry, looking at this fuckin' pile of metal coming down, and I'm thinking, *That's the guitar I want.* So I called up my cousin who had the music store and said I wanted a gold-top Les Paul as soon as humanly possible. It turned out that was the only kind they were making. Jeff was actually playing an old 'Burst, a '59, but they were just starting to reissue the gold ones. So I got one of the first ones they reissued, with the cream-colored single-coil pickups. I ran it through a couple of Fender amps that I piled up. I blew out my amps constantly and had to get new ones, but I had the money because I saved a little every week after spending the rest on my car and gas.

I ended up working in this horror show for two years. I got my high school equivalency diploma. If you can't pass that after five years of high school, you're in deep shit. Anyway, I got it. That winter I got a slightly better job in the paint shop—a dangerous, vicious place because it was piecework and you had to move fast. You were dealing with acid baths and bad fumes in there, jagged metal, people getting maimed. Some of the poor guys are walking around half-blind, and meanwhile I'm walking around thinking about being a rock star, about being in a band. I'd wake up in the morning to go to work and I wouldn't even drink a cup of coffee to get going. I'd put my Ten Years After album on the turntable and drop the needle on "I'm Going Home," and I'd be up and pumped for the rest of the day, thinking about doing what they did, having this music in my head and being able to control the output myself.

All this reminds me of when I had my first "medicinal" drink before going onstage one night when Flash played the Hopedale town hall. I had a couple pulls of Southern Comfort and all of a sudden I felt like I could do anything, as long as I had this bottle nearby. This *dawned* on me, because I'd always been the quiet kid hanging around in the back, and the stuff in this bottle just pulled me out of that so I could *perform.* This was something I could use. Now I had the three things I needed: a guitar, an amp, and a bottle.

When the summer of 1969 came, I quit the factory to go up to Sunapee to play with Tom. I told my foreman that I'd be back in the fall and he just laughed.

That was the summer Steven came to see us at The Barn.

Steven Tyler: I can't remember why I went to The Barn that night to see Joe's band. I wasn't expecting much and neither was the chick I was with. Anyway, I saw them, and I'm listening carefully, and I'm thinking, *That's it. They suck.* They couldn't sing, they couldn't tune their instruments, they were sloppy, and they just sucked.

But . . . *they were great.*

They had a groove that was better than any sex I'd ever had up to that point. They were playing all my favorite licks, stuff from "Route 66" in the middle of "Let Me Love You Baby." Joe would start playing the stutter from "Whole Lotta Love," but it would turn into "Shapes of Things." I actually experienced what I can only describe as an epiphany during a song called "Rattlesnake Shake." There was just something about the way Joe played it, this whole fuckin' *train* feeling. The energy was just so intense. I looked and it was like Joe Perry *was* the electric guitar. I thought, *If I can put that energy together with something that my father gave me, that classical influence, we might have something.*

Look at this guy . . . I knew a kindred spirit and fellow traveler when I saw one. Something in my deepest being knew instinctively that if I could get into a groove with him and start writing songs, we could combine what I knew with this *looseness* that they had.

I listened even harder as they went into "Milk Cow Blues," which they got from a Kinks album. They were horrible! It was so bad it was good. These guys didn't care, weren't interested in playing the right notes. It was just this feel they had. I knew they had probably practiced maybe thirty songs in their not-very-long lives; out of them they pulled maybe ten to do a show: "Red House," MC5, "Gimme Some Lovin' " with a wild Joe Perry solo that *shook the building*. They did Jeff Beck stuff from *Beck-ola*. Joe did "Goin' Home to See My Baby" and it was better than Ten Years After. They were just so far out. After the show I thought, *I've been playing with rigid pros for years, doing other people's songs, but these guys are newcomers and they might be open to new things, which is what I'm looking for.*

Next afternoon I'm mowing the lawns at Trow-Rico Lodge. The big Gravely mower was real loud, but I heard a noise and when I looked up I see Joe Perry sitting in our driveway in his little sports car. He's got dark glasses on. I killed the motor and went over and I blurted out, "Hey! Maybe someday we'll have a band together!"

I'll never forget saying that to him for the rest of my life. Those words are still in the trees and rocks around Trow-Rico. They heard me say it. Those words are still echoing there in the woods by the lake.

I don't remember what else was said, except I told him I really liked his band and that maybe we should try to do something together someday. I don't know why we didn't start then, but I still had a band with Don Solomon and Joe told me he was waiting for Tom to get out of high school so they could start a band in Boston. But by the time Joe drove away, we had agreed to do something together one day, down the road.

Pudge Scott: The Jam Band made an album. On August 30, 1969, we hung two Shure microphones over the audience at The Barn and Bob Grasmere recorded our set on my father's Concord two-track reel-to-reel tape recorder: "Shapes of Things," "Let Me Love You Baby," and "Blues Deluxe," all Jeff Beck songs; Jimi Hendrix's "Red House"; "Ramblin' Rose" by the MC5; "Gimme Some Lovin' "; and "Milk Cow Blues." The album actually opened with Jeff Beck's "Rice Pudding," taped by Elyssa Jerret during a rehearsal at the band house behind The Barn. We had the tape mastered and transferred to acetate at AAA Recording in Boston. The psychedelic cover art [flames, eyeballs, acidic whorls] was drawn one stoned night by Joe. We pressed about four copies. Highly collectable, to say the least. No, you can't borrow mine.

5: Doing the Willie

Steven Tyler: After the Chain broke up, I had a band called Fox Chase with Don Solomon and a bunch of different people, but after six years in the bars the bloom was off the rose, so to speak. This band broke up late in 1969 and it must have been early in 1970 that Don and I started another band called William Proud. The name came from a guy named Willie who worked at the Troc-Mar in Tuckahoe, New York; he had a harelip, so all the kids in Yonkers would get stoned on pot and make this guy's face. It was called "doing the Willie." The band was me on drums and singing, Don Solomon on keyboards, Dwight "Twitty" Farren on guitar, and Ray Tabano on bass.

Ray Tabano: After I got out of high school a few years earlier, I bummed around California for a while. Then my wife and I saw the

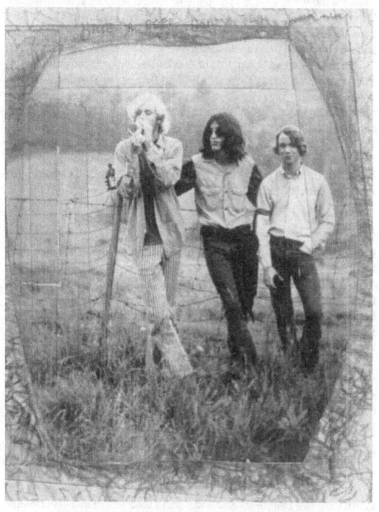

The Jam Band: Tom Hamilton, Joe Perry, and Pudge Scott
in Georges Mills, New Hampshire, 1969
(PERRY COLLECTION)

movie *Alice's Restaurant*. The Berkshires in western Massachusetts looked great and we said, "Let's move there." So we landed in Stockbridge and, like the good hippies we were, we started a leather business. Then we moved to Boston and opened a leather shop on upper Newbury Street in the Back Bay called the Yellow Cow. We got involved with Mel Lyman's famous commune and their underground newspaper *Avatar* and just sort of melted into the Boston scene.

Then Steven and Don got rid of Frankie Ray, who played guitar in the Chain, and hired Twitty Farren, "All-Night Dwight" as Steven called him, who could really play. He'd do "Come On" by Jimi Hendrix and get a standing O every time. I was the bass player, and we played this weird circuit in New Hampshire and Long Island, cranking out "Back in the U.S.S.R.," "Love Me Two Times," "Bring It on Home to Me," "Bitch," all those songs. It was a good band, but it just wasn't what Steven wanted anymore. He wanted a harder sound, to rock more like Led Zeppelin. He was tired of that Beatles shit.

Steven Tyler: William Proud was like our third and last try at having a career. We'd been playing in bars and trying to do something for seven years and nothing had happened. We played the Cheetah in Times Square, five sets a night for $500. We played at Salvation, which by then had moved up to Central Park South where the Nirvana restaurant is now. Then when the summer [of 1970] came, the people that owned Salvation opened a club in Southampton, out on Long Island, and hired William Proud as the house band.

It was fun being out at the beach and it was a big "Mrs. Robinson" scene, with all these sexy divorcées hitting on me, hitting on the band, even though their boyfriends were around. Then the band started to burn out and I blew up one night. I was snorting this blue crystal methedrine we were keeping in the freezer. We had rehearsed all day, trying to write songs with a guy named Steve Emsback, who had gotten us this gig. Me and him had written a song called "Somebody" that was just beginning to jell.

The band had been up partying the night before and we were on our fourth forty-five-minute set and it was just a complete drag. I kept looking over at Twitty Farren and he was *yawning*, like he was bored or something. Then "Beulah," our sound system, was fucking up and I looked over and fuckin' Twitty's yawning again and I'm thinking, *This sucks. It's so going* wrong. *I'm angry. No, I'm furious. I'm at the end of my rope. How the fuck do I get out of this—I-am-the-hell-outta-here!*

The next time Twitty yawned I climbed over the drums and tried to smack him because it was unprofessional to yawn. He should have been snorting that blue speed like I was: so, so good, it melted if you kept it out of the icebox, but it burned so *gooood* going down. I had my hands around his neck and was trying to strangle him when they pulled us apart. And that, my friends, was the end of William Proud. I literally packed my suitcase, left that night, and hitchhiked up to Lake Sunapee to see if I could find these guys I'd seen playing at The Barn the summer before.

Ray Tabano: Before he left, Steven told Don Solomon, "Listen, Don, I don't want to play drums anymore. It's just not my bag anymore, man. Fuck it. I wanna be the lead singer and that's it."

"No, you can't," Don said. "You gotta play drums. No other drummer besides Charlie Watts could work with you because you're so uptight."

And Steven goes, "Hey, who needs this hassle? I'll make it on my own! I'm splitting!"

Steven goes, "Listen, Ray, we'll do our own fucking band with these guys from New Hampshire, Joe and Tom. I heard them last year and they're tighter than a crab's asshole in mating season. Meet me in Boston in September and we'll put this together and it'll be fucking intense."

And that was it. He left in the morning on this mission to New Hampshire to put something together with these two guys.

6: Summer 1970

Joe Perry: I quit my winter factory job again and went up to Sunapee, where the Jam Band spent the summer as the house band at The Barn. John McGuire was gone, so it was like a power trio with Pudge and us. John Conrad gave us the old farmhouse on the property to live in on the condition that we clean up The Barn and mow the Conrad Manor lawn, which we never did. The house was a totally decrepit hovel.

I had a serious plan with Tom Hamilton. I had saved plenty of money, I had my MG, and the plan was to go to Boston and rent an apartment as soon as the summer was over. We had a friend named Mark Lehman, who owned a van, which automatically made him the roadie. Our drummer Pudge was only fifteen, so we couldn't take him and this created a certain amount of heartache, but this is also where Steven came in, not that he was ever going to be our drummer. But this is the summer he came up and we got together for the first time.

Steven Tyler: You wouldn't believe the house they were living in. There were holes in the floor, broken windows, no insulation, just wood and broken plaster. Upstairs was for fucking, downstairs was for smoking pot and drinking beer. It was very basic, not much more than a place to put your equipment when it rained. And it smelled bad. I can still smell that place sometimes.

Joe Perry: One of the first times we played with Steven was when Henry Smith arranged for Steven to audition for the Jeff Beck Group. Rod Stewart had left and Henry said, "Jeff Beck is looking for a singer, Steven. Better get a tape to him as soon as possible." Steven asked us to come over to The Barn, Henry set up a tape recorder, and we were the backup band for this tape. Nothing ever came of it, except that after it was done, me and Steven began to jam. And a couple of days after the tape we were really into it, saying, "Yeah, let's play together. That would be really cool." There was a lot of politics going on because Steven was a drummer and I didn't want Pudge to get upset, so another few days went by and then we began to hang out and play a lot.

Tom Hamilton: By the summer of 1970, Steven's band no longer existed. That's when Steven really started to hang around The Barn a lot and hear us play. Joe and I were headed to Boston that fall, with or without Steven, but he said he wanted to do it and Joe and I told him, "You should be singing lead, be the frontman." Pudge wasn't coming and we'd find a drummer in Boston.

And Steven says, "Great." We say, "Great." At this point, Steven says, "If I'm gonna be in the band, we gotta have Raymond [Tabano] too." Joe and I go, "Uh, well," and Joe tells Steven that if Raymond comes, Tom comes too. You have to remember that Steven was an experienced professional musician and I just graduated from high school. My playing and knowledge were limited, and my ear was nonexistent. All I had was my energy and my ambition. That's what got me through the early days of the band, just wanting it so bad.

Steven bought it. Steven was very taken with Joe, taken with Joe's fire. He seduced Joe with his music and his personality. I remember that suddenly these guys were developing a relationship, and I was part of it

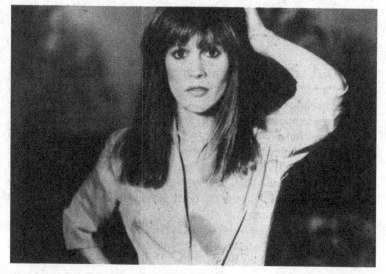

Elyssa Jerret
(COURTESY MAXANNE SARTORI)

but not really there. It was a case of two very kindred spirits getting together, and all you could do was stand there and watch in awe.

Joe Perry: It was an exciting summer at the lake. The weather was hot and beautiful and we knew we were on the cusp of something with the band. Elyssa Jerret had come home for the summer and I was escorting her around. She wasn't my girlfriend at that point, but it's a complicated story that goes way back.

Elyssa was from a musical family. Her father, Nicholas Bertocci, changed his name to Nick Jerret and played jazz clarinet in his own combos and with Billie Holiday and Dizzy Gillespie. His sister, Elyssa's aunt, was singer Frances Wayne, who worked with the big bands of Woody Herman and Charlie Barnet. She was married to composer Neal Hefti, who wrote the theme music to the *Batman* TV show that was big in 1966. Elyssa's parents had a house on the lake, so her father and Steven's father knew each other and she and Steven kinda grew up knowing each other at a distance.

I was hot for her, but we were just friends. She had this guy Joe

Jammer in London, and she was just home for the summer. My job at this point was to drive her to dates with other guys.

Elyssa Perry: My thing was water-skiing on the lake and playing pinball at the Anchorage. I was the pinball princess of Sunapee, New Hampshire. One day when I was thirteen, I noticed Joe making pizzas. He was supposed to be washing dishes, but the pizza guy got sick. Joe was really quiet, with little glasses and a Beatle haircut, and he looked like he didn't want to know from pizza. I started talking to him and found out he was just starting to play electric guitar. I waited for him to get off work and just started to hang out with him a lot. It wasn't romantic—we were like best friends. In the fall we'd say good-bye and not see each other until next summer.

I graduated from high school in 1969, and after that summer I went to London to hang out and look for work in the fashion scene. I got hired at Kensington Market as a model.

I met a guitar player from Chicago named Joe Jammer, who was managed by Peter Grant, who worked with Led Zeppelin, and we went to dinner at Jimmy Page's famous house on the Thames at Pangbourne and I met Jeff Beck and I sort of fell in with that whole London scene. I lived there for two years, but I'd come home for Christmas and in the summer and hang with Joe again, which was why I had a front row seat watching Joe and Steven get together.

I knew them both, but separately. I knew Steven as a little boy at Trow-Rico because my family would go there when they were playing music, and little Steven was always running around like a maniac. He was the same way when he grew up. Steven was *nuts*. He had a rocket up his butt, big-time high energy, very hyper. The whole town would come to The Barn to hear Steven's band. I was always in the audience.

The summer after that I came home and found Joe living by himself in this empty farmhouse behind The Barn. He wouldn't talk to anyone; he preferred to play his guitar along with *Truth* and *Beck-Ola*. He wouldn't even eat. I'd take him some food or he'd come over to my house for dinner and my parents would feed him.

Tom Hamilton: That was our last summer as kids in many ways. We spent it going back and forth between The Barn and the house, playing, cleaning, rehearsing, getting high, and even sleeping sometimes. I remember smoking some hash, putting on Deep Purple's ''Hush,'' and drifting off to sleep with these great English guitar and keyboard sounds tunneling into my unconscious.

The summer of '70 was also our first encounter with cocaine. Elyssa was home for the summer and Joe took her to this party in Sunapee. The next day he told me someone had turned him on to a couple of lines.

"What was it like?"

"Like God's breath," Joe said.

One day that summer I went up to Trow-Rico, trying to graduate to that level of worldliness. An old friend of ours named Twitty Farren was playing with Steven. He was an incredibly talented kid from Massachusetts whose parents had a house on the lake.

So Twitty's around but not realizing that there's writing on the wall that said that Twitty was out and Joe was in. So we're over there and Joe goes up to him and asks what it's like being in a band with Steven and Twitty told him, "You wouldn't believe it. Don't ever—*ever*—be in a band with this guy because he'll tell you how to brush your teeth. He's uptight, a total control freak, he'll make you crazy."

And I'm thinking, *What an exaggeration!* (Little did I know.)

Steven had his own cabin by then. He was a real mountain man and loved nature. I went over there and found him on his porch, reading a book. I remember thinking how out of character it seemed for this ultra-hip pop star in bell-bottoms to be sitting in a wool coat, reading a book with his glasses on. Steven was friendly, engaging, and the moment I realized that he might join our band was the moment when I knew we were going to make it someday.

Because Joe and I were saying that we were going to go to Boston and get an apartment, but meanwhile I had been accepted at a couple of colleges and my parents wanted me to go. My parents freaked when I explained that I was going off with Joe to do my own thing. My mother was really worried, but they couldn't force me to go. They tried to reason with me, telling me the odds against the band working out was one in fifty thousand. (Actually, the odds were even worse.) They told me that I had a year, and when the band failed I'd be back in school. That's how we left it.

I was on the path. I knew it was gonna happen for us. When we got Steven, I *knew* it.

Joe Perry: It was an unreal time. We were totally psyched we were leaving Sunapee to put this together. I wasn't twenty years old yet and Tom was maybe nineteen. I had that drive that I'd always felt, this urge to organize and make things happen. It was pure momentum carrying us forward. I told Steven to sit tight in Sunapee, and Tom and I went to Boston. Mark Lehman drove us in his step van, with a big cartoon of him painted on the side, like R. Crumb's famous character Mr. Natural: KEEP ON TRUCKIN'! I had some money, and my mother gave us enough for a deposit on an apartment when we found one. We were like thousands of college students moving into town in September, but we had other plans.

The Monkees on Drugs

3

> Aerosmith didn't really come from Boston. They came from the transatlantic daydreams of American dudes hell-bent on becoming English dandies.
>
> —*Hit Parader*

> It started from a single premise: "Rock till I drop."
>
> —Steven Tyler

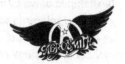

When you drive from New Hampshire down to Boston, I-93 climbs this big hill north of the city and you can see the whole town laid out before you—1970's Boston, Hub of the Universe, City on a Hill, Capital of New England, Home of the Bean and the Cod, playground of half a million students attending the area's seven major universities and countless colleges, land of the Boston Tea Party and pioneer rock station WBCN-FM, as well as three Top 40 AM stations, several other progressive rock FM stations, and a few dozen college stations.

Across the Charles River from Boston, the city of Cambridge seethed with resident hordes of hippies and Vietnam-era dropouts ready to rock at the drop of a bong. The suburbs were packed with kids who bought every album by every English band that came out. This giant youth population's unslaked craving for English rock was even famous in London, where Boston was known as the breakout market for new bands. The Jeff Beck Group, Led Zeppelin, Fleetwood Mac, and later the Faces played some of their earliest American shows at the Boston Tea Party, the Music Hall, and the Orpheum Theater on Tremont Street; the biggest headlined Boston Garden down by North Station, home of boxing matches, the Boston Bruins hockey franchise, and the Boston Celtics basketball team.

But Boston was a terrible place to start a rock 'n' roll band. If you were a band, you better not be from Boston. In the music business it was called the "Boston curse."

There were a lot of reasons rock bands weren't encouraged to develop in Boston. Rock 'n' roll was actually banned in Boston for most of its formative years in the late fifties after New York disc jockey Alan Freed booked his touring rock 'n' roll revue into Boston Garden in 1956.

Boston had been a Puritan city since its founding 300 years earlier, and little in the city's attitude toward public entertainment had changed in the intervening years. The old burlesque theaters of Scollay Square had been ripped down by urban renewal in the early sixties. The all-night strip joints had relocated to an area near Chinatown and Park Square known as the Combat Zone. The city of Boston employed an official censor to monitor entertainment, and the all-powerful Catholic Archdiocese made sure that the phrase "Banned in Boston" remained a national joke.

The Church's warnings about Freed's show at Boston Garden made sense to local officials after a teenage gang fight erupted during the performance, resulting in a melee and some thrown chairs. Freed was detained by the police and told to get out of town. He was back the following year, and the mayor officially banned rock 'n' roll shows when some hopped-up kids in black leather motorcycle jackets attacked subway passengers after the show.

The ban was lifted the next year so Freed could present his Rhythm and Blues Cavalcade of 1958 at the Boston Arena, a grimy hockey rink near Massachusetts Avenue. The lineup included Chuck Berry, Jerry Lee Lewis, Buddy Holly and the Crickets, Danny and the Juniors, Larry Williams, and Screamin' Jay Hawkins.

The show took place on May 3 in front of a sold-out house, and all went well until Jerry Lee Lewis, angry because Chuck Berry was closing the show, went wild during "Breathless" and then berserk during "Great Balls of Fire." The young audience rushed the stage and the Boston police threatened to stop the show. Alan Freed had to tell the kids to take their seats while Jerry Lee sat at his piano, glowering menacingly.

The police intervened again after Chuck Berry started "Johnny B. Goode." The kids went wild and the cops turned the house lights on. Freed stopped the show and said, "Well, kids, it looks like the Boston police don't want you to have a good time." Two local teenage gangs, the Band of Angels and the South End Barracudas, chose this moment to rumble. Chairs and bottles were flying and Chuck Berry ran off the stage. The violence briefly spread outside the hall, a sailor got stabbed, and rock 'n' roll was through in Boston, at least until the clean-cut Beatles came through in 1964.

Instead Boston and especially Cambridge embraced the folk music revival of the early sixties. Joan Baez began her career singing barefoot at Club 47 in Harvard Square. Coffeehouses sprouted like mushrooms on Charles Street. Bob Dylan was a regular on a scene that would spawn Jim Kweskin's Jug Band, Tom Rush, and later James Taylor and Bonnie Raitt. WBZ beamed Dick Summer's folk-rock radio show Nightlight over its 50,000-watt clear channel, introducing new talent like Joni Mitchell and Leonard Cohen to the entire Eastern seaboard. Boston's preference for folk music and country blues was so strong that when Bob Dylan returned in 1965 with an electric band, he was booed off the stage of Symphony Hall.

If Boston was snobby about rock 'n' roll in the mid-sixties, it didn't mean that there weren't any good bands around. Barry and the Remains played really hard rock and were often compared to the Rolling Stones. (They were good enough to open for the Beatles on their 1966 American tour.) The Barbarians were famous for their one-handed drummer, Victor "Moulty" Moulton. The Rockin' Ramrods packed the Surf nightclub on Nantasket Beach on weekends. The Lost were regulars on the college mixer circuit, along with Teddy and the Pandas. Blues bands were big, like the Siegal-Schwall Blues Band, the Colwell-Winfield Blues Band, and the J. Geils Blues Band.

The Boston Tea Party opened in January 1967 as a typical psychedelic ballroom featuring a pulsating light show and national acts and English bands. The best local bands were booked as openers—the Hallucinations, the Lost, Street Choir, Grass Menagerie, and Ill Wind. The Psychedelic Supermarket opened in a former basement garage the following year, booking mostly San Francisco bands.

In 1967, the San Francisco sound took over American popular music. The sound had a powerful base in the Jefferson Airplane, the Grateful Dead, Big Brother and the Holding Company, Country Joe and the Fish, Moby Grape, the Charlatans, and Quicksilver Messenger Service. After the 1967 Summer of Love, executives at New York record companies began searching for the follow-up to the San Francisco sound. Alan Lorber, a producer at MGM Records, dashed up to Boston, signed three local bands, and generated the notorious marketing fiasco called the Bosstown Sound.

The bands were the Beacon Street Union, Ultimate Spinach, and Orpheus. They were encouraged to churn out pretentious psychedelic art school rock that MGM marketed under the Bosstown sound umbrella. Other companies, afraid of being left out, signed the Orphans, Eden's Children, and Bagatelle (which had been the Lost; an indication of the lameness of this scene was that the Rockin' Ramrods changed their name to Puff).

MGM brought out the first three Bosstown sound albums in early 1968, hyping it as "the sound heard 'round the world." There was some initial national press interest and WBZ jumped on it, but soon it was obvious that the Boston acts didn't rock with the wild abandon of the San Francisco bands, an organic movement unto itself that was playing with a visionary artistic cohesion. The Boston bands suddenly found themselves in the national arena without having jelled in Boston. The records didn't sell. The local Underground press (Avatar, Boston After Dark, Vibrations, Broadside, Fusion) dumped on the bands and the cynical hype of the record companies. The Bosstown sound backfired so badly that it actually hurt Boston bands for the next several years. After 1968, conventional wisdom in the record business was that no band could break out of Boston.

The only group to try was the J. Geils Band. The singer and drummer from the Hallucinations and the guitar, harmonica, and bass players from the J. Geils Blues Band put together a powerful quintet that was easily the best rock 'n' roll band in Boston as 1969 turned into 1970. They covered the same funky R&B territory as the early Rolling Stones, and singer

Peter Wolf's jive-talking personal flash put the band over well enough to land a recording deal from Atlantic Records.

As Joe Perry and Tom Hamilton were driving down from Sunapee, J. Geils was actually vacating its role as the best bar band in Boston and was preparing to get out of town, which is what a Boston band had to do to survive.

Joe and Tom arrived in Boston in early September 1970 and crashed at the Smith brothers' basement apartment on Kent Street in Brookline for a few days before they found a two-bedroom apartment for $160 a month at 1325 Commonwealth Avenue in the student ghetto of Brighton, near Boston University's campus. They moved in September 15, 1970. Three days later Jimi Hendrix died in London of a drug overdose. Janis Joplin died the same way three weeks after that.

The Beatles had broken up only five months previously when Paul McCartney left the band. In England a poll in the music weekly Melody Maker voted Led Zeppelin as Britain's most popular group, the first time in eight years the Beatles hadn't been #1. The Stones were inactive. Eric Clapton's band, Derek and the Dominos, was playing the Music Hall, and Sly and the Family Stone sold out Boston Garden on September 22. Buddy Miles's band was at the Sugar Shack, and the Faces featuring Rod Stewart were about to make their Boston debut at the Tea Party. Radcliffe student Bonnie Raitt was playing slide guitar at Jack's Bar in Cambridge.

There was a Jean-Luc Godard double bill at the Orson Welles Cinema and Performance had just opened at the Cherie in the Prudential Center, featuring Mick Jagger as Turner the decadent rock star who sent his famous memo. Also playing or about to open: Five Easy Pieces, Catch-22. On September 15, Vice President Spiro Agnew gave a speech asserting that American youth were being "brainwashed into a drug culture by rock music, movies, books, and underground newspapers."

Thirteen twenty-five was one of countless attached four-story brick apartment buildings that ran along Commonwealth Avenue from Kenmore Square to the suburbs of Chestnut Hill and Newton. Half the population of this Brighton neighborhood were students and the other half elderly immigrants from Eastern Europe. Across the street from the apartment was a package store with a large neon sign that advertised BOTTLED LIQUORS all night. The Boston College trolley line ran down the middle of

Commonwealth Avenue, and in the early days the Aerosmith musicians would know it was time to go to bed when they heard the first trolley of the new day roar down the tracks toward the sleeping city, just at the break of dawn.

1: Mr. Kramer

Ray Tabano: Joe Perry and Tom Hamilton showed up at my leather shop on Newbury Street and said they had found a place to rehearse in the West Campus dorms at Boston University. I'd jammed with them in New Hampshire with Pudge playing drums, so I got out my Epiphone guitar that I'd bought for the William Proud band, and my Vox Super Beatle amp, and lugged them over to this basement room with about twenty sets of drums in it, and the three of us played a little. Joe didn't really want me in the band. He wanted a Zeppelin-style three-piece with Steven as lead singer. But Steven insisted on having a second guitar, so I was in.

One day a few weeks later, maybe early October, I'm in the leather shop and Joey Kramer comes in. I knew him from Yonkers because he was in the King Bees with Henry Schneiderman's brother. Joey hands me a pack of Camels, which he knew I smoked, and says, "Hey, Ray, I heard you and Steven are putting a band together. Can you get me an audition?" "Sure, man, I'll back you up." Next day Joey shows up at West Campus in a Captain America flag shirt like Peter Fonda wore in *Easy Rider*. I don't think any other drummer even auditioned.

Joey Kramer: In 1970, I was in Boston going to Berklee College of Music and basically wondering what I was gonna do next. My family didn't approve of me being a professional musician, and we had this understanding that Berklee was the last stop before I was going to decide what to do with my life. The funny thing was that when I met Joe and Tom the first time, I didn't think it would work out . . .

My father, Mickey Kramer, was a young infantryman from New York City who landed on Normandy Beach during D-Day. He was hit by a grenade and for him the war was over. My mother, Doris Schwartz, was an Army nurse. They got married after the war, and I was born in the Bronx in 1950. I have three sisters, all younger than me.

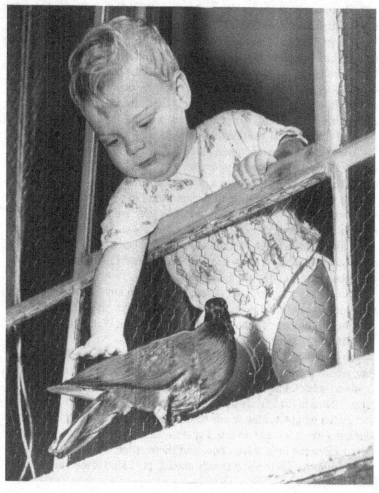

Joey Kramer, 1951
(KRAMER COLLECTION)

My dad was a salesman, and when I was about four we moved to a house in Yonkers. I was a typical kid—not specifically interested in music at all—preoccupied with cars until I was about fourteen, when I saw the Beatles and music came into my life in a big way. That's when my problems with my father began.

My father was a strict disciplinarian. He wanted me to do well in school, not confuse things. When I was in school, he told me, I should only be thinking about school. He didn't want me to intertwine things, and I looked around and realized that the whole world was intertwined, so of course I just rebelled. He would hit me, and I'm sure you can imagine I just loved that. All this must have to do with the reason I picked out the drums. As I look back—and I long ago made my peace with my dad about this stuff—it makes a lot of sense to me that I was afraid of him and his disapproval, and I was looking for an outlet for my feelings. It had a lot to do with the physical relationship, the physical *aggression* I could have with a set of drums. You couldn't hit your dad, but you sure could hit the drums. I sure as hell needed something.

Until the sixth grade, I was a nice average suburban kid. Then I went to Walt Whitman Junior High in Yonkers and I met a bunch of older guys who were still in seventh grade because they were basically derelicts who just wanted to play instruments. I had never been exposed to anything like these juvenile delinquents and I just zeroed in on them, in part for protection. Most of the school was Italian, and I'm Jewish, which automatically meant I got picked on a lot.

But I wasn't in the habit of taking shit from anyone, so even when the biggest guys would come after me, I'd always give it back to them and get the shit kicked out of me. But that was life at Walt Whitman Junior High. Steven went there too. He knows all about it.

So these were the guys I started to hang out with, especially Frankie Ray, who was into being cool. He'd wear gray sharkskin suits with black lapels to school, and he played the drums. The first time I went to his house, there in his basement was this new set of drums and I would sit and watch him play. Slowly but surely I began to tell myself, *This looks like fun. I like it. I could do this.* I spent a lot of time at his house and he would show me little things here and there. Then my parents rented a set of drums for me to see if I really liked it, but I kind of lost interest and gave them back.

The following summer I got in an accident on this minibike I bought out of the back of a comic book with my friend Sandy. I bruised the side of my face and was in bed for a while, then around the house. So I sold the minibike. My father loaned me the difference and for $85 I bought my first set of Ludwig drums. I wish I still had them today. It was a three-piece kit. The bottom head was tacked on to the tom-tom, which was hung on a clamp. Tom-tom, snare, and bass drum, and I was off and running. My parents were OK and supportive. My dad knew I liked the drums, knew it was something I wanted. And he *really* wanted me off that motorbike because he could see that I was gonna kill myself. My mother gave me certain times when I could set up in our den to play, because she had a hearing condition and didn't want me to play when she was around.

It was funny how this condition disappeared when we headlined Madison Square Garden.

I started playing along with records: the Beatles, the Dave Clark Five, the Kinks. When I saw the Beatles on *Ed Sullivan* on a Sunday night in 1964, that was it. Next morning I'm standing out in front of school with my friend and he's telling me he's gonna grow his hair so he can be like the Beatles and I said to him, "Not me, man, I'm gonna *be* the Beatles." He laughed and I just said, "Wait and see."

My parents, meanwhile, wouldn't let me have long hair. I was always the guy in the band with short hair, which I really was unhappy about, but back then it was war.

I was *into* the drums, man. In ninth grade I got a job at the Eastchester Music Center to make money so I could add to my drums. Most guys my age had pictures of *Playboy* bunnies in their rooms. I had a centerfold pinup of a set of Ludwig drums I really wanted. So I worked and bought a hi-hat cymbal and something else, then I sold the kit for something a little bigger, a little better. I kept doing this until I finally got what I wanted.

My first band was the Dynamics. This is before the Beatles, before I met Frankie Ray, when I was in maybe sixth grade. We played Ventures stuff and "Louie Louie" at the Optimists Club in Mount Vernon. In 1964, my group, The Medallions, played the New York Pavilion at the World's Fair in Flushing Meadow Park in Queens. We were a junior high quintet that covered the Ventures, Jan and Dean, the Beach Boys, and the Surfaris.

Later in junior high, I was in a band called the King Bees, which you may have heard about. We were the younger version of the Dantes, which Steven and Raymond were in. They were doing the Stones and the Pretty Things for an older crowd. We did the Kinks, the Animals, the Dave Clark Five. They were the varsity, we were the junior varsity.

Steven's other band was the Strangers. I think I saw them for the first time at a place called Jabbo's in White Plains. He was singing, man, wearing a black turtleneck and a fur vest, long hair, Beatle boots, checked trousers, doing "Everybody Needs Somebody to Love" and "Little by Little." *Performing.* There was this guy playing clavinet with his right hand and Fender bass box with his left—Don Solomon. They were one of the best bands I ever saw. I couldn't believe how good they were. In high school I used to think about how great it would be if I could play with him in the distant future.

Then the King Bees ended. In high school I came back to playing with

Frankie Ray, the guy I started out with. He was playing guitar and I had a trio, Strawberry Ripple, with him and a guy named Elliott Goldman. We were trying to think of a name for the band and I came up with this idea we ended up not using:

Aerosmith.

It was a word I was writing compulsively all over my textbooks and ring binder. My old girlfriend Patty Bourdon keeps telling me that she and I came up with the name together while we were sitting in her room listening to Harry Nilsson's album *Aerial Ballet*, which had "Everybody's Talkin' " on it. We were thinking of cool names for bands and the whole Aero-something got hatched. It had nothing to do with *Arrowsmith*, a novel by Sinclair Lewis [published in 1925] that everyone hated to read in high school.

I went to Roosevelt High in the tenth grade, then my parents moved to Eastchester, where I had to repeat the grade because of truancy. Everything was fine at Eastchester for the first two months. There were only 700 kids in the school, and they'd been together since the first grade. It was very clique-y and very Italian. You had to be in a gang and I wasn't. It was murder. I started skipping school again, forging my mother's name on notes.

Soon I found myself in the tenth grade at New Rochelle Academy, a private school. I made friends with the other kids who got thrown out of public school, and that was my introduction to smoking pot.

The headmaster's nephew was a kid fron Newton, Massachusetts, named Arnie Pinstein and we became good friends. During Christmas and other vacations, I'd go home with him. We'd hang out in Harvard Square and that's when I fell in love with Boston and the whole scene there, which was much more laid-back than New York. This must have been in 1967.

I graduated in June 1969 from the Thornton Donovan School in New Rochelle and got in Arnie's orange Corvette and lit out for Boston with the top down, smoking joints. Tell me: Could life get any better than this?

We went to shows at the Fillmore East. I saw the Who do *Tommy* there and watched the Allman Brothers record their live album with Johnny Winter from Texas as the opening act. I went to the last Newport Jazz Festival that summer, when they booked Led Zeppelin, Jeff Beck, and Jethro Tull. I saw Clive Bunker play with Tull and Mitch Mitchell play with Hendrix.

Then there was Woodstock. I went with some friends for the express purpose of seeing the Who, but ended up taking some acid and downers and almost slept through the performance. Suddenly Jerry Elliot and

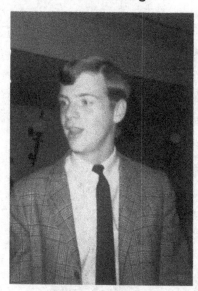

Joey Kramer in prep school, 1969
(COURTESY PATTY BOURDEN)

Howie Brooks are holding me up and slapping me. "Joey! Wake up, man, the Who, they're on!"

Next morning I came upon a hundred people banging kitchen utensils and chanting. In the middle, leading the chant, was Steven Tallarico, as out of his mind as I was.

I'd take every opportunity to go to Boston. It was a way to get out of the house and my friend Arnie was living with his uncle so we had a lot of freedom. We saw the Yardbirds at the Tea Party, the Hallucinations, the Peanut Butter Conspiracy, the Beacon Street Union. I was just starting to get high, beating the shit out of the drums, trying to get laid. It was music, smoking dope, sex, and *I couldn't get enough.* I didn't want to go to college. I wanted to do music.

In the fall of 1969, I went off to Chamberlain Junior College in Boston and took my drums with me. I used to set them up in the lobby of 232 Commonwealth Avenue and guys in the dorm would listen to me practice. Then I met a girl named Gracie, the roommate of a girl who was going out with my friend Jerry. She was fast-paced, kind of brought me along. She was a real friend to me. Then we had a student strike like every other college in Boston that year. But Chamberlain was an old-fashioned, Bostonian straitlaced place, and when Jerry and I started a protest, they threw us out.

So we got an apartment at 855 Beacon Street and put an orange peace sign in the window. We sold some pot and mescaline on a small-time basis to make our rent. Gracie and her friend came over to see us all the time, and then we each got jobs at the Prudential Insurance Company, in this giant skyscraper that totally dominates the Back Bay where we lived. I was working in the duplicating department, sitting by an A. B. Dick machine all day, bored out of my mind. I brought home $56 a week and still managed to live well, even though the drug thing didn't work out because we always ended up taking more than we sold.

Tiny was this tall black guy who worked with me. I met him through

Walk This Way

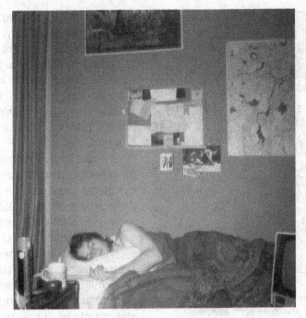

Joey Kramer asleep at college, Boston, 1970
(COURTESY PATTY BOURDEN)

the drug underworld of the company. I heard that he was a musician, but then I found out he didn't play in a band, he sang in a group called the Unique Four. They had a six-piece band, the Turnpikes, playing behind them. I had mentioned that I played the drums, one thing led to another, and one day Tiny told me they thought it would be real boss to have a token blue-eyed soul brother playing drums.

So I started to rehearse with these guys and play some gigs, even though at the time I didn't think they knew what they were doing. But they were turning me on to a new world: James Brown, the Persuasions, Kool and the Gang. They took me around with them and contributed to my higher education. We went to see James Brown at the Apollo and the O'Jays at the Sugar Shack in Boston. It was a heavy dose of rhythm and blues, much different from the British stuff I was into.

They taught me so much. We'd have rehearsals with just me and the singers and I had to accent certain steps inside the time I was playing, to accommodate their choreography. It was black music and it really grabbed me, big time. [The Turnpikes later became the disco-era band Tavares.]

After working for them for a while, I got really sick with infectious hepatitis. I had driven myself into the ground and turned yellow with jaundice. I was on my back for thirteen weeks and spent my nineteenth birthday in bed. After I got out of the hospital, I had to rest in my parents' house for three weeks. It was the summer of 1970 and my family had gone off to Europe, so my grandmother came and fed me chicken soup until my health slowly came back.

I had some time to sit and think about what I wanted to do. When my parents came back, I told them I wanted to go to the Berklee College of Music in Boston, and if they loaned me the money I would pay them back. My father told me to apply, and if I got in he would help me with it.

Well, I got in, and I was there for about three weeks, beginning in September 1970. I was living near Berklee with a saxophone player and a guitar player, practicing with them about six hours a day. It was all we did and very disciplined. I was in the guitar player's band. He had a metronome over the toilet, one over the kitchen sink, one in the bedroom, in the living room. The whole house was tick-tock and we did everything in time.

I tried to fit in at Berklee, but it quickly got to the point where it was hurting rather than helping me. I was playing with a matched grip because I was self-taught and they wanted me to play with a conventional grip. I wanted lessons on the vibes and they wouldn't let me, so I was frustrated and lost interest.

This was when I heard that Ray Tabano was in town, and I told him I was looking for a gig. He says, "I know some guys up in New Hampshire starting a band. They're good."

So we arranged for them to come pick me up, and we'd go to their place and play a little. I remember the first minute Joe Perry walked into our apartment. We were rehearsing. He wore black glasses, red bell-bottoms about four inches too short, and a short shag haircut. He came walking over, stood behind me for a moment, and all I can remember is him smiling and nodding his head. We packed up my drums and went over to their place in the basement of West Campus at B.U. I was into Mitch Mitchell and being a technician and showed them what I could do. I played a while with Joe and Tom and I think there was a keyboard player. Steven had nothing to do with it at that point.

After we said good-bye at the end of the day, I figured I'd just let it go. I wasn't that interested.

A few days later, Joe called me and told me that something had come through for them: This guy from New York was gonna come up and be in the band. I said, "Who is this guy? Maybe I know him."

Joe says, "His name's Steven Tallarico." I told them I had gone to school with him. So here was a chance to be in a band with Steven—it was my dream coming true.

Then they told Steven, and he realized that if I was good enough, it would free him to do what he really wanted to do, to be out front and fucking *perform*. He was the guy who was gonna be what he is today, whereas I had a solid reputation. "I know Joey Kramer," he told Joe Perry, "and I know he's a good player. OK, that's it. He can be the drummer."

That's how it started. By early October, I moved into 1325 Commonwealth Avenue.

2: Aerosmith Rising

Joe Perry: I remember going back to Steven's house in Sunapee to talk to him. I said, "Look, just come and play."

And he said, "I don't really want to play drums. I want to be up front."

"Great. You be out front and we got this guy Joey Kramer and he's talking about playing drums."

"Joey Kramer from Yonkers? I *know* Joey. What a fuckin' coincidence!" Then Steven said, "I don't know about Tom Hamilton, maybe I'll get Don Solomon," or one of the other guys that had been in Steven's bands. But I didn't like Don or any of those guys, any of them. I didn't dig that whole professional cover-band thing and never wanted to be in a band like that. And besides, I really liked Tom as a friend. I didn't even think about whether he was good or bad, because he was good enough and he was a good guy. So I said, "No way. Tom is in the band."

And Steven said, "OK, then I definitely want Ray Tabano to be in the band and play rhythm guitar."

I said, "Well, man, if that's the deal I gotta make, I'll do it, but I don't really see the need for another guitar player."

"C'mon, Joe," Steven said. "You know you can do a lot more with two guitars. Look at the the Beatles, the Stones, Fleetwood Mac."

So I compromised. I could've said, "Yeah, but what about Hendrix, Jeff Beck, Ten Years After—all these other bands with one guitar player?" I went back to Boston and told Joey that Steven was in the band. Joey said, "I'm in."

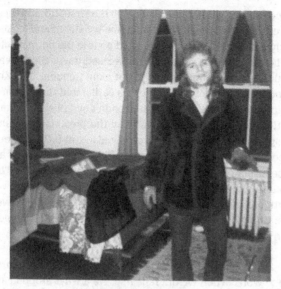

Joey Kramer in Boston, 1971
(COURTESY PATTY BOURDEN)

Tom Hamilton: It was Ray Tabano who said, "Let's get this guy Joey." The fuckin' guy could *play*. He'd gone to Berklee but left to join us. He was still recovering from hepatitis; when he started with us, he was the only one who didn't drink or get high. He knew how to take care of himself, which was more than any of us did.

So Joey moved into 1325, sharing the back room with Steven. I was in the living room with Steven's piano and the couch, which meant I'd always come home and find people sitting in my room, smoking joints, and farting on my pillows. Joe Perry and Mark Lehman had the other bedrooms, and that's how we lived for the next two years, five of us squashed in this apartment with absolutely no money. Steven cooked brown rice—he was fanatic about it—it's what we lived on, along with Campbell's soup and peanut butter and jelly sandwiches. When we were desperate, we'd go to the Stop & Shop (we called it the Stop & Steal) supermarket and stuff a couple steaks under our jackets. It was survival. You didn't call it stealing in those days. "Liberating" was the politically correct term.

Someone knew a guy named Jeff Green, who was the director of the West Campus dorms at B.U. These were three high-rise tower blocks overlooking the football stadium, just down the street from our apartment. Jeff gave us this great rehearsal room in the basement and looked out for us. He'd give us meal tickets so we could go into the dorm cafeteria and stuff our faces. So we practiced and rehearsed down there, which was great until the bomb scares started to get more frequent. The Kent State killings had happened only a few months earlier and the Boston colleges were basically in turmoil. Most of them hadn't even held graduation ceremonies the previous June because of all the protests and demos, and this atmosphere was exactly what we walked into at B.U. We'd be playing and someone would call in a bomb scare. The bell would go off and we'd haul all the fucking gear up the stairs so it wouldn't get stolen. Then we'd have to stand around with 5,000 stoned and sleepy students while the fire department determined there really was no bomb. Then we'd have to set everything up again. This went on for some months. Someone had to sleep in the van every night so we wouldn't get ripped off.

Joey Kramer: Certain days we rehearsed, certain days we had to go to work. When we did rehearse, we always stopped at exactly four-thirty and hitched a ride back to the apartment so we could watch *The Three Stooges* at five on Channel 38. The whole band piled into Joe's room where the TV was, glued to the set, paralytic with laughing so hard. A bong full of brown Mexican marijuana made the Stooges' thirty-year-old comedies seem like the funniest thing in history. A lot of our early group interaction was definitely Stooge-like. I went around saying, "Coitainly! Coitainly!"—until I drove everyone nuts.

One day we were sitting around after watching the Stooges and we had a meeting about finding a name for the band. For the first time in years, I remembered writing these words all over my math and bio textbooks in high school, and that's when I pulled the concept of Aerosmith out of the old memory bank.

Tom Hamilton: We had to find a name that somehow matched the power of the band and gave you the same sense of *lift* that we got when we played together. Everyone's in the room trying to think of a name. We had Spike Jones and the Hookers. But a "spike" was junkie slang for a syringe, and a "jones" was an addiction, so that didn't go over. Steven liked the Hookers, but no one else did.

"What about Aerosmith?" This from Joey, the newest member of the group.

I go, "Oh, no, it's that book they made you read in high school. That's too sophisticated."

"No, no," Joey said. "A-e-r-o . . ."

We liked it.

One of the first things we did with the name was have it stamped on packs of generic rolling papers. We were always driving around Boston in Mark Lehman's van, giving these Aerosmith rolling papers to hitchhikers as a primitive merchandising tool and expression of our general philosophy of life. Those papers are my first memories of seeing the name of the group in print.

Steven Tyler: I went home to Yonkers for the weekend right after Joey Kramer joined and we got the name. A few days earlier, Joe Perry and I sat down for the first time on his bed and wrote a song we were calling "Movin' Out," and I just had this feeling. First thing I said to my mother when I walked in was, "Mom, we're gonna have to move out of this house, because this new band of mine is gonna be so big there are gonna be kids in the bushes, kids peeking in the windows, kids all over the place."

She thought that was funny, but I *knew* what was gonna happen when people saw what we could do. Something deep inside me knew that it was only a matter of time now.

3: Showdown at Nipmuc Regional High

Joe Perry: The first Aerosmith rehearsals were in the basement over at B.U., and it was like we were the students and Steven was the teacher. He taught us order and discipline and we taught him energy and raw power. That's what drew us together at the start; it forms the basis of the love/hate relationship we share to this day.

What I knew how to do was get up there and rock. What Steven knew was songwriting, craft, pacing a song, a set, a whole show. We started writing our first song, "Movin' Out," and that's how I learned to write, from working with him. He gave us the tools to work with, and he wasn't shy about getting what he wanted from us. There were a lot of arguments.

Tom Hamilton: I was very raw when we started the band, not very experienced, and Steven was fuckin' Stravinsky. He had an uncanny ear and caught every one of my mistakes, and there were a lot of them. His way of criticizing you was harsh and intimidating. It was like rock 'n' roll boot camp directed by a sadistic drum major. In a matter of days, I developed a definite inferiority complex. And he almost drove Joey Kramer nuts.

Steven Tyler: When we formed the band, we started out using Stones songs as exercises, everybody playing the same notes. They didn't know how to *cook* and sustain the thing, so I had to teach them how to cook and keep time. We'd do parts of "Route 66" over and over again as an exercise, which eventually turned into the song "Somebody" on our first album.

Yes, I'd been a drummer, and yes, I worked Joey Kramer very hard. I taught Joey to open up the hi-hat [cymbal], had to work him very hard at that. I'd say to the band, "You know why Led Zep is so good? 'Cos everybody in the band is playing the same notes, the bass and the guitar, so let's get into that." Those guys would fight me on this, but I'd make them do it as an exercise. " 'Oklahoma City looks oh so pretty . . . Oklahoma City looks oh so pretty . . . ' "

I wanted to turn the guys on to the fact that *this is the way bands fucking make it!* This is what you gotta have. We didn't know about click tracks like we have today. Back then the drummer would just *play*, and he was only human, so you had to work on him getting the groove. And that was hard for the young Joey Kramer to do. He tended to speed up, especially after the solo. He'd come back in and speed up. Big problem for him, even today.

Anyhoo, I taught them how to be a band. They've hated me for it ever since. You laugh, but there's been lots and lots of therapy over this.

Joey Kramer: Steven made my life fucking miserable. Granted, it was because I let him.

Steven and I had a very heavy connection when we started. We'd known each other in Yonkers and had a lot of history in common. He was a very good drummer and I had lots of respect for his musicianship and in general was very impressed with the guy and amazed to be in a band with him.

He picked on me all the time.

I had what was needed and what he wanted—chops and the talent, but it was in a different direction from where he wanted to go. I was thinking Mitch Mitchell and he was thinking John Bonham. Steven saw that I loved to play, he told me so, but he thought I was lazy and he was mostly interested to help me to get to his place.

He was a total fuckin' monster about it. There were many nights, sitting in the back of the car going to a gig, being told how much I sucked and needed to get my act together. He was verbally abusive, very much so, but that was his personality and I just wouldn't let him grind me down.

Tom Hamilton: "Play it from the root," Steven would yell. "Play the fuckin' root!"

It wasn't long before we were formed up and meshing pretty well. We all started learning from each other. Steven learned how Joe had to crank up his Marshalls really loud to get the right sound. What we mostly learned from Steven was dynamics. I'd never even heard the word before. Dynamics meant loud during the breaks and then bring it down during the verses. I had been having fun for years just blasting away, my sonic crayons going way outside the lines. Steven brought us harmonic discipline for the first time.

Typical conversation between Steven and Joe:

"Joe, you can't play that note there."

"Why not?"

"It isn't right."

"But I like the way it sounds."

"You can't go there from there. It isn't right!"

"What the fuck!?!"

Actually, it hasn't changed that much.

Joe Perry: We were never a Boston band in the sense that you could see us in any given week in a club in Boston. We saw too many bands trapped into the $800-a-week, four-set-a-night syndrome. We were

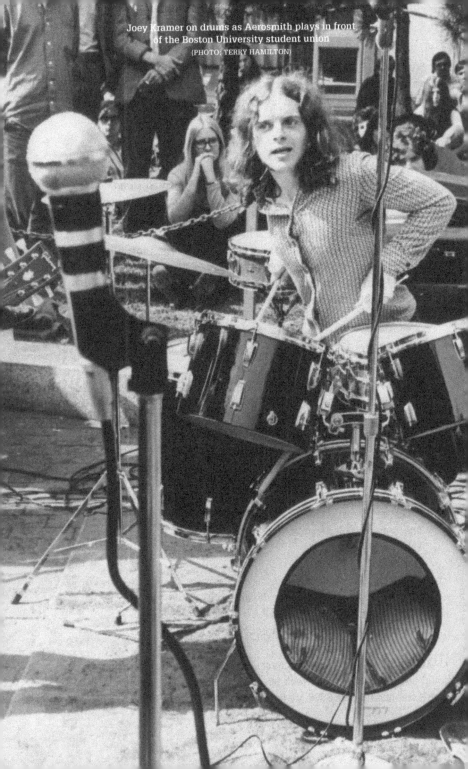

Joey Kramer on drums as Aerosmith plays in front
of the Boston University student union
(PHOTO: TERRY HAMILTON)

ambitious enough to want to be a concert band, playing our own material. So we started out playing at out-of-town high schools on Friday and Saturday nights, and we did our own show. There were two sets, half our own material and half covers like "Train Kept A-Rollin' " and "All Your Love," which we took from the John Mayall record with Clapton. We played "Peter Gunn" and "Honky Tonk Women" because we got so many requests for them all the time.

Steven Tyler: The last thing I wanted was to be in a Boston band. If you were from Boston back then, you were either a folkie into blues or you were into more intellectual rock, which I thought was pretentious. The records we had in our apartment were Jeff Beck's *Rough and Ready* and *Machine Head* by Deep Purple, *Let It Bleed*, *Led Zeppelin II*.

We also had an agent, Ed Malhoit, up in New Hampshire, who booked us at colleges and ski lodges and roadhouses up there, which was good because we failed most of the auditions we reluctantly played around Boston. The club owners complained: "It's too loud and people can't boogie to it." They said, "Don't you guys know any Credence songs?" and we'd say, "No, we don't." It was fine with me. I'd been in the bars for seven years—been there, done that. I didn't want to cover other people's songs, but when you're starting a new band, you got to fake it until you make it.

Tom Hamilton: Aerosmith's first gig was at Nipmuc Regional High in Hopkinton, Mass., near where Joe grew up. Over the next two years, we played at every high school in Massachusetts and New Hampshire. We'd play anywhere fifty people would show up to hear us.

We drove out to Nipmuc Regional in Mark's van and set up the gear and played three forty-minute sets of Yardbirds, Beatles, Led Zep, "Walkin' the Dog," "Cold Turkey." We did "Live with Me," "Shapes of Things"—everything we knew and some we didn't.

Ray Tabano: Before we even played the gig, I went down to the basement where they had a community center or something. I saw these beautiful marble and wood pedestals, really nice antiques, so Steven and me stole a few, loaded 'em right into the van with the amps after the gig. Then we noticed some nice green Nipmuc T-shirts in an open storage locker and we liberated a bunch of those as well. We must not have thought they were paying us enough.

First gig, big debut, we opened with "Route 66":

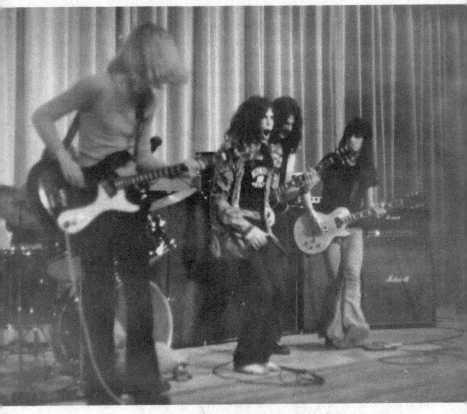

Aerosmith's first show, Nipmuc Regional High, 1970;
Tom Hamilton, Steven Tyler, Ray Tabano, and Joe Perry
(COURTESY ED MALHOIT)

First Set List

Route 66

Snake [Rattlesnake Shake]

Happenings [Happenings Ten Years Time Ago]

Movin' Out

Somebody

Think About It

Walkin' the Dog

Live with Me

Great Balls of Fire

Good Times Bad Times

Train Kept A-Rollin'

Tom Hamilton: Joe and Steven had their first big blowup in the locker room after the gig. Steven goes, "Joe, it's way too fuckin' loud. I can't *hear* myself to sing right. Turn down, you gotta turn down."

"Look," Joe said, "to get this kind of sound, these amps *need* to be loud. They don't even really start to sing until you get them up into distortion mode. That's just the way it is."

This got to be another of those big problems that's still not quite reconciled even today.

Joe Perry: I was always playing too loud for Steven, because if you're playing with Marshalls you had to get them going at a certain volume to sound good. It still goes on today, this war between the volume of the instruments and the vocals. I'm doing my thing, and to do it I have to be loud.

"Turn *down!*"

"I can't turn down."

"MY EARS ARE BLEEDING!!"

I didn't want to hear it. I was pissed off anyway because Steven stole a T-shirt from some kid's locker, pulled it through the wire mesh, and I said, "Where'd you get that?"

"I got it from that locker."

"You stole it?"

"Yeah."

"That's really fucked up," I said. "It's gonna look bad, you know?" A couple of weeks later, we're playing a dorm gig at Dartmouth and I caught him and Raymond rifling a kid's stuff and I yelled at them and they stopped. We had plenty to fight about besides volume. Plenty.

Steven Tyler: My first paycheck? I bought a big bag of Zaloom pistachios, a bottle of Boone's Farm, and a little bag of blue crystal meth, which I hid in the back of our freezer.

Ray Tabano: Boone's Farm apple wine. Joe Perry *lived* on Boone's Farm. It gave you a very bad head, but if you did enough coke the headache went away. I mean, we were doing a lot of drugs in those days. I'm amazed at the amount of drugs we took. It would've killed ordinary people. We were dropping LSD, smoking pot, drinking wine, taking pills. Steven and I started shooting cocaine because we knew this guy named Porky who was diabetic and taught us all about needles. We even shot LSD, which was highly not recommended. The dosages were so high it was incredible we were able to bounce back and be human again.

4: The Cabozzi Chronicles

Joe Perry: When I moved to Boston, my parents told me I had to be self-supporting; since nothing was coming in from the band, I had to get a job. So when I ran out of money that fall, I looked around and an Italian family that owned a cleaning company hired me to be the janitor at Temple Kihalleth Israel on Harvard Street in Brookline. I cleaned this synagogue for months, which was a lot saner than working in the factory. Steven got a job at the King Bagel bakery down the street but didn't last that long. I know he had the hardest time of all of us working at an outside job, and I'm sure he worked the least.

My parents helped a little. For Christmas 1970, they gave me $60 in the form of twelve $5 checks mailed out once a week so I wouldn't spend it all in one place.

Tom Hamilton: I got a job by going to the Roxbury Area Planning Action Council, which was a Great Society/War on Poverty office that channeled people into federal programs. I fudged my dad's income on the application and got hired into a paid training course for mechanical drawing in Roxbury. So I went over there and learned to be a draftsman. Joey didn't work because he was recovering from hepatitis.

I got really sick myself toward the end of the year. I didn't go to a doctor, but I think I had pneumonia. I was coughing badly and didn't feel right, and I said to Joe, "Man, I think I gotta go back home for a little while."

"You *can't* go back now," he said. "I mean it. There's no going back."

"But, Joe, I'm out of it. I think I've got some kind of bug in my lungs."

He looked at me. "You go back to New Hampshire now, that's gonna be *it*."

"C'mon, man."

"I'm serious. It's a feeling I have."

I knew Joe meant that the whole momentum we were building would be stopped. The train done left the station and there was no getting off now. So I didn't go. For a week I suffered through a heavy chest cold, coughing, gasping for air. (I can't wait for my mother to read this. She'll call me up and say, "I *knew* it!")

Ray Tabano: It's hard to stress enough that Joe Perry had a clear picture. He knew where he wanted to go and what was going to happen if he kept at it. He had such incredible drive in addition to his talent, which is why I'm still a Joe Perry fan to this day. Him and Steven dragged the rest of us up with them, as far as I'm concerned.

Joe Perry: We started to promote our own shows because back then, if you couldn't play a whole set of what was on the jukebox, nobody wanted you. So we'd hire out the local town hall and put up posters. We played high schools and colleges and rehearsed during the week. Some days we set up outside the student union at B.U. and played for the kids milling around during lunch hour. We did that a lot, and it was very good word of mouth for us.

Joey Kramer: I handled the business end of the band in those days. This simply means that I spoke to the booking agents, collected the money after the show, paid the expenses, and distributed anything left over among the five of us. If we got paid $300, which was a good gig for us, we might have $150 between us, which meant we could eat good that week. More often, we each ended up with $8 after a night's work.

The main thing was that I collected the money, because nobody could give me a hard time. You know, if someone owed me $300, I was gonna get $300.

Tom Hamilton: One of our main gigs in early 1971 was the Lakeview Ballroom in Mendon, Mass., a big hall that could hold a few hundred kids for two bucks apiece. It might have been a regular teen center they were operating. We got $300 and a box of malted milk balls in the dressing room, and we'd dress up and put on a rock show. We never played in our street clothes. I've always thought changing clothes and putting on something special was part of the magic of the whole thing. We'd play there with a good band from Worcester, the Joneses. Another band we liked was RGF [Real Good Fuck], who had cool clothes and were very professional and great-looking. We didn't have much dealings with the other Boston bands. J. Geils ignored us completely and other groups like the Modern Lovers and James Montgomery were just starting out like we were.

One day at 1325, Steven ran up to me and said, "Tom, you won't believe what I found downstairs in the basement. Somebody *lives* down there. I went down the back stairs and looked through a crack in the door and I see this foxy blonde lying on a couch with no clothes on and she's fuckin' looking back at me and playing with herself!"

It took me a few seconds to access this information. We thought there was nothing but a furnace and some storage down there. It turned out the blonde's name was Millie and she was the wife of one of the most amazing characters we ever met.

Gary Cabozzi.

He was the super and he lived in the basement with Millie, his father, and his little brother. Cabozzi was basically very huge, well over six feet; his arms looked like someone had torn the hind legs off a wild boar, shaved the hair off, and stuck them onto Cabozzi's large biker-type body. The whole unit looked like it was designed solely for the purpose of kicking the shit out of whoever he was up against, which fortunately was Cabozzi's main hobby and pastime. He had a big round head with longish black hair that was either greased back or hung loose, depending on whether Gary was in biker mode or in a semi-quasi-blend-in-with-the-hippies mode. His dark-eyed persistent glare combined with missing upper front teeth to hint of extraordinary violence, just a kiss away. The whole package came wrapped in authentic pissed-in biker denim over a Harley-Davidson T-shirt.

After he and Steven got straightened out about Steven seeing his wife naked, we got to be good friends with Gary. He was one of those guys who, if he's your friend, he'll do anything on earth for you. (If he's pissed off at you, leave town.) As time went on, he began to be available to help us out when we needed it.

When we couldn't use our rehearsal room at B.U., we were without a place to play. Cabozzi said, "Hey, you can rehearse in my living room. I don't care."

"Are you shitting us?"

"No problem. C'mon, let's hump the gear down there."

Cabozzi had converted one of the back basement rooms into his version of a swinging hangout: pool table, little bar, electric Budweiser signs, colored lights to give it the classic tavern atmosphere. A very funky and classic space. We moved some small amps and drums down there and got to work. Rehearsals became like a party, with pot and incense and beer nuts and a new malt liquor called Maximus Super, basically a can of alcohol with some foam on it. We'd polish off a couple of these and go into our James Brown phase, which we were very into at the time. Cabozzi happened to be a James Brown fanatic. We'd rip along on "Mother Popcorn" or "Hot Pants" and he'd go into action, dancing that big body around the room, leaping up on the pool table and then back down into a perfect split on the floor!

He soon become our *ex officio* roadie, helping us to load the gear into the van for gigs at B.U. We'd be there in the George Sherman Union, blasting away, and when we slid into "Hot Pants," Cabozzi would appear in the center of the stage and leap into the audience, landing in a split and then launching into his Jamesian dance routine. I can never forget the look on the faces of these long-haired students as they scattered, terrified and laughing at the same time. We knew just how they felt.

Gary Cabozzi: When I came back from Vietnam and got out of the Marines, I went home to Brighton and became the rent-free super of 1325 Comm. Ave.

Anyway, I took a liking to the guys and then Steven hired me as a roadie with my buddies Pat Morocco and Mike Montague. We'd load up their van and get paid in beer. We'd go down to the B.U. Boogie with them and from the first time I heard them down there, I couldn't believe how great they already were. You had to hear this to believe it, because it was like a full-blown thing right from the start.

Then they needed a place to rehearse and I gave 'em the basement. We had an honor system with the fridge where you had to check off next to your name if you took a beer. For the next year, they worked out the songs on their first album in my basement.

When the weather got warm again [spring 1971], we opened up the windows in the daytime and the music went out to the street. You saw these old Ukrainian and Greek ladies dancing on the sidewalk while Aerosmith blasted out "Write Me" and "Make It" and "Honky Tonk Women." The little old ladies in the neighborhood really loved the band. The guys were great.

Then I started to look out for the guys. I took them to Providence [Rhode Island] one drunken night so they could get their tattoos. We went to famous Ronnie's on Eddy Street: me, Steven, Tom, and Joey. Joey didn't want to do it, but we made him. On the drive down, Steven is nervous. He took three Quaaludes before we left and during the trip he smoked three bones and drank two Heinekens. Instead of heading to the tattoo parlor, he made us go into the bar next door and he put back four martinis. Steven was feeling no pain until he got hit with that needle. And then—oh, boy.

Tom got a diving swallow on his chest, Joey got a scorpion on his right arm, and Steven got a winged heart on his left bicep. The lettering under the heart read MA KIN, which was the name of a song Steven was working on. He told me it was gonna be the song that would make them rich and famous. He loved this song and had so much faith it, he tattooed it on his fuckin' arm.

5: The Suitcase

Joe Perry: We had a lot of little busts in those days because we had an open-door policy: Almost anyone was welcome to hang out if they brought some dope with them. This eventually attracted the attention of the authorities and got us into trouble.

One night some guys came over with some Colombian pot, and we were all crammed in Tom's room when we heard this strange noise and smelled something. Someone said, "Joe, man, I think like your room is burning," and sure enough the hippie candle on my spool coffee table burned down and set some song lyrics on fire. The flames were licking up toward this Indian cotton spread I'd rigged under the ceiling like a tent, and now the whole room was blazing and crackling. We had five seconds to decide whether to evacuate or fight the fire. We couldn't call the fire department because we would've gotten busted, so we had this whole bucket brigade going from the kitchen to my room and managed to contain the damage. Stuff like that was always happening.

Tom Hamilton: The suitcase incident happened on one of those cool autumn evenings that remind you that the seasons are changing and winter's really coming on. We finished rehearsing around dinnertime and our B.U. benefactor Jeff Green invited us to eat in the dorm cafeteria. We piled our plates high with the bland institutional chow because we were so broke that our next meal was going to be nonexistent, stolen property, or more brown rice and carrots.

When we got back to 1325, we hopped out of the trucks and noticed a man jump into a yellow taxi and speed away. Next we saw a small light-brown suitcase next to the big tree in front of the building. We began unloading the trucks in the daily drudgery of bringing our gear up to our second-floor apartment. In the middle of all this, Steven invoked the ancient law of finders keepers and scooped up the suitcase and disappeared into the building. As soon as all the equipment was neatly stacked in our hallway, we all made a beeline for Steven's room, where he was already sitting in front of the open suitcase.

"Whoa," he said. "Looka here." Dangling from his fingers was a baggie full of some decent-looking pot.

Joey Kramer: I actually found the suitcase first because I hitched to 1325 from rehearsal and saw this guy pull up in a cab, put the suitcase on the sidewalk like it had a bomb in it, and then take off. I looked around: no one in sight. So I took it upstairs, and—just out of curiosity—rummaged through it. Nothing but old clothes. So I put the suitcase back on the sidewalk. Next thing I knew Steven was walking in with it.

"Look what I found!"

"I already did. There's nothing in it."

"What the fuck, I'll just go through it." Steven had found something: a little reefer, which he gave us, and hundreds of dollars in cash, which he didn't. He didn't tell us about the money. Then he put the suitcase back on the sidewalk and we forgot about the whole thing until that night.

Tom Hamilton: The evening wore on, and we were blissfully vegetating in front of Joe's TV, pleasantly stoned on our ill-gotten pot. A couple of girls were over; a quiet, typical evening at home for Aerosmith. Then the phone rang. It was Cabozzi calling.

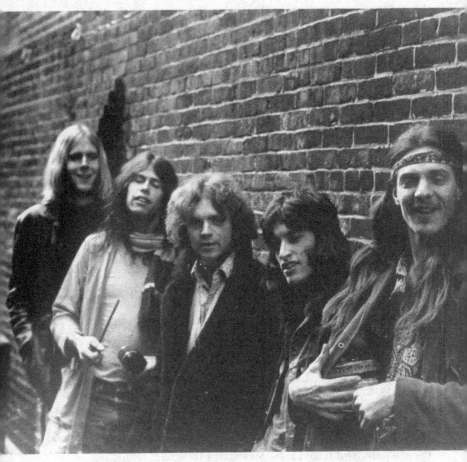

**Aerosmith in the alley behind Kent Street, Brookline, Massachusetts, 1970.
Ray Tabano, right, holds the band's stash.**
(COURTESY RAY TABANO; PHOTO BY CHRIS SMITH)

"Hey! You fuckin' guys better get down here for a minute. I needa
talk to you about something."

A couple of us went down to the sidewalk, where Cabozzi and his
father were talking to some greaser, who was upset. Cabozzi turns to us
and says, "Did any of youse guys see a suitcase here a while ago?"

"I, uh, well, duh, um, I don't think so," I asserted lamely.

"I paid this old man ten bucks and he told me you people took it," said the greaser.

"That's bullshit!" protested the senior Cabozzi.

"No way, you old piece of shit."

Cabozzi Jr. grabbed the greaser's shirt. "You calling my father a liar, you fuckin' scumbag?"

"Yeah, man, I am," said the greaser and a long knife seemed to grow out of his hand as the blade opened with a slash. Cabozzi's eyes lit up.

"All right! You're singin' my song now, asshole," said Cabozzi, whipping off his black garrison belt and wrapping it around his hand to fight with. The other guy took off down Commonwealth with Cabozzi in hot pursuit, his black jeans riding low on his commodious behind. It looked like a cement truck with a nitrous oxide hook-up doing zero to sixty in seven seconds flat.

We went back upstairs and settled into our nightly routine. Everybody hung out in his respective room. Joe was watching TV with the sound off while the stereo played a Deep Purple album. Joe liked to stare at the tube with a guitar in his lap, running off notes at a high rate of speed, showers of sparklike notes drifting from his room that betrayed the pent-up, smouldering energy inside of him. Steven was in the room he shared with Joey, arranging things in exactly the meticulous way he liked to have them. Somehow they had crammed a pair of bunk beds in there. Brad was with his girlfriend Lori and her sister, who had come over to visit. The heat in our building was always too high, which tended to cast a mellow, drowsy glow over the place. Suddenly there were three sharp bangs on our door. Ever ready to help, one of the girls ran over and asked brightly, "Who's there?"

"We wanna talk to Jim right now."

She opened the door a crack and said, "There's no Jim living here."

"You know, the tall blond guy."

"Oh," she chirped. "You mean *Tom*. Tom, there are three men who want to see you."

I went to the door and found three mean-looking, ugly guys. One looked like a college student, the others looked like Mafia recruits.

"I want my money now," said Joe College.

"What money?"

"You know, asshole. The money in the suitcase."

The college kid put his hand in his pocket like he was reaching for something. My stomach went light. "I'm not fuckin' around," he said. "I want the two thousand bucks that was in the suitcase."

Gary Cabozzi: I got a call from upstairs—I'm the tough guy in the neighborhood, everybody comes to me—and it's Steven and he's whispering, "Gary, get right up here now, because there are a couple of guys hassling us and one of 'em maybe has a gun. Come quick, good-bye."

I grabbed this curved Spanish sword and ran up the back stairs and kicked the back door open and jumped in the kitchen with this sword, ready to do battle. These two guys are standing in the hall and they both drew on me.

Honest to God, I almost shit myself.

"Drop it!"

"No, you drop it, asshole."

"I said drop it."

"You can fucking shoot me, but one of you is gonna *die*."

Tom Hamilton: Cabozzi blasted through the doorway with a gleaming five-foot military dress sword and roared like a raving beast, "WOT THE MOTHERFUCK IS GOIN' ON HERE??" Immediately the two guys pulled out pistols, cheap Saturday night specials that could kill you real dead anyway.

"You both better use those things," Cabozzi told 'em, "or I'm gonna be on you like stink on shit."

"I'll shoot you!"

"Go ahead, fuckhead. Won't be the first time, and my wife is on the phone and the cops'll be here in five minutes."

The cheap pistols sagged to the floor. I took this lull as a chance to talk to the college boy again. My voice was full of sympathy when I told him we didn't have his money and was this really something he wanted to discuss with the police? Right then the situation seemed to evaporate.

Gary Cabozzi: Those guys? I kicked 'em the hell out of the building and kept their guns. Twenty years later, I found out that Steven took the money. Fuckin' guy . . .

6: The Savage Breast

Joe Perry: Our best friends were drug dealers. We identified with them because we felt like outcasts, outlaws, menaces to society ourselves. We all liked drugs, so it seemed natural to gravitate to the dealers, like a kinship. We were doing our thing and they were doing theirs. We saw nothing wrong with it and even thought it was a respectable and even righteous profession.

Zunk Buker was our local bad boy in New Hampshire, who went to California and started running Mexican pot to New England, first in an El Camino, then in a camper, then in airplanes when it got more sophisticated. He'd regale us with tales of the money he was making and the cars, bikes, and girls that went with the outlaw life in La Jolla, where he and his partner set up after they made their first million.

Zunk Buker: That summer Joe and the guys were as broke as you could get and not be on the street. I flew Joe out to San Diego first-class and then took him home to La Jolla for a taste of this life we were living. On his first day with us, I sent a young woman to Tijuana for some blow. We're sitting around the living room when she came back, this beautiful blonde like out of *Baywatch*, and she reaches into her pants and slowly pulls out this huge condom full of blow that she's smuggled across the border, inside her. She gave us a big smile, totally unselfconscious, and plunked it down on the table.

Joe Perry: It was the most coke I'd ever seen and it got snorted up pretty quick. It was my first nosebleed—and not the last one either. Not long after Zunk sent me back to Boston, the Feds came in and busted Zunk's operation. It was terrible, and I missed being in it by less than a week.

Instead of going to prison, I spent the rest of the summer trying to figure out where we should be going with the band and whether Ray Tabano was right for us.

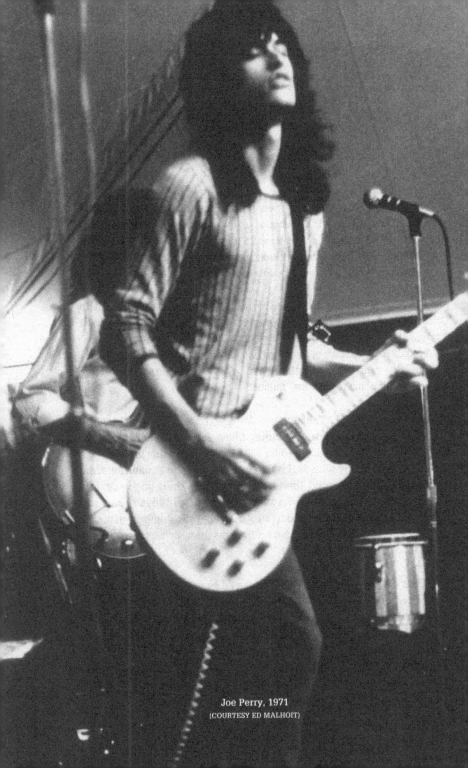

Joe Perry, 1971
(COURTESY ED MALHOIT)

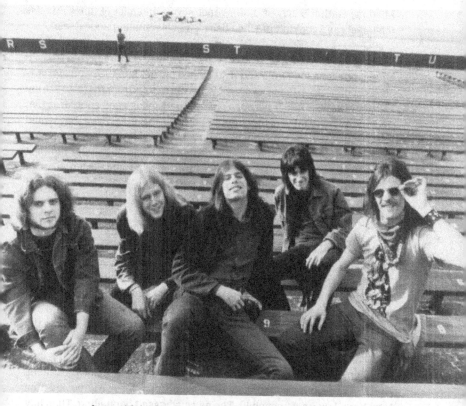

Aerosmith in the bleachers, Boston University, 1971
(COURTESY RAY TABANO)

Steven Tyler: Raymond was just too wild for the other guys. Raymond scared the shit out of them. They felt threatened, like he was gonna hit them. Joe wouldn't even talk to him and Tom was scared to death, because if they complained about his playing to his face, he would call them out.

Ray Tabano: That summer was when my inadequacy as a musician really came to the surface, 'cause I knew those guys were a lot better than me, music-wise. I was struggling and fighting to survive and Tom would tell me, "You really don't play that good, man," and I'd want to murder him.

You gotta realize that I was the only one with a life outside the band.

I had my leather business and my motorcycle and a lot of times I'd miss rehearsals and couldn't practice because I was running dope deals.

Joey Kramer: I wasn't into Raymond getting fired. Why? I'd known him for a long time and he'd helped me get into the band and was always supportive. For instance, Steven was always after me to do a drum solo, but I wasn't into it because I didn't think I was good enough at that point. But Raymond was like a buffer between me and Steven. Ray would say to me, "Hey, man, I see you doing great things when we're rehearsing, fooling around. If you got ten of these great things, take the best three or four and construct them like a fuckin' song. Build it up, plateau it out, build it up again a little higher, then take the best trick you got and do it the best you can, and then stop. And leave 'em hanging." No one else was saying this kind of thing to me.

Tom Hamilton: One weekend late in the summer we went up to Sunapee to play at The Barn. The night before we went to see Twitty Farren's new band at Larry's Playhouse in Sunapee Harbor. After William Proud broke up, Twitty had started this new band with a guitar player from Reading, Mass., named Brad Whitford. Anyway, we went and we're listening to Brad and we're like looking at each other and mouthing the word: *Wow!*

Next day at The Barn Steven and Ray had a fight that was really a big drag. By then we were frustrated by the constant war between them. And I was totally intimidated. Ray was a tough, aggressive street kid from New York. I was a flower child. The mix just wasn't happening. Then Ray gives the band this Looney Tunes ultimatum that he was taking over. He said, "Either you line up behind him [Steven] or line up behind me."

This was really out of touch, because Raymond couldn't really play. From that moment on, Ray was *gone*.

Zunk Buker: I came back from California that summer. On a Friday night, I went to Larry's Playhouse to see Twitty Farren's band. I walked in and Elyssa ran up to me. I hadn't seen her in a couple of years and she was now more beautiful than ever. She was home for the summer and introduced me to her boyfriend, Joe Jammer, this guitar player she had met in London. Then Twitty's band, Justin Thyme, began to play. It was Twitty, Guy Williams, and Brad Whitford, and they were rocking the place. Brad basically knocked everyone out.

Later that night, at a party, I ran into Joe and found out for the first time that he had a band with Steven.

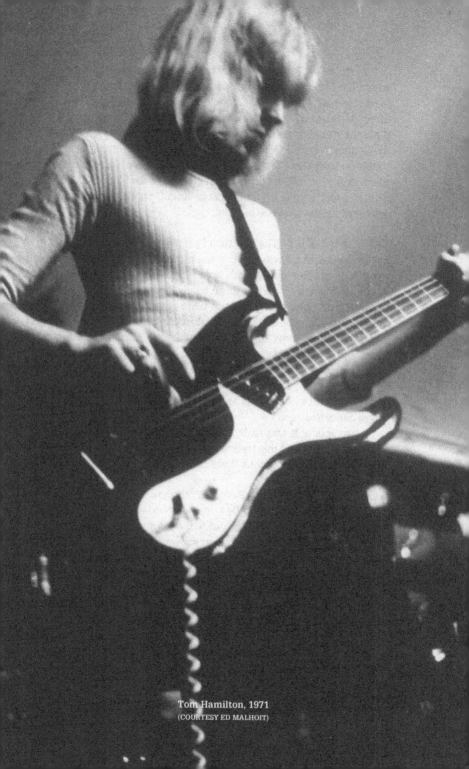

Tom Hamilton, 1971
(COURTESY ED MALHOIT)

Next day at The Barn, I heard Aerosmith for the first time. At one point, Joe Jammer jumped up with his guitar and began to play with them. He had a couple of albums out and just was great. Joe Perry—insecure—just laid his guitar on the stage and left. Out of nowhere Brad Whitford picked up Joe's guitar and starts to play, and soon he's cutting Joe Jammer! *Yeow! Whoa!!* Brad and Joe Jammer, going at it. Steven stands on the side of the stage with his mouth open, harmonica hanging silent at his side. The sun is shining through the cupola of The Barn, bathing everything in bright beams of light. It was a magic moment, the day that Brad became one of them.

Joe Perry: The first time I played with Brad, it just seemed to work. The chemistry was right. In the beginning we had an understanding that I was the lead guitar player and Brad was coming in to play rhythm. Almost immediately those labels lost their meaning. We would very rarely sit down and talk about what we were going to play. I never could say anything like, "I'll play the descending fifth," none of that stuff, because I didn't know that much about music anyway, and we didn't know how to put our ideas into words. I'd just play my lead part, and he'd put something on top that fit perfectly.

Back in Boston, I took Raymond to lunch at Ken's Pub, down the street from 1325. After a hamburger and a few beers, I just told him, "Raymond, you're out of the band."

It was tough. It was really heavy, but I had a Machiavellian attitude about the band. I had this feeling of optimism and momentum and drive. I knew it could happen for us if we worked really hard.

Tom Hamilton: Raymond didn't really believe we would fire him. Sometime around Labor Day, we were booked into a club called the Savage Beast in Ascutney, Vermont. This was supposed to be Brad Whitford's first gig with us, but Raymond showed no sign of actually leaving the band. He told us he'd see us at the Savage Breast, which is what we called the place. So Joe and I told Steven that he was going to have to confront Ray and tell him that he was out of the band.

So we drove up to Vermont. The club had a little house out back for the band to sleep in. I got my first case of crabs there, but I dug it anyway because it felt like we were on the road. I remember Steven proudly showing me his stash of pot he had grown that summer, two big baggies full of male and female plants. Brad came up and fit in to our whole vibe. He was nineteen years old, the baby of the band.

"So, Brad," I asked him, "you smoke pot?"

"Yeah! Are you kidding? I love it!"

"Good," I sagely advised him. "That's important."

Zunk Buker: They were scheduled to play five nights at the Savage Breast. On the first night, I gave Joe Perry a ride over from Sunapee. And Joe says, "We're gonna have Brad Whitford in the band, depending on whether Steven has the balls to fire Raymond or not."

I knew this was a big deal because of Steven and Raymond's longtime friendship. When we got to Ascutney, we got off the highway and stopped at a traffic light, at least half a mile from the club. It was a real quiet summer night, and while we were waiting for the light to change we heard this noise coming from down the road. It was Raymond and Steven screaming at each other.

Joe looked at me and said, "Here we go."

When we got to the club, we drove around back to the band house. Raymond was shouting at Steven, and then he stormed off without even looking at us. Brad Whitford played with them that night and the difference was instantaneous. As soon as Brad plugged in, you *knew* they were gonna take off.

Ray Tabano: My last gig with Aerosmith was at a place called Menlo Park, before that Savage Beast thing. Steven didn't want me to go. He couldn't believe it. He kept saying, "You're not really leaving, are you, man?" Then at the Savage Beast he and Tom got the job of formally telling me I was out of the band. I got mad and went, "FUCK YOU!" But Joe Jammer told Joe Perry that I sucked, and so my career as a musician was over. I was bummed out, but my wife said, "Hey, what do you care? They'll never get out of the bars anyway."

The final straw was I asked Tom Hamilton to take my guitar back to Boston so I could ride my motorcycle home. Next day he stopped to get a haircut on his way to Newbury Street and someone stole my fuckin' guitar out of his car. I made him work it off until he payed me back $300.

7: Mr. Whitford

Brad Whitford: I was nineteen years old when I joined Aerosmith, which might seem young until you consider I'd already been in bands for six years. I wasn't in awe of these guys. I'd barely heard of them.

Walk This Way

I'm from Reading, Massachusetts, a suburban town north of Boston, where I was born in 1952. My father was from Massachusetts, and he met my mom at a dance for soldiers in Olympia, Washington. He was stationed at Fort Lewis at the time, so he began courting her and they married about a year later. When they moved back to Massachusetts, my dad got a job with Raytheon, the big electronics firm.

My older brother played trumpet in the high school band, so there was a trumpet in the house because my parents had to buy one. I took trumpet lessons in school for three years, starting in grammar school and going on to junior high. Then the trumpet teacher stood behind me in the music room and every time I made a mistake he'd hit me over the head with this big drum mallet. I wasn't exactly *encouraged* by this. I thought briefly about killing this guy, but decided to spare his life. So at the end of eighth grade, he came to me and said, "You're going to take the trumpet again next year, right?"

I told him no, my parents didn't want me to. Meanwhile, my father had bought this little acoustic guitar, a cheapo that he kind of kept in the corner and didn't do anything with. I picked this thing up and made this little connection with it. Then someone they knew had one of those Japanese things, a Winston, one of those electric guitars you could get at Sears for $25. And I just fell in love with it, this red-and-black Winston. This guitar opened a whole new door.

I'm the middle child in my family. One brother is five years older, the other brother five years younger. My older brother wanted to be a disc jockey and had a Wollensack tape recorder. I had this guitar but no amplifier. So one day I plugged my guitar into the Wollensack and then plugged the tape machine's external speaker jack into the speaker of our television, a big console model with the speaker exposed in the back. So I'm there in the living room, sitting on the couch, ready to go. I turned it on and played a chord and we were in business.

I started taking lessons at Pampelone Music in Reading. They were a little music store chain that offered lessons in the back of the shop. The teacher was so good that by the time he left, I probably played better than the guy that replaced him. I only took lessons for about a year, then I started to learn from records. When you're thirteen, you want to play what you hear on the radio. I wanted to learn the Rascals' songs, whatever was happening.

When I was about ten, I shared a room with my older brother, who always had the radio turned to WMEX. I remember sitting in my room and hearing the Beatles for the first time. It was "Please Please Me" and it was a big deal. The deejay, Arnie "Woo-Woo" Ginsberg, kept talking about how big this new sound from England was going to be.

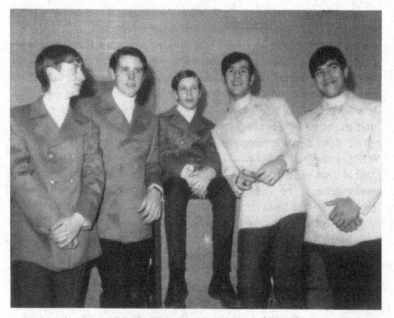

Brad Whitford, left, in Earth Inc., circa 1968
(WHITFORD COLLECTION)

My brother told me a lot about local bands like Barry and the Remains and the Rockin' Ramrods, but I was too young to go see them. He liked the Kingsmen, and I liked what he was into, so he took me to see the Kingsmen at a nightclub in Lowell on my thirteenth birthday. We had to beg the cop at the door to let me in. Around that time I went to see the Dave Clark Five at Boston Garden. They were great, did all their hits, and I immediately decided to start my own band.

The guys who worked in the music store all had bands, and they were really supportive. I remember them coaching my first band, the Symbols of Resistance, before our premier performance, probably at the Moose Lodge in North Reading. We also played at a local nightspot called the Commodore and in our junior high canteen. Then a kid who lived around the corner named Brian Beaudry played bass and sang, so we started playing together with a drummer named Ed Merullo. This was Earth Incorporated, winners of countless North Shore Battles of the Bands (usually sponsored by the Reading Jaycees) from 1967 to 1969. We had long hair, little band uniforms, the whole trip.

Why would I want to do this? One of the reasons was that when I was fifteen or sixteen, I wanted to be accepted and recognized.

My father and I never fought over the long hair thing. My parents were great. They let my bands rehearse in the house—in the dining room! Nobody else's parents put up with that, believe me. My dad was one of those guys who, before we could drive, would take us to wherever we were playing. And we got a lot of jobs because a woman who lived right near me, Mary Stafford, was a local booking agent. My high school bands—Teapot Dome, Spring Rain, Earth Incorporated—played in places like the Charlestown YMCA, a rough joint that would fill up with sailors from the Naval shipyard, most of them really shit-faced. When the NATO fleet docked in Boston, we were the band. The highlight of this era was when Teapot Dome opened for the big Boston band Orpheus down in Plymouth in January 1970.

Eventually I moved up through the ranks to play in the top neighborhood band, the Morlocks. I think I was still in that band when I graduated from high school [June 1970] and started going to Berklee College of Music the following September.

In the summer of 1969, I drove to Framingham because I heard that Led Zeppelin were gonna play in the Carousel Theater, an outdoor music pavilion on Route 9. "Sorry, kid," the guy in the box office said. "No tickets left."

Oh, man, I couldn't believe it. I called my girlfriend, Gail Brown, and said, "We're gonna go back the night of the show. We'll sit up on the hill and just listen." So that night I borrowed my dad's station wagon and picked up Gail and just as we left her driveway, the whole tailpipe fell off the car. But only partway off, so it's dragging and sparking as I'm rolling down her street. So I pulled over and just snapped the rusty thing off bare-handed and we drove to Framingham sounding like a Panzer tank.

We went up the hill and sat down and the show started and I'm going, "This is incredible! Listen to that bass!" After a while, I had to use the toilet, so we walked down to one of the police officers and asked where the bathrooms were and he pointed behind him, inside the gate. So we walked in and used the bathrooms, and then walked up the ramp and sat down in a couple of vacant seats. Led Zeppelin was playing in jeans and dirty T-shirts. Back then you looked like you were on the road. Jimmy Page was bowing his Les Paul guitar during "Dazed and Confused," and he had that Danelectro with two full stacks of Marshall amps. They did a couple of songs from their second album, which wasn't out yet, and blew everyone away. Page was just the most incredible showman I'd ever seen, just mesmerizing. His facial expressions and body movements were indescribably cool. Impossible to take your eyes off him! It was the kind of wild vibe that you don't get at many concerts these days. Before MTV, there was amazing mystery in rock 'n' roll: You had to go see a band to find out what they actually looked like. A lot of that mystery is gone. If you think about it, it was a terrible thing to have lost.

Anyway, they did a couple of encores, it was well past midnight, and the final song was "Communication Breakdown." We're talking about a major change in my life here. I got stopped for speeding on the way back, got my girlfriend home real late, and got yelled at by her parents and mine. The next day I went out and bought a Gibson Les Paul.

Berklee was on Boylston Street. The attitude that prevailed was snobby in those days, real jazz. If you were interested in rock 'n' roll, that wasn't very cool. The *in* music was fusion—*Bitches Brew*, Chick Corea, the whole jazz-rock thing. People asked, "What kind of band do you want to have?" I'd say, "I want to have a band like Humble Pie—someone who sang like Steve Marriott, two guitars, bass, and drums." Because I was a huge Humble Pie fan—*huge*. I was such a Humble Pie fan that I'd hang out with them when they came to Boston. They'd play at the Orpheum and I'd go back to the hotel with them. I was Brad, the Humble Pie groupie!

I was living at home while I was going to Berklee. After my last semester, I just took my Les Paul and my Marshall stack and I went down there and spent most of the summer of 1971 playing at Preston's on Nantucket Island. This was my wild summer and I had a great time. When we finished on Nantucket, we went up to play around Lake Sunapee toward the end of the summer. The connection was Dwight Farren, Twitty, a really talented guy who sang and played guitar in Justin Thyme and he'd also been in one of Steven's bands. When we played in Sunapee Tom and Joe came to see me play because they heard about me from Twitty and they were unhappy with Raymond. We were playing this place that was a real hole, that looked like it was about to fall into the lake, across from this restaurant Joe had worked at. That's where they ended up watching us play.

I watched them too. They looked more serious, more rock & roll than most people in bands, like they were really living it instead of just having a fantasy about it. They had the right clothes, the right hair, the right attitude. I guess I had the right gear and was playing the right notes that night. We talked afterwards. They were friendly guys, really into it, and I liked them immediately. They had the gang you wanted to be in. It was a very exclusive thing.

Next weekend I was at home and Joe Perry called me.

"Hey, man, it's Joe. Joe Perry. I'm just calling 'cause we want to hang out with you."

"Sure, man. I'd love to."

"So, Brad, what would you think about playing with Aerosmith?"

I told him I didn't know. I'd never heard the band and didn't know anything about it. Joe told me they were playing that night at the Lakeview Ballroom in Mendon and so I went to see them. They were playing Stones, Zeppelin, Lennon, all these cool covers, exactly the songs you wanted to hear but couldn't, because all the bands that played them were too big to come to your town. They had some original songs too that had a lot of promise.

That's how I found the Humble Pie-type band I was looking for. I listened to them for about ten minutes and I thought to myself, *I should probably do this.*

A few days later, I went up to New Hampshire to learn what they were playing. On my first day, I was standing outside Tom Hamilton's house. I was in the band, but I'd only met Steven a couple of times at that point, it was my first day, and Steven comes up to me with a spoon of coke. He didn't even say anything, just held the spoon up. And I'm thinking, *Ooh, what's this? What's going on here?* Because this was a whole other level in the drug culture that was going on, that I hadn't experienced. New worlds were opening for young Brad. For me, it was an indelible period, a period of "Yeah!"—an explosive era.

My first gig with Aerosmith was at this club in Vermont, the Savage Beast. Raymond is still there, arguing with Steven. As much as Joe and Tom wanted Raymond out, they hadn't gotten Steven to the point of telling Raymond until that night. The funny thing was Raymond didn't leave. After those gigs in Vermont, we practiced and rehearsed and Raymond was still there. I couldn't figure this out, because if you threw me out of a band, you wouldn't see hide nor hair of me again. Pride and ego would say, *Forget it, I'm outta here.* I still don't understand their relationship, which goes on strong today, but I do know that Steven is loyal and it hurt him to see Raymond go.

After that, I moved into 1325 Commonwealth Avenue with them. I was nineteen years old and had a little leather satchel and a guitar case in my hand.

Moving in with them was important. Raymond lived somewhere else, had his own thing happening, and so wasn't perceived as this dedicated band guy who was staking everything on making it happen. I didn't even have a room. When I first got there, I didn't even have a bed. I slept on the couch in the living room with Steven's piano. Joey and Steven had just

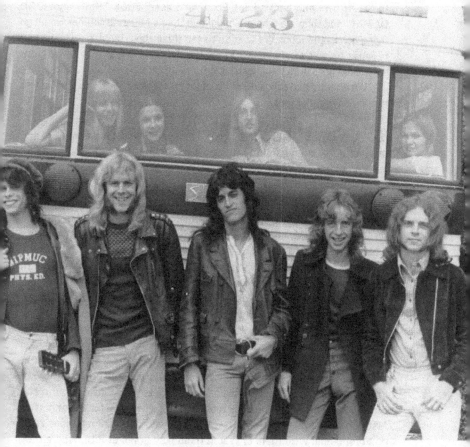

Aerosmith as Brad Whitford joins, 1971
(PHOTO: CHRIS SMITH)

moved to other apartments nearby and Tom had taken over their room, replaced by me and John Andrews, who was helping us out with his pickup truck. But right away at a gig in Hopedale, I met a girl named Lori Phillips, who was the sister of Joe's girlfriend Randy, so I'd spend a lot of time at her apartment.

Also living at 1325 was the band's crew guy, Mark Lehman, who moved all our equipment and got next to nothing to do it. It was a horrible job because we were all so arrogant that we wouldn't help him. The elevator didn't always work and Joe and I would come back from a gig, collapse into the apartment and light a joint. Soon we'd hear "FUCK THIS!" and "GOD DAMN!" and then we'd hear a crash and then a Marshall cabinet would go flying across the room. We wouldn't even *think* about helping this poor guy because he was the "roadie." When we did help, it was only to save our expensive gear from total destruction.

We already had this kind of vision of grandiosity. We were also having trouble paying the rent.

Tom Hamilton: We were lucky to have a lot of beautiful and interesting women coming into our lives around this time. We were all starting to pair off, and in my case it really took because I'm still with this foxy brunette I met back in those far-away days . . .

Terry Hamilton: I graduated from high school in Worcester, Mass., in 1969, and that summer I went to see my friend Amy Artz who was working as a counselor at Camp Kearsarge in New Hampshire. She was dating Joe Perry. We went to see the Jam Band play at The Barn and then to a party in someone's parent's big house, where I met Tom Hamilton, John Andrews, Robert Grasmere, the whole Jam Band crowd.

Then I moved to Boston to go to New England College of Art, where one of my classmates was Chris Smith, brother of Henry, who knew all those guys. Amy and I would go over to 1325 to visit or we'd bring them leftover food from waitressing jobs. The guys were great and it was a fun place to hang out. Joe was usually in the kitchen cooking hot, spicy Italian food, blasting giant cockroaches off the kitchen walls with this air pistol he had. Steven lived in the back room with Lisa Bercecki for a year or two. Mark Lehman had a waterbed we used to hang out on. Sometimes we'd go to rehearsal with them or watch them play down at B.U., where they blasted the students off the sidewalk at lunchtime.

Tom Hamilton: There was this warm afternoon where Amy and Terry came over and the three of us just kinda lay around Mark's waterbed. Terry's in bell-bottom hip-huggers and a sexy halter top: sexy, but friendly-sexy. I just looked at her soft belly and flipped out. I'm this New Hampshire farmer kid, and here's this exotic girl from Massachusetts. I tried to get something going with her, but that summer [1971] she and Amy took off for Israel. We got together as soon as she came back.

Joe Perry: Around this time I started to go out with Judy Nylon, one of the best-looking and most intriguing girls in town. Judy

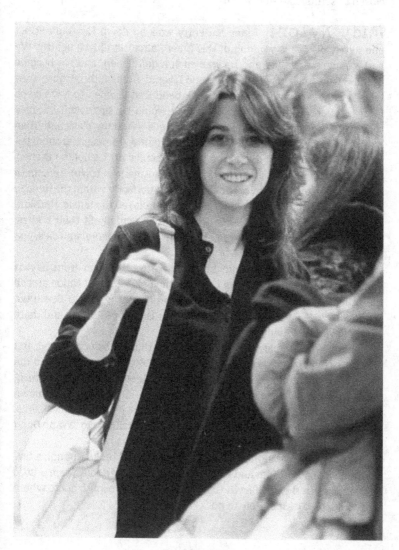

Terry Hamilton
(PHOTO: RON POWNALL)

was totally ultra-hip, and she opened a lot of doors that were otherwise closed to scruffs like Aerosmith.

Judy Nylon: I met Joe Perry walking down Newbury Street one day while I was working at this biker haircutting place nearby. We had a common tonality and he was such a gentleman, and we became friends. I was surprised the first time I heard Aerosmith because they were a fully existent, functioning rock band that seemed to have come from nowhere. I knew immediately they would be successful because they were the voice of the mills and the malls—working-class suburban kids who had grown up on English rock. There were people around, so-called hip people, who dismissed them as copies of the Rolling Stones, but they just didn't get it. Boston is an Anglo-American town; Aerosmith might have been derivative, but they figured perfectly within the lineage of an English band. They looked English, they played the music, the skin-tight velvet jackets from Granny Takes a Trip actually fit their bodies. They performed shirtless a lot and they didn't have pectoral muscles, just like the English musicians.

They were also fresh and didn't have the cynicism from having watched what happened to the Lost and the Beacon Street Union and all the other Boston bands that were decimated by the whole Bosstown sound fiasco. People said a band couldn't break out of Boston, and there weren't even that many bands around.

There were various circles in Boston back then, all self-contained, and only girls could move through them: the gay "Boston bohemians" in the South End; the street scenes on Charles and Newbury streets; the macrobiotic people; the political crowd from the civil rights and antiwar movements; art students; jazz people; the universities; and the folk people. The only thing they had in common was Howlin' Wolf's song "Wang Dang Doodle," a huge Boston song, a big jam at parties.

If I have any role in their story, it was only that I broke through a few of these circles for them and helped people to know about them a little before they met the people who could *really* help Aerosmith get to where they wanted so desperately to go.

8: The Red Bus

Steven Tyler: Man! So much happening that fall [1971] I can't remember half of it.

I do remember Led Zeppelin at Boston Garden [September 7], because we were up in Sunapee and Henry Smith drove the Zeppelin gear up to the lake while Zeppelin was on a break. The truck was just sitting there in his parents' driveway, vibrating.

"Open it up, let's look."

"I can't, Steven."

"C'mon."

"Richard Cole [Led Zeppelin's fearsome road manager] would kill anyone who messed around with the gear."

"Hey, we just wanna look." And as I recall, I didn't even take anything, except maybe some drumsticks.

I remember the songs we were getting together a lot better. "Movin' Out" and "One Way Street" were written at 1325. We had "Somebody," "Mama Kin," and "Major Barbara." I had been working on "Dream On" for a long time already, but the first sheet music is dated May 26, 1971. What actually happened is that I took the suitcase money and bought an RMI keyboard and set it up and played "Dream On" for the first time on the road at the Shaboo Inn in Connecticut. "Dream On" and "Major Barbara" came to life on that keyboard. Then we made the mistake of staying at the Shaboo Inn that night. Me and Joe had a couple of girls and we all slept in the same bed. You know how you fuck till you're *blind?*

We both got the crabs.

Tom Hamilton: One of the first times we actually tried to get a record deal was when we auditioned for a guy named George Page at West Campus. He had an in at Columbia, so we set up and did "One Way Street" for him as a demo. The song was pretty new then, and we felt awkward about it, so we sucked.

George Page: I was road-managing Edgar Winter's band White Trash around this time and had a girlfriend who moved in with Terry Cohen on St. Paul Street in Brookline. Terry and Tom Hamilton were together and Tom stayed there a lot. He kept telling me I had to see his band, so they took me to an Aerosmith concert at some high school out in the suburbs. The show started with a drum solo, which was so eccentric I couldn't believe it. They were this full-blown rock band, and the high school kids ate it up. It was like having the *Exile*-era Rolling Stones playing in the gym.

So I started to hang out with them, which meant doing a lot of drugs. Steven and Joe were always fighting, with Joey Kramer as the mediator and peacemaker. There was so much conflict that I never thought they would stay together. Steven was incredibly confident and sure that he would make it someday. Joe was equally determined—if not more so.

I knew they were simply one of the best bands I'd ever heard, so I took this tape to Steve Paley at Epic Records in New York. He *hated* it. He also hated the band. I don't remember if he saw them or had someone check them out, but I remember him telling me that the public will *never* buy a blatant Mick Jagger rip-off. I had never experienced someone passing on a band so vehemently. He advised me to drop Aerosmith immediately for the good of my career.

It was intense, because I knew how great they were. I'd heard Steven play "Dream On" at this high school and I just knew that this was an important song.

Joe Perry: Mark Lehman's van was getting really beat. It had 100,000 miles on it and the end seemed in sight. We used to play gigs with the Joneses, two brothers who had a hot-shit local band from Worcester. They were a *great* cover band that always drew a crowd and made good money. Their father managed them and drove their bus, and soon we were saying, "Hey, we should have a bus too."

Then we ran into this hippie commune who had just traveled cross-country in their bright red converted school bus. It had a hand-crafted interior, oak cabinetry, plenty of Ken Kesey/Merry Pranksters mystique, and it converted to propane if you ran out of gas. We hung with these very impressive California hippies who tried to explain their unmarked wiring system to us.

We thought it was the coolest thing. We wanted it, but we couldn't even pay our rent. We were stealing food from supermarkets to survive. So I went out to Hopedale and told my parents about the bus. My mother noticed I was close to starving and asked if we were sure about what we were doing, but in the end they cosigned a bank loan for $2,500 and we bought the bus. I was so grateful to my parents and I remember saying,

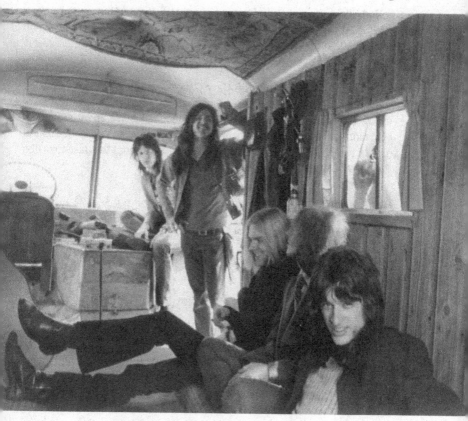

Aerosmith in the band's first van, April 1971
(TYLER COLLECTION)

"As soon as we get some money, we're going to pay my parents back."

"Yeah, sure, OK, right."

But I busted everyone's balls and we finally paid them back a couple of years later. Mark Lehman got a second-class license and we were on the road.

Joey Kramer: It was a 72-passenger Ward school bus that a guerilla theater troupe had converted to a hippie caravan. We kept it parked in front of 1325 and drove it all over New England that freezing winter of 1971–72. The wiring was ridiculous hippie shit, non–color-coded, like a huge bowl of greasy spaghetti. If something went wrong with it I'd take it over to Atamian Ford and the guys in the repair shop would just laugh at me.

Joe Perry: Later on Gary Cabozzi would spend hours out on the street trying to make the red bus go in the middle of winter. None of us were that handy, and Cabozzi was a mechanic. We spent many ice-cold nights huddled in the back of the bus on the way to and from isolated gigs in rural New England, trying to keep warm around the gas stove like the crew of some B-17 lost over Germany.

9: The Academy of Music

Steven Tyler: Just after Thanksgiving [December 2, 1971], we got a big break when Aerosmith was booked into the Academy of Music on 14th Street in New York City, third on a bill with Humble Pie and Edgar Winter's band. No one exactly remembers how this happened, but Steve Paul was managing the Winter brothers, and years before he had booked the Chain into his club the Scene, where we played with the McCoys, Rick Derringer's band, and now Rick was playing with Edgar, so there you have it. This was our first gig in New York, and our first out of New England.

Tom Hamilton: This wasn't a college mixer, a high school gym, or the Lakeview Ballroom. It was the biggest gig we'd ever done. Humble Pie with Steve Marriott and Peter Frampton in the band were like a supergroup to us, and Edgar Winter had hit records and everything. The idea seemed to be that if we did well, Steve Paul was going to be our manager and our troubles would be over.

There was a big fuck-up on my part because we got the job on short notice and my amp was in the shop getting fixed, so we had to leave early so we could pick up an amp for me in New York. We piled everything in the red bus and drove all night, down to the city, totally aware that it was either going to be a turning point for us or a disaster.

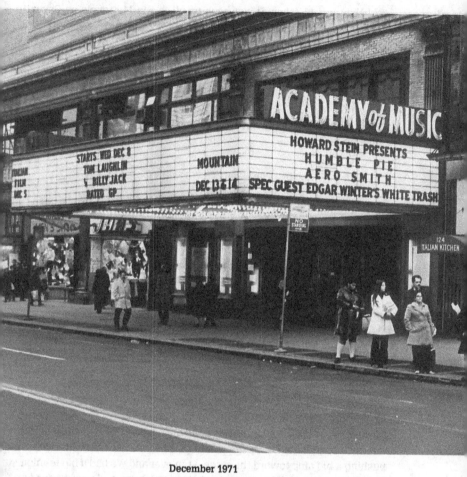

December 1971
(COURTESY ED MALHOIT)

Robert Grasmere: I had just gone to Boston to see the boys when they got word about this show and they said, "Come to New York with us." I told them they could crash afterward at my parents' house in New Jersey because my folks were out of town. I think we left late at night or early in the morning because I remember driving all night in this old bus and everybody was really exhausted. Our first stop was in midtown, where we had to pick up an amp for Tom at Sam Ash because the Winter brothers wouldn't let us use their bass amp, even though they said they would. Then Steven took us all to the Metropole on Seventh Avenue for a couple of drinks and we studied the nude go-go dancers. Then we had to go over to legendary Max's Kansas City for a couple of drinks, just to check out the place and see if there were any famous people around. By the time we pulled up to the theater, we were all pretty far gone.

Joe Perry: We get to the Academy of Music and there's our name up in lights:

HOWARD STEIN PRESENTS

HUMBLE PIE

AEROSMITH

SPEC GUEST EDGAR WINTER'S WHITE TRASH

Right away, a cop tells us we can't park in front of the theater. The band ended up setting up the equipment because Mark Lehman was too busy finding a place to park our bus in New York.

Liz Derringer: No one had seen Steven in a couple of years. We'd heard he had a new band, but there just wasn't much buzz about it in New York.

Steve Paul knew Steven from the Scene, which had closed when Steve got tired of being squeezed by the hoods that bothered him constantly. He brought this albino blues guitarist up from Texas in a famous deal and now managed both Winter brothers and my husband Rick. So I'm hanging out backstage listening to the sound checks and I see Steven Tallarico pushing a big amp toward the stage. I ran over and we had a big reunion. He'd lost a lot of weight, grown his hair even longer, and was dressed in a combination of tights and flowing rags—and these were his street clothes! He was so excited about his new band Aerosmith and we just had a great time.

Steven Tyler: I was in awe of anyone who actually went out and toured, and here was Rick, who'd already had a band when I was in high school, the McCoys, playing "Hang On Sloopy" and "Fever" and being famous, which was what I had in mind as well. I'm hanging out with them backstage and I'm going, "Duh, what's it *like* to tour? What kind of hotels? When you get paid, do you get a lot of money?" The *mys-*

tique of just going out and playing was still a big dream for me. They must have thought I was so naive. I guess I was. Anyway, I became friends with Rick and Liz again. Just being invited to their house was a big thing.

Another thing that happened was we learned how to tune. Our band couldn't tune to save its life and we were always fighting about this. Rick had this new thing that tuned the guitar electronically: the closer you got to the note, it showed a standing wave. Joe came in and Rick showed him this trick and that's how we learned to tune. This was a big deal at the time.

Robert Grasmere: Steve Paul put them on the bill and insisted that Aerosmith play three songs only and get off the stage. So there was a big argument over which three to do. They came out and at first the audience was bored and I thought, *Oh, no.* But then Steven turned up the heat and the audience began to respond.

Tom Hamilton: We did "Make It," "One Way Street," and "Major Barbara." The audience liked it and applauded. Then, instead of saying good night and walking off, Steven and Joe started "Train" and just kept going.

Robert Grasmere: I'm in the wings as Aerosmith started its fourth song, and Steve Paul starts shouting, "They were only supposed to play three fucking songs! Get off! Get them off!" He was practically ripping my arm off, apoplectic with rage. But the kids down front were loving it and I think they finished with "Walkin' the Dog."

Tom Hamilton: I was surprised how much the audience liked us. There was a lot of applause, but as we came off I hear Steve Paul yelling at Steven and Joe because they sat down to play "Major Barbara." Only big stars like the Stones or Zeppelin were supposed to sit down and play acoustic music during a rock show.

Steve Paul shouted, "How can you have the *balls* to sit down?? You're two *unknowns*, two fucking guys off the *turnip truck!*"

Robert Grasmere: They sent me upstairs to collect the money, so I made my way through a backstage labyrinth to the manager's office, where they counted out $700 in one-dollar bills. Then they said, "Now *you* count it." But I was too drunk to focus on this and just pre-

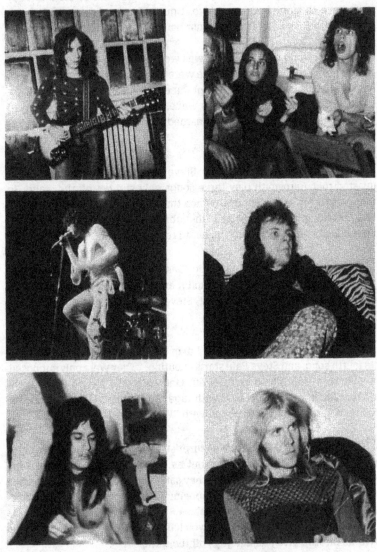

On and offstage at the Academy of Music
(HAMILTON COLLECTION)

tended to count it. Later Steven got mad at me because he said all the money wasn't there.

I did manage to recruit three very pretty girls from Yonkers and we all got back on the bus and headed to my parents' place in New Jersey. But they wouldn't let the bus through the Holland Tunnel, so we had to drive all the way to the George Washington Bridge to cross the river. At my parents' house, the band was still so excited by the show that everyone stayed up all night talking and no one paid any attention to these three very willing and pretty girls, who I then had to drive back to Yonkers the following day. Later we drove back to Boston and the next night they were playing again in some high school out in the far suburbs of Boston.

10: John O'Toole

Joe Perry: By the last days of 1971, we were really low on money and there were unspoken questions about whether we could actually afford to stay together. Gigs were few and far between and we were stealing to survive. We saw other bands making $1,000 a week playing other people's songs, four sets a night, but we looked down on them because they were trapped. You have to rehearse, you have to do new material of your own, or you're just fuckin' *dead*. So we stuck to our $300 high school dances.

We had this great regular gig at the Charlestown Naval Shipyard, but we lost it. It was a steady thing, a Tuesday night dinner every other week in the officers' mess. We loved it because we usually only played high school dances on the weekend. It was regular, we got $400, and they fed us in our own room with a big table that they set up for us. We'd get a huge roast beef dinner while 100 young officers ate in the next room, then we played two forty-five-minute sets. It was what we called a tit gig.

One night after a couple of months of this, Steven and I went into the office to get paid while our equipment was being loaded out next door. Steven saw this beautiful slide projector and maneuvered it out of the office and into the hallway, where we loaded it into the truck.

I said, "What the fuck? Don't do that." But it was too late. The projector was stolen. We got paid and left. Sure enough, next week we got a call: "Don't come back, not working out, thanks for everything, sorry." They knew what had happened and I was really pissed.

Then Mark Lehman quit.

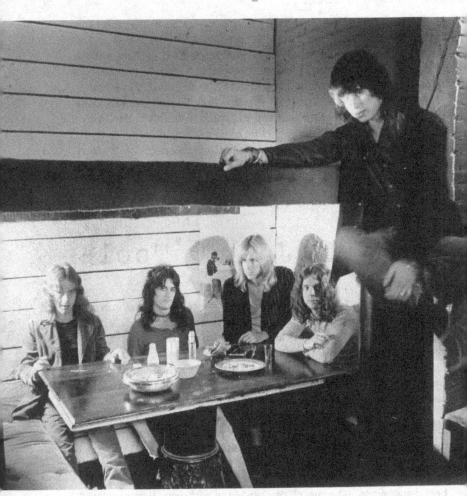

Dinner at Kent Street
(PHOTO: CHRIS SMITH)

Tom Hamilton: Our deal with Mark was that he got 10 percent of the net, a terrible deal. If we got paid $300, he got $30, plus he had to pay for the upkeep of his truck, which no one but him was allowed to drive. If we'd had those negotiating skills when we signed our first record deal, we'd all be a lot better off now. Despite—or maybe because of—his peonage, Mark used to boss us around and throw big tantrums.

After we bought the red bus, Mark took this as his cue that we didn't need him anymore. He'd complain about our chronic poverty and not having enough to eat and Steven gave him a sarcastic look and said, "Hey, Mark, you know, you could go out and *steal* food just like anyone else."

Steven Tyler: Mark was follicly challenged, which meant he didn't have much hair. That's him in the lyrics to "Mama Kin":

Bald as an egg at eighteen,
and workin' for your daddy's a drag.

Joe Perry: So Mark left the fold. He took his step van and went back home to Amherst, where he started a furniture company. We never saw him again. He's the only person who never came back to see us. Gary Cabozzi helped us on our local gigs, but for a while when we went up to New Hampshire, we were on our own.

Gary Cabozzi: So I fixed their bus as best I could and started to drive it for them. Steven taught me how to be a roadie—fixing cords and cables, stage-managing, eyes open all the time, duck down when onstage, don't get in the way, make a clear path from the dressing room to the stage, drive to South Boston for illegal beer on Sundays when the stores were closed and the band got thirsty. (Joe Perry and I almost got killed in tough fuckin' Southie when some of the locals took a dislike to us and wrecked a friend's pickup, which we had borrowed.)

My first show with them was at Marlborough High out in the 'burbs. The place was packed with kids because Aerosmith already had that kind of reputation as a band that brought the house down every time. But they had two main problems. One, they were broke. Two, they got thrown out of B.U. and had no place to rehearse.

Tom Hamilton: The first eviction notice came in December. Steven had moved to Kent Street and Joey was living with his girlfriend Nina on Hemenway Street, but it was a blow for the rest of us who were still living at 1325. The eviction notice gave us thirty days to get out. The band's bank account had $19 in it. There were no gigs because we'd saturated the local market. We couldn't rehearse. Time was running out for us.

One day Brad and I went to E. U. Wurlitzer's to do some errands. It was Boston's main music store and had been like going to Disneyland for me since I was thirteen years old. Brad and I were hanging around the counter when a friend named Scott Baerenwald walked over. He played with Ready Teddy, a good local band. He asked what was up and we told him we had no place to rehearse. He told us his brother was the assistant manager over at the Fenway Theater on Massachussetts Avenue, right down the street. Maybe we could use the stage to rehearse in the daytime.

I thought this sounded far-fetched, but Brad said, "Call the other guys and tell them to head over there."

"Just ask for Swine," Scott said.

Swine? I wanted to make sure I heard him right. No point in accidentally calling someone a pig. An hour later, the whole band converged at the Fenway. It was a small theater, about 1,500 seats, but it had a big stage and a balcony and was exactly the kind of place we wanted to play in. We wandered around until we found a little wood-paneled manager's office and came face-to-face with two of the toughest guys we'd ever seen. Steve "Swine" Baerenwald was about six-five with long hair pulled back, narrow eyes that had seen their share of mud and blood, decked out in classic biker's denim. His no-shit face was hidden behind a huge bushy mustache that made him look like the old-fashioned ice cream man. He introduced us to his boss, John O'Toole, who looked like an especially mean longshoreman. O'Toole made Swine look sweet. His voice was a long, low rumble: "So I hear you're lookin' for a place to practice. Well, it'll be fifty bucks a day, plus fifty for an engineer to run the soundboard."

We just stood there, another opportunity blowing away like a fart in a breeze. O'Toole may as well have asked us each to cut off a left nut and put it on the desk. (Actually, that would have been more feasible, since we at least *had* a left nut apiece.) He didn't wait for a reply, because our stunned faces had *No deal* written all over them. So after letting the value of the favor he was about to do us fully sink in, he said: "Well, I'll tell you what. I don't have anybody coming in here this weekend. You can set up here for the next three days, and if I like you, maybe we can work something out."

Bam! Just like that, we'd had our first taste of the flip side of John O'Toole's personality. It was only a rehearsal space, but we were elated.

Aside from the occasional concert [T. Rex, Traffic, Santana, Captain Beefheart], nothing much was happening in the theater. So there was basically no heat and it was winter. We plugged in some space heaters and wore our overcoats. We'd set up the gear on the stage, but it was so cold that we kept the big stage curtain closed to conserve any heat coming from the amps. It was probably fifty degrees in there on the warmest day. So we piled on the layers and rehearsed, working on our new songs. Joe wore woolen gloves with the fingers cut out, and we'd see our breath in the air. At four-thirty sharp, the five of us and Tiger, Joey's huge Great Dane, would pile into Steven's black VW Beetle like a bunch of circus clowns with guitar cases on our laps and this giant dog. *The Three Stooges* were on at five and we didn't want to miss them.

"Shit, man," Steven protested. (He hated the Stooges and didn't watch them unless we made him.) "There's too many of us for this little car. We're gonna blow the fuckin' engine. Can't some of you take the trolley?"

I tried it once or twice, but after watching the car disappear down Commonwealth Avenue and waiting in the wind chill of a Boston winter, I decided it was worth whatever it took to get in that backseat.

Meanwhile, we still weren't working, and the eviction notice loomed over our heads like an evil spirit.

We started getting a really good core of original material together at the Fenway Theater. Constant rehearsals, an astonishing luxury to most working club bands, allowed us to polish songs until we were ready to play them for whoever would listen. We'd get there early in the morning and stay until the Stooges were on. Once in a while Steven or somebody would disappear and come back wide-eyed and talking about John O'Toole taking out his gargantuan Buck knife and shoveling premium blow up their nose. It wasn't long before we were all sneaking up to John's office.

"You fuckin' guys are getting pretty good," he told us one day matter-of-factly. "But you need to get out more and hear what other bands are doing. Listen, Cactus is playing here on Saturday. Here's some free tickets and I wanna see you there."

Cactus was a big band, so of course we wanted to go. That Friday we stowed all the gear down under the stage, ready to share our new-found turf with one of the name acts of the day.

It snowed the night of the show. I brought some pot and a couple hits of speed, and we marched up to the balcony and took possession of the first row. We put our feet up, fired up the first joint of the evening, and waited. And waited. Nothing. No show.

I'm just getting off on the speed. "Hey, you guys!" Someone's talking to us. It's Prew, who ran errands around the place. "John's gotta see you in his office right now, OK?"

We jumped up and ran down to see what was up.

"Bad news. Fuckin' Cactus can't get in because of the snow, so they canceled. You guys are gonna have to play."

He whipped out his big Buck knife and we lined up. One by one he told us to lie down on the couch with our heads hanging back over the edge and he packed all ten gaping nostrils with gigantic hits of the devil's dandruff. We humped the gear onto the stage, the lights went down, the curtain went up, and we were off:

Good evening people welcome to the show.
Got something here I want you all to know.
When life and people bring on primal screams,
You gotta think of what it's gonna take
to make your dreams—
Make it. Don't break it.

We played "Movin' Out," "Mama Kin," "One Way Street," and every-thing else we knew. There were only 100 people there, but they were rockin'. It felt so great to feed on this. We settled in and for the first time were able to squeeze their energy to recharge our own performance in a concert hall. It was a whole new experience, but it also felt like we had done it many times before. After the show, we went to see John O'Toole.

"You were fuckin' *great*," he bellowed. "It was like watching a major act. I just wish Frank could have been here."

We'd heard him mention this guy Frank before with awestruck ad-miration. Someone asked who he was.

"Who's Frank Connelly? Are you shittin' me? He's only the biggest promoter in Boston. He's only the fuckin' guy who put the Beatles on at Boston Garden. He owns the fuckin' Carousel out in Framingham where Hendrix and Zeppelin played. He brought the Stones to town last time. Frank Connelly is hot shit, baby. And he never managed anyone that I knew of. If he heard you and decided to manage you guys, take my word for it, you'd be making five hundred bucks a night in no time."

We looked at each other and thought, *Holy shit.* The most we usually got was $300.

Next morning we got another eviction notice. If we didn't get some-thing together quick, we were gonna be out in the freezing cold.

Late that afternoon, we were hacking away at arrangements on the stage at the Fenway when suddenly the curtain opened and the stage lights came on. Frigid air from the dark auditorium washed over us like an icy wave, and John O'Toole appeared in the aisle downstage and yelled, "Hey! Play some of your songs." We had an idea what was hap-pening but couldn't see who was out there because of the stage lights.

Joe Perry: The curtain goes up, cold air slams us, and the house is black. We're standing there playing our set to an empty theater.

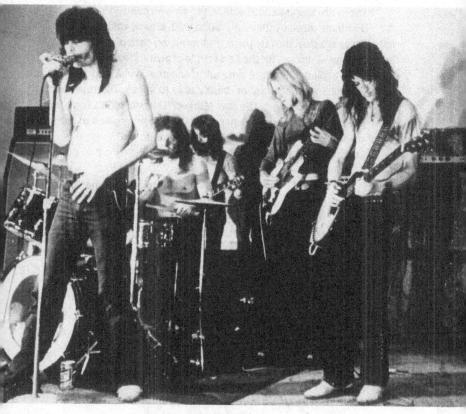

Rehearsing at the Fenway Theater, 1972
(TYLER COLLECTION)

Then the curtains closed again. Steven says, "What's happening? Is this weird or what?" But then we peeked through the curtain and no one was out there.

Tom Hamilton: Someone had been smoking a cigar. We could smell it. But when we looked, no one was there. A mysterious presence had been and gone, like in a movie. That's what it felt like. We put down our microphones, sticks, and guitars and made our way up to John's office. He was sitting at his desk with nothing on it but some papers. "Frank left this paperwork for you boys to look over when you have a chance," John growled.

"These are management contracts," Steven said.

"Goddamn straight they are," John said, almost smiling. Our mouths fell open as we read the last page, guaranteeing each of us an implausibly large amount of income for the first couple of years. It said that if we didn't make this implausibly large amount of income, we would be free and clear. We looked at each other, barely able to speak. Did this mean we could stop stealing food at the Star Market? That we didn't have to book our own gigs? That we didn't have to worry about a place to rehearse? Did it mean that someone would be looking out for us?

Out came the Buck knife!

Joe Perry: We took the contracts back to our apartment, and we sat down at the kitchen table with the contracts in one hand and the eviction notice in the other. We just looked at each other and shook our heads in disbelief. That's how close it was.

Really Rockin' in Boston

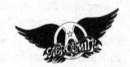

We believed that anything worth doing was worth overdoing.

—Steven Tyler

The early 1970s were weird times for rock 'n' roll. The big late-sixties American bands—the Velvet Underground, the MC5, and the Stooges from Detroit—were history. Jim Morrison died of a heroin overdose in 1971. James Brown had the best band in the world. Alice Cooper, another Detroit band, got a lot of attention with a stage show featuring a live snake and a working guillotine.

In England, the Rolling Stones were in exile and Led Zeppelin IV hadn't been released. Jamaican reggae was breaking out of Brixton. In the London clubs, a new movement was hatching. David Bowie's androgynous persona was an underground sensation and the #1 record was *Electric Warrior* by Marc Bolan's band, T. Rex. It was a new era—glitter, glam, trash—and the final stake in the heart of peace and love.

The glam rock scene in London started happening in 1971 when rock musicians like Bolan and David Bowie's Spiders from Mars began mocking sexual taboos while churning out throbbing hard rock. Bowie, T. Rex, and their American counterparts (Lou Reed, Alice Cooper, and the New York Dolls) built on the cool primitivism of the Stooges and the Velvet Underground and evolved into Warholesque collages of cross-dressing and gay impersonation that proceeded to take over the rock world, the fashion industry, and the avant-garde on both sides of the Atlantic.

Cut to a white-hot new rock band that storms Lower Manhattan in early 1972. The singer has big pouty lips and he minces across the stage like Mick Jagger's kid sister. The dark shag-cut guitar player slouches; he roars like Keith Richards. A tall blond guy is playing the bass. But we're not talking about Aerosmith. Look closer: This band's from New York City. The bass player is wearing a tutu. The singer's in high heels. The guitar player wears a dress. The rhythm guitar player isn't wearing pants. They have terrorist energy and addictive charisma, but they can't really play because while hardworking Aerosmith is rehearsing in Boston, the New York Dolls are flitting from shop to shop just like butterflies on the Lower East Side, buying frocks and eyeliner.

However, in the Oscar Wilde Room at the Mercer Arts Center or a bar called Nobody's on Bleecker Street, where 484 kids are packed like goats in a space meant for 150, the New York Dolls look and sound like the Second Coming of Christ. Singer David Johansen, an alumnus of the East Village anarchist street gang the Motherfuckers, floats on stiletto heels like a drag queen. Guitarist Johnny Thunders, name taken from an old Kinks album (real name: John Anthony Genzale), blasts out adrenalized Stones chords through a haze of 'ludes and tulle. The rest of the band [Billy Murcia, Sylvain Sylvain, Arthur Kane] staggers in their London-made stacked-heel boots and their parody movie-harlot drag and drunkenly blasts out their songs—Bo Diddley's "Pills," "Looking for a Kiss," "Personality Crisis"—for enraptured audiences of downtown superstars and rock critics, who en masse anointed the Dolls as the Next Big Thing and the Wave of the Future and the biggest thing to hit New York since China White.

"It was the Rolling Stones on acid," Steven Tyler says admiringly. But eventually, Aerosmith would watch the Dolls snatch defeat from the jaws of victory and collapse into oblivion and death, while they soldiered on through the dangerous 1970s . . .

1: Father Frank

Joe Perry: So we signed the contracts with Father Frank, as we called him. It was like a bolt from the blue. We'd just played in New York and been pissed on. We had no bites or even nibbles, so it was almost like magic. We each got a little money when we signed, which we used to buy some groceries and try to put our lives together after two years of grinding poverty.

Frank Connelly was forty years old, the big promoter in Boston. We were totally in awe of him, and he became our father figure and coach and inspiration. He never missed an opportunity to tell us how great we were. In our first meeting with him, he looked each of us in the eye and said, "You boys are the next Beatles or else I'm a moron! When that goddamned curtain went up, I heard the war drums pounding and saw the goddamned Indians running over the hill! Your whole damned thing, it's *majestic!*"

Frank was a tough ex-Marine with gray hair and a red nose, well dressed but casual, the type who wore an ascot instead of a tie. He had the grand manner of an Irish poet and an incredible gift of the gab. He was originally from Providence, but he did the whole Boston Irish blarney—very authentic. When it came time to sign his contracts, he met with each of us, one at a time. It was like, "NEXT!"

Within days, he had nicknames for us. Steven was L. M.—or Loud Mouth. I was the Flash. Tom was the Brain. Joey was Coitainly! Coitainly!—after Curly in the Three Stooges. Brad was Lighthorse. Frank completely took us under his wing, like we were the family he never had. He brought us out to his house in the suburbs in his Delta 88 and cooked for us or took us to dinner in the back room of Giro's Restaurant in Boston's North End, where he drank with his shady pals. That's where he taught us to drink bourbon whiskey like gentlemen instead of shooting cans of malt liquor until we collapsed.

I spent many a night in Giro's, getting shit-faced with Father Frank, listening to his tales of the Beatles, Hendrix, Janis Joplin, Tom Jones, Diana Ross and the Supremes, and Simon and Garfunkel, who he first booked into the Carousel Theater as a $250 opening act for the Lovin' Spoonful. He told us how his driver had gone to pick up Brian Epstein, manager of the Beatles, at Logan Airport in 1964 and made derogatory comments about homosexuals to Epstein, who was gay. Epstein kicked the guy out of the car in the middle of the tunnel under Boston Harbor. When the Beatles came to town to play Boston Garden a few weeks later, they only stayed fourteen hours and left.

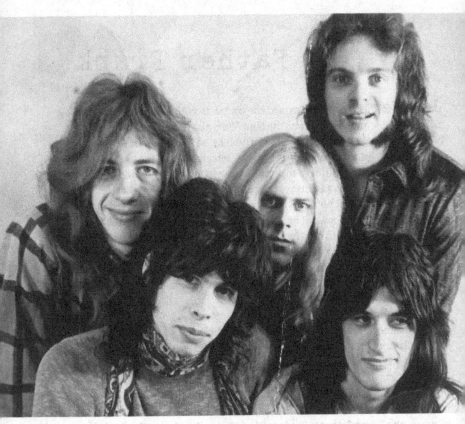

(HAMILTON COLLECTION)

Our first gig was typical Frank. He calls and tells us that he's got us a gig and that we should meet him at his office at 10 o'clock the next morning. We, of course, think that this means we'll be playing somewhere—our first show with our new manager—and that we'll be making some money, even though we weren't sure what kind of show he could have booked at that time of day. So we get there, only to find a Ryder truck parked in the lot, filled with scenery from an H. L. Mencken one-man show that Frank was producing, which had just closed in Washington. Our *gig* was to help John O'Toole unload all this stuff—for which Frank paid us $10 each. He had his fingers in all kinds of pies—concerts, clubs, touring shows, legitimate theater. Around the time he met us, he was bringing the rock opera *Jesus*

Christ Superstar to town. One of the first places he put us in to rehearse was the Charles Playhouse in Boston's theater district, where he knew everybody.

He even talked like Mencken, or Will Rogers, or Mark Twain. Just hanging out with him was an adventure. Once we were driving in his Delta 88 when his transmission dropped out at the intersection of Beacon and Park streets in Brookline. "We'll handle it," Frank said, guiding me into a convenient bar. When we emerged six hours later, dead drunk, the car was gone. Next morning Frank had a new Delta 88.

Steven Tyler: When Frank Connelly came along, he sat me down and told me he was going to book us into the Galaxy Room in the Neponset Holiday Inn and then we could do four shows a night at the Manchester Sheraton for seven weeks. I hit the fuckin' ceiling. "Frank," I said, "I'm a veteran, I've done so much damage before Aerosmith came along, I'VE BEEN IN THE BARS FOR THE LAST EIGHT YEARS, YOU FUCKING IDIOT!"

"Ah, Steven, m'boy, Steven. Just shut the hell up and listen to me. You want to be famous, right? Well, getting famous is like going to the beach with your parents. The ride home is short, but it takes a long, long time to get there.

"Of course, you're absolutely right, you don't want to work in clubs anymore, but the other guys have never done clubs, and that's where you have to start out, so you're tight. We have to have it so everyone in the band gets really tight."

And on and on like that in his charming, lilting brogue until he even had *me* sort of convinced that, yes, this isn't about *me*, and yes, we *needed* to play the Starlight Room of the Manchester Sheraton. The guy could talk a dog off a meat wagon.

Joey Kramer: Frank had a classy side, his theatrical business, and a dark side, his Connectedness. For instance, he introduced us to some guys who ran what was supposed to be a greeting card shop down by Boston Garden. They'd loan us money and do other favors. I used to go into this shop and make snotty remarks about how the candy bars were ten years old and the cards were all yellowed and out of date. They just looked at me and shook their heads. It took me a while to realize the shop was actually a bookie joint and that they were basically gangsters. I think they loaned Frank money to finance our management, and I remember if they were looking for Frank and couldn't find him, they'd lean on me!

Brad Whitford: The main thing was that Frank was a real old-fashioned *promoter*. He knew how to take something small and make it big. So we put all our faith in him. He took care of everything so we could concentrate and focus on the new material we were developing. We didn't have to worry about the gigs anymore or getting the rent paid. He put us on salary, a hundred a week, what he called "walking-around money." He wanted us to feel good about what we were doing.

Steven Tyler: All this time we're still going to gigs in our bus. Dead of winter, fourteen below, Cabozzi at the wheel, four-hour trip to Newell's Casino deep in the Maine Woods, three miles off the main road in an old barn. Really the pits, but by eight o'clock there are a thousand kids. The place was so remote that no one could believe it or understand where they came from. I remember this gig because Joey got sick and didn't make the trip, so I had to play the drums—the only time I ever subbed. But I'd only gotten off the drums a year before that, so I could still play enough so that we got our $300, which to us was a lot of money back then.

Joe Perry: Frank Connelly was friends with the manager of the Charles Playhouse, a small theater in downtown Boston, which is where we began to rehearse next. We'd practice all night, and in the morning we'd lock it up and leave. Next day we'd come back and climb up to the projection booth and slam on the light switch, and in that second before the lights came on, we'd pray that our equipment was where we left it.

Frank was already talking to New York about us. He was experienced at booking and promoting shows but not in dealing with record companies. So he was casting around his New York contacts for people to work with us. One of the first to come up was Bob Ezrin, who'd worked with Alice Cooper. He came to the Charles Playhouse to hear us.

Joey Kramer: Bob Ezrin was brought up to see if he wanted to produce us, but he passed. It was: "Keep rehearsing, boys. You're not quite ready." We weren't that disappointed because Frank had put some money where his mouth was and we'd gotten new equipment and we thought we had a good momentum going.

A couple of days after this, we got to the theater late in the afternoon, ran upstairs, and threw on the lights. There was a collective gasp of horror as we saw the empty stage. Someone had stolen everything. All our gear was gone, except for the blue carpet where my new drums had been, some broken sticks, and two packing crates, one of which had held Tom's brand-new bass and amp. Brad's vintage Marshall amps, Steven's scarf-draped microphone—everything gone. We had to start all over again. Frank fixed it somehow and we kept rehearsing.

Joe Perry: A lot of dealers hung around 1325, because in order to be near us, to hang out with us, it was good to have drugs. It got you in the door. There was a guy called Casey, who was like our mascot. He always had good pot and a little coke and drove a '47 Ford coupé and a 500-cc. Kawasaki. To show how loose we were about all this, one after-noon I'm riding on the back of his bike when a couple of bricks of pot he had under his coat just fell out and landed in the middle of afternoon traffic on Memorial Drive in Cambridge. We sheepishly swung around and picked it up and carried on our business.

Brad Whitford: Then we got busted: 1325 was your typical rock 'n' roll apartment with people coming and going all the time, so much so that we didn't bother to lock our door. We had a lot of friends, and one of the guys must have been hanging out with some unscrupulous char-acter who got in trouble and dropped a name—Joe Perry—to the police.

So the cops sat outside and watched the traffic and decided to bust us on a Saturday night when everyone was out except for me and Mark. He was in the bathroom shaving and I was in Joe Perry's room and had actually just gotten stoned. I was trying to focus on the TV and someone flashed a badge in my face and said, "Get up." I immediately got frisked by the plainclothes police and narcotics detectives who were all over the apartment, going through everything.

Then it was Good Cop/Bad Cop for a while. Good Cop goes, "Hey, man, where do you keep your stuff? Where do you live?" I pointed to the living room and managed to say, "*Couch*. I live on the couch. And I'm not a dealer." I even showed him this little baggie of marijuana I had. I showed him my imitation switchblade, which he pocketed and then gave back. Meanwhile, Bad Cop is opening the vitamins in the kitchen and asking, "How much of this LSD you got?"

"It's not LSD, officer."

"Yeah, right. Where's the main stash?" And so on.

Now I'm sitting in the kitchen while they're grilling me. I'm chain-smoking Winstons from a box also holding a big joint rolled in yellow wheat-straw paper, which is plainly visible every time I take a cigarette out, but they don't seem to care. But then they thought they found some residue of LSD, so they collected all the bongs and paraphernalia and cleaned the place up a bit and took us downtown.

While they were booking me, the Boston cops were passing around one of those mimeographed office jokes, which they handed to me. I was shocked. It was a cartoon of a black man tied to a post, like a gallows. There was a string tied to his dick and the other end was tied to the trigger of a pistol that was pointed at his head, so that if he got an erection he would shoot himself. Standing in front of him was a buxom bimbo with everything hanging out. The caption was: HOW TO FIX THE BLACK PROBLEM. The cops were all laughing at this, and I'm like, *Oh my God, I'm going to die tonight.*

We used the $70 band kitty to bail ourselves out. We went back to 1325 and smoked the yellow joint, which they had never found. We hooked up with a young lawyer fresh out of Harvard Law and he got us off, even though they tried to nail us for selling LSD. Joe Perry moved into Cabozzi's basement for a week in case the narco squad came back, but they never did and the charges were later dismissed.

2: Max's Kansas City

Joe Perry: In the early spring of 1972, Frank said he was looking for a partner in New York to help us with the record companies. We made a demo tape of one of our rehearsals and played three different dates at Max's Kansas City in Manhattan over the next six months. That's where we met David Krebs and Steve Leber for the first time. They would manage Aerosmith for the next twelve years.

Steve Leber: I knew Frank Connelly because I had worked my way through Northeastern University in Boston during the very early sixties booking local bands in Mafia-connected clubs.

I got to be so successful as an agent that eventually [the] William Morris [Agency] in New York offered to either give me a job or put me out of business. By 1968 I was the head of the music division at William Morris and David Krebs was a young lawyer who worked in my department. So did a young guy just out of the mailroom named David Geffen. When the Rolling Stones toured in 1969 without management, David Krebs and I booked the tour. My wife and I went along on every date and David Krebs did their day-to-day management out of our office, which is the way we learned to manage.

Eventually David Geffen left William Morris to manage Laura Nyro and later founded Asylum, his [first] record label. David loved Krebs and wanted me to be his partner in his new company, but I wanted to go out on my own, into management and the record business, and I wanted Krebs with me. I considered myself the more serious music person, while Krebs was good with contract work and he ran a little mail-order poster business on the side—he wasn't really a music guy. But I had this instinct that David would be a good partner, that he could take an Aerosmith and make it a really big band.

Then we got an incredible opportunity from [producer] Robert Stigwood, who came in one day with *Jesus Christ Superstar*, the first Andrew Lloyd Webber musical, actually the pre-Broadway concert version that he wanted to put on the road. He said, "Do you want to handle *Jesus Christ Superstar* on your own? Produce it, tour it for me?"

It was the greatest opportunity in the world because it was foolproof, not like an act or a band. *Superstar* didn't talk back, you could have four companies out on the road that wouldn't get sick or drugged out. I didn't think a rock musical about Christ would appeal to the Hadassah ladies who bought tickets for Broadway shows, but out in so-called Middle America they loved it, and Stigwood made the money that enabled him to go on and do things like *Saturday Night Fever* and *Grease* later on.

So David Krebs and I left William Morris, using the touring rights to *Jesus Christ Superstar* to pay our bills. We formed a company called CCC—Contemporary Communications Corporation—and within a few months had signed John Lennon's backup band, Elephant's Memory, and a new group called the New York Dolls.

David Krebs: I was born in Brooklyn in 1940 and went to Columbia University, where I also got law and M.B.A. degrees. When I got out of the National Guard, I went to work in the mailroom of the William Morris Agency at 1740 Broadway for $55 a week. After two months, I went to the legal affairs department and then to music, because it was only a two-step department. You were either an agent or the head, which happened to be Steve Leber, a genius agent. Then Steve developed the rock opera *Jesus Christ Superstar*, which was a big hit, and in late '71 we left the agency and went out as managers.

On Valentine's Day, 1972, a guy named Marty Thau called and said he had a band called the New York Dolls playing at the Waldorf-Astoria. We went to see them and found that the hotel was so appalled by this punk band in dresses that they fired the guy who booked the show. So I took the tickets.

Nine out of ten shows, the Dolls were the worst band in the world. But in one out of ten, they were the best rock 'n' roll band anyone had seen in years. If you crammed 300 people into a small room, the Dolls created a lot of heat. They looked like nobody else and the press literally worshipped them. If you looked at the early press on the Dolls, you'd say, "They're going to be the biggest superstars around." If you looked at the early press on Aerosmith, you'd say, "They're gonna have day jobs."

So we went partners with Marty Thau and signed the Dolls. Not long after that is when Frank Connelly called and told us he had signed this fabulous band he'd found in Boston. Frank was the top promoter in Boston and a very special person, so we took him seriously. He said we had to see them, so we booked Aerosmith into Max's as a showcase for ourselves before the labels got a chance to see them. We got down there and saw this beat-up red bus parked outside the club on Park Avenue South and we thought, *Oh, no.* Then we heard them play and Steve Leber whispers, "This is a *phenomenal* band. They could be as big as the Dolls. Let's do it." So he primarily oversaw the Dolls and I concentrated on Aerosmith. Sometime in May or June of 1972, we brought them back to Max's for a second time to show them to labels, and we invited Atlantic Records and Clive Davis, the president of Columbia Records, to come to see them.

Steve Leber: I played Aerosmith's tape for two people: Jerry Greenberg, president of Atlantic Records, and Clive Davis, president of Columbia Records. By now the Dolls were hot and they were interested in other things we were doing. Then we arranged for Aerosmith to play at Max's and invited them down. Jerry Greenberg brought Ahmet Ertegun, the founder and chairman of Atlantic. We knew that either Columbia or Atlantic would sign the band. We thought it would be Atlantic because they were *the* rock 'n' roll company, with the Stones, Zeppelin, and all their bands. Clive Davis had built Columbia more on music he liked—Paul Simon, Barbra Streisand—but he had also signed Janis Joplin and wanted to get more into rock 'n' roll.

So we're at Max's Kansas City, everyone drugged out of their minds, and we're having a few drinks, and Aerosmith comes on, this young band, loud, strong, tough, Steven Tyler at twenty-four, *phenomenal!* They played a forty-minute set and were terrific.

Steven Tyler: Halfway through the show, I stop and say, "Ladies and gentlemen, thank you very much. Right now we wanna do a little instrumental thing for you, Joe Perry and Brad Whitford on guitars extraordinaire. We call it 'We Don't Wanna Fuck You, We Just Wanna Eat Your Sandwiches.' " Silence. Nobody laughed. But after the show Clive Davis put his arm around me, gave me a little squeeze, and said, "Steven, you want to know something? You're gonna be a big star." He actually said that.

Steve Leber: Afterward Jerry and Ahmet come over to me. I assumed they loved the band, but they said, "Steve, come here. This band sucks. We don't like this band. But we're going to spend ten minutes talking to you as a favor, because Clive Davis is going *bananas* over this band and the more time we spend talking to you, the more nuts Clive's going to get."

So Atlantic passed on the band, but as a goof they did a number on Clive and sure enough in a few days he was eating out of my hand. He went after Aerosmith big time, signing them personally to Columbia Records. John Eastman, Paul McCartney's father-in-law, became Aerosmith's lawyer, and we did one of the first big rock 'n' roll production deals. The band was signed to CCC, and we got a record deal that called for two albums a year. We got an advance and a royalty rate of 75¢ a record, which we of course later renegotiated.

Steven Tyler: We thought, *This is it! Signed by Clive Davis! Aerosmith has arrived!*

Joey Kramer: Aerosmith was never a huge groupie magnet, even in those days before anyone was married. We all had girlfriends and often they were with us at shows, so there wasn't that much going on. But this beautiful girl had been hanging around Max's and late that night John O'Toole brought her to the hotel and let her into the bedrooms. I woke up and realized I was being *done* by this girl and that John was doing her from behind. When she was finished, she crawled up—*What now?*—and whispered into my ear, "Where's the rest of the band?"

There was another girl who liked us a lot. Her name was Silverbird, but we called her the Glitter Queen because she liked to sprinkle glitter over herself. You could always tell someone had been with the Glitter Queen if he came out of a room all sparkling and covered with the stuff.

David Krebs: Now we had to work out a deal with Frank and sign new papers with the band that superseded whatever he had with them. I think this happened up in Boston.

Zunk Buker: David Krebs and Steve Leber came up to Boston to see the band play at K-K-K-Katie's. I got there late and found the band fighting in the dressing room. Joe Perry said, "The first set just sucked. We're trying to do a deal with these guys and we just blew it. Maybe you're our good luck charm." He shouldn't have worried, because they redeemed themselves with a blistering second set.

Gary Cabozzi: While they were playing, I overheard a couple of drunks in the men's room talking about how they wanted to kill Steven and Joe for wearing makeup and just looking like that. I told Frank, and he said, "As soon as they're offstage, get 'em outta here." So we ran them out the back door and into a cab and as I'm heading back up the alley these two morons started hitting me with lead pipes. I could hear my cheekbones breaking inside my head before everything went black.

Zunk Buker: Everyone went back to the Kent Street apartment and that's where they did the deal, in the kitchen. There was a lot of negotiation, and a lot of trips to the living room, where the blow was laid out in lines on a mirror. They did the deal with Leber-Krebs that night.

David Krebs: That's where my friendship with Steven Tyler began. He looked at me and said, "Hey, man, go get me a turkey sandwich." I told him to get it himself, and that established our relationship. He may have a weird personality, but he was and is, singularly, the most talented rock artist to come out of this country. He can sing, dance, move, write songs, and play half a dozen instruments, one of those enchanted people like Peter Pan. Joe Perry was also in a class by himself. Joey Kramer was a great drummer and Brad was an excellent guitar player. Tom Hamilton looked cool on stage with that tall blond head sticking out and he was a more than adequate bass player.

But Steven Tyler and Joe Perry were the real show. I always told the guys not to worry about this, because if you had five stars in the band, you'd have nothing. Too much on the charisma level *never* works.

And so we signed them, in partnership with Frank Connelly, in July 1972. Columbia Records paid Aerosmith an advance of $125,000. It turned out Aerosmith was the last act Clive signed to Columbia.

Tom Hamilton: When the contracts were drawn up, we went to the Leber-Krebs office in New York to sign them. David Krebs was sitting at his desk in his trademark blue polo shirt, smoking a joint. He explained that $125,000 would be divided between two sets of managers and then divided five ways, with our royalties going to pay off the advance, recording expenses, and other reimbursable costs. It would be a long time before we saw any more money from records, he told us, which meant we had to really hit the road and just go out and play. He told us what was in store, that Aerosmith would have to become the hardest-working road band in America.

David Krebs was right. It would be three years before we saw any more money from our record label.

After we signed, Frank Connelly seemed uneasy. "Krebs, he's a nice guy," Frank told us. "But watch out for Leber, he's a snake. All these record guys—serpents."

Gary Cabozzi: When I got home from the hospital, Frank and the boys gave me this big fake newspaper they had printed, with the giant headline GARY CABOZZI KICKS ASS FOR AEROSMITH!!!! I framed it and it was on my wall until my house burned down a couple of years ago.

3: Movin' Out

Joe Perry: That summer, after we got our record deal, Frank got us rehearsal space in the visitors' locker room at Boston Garden. This came through Frank's North End connections.

Boston Garden was like a holy place. It opened in 1928 as a boxing arena and was the home of the Celtics and the Bruins, whose many championship banners hung from the rafters. When we first started, it was being used for summertime pro wrestling, and we'd walk through the locker rooms and Haystack Calhoun would be in the whirlpool and he'd yell at us, "Hey, you guys! How ya doin'!"

On July 18, 1972, the Rolling Stones played the Garden. It was like a papal visitation for us. Keith had got himself arrested when he flew in and the Stones didn't go on until one in the morning after the mayor of Boston had pleaded with the crowd for peace. The next day their stage was still set up for the second night's show, and Steven and I walked out on it. The big hall was empty and black. We had been playing to maybe 400 kids at high school dances. Steven said, "Wow. Wouldn't it be great to play here someday?" And I just thought, *Well, man, someday.* In three years, that was *our* stage.

We also rehearsed at a club across from a theater called Caesar's Monticello, where actress Judy Carne was playing in some summer stock production. She was a former member of the cast of *Rowan & Martin's Laugh-In* during the late sixties, an English dolly bird gone Hollywood, and she liked to come over to this club after her gig and flirt with the guys in the band. We were introduced, she latched on to me and I learned a lot from Judy.

She was something else, with a cool car, money, a house, and a doctor's bag full of fresh drugs from L.A., the most amazing thing I've ever seen: the best cocaine, needles, ups, downs, ins, outs. B-12 syrettes. Best coke I'd ever seen in Boston. She had an incredible make-up girl, a tall redhead who went everywhere with her. Guys would hit on her and try to pick this makeup chick up, she was so hot. Judy had to tell me that she was a man.

When Bob Ezrin came up to see Aerosmith, in the middle of rehearsing with him, Judy insisted I leave and go to Philadelphia with her. Then we had a car accident where I rear-ended someone and Judy's foot was injured. We made it back to Boston, checked into the Copley Plaza Hotel where she was living and started smoking cocaine. I think this was also the first time I ever tried heroin.

Toward the end of the summer she got tired of me. She came to see us rehearsing at Boston Garden and some of the other guys in the band overheard her talking on the pay phone promising some guy in L.A. the fuck of his life when she got there. We spent a week together at Kent Street, then she said goodbye and left.

Shortly afterward, we left Boston and headed for Lake Sunapee, where we had some gigs. This is when Elyssa Jerret and I got together and set in motion some stuff that would change everything for Aerosmith.

Elyssa Perry: I was living in England with Joe Jammer, the guitar player, right? And I'm getting letters during all of 1971 from Joe and Steven, saying they got together and formed Aerosmith. I still have these letters; Steven spells every word wrong except his name and mine. Then in the summer of 1972, I had a fight with Joe Jammer—a big fight. I was tired of him anyway, so I went back home and started with Joe Perry.

Joe Perry: After we got signed to Columbia, Elyssa and me, we started to be together constantly, and I know the rest of the band felt excluded. I'm the type of person that gets very attached to the woman I'm with. I know Steven had this thing for her too. They'd grown up together on Dewey's Beach in Sunapee, so now there was this unspoken triangle going on between me, Steven, and her. Steven wanted to get in her pants, but she was having none of it.

So now there was jealousy. All of a sudden I had this girlfriend that I was madly in love with. What happens to two guy friends like me and Steven when they're bonded in their work and something like this happens? We would play and he would complain about the volume or the tuning, but there was always this undercurrent humming along: it was always "Oh, Joe, he doesn't care about the band."

Tom Hamilton: We were playing at the Lake Sunapee Yacht Club and that's where Elyssa all of a sudden—after Joe wanting her so bad for so long—finally decided that she was going to come around and be with him. It was right when we got our recording contract, and her timing was noticed by one and all. The train was pulling out of the station.

Boy, everything changed. For one thing, the lease was up at 1325 and we were moving out. It was September 1972, and we'd been there for two years. An era was over and we all felt it. And I felt incredibly rejected and alienated by Joe's relationship with this girl. We were in the Jam Band together and had these dreams together and had come to Boston together to make them happen, but the minute she came along, I was all of a sudden not Joe's friend anymore.

There was one climactic night when we were moving out of 1325. He was moving to Kent Street and I was moving into my girlfriend Terry's apartment on St. Paul Street nearby. I took too long with the truck, which somehow meant that Joe wasn't going to be able to spend the night with Elyssa on Kent Street, and he was furious with me. Fuckin' *furious*. And he really—spitefully—let me know how he felt. It was a big event that ruptured our friendship.

I felt rejected, and for years it was reinforced by Elyssa fostering an atmosphere of: "Me and Joe, we're hip, we're the elite club within the band, and you're either in or you're out." I was very insecure about myself back then. If it wasn't for Terry, I might have sublimated my better judgment and tried to stay close to Joe. But Terry was so strong herself that she couldn't allow any of Elyssa's behavior to go by, and so it was like a standoff for years. No wonder we got the reputation as a fighting band.

Joe Perry: So Elyssa and I moved to Kent Street together. The Smith brothers were upstairs, and Henry Smith left Led Zeppelin and came to work with us. Billy Brigode, a sailor friend of ours, was across the alley, and Steven and his cousin Augie were there. Billy and his sailor pals got great drugs, which is how our friendship began. Henry and Chris Smith had fixed the downstairs up beautifully with barn boards and a bar in the front room. I ended up living in the loft. It was great and we took it from there.

Gary Cabozzi: There were a lot of changes around that time, fall of '72. The red bus finally died and they moved out of my building for good, which was a relief because I didn't have to listen to no more homicidal arguments over a missing hard-boiled egg that later turned up behind a bottle of milk. But I kept working with them and they kept fighting even more because now Elyssa was on the scene. She was horrible, unbelievable, out of control. One time we did a gig at Tufts University and Terry Hamilton kicked Elyssa over something she'd said to her, and she took it out on Joe and beat the shit out of him. If any guy ever had a reason to turn around and whack a woman, Joe did. But of course he never touched her. He was crazy about her.

4: Steven Tyler

Steven Tyler: We played Max's three times that year [1972]. The first time we got our management, the second time we got our record deal, and the third time was for the booking agency.

There were no kids there for that last show. It was all corporate people from record labels and agencies, so the business could get a look at the band. I was changing for the gig, looking out the window, and I saw all these limousines and I thought, *Holy shit! What if John Lennon's here!* There was a buzz going on, finally the word had gotten out. We did our set and once again Clive Davis came back and said, "You're gonna be big stars someday," just like it was the real thing, like something you'd read about in a book.

People still ask me about Max's Kansas City. They say, "We wanna start a real rock club, not a theme park operation like the Hard Rock Cafe. What was Max's like?" It was a dive. You could cop drugs at the door. It held

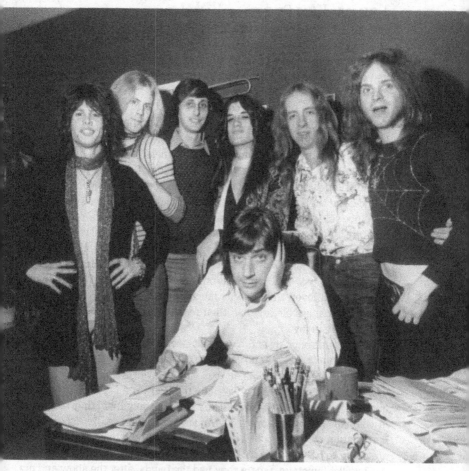

**Aerosmith and manager David Krebs (standing third from left) sign with first
booking agent, Herb Spar, seated, 1972**
(TYLER COLLECTION)

maybe 50 people. It wasn't what the place was like, it was what the talent
made it. We'd be unloading the truck and the guys from the Dolls would be
hanging out, tripping over their hair, along with the truckers and transvestites and street people. That was the scene.

This third gig at Max's was when we met Laura Kaufman, who worked
for Leber-Krebs and became our publicist.

Walk This Way

Laura Kaufman: I had just started working for David Krebs and Steve Leber as a secretary. I'd been hanging out in the Village since I was a kid and I knew all the bands and people in the business, and by 1972 there was a scene at a bar called Nobody's on Bleecker Street, which had been the Tin Angel, and that's where I met David Krebs, who hired me to work for CCC, better known as Leber-Krebs, also the corporate umbrella for their publishing companies DAKSEL, the initials of David A. Krebs and Stephen E. Leber, and SELDAK, the other way around. Steve Leber was president and David Krebs was executive vice-president.

The company hadn't even been in business for a year, but they had signed a bunch of people—Elephant's Memory, the Dolls, a band called Bulldog, Supa's Jamboree, which was Richie Supa from the famous Long Island band the Rich Kids, and this new band from Boston. Everybody at the office said to me, "Wait till you see this band Aerosmith. You're gonna love 'em." I got my chance on October 7, the night they played Max's to get their deal with IFA [International Famous Agency, which later became International Creative Management, today's ICM]. Herb Spar, who was head of music at IFA and was one of David Krebs's best friends, came to Max's and loved the band as much as I did and signed them up as clients. Aerosmith already had their record deal, and so they were now really on their way.

They came onstage and it was just electric. You saw the microphones draped with silk scarves and you said, *What is this?* Then the band played "Mama Kin" and it was like an explosion. Steven's wearing metal-flake eyeliner and dancing during "Walkin' the Dog" and I was just riveted. I immediately realized that the big lips were the only thing they really had in common with the Stones. The music was more Yardbirds/Zeppelin, hard, hard rock, really skilled and thought out. And I thought, *These guys are going to be very big, and I want to work with them.*

I walked upstairs, where they had the bands, after the show and my first glimpse is Steven telling David Krebs that he was changing his name, that he didn't want to be Tallarico anymore because it was too long and he didn't want his family bothered when they got big.

David said, "That's cool. What name do you have in mind?"

"What do you think of Tyler Britt?" Steven asked.

"Tyler Britt. Tyler Britt. No, no, doesn't work for me. Do Steven Tyler instead."

That's how that happened.

I was supposed to take the band over to the Mercer Arts Center afterward to see the New York Dolls play. We got in the limo: the five guys in the band, Joe's girlfriend Elyssa, and me. The entire ride to the club, Steven and Joe argued over who would drive home to Boston. It got really bitter, and I soon realized they fought constantly. You just had to get used to it if you were going to hang around them.

Joe Perry:
People always talk about how much we fought with each other back then, because there was a battle in our dressing room after almost every show. Steven complained about the volume or the monitors and that would set it off. But they don't understand that we all had this objective and didn't care about being friends as much as making the music right. They'd hear this ungodly yelling in the dressing room because we didn't mind offending each other if someone's playing wasn't up to par. After spending so much time together, we all *knew* there was no way we were ever gonna break up. We were confident and idealistic and felt superior to the competition. So, yes, there were times we weren't speaking to each other. We were heavy into fighting. A good fight was just part of our normal workday. If someone got really offended, I'd tell them, "We'll be friends later. Let's be rock 'n' roll musicians first."

Seeing the Dolls in New York just reinforced this feeling. We were reading about them in the press, where they could literally do no wrong. And we're going, "Hey! What about us? We can actually *play*." We took pride in having roots and tuning our instruments and rehearsing. They came to check us out on their own turf, Max's Kansas City, and they're fucking wild-looking, like *bizarre*. I thought to myself, *What the fuck is this*? They were in drag, the real deal, hair sticking out, high heels, spandex pants. Then we went to see them and eventually I fell in love with the Dolls. Elyssa and I got to be good friends with David Johansen and his wife Cyrinda. But the rest of Aerosmith hated them.

Steven Tyler:
We get to the Mercer Arts Center and the Dolls are on and I'm thinking, *Why is the singer wearing hot pants?* It was an improvised psychodrama tarted up in fake leopardskin, black nail polish, bouffant hairdos, feather boas, six-inch platforms, and panty hose, reeking of heroin. They did "Looking for a Kiss" and "Pills" and all their cool stuff. The Dolls couldn't tune their instruments or even sing that good, but it didn't matter because they had attitude. I loved them because of the attitude, the clothes, and because they were just so fucking high. They were twice as stoned as we could ever think of being, and they believed in it.

It wasn't an act. They believed in their grungeness, their outlaw cross-dressing thing. Before a show, they passed around a lipstick the way other bands passed a joint. They believed in that saw-toothed part of their act so much that it brought them down. A month after we saw them, their drummer [Billy Murcia] OD'd in London and died. They were so nuts they never had a chance to grow. When people used to ask me about Guns N' Roses, I'd start talking about the New York Dolls and their attitude. Same with the Sex Pistols. They were in synch and out of it at the same time. They existed on their own *planet*. It was genius, perfect for its time, all about the moment.

The funny thing was a couple of weeks later, Aerosmith played at the Mercer Arts Center, home of the Dolls, and the next day after we played, the exterior walls collapsed and the building was condemned and nobody ever played there again. Aerosmith literally brought the house down.

5: Live at Intermedia

Steven Tyler: In October 1972, we started work on the first Aerosmith album at Intermedia Sound on Newbury Street in Boston. It took maybe a couple of weeks to record, but we'd been playing the songs for a year.

Frank Connelly was always saying, "We gotta get the guys out of the house and away from their girlfriends and put 'em all together in a hotel or rent a house for 'em, and they'll be creative." So he booked us into the Sheraton Manchester north of Boston, where we lived and worked that fall. Then he put us into a couple of suites at the Hilton near the airport, and then there was a house in Boxboro, Mass., where we did a lot of rehearsing, just the five of us and Tiger. The songs for the first album were worked out in all these places.

Joe Perry: Frank had us living in all these places for a few weeks. At the Sheraton Manchester, Brad Whitford and I would get up, have a couple of martinis for breakfast, walk over to the [tax-free] New Hampshire liquor store for a fifth of vodka, drink and rehearse all day. We got to know all the waitresses pretty well—too well. We'd sleep it off and then do our show in the Galaxy Room that night. Then we lived at the Logan Hilton while we were recording. I went home with the Intermedia receptionist and stayed out all night. Back at the hotel next morning, Elyssa's on the phone: "Where the hell are you?"

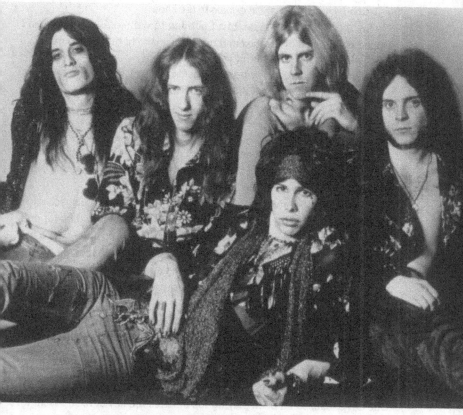

First official Aerosmith publicity photo, 1972
(HAMILTON COLLECTION)

The house in Boxboro was empty because Frank's sister got divorced and moved out. So we moved in to write songs. We were comfortable moving around like this.

Steven Tyler: I wrote "Make It" in a car driving from New Hampshire to Boston. There's that hill you come over and see the skyline of Boston, and I was sitting in the backseat thinking, *What would be the greatest thing to sing for an audience if we were opening up for the . . . Stones? What would the lyrics say?*

Good evening, people, welcome to the show.

(*Ah!* Of course, as usual, I had nothing to write on—no paper—so I ripped open a box of Kleenex and used the inside of the cardboard.)

Got something here I want you all to know.
When life and people bring on primal screams,
You gotta think of what it's gonna take
to make your dreams—
Make it, don't break it.

Back at the house, I looked at what I'd written and picked up a guitar and—as I often do when I get pissed at somebody—wrote the song, which ended up opening the album.

"Somebody" grew out of a lick that our roadie Steve Emsback used to play on his guitar during the days of William Proud. I grabbed it and wrote the lyrics. The whole story of me and songwriting begins with me saying, "Stop. Stop. What was that? Wait a minute. Do that again." I'm a guy panning for gold. They're playing along and I hear a nugget in there when they don't know enough to stop because they don't hear it. That's my job.

The music for "Dream On" was originally written on a Steinway upright piano in the living room of Trow-Rico Lodge in Sunapee, maybe four years before Aerosmith even started. When I was seventeen or eighteen, I used to come home and crash there, Napoleon Blownapart on some trashy New England weed. I'd have a pipe, go in there, and play the piano. One day I realized I'd been playing too much in the key of C, so I went to F. When you're a kid, F is the greatest. That's where it started. It was just this little thing I was playing, and I never dreamed it would end up as a real song or anything.

I wrote the first verse in Sunapee, the second verse at the Logan Hilton. The first time I brought the song to the band was at this house in Boxboro. Frank put us in there because we had six songs for the record and needed four more. There was a piano in the basement and I played it for them. Right away, Joe Perry started playing my right hand on his guitar, while Tom Hamilton played my left hand on bass. And it was the first time I got the band to play the song, because Joe didn't like it and he's so fuckin' stubborn. A little later, I remember working on the bass line with Tom and I got emotional. I started to cry with relief because I was so sure of this song, so sure that it could really work for us and take us places we wanted to go.

People ask me all the time what "Dream On" is all about. It's simple. It's about dreaming until your dreams come true. It's about the hunger and desire and ambition to be somebody that Aerosmith felt in those days. You can hear it in the grooves because it's *there*. It was "Make it, don't break it" for real.

What else?

"One Way Street" was written on piano at 1325, with the rhythm and the harp coming from "Midnight Rambler." "Movin' Out" was the first song I wrote with Joe, the first experience of coming up with something and saying, "See? I *can* do it." Who would've thought writing could be that easy or so much fun? It sealed the bond between me and Joe, and we didn't waste a lot of time with the rhymes. Joe quotes Jimi Hendrix's "Voodoo Chile" the way he quotes the Beatles and Stones elsewhere on the record. "Write Me" was originally "Bite Me," something we'd been working on for five or six months starting in the Bruins' dressing room at Boston Garden, but it just didn't make it. Then one day I said, "Fuck this," said something to Joey, who started playing like a can-can rhythm thing, and suddenly there it was. The intro comes from the Beatles' "Got to Get You into My Life" because we didn't know how to write hooks of our own yet.

"Mama Kin" was a song I brought with me when I joined Aerosmith. One day I grabbed this old guitar Joey Kramer found in the garbage on Beacon Street, an acoustic with no strings. It had snow on it and was so warped you could shoot arrows with it. I wedged it between the door and let it dry out for a week. I looked at it for about two days, put four strings on it, which was all it would take because it was so warped, gobbled two Tuinals, and went down to the basement of 1325. I stole the lick from an old Blodwyn Pig song.

Lots of times Joe Perry would be playing a lick and I'd pop a couple of pills and put headphones on and just be scatting. Then we'd play the tape back and I'd find words to match the scat sounds. I took lyrics, from scat, like automatic writing:

Keep in touch with Mama Kin
Tell her where you gone and been
Livin' out your fantasy,
Sleepin' late and smokin' tea.

I loved that song so much. I had so much confidence in it that I had MA KIN tattooed on my arm.

There were two guys at Columbia Records who believed in the band. Ray Colcord was the A&R guy and Arma Andon was our product manager. They huddled with David Krebs and picked Adrian Barber to produce our record. Adrian was an English engineer who had worked with Cream, Vanilla Fudge, and he produced the Allman Brothers Band's first record. We thought, *Far out. He's English.* So we brought in our songs and went to work.

Joe Perry: The album was recorded on sixteen tracks, with those real big knobs. Today everything's computerized and digitized. Back then we just had this reel of tape. It was my first time in the studio and Steven's first chance to make an album. You can hear how uptight the band was, how little confidence we had. Steven even changed the way his voice sounds.

We were uptight, afraid to make mistakes. No one was hounding us. It was pressure from within ourselves, so much pressure that the record came out sounding thin and sterile. We were total novices with no idea what to go for. A lot of the songs already existed because Steven had them from previous bands or had written them while we were together, like "Mama Kin," and we worked them into our shtick. I didn't even know or give a shit about songwriting. So we just went in there, pushed the knobs up, and said, "Go for it." Then the red light came on and we froze up like fuckin' Eskimos. It was a big drag.

Steven Tyler: It got so bad that eventually I got a stepladder and just unscrewed the red light so we could get on with it.

I don't want to take anything away from Adrian Barber, because he was great for his time, but we got very little help in the studio. It was like being with a retarded child in there, and I'm not sure if it was because he was so high, or because we all were. It was Adrian and an assistant. They'd do things like putting the echo right on the tape, and then when you get ready to mix, you're stuck with the echo. Can't get rid of it.

Joey Kramer: Intermedia Sound was a studio where they did a lot of TV commercials. First time I'm ever in a recording studio in my life and I'm scared shitless, really excited to be doing this, and I made *hundreds* of mistakes. Oh, God! And it was so simple. We set up the instruments, put mikes in front of them, and played our songs live a couple of times. That was it. That's how we did the first album. If we were good, Adrian would yell, "Yes! It's got the fire. It's got the bloody fire" in his priceless English accent that we made fun of. That's how we knew we had a take.

Steven and I almost killed each other because I had problems with my timekeeping. I hated playing in a confined area.

Tom Hamilton: The album was done so fast I barely remember anything but overdubbing some tracks and running to the bathroom for a hit of blow, good-tasting *strong* blow like we hadn't seen before, a better class of blow that we all got into, like the Peruvians we were at heart.

Brad Whitford: I actually loved recording our first album. I played my old Les Paul and did the solo on "One Way Street," still one of my favorite moments. Then the neck of that guitar gave up the ghost and I got another Les Paul, but it never sounded quite the same. We recorded on equipment that now seems to have come from some archaic era. The mixing board looked like it was made out of cardboard. But we just thought it was so exciting, so incredibly cool to be making our first record.

Steven Tyler: You can tell that it's a very basic album. There's nothing on it. It's bone dry—two guitars, bass, drums, a singer, and a mellotron for the *coup de grace*. A musician named David Woodford plays a little sax on "Mama Kin" and "Write Me" and that's it. It was history. I mean, it was bleak and barren. We had to walk into that building and create life.

Yes, I changed my voice when we did the final vocals. I didn't like my voice, the way it sounded. I was insecure, but nobody told me not to do it. I thought I didn't sound right on tape. To me, it sounded like a neutered or *castrato* voice and I wanted to sound a little bit black because I was from Yonkers and back then James Brown and Sly Stone were the only ones saying anything in music, so I put that shit on.

I got a lot of shit for it, too.

I used this voice for "One Way Street" and all of that stuff except "Dream On." "Dream On" is the real me.

When I had found the $1,800 in the suitcase in front of 1325, I took some of the money and bought an RMI electric piano so we could play

"Major Barbara" and the early "Dream On" at the Shaboo Inn down in Connecticut. Then the piano was stolen in New York, so when it came time to record "Dream On," we called E. U. Wurlitzer's and got a mellotron, early icon of "progressive rock."

Think of the flute at the beginning of "Strawberry Fields Forever," the string section on the Moody Blues' "Nights in White Satin," Traffic's "Hole in My Shoe." The mellotron was a tape-driven English keyboard that looked like a Hammond organ and was actually an early sampling device, *not* a synthesizer like the Moog. The thirty-five keys activated tape-recorded notes. It came with a standard set of tapes that included brass, flute, violins, cello, and an eight-voice choir. By overdubbing you had a cheesy-sounding orchestra at your fingertips.

So I put the string section on "Dream On" sitting at this mellotron while a friend of mine kept laying out lines of crystal THC that I was snorting while I was playing. That's my memory of the mellotron, except that we used it for the flute of "Dream On" too.

6: Revere Beach

Laura Kaufman: After they finished recording in Boston, Joe Perry and Steven Tyler started to come to New York to do overdubs and the vocals. They both slept on my roll-away couch. Steven brought along his laundry, which I did, and we ate a lot of take-out Chinese food, which I paid for. They were funny and always ranking on each other, and it was the only time I ever saw Joe without Elyssa.

Steven Tyler: At the end of recording, we had eight tracks. Then we decided not to use "Major Barbara," which made it seven, so we cut Rufus Thomas's "Walkin' the Dog" and made it eight songs for a running time of just under thirty-six minutes. We went down to New York and met with a CBS heavy named Kip Cohen, and we played him the album track by track. He looked at us and said, "There's no single on this album."

That's when my heart sank and I knew we were in for a rough ride with our record company. Nobody gave a fuck. They were all excited about another first album they were releasing at the same time as ours by a new guy from Jersey named Bruce Springsteen. And they had Blue

Öyster Cult from Long Island, which was like New York's local rock band after the Dolls. So we knew it wasn't even gonna be easy to get noticed at our own label.

I think the meeting at Columbia ended with them saying that *if* they put out a single (had to see how the album did first), it would be "Somebody." That's what they wanted.

Across Newbury Street from Intermedia Sound was an antique boutique called Caprice, where we bought all our clothes, jewelry, earrings, feathers, whatever we needed in the way of looking cool. If it was on the racks at Caprice, Aerosmith wore it—black lace, feathers, whatever. Our album cover was shot on the steps of the store by an English photographer named Robert Agriopolis, who captured our air of snotty defiant arrogance, as well as details like our hippie clothes, indecently long hair, the blond streak in Joe's mane, Tom's tattoo, my painted nails, the whole *look* we had, and a lot of cleavage.

Joe Perry: Then Columbia decided we needed some liner notes, which was a problem because no one had ever written anything about us. The Boston media ignored us because we didn't play much in town. I talked to Judy Nylon about this and she made the connection with the guy who wrote them.

Stu Werbin: I was an associate editor at *Rolling Stone*'s New York office when I heard from Judy. I'd started out as a rock critic in Boston and had a lot of contacts there, and maybe a year earlier she told me I had to go over to B.U. and check out something called the Weekly Boogie. She told me I'd see something I hadn't seen for a long time. And there was Aerosmith set up outside, wailing as if this music had just been discovered and they had the patent. Hundreds of kids were dancing and even a jaded rock critic began to shake with how cool this was. They were a street band, pure and simple, young punks five years before the term "punk" meant anything in music. They were so good and brash and trash that I knew everybody in the music business was going to hate them with a passion, but that eventually it wouldn't matter because Aerosmith were their own audience. They were the same people that loved their music. All they had to do was please themselves and sooner or later the millions would follow.

"That was my introduction to the Big Get Off," I wrote in my liner notes, "and this album will probably be yours. . . . It's for the young, and the young in the head, and for anybody who can still take it raw."

Terry Hamilton: I think they shipped a test copy of their album to Boston, and the band gathered at Joey's apartment at 203 Commonwealth Avenue to listen to it, and the general feeling was dissatisfaction. But it didn't get anyone down, it just made them all the more eager to make a new record. This was right at the end of the year.

Joe Perry: We finished the tumultuous year of 1972 playing a New Year's Eve gig at Scarborough Fair. Frank had us play there so many times that we thought we owned a piece of this club, which was always jammed with guns and gangsters and bikers from the bucket-of-blood hole-in-the-wall bar next door. It had fighting, gunshots, the whole scum-of-Revere atmosphere.

Gary Cabozzi: We had gone out early in the day with some lumber and plywood and nails and Steven and Joe Perry actually built a stage for them to play on.

That night it turned out that the Ladies Room was next to the band's upstairs dressing room. There was this one very noisy lady, really loaded, and she got on Steven's nerves. He asked her to pipe down and she cursed him out like I've never heard. This got Steven going.

"Hey, lady, watch your mouth—your string's hanging."

It was a nasty thing to say, I admit, but this was a major bitch so it was appropriate. Except she was the girlfriend of the president of the Trampers, a motorcycle gang with a reputation for serious violence. These were the guys who couldn't get accepted into the Hell's Angels. Pretty soon the stairs were full of crazed-looking Trampers in full colors, looking for the guy who swore at the girl.

John O'Toole was a very tough man. As tough as I ever met. He'd been in prison, the whole deal. He was a veteran bodyguard and roadie who had worked with the Beatles and had seen a lot of shit happen. We checked out the scene with the Trampers and each of us ordered a double bourbon.

"We can handle this," I said.

He looked at me like I was stupid. "No, we can't."

In the end O'Toole persuaded Steven to apologize, which saved all our fuckin' lives.

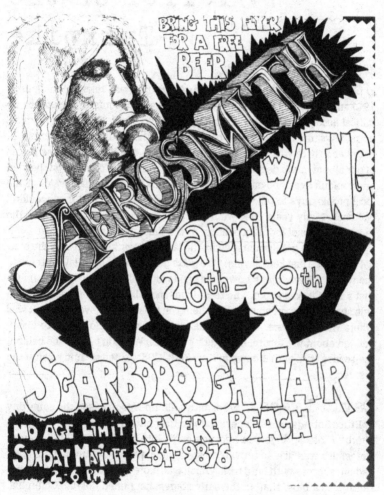

BRING THIS FLYER
FOR A FREE
BEER

AEROSMITH

w/ING

apriß
26th - 29th

SCARBOROUGH FAIR

NO AGE LIMIT
SUNDAY MATINEE
2-6 PM

REVERE BEACH
284-9876

(TYLER COLLECTION)

7: Terror on the Turnpike

Joe Perry: So our album, *Aerosmith*, was released in January 1973 amid less than total national joy. There was no fanfare, no parades, no critical accolades. There was nothing at all: no press, no radio, no airplay, no reviews, no interviews, no party. Instead the album got completely ignored and there was a lot of anger and flipping out. We saw review copies of our album in the deejay bins at the record store. We'd go out on the road and couldn't even find our record in some markets. Sometimes we'd call the local promo guys to tell them we were coming to town and they wouldn't call back. Many years later we heard that *Rolling Stone* didn't review the record because of industry politics. At the time, this was a real killer.

Some of us got discouraged by the lack of attention, but I was the eternal optimist. I just kept saying, "We gotta get out there and play and spread the word." I knew that's how most bands did it. They toured and toured—that's what it was about. The record was more like this thing you did as a side show to support your touring. Being on the road was everything: It was where the girls were, the food was, the money was. So we were disappointed about the record, but it didn't stop us. We didn't know the behind-the-scenes stuff or that down in New York, CBS wanted to drop us after the first record.

David Krebs: Aerosmith's album was released the same day as Bruce Springsteen's. For every dollar they put into Aerosmith, they put a hundred into Springsteen because he fit into the folksier CBS essence. Aerosmith was like an unwanted stepchild because Columbia had never had big success with hard rock, which was more Atlantic's thing. So Aerosmith was a band that, in the early stages, happened *despite* Columbia.

Our strategy was: "If you're a hometown hero and can also do it somewhere else—wow! Not every band can do that." So Aerosmith became like the Marines, having to challenge every city, beachhead by beachhead, play live, command respect, play live again, create word of mouth, play live, get people to buy the record and turn the radio on. It was Aerosmith going in and creating excitement as a brilliant, *magic* live entity. It was an extraordinary achievement, and we're talking B.D., Before Drugs, or at least before the drugs totally took control.

Joe Perry: We started out doing station wagon tours of clubs and colleges around the Northeast. John O'Toole drove or we took turns driving, except that everyone wanted to drive so that Steven wouldn't. He'd go thirty miles per hour on the interstate and then come to an off-ramp and do ninety, which drove us all bananas. We had the band car Frank Connelly had gotten for us, this Delta 88 we were driving down to a college concert in Pennsylvania when the state police pulled us over on the New Jersey Turnpike in the rain.

Brad Whitford: I was driving the band car and we were all goofing and talking. I went by this state trooper as we came over a hill and he looked at me and I just *knew*. He pulls onto the road and I said, "Sorry, guys, but we're busted."

Joe Perry: I was trying to get some sleep in the back when I figured out what was going on. I wasn't a big pot smoker, but I'd been at Joey's apartment and some guys had given me some joints, which I now stuffed under the seat.

Brad Whitford: The trooper asked if I had any drugs and then ordered us out of the car. The rain is pouring down and giant trucks zooming by on the turnpike are covering us with cold, gritty spray. Then he goes, "What's this marijuana seed doing in your car, Brad?"

"Well, officer, I don't know because it's a rental." He wasn't impressed. He searched the car and us. I had two ounces of pot stuffed in the right pocket of my jeans, but the cop only searched my left pocket. But he found the joints in the car and turned to us—we're dripping wet by now—and tells us he's taking us in.

Joe Perry: They chained us to a bar in the hallway of the state police barracks where we watched in awe as reports of a rumble with the Black Panthers in Newark came in and all these state troopers started running out with shotguns. Meanwhile, we were shitting bricks because Brad—the designated pot smoker, along with Tom—had a couple of fat lids in his pants. Steven goes, "Something tells me we're not gonna make it to the gig."

Brad Whitford: I'm chained next to Steven and I whisper, "I've got two ounces in my pocket. Are they gonna search us again?" He goes, "Definitely!" Then he hisses, "Give 'em to me. Quick." And he threw these baggies in a dark room off the hallway, which turned out to be the fingerprint room. They took us in to get printed, turned on the light, and there was my pot just sitting there on a table. My heart sank, but the cops either ignored it or thought it was old evidence. They never searched me again and I could have walked out of there with the stuff.

Joe Perry: Eventually they found my pot, Tom's film canister with a couple of roaches in it, and Steven's hash coffin, this tiny metal box with some dust and a Nembutal in it. Joey got off because they didn't find anything. They interrogated us, and the cop that talked to Steven knew him from high school. He'd even been the drummer in a band that played with one of Steven's. They booked us, let us go, we got to the gig—"Wow, we *made* it!"—and there were twelve people there.

Brad Whitford: We drove home that night, stopped for food somewhere in Connecticut, and I locked the car keys in the trunk. It was just one of those days.

Tom Hamilton: Frank Connelly fixed us up with a lawyer and we had to go to court. But the judge was in a good mood and continued our case without a finding. This meant that we could do whatever we wanted for six months as long as we didn't get caught. At least that's how we interpreted it.

8: Mondo

Steven Tyler: Little by little, we began to hear bits of the album on the radio. It started at WBCN in Boston and then slowly spread. The first person ever to play our record was Maxanne, who was on BCN in the afternoons.

Maxanne Sartori: I came to Boston in 1970 from KOL-FM in Seattle, where we were doing progressive rock in the same format as KSAN in San Francisco, KMET in L.A., WNEW in New York, and BCN, which was generally considered the best station, with the highest production values. The guy that owned the station [T. Mitchell Hastings] had actually invented the FM stereo process. In 1967, he went into the hospital for surgery with WBCN as a classical music station (the call letters stood for Boston Concert Network). When he came out of the hospital, it was an FM rocker. Peter Wolf and Ray Reipen and those guys just changed the format.

One day their top jock, Charles Laquideira, announced that the station needed some chicks to come in and type and the next day a radical feminist group called Bread and Roses sent the station a box of baby chickens and an ultimatum to hire a woman deejay fast or there would be problems for the radically chic station. So they scoured the country and I got hired to do afternoons, two to six. I went on the air November 13, 1970. We were playing the Faces; the Stones; Zeppelin a distant third; Cat Stevens's *Tea for the Tillerman*; J. Geils; bootlegs like *Great White Wonder*; Crosby, Stills, and Nash; and the Moody Blues. I was the only woman deejay, and J. J. Jackson (who later became one of MTV's founding veejays) was just leaving, so that was it for diversity.

In 1971, someone named Ray Tabano called me at the station and brought over a live tape of Aerosmith. I think he was working as their roadie at that point. I could tell the music was great, but the sound quality was horrendous, like underwater. "Too rough to play on the air," I told Ray, "but great music."

That Christmas Danny Klein from the J. Geils Band came over to the station with a bottle of Scotch and we played heavy R&B all day, for which I almost got fired. So they moved me to nights. Around this time I moved into a house with some of the Modern Lovers. The drummer, David Robinson, who became one of the Cars, kept talking about Aerosmith. The whole group loved Aerosmith; they kept telling me that Aerosmith was the best band in Boston. I had never even seen them.

Nobody at BCN wanted to play their record except me, and the guy deejays put me down for playing them, like I was doing it because Joe and Steven were cute. There was a line on Aerosmith: they were a rip-off of the Stones, a bubble-gum act for high school kids. (The same attitude applied to Queen when they came along just a little later.) No one got the fact that every generation of high school kids needs its own bands, and Aerosmith was that next generation. They would be the great hard rock band of the 1970s, bar none.

So I kept playing them. Then a guy named Charlie Kendell at WVBF-FM [in suburban Framingham] heard my show and started playing "Dream On" and "Mama Kin" and soon their phones started ringing. Then WVBF had a Battle of the (local) Bands—J. Geils versus Aerosmith—

and Aerosmith mobilized their forces and their fans and won! It was considered a big upset and every other station in the area noticed.

I had been talking on the phone to Steven all this time. We had a phone friendship, but I'd never met him or seen the band yet. Then Kenny Greenblatt, who was our station's account executive for music, staged a benefit at the Orpheum Theater for the Warehouse Cooperative School in Roxbury and Aerosmith agreed to play the benefit, along with some other artists recruited by the local CBS branch—Doug Sahm, David Bromberg, and Eric Weissberg and Steve Mandell, who had a current hit, "Dueling Banjos," from the soundtrack to the movie *Deliverance*. Aerosmith was at the bottom of this bill and this is when I met them [March 3, 1973].

I was backstage because I emceed all or part of the show. This was the first time Aerosmith had played the Orpheum, so it was a big deal. Elyssa's guarding things backstage, wicked beautiful, greeting people and sorting things out when I introduced myself to Joe Perry, thinking it was Steven Tyler. They did a short set and I was just gone, they were so good. Afterward Steven took me to this after-hours club in the North End that he knew about. It was raining and he didn't want to get his velvet boots wet, so he jumped on my back and made me carry him across the street. He was so thin he didn't weigh anything.

Gary Cabozzi: They played with Doug Sahm and the fuckin' "Dueling Banjos" guys at the Orpheum and no one wanted to go first. But "Dueling Banjos" was the #1 record in the country and Doug Sahm wasn't even there. So Steven goes, "Gary, we ain't playing if we have to go on first, and if we don't play you don't get paid." So I went over to the guy and said, "If you don't go on in ten minutes, I'm gonna break all the equipment and then I'm gonna snap your fingers off so you won't play the fuckin' banjo no more, because if you don't go on in ten minutes I don't get paid and I got hungry bambini at home, can you dig it?"

So "Dueling Banjos" went on first, swearing never to play Boston again. "Who fucking cares?" Steven shrugged. "I don't even like that fuckin' song anyway."

After that show, we went over to Giro's and had a few drinks. Then to Ralph Mormon's apartment building, which had a pool on the roof. Ralph was the lead singer of the local band Daddy Warbux and a good guy. Steven would show up very late with strippers from the Combat Zone clubs and there was nude swimming until dawn. I don't know how he attracted these girls—he was nothing but bones—but they loved him and let him get very rude and gross with them, farting in their faces, eating them in the pool. That was Steven. The other guys in the band called him Mondo. That was their nickname for Steven.

Maxanne Sartori: After that Orpheum show, I started to get friendly with Steven, with whom I had a little fling, as well as Joe and Elyssa, who were basically about the coolest couple in Boston. She was dressing him and they were always right on the cutting edge, very stylish. They were living downstairs at Kent Street. Frank Connelly would kidnap Steven and take him out to his house in Sudbury to keep him out of trouble. I'd get these 2 A.M. calls. "Help, save me, I'm stuck in the 'burbs without a car. Can you come right now?"

Aerosmith was working and sometimes I'd go along to these dives like Scarborough Fair, where I'm in the dressing room with Steven and gunshots break out and suddenly one of the road guys bursts in and says, "OK, we're leaving *right now*. Quick, please. Everyone in the cars." Down the stairs and out the back door and we heard that at least one dead biker was on the floor of the bar that night.

That's the kind of scene Aerosmith put up with.

9: The Inner Mounting Flame of Mahavishnu

Joe Perry: We were about to go on the road in a more serious way and realized it was time to get a proper road manager. We'd been doing station wagon tours and gigs around Boston, but now we heard we were going out with the Kinks, maybe Deep Purple, Mott the Hoople. Gary Cabozzi was our roadie and bodyguard, but his boundaries weren't so hot and he often ended up onstage. He couldn't help it because he wanted to be part of it.

So we ended up firing him. Frank must have told him not to come around anymore. Gary went apeshit. He told us he was going home to get his shotgun and would be right back. Frank goes, "Get in the car. We're getting out of town." He checked the band and himself into the Marlborough Sheraton Tara and ordered up a bottle of Jameson's. Then John O'Toole shows up with a loaded .44 Magnum, which he handed to Frank.

So we're drunk, hanging out, and after a while it got boring. We drove

Walk This Way

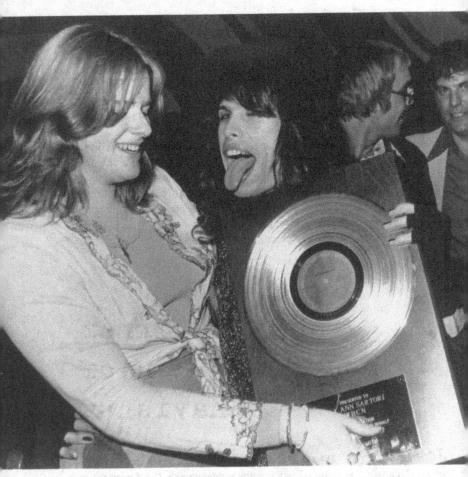

Maxanne with Steven Tyler, 1974
(COURTESY MAXANNE SARTORI)

back into town and went to Giro's, where it was all these shady-looking guys going, "Hey! Paisan!" because they knew that Steven and I had Italian blood. Now it's 1 A.M., the after-hours crowd, we're all shit-faced, and who swims into view but Ricardo Montalban, the actor. Frank gets up to greet him with the gun sticking out of his waist, and of course the .44 falls to the floor and discharges with a deafening flash, and all the shady-looking guys hit the deck like it was a Mafia hit going down.

Cabozzi eventually calmed down and now we're friends again. Just don't give him your phone number.

Then we met two Italian brothers who owned two limos, and that's how we went on the road, a couple of weeks at a time in Ohio, Michigan, the Midwest. The brothers drove: We'd pile in and smoke pot. If someone found a girl, she could come along. Then in Ann Arbor a girl started following us in a new white Corvette with two pounds of Thai sticks in the trunk. I rode with her for a while.

We broke in our new road manager, Robert "Kelly" Kelleher, at home in Massachusetts. Kelly was a big guy with a gut who liked beer as much as we did. We'd have contests shooting beers backstage—hold a can upside down, pop the top, and chug. Early on, he and Steven were shooting beers and Kelly was a big guy with a lot more capacity and I think he had Steven up to twelve beers at one point. After the show, we poured Steven into bed at a Holiday Inn to sleep it off, and while he was resting, Joey and I went in and smashed the furniture and threw it over the balcony. We broke everything we could break in two minutes and took off. Steven woke up with a hangover and two state troopers outside his door. He had no money and the cops wouldn't let him go until the damage was paid. Steven went out the bathroom window, shinnied down the drainpipe, and hitchhiked to the next show.

Brad Whitford: The first night Kelly came to work with us we were playing up in Salisbury Beach, New Hampshire. The place was packed to the rafters and we were licking our chops because the band had a big piece of the door. After the set, Kelly went up to the office to get paid. He meets three huge guys he never saw before and they reached into the safe and came up with a snub-nosed .38 special, which they put on the desk and told Kelly to get out. He came back to the dressing room, literally shaking. "I don't fuckin' believe this—my first night and someone's already trying to kill me."

Joey Kramer: Our first real tour was opening a few dates for the Mahavishnu Orchestra, which was so incongruous, but it was either go out with them or not go on the road.

On the first night, I was sitting behind the stage watching those guys play and I got depressed. Mahavishnu was a spiritual jazz-rock fusion band led by John McLaughlin, who had been playing with Miles Davis and was one of the best electric guitarists in the world. Jan Hammer was on keyboards and Billy Cobham was the drummer—so good that I could not really believe I was playing the same instrument as he was. Their audience was there for loud but somehow meditative music—an electric violinist named Jerry Goodman tied all this together—and we were there to kick ass and prove ourselves to our usual audience, who of course didn't show up. We'd play and Mahavishnu's audience was just aghast. There were nights where they paid us not to play because we were causing too much excitement.

Brad Whitford: John McLaughlin? Are you kidding? *Incredible.* I still think about it. He had two stacks of Marshalls, so loud, too loud for the bass player [Rick Laird] so part of the cabinet was facing backwards. We used to sit behind Billy Cobham, and next to him was one of John's cabinets facing us, so we could hear every note perfectly from behind. Man, this was a great band. It was a mystical experience. They would go places.

Joe Perry: A brilliant move, us opening for Mahavishnu.

Steven Tyler: There was one gig where it was outrageously embarrassing. The audience was dead, stillborn. I have tapes where they're going *clap/clap/clap* in slow motion. It wasn't like Hendrix opening for the Monkees, but sometimes we felt really rejected. Right after the first song, "Make It," we'd hear them chanting, "MA-HA-VISHHHHH-NOOOOO." We'd get mad like, "Fuck you. Dig *this.*"

Laura Kaufman: I saw one of these shows at Fordham University in the Bronx. Mahavishnu's audience had no idea what was going on or how to respond to this Mick Jagger clone cavorting around the stage in motley and rags with scarves draped over the mike. Then McLaughlin came out in his white clothes, burning incense, and he looks at the crowd with great sympathy and asks for a moment of silence. Joe Perry, standing next to me in the wings, said, "I guess he figures after an hour of us, they *need* it."

Joe Perry: So that was our first tour, trial by fire. Later we realized it was good for us, because we had to play that much better to try to win his audience. We had to kick ass every night, and later we'd listen back to the tapes and it would sound almost professional to us. Meanwhile, these geniuses in Mahavishnu had been to fuckin' Mars and back, every night. We'd say to each other, "What are we doing here?"

But we stayed and did it. We didn't go home. We got booed or ignored, and it was scary. But after that everything was gravy because we'd
survived.

10: Harry Smith

Joey Kramer: Then we went on tour opening for the Kinks in
the Northeast and Midwest, traveling in our limos and putting up with Ray
Davies, who called us "Harry Smith." The guy was one of our heroes, but
was so mean he wouldn't even let us have a fuckin' sound check. The positive side of it was that up till then the band had been making an average
of $300 a night. After that our fee went up to $1,500.

Laura Kaufman: It was hard. Ray Davies was famous for
not giving his opening act anything, and Aerosmith just went out there
and really paid their dues. David Krebs said—and he was right—"This
isn't a band that will *ever* break on radio. They have to break live." There
was no MTV or any other alternative back then, and the album was getting played only in Boston and Detroit, where a deejay who was from
Boston was really pushing them.

So David kept them on the road, and once they had toured, we could
see where the sales were. So you hammer the market: play, wait three
weeks, come back and play again. You built your audience in the Midwest. Aerosmith could headline Cobo Hall in Detroit months before they
could Boston Garden. So Aerosmith went out and played and it worked.
Eventually their record got played because the only way a hard rock band
gets on the radio is if the programmers are forced to take the record because of requests. They have to play it.

David Krebs: They went out with Mahavishnu Orchestra
because I let my booking agent talk me into it. Then we learned to play
to our market. We had them open for acts that were slightly on the downside of their career trajectories, bands whose audience we wanted. Even
if we didn't blow them off the stage every night, we could at last count
on some to buy an Aerosmith album. That was the strategy.

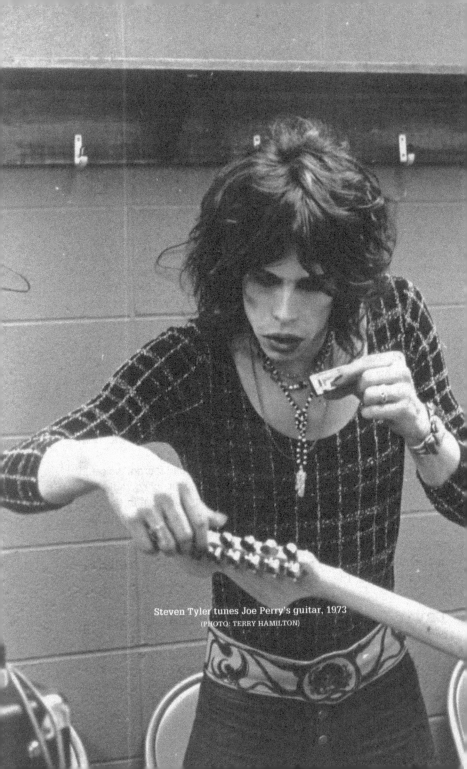

Steven Tyler tunes Joe Perry's guitar, 1973
(PHOTO: TERRY HAMILTON)

THE BOSTON GLOBE

The Kinks were in town at the Music Hall Sunday night . . . Opening were the local heart throbs and rock 'n' roll stars, Aerosmith. Led by the Jagger-like Steve Tyler and his pink-feathered tail, they churned out an almost nonstop, straight-ahead, steamroller, generator rock, twitching and fretting their time upon the stage. Although their material seemingly merges into one long medley, they would seem to have a future. Until that time they'll continue to be dwarfed by such as the Kinks, but they have the talent to make it. (April 4, 1973)

Steven Tyler: Then we played a couple of nights at Paul's Mall, a jazz club on Boylston Street in Boston; one of those nights [April 19, 1973] was broadcast live over WBCN. I did the show with a long tail made out of peacock feathers pinned to the back of my pants, and there were maybe 100 people in the club.

"Ladies and gentlemen," Maxanne says on the tape we have of the show, "will you please welcome Columbia recording artists—Aerosmith!" We launch into "One Way Street"—"Midnight Rambler"-style— my changed voice sounds weird, Stones, Humble Pie, and I'm saying, "Ooohhhh, look out!" as Brad Whitford takes the first guitar solo of the evening. "Thank you very much . . . Lord, have mercy . . . Here's something else off our album: 'Somebody,'" and Joe Perry sings the chorus along with me. We dedicate "Write Me" to All-Night Dwight, who must have been in the audience that night. Then "I Ain't Got You." Verse, harp solo, and "Mr. Whitford!" as Brad does his thing. Another verse and "OK, Joe" and Mr. Perry does his. "Would you please welcome David Wood Ford, who's gonna blow some sax" and we go into James Brown's "Mother Popcorn," totally over the top, but I always thought Aerosmith was a great funk band. Then "Movin' Out," "Walkin' the Dog," "Train" complete with our final live mike-swinging finale in which I often nearly brained band members who got too close to me, which segues into "Mama Kin."

And that was our show, except for "Dream On," which I'm almost sure we did that night, but for some reason it doesn't appear on the tape. This was supposed to be a showcase gig, and a lot of radio and press people came to see us. But did we get a lot of radio and press out of it? Nope. Most of *Rolling Stone* magazine's rock critics lived in Boston, but did we get a good review in *Rolling Stone*? Nope. Did we even get a notice, a mention, a little item in "Random Notes" at least? Nope. Aerosmith was ignored.

When we did get a review anywhere, the three words most often used were "primitive," "derivative," and "redundant." The straight press didn't like us and the feeling was mutual. Most of the critics panned our first album and said I was ripping off Mick Jagger. *Every article mentioned this.* And I think it really held us back. I felt that "Dream On" was a great song, but people didn't really start to hear it until two or three years after it came out. I still have anger at the press over this. I'd say to interviewers, "Look, if I have a physical resemblance to Mick Jagger, then that's an honor for me. But it also shows the lack of imagination of people to compare my movements to his and see nothing else." We would have been stupid to directly imitate the Stones. We would have gotten *crushed*.

Tom Hamilton: We were so starved for attention that it was a really big deal for us when Steven appeared on the cover of *The Point*, an alternative paper in Providence, Rhode Island. Inside was a shot of Steven mooning the photographer. It was our first visionary rave review.

THE POINT

Aerosmith rocks like a bitch and has all the harnessed energy of a busting supernova. They're young, they're tough, and they play like their lives depend on it. Aerosmith move like no other band I've seen. Black Oak Arkansas comes close, but Aerosmith is closer. They are the answer to what is perhaps my ideal band. Rock 'n' roll lives, a phenomenon is born, the circle widens. (April 1973)

Laura Kaufman: *Rolling Stone* ignored them, which was a big disappointment, not having their record reviewed. It just made them mad and even more determined. They got their first national record review from *Creem*, which was published in Detroit.

CREEM

Aerosmith is as good as coming in your pants at a drive-in at age twelve with your little sister's babysitter calling the action . . . they seem to be true to themselves; no imitation country or superhip posturing or frosted hair and beauty marks, just a few pimples and an LP of screaming, metallic, creative rock 'n' roll . . . Sure you'll hear influences, some quite obvious at that, but we all had to suck somebody's tit, and whatta buncha tits these chubby-lipped delinquents have gone after! . . . (April 1973)

Mark Parenteau: Aerosmith was big in Detroit from the beginning because Detroit is much more of a rock 'n' roll town than Boston. Detroit had that heavy black influence from Motown, and it had a heavy industrial vibe that liked its music loud, flashy, gritty—in other words, Aerosmith. In Detroit, a band had to cut through the din of the assembly line, the paint shop, the foundry. People lived a dark, dank factory life, and if you were a band, you just had to fucking *sparkle*.

I was one of the top disc jockeys in Detroit when "Dream On" came out, but I'm originally from Worcester, Mass. Early in 1973, I moved to WABX, Detroit's original underground rocker, where I was the music director and did the afternoon show, championing Boston bands because by then I was a little homesick. I helped J. Geils break in Detroit, and now I kept hearing from my friend Maxanne, who did afternoons at WBCN. "Hey, man, there's this young band you gotta hear from up in Sunapee, of all places. They're on fire, man."

I was at the station when the Columbia promo mailing came in with the first Bruce Springsteen and Aerosmith records in the same package. We put on *Aerosmith* and . . . *Wow!* We liked "Dream On" best, but thought it wasn't rocking enough for Detroit, so we played "One Way Street," "Make It," and "Walkin' the Dog."

Then Steven Tyler and Joe Perry came through on tour and I interviewed them at the station. It was their first Detroit concert (at Michigan Palace), as well as one of their first interviews. Their album was happening as far as we were concerned, the buzz was on, and Steven was great. I had him singing along with the record and he was just a natural on radio. I thought, *This kid really has it. He's the most charismatic person I've met since Mick Jagger.*

He was also scary. "C'mon," he says to me after the interview. "We'll go out tonight and get into *trouble*." He was so open about scoring some heroin and meeting some hookers that I went, "Whoa, not tonight, man." I was scared because Steven just had this total no-limits vibe.

But the bottom line was that Aerosmith was perfect not only for Detroit but for all the so-called Rust Belt towns that embraced them as the American Stones or the American Zeppelin: Toledo, Cincinnati, Cleveland. Dirty Midwestern auto-based towns where Steven got to try out his rock star persona in a way he couldn't at home. These were tough working-class places that accepted Aerosmith early on.

Steven Tyler: We thought we were on our way, but Frank Connelly showed up one day and told us that Summerthing, a series of concerts on Boston Common that summer, had refused to book Aerosmith. All the other local acts—the Modern Lovers, James Montgomery's band, Daddy Warbux, Ready Teddy, Orchestra Luna, Liv Taylor, Seatrain, Jonathan Edwards, Loudon Wainwright III, J. Geils, the Sidewinders, Bonnie Raitt—got booked except us. That wasn't all. Frank told us Clive Davis wanted to fire us because we hadn't sold enough records.

Maxanne Sartori: Aerosmith sold about 30,000 records out of Columbia's Boston branch. Under the branch system of record distribution, if there were eight branches around the country, this should have represented about 12.5 percent of Aerosmith's national sales. They needed to sell a quarter of a million albums to stay on the label. Outside of Boston, they sold something like 10,000 albums in Detroit, and that was basically it. When that happens: "good-bye, so long, you're gone!"

11: Aerosmith
Rocks Natick

Steve Leber: The album died because the young promotion people at Columbia hated us. They were either stoned or lazy, and we told them we knew Clive and the top management. We busted their chops and threatened them. If we didn't break Aerosmith's record, no one was gonna feed my three kids. We were terrorizing them to kick ass because no one gave a shit. Then Clive issued a release to the band. He sent notice he wasn't picking up our option. There would be no second Aerosmith album from Columbia. Clive said, "You're out!"

David Krebs: Our option came due and they didn't want to pick it up because we'd had an unsuccessful record—30,000 units, 20,000 in New England. So I made some moves. I don't know why, but I think my instincts proved to be valid and smart. I called Larry Harris, vice president for business affairs at Columbia. I said, "You're not gonna pick up their option, so I'm going to *give* you an extension so we can have more time to prove ourselves." I'd never heard of anybody ever doing this before, but it didn't mean it couldn't be done. I knew we'd have a hard time getting another record deal, so we gave them additional time for free so they didn't have to pick up the option.

Steve Leber: I called Clive. I begged him. I said, "Clive, *please* release 'Dream On' for me [as a single]," and he did. It went to something like #60 and got them some momentum, so CBS at least understood something was there. They had lost faith in the band because Aerosmith was the antithesis of what CBS was, a company Clive Davis had built on Streisand and Paul Simon. So we did that and extended the option period so we could get the second album recorded.

Steven Tyler: Late in May [1973], Columbia fired Clive Davis for supposedly using company money to pay for his son's bar mitzvah. At least Clive had given us our break.

They released an edited and remixed single of "Dream On" that June, with "Somebody" on the flip side. Maxanne had been playing "Dream On" all along, as if it had been a single. Then Ron Robin started to play it early in the summer at WVBF out in the burbs, where it went to #1. VBF took requests every night for their *TNT [Top Nine Tonite] Show*, and "Dream On" would be #1 almost every night for the next four months. We started to see the graffiti painted on bridges going over the Mass. Pike in huge block letters: AEROSMITH ROCKS NATICK!

We kept working all that summer. With "Dream On" on the radio, we got booked into Summerthing after all. We headlined a free concert for Boston's Top 40 AM station WRKO at Canobie Lake Park in New Hampshire and drew 7,000 kids. Then we got really pissed off when RKO listed *Aerosmith* as the #1 album in Boston on their survey sheet without ever playing "Dream On." I even did an interview with them, but they still didn't play the record. Everyone knew us in Boston, but RKO had a strict playlist from hell and they still wouldn't add "Dream On."

We played Hopedale High's senior prom on June 16. On June 23, we headlined at Cape Cod Coliseum, drew only 1,500 people, got four encores, and had to pay the local cops $400 in overtime.

The national label didn't care, but in Boston the two local CBS promo guys, Sal Ingeme and Ed Hynes, really started to push for us. In July, John Garabedian, who programmed AM station WMEX, broke "Dream On" nationally when he played it like it was a hit record. Then WRKO, the big AM powerhouse in New England, started to play it and it was #1 for the next eight weeks, until even I got sick of hearing it. (It was finally knocked out of first place in October by the Rolling Stones'

"Angie.") I was walking around like I was God, except that God probably never got as high as I was.

Now it felt like we were happening. We played a week at Caesar's Monticello in Framingham and drew 2,000 people a night. We played to capacity, about 1,000 people, for a week at Frolics in Salisbury Beach and 1,000 people were turned away every night. We were working five nights a week and we heard that "Dream On" was starting to do well in the Northwest and upstate New York.

You could feel it starting to build, and the kids out there were a little nuts. On August 10, we opened for Sha Na Na at Suffolk Downs racetrack near Boston. These summer shows usually drew about 10,000 kids. When we played, 35,000 showed up and the kids were so rowdy that they had to stop the show.

Tom Hamilton: Suffolk Downs? Oh, God, all I remember is a fuckin' *fog* of beer bottles suspended at the top of their arc before they fell on the stage all around us in a storm of shattering glass.

THE BOSTON GLOBE

FANS HIT NEW LOW AT SUNSET SERIES

. . . As the sun set over the right side of the stage and clouds moved in from the west, Aerosmith began their set with "Make It."

Into the third song a barrage of beer cans filled the air, sending people to the ground seeking whatever shelter they could find.

The show was stopped at least twice as Steve Tyler, pseudo–Mick Jagger lead singer for Aerosmith, scolded the bubbly little teens, trying to make them behave. It didn't work and the show went on.

Aerosmith is a local group catering to the bubble-gum set. They put out a sound that will never grow away from the AM radio Top 40. (August 12, 1973)

Joey Kramer: That summer we were all living together again in an apartment on Beacon Street near Cleveland Circle in Brookline, the five of us and Tiger, working on songs for the next album. Every day at five we'd crowd into Brad's room, which was the size of a large closet, to watch *The Three Stooges* as in days of yore. Every show was a religious experience for us.

I'd always wanted a Great Dane since I was a kid. Tiger came from one of my girlfriend Nina's friends who couldn't afford to feed 130 pounds of dog. Tiger was emaciated when I got him and he needed a lot of res-

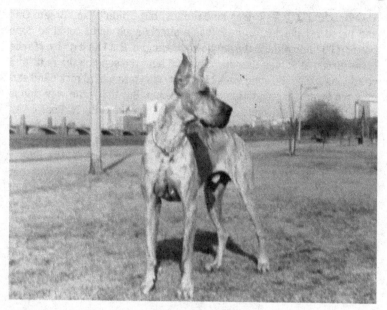

Tiger
(KRAMER COLLECTION)

toration and care. Tiger really became our mascot, the source of a lot of hilarity. On my birthday that year [June 21, 1973] someone brought over a tray of pot brownies for me. We put them in some foil on top of the fridge, and went to the gig in Worcester. We came back early in the morning to find Tiger comatose on the kitchen floor, lying in shredded tinfoil. We couldn't even move him. "Poor fuckin' dog," says Tom, and we all started to giggle. Someone made me a huge chocolate cake, and I happen to hate chocolate cake, so Steven dared me to put my face in it. What else could I do, drunk and stoned as I was? I plunged my head in the cake amid great applause, then lay down next to Tiger, who managed to come to, roll over and lick all the chocolate off my face.

Good thing we didn't have video cameras back then.

And my birthday wasn't even over yet. I'd had a big fight with Nina at her house after the Worcester gig, and then went home and slept with another girl that night. In the morning Nina tiptoed in with a birthday cake and found me sleeping with this other girl. She just closed the door quietly and left. Next afternoon I go outside and my car—this little Vega station wagon—was completely covered in smeared cake, which had baked in the sun and now formed a hard crust all over the car. Everyone thought it was a pretty cool thing to do, but that was Nina.

Joe Perry: It was kinda funny, but I didn't like "Dream On" and hated my playing on it. It was a simple song and I could've done better if I'd hung around the studio a little longer. But I let it go by. Maybe I was pissed at Steven that day. Then I'd hear the song on the radio and cringe. As big as the song was, I hated it. We were a hard rock band and now we owed our reputation to a slow song. But that's the way things were then. A couple years ago, you had to look like Guns N' Roses. Ten years before that, you had to have hair like Bon Jovi. In 1973, you had to get your songs on the radio and the only way a band like us got on the radio was by having a ballad.

We're still playing the same games. The numbers are bigger, but that's about it. I've heard more bad songs that have made it because of MTV than good songs that haven't.

I just remember that it was pretty cool to hear Aerosmith back-to-back with a Stones record like *Goats Head Soup* on the same radio show. I felt great for a couple of minutes before I realized, *It isn't quite as good as them.*

Hey, like Steven says, it's the journey.

Elyssa Perry: "Dream On" was really a big bone of contention. I hated this song so much it became my bathroom song. They'd start playing it at the shows and I'd go to the bathroom.

Steven Tyler: We went back to New York early in September and played a showcase at Kenny's Castaways. We went around to the offices of the trades—*Billboard, Cashbox, Record World*—so the chart people could get a look at us. And believe it or not, we started to get some good reviews. We went to Max's Kansas City, where Columbia promo man Mike Klenfner had put "Dream On" into the downstairs jukebox, where it was a big closet hit with the music crowd who hadn't heard it on the radio yet. It got played all the time, every night, on Max's jukebox for the following year.

VARIETY

Boston is enjoying an up period as a center of rock 'n' roll and this combo of nineteen-year-olds is one of the reasons . . .

Lead vocalist Steve Tyler, with plenty of pelvic action, is garbed in black net shirt trimmed in glitter and multicolored tights. His vocals are strong, sometimes screaming. He usually is the focus onstage . . .

Standing out are lead guitarist Joe Perry and drummer Joey Kramer with solid assists from rhythm guitarist Brad Whitford and bass guitarist Tom Hamilton. (September 12, 1973)

CASHBOX

Aerosmith is bursting with rhythm and raunch, carrying on the tradition of the Stones but with the innuendos of the 70s. The sound radiates total energy. Want energy more total than total? Try the new Aerosmith album! (September 20, 1973)

12: American Bandstand

Joe Perry: During this time, the band was living on Beacon Street in Brookline because Frank Connelly wanted us to move back in together to write the second album. Steven and I were writing "Same Old Song and Dance" and he was working on "Seasons of Wither." There was a party every night we weren't playing somewhere, lots of Quaaludes and blue crystal meth we kept in the freezer (stick a little up your nose and it was really vicious, really good speed), plenty of hash, joints rolled like massive Jamaican spliffs, the whole 1973 trip.

For four months that summer and fall, we rehearsed the songs for our second album in the basement of a store called Drummer's Image on Newbury Street. That's where *Get Your Wings* really came together.

Steven Tyler: We used to practice in a closet in the cement-walled basement at Drummer's Image—amps, no chairs, I'm sitting on the floor, and one day I had this paranoid vision that this was the way the Beatles, Stones, Led Zep started—all the big bands started as little bands with a vision—but the only trouble was that we're *not* gonna make it, we're gonna get *beat*, because we're not a big band and our record company doesn't get us, we fight all the time, and this is just never gonna work.

So I'd start a conversation. "This'll never happen. We'll probably get beat, but if we had $300, we could buy ten twenty-five-pound bags of peanuts—enough peanuts to fill a small room waist-high and have the instruments and lots of naked girls' legs sticking out of the nuts, girls'

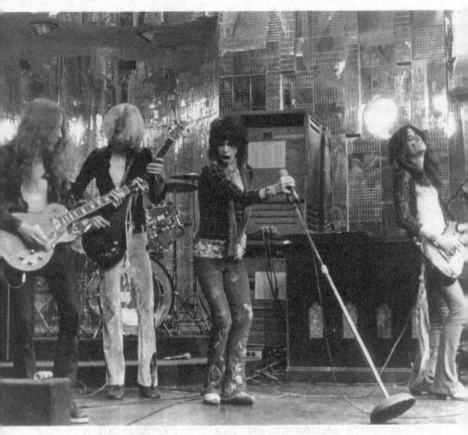

Aerosmith plays Lucifer's, Kenmore Square, Boston, 1973
(PHOTO: TERRY HAMILTON)

arms holding the guitars, and the band just sitting there in the nuts, and we call the album *Night in the Ruts.*"

"Nah, that sucks, and we don't wanna spend money on peanuts anyway."

"Yeah, you're right. Fuck it."

It got passed on.

Tom Hamilton: The first Aerosmith band profile was published that fall after the *Boston Herald* sent a reporter and photographer to our apartment to interview us. I go back and read these old clippings today and I realize that I was playing dumb for the press because that's what I believed our audience wanted.

BOSTON HERALD

BAND IN LIMBO
CAN BOSTON'S YOUNG AEROSMITH
FIND ROCK FAME AND FORTUNE?

The last time Steven Tyler walked into a plush restaurant, the hostess ushered him out because of the shabby-looking rags he was wearing. Rushing outside, the proprietor—an old friend—apologized and invited him back in.

The incident illustrates the predicament of Aerosmith, the five-man rock band for which Tyler sings, now perched in that limbo between obscurity and fame . . .

Their name is far from a household word. The $1,500 they receive for an engagement is far less than star quotient. Each member is salaried a modest $100 a week. And the editors of *Rolling Stone* are hardly beating on their apartment's front door . . . What they are is an exciting, tight group waiting for their next break, preparing themselves to capitalize on it.

But what manner of men are these musicians, poised on fame's brink, who might be catapulted into the role of cultural arbiters, inspiring standards of conduct and taste for our vestal youth?

. . . Hardly stereotypical left-wing anarchists, no member of Aerosmith has ever even worked in a political campaign. "The guys are quiet about their politics," says Hamilton. "We're apolitical. I guess I lean a little to the right, maybe because that's where I'm from. Nixon's generally doing things right. His meeting with Brezhnev, going to China. That's the way things have got to go . . . But I also think Nixon's a lot of lies. It didn't help that those [Watergate] people led him on." (September 16, 1973)

Steven Tyler: In October 1973, we went on tour opening for Mott the Hoople, the English pub-rock band fronted by Ian Hunter turned glitter rock stars under the auspices of David Bowie, who had written their hit record "All the Young Dudes." Mott was so cynical about this glam and glitter shit that they hired a new guitarist, Luther Grosvenor from Spooky Tooth, bought him some new clothes and eight-inch platform boots, and renamed him Ariel Bender. ["Bender" is Cockney slang for a homosexual.]

Mott loved us because we got their audience crazed. Soon Ian Hunter was complaining the cut of my low-slung trousers was cooler than his. They were. (David Bowie: "Basically, rock stardom comes down to the cut of your trousers.") Working in larger places—coliseums, theaters, mu-

sic halls, auditoriums, Massey Hall in Toronto, Syria Mosque in Pitts-
burgh—we learned even more how to put Aerosmith over as a live band.
On October 27, the tour hit Boston.

THE [BOSTON] REAL PAPER

Last weekend's two concerts at the Orpheum were set to be the
high point of the glam rock season, with headliners Mott the Hoople
premiering their new guitarist, Ariel Bender . . . who looked like
David Bowie's maiden aunt and had a hard time prancing around
ungracefully on his new platforms . . . The rough-hewn performance of Aerosmith was much more of what rock is all about.

. . . The reaction of the Orpheum crowd was tumultuous . . . It
was . . . like *The Ed Sullivan Show* in 1964. They're really rocking
in Boston. (November 5, 1973)

Steven Tyler: David Krebs was always saying that Aerosmith had to break on the road, which proved to be true when we finally
got on the charts. "Dream On" went on the *Cashbox* singles chart in October, getting to #43 during an eleven-week run. In *Billboard* we got to
#59. Our album finally got on the charts ten months after it came out and
got to #166.

AEROSMITH PRESS RELEASE

. . . The next album has been pushed up until early next year. The
album is tentatively titled *Night in the Ruts* and will be recorded in
New York at the Record Plant this month. Steven Tyler describes
the album as "Crystal." He says the LP is penned by "me and the
boys" and will have eight tracks, including "Pandora's Box" and an
Aerosmith arrangement of the traditional "Train Kept A-Rollin'."
Steve thinks "Train" will be live and adds, "We ain't gonna do it
like the Yardbirds."

. . . The five boys from eastern Mass., Yonkers, New York, and
New Hampshire will go on national tour again sometime in November or January. The five-piece "Schlamoon . . . orrgaaassmm . . .
massive ventricle thrombosis . . . whatchamacallit" as the boys describe themselves have one major obstacle to overcome: "Our
Three Stooges syndrome; but then, *look out!*" (Laura Kaufman,
circa November 1973)

Steven Tyler: We ended the year in Los Angeles, where
we played a showcase at the Whisky [A Go-Go on Sunset Boulevard] that

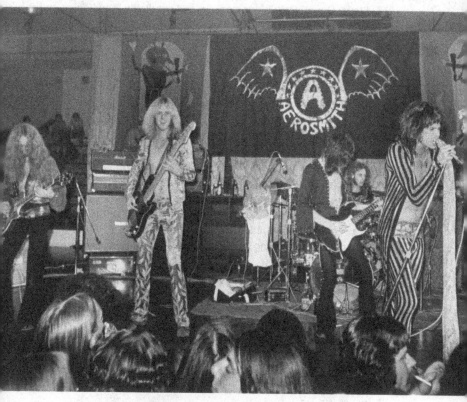

Aerosmith at Boston College, 1973.
Note original bat-wing logo banner and Woodstock demon banners.
(PHOTO: RON POWNALL)

filled the club on normally dead Monday and Tuesday nights. People told us we were a hot rumor around town. We also taped "Dream On" for *American Bandstand*, the longest-running music show on TV. (We were on with Billy Preston.) I'd always wanted to know what Dick Clark did while the kids were dancing, and there he was shouting at the director through a head mike.

We also endured some interviews with some of L.A.'s totally hostile music writers. Here's an example from the old scrapbook:

Q: How did you get mixed up in this mess?

Steve *(lead singer)*: We were in other bands.

Joe *(lead guitarist)*: We were in worse messes.

Q: Are you living at home with Mommy and Daddy or is this gig for real?

Steve: Our mommy is our manager and our daddy is our jonses and our jonses is our music.

Q: That's profound. How old are you?

Steve: How old do you think?

Q: Fifty-three.

Steve: Funny. I'm twenty-five.

Q: Why are you making rock? Haven't you heard it's dying?

Steve: Rock's not dying if you know what you're playing, what you're communicating. Songs have character, and a minor chord is sadness. Are you into music?

Q: No. You guys seem to be stealing the visual trip from the Dolls.

Steve (stunned): We steal from the Dolls?

Q: Sure.

Steve: That's a load of shit! Maybe there's a bit of resemblance, but that's a very low-class opinion.

Q: You're not imitating David Johansen?

Steve: Oh, fuck . . .

Q: Would you be disillusioned if you were compared to the Stones?

Steve: Hell no! Today, maybe, but not the early Stones, music being the cell doors closing as opposed to the opening of a rose petal.

Q: Are you guys punk rock?

Steve: No. A punk is a wise guy who doesn't know how to wipe his ass.

Q: I always thought a punk was a guy who thinks he knows more than he does.

Steve: What?

Q: Never mind. When's your next album coming out?

Steve: March. No, January. Hey, I gotta take a whizz. Talk to you again, OK?

Q: You bet.

Joe Perry: I always thought that one of the reasons we didn't get good press was that we were actually hard to figure out for them. The Beatles had been the light side and the Rolling Stones were always their shadow side. But Aerosmith tried to play both sides, dark heavy songs and funny dance numbers. It was hard for people to categorize us. People our age doing the magazines and radio just didn't get it. We used to laugh about how they considered themselves rebels in the sixties.

As far as we were concerned, if a kid read a bad review of us in *Rolling Stone* and he's a fan of ours, the kid was thinking, *This paper* sucks. *I* like Aerosmith.

The Blue Army

5

There's no substitute for arrogance.

—Joe Perry

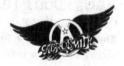

RECORD WORLD

AEROSMITH SMASHING

Los Angeles—It is a rare treat indeed to have the opportunity to see a first rate act before it is picked up and marketed like a candy bar or laundry soap. But a recent evening at the Whisky was such an occasion. A Boston group, Aerosmith (Columbia), staged one of the best performances this reviewer has seen in some time. The lead singer, Steven Tyler, came on with polish and charisma a cut above even some of the best of today's upper echelon of rock . . . Joe Perry, the group's lead guitarist, also performed admirably, with solos reminiscent of the early Stones—not too long, basic, accessible. (S. L. Smoke, "Club Review," December 29, 1973)

1: The Legend
of Jack Douglas

Joe Perry: We had such a strong feeling as a band when we started to record our second album. We believed in our music, what we were doing. Besides, all of a sudden we're in New York, making an album at the Record Plant, sitting in the same seats Mick and Keith were sitting in a few weeks previously. Jimi Hendrix. "Room Full of Mirrors." And we're pretty much in awe of this.

Jack Douglas produced the record, the start of a long association. He's a cool guy and we all liked him personally. He had that New York edge but wasn't a snob about it. He wasn't like one of those record label jerks; instead he was someone you could laugh with. Bob Ezrin came in and had this fuckin' attitude like he was God. Jack came in and said, "Let's have a drink." He became like a member of the band. We worked with a lot of people and never had the same feeling about anyone else.

Jack Douglas: I'm from the Bronx and grew up in Rockland County, north of New York, so I have similar roots with Steven and Joey Kramer. I had piano lessons as a child, some classical guitar and music theory in high school. I was playing folk music and worked in Robert Kennedy's campaign when he was running for the Senate in 1964, traveling around with him, singing songs. At Tappan Zee High, I put a band together with some other folkies: the Talismen. We got a manager and started playing gigs at some of the same places Steven's bands were playing at around New York.

In December 1965, my friend Eddie Leonetti and myself decided that where it was happening was Liverpool, home of the Beatles and the Mersey sound. So we caught a tramp steamer bound for Europe with a load of bananas and tarantulas and set sail. At night we'd entertain the crew and the officers. We're on board for like twenty-six days in a December gale in the North Atlantic, unloading bananas in Belfast, Dublin, Glasgow. Finally we get to Liverpool. Immigration comes aboard and sees these two young kids with Les Paul guitars and a couple of small amplifiers, two bloody Yanks without work permits. "Return ticket? Why would we have return tickets? We just got here!"

They just shook their heads and told us not only were they *not* gonna let us into Liverpool but that we were deportees and had to stay on the ship as prisoners until it left. That night I escaped. I said, "Eddie, cover for me. I'm gonna get us outta here."

So I jumped ship in disguise. It happened to be the day that the Beatles' *Rubber Soul* album was released. On the following day, the Beatles were coming to Liverpool to do a welcome home concert, and the whole city was rocking. The buzz was almost more intense than I could ask for. I went into a record shop to buy *Rubber Soul* and the listening booths were packed with people listening to the album, analyzing it. I put it on and the first cut was "Drive My Car." [A different version of *Rubber Soul* was released in the United States.] I'm going crazy because this was a milestone album for them and totally new to me. I'm thinking, *I can* not *leave this place.*

Walking the streets, I pass the office of the *Liverpool Daily News*. I went in, asked to see the editor, and told him my story: two stranded Yanks in Liverpool harbor. He loved it. "Nobody *comes* here," he told me. "We all *leave* here."

That night I snuck back on the ship. One of the crew had a record player and we had a big *Rubber Soul* listening party. Next day there were a dozen newspaper reporters at the gangplank to cover our story. London papers, Northern papers, Midlands, Scotland. The day after that, when the Beatles were in town and every front page in Liverpool should have been screaming this, there were pictures on every front page of me and Eddie Leonetti on the deck of our prison ship. We had, without meaning to, upstaged the Beatles in their hometown. The next day we had a fan club—teenage girls with placards marching up and down in front of the ship. We finally got in after agreeing to let them send our instruments home so we couldn't make a living in England. So we stayed in Liverpool, got other guitars, and joined a band called the Richmond Group almost immediately. We were there for about six months until someone ratted us out. Immigration came to our flat, hustled us off to London that night, and threw us out of the country.

Back in New York, we were like mini-celebs, just off the boat from Liverpool! We joined a good band called Wild Child and the Violations—I was playing bass—and then the rhythm section got a job backing the Angels of "My Boyfriend's Back" fame. After that we worked a shady club in Miami fronted by Wayne Cochran and the C. C. Riders. Wayne was the white James Brown, big hair, real R&B and soul. That's where I really got my chops because if you were the bass player in that kind of band, you had to be *married* to the drummer, married to the snare drum, the bass drum, the hi-hat. Wayne used to punch the ceiling when he got excited, with his big white pompadore, and then he'd start preaching, really wild. It was an all-white Southern band, totally racist, and I wasn't into that scene at all, so we split.

My recording career started with an English group, the Liverpool Set, who were working in Canada. I stayed with them for two years. Then I heard from Eddie Leonetti, whose group the Soul Survivors had a hit with "Expressway to Your Heart." They were breaking up, so we put together a "heavy" band called Privilege. One night the Isley Brothers came in because they'd heard about us and wanted to sign a white rock band so their T-Neck label wouldn't be all black.

They sent us to A&R Studios with their engineer, Tony May, a black guy. To do an eight-track heavy rock album was a really big deal back then, but they left us alone. We cut some tracks and vocals, very sparse, very heavy, a lot of space, and I was happy with it. Then they said, "OK, next week, we're gonna do some overdubbing. We don't need you anymore." This was the Isley Brothers so we thought, *What can they possibly do? They can't fuck it up. They only have to mix it, right?*

What we got back was an Isley Brothers record—horns, black girls singing harmony with us. I got really irate and told them it was all wrong and wouldn't sell. They said they didn't want to remix it, so I told them I would. So Tony May and I went back to A&R and I started to mix and I'm thinking, *I like this. I like it on this side of the glass.* This was 1968, and there was Phil Ramone, the master sound guy of his generation, puttering around, doing his thing. Tony May started to tell me, "I think you've got a talent for this. Maybe this is your bag, man."

The Isleys put out our album, but they didn't know how to market it and it died. Then a new thing called the School of Audio Research ran an ad in *The Village Voice*: LEARN TO BE A RECORDING ENGINEER! The school was in a small room at the Wellington Hotel on Seventh Avenue. There were thirty people in the first class before the guy came out and said, "If anybody doesn't know basic algebra, we'll give you your money back right now." There were five people left in the class after that. The first six weeks was nothing but math and theory. *When are we gonna see a microphone?* They crammed it all into us: wave theory, wire maintenance. Ohm's law was coming out my fingertips. After six months, when I looked at a recording console, I could see through it, like an exploded diagram. They didn't teach me how to do a mix. They told me how to pull a pan pod and fix it. Frequency response, how a compressor worked, which equalizer was what.

Then Tony May called and said a lot of the A&R guys were defecting to a new studio called the Record Plant. "Run down there. You might get a job." I wound up with a job as the janitor.

My job was to clean the toilet bowls, empty the ashtrays. Two months later, I moved to tape librarian, and that's when I started sneaking into the studio with my own set of keys. I'd take people's tapes, remix them, and leave them for Roy Cecalla, who was chief engineer. I'd come in on Monday and Chris Stone, who managed the place, would fire me—every week. Next day I'd be hired back by Roy, who was saying, "I think this kid might make some money for us. He has ears. Move him along." That's how I became an assistant engineer.

I worked on countless records: Miles Davis, Judy Collins, Mountain, the James Gang. I'd do a jingle in the morning, a jazz date in the afternoon, and then a rock band at night. I'd sleep for three hours and then come in and do a jingle. I got tons of experience engineering.

The first real rock date I did was assisting a guy named Jack Adams, who did the R&B dates. I look in the book and see that the Who are coming in and that Jack Adams is doing it. Jack hated rock dates with a passion, so I begged him to get me on the date. This is right after *Tommy*. He asks, "Who are the Who?" I said, "Don't worry about it. Just get me on the date."

The Who comes in—Townshend, Daltrey, Entwistle, Moon—with Kit Lambert producing. Total drug addicts, total maniacs, total rock 'n' roll. I set up all their stuff: big Coliseum bass amps, Marshall stacks. Jack Adams comes in and groans. I said, "Jack, it's the Who!!" He says, "Fuck the Who. Go to the house phone, call me up here in the studio, and say my houseboat's on fire over at 79th Street, so I can have an excuse to get out of here." So I called him up and he started screaming. I walked back in and he's telling Townshend and Kit Lambert that he's leaving them in the capable hands of his assistant—me—except I'm really a great engineer.

And Jack leaves. Townshend takes a look at me and goes, "Fuck all. Go ahead." They went in and did "Won't Get Fooled Again" and my hair's standing on end! They had that preprogrammed thing, a Peevee synthesizer which was a riot, an English machine that had pins in it like an old telephone exchange. These turned out to be the sessions for *Who's Next*, a great album.

I started going out at night with Moon and Entwistle. Moon would wreck every club he went to. He was dangerous, a real madman. He played totally nude in the studio. If he was out at night and disappeared for a second, it meant something was going to fly around the room shortly. Townshend would literally get under the table if he lost track of Moon, because he knew there would be trouble.

I would just climb into the limo with them after work. One night we ended up in a private club in a high-rise building, palm trees everywhere. After a couple of drinks, Moon disappears. I see Townshend getting under the table and within seconds a palm tree comes crashing down on the table with Moon riding it. When he died, I was sorry to see him go, but it was inevitable after so many years of abuse . . .

2: The Record Plant

Jack Douglas: When I heard John Lennon was coming to the studio to record what would become *Imagine*, I asked to be the third engineer because John wanted to run two rooms at once, twenty-four hours a day, to do this record. They had a lot of tapes already, but they needed sweetening and none of the vocal tracks were done. Roy Cecalla had a room and Shelly Yakus and I were working shifts in another room. Phil Spector was producing. He was one of my heroes, but I was so disappointed. Every day he'd come in and fall asleep. Once in a while he'd wake up and say, "More echo" and then go back to sleep. His bodyguards would carry him out of the session and put him in his limo. John Lennon and Roy Cecalla were actually doing the record.

John Lennon was a guy who made you feel comfortable immediately. I had been such a Beatle fan that I used to fantasize that they were my friends. I used to listen to the *White Album* on acid, communicating with them and their producer, George Martin. I was so nervous when I heard John Lennon was coming in. First Yoko came in and scared the shit out of me. She was completely like what I thought she'd be: crazy, really paranoid. She looked at me and hissed, "Who are you?" Then John came in and it was a casual "Hi" and a big relief. He introduced himself to everyone in the room, asking who they were, chatting with us about what he wanted to do. And we got to work.

Three days into the project, I told him about my adventures in Liverpool, and he did a double take because he remembered the newspaper headlines. "Crazy fookin' Yanks," he goes, "and it was bloody *you*?" He started to laugh every time he looked at me, laughed with a lot of warmth, a sound that no one who heard it will ever forget.

After that he asked me to go out with him, because he didn't know New York and a lot of people were looking to get something out of him. He was thrilled to be in New York, living in a basement flat on Bank Street with the door basically open to the street traffic. We went to parties at night. There was one for the avant-garde Living Theater where John pulled a knife on a girl who was talking carelessly about killing people during the forthcoming revolution. He put the knife to her throat and asked, "You really wanna take somebody's life?" It was the first time I ever saw that side of him. He was crazed and I had to get him out of there. It scared the shit out of me.

I started hanging out with John, and he asked me if I'd get involved with Yoko's records. I said sure, as long as he was producing. So we started with the end of *Fly* and then did *Approximately Infinite Universe* and a couple of others. This went well until one day Yoko was in the studio yodeling one of her trademark vocals, really out there, and I must have given John a look because he started laughing and couldn't stop, couldn't control himself, his head bobbing up and down on the console while his wife was wailing away like an air-raid siren. He tried to suppress it, tried to hide it, but then I lost it too and we both ended up under the console. John was banned from the studio after that.

In the early seventies, I got a relationship going with a guy named Bob Ezrin, and we started doing Alice Cooper records. When I met him, he dressed like an old man and smoked a pipe and one day I said, "Bob, how old are you?" I was twenty-seven, twenty-eight at the time. I had so much respect for this guy as a producer, arranger, musician. I appreciated him because I looked at Alice's band and saw that what Bob had to work with was horrendous. And they sold millions of records based on Bob's arrangements, musicians, everything. And he looked at me and said, "I'm twenty-two." I was laughing so hard. I couldn't believe it, how mature his work was.

We got to be close, doing *School's Out, Billion Dollar Babies*. I worked on Lou Reed's albums—*Berlin*—brilliant but depressing. Anyway, around that time Warner Bros. bought the Record Plant and the one on the West Coast. They had a contest among the engineers to see who could book the most studio time. By that time my name was out, I got a lot of work, and I won. They gave me an incredible amount of then nearly worthless Warner stock, which I still have, ha-ha . . .

My work came to the notice of the people who worked with the New York Dolls—David Krebs and Todd Rundgren, who was producing their first album. This was a very extreme group for the time and they needed my city/street thing. Meanwhile, Bob Ezrin was downstairs and he kept coming up to see what I was doing. After the Dolls, he said I should be producing and hired me for his company, Nimbus 9. He told me I had to open out of town, so I went to Canada and produced a group called Crowbar for Columbia. Then I did a Sha Na Na record. I was the producer, Bob was executive producer. That's when he got a call about a group called Aerosmith. It must have been late in 1973.

They'd just had an album out, with a single about to take off. They'd had a problem with their first producer and David Krebs wanted Bob Ezrin.

Bob went to see them and was totally turned off because he thought it was going to be another Alice Cooper, and he was tired of that. He didn't even want to do Alice's *Muscle of Love*, the last group album, which I ended up producing. So now I had a platinum album under my belt. Bob Ezrin says, "You liked the Yardbirds, so you'll like Aerosmith. Go see this band in Boston."

I took the train to Boston the next day and got picked up at South Station by Frank Connelly. What a character: a wild man, an old-fashioned Irish rogue promoter, who could have been promoting a circus or a fight. It didn't matter. He was something of a gangster, but he had wonderful eyes, loved the band, *really* believed in Aerosmith. He was 50/50 partners with Leber and Krebs, and he was mostly promoting them in local high schools. He drove me out to a gig at Framingham High in the suburbs and the place was *packed*, three-to-one girls and hard-looking guys, all 15, 16 years old.

Aerosmith came out in stage clothes, very glam but still very street, scarves draped over the microphone, and put out this amazing raw energy. I'd seen the Jimmy Page Yardbirds at the Village Gate in New York, and that night I thought I saw the American Yardbirds—not a copy, not an imitation, but the real thing, a hard-rocking blues/R&B rock group. They played "Train Kept A-Rollin' " and I was just floored. *This*, I'm thinking to myself, *is the Great American Rock Band*.

I went backstage to see them and they were hostile. *Very* hostile. Which was OK with me. I liked people with an attitude. Brad was friendly and forthright, and Tom was a real New England gentleman, but Steven, Joe, and Joey were like a bunch of toughs, and that made it even more real. You knew it would come across in their music and on their records.

I told them I enjoyed the set and then we started talking about guitars. Joe warmed up first, and that was a signal to them. You could see Steven thinking, *Well, OK*, and so I started talking to him and found we had so much in common. Very much alike. Really something there.

They were initially hostile because they'd been told that Bob Ezrin didn't want to do it and they thought he was sending up a lackey. But because of the Dolls, both the band and Leber-Krebs were receptive to my doing the second Aerosmith album. I told them up front that I didn't like the sound on their first album at all. Some of those first and second takes are great if they're in the spirit of "raw first album" rather than "I just want to get outta here," which is the impression I got from the band of how *Aerosmith* was done.

So, to the best of my memory, the preproduction work for *Get Your Wings* started in the back room of a restaurant that was like a Mob hangout in the North End. I commuted there from the Copley Plaza Hotel and they started to play me the songs they had for their new album. My attitude was: *What can I do to make them sound like themselves?*

No one had ever worked with them before. There were many long hours of practice to get them to sound professional by my standards. They were a young band and they were afraid of the studio. They'd see the red light come on and choke. Plus, we had the usual hassles when the dealers showed up. They tortured each other. There were a lot of fights.

3: Studio C

Joe Perry: Like I said before, we were recording in New York City for the first time and we were so in awe of the Record Plant that we just did what Jack told us to do. He really produced that album, along with Ray Colcord from Columbia, who was there to see that the trains ran on time.

We were still pretty much recording the band live, and we were very wet behind the ears. It was all we could do to get the basic tracks down and worry about getting a good take all the way through. Jack worked us very hard over the two weeks it took to record, and I remember many mornings with all of us walking up Eighth Avenue, guitars in hand (minus my black Strat, which got stolen at the Record Plant), threading our way through the hookers and pimps and derelicts just before dawn to get to the Ramada Inn on 48th Street, where we were staying.

The tracks were the stuff we'd been working on at our apartment on Beacon Street in the summer of '73. I wrote the riff to "Same Old Song and Dance" one night in the front room and Steven just started to sing along. "Spaced" happened the same way in the studio, with a lot of input from Jack. "S.O.S." meant "Same Old Shit" and came from the rehearsals at the Drummer's Image. "Woman of the World" was a song that Steven had written with Don Solomon, a real rocker that we developed playing the middle section of "Rattlesnake Shake" from our live show. We thought it was gonna show people who liked "Dream On" what Aerosmith was really about. "Lord of the Thighs" and "Seasons of Wither" were Steven's songs. Of all the ballads Aerosmith has done, "Wither" was the one I liked best. I never thought Aerosmith should do any ballads at all. My philosophy was the only thing a hard rock band should play slow was a slow blues.

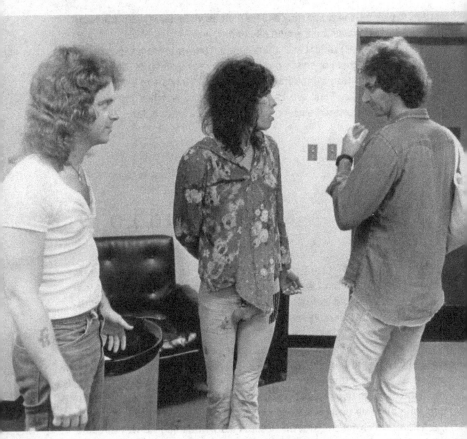

Joey and Steven with Jack Douglas
(PHOTO: RON POWNALL)

Steven Tyler: "Seasons of Wither" was about the winter landscape near this house I was living in with Joey near an old chicken farm [in Needham, Mass.]. I used to lie in my bed at dawn, listening to the wind in the bare trees, how lonely and melancholy it sounded. I was pissed off about my taxes and getting mad helps me to write, so one night I went down to the basement where we had a rug on the floor and a couple of boxes for furniture and took a few Tuinals and a few Seconals and I scooped up this guitar Joey gave me, this Dumpster guitar, and I lit some incense and wrote "Seasons of Wither."

Joey Kramer: The summer before, we'd rented a farmhouse in East Thetford, Vermont, while we were rehearsing in New Hampshire, and that's where I wrote the melody of "Pandora's Box." Steven wrote the lines about women's liberation, a big new issue in those times, and we used it to close *Get Your Wings*, a huge thrill for me, the first thing I'd ever written.

There's no sane way to describe my relationship with Steven Tyler. He was my teacher, friend, enemy, buddy, mentor, tormentor. Someone even put out a rumor at the beginning of the band that we were gay. The truth is that Steven and I have this very basic soul connection. That said, it was more like I was under his control until one night around the time we were making the second album.

It started when the phone rang at my girlfriend Nina's house, where I was sleeping. It was Steven calling from Kent Street to say that he desperately needed a ride to the house in Needham and it couldn't wait. I looked at my watch: 3 A.M. I staggered into my clothes and drove over and there's Steven waiting for me with a huge bass fiddle that he stole. "No questions, man," he whispered as I pulled up. "Put down the fuckin' seat and let's go."

So we're driving down Route 9. When we get to Newton Lower Falls, he starts in on me, as usual, because Nina and Steven didn't get along. He goes, "Fuck, Joey, you shouldn't be with this girl Nina so much, man, she's distracting you from the work you should be doing with the band, and you can't afford to let up," and all this shit. So I finally had enough and told him, "Hey, man, it's three o'clock in the morning and I was nice enough to get out of bed and give you a fuckin' ride, so would you please cut it out!"

It was like he didn't hear me. He just kept it up about Nina, about my playing, my supposed faults, and I finally told him, "Steven, if you don't shut the fuck up, I'm kicking you out of the car."

"Never happen. Keep going."

OK, now I'm pissed off—*furious*. I pull over. "Steven, get the fuck out of the car."

"What? You're joking. Let's go, man. I'm fuckin' beat."

"No way." I got out, unloaded the bass fiddle onto Route 9, helped Steven out of the car, and left him and the bass on Route 9 at three-thirty in the morning. My declaration of independence, and it worked because Steven stopped bothering me . . . a little.

Tom Hamilton: The sessions were almost over and we needed one more song. So we locked ourselves into Studio C of the Record

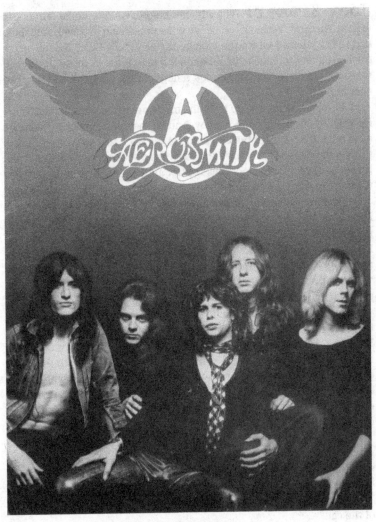

Get Your Wings
(TYLER COLLECTION)

Plant for a night and came up with "Lord of the Thighs," a portrait of the street life we used to encounter walking up Eighth Avenue at dawn after work. Did you ever see that movie *Taxi Driver*? The girls in the satin hot pants, the pimps with the big velvet hats. That's what it was.

Steven Tyler: The title is a joke on [William Golding's novel] *Lord of the Flies*, which came out as a movie around that time. The critics hated us for this. We weren't supposed to be smart enough to use literary references.

Joey Kramer: We were all under pressure—from Jack and each other—to play better, more professionally, more consistently. Everyone was telling me, "Harder! Play harder!" Henry Smith, who had worked with John Bonham, started me wearing a glove in the studio because I hold my left stick from the opposite end to get more volume with the butt end. That hand started to swell and get blisters because I was hitting the drum so hard—and still they told me it wasn't enough. We were out for blood that year.

Jack Douglas: Jay Messina engineered the sessions, and he and I worked on the tracks through most of January 1974. We got the Brecker brothers and Stan Bronstein from Elephant's Memory to put horns on "Same Old Song and Dance" and "Pandora's Box." The clarinet doodling "I'm in the Mood for Love" at the beginning of "Pandora" was played by a union engineer. Work rules required him to be in the studio, but he had nothing to do except fool around on his clarinet all day, and we used a snippet on the track.

One of the last things we worked on was "Train Kept A-Rollin'." Tiny Bradshaw wrote and recorded it in the forties, the Rock and Roll Trio had a hit with it in the fifties, and the Yardbirds owned it in the sixties. Now Aerosmith had taken it over and wanted to show how it should be done in the seventies. It was their signature song. They wanted to record it live in front of an audience because it was their big showstopper, but that was really impractical at the time.

So I took the track we cut in the studio and some really big speakers, Joey's PA that he used for his drums, and I blasted it into the famous stairwell at the Record Plant. We were on the tenth floor, and I put microphones on the eighth, sixth, and second floors so we'd get various delays and make it sound live. A couple years earlier, I had worked with George Harrison on the film mix of *The Concert for Bangladesh*, and I had all this applause from Madison Square Garden on wild tracks. I just slowly moved this out to the stairwell and brought in the crowd. Sounds pretty live. Most people were fooled.

4: Bobbing
for Piranha

Steven Tyler: *Get Your Wings* came out in March 1974. I wanted to call it *Bobbing for Piranha*. Here's the album cover: little kids around a barrel, hands tied behind their backs, flesh-eating fish hanging off their faces, graphically detailed noses and chunks of flesh missing completely, a bloody mess. No one else liked it.

Joe Perry: *Get Your Wings* worked on two levels. The first was the old biker ritual where a guy had to go down on his menstruating old lady before he could get his wings, the colors that every biker worth his Harley wore on his back. The second thing was our new logo, which made its debut over a black-and-white picture of the band on the album cover. The logo was basically a winged "A" with a shag haircut and either a clitoris or a pair of tonsils in the middle, depending on which of the many people who claim to have designed the thing you talk to. I remember that we thought the original wings looked too much like bat wings, and when we changed the logo a few years later, we made them more like the wings from Harley-Davidson.

Laura Kaufman: *Get Your Wings* wasn't only a make-or-break album for the band but for management too. By 1974 Leber-Krebs had lost *Jesus Christ Superstar*. The Dolls' album bombed. None of the other acts were happening yet. There was no money coming in except for David's mail-order poster business. Steve Leber was floating bank notes to keep the company going. The press had ignored Aerosmith's first album and didn't care about the second one. There wasn't much support from Columbia, who always released a Springsteen record at the same time as Aerosmith.

David Krebs told me one morning, "If this album [*Wings*] doesn't happen, we're out of business." So he wrote a letter to Columbia, a ten-pager that took days and days of dictation and rewriting. We sent it to Bruce Lundvall, who had replaced Clive Davis, and it worked. We got a little better promotion and advertising budgets, and they released "Same Old Song and Dance" as the first single.

Steven Tyler: The single didn't make the charts, but the album did, peaking at #100 and staying on the charts for almost a year because we were on the road constantly throughout 1974. We opened all over the country for Deep Purple, Black Sabbath, Blue Öyster Cult, Argent, Slade, REO Speedwagon, the Guess Who, Santana, Mott the Hoople, Kiss at the beginning of their career, and the Dolls at the end of theirs. When we played our strongholds in New England and Detroit, we headlined, and as our grass roots kept growing, *Aerosmith* even went back on the charts for six weeks that summer.

But we couldn't break on the radio. Columbia released ''Train'' as a single in September and ''S.O.S.'' after that, and neither of them got played, although FM radio started to play ''Train'' in various markets—or so we heard.

Mostly we just worked our asses off. I was starting to come home off the road, pick up the phone in my apartment, and order room service before I realized where I was. But the touring worked. A year after it was released, *Get Your Wings* had sold half a million copies and became our first gold record.

Ray Tabano: Around that time I started working with the band again. After I was fired, I sold my leather store and went to Mexico for a while. Then I moved to Maine, where I got a call from Steven after the first album came out. ''Ray, man, I'm goin' fuckin' nuts with these guys. You gotta come back to the band.''

''What about Brad?''

''Not to play, stupid. Just hang out. We'll give you $125 a week.''

So I went back and hung out with Steven. The other four guys hated me for not doing anything, so I started working backstage with the crew. My first night doing this, Nick Speigel, the crew chief, made me drive the truck back from Washington. But I didn't lock the rear door right and the entire toolbox—spare fuses, wires, cables—fell out of the fuckin' truck and was lost. My fault.

Steven Tyler: We were all over the Midwest that winter: East Lansing, Michigan; Fort Wayne, Indiana; Columbus, Ohio; Detroit. We were getting $2,500-$3,500 per show where they knew us, $750 a show where they didn't, like Seattle and Spokane. We played in the South, Richmond and Atlanta, five nights opening for Hawkwind, the English space-rock band, at Alex Cooley's Electric Ballroom. Going to Atlanta was a big deal for us and the local girls certainly made us feel at home. We had naked teenagers doing backbends in the dressing room, and we all remember the indelible sight of Raymond pouring a bottle of Jack Daniel's over his dick in the belief that it would prevent infection after a blow job. Some things you never forget.

This was in the spring of 1974. We headlined our first sold-out shows [7 and 9 P.M.] at the Orpheum Theater in Boston, with Blue Öyster Cult opening. We kept playing at local colleges, usually with Ready Teddy opening. We played at Boston College for 6,000 and there was a riot. The cops fought with 600 kids without tickets who smashed the doors and tried to crash the gates. We opened for Suzi Quatro, REO Speedwagon, and Argent in California, Missouri, and Washington. On April 27, we played a college blast at UConn with Springsteen and Fairport Convention. The J. Geils Band had faded, Peter Wolf married Faye Dunaway, and Aerosmith became the undefeated champions of New England rock that spring.

In June 1974, Richie Supa and I sang "Desperado" at David Krebs's wedding in New York. It was David's theme song.

On June 9, we were in Memphis, and I was talking dirty onstage, fucking this and motherfuckin' that, and soon cops showed up backstage, intending to stop the show and take me away. Kelly tells them they'll have a riot on their hands. "Hey, let him finish the set and then take him to jail." I told Kelly that during the last song, "Train Kept A-Rollin'," our lighting guy should black out the house and I'd run up the middle aisle and out the front door and they should have a car waiting to get me the fuck outta there.

Halfway through "Train," the lights go out and I jumped into the audience, tore down the aisle and into the lobby . . . where a dozen Memphis cops are waiting with drawn guns, pointing at me. "HOLD IT RIGHT THERE!" They dragged me backstage, kicking and yelling, and handcuffed me. Shit! They were mean bastards. With all these black cops around, the sergeant says, "Let the niggers take him down to the station." In the car, I asked this black cop, "How can you let them talk this way?" He turns around and says, "This is Memphis, Tennessee, motherfucker, and you want to watch what your ass is doin' down here."

Tom Hamilton: At the end of June, we flew to Los Angeles to tape *The Midnight Special*, an early rock concert show broadcast on NBC at 1 A.M. on Friday nights. We got up before dawn so we could be as loaded on Jack Daniel's to play "Train" at the 10 A.M. taping as we were for a regular 9 P.M. show. I never drank during the day and we really sucked. (Little Richard was the host, Wolfman Jack was the announcer, and we were on with Kool and the Gang, Golden Earring, and David Clayton-Thomas. The show was broadcast on August 16, 1974.)

Then we got a week off, our first since March. On July 2, we played My Father's Place in Roslyn, Long Island; Ocean City, Maryland; Asbury Park, New Jersey; the Schaefer Music Festival in Central Park; and a big ranch in Escoheag, Rhode Island.

Then, in late July, we went on the road with the New York Dolls: Sedalia, Missouri; Lincoln, Nebraska; Minot, North Dakota; Normal, Illinois; and Marion, Ohio. The Dolls were at the end of their rope, an awful thing for us to see.

Joe Perry: That's when we saw them die. They'd go out and play and we'd see they weren't getting the audience off. The Dolls looked incredible, but in the Midwest, in Florida, the kids just sat there. I loved them and their great rock 'n' roll energy, but they just didn't give a shit. Their thing never translated out of New York and they never did anything to change that. The kid in Chicago didn't get these weird transvestites the way he got David Bowie, who at least had great songs. If the Dolls didn't have the audience feedback they got in a little club in New York, they sucked. They couldn't play very well anyway, or even tune their guitars, so they bombed everywhere. Plus they were always very late and would pull shit like refusing to go on unless they got a case of champagne. When we played Chicago, where their record company [Mercury] was, they were worse than usual. We were embarrassed for them; it was depressing because we loved the Dolls and this attitude of theirs.

Despite all this, they had a press book you would kill for. We were mad. We kept saying, what about us? The Dolls' record hadn't done well. Why do they get all the attention?

Because David Johansen was a cool guy, hanging out with Andy Warhol. He actually *knew* David Bowie. He was cooler than cool, hipper than thou, and I know he looked down on us. One night his wife Cyrinda Foxe was laughing at Steven from the side of the stage, and David called Steven a hick. We heard that he said that. It got back to us.

This was the first time we saw drugs kill a band. Their first drummer had OD'd in London. Johnny Thunders was a heroin addict who was always shooting up in the back of wherever we were. He'd trade his guitar for drugs when he ran out, and I kept thinking, *Boy, that'll never happen to me.* Arthur Kane was so in the bag all the time that he was the first person I was ever able to positively identify as an alcoholic. He lived on blackberry brandy. We were healthy next to these guys. I have this image of Arthur somewhere in Florida, tottering around in knee-high leopard platform boots, pink tights, and a ripped T-shirt, waiting for a liquor store to open so he could get his morning drink.

They'd cancel gigs when they ran out of drugs, fly back to New York, and score. Seven days on the road was all they could do because they'd get sick. We'd hear that Johnny and the drummer had to go back to New York because they were "tired."

Yeah, right.

Joe Perry: We played with Kiss a bunch of times. They're doing heavy makeup, smoke, and firebombs. And we're going, "What the fuck is this? Are we gonna have to dress like this? What is *happening* in this fuckin' business?" We saw the response they were getting, putting on this show. People went nuts because it's impossible not to when some guy is breathing fire. It wasn't about music at all. We were flipping out because we were struggling.

We played with Kiss in a parking lot in Marion, Ohio. They'd have their pyro and smoke and then we'd come out, five drunk guys arguing between songs about what to play next. Plus, Kiss had this fuckin' attitude. Our road crew got in fights with theirs. Knives got pulled backstage over times or stage room. They had a cutthroat scene going. The competition was intense, but there was also more camaraderie. Ace was in the bag all the time, Gene was the businessman, the drummer was a nice guy who liked to do coke. They were good people surrounded by shit. That was Kiss.

Tom Hamilton: Our favorite gig that summer was our first big outdoor show as headliners at the Westboro Speedway near Boston on August 18, with Duke and the Drivers opening. We were guaranteed $10,000 and 60 percent of the gate and the place held 35,000 people. At the end of the show, a good-looking redhead wearing only shades and panties jumped on the stage and danced topless.

After that there were no more weeks off that year.

Steven Tyler: That fall we went out opening for Lynyrd Skynyrd and Blue Öyster Cult, playing all over the country, except that we played Ohio a thousand times—Toledo, Bowling Green, Cleveland, Columbus, Akron—like my grandfather and his brothers fifty years before. David Krebs kept us hitting our strong markets over and over again.

Then we started noticing that the press was getting less hostile. We started to get some attention. *Rolling Stone* gave *Get Your Wings* a good review. ["Maintaining an agile balance between Yardbirds- and Who-styled rock and seventies heavy metal, Aerosmith's second album surges with pent-up fury . . . They think 1966 and play 1974, something which a lot of groups would like to boast."] Younger-oriented rock mags like *Creem, Circus, Raves*, and *Hit Parader* started to interview us and splash Aerosmith pictures on their color pages. I was very distrustful of reporters because I'd been burned by so much bad press. I was nervous in interviews and when I read the old clips today, I see that I used other people's anecdotes about hanging out with Jimi Hendrix and things like that. I was insecure, couldn't remember clever stuff on demand, and needed to fill the interviewer's space.

What else could I tell them—how fuckin' stoned on pills and blow I was all the time? Because those were the days when I had to do as much as I could to keep that buzz going every waking minute of the day. I had to be in that buzz. It was secure, cozy, comfortable, and I wanted it all the time or I'd be jumping out of my skin. Wherever we went, we brought the party along with us.

The other thing that got noticed in the press was how we looked, what I was wearing—the scarves, ragged sleeves, streamers, laces, open shirts. I explained that the rags developed out of poverty. I couldn't afford stuff and so my girlfriend at the time started making things for me on her sewing machine. Then her sixteen-year-old sister Francine [Larnes] quit Framingham High to come and work with us, making clothes. We used to sit down and design stuff together for hours. The scarves—the whole Gypsy look—evolved because I'd get trashed at the shows when the little chicks and some of the guys would grab at me and I'd come up ragged. Then we noticed the movement involved with ragged clothes, so I started to wear the ripped stuff instead of throw it away. Some nights my whole stage costume was held together by a couple of big diaper pins in the back. Soon Francine was going to New York to buy expensive imported fabric and we'd turn that into rags.

As for the scarves draped over the microphone, some of them had little pockets sewn in, and I'd weight them with Quaaludes and Tuinals. That way I wouldn't run out.

Joey Kramer: We literally fought our way into the business that year. One of the people that watched us do it was an old friend of mine, Scott Sobol.

Scott Sobol: New York, late summer, 1974. Aerosmith co-headlining the Schaefer Music Festival in Central Park with Irish rocker Rory Gallagher.

Rory put on a killer show with long, multiple encores. As his roadies strike the stage, people start booing and throwing things. This continues into Aerosmith's set and escalates during their show. "Somebody." "Lord of the Thighs." "Seasons of Wither." Cans, bottles are flying. Brad's hit on the arm and there's offstage chatter about pulling the plugs out and leaving. David Krebs is shouting at everybody. The stage is covered in shit, but Aerosmith keeps playing. In fact, Steven just lets it *rock*, giving a blistering performance. "Walking The Dog." "Mama Kin" just kills 'em. As they go into "Train Kept A-Rollin' " and Joey starts his drum solo, a bottle hits his drum riser and sprays glass over Joey. Joey puts down his sticks, stares at the screaming crowd, and doesn't start the bare-handed part of the solo. Instead he pulls a microphone off his floor tom and yells, "Who threw that bottle and cut my arm? Huh? Got blood all over my tubs!! Huh? *This is for you, fuckhead!*" Joey then begins with his bare hands, tabla-like inflections, then the mock head-butt he used to do. By the time he finishes the solo, the crowd is his.

When he brings the band back in, always a dramatic moment, Steven is in midair when the lights come up. He hits the stage on the one when the whole band kicks in. Explosive! The pelting of the stage has stopped, the crowd is won over, and most people I could see from the wings have their mouths hanging open.

I always knew they'd make it big, but that night I knew they were unstoppable and would be huge when their time finally came.

5: Feet Flying
Up in the Air

Joe Perry: We'd been away from home for most of the year, playing in the Midwest with Mott and the Dolls, and we came back in late

'74, early '75, to find that Frank had booked us into a gig at Shrewsbury High near Boston. I knew things had changed because the kids went *berserk* for us to a degree we hadn't seen before. Frank pulled out a choke-a-horse roll of money, and I got the feeling that this is the way it could be. At Boston College, we played the field house and there was a riot. Frank booked us into a new club called the Box, where the Psychedelic Supermarket had been in the sixties. We did a sound check and they were still painting the old garage. That night 5,000 kids showed up to see us, the police panicked, and the city pulled the club's operating license the next day.

These were the first previews Aerosmith had of how it was going to get.

Terry Hamilton: Tom and I got married early in 1975 at my parents' house in a terrible blizzard—just family. We had a reception a month later and there was another blizzard. We moved upstairs to a bigger apartment at 1482 Beacon and paired off like everyone else. Joe and Elyssa were in another apartment on Beacon, Brad and Lori were in Framingham, Joey was a cool bachelor living in Newton with several girlfriends, and Steven was living with a very young girl named Diana Hall [Editor's note: This is a pseudonym.] in a little carriage house on Goddard Avenue in Brookline.

Diana was a sweet little girl, fifteen years old, whose parents had signed her over to Steven as her legal guardian so she could be with him. What kind of parents would do this? I don't know. When Steven would overdose, Diana would call us and Tom and I would rush over. It was a pretty strange relationship all around.

Laura Kaufman: Steven met Diana in Portland. She was cute, innocent, fourteen, way too young. But he fell for her and I truly believe Steven was really in love with her, because he had to sign guardianship papers for her to come and live with him. Her parents had to agree to this and I remember it took lawyers and cost real money. I remember thinking, he must really love her to go through with this in order to be with her. She was no piece of meat to him. Girls threw themselves at him twenty-four hours a day. He could have been with anyone. But he wanted Diana, and they were together for a long time, maybe three years. He dressed her up as Little Bo Peep, made her wear *outfits*, for God's sake, little schoolgirl frocks. No one could believe this, it was so outrageous.

Steven Tyler: Diana. You heard about her? She was a skinny young malchick, much younger than me, like fourteen when I met her in Seattle backstage after a show. She was there with a bunch of her girlfriends and they were being bisexual to get my attention and I was aroused to no end. Because nothing turns me on like being in a room with two women. All guys think about it, but few have done it. It's the most beautiful thing, immersed in *yoni*, like being between Mother's breasts again.

I brought her back to Boston because I was so in love with her. She was so young, so skinny, really beautiful; she had more legs than a bucket of chicken. She was mysterious and as sexual as I was. She just wanted to hang around all day and do it and then talk about it afterward. It was like incredible—and so delicious.

Her parents wouldn't let her leave at first. So I went to her house one night and her parents said it was OK for me to sleep over and I just thought, *Wow*. Eventually she moved to Boston and we carried on for three years, although it seems much longer to me because we were getting real high too.

Jack Douglas: Aerosmith was a different band when we started the third album. They'd been playing *Get Your Wings* on the road for a year and had become better players—different. It showed in the riffs that Joe and Brad brought back from the road for the next album. *Toys in the Attic* was a much more sophisticated record than the other stuff they'd done.

I think we did preproduction in the attic at Angus Studios in Ashland, Mass., where we rehearsed until we could do it in our sleep. *Toys* was the first time the band came off a tour prepared to record. They had a lot of energy, road energy, and they didn't have to go on sabbatical or take time out to play with their new toys. They wanted to get into making a record.

They had ideas from playing in hotel rooms. Tom had an incredible lick. They had the riffs to "Walk This Way" and "No More No More." All this stuff came from the road. We had an acoustic piano and wrote everything out on a chalkboard, so if we lost an idea in the purple haze of the studio we could get it back. We created our own alphabet and language. Joey wrote his own arrangements so every cymbal crash was orchestrated, but there was still room for improvisation. We worked hard and preproduction lasted a long, long time with rough, challenging rehearsals.

Steven's lyrics always came last, after we had the instrumental tracks. Steven had a good work ethic that he'd gotten from his dad, but the other guys didn't take him seriously because they knew he'd be the first guy out of there. When we were working on vocals, I always had Steven live with me. Steven would work on lyrics and we'd feed off each other. I'd try to compete with him and see who could come up with the best line. If mine was good, he'd always top me. We were looking for humor, irony, sex, drugs, in a way that could get on AM and FM and kids could dig, without it being lewd. Like on "Walk This Way": We had that funky track, we loved it, but it was so tough to get lyrics.

Joe Perry: When we started to make *Toys in the Attic* [in January 1975], our confidence was built up from constant touring. I don't feel great about saying it was drugs, but the plain truth is we were beginning to make money and could afford better dope.

On our first two records, we were low on the food chain of drugs. Then we started to get hold of high-velocity un-stepped-on Peruvian cocaine and the whole thing kind of took off. Some of us were quiet, insecure kids from the suburbs who got ahold of this ego enhancer and just went with it *in extremis*.

Tom Hamilton: Something happened during the *Wings* sessions that really got to me. I was stoned on a joint, a little blow, a couple of beers, and something led to Jack telling me I was an asshole. "Tom, you're an asshole." I was freaked and humiliated, and this became an event that went into the bank and started earning interest.

When it came time to practice for *Toys*, I was still in shock, mostly about my playing. So I got a little coke and started to practice for hours every day, major calisthenics, so my fingers got really strong and nimble. It was one of those instances where I used coke responsibly, the way it could be used if it weren't so addictive; as an energizer and mind-clearer. When we started *Toys*, I felt better about my playing for once, that it was up to this higher level where the rest of the band had already progressed.

We were rehearsing in an old barn west of Boston, and Jack was staying at the Copley Plaza in town, so every morning I picked him up and drove him to work while he read me the *New York Times* he always had under his arm. The rehearsals were great because Jack was lots of fun, always laughing, totally open to new ideas. If I had the germ of something, like the bass line to "Sweet Emotion," he'd encourage me to develop it. That's how that whole album got done.

Joe Perry: I wrote the original riff to "Toys in the Attic" at Black Angus Studios, Andy Paley's converted barn off Route 9 in Ashland, which is where we worked with Jack on that album before we moved to the Record Plant. This is where we started to come into our own in the studio, using it as our palette, writing more in the studio as opposed to them just turning on the machines for us to play. We started to become recording artists instead of having our albums being a record of us playing live.

"Walk This Way," for example.

I was into funky stuff, had played James Brown songs over the years, and at the time was listening to lots of the Meters from New Orleans, one of the best bands in the country, and I was asking, "Why don't we write our own songs that have that feel to them? Let's try to write something funky so we don't have to cover James Brown." At the sound check in Hawaii, I came up with that riff, added it to another one I came up with while watching a Godzilla movie—one of my favorite compositional methods—and Steven wrote the lyrics in the stairwell of the Record Plant.

Jack Douglas: We worked on the track for four fucking nights and Steven couldn't come up with anything. People were ready to give it up, dump the track, anything. So I said, "Let's take a break and walk around the block." We used to walk out of 44th Street, down Broadway, across 42nd Street, and back up Eighth Avenue. Steven would chat with the hookers and the street guys, and often we'd leave the studio with nothing but phonetics and come back with lyrics, hot off the street. So we went out and noticed that *Young Frankenstein* was playing and we all wanted to see it.

Tom Hamilton: We were working on this song and we took a break to go to the movies in Times Square, *Young Frankenstein*, and we came to the part where Marty Feldman as Igor limps down the steps of the train platform and says to Gene Wilder, "Walk this way," which Gene does with the same hideous limp. We fell all over ourselves laughing because it was so funny in a recognizably Three Stooges mode. The next day at rehearsals we tell Steven, "Hey, the name of this song is 'Walk This Way.' " He says, "Whaddaya mean, I didn't write the lyrics yet!" But we said, "Trust us."

Steven Tyler: So I went back to the hotel, popped a Tuinal, sat down, and wrote out some lyrics until 11 P.M. the next night. I had them all written down, one of the few times in my life I've had a notebook going, an incredible thing, I'm so fuckin' proud, seventh heaven. I was gonna walk in and go, "Look what I got!!" I took a cab to the studio, got out of the cab, paid the guy, ran upstairs, and—"What the fuck! Where's my lyrics? Left 'em in the cab! I left my lyrics in the cab." And everyone looked at me and said, "YOU LIAR!"

As it was, they couldn't wait to yell at Steven anyway. "FUCK YOU!" They nailed me again, we got into a fight, "FUCK YOU!" I got really pissed off at how helpful to the situation their comments were. I couldn't go back to the hotel, so I grabbed a pencil and paper and took the elevator to the sixth floor stairwell, where I could be alone and sing and yell. But it didn't feel right, so I went down two flights. *Yeah, this is the place. No one's gonna hear me.* I put the headphones on—*Fuck! I left the paper upstairs!* I had the pencil, so I started writing on the wall:

Backstroke lover . . .

Yes. A kid playing with himself, "backstroke lover." And his father caught him and said, "Ain't seen nothin' till you're down on the muffin," which meant, "You won't be jerking off anymore. You'll be gettin' pussy." And so on, my whole sexual trip—

I met a cheerleader was a real young bleeder,
oh the times I could reminisce,
'cos the best things of loving
with her sister and her cousin
only started with a little kiss,
like this:

—my fantasies of having two girls, the most sensual experience you will ever have on this planet, unbelievable, like melting into the soil before your time. God! Then there were the old make-out parties and the girl who was just a little older than you and showed you where to put your finger. This was called showing you how to walk. Walk this way.

Camille Paglia is one of my heroes. Her finger is not on the pulse, it's up the vagina of today's sexuality. She is so smart, she's got it all down. It is true: Men are afraid of women!

6: Sweet E.

Steven Tyler: I was going through hell all this time, trying to write lyrics. Most of the time the whole idea overwhelmed me and I always put it off till the last minute. Now I had to write new stuff. No one else wrote lyrics.

On a song like "No More No More," the lyrics came from my verbal diarrhea, a mishmash that I made up and eventually changed the lyrics to something cool.

Blood stains the iv'ries of my daddy's baby grand
Ain't seen daylight since we started this band.

"Write what you know," they told me, and "No More No More" is about life on the road: boredom, disillusion, Holiday Inns, stalemate, jailbait. My diary.

I was writing about what was happening to us, but when I'd burn out on this, I'd start checking out my resources. That's how we got "Big Ten Inch Record."

Joe Perry: Zunk Buker, our family dealer, heard Dr. Demento's famous radio show on KLOS one night and sent us a tape with Bullmoose Jackson doing "Big Ten Inch" from 1953. We go, "Wow, what a great fuckin' song." It was an R&B big band thing that we just reduced and did the old "white boys from suburbia do their version." It was the first time I remember working with a big horn section—the Brecker brothers, Stan Bronstein with his bass saxophone.

Jack Douglas: Steven brought the song to the band and we loved it. It needed a boogie-woogie piano, so I brought in Scott Cushnie, who had been the piano player in the Liverpool Set up in Toronto when I was working there. He was a great player who learned his craft in Ronnie Hawkins's legendary band, the Hawks. He was legally blind, couldn't tell a passing truck from a bus, and was just a great player. Scott Cushnie ended up touring with Aerosmith that year [1975], the first outside musician they ever had. He would double the harmonies too, because he had a great voice.

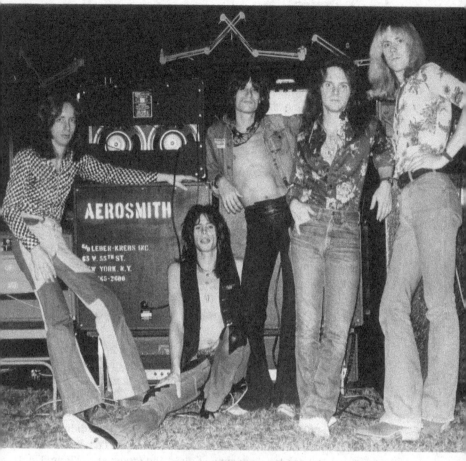

At the Record Plant, 1974
(PHOTO: RON POWNALL)

Steven Tyler: One thing that impressed me when we were working at the Record Plant was that Bruce Fuckin' Lundvall used to drop in on the sessions. Bruce had succeeded Clive Davis as president of Columbia. He was a jazz guy, hip, laid-back. "You guys got an incredible thing going here," he told us. "I just came from a Herbie Hancock session and this is much more fun." This was when we had a string orchestra in to work on "You See Me Crying," which I wrote with Don Solomon, a big production conducted by Mike Mainieri.

Maxanne Sartori: I went to one session where Steven and Joe were doing the harmonies on "No More No More" and Steven was screaming at Joe: "Don't you fuckin' know when you got it right? C'mon, man, it's like sex—you either know it or you don't." It was really embarrassing. It was a very weird vibe, a lot of blow being done, but discreetly because there were all these union engineers that had to be there, doing nothing, chomping on cigars, and getting in the way.

Steven Tyler: "Uncle Salty." Tom Hamilton comes up with these great fucking lines. The rest of it was just a fantasy I had of being a madame, the boss of a bordello: work with the girls, hire and fire, keep things running. Salty worked in a home for lost children and had his way with this little girl. That's what it's about. I'm the little girl, the orphaned boy. I put myself in that place.

I'm Uncle Salty too.

"Adam's Apple." I don't remember anything except I arranged it and must have fought for credit. And I originally wanted to call the album *Love at First Bite* after the line in the song.

Joe Perry: My original title for *Toys* was *Rocks*. I was adamant about it but got outvoted.

Jack Douglas: When I was working with Aerosmith in Boston, we'd work all day on preproduction, and then at night I liked to have a band member come over to my hotel. He'd bring an acoustic guitar and a recorder and we'd bullshit, listen to some ideas. Maybe he'd be reluctant to bring up this little lick during rehearsals because maybe he didn't think it was cool. I was open to anything. If they had three notes, I'd tell them it was a song that just needed development. Brad and I worked on "Round and Round" this way, and it's also how I first heard "Sweet Emotion." Tom drove me to work one day and he said, "I've got something. You've gotta hear it." It was the bass line of "Sweet Emotion," the basis of the song.

Tom Hamilton: I had this original bass riff in high school. It got revived when we were doing *Get Your Wings* and living near Cleveland Circle. I showed it to Steven, but I had the riff a little different and Steven said, "That's backward, man." He didn't like it. Then it got to the end of doing tracks for the *Toys* album, and we had the extra day that Jack called Jam Day, where he asks, "Does anyone have any spare riffs lying around?"

"Yeah, I have this riff."

"C'mon, let's hear it . . . Man! that sounds pretty cool." I had turned it around, a little like Jeff Beck and Clive Chapman, the bass player on *Rough and Ready*. I smoked a bowl or two and wrote the arrangements, the guitar parts. Steven took the intro, turned it around, changed key, and we used it as the tag, the resolution of the song. Brad, Joey, and I went home. Next time we heard "Sweet Emotion," it had the overdubs, the vocals, and I flipped out. I loved what they did with it.

Joe Perry: While we were making this record, Frank Connelly was getting sicker. I think he knew he had cancer when he signed us, and we'd go out on the road and not see him. Gradually we noticed that David Krebs was getting more and more involved. I thought Frank was losing interest because he was also managing Daddy Warbux and trying to bring them along. Then we heard he was really sick, and David and Steve Leber ended up buying Frank out.

Steven Tyler: Frank Connelly sold us to Leber-Krebs for what—I don't know. He said, "Boys, I've got the cancer and I want to give you to these guys in the city that can do a better job than me." That's what I like to think he said. On "Sweet Emotion," we used these backward handclaps and four of us in the studio chanting, "Fuck you, Frank." If you play it backward, you can hear this.

David Krebs: Frank Connelly was a magical guy in many ways, but he was so disorganized that money was falling through the cracks. He was also a mean drunk who would make us sit through his vaguely anti-Semitic jokes. We bought him out. [Frank Connelly died of cancer in 1977.]

Jack Douglas: The sucking sound on "Sweet Emotion" is a combination of hi-hat cymbal, backward clapping, and "masking" the words "Thanks, Frank." We used to take a guitar riff, play it backward, and learn it, a Beatles technique that John Lennon taught me. Being an engineer, I got to steal from the best guys. Kit Lambert conducted the Who, so I'd conduct Aerosmith with a cowbell to keep the meter running.

Joe Perry: "Sweet Emotion" came along near the end. Tom brought the riff in and Steven started singing over it. Jack and Jay Messina put the bass marimba in one night and I used an air bag to say,

"Sweet Emotion." You moved your mouth, the air runs down a tube that takes the place of your voice box, and you can make guitar sounds with it. It's fun. Anybody can do it.

Steven Tyler: "Sweet Emotion" is all about Elyssa, Joe's soon-to-be wife. It's all about my negative feelings for her because I couldn't get next to Joe when she was around, which was all the time. She was doing all his drugs. Before she came along, I was doing all his drugs. It was a big problem.

Tom Hamilton: At the end of *Toys*, I had become a different player and Aerosmith was probably a different band. We knew this album would launch the band like a missile. I'd written two of the songs and finally was able to feel like I wasn't fooling anybody anymore. It was an incredible time.

Steven Tyler: We put the cover to *Toys in the Attic* together with a design company Jack brought in, Pacific Eye and Ear. My original concept was to have a teddy bear sitting in the attic in a dusty beam of light with his wrist slit open and stuffing all over the floor. "Too off-the-wall," they said. So we had all the toys—bear, rocking horse, drum, toy soldiers—wondering where the kids who used to play with them went to, and when would they come back? But if the kid can find the key to get back to the attic, he regains the innocence and wonder of childhood. The keys were very important to the whole concept. The keys were the icon.

Eventually you grow up anyway. The teddy bear becomes whoever you're with. The rocking horse becomes your car.

In the attic's lights,
voices scream,
nothing's seen,
real's the dream . . .

Steve Leber: In 1975, we started to do very well with Aerosmith, Ted Nugent, other acts we had. David Krebs handled Aerosmith day to day. He was in touch with them every minute, the guy who would go smoke a joint with the band. I was wheeling and dealing with the lawyers, accountants, and CBS, trying to figure out how to survive for the next three months because royalties for publishing and record sales ran three to six months behind and the band needed clothes, gear, staff, expenses, and we're always cash poor. That year Walter Yetnikoff became president of Columbia Records and we started renegotiating Aerosmith's contract with him.

Our contract had given CBS the right to call for two albums a year, but Aerosmith was lucky if they could deliver one. The contract was renewable and should have expired, but it didn't and CBS acted as the bank for the band when they got in trouble and needed money. So we're negotiating and I said to Walter, "Why don't you give us reversion of the masters [Aerosmith's actual master tapes] after twenty years? Aerosmith won't be around, you won't be here anymore because it'll be 1994, for God's sake, and no one will care. Come on, Walter. They might be worth something. You'll be doing me a favor."

He says, "Yeah, you're right! Who'll give a shit? Nick! Give him the reversion!"

They raised our royalty rate from 75¢ a record to $1.25. Then $1.35. We kept renegotiating it and it kept increasing. Twenty years went by and sure enough, in 1994 we got back the masters! No one else in the history of the business got this, because without the masters you've got nothing.

7: The Blue Army

Joe Perry: *Toys in the Attic* was released in April 1975, got niggling reviews, and started selling literally millions of copies for the rest of the year. It pulled *Aerosmith* and *Get Your Wings* along and soon we got gold albums [awarded for sales of half a million LPs, eight-track tapes, and cassettes] for them too.

We spent the rest of that year on the road.

There's a point when you're a baby band when people start coming to your show and you feel like you're on a ride. It's bigger than you, it's out of your control, but it's cool because you're going with it. First it's friends, then friends of friends, then the real word gets out and suddenly there's something magic about the band and you hear that people are lining up for tickets, fighting for tickets, scalping tickets. Then you start playing places that are never big enough.

This is when all that shifted. We didn't headline every show. We opened five shows for Rod Stewart and the Faces and found ourselves playing to 80,000 people in a ballpark in Cleveland. We could headline in Boston, Detroit, all over the Midwest. Ted Nugent, recently signed to Leber-Krebs, usually opened for us, along with Kansas, Mahogany Rush, Slade, and Blue Öyster Cult. Our touring statistics were listed in the trades with the big boys—Zeppelin, Alice Cooper, Jethro Tull, Rod and the Faces, and Queen in their first tour as headliners. *Hit Parader* wrote that "Aerosmith became America's official Led Zeppelin substitutes in 1975, winning over heavy metal fans by the thousands."

We started to get the feeling that we were America's hometown band. We weren't pushing it anymore. It was pushing us.

We called the kids who came to see us the Blue Army. The first time we saw the Blue Army was in Toledo, Ohio, when we played there with Ted Nugent in April. We drove up to the gig and the line went around the building, long-haired teenage boys wearing blue denim jackets and jeans. An army of blue jeans. Our people. They were so loaded and would get so crazy that we had to build a portable steel-mesh barrier to keep them from overrunning the stage. Aerosmith back then was definitely a guy thing. It used to be the only girls at Aerosmith shows were the ones hoping to blow us on the bus.

As for us, we were flying commercial. Kelly, our road manager, kept us under control with Kahlúa and coffee. You want to go to sleep because you're so shit-faced, but you're buzzed by the sugar and the caffeine so you can actually get on and off the plane when you have to.

Aerosmith sold out two nights at Boston Garden [April 18 and 19, 1975, with the British band Foghat opening both shows], which was a big deal for us. Also backstage—and not too happy—were some of Frank Connelly's North End business partners, who said they hadn't been paid by Father Frank and who thought they had a piece of the band and who had made explicit threats concerning the future health of Steven Tyler's legs and knee-caps. There was a big meeting behind closed doors between them and Leber-Krebs. They made a deal and we got out of it for a lot of cash up front. At least that's what we heard.

Tom Hamilton: After the gig, Joe Perry and I were in the back of the limo going along the elevated part of Storrow Drive and we were looking back at the Boston Garden the same way we used to when we were kids hitching into town. Joe says, "Hey! We just *played* that place." It was a tingly feeling, I'll tell ya.

Steven Tyler: Joe Perry looked cool—black pants, black vest, black shirt, white tie, white broad-brimmed borsalino hat, hair cut

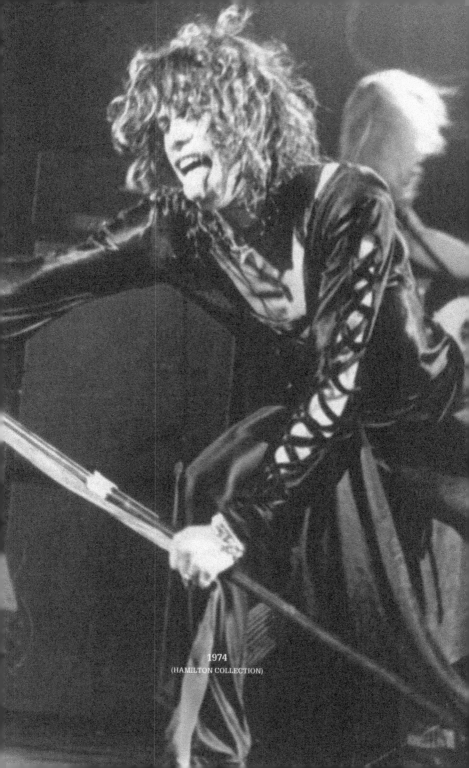

1974
(HAMILTON COLLECTION)

long with a blond streak in it. Laura Kaufman brought some press people up from New York and they somehow persuaded Kelly to let them on the side of the stage, which Joe doesn't like because it distracts him. Later they came to the party we had at the Orson Welles Cinema in Cambridge and they asked me dopey questions. "What's with the scarves on the mike? Why don't you ever take the mike off the stand? Do you know you wear more makeup than any American lead singer? Did you ever see the play *Toys in the Attic* by Lillian Hellman? Why do all your roadies wear those sweaters with the ties painted on?"

Laura Kaufman: Getting Steven to do interviews was just awful. Finally I scheduled an interview with *Creem*, a big story for them, and Steven kept canceling the interview. I'd have to call and lie: "He's sick!" "He's recording!" "He's playing a gig!" This went on all the time. I'd cry. I'd beg. Then I'd say, "OK, I'll get Joe to do it."

Ten minutes later, Steven would knock on my door, ready to do the interview. He didn't want Joe to get too much attention.

The writer who got the best access was Lisa Robinson. She went out of her way to make friends with Elyssa and Joe and the rest of the band. She wrote feature stories on Elyssa, traveled with the band and even got Elyssa to bad-mouth "Dream On" and put it in an article.

Steven Tyler: By May I'd been home six nights in the previous four months. We were all worn down—no rest, no privacy, too much room service. When we flew in to Kalamazoo, the airline lost a trunk with all the new costumes Francine made for me and I played two sold-out headlining shows at Cobo Hall in Detroit in my street clothes. It was around Memorial Day, tornado season, wet and humid and really hot. To win a bet with Kelly, I put a thermometer onstage and by the middle of the show it read 110 degrees. It was like getting into a locked car in the summer and then singing and dancing for two hours. I had trouble breathing in this atmosphere, and I'd hyperventilate to get back to normal.

We played a lot with ZZ Top that June, selling out the Los Angeles Forum on June 19. There was a big problem with the stage monitors at the sound check and I was screaming that our hopes for long-delayed recognition in California, where we hadn't played much and hadn't sold many records, were about to be wrecked if we sucked at the Forum. "I can't play!" I shouted. "I'm not going on!" No one paid any attention, so

I went off and changed into my white satin stage clothes and did the show.

We had the same problem a couple of nights later at the San Diego Sports Arena and later people told me I wrecked the buffet in the dressing room after the show. But this was probably because I found turkey loaf on the table, and our contract rider specified roast turkey on the bone.

Maxanne Sartori: There was a lot of tension going on between Joe and Elyssa, who I was hanging with in their suite at the Beverly Hills Hotel, and Steven, who was out of his mind in his lovable way. I remember after they played the Forum that Joe's dad was coming for breakfast the next day, which was a big deal. Steven was going nuts playing mumblety-peg with the knife from the melon tray and Joe was in no mood to have Steven throwing knives and there was a big fight with Steven holding this knife . . . I don't even want to think about it. They were under a lot of pressure, and the drugs were starting to take over all our lives.

ROLLING STONE
Aerosmith, which opened the show, takes itself very seriously onstage, even though its act has been lifted in equal parts from the Stones and the Yardbirds. It had the same instrumental lineup, a look that's strictly Mick and Keith, dazzling guitar work as complex as Clapton's, Beck's, and Page's and a prancing, pouty lead singer . . . (July 31, 1975)

CREEM
It is Tyler's ability to project crude, leering sexuality that makes Aerosmith attractive. Coming after a brief era when rock 'n' roll fans in their adolescence were bombarded with the exaggerated sexual ambiguity of Alice, Bowie, and Reed, it must be reassuring to have a band that knows everything we've wanted to know about sex all along: It's dirty. (September 1975)

8: A. Wherehouse

Joey Kramer: Now the pace was accelerating and we started to see some real action on the road. In Philadelphia a few hundred kids trying to crash into the Spectrum broke down the doors, beat up the guards, and set the seats on fire. The papers called it a riot. Then on June 15, Steven and I were arrested in Lincoln, Nebraska, when, after the gig at Pershing Memorial Auditorium, we put on a premature Fourth of July fireworks display out my window at the Hilton Inn and management called the police. They wanted to charge us with arson, but I think we got off with a misdemeanor for disturbing the peace.

Jack Douglas: There are so many good bootlegs of Aerosmith in those days because we'd do the live broadcasts, Jay Messina and myself. I'd bring my Sony box with me and mix live over the radio, using the station limiters with the big console to make it jump more. We did Central Park in New York, Detroit, Chicago. They were hot and did just great shows and really entered the Big Leagues that year.

Tom Hamilton: On July 7, we flew from Seattle to Hawaii, where we took some time off, did some sailing, played a show, and had a big meeting in Maui with David Krebs about Joe and Elyssa. It was very delicate because we were considering confronting Joe about her behavior toward the rest of us, and we knew it might add up to him leaving the band.

Steven Tyler: We had lost Joe to his girl. This is hard to explain. When you're in a band and you lose a member to a girl, it's not easy to explain because nobody will or can hear it with a clear, open mind. I'd go, "Joe, c'mon, you're the most pussy-whipped guy on the fuckin' planet."

"I am not. I *love* her. What's the matter with you? Can't you feel anything? Don't you have a girlfriend?"

"Yeah, but it's like you're not *here* anymore. You never turn me on

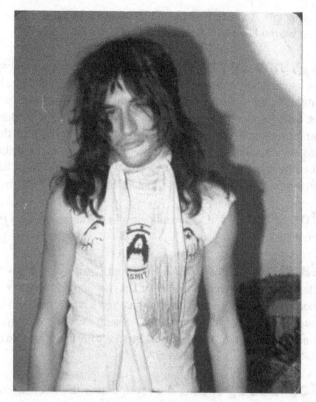

Joe Perry after being bitten by Elyssa, 1974
(KRAMER COLLECTION)

anymore, you're always off with her. What the fuck's up? You're always going away from me. I never see you!"

I confronted Joe with this. I was upset and made the mistake of baring my soul to him, because there was a certain amount of anguish. One of the most important bonds in my life was breaking before my eyes. It was a mistake because now Joe and Elyssa had a joke. Every time I came around, they would mimic me and make fun of what I said. I even confronted Elyssa. I said, "Elyssa, all right, I love you. But I also love Joe and he's my comrade and I never see him anymore because you guys are always together and it's interfering with our work."

They would look at me and listen, but when I'd leave they'd have their laugh. It was pretty painful. They got married a couple of weeks after we got back from Hawaii.

Elyssa Perry: We were supposed to get married earlier, but we had to keep changing the date because they kept adding shows and extending the tour. We finally settled on August 5 and booked the Ritz, the most elegant hotel in Boston, overlooking the Public Garden. We had our four parents, our two sisters, my cousin Cosmo Taglino the lawyer, and Mr. Whitehorn, a justice of the peace we found in the Yellow Pages. The Ritz was totally horrified by our guests, who arrived in full rock 'n' roll regalia. They totally lost it when Steven arrived in feathers.

Joe Perry: I had to talk my way upstairs, and I was the fuckin' *groom*.

Maxanne Sartori: Joe and Elyssa's wedding was a formal affair and people were dressed for the evening and there was a lot of good champagne. Elyssa's mother had had a couple, and when the guy asked Elyssa, "Do you take Anthony Joseph as your lawful wedded husband?," Mrs. Jerret, who'd never heard Joe's full name, blurted out, "Who the hell is this Tony guy anyway?"

Joe Perry: After the vows, during the champagne toasts, I slipped upstairs with Steven and snorted some heroin. Really strong heroin. We went back down and it was all I could do to keep from throwing up on the cake. Our families were there, my father. It was a weird scene.

Elyssa Perry: Joe's dad was very ill with cancer by then and died that fall, which was a real blow to Joe and probably explains what happened to us with heroin afterward. Anyway, they might have had a couple of days off. Our honeymoon had to wait. They had a hit record and were back on tour immediately.

Steven Tyler: Come live with us for a week on the road at the end of August 1975, as *Toys in the Attic* is certified a gold album and reaches #11 in *Billboard*. "Sweet Emotion," released as a single in May, is a Top 40 record.

On August 23, we take United Flight #217 from Boston to Cleveland, where we open for Rod Stewart and the Faces before 80,000 fans at sold-out Cleveland Stadium. Also on the bill: Uriah Heep and Blue Öyster Cult. We do our show. I played my harp, shook my maracas, walked the dog, swung the mike stand, pointed, pranced, and danced. At nine that night, we caught Northwest Flight #28 to Philadelphia and limoed to a Holiday Inn near Trenton. At ten the next morning, we did a sound check at the New Jersey State Fairgrounds, where we headlined that night in front of 20,000 kids with Poco, Slade, and Nils Lofgren opening.

We stayed that night at the Holiday Inn and flew back to Boston on Delta Flight #270 the next day, August 25. I got home to find the apartment Diana and I shared at 1736 Beacon Street totally burned out. I think she fell asleep and her cigarette caught the mattress on fire. Diana was badly burned on her arms and in the hospital. She was really too young to leave alone at home, but I couldn't take her on the road with me either.

Two days later, we boarded Eastern Flight #567 to Richmond, Virginia, where we played to 12,000 in Richmond Coliseum with Slade and REO Speedwagon. I blew harp, swung the mike, walked the dog, did somersaults, did two encores, and then back to the Holiday Inn. Next morning, Piedmont Flight #952 to Washington, D.C., where we played to 18,787 at the Capitol Center in Largo, Maryland, with Slade and REO. Blew harp, walked dog, played maracas, swung mike, almost catching Tom Hamilton in the face I was so out of it.

We "slept" at the Sheraton Northeast in Largo and at 1:25 the next afternoon [August 29] caught American Flight #506 to La Guardia, where we played Wollman Rink in Central Park with Ted Nugent opening. We did a sound check because the show was broadcast and Jack Douglas wanted to get it right. We stayed at the Warwick Hotel for the weekend and on Monday [September 1] flew to Toronto on American Flight #354. We played a show at the famous 2,700-seat Massey Hall with the Canadian band Thundermug. Walked dog, blew harp, shook ass, swung mike, almost hitting Brad at the side of the stage, crashed at the Harbor Castle Hotel, and flew back to Boston the next day on Allegheny Flight #508.

Two days later, we flew to Chicago and the whole thing started all over again and we stayed on the road for the rest of the year.

Ray Tabano: In the fall of '75, the band decided it needed a headquarters, like a place to rehearse and hang out in. I was deputized to find, design, and build a clubhouse for Aerosmith. I found an empty warehouse at 55 Pond Street in Waltham, near Boston. David Krebs flew up and approved the deal, with a budget of $40,000. We leased the place, built a little stage, put in a $3,000 wiring job—every box grounded separately. There was an upstairs area like a lounge, some offices, a spiral staircase. Joey could drive his Corvette right in and park inside. The official name was A. Wherehouse. We had a big party on Halloween to open it and hundreds of our best and most intimate friends came. It was a great place with good vibes. Not long after we opened it, the band Boston borrowed the room, auditioned for Columbia, and got their own famous record deal.

I used the upstairs offices for the band's T-shirt business. I started out in 1974 putting some Harley wings around an "A" inside a circle with AEROSMITH in block lettering underneath. David Krebs changed the name to script lettering; we put this on 100 yellow T-shirts, took them to Westboro Speedway, and sold them in half an hour. This was the beginning of Aerosmith merchandising. Two years later, we were selling hundreds of thousands of T-shirts at the shows. David Krebs made me sign away the credit for the logo and T-shirt designs for $1.00 or I'd get fired. I signed.

Years later, the band's lighting guy, Richie Ocean, who had actually painted the logo on the scrim that hung behind the band during the shows, claimed that he had drawn the wings logo and threatened to sue. But by that time I was long gone. I got in trouble later on, and Krebs accused me of stealing. But I know who was really stealing from who.

Brad Whitford: At that point, my bank account started to grow and I felt very wealthy all of a sudden. I wasn't, but to me $10,000 felt like a million. I was twenty-two. I thought, *Man, I can buy the kind of car I've always dreamed about.* That's when I got my first Porsche. I think that's when we all got our first Porsches.

I picked up a '71 911T from a guy in Lincoln, Mass., who raced a little and told me what to do, how to drive and feel the car. We had a couple of sessions, I gave him the cash, he gave me the car. I've had a couple of Porsches in the garage ever since.

When the royalty checks for *Toys* came in, I went right to the top and bought a Ferrari.

I could do this because by the end of 1975 we'd sold 3 million albums. All our records were on the charts. *Toys* was a gold record. After a single

of "You See Me Crying" [released in November] didn't make the charts,
David Krebs persuaded Columbia to rerelease "Dream On" as a single in
December, two years after it first came out. By early 1976, "Dream On"
was #6 in the *Billboard* singles chart, Aerosmith's first Top 10 hit record.
It had taken five years.

BOOK TWO

To regenerate love in the absurd world amounts in fact to regenerating the most burning and most perishable of human feelings.

—Albert Camus, *Notebooks*

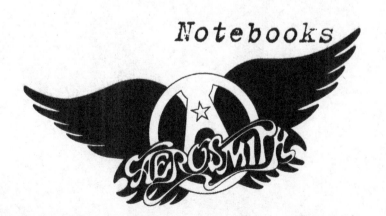

The Wonder Years

6

> We call them "the wonder years"
> because we wonder what happened
> to them.
>
> —Steven Tyler

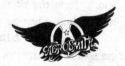

In early 1976, Aerosmith woke up to find itself one of the most successful bands in America. Tireless road warriors, Aerosmith was beloved by millions of kids as the band you could actually see. Led Zeppelin, its empire in collapse, was injury-plagued and off the road, while the Rolling Stones were in a creative eclipse. John Lennon had retired to Central Park West. New bands like Boston took over album-oriented FM radio with "More Than a Feeling," while Lynyrd Skynyrd's "Free Bird" challenged "Dream On" as an American radio anthem. Two sisters from Washington State formed a band called Heart that outrocked everybody except maybe Aerosmith. Little Feat and the Meters from New Orleans were the most respected bands, at least by their peers and the critics.

But the biggest successes in 1976 would be Peter Frampton's live album and Aerosmith's old idols Fleetwood Mac, former Brit blues scholars transplanted to Southern California in a later incarnation. The new thing was called soft rock and it began to sell, big time. Radio stations changed their formats to play Frampton, Fleetwood Mac, the Eagles, Elton John.

The rebellious spirit of rock 'n' roll lived on in unreconstructed hard rockers Aerosmith and Ted Nugent, who sold out almost every show they would play for the next three years. "In 1976 only Kiss and ZZ Top can rival Aerosmith's claim as the hottest new band in America," opined Circus magazine. "What sets the five Yankees from Boston apart from the other sensations of '76 is the purity of their roots. They are virtually the only natural heirs to the hard rock tradition founded by the Yardbirds and passed down into the seventies through Led Zeppelin."

Meanwhile in London, underneath the complacent, drug-soaked pop music structure, there was a new current of young bands that hated Elton, Zeppelin, the Stones, and other big rock icons, reviling them as rich, totally irrelevant junkies and Boring Old Farts, completely out of touch with youth. Soon the punk bands—the Sex Pistols, Clash, Generation X—would stage a revolution of their own.

In January, with the three-year-old, rereleased "Dream On" a Top 40 single all over America, Aerosmith and Jack Douglas began preproduction on the band's fourth album at the Wherehouse. In February, Brad Whitford married his girlfriend Lori at her family's home in Florida. Then the band moved to the Warwick Hotel in New York to begin recording the tracks that would ship platinum three months later under the title Rocks.

1: Back in the Saddle

Brad Whitford: We started working on *Rocks* by backing the Record Plant's mobile recording truck into our Wherehouse and just letting it fly. The Wherehouse was just a good place to hang out and rehearse; a long white corrugated steel building that you could drive right into. Local kids spray-painted messages to us on the outside walls. Inside there were pictures of Chuck Berry, Rod Stewart, and Mick Jagger. One whole wall was a photomontage composed of Mick and Keith's faces. There were five trays for fan mail in the office—four usually contained five or six letters. Steven's tray was always overflowing.

When the other guys were late for rehearsal, Joey and I could wash our cars. The place was our clubhouse and lab. We could get a real organic sound from the Strats and the Les Pauls and Nick Speigel, our crew guy, was building the switching systems for our guitars and effects that we later used all year on the road. Our fan club was upstairs, with Raymond selling T-shirts through the mail, people designing things and spending our money, stealing us fucking blind, people padding bills, stuffing their pockets. Poison was running right through the system, from Leber-Krebs down to the lowest guy on the totem pole.

We were living the high life and not paying attention to anything except making this record. I had the beginnings of "Last Child" and "Nobody's Fault." Tom had "Uncle Tom's Cabin" that became "Sick as a Dog." We had "Tit for Tat," based on "Searching for Madge," which turned into "Rats in the Cellar." We cut all the basic tracks except two there.

Joey Kramer: That's when it all happened for us. There was a lot going on. We were beginning to get into drugs, the meat of getting high as a way of life. We weren't overwhelmed yet and I was living my fucking dream. I felt so content. How could I ever ask for anything more? But that's what I did, and that's what I got—more. Even "Dream On" was a hot record! Now I listen to *Toys* and *Rocks*, and they reek of the time and the fun we put into them.

Preproduction was me, Tom, Brad, and Jack Douglas at the Wherehouse. We worked hard and we laughed all the time. Jack would say or do something and I'd fall off my drum stool from laughing so hard. Example: Jack convinced me that if I ate nothing but greens for two weeks, I'd smell like a freshly mowed lawn. This went great until I got really constipated, so Jack had me drink a quart of prune juice to push it all through. He hid a new prototype sound-activated tape recorder in the bathroom. When he rewound the tape, there was a full day of horrible gas and flushing toilets. We laughed ourselves sick.

There were constant practical jokes around the studio all the time. One of the classics happened in the Record Plant, where the engineer had to cross the darkened studio to switch on the light to start the sessions. So Jack hung dozens of live crabs from the studio ceiling so Jay Messina would get clawed as he fumbled toward the light switch.

The main thing for me was I was really beginning to establish my style of play. "Nobody's Fault," "Combination," "Get the Lead Out"— they were just so much fun to play on.

Joe Perry: There's no doubt that we were doing a lot of drugs by then, but you can hear that whatever we were doing, it was still working for us.

We were experimenting and getting into heroin. We got good dope because now we could afford it. All the big dealers started hanging around us, so we only got the best stuff. We found good, steady connections, at least until our guy in New York got murdered. I snorted the stuff, and it felt great. I'd be lying if I told you anything different.

Then my father died. Elyssa and I were living in a condo her mother set up for us at 135 Pleasant Street in Brookline. I was depressed, in great emotional pain over losing my dad at too young an age—both for him and for me. Anyone who's gone through this might be able to understand. I knew these two coke dealers who had just come back from Thailand with twenty-eight ounces of Golden Triangle pure heroin for their own use. It was the kind of shit you could step on four times and it would still be good. They turned me on to their stash and I was gone. When you first fall in love with heroin, it's like discovering God. I started studying the folklore of opium as a sacrament and really got into it. It helped me to concentrate on my work and became a good writing tool for me at the time . . . before it turned into this fucking monster.

For me, the agony you put up with when you don't have it was worth the ecstasy you felt when you did have it. Paying the piper when you're dope-sick was something I learned how to handle. I preferred to withdraw painfully rather than trying to cop on the street. I bought grams and half-ounces. I'd take a couple of hits on the road with me and just get sick and stay in the hotel when I ran out. That's how I managed it for a few years. I never even saw a dime bag until 1980.

I wrote the main riff to "Back in the Saddle" on a six-string bass guitar I'd just bought, lying on the floor, stoned on heroin. Quite a few of the songs that Steven and I wrote for the *Rocks* album started out that way. When it came time to record the song later that year, Elyssa and I had moved to a big house on Waban Hill Road in Newton, and I drove over to the Wherehouse in Waltham and played this six-string bass like it was a "lead bass." We had so much fun rehearsing at the Wherehouse we figured: Why not try to record there too?

Steven Tyler: When we're doing our albums, I listen to Joe. *Rocks* comes from a time when we used to jam and I'd hear something and go, "STOP! WAIT! WHAT WAS THAT? PLAY THAT AGAIN!!" I'd hear something really good and I'd write the lyrics down right there. It

doesn't happen that way anymore and it hasn't since we put the drugs
down. We were more free then, more creative as a band. We still haven't
solved some of the problems that the drugs cloaked.

Then we'd do thirty takes—forty!—because we were *gacked*. Jack
Douglas would then take half of this take and half of that take and the
bridge from Take 23 and put it all together and nobody knew what was
what when we finally heard the record. Today I listen to those albums,
some of our best, and all I can hear are the drugs.

Jack Douglas: *Rocks* was the album where Tom and Brad
had a lot more input and songs. I just told everyone in the band that they
were good writers and they went and did it. Tom could come up with a
lick that could kick off a whole chorus. Brad really came out with "Last
Child." Joey's only credit was "Pandora's Box," but there should've been
more because he was a rhythm master who'd say, "I've got the rhythm
and it could be a song." Meanwhile, the guitar players had decided *who*
was going to be *who* in the band. Joe was the improvisor; Brad was the
technician, the guy who would stay in the studio with me and work all
night. Joe would come in, lay down six tracks, and know he could leave.
Then Brad would work on a specific part, and if it took all night of constantly punching in, no problem. He loved doing it.

This was a big album for Aerosmith. It had to make a big statement
about how loud and hard they were, how unapologetic they felt about
being who they were—this brash, rude, sexual, hard-core rock band. We
recorded "Back in the Saddle," the opening track, to have this larger-than-
life vibe, to bring the band right into the middle of the kid's head when
he put on his 'phones in his bedroom late at night. So we had this great
kick-ass track that had to be the first thing you heard on this album. And
of course we had no vocals, which wasn't really a difficulty then because
that was the way we worked. We had a melody line and phonetics and
we knew the best was yet to come.

So at the Record Plant we were talking about Gene Autrey's "Back
in the Saddle Again" and Steven said he thought it was about fucking
your girlfriend again and I'm saying, "I wish we could use this saddle
image as a way of saying, 'Here's another album, folks, and we're gonna
rock out and I've really got my spurs on.' " Steven went into the stairwell
for two hours and came back with reams of paper with ideas on them,
and we cut the vocals.

On "Saddle" I used a Neumann "shotgun" [directional] mike instead
of a conventional microphone. The Neumann was ten inches from

Steven's mouth, so we had him just blasting. I could feel the warmth. When you blasted it—"I'm BAAACKKK"—you'd hear every edge from his throat, his mouth, his breath. So we had this big fat vocal and I'd start doing extreme stuff to it. Then Steven heard it on his headphones and started to play with the effect on his mike, singing from under it, moving to the left. That's where that famous raspy vocal comes from.

We wanted to have a whip at the end of the song, as the horse rides off. We brought in a bullwhip and spent hours getting it to crack; we got cut up and hurt and it sounded like nothing. Totally lame.

Steven Tyler: So we got a thirty-foot cord and I whirled it in the middle of six Neumann mikes in this seventy by eighty studio—*WWWWWWRRRRRRR*—and that was the whip. We got a cap gun to make the cracking sound. Joe Perry and David Johansen gaffer-taped tambourines and bells to my boots and I stomped on a wooden board to get the Western feel we wanted.

We had this drug dealer in New York named Lance, who got killed while we were at the Record Plant making *Rocks*. That's the "losin' my connection" line in "Rats in the Cellar," which was the shadow side of "Toys in the Attic."

Joe Perry: We needed an answer to "Toys in the Attic." The band was getting lower, downer, and dirtier, so the cellar seemed like the best place to go. That's where we found the rats.

Tom Hamilton: The end of "Rats" is this fuckin' thing that builds and builds; it's us doing the Yardbirds' trip because we were so blown away by the idea of taking this music and making it balls to the wall.

Henry Smith: The band was playing shows at the same time they were recording. So they flew to Toronto to play, and Steven was supposedly doing the words for the album in his infamous notebooks that always seemed to disappear, always a problem, because you just couldn't push him to do it. We flew back to New York, and Steven claimed he'd left all the lyrics on a clipboard back at the hotel.

Krebs and I talked about it. David thought that Steven was lying, because he always lied about this stuff, and I said, "David, maybe this'll be the one time he really did do them." So I flew back to Toronto. The room had been cleaned, so I spent the afternoon wading through a Dumpster until I found the clipboard—empty. No lyrics.

Brad Whitford: After rehearsal one day, I played this riff and Steven yells, "I love it!" and started playing the drums; he plays very different from Joey with a more jazzy approach, fun to work with. Joe threw in a couple of chord changes, a D chord to an A, and then spiced up the chord a little. That's where "Last Child" came from. We still play it live. When we got to New York, Jack Douglas had Paul Prestopino put a banjo track on it.

Jack Douglas: Paul was a maintenance engineer, but he was a great guitar player who had played with the Weavers [the early folk music group that featured Pete Seeger]. He also played banjo, mandolin, Dobro, so we used him all the time on Aerosmith records. There's a slide guitar part on "Last Child" that I had Paul double with what we called "slide banjo." There's not supposed to be such a thing, but this metallic sound gave the song a subtle, organic feel that sounded great on a rock 'n' roll record. Steven just loved that kind of stuff.

Brad Whitford: Jack worked with me on "Nobody's Fault" and I ended up playing both rhythm and lead guitar. I had this one lick that lasted about a minute. We recorded it and Jack wrote SOUL SAVER on the box. We kept changing it until we had a different-sounding take on this cool lick. The thing about Jack was that he was *there*, living with us in Boston, working, playing drums, a little pot/blow/beer, pushing us in a good way. He'd try anything, and it inspired us. He was a mad genius but so solid. When you're in the studio with Jack, you laugh, *roar*, do silly shit, tell jokes—it's loose. I'd throw ideas back and forth with him and then leave it up to Steven to come up with a great lick and a vocal.

Steven Tyler: The lyrics have to do with earthquakes, which we were all scared of, along with flying. There had been a huge earthquake in Nicaragua and a little one in California. Then we heard there was a fault line in New Jersey that ran near a nuclear power plant.

Joey Kramer: "Nobody's Fault" was almost totally recorded at the Wherehouse. It was never a popular Aerosmith number and we didn't play it live, but I still think it's some of the best drumming I did.

Joe Perry: Tom Hamilton wrote "Sick as a Dog" on guitar, so when we recorded it, he played it on guitar with Brad. I'm in the control room playing bass so I could hear what I was doing. Then it needed a solo, so I gave the bass to Steven and went back in the studio to play guitar. So the end is three guitars and Steven playing the bass. We did this whole routine a bunch of times until we got the take. I think it was the last thing we recorded for that album.

"Get the Lead Out" was another delve into the funk, except we got this Pavarotti-type tenor to sing on it.

Jack Douglas: Steven wanted another voice, an opera singer, to double his vocal on the descending part of the song that goes, "NO NO No No no no." So we got this guy from the Met[ropolitan Opera]—no great star but a great voice—to come in, but he couldn't anticipate the note because in opera there's nothing before the downbeat. We worked with him all night, blew his voice out, and in the end I had to move the vocal up by playing it off the synch-head instead of the playback head. I think we traumatized the poor guy.

Joe Perry: "Combination" is about heroin, cocaine, and me. It's also my debut lead vocal on an Aerosmith record.

Walkin' on Gucci, wearing St. Laurent,
Barely stay on 'cause I'm so fuckin' gaunt.

(Except that most of my shoes actually came from the Chelsea Cobbler in Manhattan and I'd found this Moroccan guy, Michel Azran, to make my leather suits.) I wasn't a pretty sight at 129 pounds. In fact, my mother was so upset by what was going on, she moved out to Arizona. She said that when I needed her, I'd know where to find her.

Steven Tyler: "Lick and a Promise" is about going out and winning an audience, a very hard thing to do. That song is such a snapshot of us in those days, a clear moment in time for me.

Jack Douglas: It was supposed to sound like the band playing live, so we needed a crowd yelling, "MORE!" We took six guys—Paul Prestopino, drug dealers, assistants—and kept bouncing it to another track and boosting and losing generations until we got six guys to sound like a thousand.

Joe Perry: The last track on *Rocks* was "Home Tonight." Steven could always be counted on to come up with some little piano riff that would be our ballad for the record. And that was it. People ask me about "outtakes" from this record, and I just tell them, "There are none because there was too much happening to record extra stuff." As soon as we had enough songs for an album, we stopped recording and went back on the road.

2: Fire in the Ballpark

Joe Perry: We spent a lot of time waiting for Steven to write lyrics, which held up the albums because we had to have vocals before Brad and I could add the overdubs and backing vocals and we could turn it over to Jack for mixing. When Steven was slow, the sessions could drag on for weeks and we had to cancel or push back ten weeks' worth of gigs that spring [of 1976]. As late as early May, Steven and I were chartering planes in New York, flying up to Boston to rehearse for the summer tour, then chartering back to New York the same night to mix the record. We had one day off in four months.

In April, the band took a break. Elyssa and I went to Jamaica and stayed at a Great House just vacated by the Queen of England, tended by eight servants, because of a booking mixup. When I got back to my apartment, it felt too small. My mantra was: "When you're staying in nicer hotels than where you live, it's time to move." I wanted to have some land to walk around on. So we went house-hunting and bought an Italian-style villa in the Chestnut Hill part of Newton. It was the first house we looked at, an ivy-covered mini-estate with fountains, statues, stained glass, a library, a two-story living room surrounded by a balcony/gallery, and room to build a recording studio in the basement. The place, known locally as the Sears Mansion, was quiet, a little weird, perfect for us. It was secluded enough that you could swim naked in the pool.

So we moved in with our dog Rocky, the Porsche, the Corvette, the Bentley, the old Buick, my gun collection, my guitars. We filed a change of address for my subscriptions to *Soldier of Fortune* and *Crash* and *Burn*, which featured gory pictures of fatal motorcycle crashes. The road crew called the place Villa Elyssa.

We knew that *Rocks* was our best album, so it was no surprise when it came out of the chute fast. The black album sleeve with the five white diamonds carried a dedication to the memories of Anthony D. Perry, my father, and our agent, Herb Spar, who had died of cancer a few months earlier. There was a *Rock Dreams*-style painting of the band on the inner sleeve by Atlanta artist Teresa Stokes. A version of this was supposed to be the stage backdrop for the tour, but Steven hated it. It cost us a fortune and was never used. The band also received a producer's credit for the first time, along with Jack Douglas.

Rocks was released in early May to pretty good reviews for us. By May 21, it was our fourth gold album, peaking at #3 and staying on for a year. The first single, "Last Child," made it to #21. It was the biggest year of the booming record industry of the 1970s, and so many albums were being sold they created a new award—platinum albums for sales of 1 million copies or more. (We were told that *Rocks* had actually *shipped* platinum.) The following July they gave us our first platinum record for *Rocks*. We were on tour and the record was said to be selling 10,000 copies or more a day. We had some 100,000-unit weeks.

On May 10, we played Madison Square Garden for the first time, opening for Black Sabbath. Eventually it got to be commonplace to play there, but this first time was very big for us. There was a band plane leaving for New York that afternoon, but Elyssa and I missed it because we'd gotten a bunch of cocaine and Tuinals and got really fucked up. Kelly thought we'd taken the Eastern shuttle earlier in the day, so they took off without us.

At 6 P.M. we hadn't shown up in New York, so some calls got made. We were still asleep in bed in Newton. Elyssa's mom came over but couldn't get into the locked bedroom and started crying at the bottom of the stairs because she thought we were dead. They broke down the door, roused me out of a Tuinal coma, got me dressed, and I caught the 8 P.M. shuttle. I walked into Madison Square Garden, started tuning, and played the show, which began with "Mama Kin" and finished two hours later with a final encore of "Toys."

ROLLING STONE

"Everybody get back and give the boys plenty of room!" shouts Aerosmith's tour director [Kelly], a burly Irishman who looks like Jimmy Breslin in a Beatle wig. The procession that follows can be compared only to certain papal rituals. First to emerge are Joe and Brad, cradling their instruments like carbines; then Tom Hamilton followed by Joey Kramer, stocky sweathog drummer, jauntily clicking his sticks in a "V for Victory" like some amiable Fonz imitator. The whole point of this display, Steven Tyler, brings up the rear, a little ragamuffin in cockamamie haberdashery complete with cape and a plumed hat and the fair maiden [Diana] on his arm. After witnessing this progress from dressing room to stage, the show seems almost anticlimactic. (Ed McCormack, "Aerosmith," August 26, 1976)

Joe Perry: Steven's parents were in the first row—it was the first time they'd ever seen Aerosmith. Joey's whole family was there too. The record company party afterward was at the St. Regis Hotel—very posh. Joey and his girlfriend [Nancy Carlson] were wearing matching crushed velvet jumpsuits. Linda Blair, the teenage victim of *The Exorcist*, showed up to have her picture taken with us. There was another party after that at Rick Derringer's. He had a studio behind his house and when it came time for a jam a young TV actor named John Belushi, fresh from the first season of *Saturday Night Live* and not yet a star, sat down at the drums and started to play.

Steven Tyler: A few days later, I'm drunk and eight miles high over cornfields and prairies on a bumpy flight to Los Angeles, where we're headlining the Fabulous Forum. Lisa Robinson, a writer for *Hit Parader*, is sitting next to me. I'm holding one hand over an eye so I don't see double when I look at her. Two tape recorders, mine and hers, are on the fold-down table in front of me, and I'm going . . .

Yeah, I don't have that much fun on the road anymore. It used to be pussy, cars, and money, but you can't write that, can you? No, not much fun, because I'd like to ball everything I see—well, not everything, but at least once a day. But I've had the clap twice now, so . . . you really have to be careful, you know? Hard to have fun anymore . . . I'll tell you what's fun: finding the right stewardess and turning her upside down in the back of the plane. Ever done it? You come so fast, it's the greatest, just knowing you might get caught . . . This pace is ruining me. Look at my face. I fly every day of my life. I put on three coats of moisturizer in the morning so my face doesn't dry out . . . Whaddaya mean, settle down? Are you nuts? Have kids? Do you see the way I'm living now? I'd make them insane . . . [Big swoon as plane hits air pocket.] I don't like to fly. I'm always like, "Hey, when's it gonna happen?" I'm on a plane every day for three years. Flying first-class—big deal. All it means is that you'll hit first. That's why I keep this tape recorder with me. At takeoff and landing, I have my finger on the button. If there's a big fuckin' problem, at least my mom will hear me say good-bye.

This drunkologue was published, almost verbatim, and it got back to our families. My mother didn't much care for my comments about the stewardesses. No one else's mother did either. I heard about it.

I had a bungalow at the Beverly Hills Hotel, but the crew was at the Hyatt House on Sunset Strip. The billboard over at Tower Records was for *Helen Reddy's Greatest Hits*. The marquee on the car rental said: WELCOME, AEROSMITH. Diana was with me, sixteen years old and pregnant. People were talking about me marrying her. It was in the air. I was thinking about it. There'd already been abortions with her. Tricky situation all around.

I felt sick backstage at the Forum as I checked out the opening bands: Mott and Montrose. I felt exhausted. I felt like an old shoe. I was twenty-eight years old and felt fifty years older. We had fifty-eight cities left to do. There was so much complaining that we decided this would be the last Aerosmith tour this big. David Krebs was telling the press that after this, touring would be limited and we could concentrate on our records.

We played our show at the Forum and in the middle of "Write Me" I just stopped dead and looked out at the 18,000 kids and didn't even know where I was. *What is this? What am I doing here?* I could sense danger, chaos. Some kid in the audience had pointed a loaded .45 at Ted Nugent not long before. A lot of the M-80s and cherry bombs that kids lit off at the shows sounded like gunfire. I'd see Joe Perry flinch when one of them went off onstage.

I faked the rest of the show, trying to figure out what it was that kept me going. I faked the party afterward at the Forum Club, too stoned on heroin to do anything except wink at Bill Graham and Richard Cole, Led Zeppelin's road manager, who kept insisting that we were the best band in America. Eventually our road manager, Kelly, took a close look at me and got us out of there. There was San Francisco the next day, Seattle and Portland after that.

LOS ANGELES TIMES
Persistence, youth, and attrition among the front-runners, rather than any distinctive musical style or extraordinarily exciting image, seem responsible for the continued prominence of Aerosmith in the heart of the teenage rock audience, which has apparently transcended the threshold of boredom. (July 1976)

Steven Tyler: We headlined our first stadium show: 80,000 kids in Pontiac Stadium in Michigan [on June 12, 1976]. The place had sold out within twelve hours. They put us into this apartment with lots of food, booze, champagne—all the essentials. Then they took us to the stage through this long tunnel so kids couldn't throw anything at us. You leave this enclosed tube and come out into this giant *whooosshhh*, a huge space you could fly a stunt plane around. The stage was so high and so far from the audience, you couldn't even see any kids, just lines of bullet-head security guys with their backs to us. The whole thing was too abstract. We were in, like, surrealism shock.

ROLLING STONE
[The audience] came staggering across the parking lot in the still, brackish Michigan dusk and advanced on Pontiac Stadium like a boozy army of hard hats coming to dismantle the place. They looked like hell. Nobody dresses up for concerts anymore.

They gobbled reds and chugalugged beer. They fell on their faces and tumbled down the hill. The oldest among them could not have been more than eighteen years old . . . You had to get close enough to see the red of their eyes to realize that this was a generation whose rock 'n' roll rituals had been raised up out of the ashes of Altamont rather than the bright muck of Woodstock.

Meanwhile, behind the big black curtain [the truss-mounted scrim depicted a giant locomotive], guitarist Joe Perry plugs in his guitar like a grease monkey getting ready to tune a carburetor. Outside the scoreboard flashes FOGHAT LOVES PONTIAC as another of David Krebs's carefully chosen tired-blood opening acts finishes up. Steven Tyler looks like an acrobat in black pajamas.

It's pandemonium out there when Aerosmith's set finally begins with "Mama Kin." The predictably criminal acoustics of the oversized hall hardly matter. The faithful seem satisfied watching the tiny figure of Steven throw an impressive temper tantrum, pointing an accusing finger, and shouting, "WOT'S WRONG WITH THE FUCKIN' PA!!!???" (Ed McCormack, "Aerosmith," August 26, 1976)

Joey Kramer: My first drum solo was at Pontiac, in front of this crowd. The band kept bugging me to do a long solo, so I planned it out and rehearsed for a long time. It blew the band away and got this ovation-type response from 80,000 people. When I stood up behind the drums at the end, I couldn't believe what I'd done.

I was really starting to get some confidence after years of feeling weird and unsure. We played with Jeff Beck a lot that summer, and his drummer was [Bernard] Pretty Purdie, who was about the best soul-style drummer in the world. One night he stuck around after their set (Jeff Beck was *opening* for us because he was now into his jazz-rock thing) and he told me that he liked what I was doing. Having Pretty Purdie say he dug me really meant a lot.

Joe Perry: Jeff Beck made *Blow by Blow* with George Martin, the Beatles' producer, and it was a hit, his first gold record. He came to Boston to rehearse with Jan Hammer's band and since Elyssa knew him we took him out to Paul's Mall to see Muddy Waters play.

It was like me and Brad watching a guitar lesson every night. We'd watch this insanity go on and then have to follow it. To me, it wasn't headlining, it was following. Jeff knew it. A lot of people of his stature wouldn't have opened for us, but he did it that summer, twenty-six shows worth, mostly outdoors.

This was the height of the whole thing for us, and all I remember is how much fun we were having, all the good times we were living through, and how much we loved to play and get people off. It was really a huge rush.

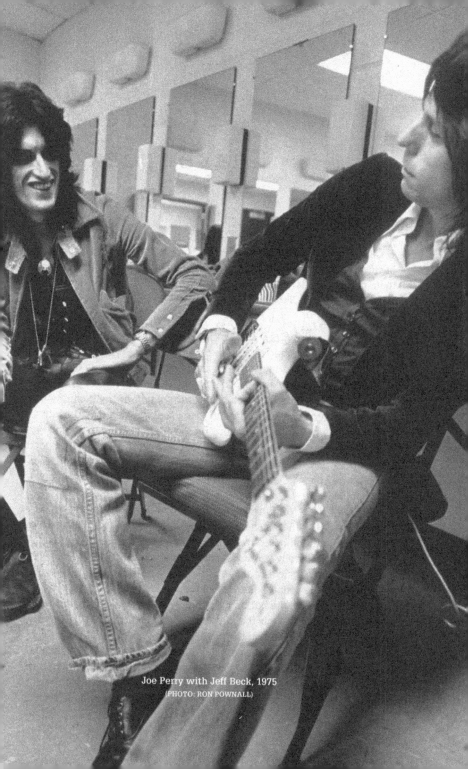

Joe Perry with Jeff Beck, 1975
(PHOTO: RON POWNALL)

3: Welcome, Shakespearean Players

Joe Perry: Back then we had one of the best road crews in the business, a bunch of guys who got to be semifamous on their own. Most of them got more girls than anyone in the band ever did. They called themselves the Country Club Crew.

Robert "NightBob" Czaykowski: In the early seventies, I was hanging around the scene in New York, playing a little, until I realized I could make more money working for bands than being in a band. So I opened a rehearsal hall on Grand Street in Soho, which is where I met the Dolls. A great band that nobody in the business got, because the audience had shifted to these younger kids who thought all the older acts were stodgy. Leber-Krebs were managing them and one day we saw these pictures of Aerosmith from Boston, supposedly a good band, but we thought they were ripping off the Dolls. I went to see Aerosmith play at Bananafish Park in Brooklyn and thought they were good. Nice people too.

A few years later, I'm working for IES, an English sound company that got hired to do Aerosmith's 1975 tour. So I come off an Emerson, Lake and Palmer tour and go up to Boston, where I set up monitors and a PA system at this Wherehouse, and in comes Aerosmith. But they were really tense and I stayed one day and left because they had this manic perfectionism about the sound—stage monitors were a big issue—and I didn't want to deal with all the fighting. But it was either work with them or be fired, so I went back to mix their live show. This is the fall of '75. I did five shows with Scott Cushnie in the band, then he was gone.

We did all these way-out gigs at 10,000-seaters and 2,500-seaters, whatever they could get. The band's gear—two tons of PA, lighting, sound equipment—traveled in a forty-foot tractor trailer driven by Gil McNeil. We'd get to a town, set up this big rock show, the band would

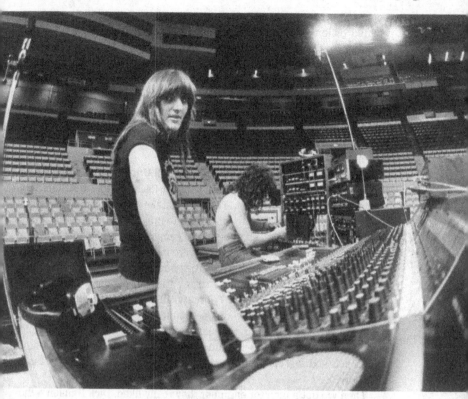

NightBob
(PHOTO: RON POWNALL)

come in and have a bad sound check with much yelling. We'd set up a support band or two, have a bite to eat, put on a big rock show, pack it up, load out. No equalizer, no compressor, twenty-four channels of English-built mixing console, some power amps, crossovers, some boxes, speakers, and miles of wire. You moved and fixed this junk every day. Then on through the night, five hundred miles to the next gig, me and Dick Hansen and three lighting guys and three band crew guys, eight guys in the little blue van.

The band flew commercial or in a private plane by the end of the year. They were big on trashing dressing rooms, yelling, throwing food, demanding their money in hand before going onstage. There were constant caterer freak-outs because their contract rider specified turkey on the bone; if they saw turkey loaf or turkey roll, they'd go ballistic. They wanted gallons of fruit juice in glass bottles because it made a better sound when they smashed them in the shower after the show. But then they were the golden boys. Them and Kiss were the big American bands in an era that up till then had been ruled by English groups. Aerosmith were the hometown guys and the kids just loved them. They worked harder than anyone else. When Aerosmith went out, they stayed out a long time. They had built an incredible touring fan base in the Midwest, the heart of where the rock 'n' roll audience is, and people came out to see them again and again.

For me, it was like going to Rock 'n' Roll University. I learned a lot from that band. A lot of people did, but a lot of people got hurt too, trying to keep up with them. The drug intake was outrageous, unbelievable. And they were a tough band, tough to hang out with. They burned through monitor engineers like cannon fodder. By the end of a tour, you were fried, hanging on to your sanity by a thread. Road crews were chewed up and spat out, trying to live the Aerosmith lifestyle—plenty of dope, constant work, no friends, isolation, the final bill of stardom. I tried to quit in February 1976 when Steven, unhappy with the monitor mix, shoved his monitors off the stage and they landed on a security guard, knocking him out. I left the tour and hid out for a few days, but Kelly found me and said they were sorry, so I went back and we just kept fighting over the sound after every fucking show.

Then we got a monitor engineer they really liked, Dick Hansen, who was called Rabbit. When Joe Perry's guitar tech died of leukemia, and the guy who replaced him OD'd on heroin and also died, Rabbit was hired to replace him.

Dick "Rabbit" Hansen: I started working with bands when I got out of high school in Chicago. I started out with [the British group] Yes and worked for a whole lot of other bands. In fact, Aerosmith were the first nonheadliners I ever worked for. I started out baby-sitting Joe and Steven at the Wherehouse in the fall of '75. They were nice guys, *wild* guys, fun to be around. When they went on the road that fall with Nugent and REO Speedwagon, I did the monitors and NightBob did the outside sound.

My first show with them was in Detroit. They invited me to fly to the next gig in Indiana with them on their chartered plane: Steven, Joe, Elyssa, Kelly, NightBob, and me. They were chopping coke and passing a mirror around the cabin. Kelly snorted the whole thing and when Steven yelled at him Kelly blamed it on an air pocket, which got to be a big joke. "Sorry—air pocket." We all had luggage tags that said WTB in big letters. This meant "Where's The Blow?" (To outsiders, it stood for "World Touring Body.")

Kelly was a great road manager, the best in the business, with a great sense of humor. He took care of the band and crew and knew how to get what was needed out of promoters. He'd book the tour into hotels as the Shakespearean Players or the Globe Theatre Company. We'd get to a town out in the boondocks and the motel sign would read: WELCOME SHAKESPEAREAN PLAYERS.

It was Steven Tyler who started calling me Rabbit, because I was a vegetarian and liked what he called "rabbit food." Soon no one called me anything else.

They were a pleasure to work for because they had the most advanced equipment in the business, everything custom-built and way ahead of its time. Joe and Brad had these rack-mounted effects with foot switches for their phasers, phlangers, digital delay, color sound, distortion, graphics, the air bag, whatever. There was another set of switches at my station, so an effect could be deployed by me if Joe forgot to turn his on.

They always played music through the PA before they went on. When I started it was [Bernard Hermann's] music from the shower scene in the movie *Psycho*, but we also used *The William Tell Overture* and *The Ride of the Valkyries*. The stage was always set up a certain way. Naked pictures of groupies in hotels were pasted to the amps; an old doll was on Joey's drums; a model of the Starship *Enterprise* had its own place. I kept a straw in a vial of coke so Joe could snort during the blackouts between songs, while Steven would leave lines on the amps. If a roadie put his flashlight down on the lines by mistake, he was fired.

You had to be careful around Aerosmith.

There was always a bottle of Jack Daniel's on the drum riser, as well as a bottle of 150-proof white rum, a total mind-fucker. Steven's little joke was to take one hit off this bottle and pass it down to the teenage kids in the first row. Five minutes later they'd all be vomiting because they weren't used to the overproof firewater. Nothing more hilarious than a row of puking fans.

The great thing was how close the band and the crew were. We called ourselves the Country Club Crew—Kelly, Nick Speigel, Henry Smith, NightBob, and myself—because we always wore these neat little Lacoste polo shirts and Gucci belts that Elyssa bought us. When we got sick of the road and had a few days off, we'd spend our per diems on drugs and take the crew bus to a campground by some lake and just spend our time water-skiing and live on the bus while the band went home. We called them "camping trips."

The crew got a lot more girls than the band, who were more inter-ested in dope than the girls who showed up backstage to blow them on the bus. So we got them instead. A day where I didn't have two girls was rare. The rule was, of course: "No head, no backstage pass."

Another rule was nothing but blowjobs ten days before coming home so you wouldn't pass on the clap to your girlfriend. This was the Ten Day Rule, alluded to in "Last Child" on *Rocks*.

The Country Club Crew's 21 Rock 'n' Roll Lies for All Occasions

1. Of course I remember you.

2. It sounds great out front.

3. I'll fix it in the mix.

4. They're prepaid at the airport.

5. I'll call you on Monday.

6. I only use a third of a bottle.

7. One more line, and we'll go to bed early.

8. There'll be bonuses at the end of the tour.

9. Ask me.

10. I won't get drunk onstage tonight.

11. I usually don't do this with girls.

12. Your name's on the list.

13. I'm all packed.

14. I'll turn down tonight.

15. We'll have a sound check tomorrow.

16. There's enough T-shirts for everyone.

17. I'll be down in five minutes.

18. I've got some in my room.

19. Yes, I turned you up.

20. I'll do it in the morning.

21. The check? It's in the mail!

4: No Turkey Roll

New Orleans: *City of mystery. Intrigue. "Back in the Saddle" blasting from the radio. Also Boston's "More Than a Feeling" and Blue Öyster Cult's "(Don't Fear) The Reaper." Joe Perry toting a Super-8 movie camera everywhere. Ex-Doll David Johansen and beautiful wife Cyrinda Foxe hanging out. Joe and Elyssa join the Johansens at David's gig at a club called Cord's, full of Bowie impersonators and transvestites. The owners send magnums of Moët & Chandon and pitchers of margaritas. Joe and Steven get up to jam and everyone stays up all night.*

Next night: big outdoor stadium filled to capacity. Backstage talk of a girl, a professional called Jaws, rumored to be more skilled than Deep Throat, hired by the promoter to service the bands—Nazareth, Earth Wind and Fire, Nugent, REO—playing this two-day festival. (Aerosmith passes on Jaws.) Steven in a leopard-spotted stage suit with a heavy silver cross and a gold razor hanging around his neck. Tom Hamilton in black, long blond hair blown back by the stage fans. Joe Perry in leather pants and ruffled white shirt open to the waist. Brad in jeans and a shirt, with the longest hair in the band. Joey in a pink leotard.

Milwaukee: *Lori Whitford and Elyssa Perry arrested for jaywalking.*

Detroit: *Joe Perry's T-shirt:* GET OUT OF MY WAY. *Steven Tyler's:* I CAN'T HEAR THE MONITORS.

South Bend: *The band always eats at Denny's because it's always open. This one's on Knute Rockne Boulevard. Steven asks the waitress if the fish is fresh. "Yes," she says with pride. "All our food is fresh-frozen."*

Chicago: *July 10. Rick Derringer, hanging out of seriously ripped jeans, finishes his set at Comiskey Park, which catches fire when firecrackers and cigarettes ignite the old tar roof. Jeff Beck takes the stage with Aerosmith watching from the wings. 65,000 in the house. Smoke pours out of the upper bleachers. Thousands pour out of the ballpark as huge flames lick the sky. Beck keeps playing "Freeway Jam" and laugh-*

ing. Bill Veeck, owner of the Chicago White Sox, is freaking out backstage as Rabbit tries to calm him down. A kid jumps from the upper deck (and miraculously survives). Road crew hustles Aerosmith into their trailers. Steven Tyler continues applying makeup, confident show will go on. Krebs and Kelly frantic for Aerosmith to get onstage before the cops call off the concert. Beck keeps playing. Elyssa thrilled because Beck promises her his incredibly cool vintage Yardbirds T-shirt.

Someone remarks on how calm the crowd stayed during the fire. "Calm?" Tom Hamilton observes. "They're all too stoned to move." The fire gets put out. Aerosmith plays for two and a half hours. The band bails out of the swank Ambassador East because room service stopped at midnight and winds up at the shag-carpeted O'Hare Hyatt House, partying all night with the Derringer band.

Laura Kaufman: Steven could be really brutal when he got pissed off. He'd make you suffer. I'd see him on a stepladder in the dressing room, holding a piece of meat up to the lightbulb and screaming, "THIS IS TURKEY ROLL!" at some hapless promoter. "THE FUCKIN' RIDER SAYS SLICED TURKEY!!!" This was the summer when Steven started shouting at me about the pictures that got published. He'd rake me over the coals if you could see his gold tooth. He'd wave a copy of Hit Parader in my face and yell, "What the fuck is this, Dental Daily? It's like looking at Oui and you got this naked little potato cake, nice negligee, and her string's hanging out."

So I learned to cover my ass. Our contract rider called for no unauthorized photographers and Kelly helped me rip them out of the pit all the time. Then we had slide shows for the band so pictures could be approved or destroyed, which helped somewhat.

There was a lot of tension on that tour because Rolling Stone was doing its first cover story on the band and they told us they didn't want the band on the cover, they wanted Steven. Annie Leibovitz insisted it was impossible to get all the band looking good on one shot. Couldn't be done. Threats. Promises. Excuses. Lies. CBS executives dragged in. Phones buzzing. No one happy. I said to him, "Steven, when we go to Los Angeles in a couple of weeks, Annie Leibovitz is gonna be hanging around, trying to get a cover picture of just you. Don't go near her. She'll get something from you that you don't want."

Of course Annie knocked on the door of Steven's bungalow at the Beverly Hills Hotel at six in the morning and took the picture when he opened up, bleary-eyed on two hours' sleep. That was the picture they used. Krebs freaked and screamed at Jann Wenner, but it did no good. Plus, they hated the story ["Aerosmith's Wrench Rock" by Ed McCormack], which portrayed them as a bunch of greasers. I thought I might get fired.

San Francisco:

The Cow Palace. Joey in black shirt, knicker-cut jeans, short socks, sneakers. There's a mini-riot when he starts throwing drumsticks to the fans during his solo as the band goes backstage for a rest and a line or two. Joe tells a reporter, "At least we don't return to the hotel during the solo, like some bands I could name."

Seattle:

Edgewater Inn, seaside hotel where you can fish out the window. Scene of Led Zeppelin's famous dead-shark-and-groupie story. The band goes fishing for sharks. One is left propped up outside Steven's door all night. Aerosmith, Jeff Beck, Derringer, and Starz [an English knock-off of Kiss] sell out the Kingdome in ninety minutes.

Boston:

Aerosmith wanted to play the local football stadium on the Bicentennial, July 4, 1976, but the town of Foxboro, where the stadium was located, refused to grant a permit because the last two Aerosmith gigs in Boston turned into riots. "Banned in Boston." The band passes on Boston Garden because of no air-conditioning, settles for three nights at the Music Hall later in the year.

Maxanne Sartori:

"Back in the Saddle" was my theme song on WBCN that summer, an incredible track with a lot of power on the radio. The whole *Rocks* album was like an explosion. A great album, and people were in awe of how cool Aerosmith was. I was living across the street from Joe and Elyssa in Brookline, but when they moved to their new house they got a lot more private. They changed around then, and you could tell they were getting too high. It was when Joe started using heroin. One night I went over to the new house and Elyssa was screaming, as only she could: "Goddamn it, Joe! I *told* you if you did that much you'd get sick and now I have to clean it up!" And there's Joe on hands and knees in the bathroom, almost in tears. I knew by his eyes what he was doing and it was pretty scary.

But did I say anything? Did I go, "Hey, as your friend, this is a dead end? You shouldn't do this?" No, I didn't. I wanted him to like me and was too proud of the friendship I had with him. You just couldn't talk to people about drugs in those days. If you tried to intervene, you were dead meat.

ROCK MAGAZINE
"Before, it was a struggle to keep alive," says Joe Perry. "Now it's more like a struggle to find a sound. We can keep playing the largest stadiums in the country, but we'd never be answering the question of our basic values. Our biggest struggle now is to make an artistic dent." (June 1976)

Los Angeles: *Dar Maghreb [a Moroccan restaurant] on Sunset. Steven and Diana at dinner with Liz and Rick Derringer. Sitting on cushions, smoking dope, getting drowsy. Steven converts the lamb appetizer to spitballs, which soon stain the white stucco walls. Asked to leave.*

Anaheim: *56,000 kids in the stadium tonight, September 10, 1976. Joe Perry's twenty-sixth birthday. He drinks a bottle of Dom Pérignon in the dressing room before the show. Kelly comes in and bellows, "You fuckers ready to rock 'n' roll?" During the show, Elyssa prevails on Jeff Beck to join Aerosmith on the encores as a birthday surprise for Joe. Beck strolls onstage halfway into "Train" and then does "I Ain't Got You." Joe ecstatic at Elyssa's surprise present, as Beck rarely jams with anyone. (Beck in a good mood because he'd just been given his second gold album, for Wired.) Joe listening to the tape afterward in the dressing room, jumping up and down. It was the first time many in the road crew had ever seen Joe smile.*

Terry Hamilton: We all went to Hawaii around that time and had a lot of fun. Steven and Diana camped out on their balcony, living outside on mattresses and blankets. David Krebs rented a huge boat for diving trips, which of course was the only time we really saw the sunshine. Tom and I ate some 'shrooms and tripped out on our own balcony.

Liz Derringer: Rick was opening for Aerosmith and had a hit record with "Frankenstein," so we were all riding high. Things were so silly then. We'd be in Joe and Elyssa's suite and there'd be five trays of room service, untouched, because we were doing too much coke to eat. I remember Rick pouring a big mound on a mirror—we were on the terrace of Joe's suite at the Kahala Hilton—and chopping it in a perfect spiral, enough for four or five people. Steven Tyler walks in while Rick's in the bathroom and goes, "For me? You shouldn't have," and snorts the whole thing.

NightBob: We finished that tour outdoors on the West Coast, huge gigs, semi after semi after semi of PA, and it wasn't enough! The gigs got too big—110,000 indoors at the Kingdome in Seattle—and it became a joke. It was stupid, with kids half a mile from the stage, the band insulated from them, no contact at all.

Los Angeles: *At the last minute, Joe and Elyssa and Steven and Diana decide to attend the Don Kirshner Rock Awards TV broadcast, because Aerosmith has been nominated for Best New Group, which they think is pretty funny. Bored out of their minds (except when watching Jeff Beck's band writhe in mock agony during Rod Stewart's big number) they leave after Hall and Oates wins Best New Group. "Sounds like a cereal," Elyssa complains.*

The Perrys head for New York, where Joe will play on David Johansen's debut solo album. Steven repairs to a beach house in Malibu owned by the guy who leases jet aircraft to rock stars. The house is equipped with one-way mirrors so guests can watch the sex shows the owner likes to put on. Another guest, Mick Jagger, tells Steven Tyler, tongue in cheek, about the Stones' plans to hang parachutes around the halls of their next tour to get a better sound. Steven bothers NightBob about this for the next year.

Steven then flies to Boston, where he's met at Logan Airport by Harold Buker, Sr., Zunk's father, former campaign pilot for Jack Kennedy and now commander-in-chief of the Aeroforce, the band's flight wing. Light rain as Buker murmurs into the radio and the twin-engine, six-seat Cessna Citation clears the runway and heads north over the flaming golden carpet of New England in September to Sunapee, where Steven is living in a rented house on the lake while waiting for his new house, a former steamboat landing and yacht club, to be renovated. Exhausted after four months on the road, he dozes until Mount Kearsarge looms into view and the plane begins to fall into a steep bank as it approached Eagle's Nest, the Bukers' private airstrip in New London. Diana is there to meet him in his own red Porsche.

Steven Tyler: It was one of those houses I'd see when I was a kid driving around the lake in a little putt-putt boat that kids could rent down in the harbor. It was on Lovers' Point; it had a boathouse, a boardwalk, wooden stairs leading up the house. I'd admired this place for years, and I heard it was for sale and I had some money for the first time. "Seventy-five thousand? Yeah, I'll do it." I had this friend, a Vietnam vet who would bring up needles and coke to the house and we'd shoot coke all night. I'd get so high that the downstairs of the house always looked distorted to me, like it was elongated. When I finally got sober, I had to have the whole house gutted and rebuilt to get it out of my past.

5: Playmate of the Month

Steven Tyler: Diana and I had been carrying on for a couple of years, and it was beautiful until the drug thing got out of hand. We were living in an apartment on Beacon Street. Francine, who did our clothes, lived in the basement. I knew something was wrong when I'd stash an eighth of cocaine in the walls, something I was saving for when I got off the road, and I'd get home and it would be gone. Same with money and the bank accounts. Diana had lost her childhood and I lost my mind. The drugs were so heavy I don't even remember very much except that I was out on the road and Raymond called and said, "Steven, there was a fire." I got back and Diana was in the hospital with smoke inhalation and burns on her hands. I went to the apartment and everything was black three feet above the floor. The fire marshall said he'd never seen such thick smoke. She rolled out of bed and somehow crawled out of it.

Ray Tabano: Diana was too young. When he went on the road, he'd say, "Ray, make sure you keep an eye on her." Because the apartment would get ripped off and bad shit would go down. I went over one day to dole a little coke out to her and a half hour later I get a call that the street is full of fire engines. I told Steven to get rid of her after she burned his fuckin' house down, but she was pregnant and he still wanted to be with her. Fuckin' guy wore her dresses, for Chrissakes! I said, "Steven, if she has this fuckin' baby, you're gonna be stuck with this girl for life. C'mon, man, do the smart thing." So they had the abortion, and it really messed Steven up because it was a boy. He was there, he saw the whole thing, and it fucked him up big time.

Steven Tyler: It was a big crisis. It's a major thing when you're growing something with a woman, but they convinced us Diana was too young and it would never work out and would ruin our lives. They said, "Will you do it?" And we said, "Yeah, let's do it." You go to the doctors and they put the needle in her belly and they squeeze the stuff in and you watch. And it comes out dead. I was pretty devastated. In my mind, I'm going, *Jesus, what have I done?*

So if there's a heaven and hell, I definitely have a little hell to go through. My conscience would still be tormenting me if it weren't for the therapist who said, "Listen, your sense of moral responsibility is lessened when you're out of your mind on drugs the way you were." I went, *Wow, thank God.* But I don't wanna kid anybody, because it affected me later when I tried to get my real wife pregnant. I was afraid. I thought we'd give birth to a six-headed cow because of what I'd done with other women. The real-life guilt was very traumatic for me. Still hurts.

And that was it for me and Diana after three years.

I had a girlfriend around this time named Carole Miller. She'd been to law school and was really intelligent. People on the tour like Laura Kaufman said she was a big improvement over Diana because you could have a conversation with her. Then my path crossed with Bebe Buell, a big blonde with huge breasts who I'd seen in *Playboy*. I went out with her for such a short time—we're talking a couple of months—but our thing had some extremely heavy-duty life implications for both Bebe and me.

Bebe Buell: I was living on Horatio Street in New York with Todd Rundgren when I met Steven. I had come to the city as an eighteen-year-old model in 1972, making the rounds, signing with Elaine Ford's agency. A photographer, Lynn Goldsmith, took some nude pictures of me, which is how I wound up in *Playboy* [in November 1974]. After I saw some copies of *Penthouse*, I decided *Playboy* was more wholesome, but appearing there also tagged me for life. It was like being Miss America, but you take a lot more flak.

I actually met Steven in late 1973 when Aerosmith was looking for a producer [for *Get Your Wings*], and Todd and I flew up to Boston in the rain, thinking he might take the job. It was at a muddy outdoor gig. I was in a white dress and espadrilles and Todd was being unhelpful and yelling at me not to be a pussy and Steven overheard this. Suddenly he leaps over and carries me across this muddy field in front of everyone. Todd was not amused by this conspicuous act of gallantry.

Back then we lived the full seventies lifestyle. Fidelity wasn't a big thing, and relationships tended to be progressive, much more open. It didn't mean you didn't love your mate, but the person you kept house with might not necessarily be the one you traveled around the world with or had sex with. Todd was my mad scientist boyfriend, my anchor, who lived in recording studios under a pair of headphones, while I was a young wildcat who needed to live out all my fantasies. I was young, pretty, and lucky to hang out with boyfriends like Mick Jagger and Jimmy Page. When my flings were over, Todd was at home and I always ran back to him.

I met Steven again in 1976 when I was in L.A. and Liz Derringer took me to the CBS convention, where they presented Aerosmith with three platinum albums with lots of speeches and pictures. When Steven saw me, he said, "You again? It's not rainin' tonight, baby!" We both laughed because we were the only two people at the CBS convention dressed in leopard. He was with Diana, a young, very pretty girl. But they were on the rocks and arguing, which I'm picking up because I'm digging Steven. He was really cute, and Todd was on the road having seventy-five affairs, and the downside of this seventies lifestyle was that it could become a contest to see who could hurt the other person the most. Very unhealthy for everyone.

A month later, Derringer is opening for Aerosmith in Philadelphia and Liz calls up and says, "Let's go. You can see Steven again." That was the night things changed. After the show, Steven and I talked and flirted in his room, spent some time alone, didn't even get to kiss because Liz was going, "You can't stay. Get in the car." It was like she dragged the dogs apart before they got into it. Then Steven started calling me from the road. That's how we fell into this very passionate love affair.

One night I was in bed with Todd on Horatio Street and Steven called me at 4 A.M. He was in New York and he wanted to see me. I told him I had to go to the dentist that morning, which is where Steven found me. He was sitting in the waiting room when I was done, and we spent the rest of the day together. Very late that night he called me from a hotel—where he was alone and overwhelmed from too much cocaine—asking me to come and rescue him. So I went and got him and took him to Liz's house. The Derringers gave us their bed and went off to sleep downstairs.

We stayed there until we got on Steven's private plane and flew up to Sunapee, where we spent a few extremely romantic days in Steven's guest house while his new house was being remodeled. We went to flea markets, spent time with Henry and Gail Smith, went out on the boat, and it was just a beautiful fall season. He took me way into the woods behind his family's resort in his uncle's old jeep and we got stuck in a swamp and had to walk out for hours. Then we dried out in front of a big fire and drank wine until the morning. We were together almost every minute and it was just a real ride, if you know what I mean.

Then we flew to Boston and went to Steven's carriage house in Brookline. Diana was there, although she wasn't supposed to be, and she and Steven fought all night and then she left. Steven and I dove right in to this deep sexual trance, very heady and moving, and this is when I got pregnant. It was late September 1976.

Back in New York, I told Todd that I was going on Aerosmith's European tour with Steven. He looked at me, shook his head, and said, "Don't come home." Then back to Boston, and many suicidal calls from poor Diana as they were breaking up. It was actually a pretty sad time. The following day we left for London.

Steven Tyler: Aerosmith's first European tour began October 13 in Liverpool (where we visited the Cavern, shrine of early Beatles days), and then did seventeen shows in twenty-one days, London, Paris, the whole deal. We may have been huge in America, but in Europe they didn't wanna know. Our first album had sold 900 copies in England and the shows just weren't selling. We didn't want to get our heads chopped off in the English press, so the promoter took out ads that said: HEY, BRITAIN, WAKE UP! THIS IS AMERICA'S GREATEST ROCK 'N' ROLL BAND! Pretty lame, but at least we didn't look bad when we got to London. The tour was hell, everything disorganized and screwed up, especially the publicity. One review of our London show said I handled the microphone like a Hoovering *au pair*.

In Germany, I tried to get through major fuckin' customs with this big buxom blonde who'd been in *Playboy* and a hash coffin in my pocket. I got off the plane, really stoned, and something was out of order with the passport. "Stand ober here, pliss!" *Oh shit*. They went through our pockets and our bags. The guy opens the coffin and there's a little hash powder, enough for one hit. "Vot iss dis?" "Huh?" "Dis! Vot iss dis?" He holds the hash out, so I blew the powder in his face.

And they fuckin' went apeshit. They brought the *dogs* out. They brought a woman out to strip-search Bebe. They took me in the back room to look up my butthole. They put some chemical shit in my hash coffin

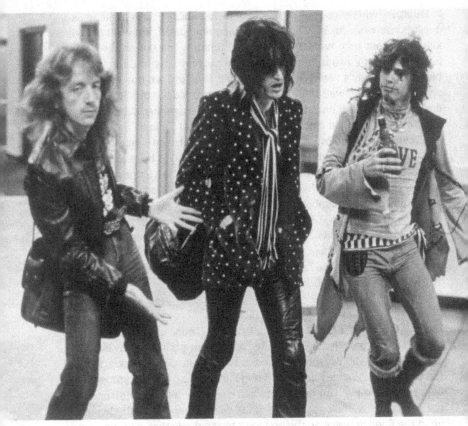

A stroll through a European airport, 1976
(PHOTO: RON POWNALL)

and it turned blue. So they arrested me. They found Bebe's birth control pills and arrested her for drugs. The promoter came in and said, "Look, he's gotta play tonight or there'll be a riot. We'll get him out of the country afterward." We ended up paying some ridiculous amount of money so I could stay and work.

It was raining in Germany and the whole tour was a mudbath. They got us some Wellington boots and we tried to make the best of it. It turned out that LEBER-KREBS, which was stenciled all over our gear, meant "liver cancer" in German and some of the local crews were afraid to handle them. We rented nine big Mercedes sedans, but only four got returned untotaled. Henry Smith got in an accident at 100 miles per hour on the Autobahn. He walked away, but the car was fuh-ucked.

MELODY MAKER

Aerosmith are a remarkable band, the first American group to successfully adopt the stances of those English bands that have successfully dominated world markets for a decade. Led Zeppelin, Yes, ELP [Emerson, Lake and Palmer], and Queen have climbed from obscurity to fame and riches. It could only be a matter of time before America would strike back.

. . . But the critics' assault on Aerosmith did not sway the fans. As the band slogged around endless tours, opening for many a British act, they gradually built a following. After four years, they have become a record-smashing band—at home. They remain virtually unknown in the land that provided them with so much inspiration. (October 1976)

Bebe Buell: Aerosmith wasn't a big band in England and there was a little backlash against them after they closed their Hammersmith Odeon show with "Helter Skelter" and they were accused of ripping off the Beatles, as absurd as that sounds. We went to see Paul McCartney's band Wings play at Wembley and Steven was impressed that I knew Paul and Linda and the guys in Queen and all the English musicians I'd met on the road. There were a lot of laughs and funny times, like Steven getting devoured by a crowd of young girls in Sweden.

There was also a lot of tension because Joe's wife Elyssa hated me from the minute she saw me. She was a real witch and told a lot of lies about me. This made Joe Perry very leery of me being around. He thought I had too many boyfriends and that I'd hurt Steven. Joe is old-fashioned and protective. He came up to me early on and said, "Listen, Bebe, don't hurt Steven or you're not gonna come out of it smelling like a rose." The whole scene was also complicated by Cyrinda Foxe, wife of David Johansen, who was Joe Perry's best friend. Cyrinda had been part of the Warhol scene and was in *Andy Warhol's Bad*. I could tell that Cyrinda secretly liked Joe, but she was Elyssa's best friend, so that was pretty weird.

Joey Kramer didn't trust me either. He and Steven would stay up all night doing coke together. They'd go to bed at dawn, just as I was getting up, so I didn't even see that much of Steven. That's when I started to get Steven's scary side. He was really crazy in Europe, totally drunk, really out of it. We had a couple of fights, one of them in public that got into the British press after Steven destroyed his dressing room at Hammersmith.

I started throwing up in Germany and that's when I realized I was pregnant. Steven said, "Bebe, that baby better not have droopy eyes and big ears," but I told him that I hadn't been with Todd since my last period and he had to be the father. Meanwhile, Elyssa—bossy, loud, mean, vengeful—decided I definitely was *not* gonna be part of the family and started this huge conspiracy against me. She told Steven that I'd slept with lots of men and that any of them could be the father of this baby.

After we got back from Europe, Steven took me to Sunapee. One night I found him on the floor of his bathroom, having a drug seizure. He was writhing in pain. I had to hold his tongue down with a pencil, totally wild. A voice inside me whispered, *Bebe, you're in this way over your head.*

We were supposed to go on vacation in Hawaii, but I decided to run. Todd had a house in Woodstock, New York. Under the pretext of going to fetch my old dollhouse, which I told Steven I absolutely could not live without, Steven had his private plane fly me to Woodstock. I got out of the plane and told the pilot to go back without me.

OK, maybe it was a mistake to leave when I was pregnant. It probably confirmed everything that Elyssa was saying about me. Steven called me in Woodstock, but I was adamant. I was only thinking of saving my own ass.

That's how I went back to Todd. I couldn't handle it. Because these boys in Aerosmith were out of control. They were like a gang of kids with their own planes, Porsches, millions of dollars, limitless resources. They were younger, crazier, and it was just nuts. Mick Jagger and Jimmy Page had control, but these boys did not care. They won the prize, hands down, for the rowdiest rock 'n' roll band in that era. No question.

To make a long story short, Todd was not too pleased, but he took me back. I said, "Todd, this isn't your baby. Are you sure you can handle this?" And he said, "Don't ever say that again." We made a pact that he would be the father and raise the baby as his own and we wouldn't tell anyone. My daughter Liv was born July 1, 1977.

Steven Tyler: Bebe and I were boyfriend and girlfriend and it never got much past that, emotionally. She was living the life of a *Playboy* centerfold, a very sexual persona, and I was spinning from the drugs and the fame.

Meanwhile, Elyssa was like, "I know something you don't know," and when I finally pried it out of her she said that Bebe was seeing Ritchie Blackmore [of Deep Purple] at the same time we were together. It was a lie and I believed it—all the hype and hoopla—so when Bebe got pregnant, I believed it wasn't mine. So I got scared and I disengaged. I thought it was just one of those spins that happen when you're up and coming—people want to attach themselves to you.

Bebe Buell: It was a very confusing time. Steven's always known that Liv was his child, but we saw each other a few times when I was pregnant and I'd tell him, no, it wasn't his child, because I was with Todd. But then I'd make love with Steven because Todd was off in Japan, and I wanted to be with the father of my child, but at the same time I couldn't *be* with him. I didn't have the heart that his wife Teresa has, the ability to stand by her man and fight. I didn't have the strength and willpower to go through a recovery like that, and that's what it takes.

Liz Derringer: My impression was that they were in love, but to be honest, Bebe was not exactly the love of Steven's life.

6: Big in Japan

Joe Perry: 1976 had been a hell of a year and we were all fried and needed to dry out. Steven had laryngitis and we had to cancel some shows. (A rumor got out that he had throat cancer.) When we got back from Europe in November, we played for three nights at Boston Garden and then took a break. Elyssa put her finger at random on a map of the Caribbean and landed on Barbados. So we took two crew guys, Rabbit and Nick, and went down for a couple of weeks. I think we only lasted seven days, but it was the only peace we ever had in that era because we were basically touring all the time.

Around that time "Walk This Way" was released as a single (eighteen months after it came out on *Toys in the Attic*) and got to #10. It was Aerosmith's second Top 10 record of the year; it would also be our last Top 10 hit for more than ten years.

Aerosmith headlined Madison Square Garden again in December, with

Ted Nugent opening. The party afterward was at the Promenade Café in Rockefeller Center with lots of friends and stars. I remember what a buzz it was to have sold out the biggest hall in New York, what a cool feeling it was to be the toast of the town for a night.

We stayed on the road until December 19. The last show of the year was at Columbia, South Carolina. On New Year's Eve, we threw a big party at the Wherehouse for just about everyone we knew.

Brad Whitford: The money started to come in and we got no help at all to manage it—not that I asked for any. Between agencies and managers, we were paying 35¢ on the dollar. We were paying 50¢ on the dollar to tour. So five guys ended up splitting 15 percent of what we were earning. There was no documentation, and management told us they were deferring their commissions to put more money in our pockets, which meant we were always pretty much in debt to them. We were handed American Express cards that got billed to Aerosmith Productions. It felt like free money, so everyone went shopping.

Then one day CCC sent me a check for $175,000 and I figured I was set. I bought cars, vintage guitars, a couple of ounces of pot. I had a fridge filled with Heineken in the house that Lori and I bought in suburban Walpole, a freezer full of frosted mugs, and I thought everything was pretty cool. I went to the Ferrari dealership in snooty Cohasset and they showed me a three-year-old Daytona, one of the finest production cars ever made, and I said I'd take it. They looked at me, this long-haired hippie, and went, "Sure, kid. Right." I was back the next day with a cashier's check for 22K, which was a steal considering that for a while in the eighties the car was worth half a million. It was really a toy, because you basically had to drive it in a big circle because it was too valuable to leave on the street. It wasn't just me. Tom and Joey went out and bought Ferraris that year too.

Tom Hamilton: In early 1977, we all had a new dose of fantasy fulfillment when we were asked to come to Japan and tour. We had heard we were "big in Japan," and from the beginning the whole journey had a Beatle-esque vibe to it.

Terry and I had bought a house in Newton, not far from where Joe and Elyssa lived. Joe would come by to see us in his blue Bentley, and Joey would invariably get his huge Mercedes stuck in our narrow driveway. One day in January, we got on a plane in New York and flew fifteen hours to Tokyo. The flight went pretty quickly because Terry and I were well equipped for the ride, although we all made sure we weren't bringing anything into the country. The Japanese are well into sake and other elements of the spirit world, but they definitely frown on everything else we were interested in. So we're blitzed when we landed, bewildered by the signs in Japanese directing us toward customs, dragging our carry-on baggage. Smiling customs agents show us little pictures of drugs, bombs, guns, booze, vegetables, and other contraband. "Anything to declare?" "I don't think so."

Past customs we were met by a staff of guides from Udo Artists, the promoter. [The legendary Mr. Udo had booked the Beatles into the Budokan martial arts arena in 1966 despite death threats from the judo fighters, who didn't want their hall, which had been built for the '64 Olympics, polluted by Western pop. Mr. Udo is still *the* Japanese promoter and a longtime friend of Aerosmith.] Our guides led us into a hallway packed with young fans, mostly teenage girls in blue school uniforms, who exploded into a screaming, squealing, crying, flashbulb-popping mob the minute they saw us.

I asked Brad, "How long do you think that line of skinny little cops is gonna be able to hold those girls back?" And Brad says, "About five seconds." Sure enough, the girls broke through, and we woke up real quick as they came at us at full charge. Someone yelled to retreat down the hallway behind us and then I was propelled by this tidal wave of kids, literally out of control, flowing with the mob like a canoe loose in rapids. I lost track of Terry and most of our bags.

I got free when the hallway took a right turn as the kids surged after Steven and Joe. I hugged the wall until the human flood washed by. Still no Terry. I started backtracking until she came around the corner. "Where the hell did you go?" I felt dazed, confused. I heard myself saying, "Man, what happened?" We turned the corner and found the empty hall littered with strewn baggage, jackets, and other stuff that had been ripped loose when we were mobbed. That's when I learned how dangerous it can be. Your clothes are torn, your hair is pulled, your skin is scratched, you could lose an eye to a long teenage fingernail. It ain't no picnic.

So I was pretty impressed by the enthusiasm of the Japanese fans. I was so grateful that they made us feel like the Beatles must have felt. Mr. Udo's people looked after us, down to the last detail except for drugs. (Some of the crew got so antsy that they bought antique opium pipes and tried to smoke the residue inside the bowls.) The promoter and the record company people vied for the honor of taking us shopping and out for dinner at the best restaurants. There was a press conference and photo opportunity where they put us on a raised platform, and after countless toasts slugging down sake out of little wooden boxes, hundreds of photogs blinded us with their masses of flash.

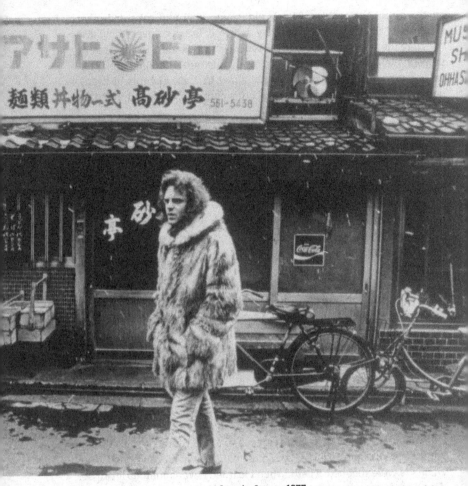

Joey in Japan, 1977
(PHOTO: RON POWNALL)

The fans that jammed the hotel lobbies were always well equipped with pens and neat little pieces of white cardboard with gold edges, all ready for autographs. They were hysterical but always polite. If one of us would go over to them, they sometimes cried with emotion. It was impossible not to be caught up in it.

The intensity of all this would show in a different way at the seven sold-out shows (opened by Bow Wow, a Japanese band), where the kids were regimented by security and stayed put in their seats. Between songs, the clapping and cheering would quickly build to a peak and then drop into virtual silence, with none of the movement and expression that we usually saw at concerts. We were told the fans were really into it and didn't want to miss even the smallest thing. It took a couple of shows, but we got used to it. Any doubts about their enthusiasm were obliterated when we'd leave the halls and it seemed like half the audience was waiting for us at the stage door. We could only stare out the car windows as the kids chased us for blocks down the dark, wet nighttime streets of Japanese towns. *Domo Arigato*.

Rabbit: One night in Tokyo, two white Rolls-Royce limos pulled up to the hotel to take some of the band to a geisha house in Kawasaki. I got to go because Joe was married and never cheated that I ever saw, not even once. Steven, always in a good mood because his drugs got smuggled in the bottoms of roll-on deodorants, liked the geisha girls so much he treated the whole road crew to a less classy place the next night.

We left Japan on February 10 [1977], flew to Hawaii, and checked into a good hotel in Maui to begin preproduction on the next Aerosmith album.

7: The Cenacle

Brad Whitford: We had a new album to make, the follow-up to *Rocks*, and so the pressure was definitely on. We wanted to do a remote recording, out of the normal studio grind, and so through the Record Plant people we found the Cenacle, an isolated estate on 100 acres in Armonk, New York [in Westchester County, north of New York City]. It was built by Broadway showman Billy Rose in the 1920s and was reached by a half-mile-long driveway up a small mountain. Its most recent incarnation was as a nunnery; the mansion had these wings for nuns' dorms, libraries, chapels, refectories—the whole convent scene.

By the time we got there, Jack Douglas, Tom, Joey, and I had been working for a month in Boston without Steven and Joe, who were both three sheets to the wind. We just kept working when we got to Armonk, figuring that (hopefully) Steven and Joe would start writing in the studio.

Tom Hamilton: The Cenacle [the name was the French word for the Last Supper] was now owned by a psychiatrist who wanted the place to become a treatment center for disturbed adolescents. Instead he got us. We had to build a studio but weren't allowed to drive any nails into the walls, so they built a room within a room. They laid down a lot of cable and we recorded in the chapel and various other rooms of the big house.

Brad Whitford: We explored the house and picked out our rooms on the second floor, each a little suite with its own bathroom. We looked at all the old cubicles for the nuns and listened to the caretaker's innuendos about their nocturnal habits. We brought in cooks to do the catering—the place was so big the food was about a quarter mile from the bedrooms—and settled into a routine of eating, driving our Ferraris and motorcycles on the Merrit Parkway, playing with our various toys, and getting high. One night early on, we turned out the lights and had a huge squirt gun fight. Jack went crazy and took it to extremes, stalking us on hands and knees in the house's giant attic, pitch-black, lit only by the lights of a digital watch. It was nuts. We were all soaked.

A couple days later, Joe Perry arrived in his black Porsche Turbo Carrera, toting one of his new toys, a semiautomatic Thompson submachine gun. Joe and Elyssa had driven down from Boston at a very high rate of speed with this thing in the trunk. Loaded. They went up to their room and disappeared for the next three days. Steven came in his 911 Porsche and he disappeared too. The three of us just kept working with Jack.

Jack Douglas: They came to the Cenacle almost right off the road—no rest, no songs, no ideas, talking about maybe doing some cover versions. Never a good sign. The band had a chance to solve its problems by staying off the road and out of the studio, but they wanted to work. I thought they were crazy. The idea of the Cenacle was for them to rest, play with their new toys, eat well, and supposedly stay away from drugs right off the street. Jay Messina and I designed and built a control room with video monitors so we could see the guys while they were recording. Joey's drums were in the chapel, Steven was up on the second floor, Brad was in the living room, and Joe was in this big walk-in fireplace. That's how we did the record.

Rabbit: They'd brought at least twenty guns with them, cars, motorcycles, two bodyguards. There was constant target practice. Joe Perry set up a rifle range in the immense attic and basically opened fire. They liked to blow cymbals apart with shotguns. Everyone was fucked up on coke all the time. The caterers were former cooks for the Grateful Dead, so they were dosing the food. If they ran out of dope, crew guys would be sent into Manhattan. David Johansen was bringing in heroin, so not a lot of work got done. Sometimes the shrink who owned the place would materialize out of the fog wearing a long cape. The whole trip was pretty weird, and we were there for six weeks.

Joey Kramer: The Cenacle had been built by Billy Rose in the Gatsby days, and we had our own version of the Gatsby lifestyle going. We had girls catering the meals, a big table in the hall where we ate. After dinner, they left coffee and dessert for us and we'd work and record at night, because during the day we were too busy getting high and driving our cars and having a good time.

Tom Hamilton: It was a rough period, because the band was split in two. Brad, Joey, and I would work all evening, rehearsing, tightening up. Steven and Joe wouldn't come down until midnight. So the band was fragmented. Heavy drug use was in the picture now, a really sick, very evil corrupt thing was happening. The vibe started to happen when Joe would be working on "his" songs, as opposed to "ours." We had some fun there, but no one was too happy.

Brad Whitford: One night Joe came down to play with us. He said he wanted to practice the slide guitar part for the track that became "Draw the Line." But he was way out of it, slurring, nose running. But he wanted us to lay down some rhythms so he could play over it. After ten minutes, he staggered to the nearest bathroom and puked his guts out. Then he came back, played for an hour, went back up to his room, and we didn't see him for five days.

Jack Douglas: Joe and Elyssa were just totally wrecked. Joe would show up, glassy-eyed, and I'd throw him out because he couldn't play. I told Joe he should be ashamed of himself, coming to the session in that condition. He didn't give a shit. He'd just shrug and go back upstairs—for days at a time. Steven was a less-obvious junkie than Joe, but he had his own problems. He'd done some preproduction at my house in

New Jersey but hadn't really written anything because he was on tour when he should have been writing. Most of the lyrics and vocals were done later at the Record Plant. It took us six months and half a million dollars to make that record.

Joe Perry: There was an amazing line of Ferraris and hot Porsches in the Cenacle's driveway, but I never even drove mine after I got there because I was burnt-out and didn't need to go anywhere. Joey would wash my car for me because he hated to see it look bad.

We got there—me, Elyssa, Rocky (our Lhasa)—and checked out the studio they'd built on the first floor, the drums set up on the altar of the chapel. We went into our room, did a lot of dope, and basically went to sleep because we were exhausted from being on the road for two years. Rocky pooped in the closet. He was pretty good about it.

I'd shipped down my motorcycle, a Thompson submachine gun, a bunch of .22 rifles, pellet guns loaded in holsters. When I woke up, I'd go up to the attic, pull out the Ruger and shoot off a bunch of rounds to let off steam, clear the cobwebs out. Downstairs, I'd have a big White Russian for breakfast. That's how I'd start off the day.

Rabbit: At one point we got an ounce of bad coke from some mob guys and we decided to try to return it. Steven gave it to Henry Smith to hold. Henry put it into a manila envelope, but later switched envelopes because we knew that Steven would decide he wanted the coke at 4 A.M. Next day Steven was pissed off and asked why we switched envelopes on him. I said to him, "Steven, we did it because you just don't know when to stop. You don't know where to draw the line."

Joey Kramer: Every night before dinner, Steven would go up to his room and lay out two big lines of blow to do afterward. Raymond was around and he started to poach these lines while Steven was eating. Steven would go up and we'd hear him yelling, "WHAT THE FUCK!!!" One day someone saw Ray snorting these lines, but without Ray knowing it. Steven says, "OK, I am gonna really fix his ass good." So Henry Smith scraped some loose plaster off the wall, chopped it up into little lines, and baited the trap. We all went down to dinner. Raymond slipped away. We looked at each other and waited. Soon we heard terrible coughing sounds. Raymond tumbled downstairs, screaming, with all this shit up his nose. He had to deal with it all night.

Terry Hamilton: Steven was there with his girlfriend Dory. Joe and Elyssa were off in their separate attic and rarely came down. Joey was with his girlfriend Nancy Carlson, and Brad was with his wife Lori. One night Tom and I were eating and Joe came down with Elyssa. He was out of it, and he says to me, "I'd like to introduce my wife Elyssa." It was so silly I just started laughing, because I'd known her for years. We hated each other. She ran away in tears. Then she came back and everything was "normal."

Joey Kramer: Steven and I stayed up for days at a time. Day and night was the same thing, a blur. One morning at 5 A.M. Steven wanted to shoot some .22 rifles, so he and I went all the way to the end of the yard and set up some cans. He started to line up so he was shooting back towards the house. I said, "Steven, you've been up for three days, you can't even talk, why do you want to shoot?" But he wanted to shoot. He loads the rifle, lies in the grass, and he's aiming, aiming, aiming. "Steven! Shoot the fucking gun already! Let's go!"

He keeps aiming. "Steven! C'mon!"

That's when I heard him snoring. He'd passed out. I picked him up, threw him over my shoulder, carried him up to the house and put him to bed.

Rabbit: Steven Tyler was a great guy who turned into Mondo when he did drugs. He liked to come in, piss off the crew, and walk out, having left a cassette recorder secretly running so he could hear what we said about him after he left. He was always walking around with one hand over his eye because he was seeing double. One day at Armonk he told me, "I've reached a new high—I'm seeing triple!"

Steven Tyler: We were *out there* at the Cenacle. Those were my Tuinal days where I'd buy a bottle of Tuinals, a hundred to the bottle, and I could only eat four or five a day because they were so strong, so I'd be good for a couple of months. I'd stash 'em in my scarf with a little hole in the bottom. I'd stuff twenty Tuinals in there and could go anywhere for a week. I was stoned on pharmaceutical drugs—much stronger than street drugs, which is why that period is blackout stuff.

Joe Perry: The Beatles recorded their White Album, right? Well, *Draw the Line* is our "Blackout Album."

Scott Sobol: I visited Joey a couple of times at the Cenacle and came away with an outsider's perspective. People who knew the band liked to trade Cenacle stories because it was basically one long party: lots of food and blow, driving the respective Ferraris and Porsches around quiet little Armonk, down into White Plains, and up into Mount Kisco. Lots of weird relationships going on: Steven with a girlfriend, Elyssa making everyone she came into contact with miserable, Joey breaking up with longtime girlfriend Nancy in the middle of everything.

On my first visit, I wanted to drop off some posters I'd gotten for Steven. Joey directed me upstairs to Steven's room at the end of a long hallway. The door was closed, guarded by a piece of notepaper (printed FROM THE BED OF STEVEN TYLER) with the scrawl DON'T FUCKING KNOCK IF IT'S CLOSED. I knocked, because he'd asked me for these posters.

The door swung open quickly and there's Steven with this amazed look on his face that anyone had ignored his note. He saw me and lightened up instantly as I handed him the posters. "Hey, man. Thanks! Cool!" He was like a kid getting fresh posters of his favorite band, which I guess was what was happening. Over his shoulder I could see a pair of beautiful bare female legs stretched out on the bed, a mirror with some residue on it, and a rolled-up bill of large denomination, which made me feel awkward and I said good-bye.

When I got down to the front door, I heard footsteps bounding down the hall and Steven appeared at the top of the huge main staircase, bounded down two steps at a time, and stuffed a wad of cash in my hand. "Hey," I said, "the posters were a gift." He said, "Fuck you. I didn't used to have money and now I do, so take it and when you have the money you can give it to me." Typical, unpredictable, wonderful Steven.

You hear a lot of horror stories about Steven in those days, but nobody tells the ones that show him as he usually was. If you spent time alone with him, he was just the best. I remember him showing me the endless hallways in the huge basement one afternoon before we grabbed a couple of Heinekens out of the walk-in coolers in the kitchen. (One was for food, the other was full of beer and champagne.) We went upstairs and sat in one of the small rooms off the hallways.

Steven peered out one of the castle windows and looked across the great lawn behind the monastery, lost in thought, sipping his beer. "Here we are," he said a couple of times to himself, softly, with not a little sadness to it. "Here we are." It blew my mind because it seemed like something was hitting him at that moment, that they—and he—had really made it, and now they didn't quite know what to do with it.

8: Self-Destructive with a Sense of Humor

Joe Perry: If a band is like a river, an album is a bucket of water you take out of it, a moment in a band's life. *Draw the Line* was untogether because we weren't a cohesive unit anymore. You could tell we weren't in the same room when the tracks were done. The only thing linking us together were headphones. We were drug addicts dabbling in music, rather than musicians dabbling in drugs.

A lot of people had input into that record because Steven and I had stopped giving a fuck. "Draw the Line," "I Wanna Know Why," and "Get It Up" were the only things Steven and I wrote together. Tom, Joey, and Steven came up with "Kings and Queens," and Brad played rhythm and lead. Brad and Steven wrote "The Hand That Feeds," which I didn't even play on because I'd stayed in bed the day they recorded it and Brad played great on it anyway. Tom Hamilton and Steven wrote "Critical Mass." David Johansen worked on "Sight for Sore Eyes." In the end, we didn't have enough for a whole record, so we covered Otis Rush's "All Your Love" and reached back into the Jam Band for Kokomo Arnold's "Milk Cow Blues," which had been done by Elvis and the Kinks, whose version we modeled ours on. Brad played the solo and it made it onto *Draw the Line*. "All Your Love" didn't.

Before we went to Armonk, I worked for about a month in the eight-track studio I'd built in the basement of my house, which was filled with Stratocasters, Gibson Les Pauls, a B. C. Rich Mockingbird, a double-neck, and custom guitars by Dan Armstrong. I was into an "A" tuning for slide guitar and was writing and arranging things on a six-string bass tuned that way. I was way into the energy of the Sex Pistols, which I thought was another important thing from England that we should absorb. "Holiday in the Sun" and "God Save the Queen" and "Pretty Vacant."

That's where "Bright Light Fright" came from. We'd work all night, crash at dawn, when the only thing on TV was the good morning news.

(This was before cable, right?) You write about what you know, so I put this on tape, along with some demos and various raw things. I put a bunch of these cassettes in a cookie tin, brought them to the Cenacle and forgot about them. A month later, we ran out of material and Elyssa reminded me of the cookie tin. There were all these slide riffs that caught Steven's ear and became "Draw the Line" and "Get It Up." I'm scratching my head, going, "Gee, I *knew* I had more songs." I brought "Bright Light Fright" to the band, complete with words and everything, ready to go. They didn't like it. I said, "Do you want to do it or not?" They said no.

In the end, Jack talked them into it.

Joey Kramer: "Kings and Queens" was a typical session at the Cenacle. It was recorded in the chapel with the pews out, the drums on the altar. Jack was in the confessional, hitting a snare drum by himself. We were playing a lot of practical jokes on each other, so I snuck up behind him and yelled boo and scared him so much he chased me around the house for ten minutes before I lost him in the warren of nuns' cubicles.

Jack Douglas: By the time we left the Cenacle at the end of May, I felt pretty bad. *Toys* and *Rocks* had helped me to another level of success. I had discovered and launched Cheap Trick, produced Patti Smith's *Radio Ethiopia*, and was turning down a lot of offers. I could have done Kiss and made a lot of money, but that would've been unfair to Aerosmith because by 1977 Kiss was their only competition, at least among American rock bands.

So I started *Draw the Line*, and for a while gave it my all. But because they were halfhearted about the record, I was too. Steven wasn't writing at all. The lyrics to "Critical Mass" came from a dream I had at the Cenacle. I never expected Steven to record it, but he didn't have anything else, so he used my lyrics as written. Same with "Kings and Queens." Steven and I wrote the lyrics together, which was like pulling teeth. After the Cenacle, we spent from June to October either in the Record Plant, trying to finish the album, or on the road, where we recorded some of the live stuff that came out on *Live! Bootleg* and occasionally snuck into local studios trying to finish *Draw the Line*.

Steven Tyler: Why did it take so long? Because I wasn't Patti Smith writing poetry. I write exactly to the music, and when the music ain't coming, neither were the lyrics.

Tom Hamilton: One afternoon we posed for Al Hirschfeld, the famous theatrical caricaturist, who came up to Armonk to do a line drawing of us for the album cover. *Draw the Line.* Get it? Hirschfeld was this quiet, bearded, bohemian artist, about seventy. He said he used to draw theater sketches inside his pocket during performances. I asked him if this used to get him thrown out of the theaters, but he didn't laugh. A week later, he produced this caricature that I thought captured us with wicked cruel accuracy. I liked it so much I bought the original.

Laura Kaufman: Ray Tabano and I went up to the Cenacle to work on the tour book because they were going back on the road that summer without finishing the album. By that time, the drugs had taken over all our lives. I mainly remember that I did a lot of blow and never heard a note while I was there. One night we had a slide show for the band to approve photos, and Steven yelled at me yet again about some of the photos of him that were getting into the press. I finally solved this problem once and for all by going to CBS and stealing the whole Aerosmith photo file.

Joe Perry: I couldn't wait to get away from the Cenacle. The day before we left, we had five U-Hauls lined up in the driveway for our motorcycles, amps, and guitars. I was pretty wasted, but I tried to drive my bike up the little ramp into the back of the truck. I got on the thing, gunned the engine, drove onto the fuckin' ramp and right off again, careening into some bushes. I got up, dusted myself off, looked at the crew, and said, "You guys take care of it."

Rabbit: Last day at the Cenacle, a TV crew shows up to make a promotional video for the album. This was Aerosmith's first video. Joe was so fucked up on heroin that we had to put a couple of grams of coke up his nose, just to get him to stand up. The video was never used.

Tom Hamilton: Then there was the insane ride home from the Cenacle. We'd been up all night shooting this video and drinking Jack Daniel's. Joey got in his Ferrari and left immediately after we were through. "Be careful," I told him.

A couple of hours later, I'm driving up I-86 [now I-84] without a radar detector because I couldn't plug mine into the Ferrari's weird cigarette lighter. So I limited myself to 80—nothing faster, or slower. I get on the Mass. Pike, and at Framingham I saw a black shape on the side of the road, an unmistakable Ferrari mashed against the guardrail. My heart sank when I realized it was probably Joey's.

Joey Kramer: I was almost home and doing about 135 because the car was finally broken in. We'd been filming a commercial under hot lights, and I was tired. Brad had offered some keep-me-awake powder, but I refused. At 4 A.M., I fell asleep and smashed into a guardrail. My head rammed into the glass, nicked an artery, and I started to bleed. Tom, an hour behind me in his Dino, saw the wreck and at first was afraid to call the hospital because he thought I was dead.

Tom Hamilton: I pulled into a rest stop, called the state police, and went over to the hospital as Joey was released, soaked in blood, his head bandaged, and cut up from the glass. We went to the police barracks and Joey pulls out this *deck* of registrations, because he owned nine cars and carried all the paperwork with him. I watched this cop watch this bruised and bandaged, pissed-off, burnt-out, half-stoned, Ferrari-driving punk shuffling through the registrations, and I just knew he was thinking, *Who the fuck is this guy?*

Joey Kramer: The damage report? Seven stitches and $19,000 for the car. Plus, we had to cancel some shows. Then Joe Perry completely totaled his Corvette.

Joe Perry: I was doing 90 on Route 9 in Newton, passed a slower car, swerved, hit the guardrail, spun around, and sideswiped an unmarked cop car. I walked away from the wreck without a scratch, started picking up pieces of fiberglass all over the road. The cop told me to get the hell out of there. He must have felt sorry for me. He even dropped me off at Dunkin' Donuts.

Steven Tyler: All this time we were out on the road. With the album unfinished, we played a show at Cleveland Stadium that was later voted worst show of the year by the local stations. Then Omaha. Fort Worth, Texas, on Joey's birthday [June 21, 1977], in front of a rabid, hardcore audience. In August, we started a three-week mini-tour to honor some concert dates, with the record still unfinished. Everywhere we went people told us they'd heard rumors Aerosmith was breaking up.

AERO KNOWS, VOL. 1, #3 [official fan club newsletter]
We're getting organized for the big one, AEROSMITH EVERY-
WHERE on tour '77. It should start right around Labor Day and most
major cities across the land are planned stops. Listen up, you loyal
fans out there. No matter what you hear, there is only one AERO-
SMITH, we're going to be playing everywhere constantly. "Accept
no substitutes" and let me add this! (Ahem, *Aero Knows* is about
to get heavy.) If you hear any kind of weird rumors, stories, concerning AEROSMITH as a group or the lads individually, unless you
hear it here, baby, somebody's only exercising their jaw! (Ray Tabano, July 1977)

CIRCUS
Performing their last mini-tour date at Baltimore's Civic Center,
Aerosmith had technical problems as Joe Perry's guitar amp kept
cutting out. After the fourth breakdown, Perry took off his guitar
and walked over to Steven Tyler, and the two square-danced while
waiting for the repair job.

During the group's encore, "Train Kept A-Rollin'," the amp
[quit again.] Perry walked over to the mike and held the guitar over
his head.

"This is a 1957 Stratocaster," he said. "It's been in my family
for generations, and this is how we used to solo back then." The
precious stringed relic of the pioneer days of rock 'n' roll flew fifteen
feet in to the air and crashed to the floor unattended. The group
finished the show without Perry. (September 15, 1977)

Joe Perry: I was throwing monitors into the audience. When
a string on my Strat broke, I must have snapped. But I had the presence
to grab a fake Strat, which is the one that got smashed. I mean, we're not
talking about schizophrenia here, just self-destructive with a sense of
humor.

9: Number Two's on Fire Again

Joe Perry: Summer of '77. Having a great time. Wild parties at the house every night with the crew. Unfettered hedonism. Up until dawn. *Hollywood Babylon.* Cases of vintage wines drunk like water. Cocaine in the antique silver chalices on the mantel. Series of car accidents. Got arrested. Security guys living at my house in Newton, keeping an eye on me. I'd just gotten a load of opium and literally didn't leave my room for days on end. I'd roll it into a little ball and eat it. Two hours later, you'd get off and it would last forever. I'd wake up, peek out the window at the security guys working on their tans out by the pool, and decide to go back to bed. Fucking literally vegged-out. We called the supermarket for food and steaks.

If we were playing at Madison Square Garden, I'd call up my Moroccan buddy who made our leather clothes and tell him what color suit I wanted. At the airport in New York, I'd find a bag waiting for me in the limo. I'd change into the suit, which always fit perfectly and always had a couple of grams in little hidden pockets. We'd drive up into the Garden and I'd get out in a new lambskin suit and walk onstage. The amps were buzzing and ready, the crowd was going nuts, throwing cherry bombs and shit, and we'd just play. A lot of the time, we really sucked.

But we'd stopped giving a shit.

I'd put on one of Michel's leather suits and live in it for days, playing, partying, staying up. Sometimes those suits didn't last too long.

Rabbit: After they left Armonk, they stayed on the road all summer. The tour was offically the Aerosmith Express Tour, but the crew called it "The Lick the Boots That Kick You Tour." There were thirty people in the crew and fleets of private planes, limos, tractor trailers, sound trucks to record the shows. It was very rowdy; we carried a chain saw for trashing hotel rooms. Kelly would walk into a room where Joe Perry was sawing an ugly motel armchair in half, Joe would throw the saw to me, and I'd get blamed.

We liked to wire big TV sets to extra-long extension cords so they'd be playing as they went over the balcony and actually explode when they

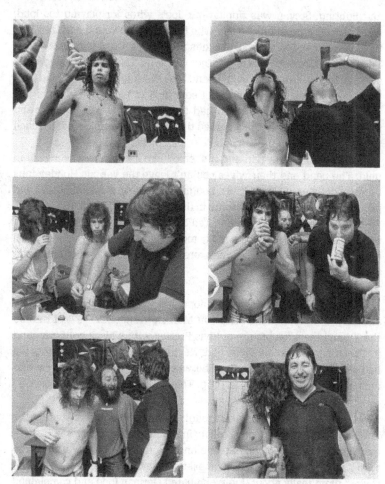

**Shooting beers with
tour manager Kelly**
(PHOTOS: RON POWNALL)

landed in the hotel pool. We'd buy $200 Jap Strats, cheap copies, which Joe would ram into the amps at the end of the show and walk off, leaving the thing sticking in the amp, filling the racetracks we played with ungodly feedback and noise. We built some of them into pyro-guitars, which Joe could swing around the stage like a flaming torch.

Then we went back to Europe, which was horrendous. Everyone on that tour hated it. We spent most of Eurofest '77 playing soggy festivals and fighting. Steven was ripping out Joe's wires for playing too loud, which set off horrendous battles. The first mudbath was the Biltzen Festival near Liege, Belgium, 12,000 kids ringed by barbed wire in the rain. They looked like prisoners of war, not rock fans. The mud backstage was over the tops of our boots, so the band took the stage soaked in mud from the knees down. The caterer had tied a goat to the coffee table; if you wanted milk in your coffee you had to milk the extremely muddy and reluctant goat yourself. This pleased the already miserable crew so much they all took shits in the promoter's trailer, on his desk.

It did nothing but rain and it seemed like all Europe was awash in mud. The band and their wives couldn't leave the various Holiday Inns because of the rain. David Krebs bought everyone green Wellingtons and raincoats, and we spent the month in them—Stuttgart, Hamburg, Munich, Frankfurt. Between our crew and Ted Nugent's we looked like a hip army on maneuvers. The army vibe really took hold when we played for 40,000 mud-soaked American G.I.s who were really up for the show and made us feel almost at home.

Joe Perry: I ran out of dope, got sick, drank the mini-bar dry and stayed in the hotel. One day in Munich [August 17, 1977] I turn on the TV and there's a picture of Elvis Presley with a black border around it. That's how we knew Elvis died. Next show, indoors at Hamburg, we had a minute of silence for Elvis between the Doobie Brothers' set and ours, and you could hear a pin drop. They loved Elvis there.

Rabbit: Conditions were tough. Steven passed out onstage at the Lorelei Festival in Germany, collapsing after three songs, which made everyone crazy. In Cologne Steven and Joe did four hours on the radio with hostile disk jockeys who kept asking what the words to "Rats In The Cellar" were really about. Everyone hated German food and complained bitterly. The crew's motto became "More Abuse."

There were some bright spots too. The band started playing "Draw The Line" and got good response. In Hamburg, just for the fun of it, Joe started wearing two guitars on stage, the Strat in front, a B. C. Rich in back. Steven thought this looked extremely cool and the look became one of Joe Perry's trademarks.

Steven's voice finally gave out at a big festival on the Rhine, near Frankfurt. The band went on at 1:40 A.M. in a freezing drizzle. Halfway through the show he started spitting up blood, which caused the cancellation of the Swedish shows a few days later.

On August 23rd we flew to London and checked into decent hotels

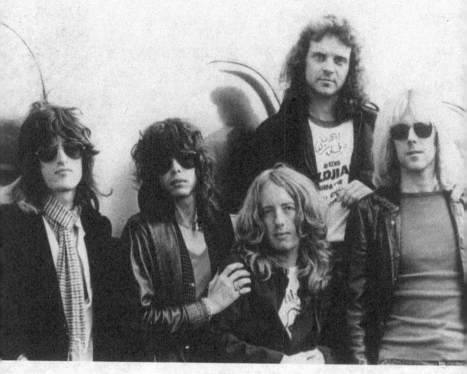

Summer 1977
(PHOTO: RON POWNALL)

[Blakes, the Mayfair] and the band went shopping for antiques and clothes. The band even did some press. Meanwhile we were dragging miles of tape and Jack Douglas and Jay Messina around Europe, recording shows and booking studio time in Germany and England to work on *Draw The Line*. They worked (illegally) at George Martin's AIR studio [Martin let them deploy an ancient compressor that had been used by the Beatles.] Brian May, Queen's guitarist, visited the studio, along with Richard Cole, Led Zeppelin's raucous tour manager. I think this is where Joe recorded the guitar solos on the "Draw The Line" track.

The Reading Festival was muddy too, but at least the promoters were prepared, unlike the members of Queen who came in white

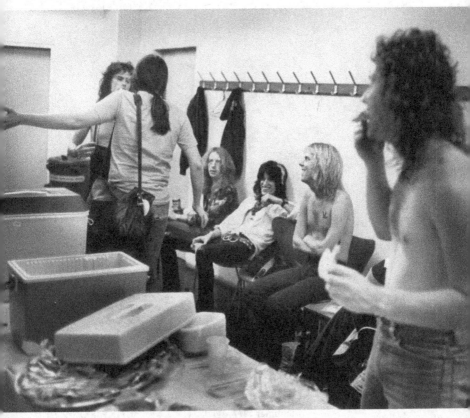

Steven fighting with NightBob about the wrong kind of salami, August 1977
(PHOTO: RON POWNALL)

shoes and velvet trousers. The limos got stuck in the mud and the band had to slog to the site on foot. Kelly was so pissed off he threw two of Leber-Krebs' English employees down the back stairs of a double-decker bus they were using as a hospitality area backstage. Then he ordered all the other English guests and the rock press people out into the pouring rain. Even though it was the height of punk in England the crowd was yelling and screaming for Aerosmith so they played the best show of the tour.

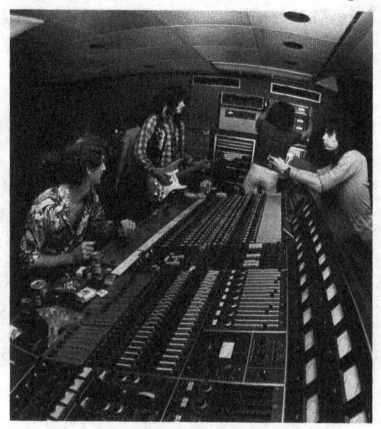

Jack Douglas, Joe, and Steven, AIR Studio, London, August 1977
(PHOTO: RON POWNALL)

Joey Kramer: I was sick the whole tour. I started to think seriously about what I was doing, and I wanted to go home.

Steven Tyler: I remember snorting heroin at Richard Cole's house. Then we went to a museum near the festival site, and while I was admiring some antique knives Richard took out a blackjack and smashed the glass case and stole a knife for me. Then we walked out.

Walk This Way

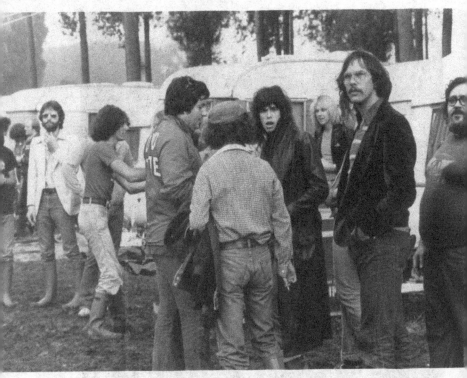

In the mud at the Reading Festival, 1977. From left: Rabbit, Paul Ahearn,
Nick Speigel, Kelly, Steven, Tom, Henry Smith, Joe Baptista
(PHOTO: RON POWNALL)

THE BEDFORD RECORD

The Reading Festival site was a no man's land, a war zone. The
mud was the consistency of a soggy quagmire. You had to throw
caution to the wind, and the rain, and just wallow in it . . .

Aerosmith is an American band, made up entirely of prats who
will insist on adding insult to injury. The heavy metal garbage this
band churns out belongs in a breaker's yard, not a '77 rock festival.
Each rock and blues number was as turgid as its predecessor and
lead singer Steve Tyler thinks it's hip to tell his audience to eat
excrement. America can keep them. (September 6, 1977)

Tom Hamilton: America did keep us. We didn't play in Europe, or anywhere else outside North America, for ten years.

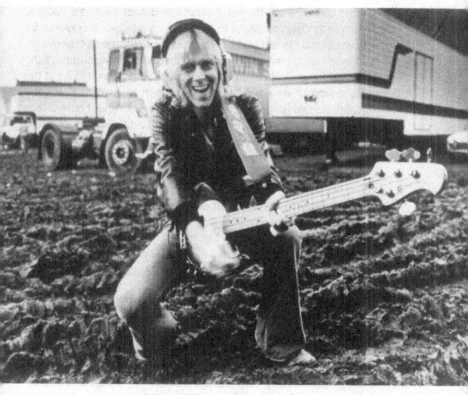

Tom Hamilton, summer 1977
(PHOTO: RON POWNALL)

Zunk Buker: In those days, I was always saying things like, "Don't worry, Elyssa. These little planes catch fire all the time." Meanwhile, she's getting upset and my father's calling the Louisville airport, which is closed because it's two in the morning, and asking them in his pilot's drawl whether they would mind opening up a runway for us and maybe laying down a little foam because one of the engines was on fire.

My dad was head of flight operations for Aerosmith in those days, which meant he flew them around in the Convair they were leasing. Steven and Dory would be shut in the bathroom for an hour. Then my dad would go in and brush all the lines of talcum powder off the sink. Steven would scream, "AARRGGHHH! It was blow!!"

Earlier that summer, the band's tour accountant called my dad and asked him to fly down to Dallas to check out an inexpensive Convair for them to charter for the rest of the year. Dad flew down and met the owner. "Yes, sir, we can do anything you want with this airplane, go anywhere, anything the band wants to do." Wink, nudge. And my dad looks at the guy and says, "All we want to do is fly concert to concert. That's it." Meanwhile, the two pilots are smoking and passing an open bottle of Jack Daniel's in the cockpit. The whole thing stank. Dad calls the accountant and tells him to forget it. "No way are we going to fly this airplane."

"Yes, we are, because it's gonna save us $30,000 on this leg alone."

"The plane isn't safe. We're not doing it."

"Yes, we are."

"OK, put David Krebs on the phone. David? If you insist on using this plane, I'm paying my own way back to New Hampshire and I'm going to resign. I'm not flying in this crate. I quit."

"You *can't* quit. The boys won't fly without you."

"If you're flying them in this airplane, I'm resigning—effective immediately."

Three months later to the day [October 20, 1977], this same plane crashed in Mississippi with Lynyrd Skynyrd on board. Half the band was killed outright and the rest were seriously injured. Five minutes after this news was broadcast, David Krebs called. "Harold? I owe you an apology."

Around that time Steven gave us a check and told us to buy a plane for him. We found a Riley Turbostream, a souped-up Cessna 310 conversion with huge Lycoming engines off a Piper Navaho. It was the fastest plane in its class. The thing went like crazy, pulling G's. You could fly across country in ten hours. I think we paid $200,000, including $10,000 for the low ID number, N42 Lima, which usually meant someone real important, like the Vice President. This impressed the hell out of control towers.

"Boston Approach? 42 Lima."

"42 Lima? Give full identification, please."

"November 42 Lima."

Instant clearance. "November 42 Lima, proceed to . . ."

We flew in and parked next to an F227. The band was just coming in from a gig and we met them on the runway, next to this wet and gleaming aircraft, and Steven's going, nonchalantly, "Yeah, this is my new airplane."

Joe and Elyssa looked at each other, disgruntled.

Joey had built a house in New London and Steven lived in Sunapee, so we'd fly out of the Eagle's Nest in New London either to the gig or to

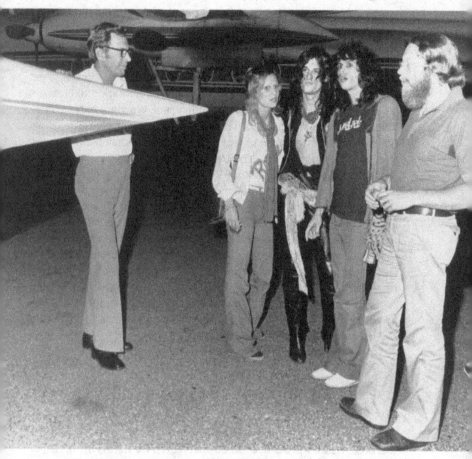

Steven gets his new plane. From left: unidentified, Elyssa, Joe Perry, Steven Tyler, Zunk Buker
(PHOTO: RON POWNALL)

a bigger airplane in Boston. Then we flew back to New Hampshire, landing after midnight. Joey Kramer had to be driven home because he was
in no shape to drive himself. He used to laugh and say, ''Hey! Let's go
over to my place and get *irrelevant*.'' And that's what we'd do.

Joe Perry: One night we're Learjetting from Boston to Syracuse when we lost cabin pressure at 14,000 feet. It sounded like someone
stuck a vacuum cleaner in your ears. Drop landing gear, down flaps, and

we go into a fighter-type dive straight down. Lights go out, huge noise, ears popping, couldn't talk, feelings of going down for the last time. One flight too many. But the pilot made an emergency landing back in Boston with fire trucks lining the runway.

We were shaken but not stirred. Kelly tried to find another jet to get to the gig and people at the airport are asking us how we could just get on another plane right then. But we didn't care. We were in the billion-mile club. But there was no plane and the gig was canceled. The crowd got mad and the crew had to wear hard hats while they packed up the gear because of the incoming bottles and cherry bombs. The gear arrived at the next show soaked in beer.

Another time Elyssa had a toothache in Florida and wanted to go to the dentist in Boston. This was a great excuse to go back and cop. I got $5,000 in cash to buy fuel and called the pilots. "Gas it up, we're going to Boston." We took off from West Palm, and they folded down the back of the plane to make a bed because it's like three in the morning. So Elyssa's sacked out in the back and I told the pilot to do a couple of totally illegal barrel rolls. We're completely upside down, Elyssa wakes up, her mind completely blown, the ground up here and the sky down there, and she goes, "That was cool. Can we do it again?" I gave the pilot the high sign and over we went again.

10: The Toxic Twins

Brad Whitford: In October [1977], we started the fall leg of our tour at the Spectrum in Philadelphia, where there was a riot the last time we played. From the moment we started "Toys," the 20,000 kids were just nuts. This time we got through the show all right, but backstage we could hear a lot of Blue Army ordnance going off, firecrackers and cherry bombs. We go back for the encore, we're on the stairs, and an M-80 goes off in our faces like a shotgun blast. "What! What happened!!" Steven's holding his eyes and yelling that he can't see. Joe Perry's right hand is spurting blood. Steven and Joe got a police escort to the hospital.

Later I called my wife and found myself crying. I hadn't cried in *years*. "Steven could have been blinded," I told her. "Joe's been, like, *maimed*. This life, it really sucks." It was something we'd been expecting for a while, but we were shocked when it happened anyway.

Joe Perry: The blast burned Steven's cornea and opened up an artery in my hand. At the emergency ward, Elyssa flipped out when the head nurse didn't jump. We'd just walked off in front of 17,000 at the Spectrum, jacked up from snorting and drinking, covered in blood. Elyssa went and knocked everything off the desk to get their attention and yelled, "You better see us *now!*" A great way to influence people.

Steven Tyler: They gave me an eyepatch and I went back to New Hampshire. The October shows were canceled and me and Joe finished up *Draw the Line* in New York. We resumed the tour in the Midwest a month later.

Rabbit: Aerosmith decided they needed the Record Plant to finish this album, which was six months overdue. People were screaming for it. They'd block out massive amounts of expensive studio time and not even show up. They were so big by then that they bumped Bruce Springsteen out of the studio so they could use it. Then they didn't show up.

When they did come in, it was in style. Elyssa was using cocaine for eyeliner. Steven and Joe would light cigarettes with hundred-dollar bills, just to fuck with the heads of the record company people visiting the sessions.

Laura Kaufman: It was very bad. I had to literally scrape Steven off the hotel floor to get him to the studio.

Steven Tyler: This was supposed to be a huge album for us, a big follow-up to our best work. "Draw the Line" was released as a single that fall and didn't make the Top 40. We finished the record at the Record Plant. I remember working on the vocals for "Get It Up" with Karen Lawrence, a singer [from the band L.A. Jets] managed by Leber-Krebs. We used her on the chorus, the first woman to appear on an Aerosmith record. The album was released in December, in time for Christmas, just as we got off the road.

David Krebs: The lyrics were a big problem with that album. The essence of Aerosmith had always a positive and very macho sexuality, totally unashamed, a little sleazy and testosterone-saturated, full of male lust, because that's what our audience wanted to hear. They *didn't* want to hear lyrics like "Get It Up," which repeated over and over again, "*Can't* get it up." Kids who went to our shows and fantasized about their girlfriends didn't want to hear "Can't get it up." The negative lyrics were a big problem.

Jack Douglas: I had my fingers crossed about *Draw the Line*.
I was working on a Frankie Miller record in London when it started out hot, the fastest-selling record the label ever had. Someone asked me how it felt to have the bestselling album in the United States.

I told him I'd never know. The album sold 1,500,000 copies in the first six weeks and went platinum and all that, but with the band off the road it fizzled and only got to #11. The boys just weren't around to give it the extra push into the Top 10. And then [early in 1978] rumors started to leak into the press that there was major strife in the band and Aerosmith was breaking up. It didn't help the record.

Draw the Line is a classic title that says it all, the coke lines, heroin lines, drawing symbolic lines, and crossing them—no matter what.

Maxanne Sartori: I was wicked disappointed by *Draw the Line*. Everybody was.

ROLLING STONE
. . . a truly horrendous record, chaotic to the point of malfunction, with an impenetrably dense sound adding to the confusion. This album shows the band in a state of shock. (March 9, 1978)

Joe Perry: It wasn't as good as *Rocks*, wasn't as hard-edged.
The focus was completely gone. Listen to *Draw the Line* and you can hear the music get cloudy. We got too into it, heard too much of it, so it was a real self-indulgent album. We had car accidents, physical abuse, break-downs, exhaustion. We were fried. What can I say?

The expensive thing for us wasn't really the drugs, it was the deci-sions we made while we were fucked up. That's what cost us, big time. We didn't want to be told what to do and we had lost any respect for someone else's advice. No one tried to tell us anything, and if they did, they were afraid they would be history. Our attitude cost us half a million dollars, which is what that album cost. Basically we ate the dessert before the main course. That's when we stopped steering our band toward a goal. It was over.

One night around that time, I was doing coke with Paul Ahearne [who managed the group Boston] and we ran out, so we went over to the Par-

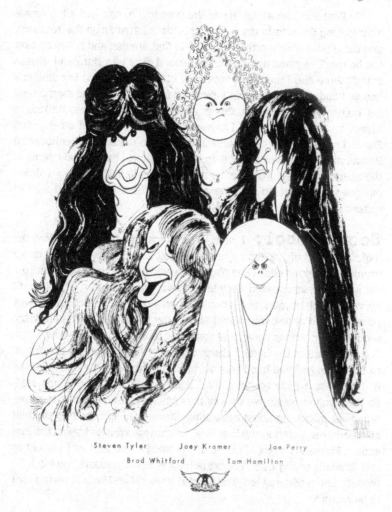

Steven Tyler   Joey Kramer   Joe Perry

Brad Whitford   Tom Hamilton

Draw the Line; drawing by Al Hirschfeld
(HAMILTON COLLECTION)

adise to try to cop some more. In those days, it was very rare for me to go anywhere in Boston. The drug dealers would come to the house, or there were one or two people I might visit. Clubs, never. Elyssa had to be asleep for me to go out of the house.

So Paul and I went out, made the connection, and had a big hassle after locking the keys in the car with his loaded syringe on the front seat, and came back after a couple of hours to find firemen and police all over the house. The place was black, the second floor was burnt-out. Elyssa wasn't there and I just went nuts until I found her safe at her mother's house. I ended up getting high over at a friend's house and sleeping on his kitchen floor. I stayed in this guy's kitchen for three days, talking to Elyssa on the phone. Then I moved into the Lenox Hotel on Boylston Street. I moved my cars to a safe place and then rented another house on Princeton Road in Chestnut Hill. In the meantime, I had armed guards at the house because burglars were trying to break in. There was a shoot-out one night between a robber and one of these guards, and a lot of rumors started.

Scott Sobol: I went to an Aerosmith show in Hartford the night after half of Joe Perry's house burned down. He was falling down drunk at the sound check and played the worst show I ever saw them do. For some perverse reason, they left Joe way up in the mix, even though he was unable to play but thought he was doing OK. The crowd was pissed off and almost got violent about how bad it was. But the rhythm section was great, as usual, and somehow they finished the show.

Afterward at the hotel, I checked in with Joey, who was in a frugal single room, and told him I was going to check in with Steven, who was in the most expensive suite they had. "You'll be sorry," Joey said. Steven's suite was strewn with clothes when I walked in, and the entourage was snickering about something. Steven's half in the bag and half slumped over, berating the beautiful seamstress who had taken the legendary Francine's place. They're in the middle of it and as I walked in and Steven's telling her, "You were born a fuckin' mutant, you bitch," I thought better of it and left. The band at its worst and ugliest wasn't cool to be around.

Night Bob: I left Aerosmith around then (my last gig was in Largo, Maryland [December 22, 1977]) because of pretty high stress. I can't think of two more intense years in my life. I watched them go from local to global in two years. The gigs were big, they were on the edge of a lot of new technology, and we were making a lot of money, but I had to get out. They had gotten big, with everything that entails. They had worked hard, would play any gig; this didn't just fall in their laps. They were tough on their crew because they were tough on themselves. I saw a lot of stuff happening, and I understood it because it's *something* to command that kind of attention, to make ten or fifteen thousand people pay to see you and focus on you when you perform. You're wielding a lot of power, there's an influx of a lot of money, and you begin to think you're indestructible.

Tom Hamilton: We started hearing the rumors that we were breaking up when word got out how crazy things were. The press started referring to Joe and Steven as the Toxic Twins. It's hard to keep this stuff secret. We'd gotten to a very dangerous point where we could afford all the vices we wanted. We had our mansions, our Ferraris, the bottomless stashes. Where do you go from there?

11: Cyrinda Foxe

Elyssa Perry: Cyrinda was kind of my fault. Is that what they told you?

Joe was a huge Dolls fan and was going to produce David Johansen's record. I got friendly with his wife Cyrinda. I kind of felt sorry for her and had her around a lot. I haven't talked to her since she went off with Steven in . . . what? 1978? I feel like she used me. I still feel badly.

It was at the end of the tour; she said she needed to get out of town and I had her fly out. Then the tour ended and we flew home to Boston. She was supposed to go back to New York on the Eastern shuttle. Then David called me. "Where's my wife?" I said, "I don't know, but she should have been home by now."

She was with Steven. I didn't even know. I felt like an idiot. She had had a game plan in mind. David was a good friend. I'd paid—*Joe* paid—for her to fly out. I was really hurt. It was a really uncomfortable situation.

Ray Tabano: Cyrinda was a New York City girl. Steven was like a rube to her. He was a ripe apple waiting to get picked. All this is magnified by drugs. He's spending $2,000 a week on heroin, cocaine, partying, and drinking. They start getting it on and Elyssa says, "Hey! I'm a *Catholic girl*. You can't do that!" So Elyssa and Cyrinda become bitter enemies. Now you had two queens in the castle.

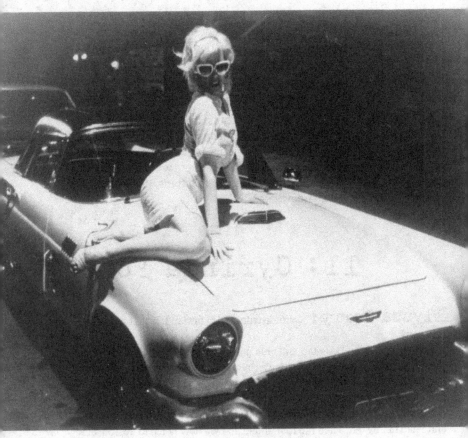

Cyrinda Foxe
(HAMILTON COLLECTION)

Steven Tyler: Cyrinda's real name is Katheleen Hetzekian. She's from Texas. She was a major starlet on the New York scene and was just back from Japan, where she promoted the Warhol movie she was in. I used to see her when I was buying heroin at David's house. He had some real good stuff and he sold it to us. I said, "What the fuck." I had to find out about it on my own.

David was an alcoholic. Cyrinda told me he used to piss in the bedroom drawers because he thought he was in the bathroom.

I never got that stoned when I OD'd.

I shot coke with Cyrinda. We did everything.

It started with the isolation of the road. Look at the situation from a thousand feet up. Take the roof off the hotel and look down at the cross section. You see Steven alone in his room and you say, "Wow, you could throw just about anybody in there and this fuckin' guy would go crazy. He's isolated, doing drugs, out of his mind."

And she's not just anybody. Cyrinda was a character from heaven. Gorgeous and glamorous. She took that Marilyn Monroe spin and had it nailed down.

You have to understand something. When I got the band together, I had drugs and I shared them with Joe because it was a good way to get close to him. Then I couldn't get near Joe because he was always with this beautiful Elyssa, who was doing heroin with him. She was keeping him away from me. I couldn't even *talk* to him. There was major jealousy because Cyrinda was their heroin connection and Elyssa didn't want me getting the drugs first.

I'm in the hotel, spinning my wheels, ready to go, and here's this stunning *fox* on tour with us. Suddenly, in the world of Aerosmith, of road managers, the plane, these two people saw their chance to get laid and took it. I started to act out with this girl, big time.

I'm like, *"Mmmeeeooowwwww. Mmmeeeooowwwww"* outside her hotel room. Joe and Elyssa bring her on the road and I'm literally rubbing on her doorpost and yowling like a cat. *"Rrreeooww. Meeoowwww."* I was really doing that, out of my fucking mind.

Rabbit: Cyrinda and I were in Joe's suite at the Plaza Hotel [in New York]. And Steven's nuts about her. At 3 A.M., Steven's pounding on the door of Joe and Elyssa's room and yelling, "Cyrinda! I love you!"

She turned to me and said, "I'm gonna take him for everything he's got." She just flat-out said that.

Steven Tyler: *"YYYeeeooowww!* C'mon! Lemme in! Please!" And she goes, "You're not gettin' any of this, honey." She just played me to the max. She fuckin' knew how, man. And I really fell for her.

Laura Kaufman: It had started on the road, in Phoenix or Denver, with David there. Then I'm backstage at the Nassau Coliseum on Long Island and I see Cyrinda and say, "Hi! Where's David?"

"Laura, I need to tell ya something. I'm with Steven now." I was shocked and walked away. Later she called me up. "Laura, listen, will you please call David for me and tell him . . . I'm not coming home?"

It was the last time Elyssa spoke to Cyrinda. Everybody paired off and didn't hang out together anymore. They wouldn't ride in the same limo together. Nobody around this could look at it and feel comfortable. People blamed Elyssa when Joe left Aerosmith a year later, but believe me, this didn't help.

Steven Tyler: There isn't a girl, from Diana to Bebe to Cyrinda to Dory, that I don't still feel for. There's a part of me that loves every one of them equally as much. I loved them. I lived with them. When I moved in with a girl, I bonded with her, living inside each other's head until it's mystical. When we make love, the gods come out. I'm in there, a sea of lubricity, sharing a thing that gods do. Normal people didn't fuck like that. They don't touch and smell and taste and lick and feel everything like we did.

So I went off with Cyrinda. I took her to my house in New Hampshire, she got pregnant that spring [1978] and we got married in Sunapee in September and had a baby girl, Mia Abagale, on December 22. It was Christmastime. I was there, helped deliver her, and it was great. Then what do you do with a baby when you're a rock 'n' roll guy? You spend some time with the baby, then you go back on the road.

Bebe Buell: Cyrinda told me and Liz that she was tired of living poor with David on the Lower East Side. It was like, "This guy has money and drugs!" She liked that stuff that begins with an H. He was more into Tuinals. I don't think he began to dabble seriously with that stuff until he met her. Anyway, she dumped David and even took the dog.

Rabbit: David Johansen wrote a song about her leaving him, a very sad song called "Flamingo Road."

Liz Derringer: Cyrinda married Steven and changed. She became a person I didn't know. She was a big New York star who became an "old lady" and disappeared. She went to Steven's house in New Hampshire and stayed there for twelve years.

7

Spilt Milk

I was in seventh grade and just going
through the whole 1978 music thing
that was happening for kids—which
was like Cheap Trick and the Cars.
Anyway, there was this chick that I
was going after that was
considerably older than
me, and she was pretty
hot. And I'd been trying
to be cool enough to take her out and
have my way with her at some point.
This went on for months. Finally I
sort of weaseled my way into her
apartment. So we're hanging out and
she put *Rocks* by Aerosmith on, and I
was mesmerized by it. It was like the
be-all-and-end-all, best attitude
fuckin' hard rock record. This was
before I had started to play guitar
. . . I'd grown up with music, but
this was like *my* record. I must have
listened to it about half a dozen
times, completely ignored her, and

then got on my bike and rode. I was totally *in there*, I was at least gonna get a decent french kiss out of it, and I completely dropped the ball for Aerosmith, and that was that. It's probably one of the records that sums up my taste in hard rock bands to this day. Meanwhile, she's out there somewhere and I missed it. But it was worth it. That was the record that changed my life.

—Slash, Guns N' Roses

1: Coliseum Rock

Joe Perry: Going crazy, needed a break, gotta get away. George Martin, producer of the Beatles, told me he was building a recording studio on the Caribbean island of Montserrat, so in February [1978], Elyssa and I flew down to check the place out and dry out for two weeks.

We went down with the best intentions. George took us out to a pasture with a tree in it and showed us where the studio would go. [The studio, AIR Montserrat, was destroyed in a 1994 hurricane after a distinguished career.] Meanwhile, I've snorted my last grain and am dope-sick and on the edge of my seat all the time. I couldn't wait to get out of there. We got home the night before the Blizzard of '78, which we spent socked in with enough heroin and cocaine so we didn't have to leave the house for a week.

My mantra used to be: "Let's do all the drugs in the drawer."

David Krebs: In 1978, Aerosmith represented the living spirit of American rock 'n' roll. To see them destroy themselves through immense disregard for anything but self-indulgence was a tragedy.

I didn't become a manager to be a doctor. If you wanna be a doctor, be a doctor.

Tim Collins was a great doctor. Without him, you'd have no Aerosmith today.

But back then the drugs had reached the point of undermining everything. Everything.

In 1977, we had reached the top, but the band was dying, so we switched from a running game to a passing game. By the end of that year, I knew I had problems. My idea was that I wanted to build a roof over their heads, to give them time to work out their problems. We came up with these giant events—Cal Jam, Texxas Jam—that would make so much money it would give them running room to deal with these problems.

Aerosmith headlined, always supported by Ted Nugent, who we put on the road with Aerosmith in 1975 and broke wide open. That's how they spent most of the year, headlining ten major outdoor festivals. I felt there was a certain mystique if you're a teenager and I bring you into a 60,000-seat stadium. You see a six-act dynamite rock show that ends with Aerosmith onstage and fireworks after. If you're a fifteen-year-old kid in 1978, very impressionable, this will go down as your most exciting experience. It was very fascistic, the whole coliseum rock thing, but it sold a lot of albums for Aerosmith and Ted Nugent.

Rabbit: Aerosmith decided that they were too removed from their audience, so during March and April they played a mini-tour of smaller theaters—the Aragon in Chicago, the Music Hall in Boston, the Masonic Temple in Detroit—as a kind of reaction to the punk idea that big bands were totally irrelevant. They hired Mark Radice, a young math whiz, to play keyboards and sing along with Steven.

They played the Cal Jam thing in the middle of this tour. [Cal Jam II, held at Ontario Motor Speedway, 60 miles east of Los Angeles, on March 18, 1978, was the biggest rock festival of the late seventies. 350,000 kids paid to hear Aerosmith, Ted Nugent, Foreigner, Heart, Santana, Dave Mason, Bob Welch, and Mahogany Rush. The *Los Angeles Times* reported the next day that 700 people were treated for angel dust overdoses. There were also two robberies, a rape, a stabbing, and countless looted cars. But no deaths.] I remember that Steven ran out of cocaine before the show and sent one of the roadies back to Boston on the Learjet to get some, telling the poor guy he was going to pick up some music that had been left behind. Also Aerosmith got pissed off at Nugent because Ted was late coming back from Africa and would probably close the show.

Joe Perry: Ted was this guy you loved to hate. We played hundreds of gigs with him starting in 1975, and I liked him because he was a stand-up guy who believed in what he said. He was a straight-ahead wild man who pursued guns as a way of life. He drank a big carton of chocolate milk before going onstage. At Cal Jam, while the opening acts were playing, he was on a Learjet returning from a safari in East Africa. He wanted to land, get on the helicopter that was shuttling bands, and drop onto the stage from a rope and start playing! When he finally arrived, he comes into our dressing room and goes, "Hey! You gotta see what I brought back!" He pulls out a bloody handkerchief full of fresh lion claws with the meat still hanging off them. We go, "Yeah, Ted, pretty cool."

Rabbit: So I bought a copy of the Byrdland guitar that Nugent played and gave it to Joe onstage. He played a few bars of Nugent's big hit "Cat Scratch Fever" and smashed the guitar to bits.

Laura Kaufman: I remember Cal Jam as being the highest day that we ever had. Everyone was bombed. The shows from those days sucked because no one was really present by the time they went onstage. Steven had arrived at 11 A.M. and they played last, so by the time they went on he'd taken so many drugs that the lyrics to the songs had to be written out and taped onto the stage because he was too far gone to remember them.

Rabbit: Cal Jam was also Kelly's last gig as road manager, a *great* road manager, who always carried four grams of coke in the pockets of his safari jacket. As Aerosmith was coming off the stage that night, Steven broke a neon sign on purpose and fired Kelly for being as out of control on blow as he was. That was pretty much the end of that era. Henry Smith became the tour manager after that.

Tom Hamilton: The next huge gig was Texxas Jam '78 over the Fourth of July weekend in the Cotton Bowl, where it was so hot that fans were frying eggs on the hoods of their cars and the crowd had to be dowsed with fire hoses. The temperature in Dallas was something like 120 degrees.

David Krebs: We had a big argument because I wanted to spend $200,000 to pay NFL Films to shoot Aerosmith in 16 mm instead of in video. That's why we have that footage today.

Steven Tyler: I look at that stuff to remind myself how sick I was. I could hardly even fuckin' move that night. I had to be carried to the stage. I remember saying sometime in '78, "It's never gonna happen to me. I'll never lose my fortune." I had a million dollars by '78. I told everyone I was damned if it was gonna happen to me. "I'm not gonna be like those fuckin' idiots, never happen to me . . ."

AND IT HAPPENED!

Tom Hamilton: Mark Radice was a shy kid, pretty young, who was the son of Gene Radice, a famous New York studio engineer. Joe Perry's singing wasn't as good as it is now; his harmonies weren't dependable, and often Joe wouldn't show up at the mike to sing them anyway. Steven would get mad, because he'd written great harmony parts. Mark was with us all the *Draw the Line* tour through 1978, but he was shy and kept to himself. On the plane, he'd be playing mind games with exotic math theories.

Texxas Jam. I look at the tapes of me onstage—what I was, how I played—and I cringe. All I hear is the cocaine. Lots of cocaine, which gave us a tendency to play too fast. It was fucked, because when we put the band together we worked so hard to learn to cook, to get that magical feel. Steven used to yell at us, "LAY BACK!" Meaning, "Lay back on the beat. Don't speed it up."

Texxas Jam featured Walter Egan, a new band called Van Halen, Eddie Money, Heart, Journey, Mahogany Rush, and Ted Nugent, who took the stage at 10 P.M. and got 80,000 kids going with "Cat Scratch Fever" and "Wang Dang Sweet Poontang" before passing out cold from hyperventilation. Aerosmith's set list included "Rats in the Cellar," "Seasons of Wither," "I Wanna Know Why," "Uncle Salty," "Get It Up," "Walkin' the Dog," "Walk This Way" (with the keyboards playing the guitar parts), "Lick and a Promise," "Get the Lead Out," "Lord of the Thighs," "Draw the Line," "Sweet Emotion," "Same Old Song and Dance." During the first encore, Ted Nugent came out and played on "Milk Cow Blues," the first time he'd ever played with Aerosmith. The show finished at 1:30 A.M. with "Toys in the Attic" and a monstrous fireworks display.

Tom Hamilton: Steven was in a rage all the time. He got angry at Texxas Jam and there was serious trailer destruction. I can still hear him heaving glass gallons of Tropicana into the shower, making a horrendous noise and sending shards of glass everywhere. Someone threw an egg just as a nosy cop opened the dressing room door to check out the noise from the breaking glass. The fuckin' egg hit him right in the eye. Three Stooges stuff, much laughter.

2: Sgt. Pepper in Hollywood

Steven Tyler: Richie Supa was an old friend of mine who'd been in the Rich Kids on Long Island and the cast of [the 1969 rock musical] *Hair* and was a very talented musician. He was also managed by David Krebs. He was a musician and songwriter and dealer who hung out with John Belushi and them. He brought us a song called "Chip Away the Stone" that Aerosmith started to play on the road in March and April [1978] while we were recording tracks for a live album. We also recorded it [on June 4, 1978, at Long View Farm studio in Massachusetts] to be a single sometime that year.

Because we weren't writing any hit records anymore. Columbia had released "Kings and Queens" in February, but it didn't do anything. So they thought that "Chip Away" might do it for us. [It appeared later on the *Cal Jam II* "live" album, even though Aerosmith didn't play it there.]

Then in March [1978], the whole *Sgt. Pepper* thing happened and we went to Hollywood.

There was a lot of Beatles revival stuff in the air back then. People missed the Beatles. Steve Leber put together a show called *Beatlemania*: four musicians impersonating the Beatles. Aerosmith were investors in that. Then we got offered parts in a movie version of *Sgt. Pepper's Lonely Hearts Club Band* produced by Robert Stigwood, who had paid the Beatles $500,000 for the rights to use their songs. Stigwood had just made all this money with the *Grease* and *Saturday Night Fever* movies and soundtracks, two of the bestselling albums in history. I don't remember why, but we did it, probably because it gave us a chance to work with George Martin when we cut our version of "Come Together" for the soundtrack.

Tom Hamilton: The Record Plant. We're blown away, doing a Beatles song with the Beatles' producer, George Martin. Jack's in heaven. George Martin is sitting there, very cool in blue blazer, crisp white shirt, regimental tie, an English gentleman, maybe a little loaded, and we're like, "Tell us what to do, Master."

"Right. Well, you've learned it from the album, so just run through it . . . 'Hear come old flattop,' . . . OK, what you've done is quite good, just what's needed in fact. Thank you very much." He turns to Jack Douglas and says, "And that, I believe, is that."

Rabbit: Joe insisted on singing the line "I shoot Coca-Cola."

The funny thing was that George Martin knew two things about Aerosmith: They took forever to record, and they loved Jeff Beck. George had produced Beck's two biggest records [*Blow by Blow* and *Wired*] and knew Beck was in town. So when they got in the studio Martin told them that Jeff was playing that night at Trax and that they could all go see him when they finished. Aerosmith cut "Come Together" in two takes, George Martin flees with the tape, Aerosmith gets to the club, and no Jeff Beck. It was a hoax.

Joe Perry: Up until then I never endorsed any guitars because I didn't want to endorse some new company whose products I didn't really love. Finally I agreed to endorse B. C. Rich guitars after I'd paid for a couple. So they gave me this solid rosewood guitar, a Mockingbird, an amazing guitar, so heavy. I did "Come Together" with it, but was less than thrilled about what I played.

Joey Kramer: The *Sgt. Pepper* movie? Are you kidding? It was a disaster. A real debacle. The Stones refused to do the part that was offered to us. Now we know why. It was just a pretty silly movie. Peter Frampton and the Bee Gees played the band, there was a girl named Strawberry Fields, and we and Alice Cooper were the bad guys, which was great because everyone looked so silly that we looked cool when we wanted to kill them. [The original screenplay, written by *New York Times* pop critic Henry Edwards, involved the Pepper Band—Frampton and the Bee Gees—becoming corrupted by the record business and the victims of a plot by the Future Villain Band, played by Aerosmith, to turn music fans into mindless drones consuming product. Eventually a weather vane comes to life (as Billy Preston) and saves the day.] The only ones to get any airplay out of it were us and Earth, Wind and Fire, who did a great version of "Got to Get You into My Life."

Joe Perry: Leber-Krebs called and said, "They want you as the Future Villain Band. You get to kill Frampton and the Bee Gees." Sounded cool, so that spring we went to California and moved into the Beverly Hills Hotel. I registered under the name Richard Burton, which made the room service come faster because they thought Elizabeth Taylor was in the bungalow. The pace was hectic: fittings for costumes, people waiting on you, huge amounts of waste. We were all really high on the set, doing hits of dope in the trailer between takes.

Brad Whitford: It took three twelve-hour days to film our part. I'd get to the studio early and wander around, hang out with the Bee Gees, who were very cool, quiet guys. Barry Gibb was rolling cigarettes out of a plastic bag full of tobacco, pot, and hash, which kept something light going all day. They dressed us in Nazi-style uniforms and gave us MP-40 Schmeisser machine pistols and we looked perfect, because we basically *were* villains. During lunch, we drank a few six-packs and passed a bottle of Jack Daniel's around. We were just being normal; if it was midday, it was time to medicate ourselves. Soon the director [Michael Schultz] was heard muttering, "Who are these *drunks* on my fucking set?"

At the end of the first day, he was very pissed off, yelling out the call times for the next morning. "I want everybody here on time." He looks over at us. "And come back sober!"

Tom Hamilton: Most of the band was at L'Ermitage in Bel Air. We started on Jack Daniel's on the way to the studio at 5 A.M. We kept an even keel, but I guess Steven looked drunk on the close-ups. The director was annoyed, yelled at us, and we tightened up. We weren't into fuckin' up when we could avoid it.

Brad Whitford: The first day was close-ups. The second day was us performing "Come Together." The third day was the fight scene with the Bee Gees and Peter Frampton, which took place on a thirty-five-foot platform illuminated by glowing dollar signs. I fought with Robin Gibb, pretty funny, and Steven fought with Frampton. There was a lot of politics about that.

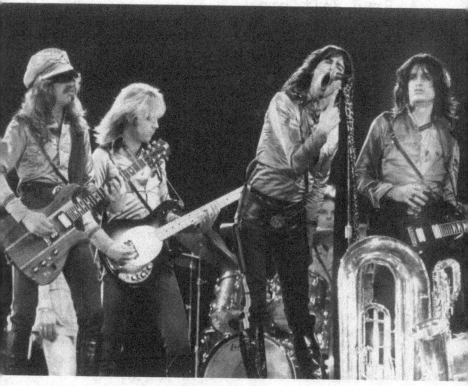

The Future Villain Band
(TYLER COLLECTION)

Joe Perry: They wanted Frampton to kill Steven, but we wouldn't have it. And we're saying, "There's *no fuckin' way* that Steven is gonna get directly offed by Frampton. No way. It's gotta be an accident, the way it was in the original script we fuckin' agreed to." So they switched it back, and what happens is we kill the Bee Gees and Strawberry Fields pushes Steven off the stage and kills him, so it wasn't Frampton who got him. Then we killed Strawberry.

We noticed it took the Bee Gees hours in makeup to get their hair right. Then we heard these three guys were getting a million dollars to be in this movie, which we didn't like, because we were getting considerably less. Joey Kramer goes, "Let's not beat them up in the fight scene. Just mess up their hair. That'll really fuck 'em up."

Brad Whitford: Three days later, I went to see the rushes at Robert Stigwood's home, this beautiful house where *Annie Hall* had been filmed. The rushes were *terrible*, fuckin' *horrible*, like they were deliberately putrid. No one could deliver a line and it was totally embarrassing. It wasn't until we went to the big Hollywood premiere that we realized they had hired George Burns to do a voiceover narration explaining this totally incoherent movie. When we came on, there was this huge roar from the audience, the only positive vibe of the night. The other cool bits were Alice Cooper's part and Steve Martin's film debut as Dr. Maxwell, of "silver hammer" fame.

Joe Perry: I'm watching this movie and I'm wondering, *Why is Aerosmith always the underdog?* I'm watching the Bee Gees smiling with their nice teeth and shit and then we get close-ups of me and Steven, and you can tell by his eyes that Steven is fried. We're both fuckin' out there. My skin is all white from being on the road all winter, my crooked teeth, my fuckin' crooked nose. I'm thinking, *They really picked the right band to be the villain. At least we didn't suffer too badly in the image department.* But it didn't matter because the whole project was in such jaw-dropping bad taste that the movie bombed and almost everyone in it was rewarded with career devastation. Peter Frampton didn't make the premiere because he was in the hospital following a bad car accident [in the Bahamas on the previous June 29]. At a press screening in New York, critics yelled "Jump" at the scene where Frampton stands on a roof, contemplating suicide after we killed Strawberry. [Rex Reed described the cast as "a parade of idiotic, egotistical rock stooges mugging before the cameras."] The film's budget had gone from $6 million to $30 million. Hollywood insiders called it "Stigwood's Folly." When the soundtrack came out, the industry joke was that it was the first album to be shipped platinum and returned double platinum.

Steven Tyler: On July 19, we played a club date as Dr. J. Jones and the Interns at the Starwood Club in L.A., which was packed. We were so locked into stadium shows that it was a pleasure to connect with a small crowd again. We booked the club and hired the equipment ourselves and told Henry Smith about it afterward. Joe Perry said it was the most fun he'd had in two years. There were so many stars that we heard even Rod Stewart got turned away at the back door.

3: The 24-Hour Rule

Joey Kramer: We were in L.A., working on the movie. My dad was always going, "Joey, what a life! Girls, cars, money—you've got it so easy." So I said, "Dad, why don't you come on the road and see how easy it is?" He said OK, flew to L.A., got picked up by a limo because we were shooting our parts all night. I rented him a Rolls-Royce convertible, a Corniche, so he could get around.

The first day he called me at the studio. "Joey, I can't go anywhere. The valet keeps bringing me the wrong car. What? A Rolls-Royce? Are you crazy? What if something happens! I can't drive that thing." He made me trade it in for a Benz.

Jack Douglas, meanwhile, is out in L.A., working with another band over at A&M Studio. He introduced me to his secretary, April, at L'Ermitage. The second I laid eyes on her something in my soul went click. *Bang!* From the day I met her I knew something was up.

She thought I was a jerk. A drug-taking fool. Which I was.

So this was a weird time for me—doing this movie, being with my dad, trying to get with April. My dad was the easiest part of it. He basically joined the party—hash pipes, lines on a plate going around. He enjoyed himself, and he didn't bother me about having an easy life anymore.

April and I started running together, became friends. I took her to an Italian place and totally fell in love with her. I was taken by her, her face, her smile, her humor, the whole thing. The restaurant closed and they asked us to leave. She told me about her four-year-old daughter Asia. I told her about my log house in New Hampshire. We parted that night and she promised to come visit me up there. Back in the hotel, I'm thinking, *How can I get this woman not to think I'm some fuckin' jerk?*

April Kramer: In early 1978, I started working for Jack and Christine Douglas. I was in my twenties, with a young daughter from a relationship that wasn't working out, and I had a pretty good background in music and theater. Right after high school, I came to New York and immersed myself in avant-garde theater, taking classes, going to workshops. I just learned and absorbed so much from this incredible group of people. For three years, I was a backing vocalist in a band called Life

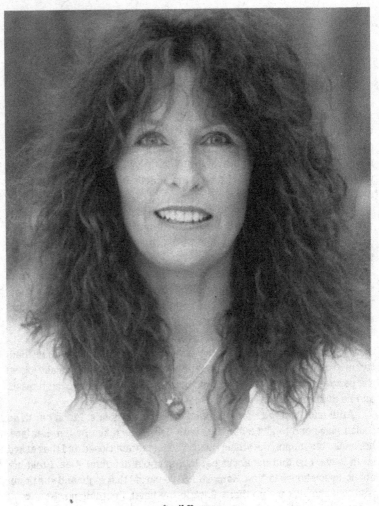

April Kramer
(PHOTO: MICHAEL FASSENELLA)

Itself. I was waitressing in a famous music club on the West Side called Mikell's where all the jazz musicians hung out. That's when I met Jack, who was helping my boyfriend's band out.

Jack was nuts, doing a lot of drugs like we all were. I started helping them manage Karen Lawrence's band, 1994, booking shows, going on the road with them. They invited me to go to California and help them out, so I flew to L.A. and checked into L'Ermitage. It was my first night in L.A., so we all piled into a car for a tour of the town. That's when I met Joey. We had a couple of bottles of wine and were doing lines in the car, thinking we were pretty hot shit. I started talking to Joey and it just kind of took off from there. We talked about everything under the sun. We got along really well and I just liked him. Back at the hotel, we made a date to go running in the morning.

That night he invited me to dinner, and we went to Chianti on Melrose. Joey was showing off, ordering a hundred-dollar wine, trying to tell me about himself because I had no idea who he was. I was more into jazz, fusion music, the stuff they played at Mikell's. So I started interviewing Joey to find out who he was, where he was from. He told me about the house he was building in New Hampshire and it sounded so enchanting the way he told it, so exciting, such an adventure.

It was hard for me to fathom it all, but as I was listening to this, I started really caring for him. He was such a good guy at heart. And I honestly think I fell in love with him that night.

We saw each other for the next three or four days. I met his dad, who'd come out to see Joey while they were working on the film. Then I went back to New York. A few days later, Joey called and asked me to fly to Billings, Montana, where Aerosmith was on tour with AC/DC. The next day I stepped off a plane after a stunning flight over the mountains and met Joey at the band's hotel. I was so excited to see him, so much in love. I met the band—Elyssa and Terry were there—and flew with them to Canada on a private jet for a concert. It was just the best time, and I was like three feet off the ground. I just hung out with Joey. We were together the whole time, which was all I wanted.

I just remember how hard it was to leave.

Summer came and went. Joey moved into his house and I visited him. In the fall, I went back with my daughter, and I got a taste of the other side of this life they were living. I flew in to the airport in Lebanon, New Hampshire, but Joey was so out of it he couldn't pick me up. Hundred-dollar taxi ride. As we're pulling in the driveway, the girl he'd spent the previous night with was leaving in one of his cars. So I freaked out. Called him every name in the book. I ended up staying the weekend because I didn't want to upset my daughter, but I wasn't happy about it.

Now I know it was the drugs, not him. And he hated being alone.

I went home to New York and wrote Joey a letter. I never wanted to see him again. He kept calling me at work, but I tried to avoid him. Then I ran into him in Chicago while I was working for Jack. He said he really wanted to talk to me, so we went for a walk. He was very direct. He just asked me, "What do you want?"

I said, "I'm tired. You ask what I want? Stability. Monogamy. Honesty. Integrity. Trust. I'm tired of all the types of relationships I've had."

He just said, "OK."

"What do you mean, 'OK'?"

He said, "I want the same thing." I was shocked. My reserve crumbled. I loved this guy. A very romantic time.

So we were together again. He wanted me to move in with him in New Hampshire. A tough decision, but I knew it was the right thing to do. I left my boyfriend, quit my job, took my daughter, and moved to New Hampshire, where we lived for five years until the shit hit the fan with the band. We were married in 1979 in New Rochelle. Our son Jesse was born in 1981. We stayed together through some terrible times for the band and for us. I watched Joey Kramer grow and change when we quit drugs later on. We went through a lot together. You know what? It was worth every minute.

Joe Perry: While we were in L.A., we got dressed as coal miners, smeared our faces with charcoal, and drove up the side of the mountain with the HOLLYWOOD sign on it to take the picture for the "Chip Away the Stone" single. It was supposed to follow "Come Together," which Columbia had released [it reached #23 on the charts late that summer].

Aerosmith was on the road for six weeks that hot summer of '78. The last show [August 6] was at Giants Stadium in the Jersey Meadowlands, with Nugent, Journey, and Mahogany Rush. Only the second concert ever at the huge football field.

CIRCUS WEEKLY

Steven Tyler's eyes are black with fatigue before he goes onstage. He is trying to save his right arm from being pulled off at the elbow by an overzealous groupie, while his pregnant girlfriend is tugging at his left arm, attempting to negotiate the last few feet to the dressing room. It's the last stop on the first leg of Aerosmith's 1978 tour, and the rain, the humidity, and the backstage crowd—which could fill a smaller stadium by itself—all conspire to make this last date as unpleasant as possible for the band . . .

In New Jersey, two giant TV screens at the ends of the stadium focus on Tyler as he unfolds his giant blue scarf. Out of the crowd of 50,000 rain-soaked kids comes a roll of toilet paper aimed at

Tyler's head. It misses, but Tyler is taking no chances. He retreats to the rear of the stage, wary that the next missile could be more lethal. "They're not really throwing at you," Tyler offers. "They just want to see what happens, how a rock star reacts—if you're a regular human." (December 5, 1978)

Needing more tracks for the upcoming live album, Dr. J. Jones and the Interns played an August 9 gig at the Paradise on Commonwealth Avenue, where the blistering "Last Child" that appears on Live! Bootleg *was recorded. On August 21, Jack Douglas and the band recorded a live version of "Come Together" at the Wherehouse.*

Steven Tyler: *Beatlemania* opened in August on Broadway. We went to the opening and then to the party at Studio 54. That was one fuckin' night I don't think I want to remember.

Rabbit: I rode over to the Winter Garden Theater with Steven and his date, and I look across the limo and this beautiful girl is masturbating. She's not wearing anything under her dress, and she's playing with herself.

Ray Tabano: She was a whore. At Studio 54, while Steven's having his picture taken with Michael Jackson, she's flashing her pussy at people. Soon flashbulbs are going off. My wife pulls me aside: "Ray, I just saw Steven's girlfriend flashing her pussy at people. She's got no panties on, and she's pulling her skirt up."

I tell Steven, who comes back and says, "No, man, she says that your wife is lying."

"What! You call my wife a liar over some fuckin' whore?" We had a big fight. Next week the *Soho Weekly News* ran a picture of this girl flashing herself. Steven told her to get the fuck out the next day.

Rabbit: We found a big batch of these pictures a year later behind the water cooler at Leber-Krebs, where Steven had stashed them.

Bebe Buell: I'd go to see Steven at the Mayflower Hotel on Central Park West. I'd flirt with him, show him Liv. If Dory or Carole Miller were around, he'd throw them out while I was there. He told me he'd played a festival in Ohio and Todd had been there with a redhead, Karen

Darben, who'd been Bruce Springsteen's girlfriend. That's how I learned Todd was having an affair.

So Todd dumped me. But he was a good father to Liv. He saw her and paid the bills. We were banished to an apartment on 58th Street. I had nobody and people felt that's what I deserved. So Steven and I had a little affair again. It was nice. He'd bring Liv toys and play with her. Then he married Cyrinda, who was pregnant, and I didn't see him for a while. I dated Rod Stewart briefly—it was the seventies, a very chauvinistic time, and girls like me were ornamental and used for publicity—and then I met Elvis Costello and went on from there.

Only a few people knew the secret of who Liv's father was. There was a lot of pain because we couldn't tell the truth. We thought Steven was going to die at any minute because he fit the profile.

Rabbit: I left Aerosmith around then because it was just too painful. People were shooting heroin, having seizures. It was tough. The crew had a rule: If you didn't see a band member for twenty-four hours, you broke down the door of the hotel room to see if they were alive.

I loved Joe Perry. I loved the guy. And I didn't want to be the guy that found him dead. So I left.

This was around the time of the Blackfriar's Massacre, when five coke dealers were murdered in the Combat Zone in Boston. They went to Florida to do a deal with Mob money, got robbed in Florida by other guys from Boston, and got killed when the people who came to collect the money pulled guns and shot them. [This incident took place in the basement office of Blackfriar's Pub on June 28, 1978.] We knew all these guys because Aerosmith was buying most of the coke in Boston. Shots got fired outside Joe's house some nights. The house itself was like an arsenal. Let's put it this way: We were always one step away from the people who were getting popped. We were on the next level of dealers.

4: Brad and Karen

Karen Whitford: I'm from Brooklyn, went to art school, started working for my sister Jayne's husband, Burt Goldstein, who was putting out a little music paper in New York. Then I started working as assistant to Bob Gruen, a major rock photographer. The first day in his stu-

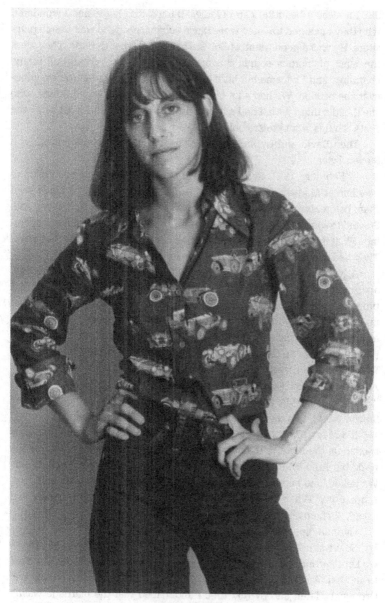

Karen Whitford
(WHITFORD COLLECTION)

dio, I noticed a beautiful pair of ladies' pumps, size large, and I wondered who they belonged to. They were David Johansen's, who was sleeping upstairs. He was a good friend of Bob's. That's how I met Cyrinda. They were the most glamorous couple downtown. She was very beautiful, funny, charming, and I became her little go-fer, doing things for her, taxes, whatever she needed. We had a lot of fun, and I got to meet David Bowie, who she'd had a thing with. I had a boyfriend who played with a local band, the Brats. Things were pretty cool.

Then David and Cyrinda began to deteriorate and she went off with Steven Tyler.

In February 1978, Bob Gruen gave me two tickets to see Aerosmith headline at Madison Square Garden. And there they were. I'd never seen them before, but it looked like they were arguing onstage. And at the end, Steven's swinging his mike an inch from Joe Perry's head and I'm wondering, *What if he hits him?* You could feel the tension and the anger in the air. They had a big skating party at Rockefeller Center afterward.

A couple of months went by. Cyrinda and Steven are in the New York apartment of the guy who made their leather clothes. One day in April, I brought them some scones for breakfast and helped them pack and clean up because they were going back on the road the next day. Next morning at 2 A.M., Steven called me and asked if I wanted to come and work with him for a month on that leg of the tour, helping him in the dressing room. "Karen," he said, "you have twenty minutes to let me know your answer." And he hung up. I called some friends. "Don't do it." "They're crazy." "You're crazy." But something inside me said, *You gotta do it.* I called Steven, said I'd be there, and flew up to Boston the next day.

It's May 1978. I met the band at the airport. There was no first-class section on the flight to the gig, so we all sat together. I was headed to the back, but Brad Whitford touched my arm and asked me to sit next to him. We talked, and he was a gentleman, very funny, and had the kindest eyes. A great guy! When he went to the bathroom, I leaned over to Cyrinda and asked, "Is he married?"

Cyrinda giggled. She said, "Yeah, but he fools around."

So we started having a secret affair on the road. Somehow—destiny—we kept getting assigned hotel rooms next to each other, and one thing led to another. And nobody knew. His wife was supposed to come on the road two weeks later, and by that time I understood that the marriage wasn't real loving. Brad and Lori had been married for a year but had been together for seven years. Brad was a rock star, but, underneath, his self-esteem was very low. He didn't even think he could play the guitar much longer.

Meanwhile, Steven and Cyrinda's relationship was so heated that he'd call me, enraged, at all hours, yelling, "Get this bitch out of my room! I never want to see her again. Just get her the fuck out!" Sounds of crying, breaking glass. Cyrinda was pregnant.

Then Lori Whitford joined the tour and we flew to Florida, where she was going to stay because her family was there. Brad told her that he had met someone and the secret was out. Both Cyrinda and Elyssa were *bullshit* when they found out this had been going on under their noses and they didn't know. Ab-so-lute-ly ripped. And naturally the other wives rallied around Lori, because there but for the grace of God . . . You also have to remember Elyssa had a fan club of her own, Cyrinda was a movie starlet; it was hard to break in.

So it was pretty tough. People wanted me to leave the tour, but Brad insisted that I stay. For a while, he was going between my room and hers—very confusing for everyone. Then the tour moved on, and Brad was arrested when he tried to get on the plane in New Orleans and they found a belt buckle knife in his carry-on bag. Henry Smith stayed behind with him and I think he made the gig in Shreveport that night.

Brad Whitford: I didn't know what to do. The leg of the tour came to an end and I'm living this dilemma of loving this girl but being married to that one. The plane lands in Boston and I'm wondering, *Where do I go?* I didn't know what to do. I'd been with Lori since 1971. I had drug and alcohol problems, so naturally I didn't handle it well.

If you want the truth, all my relationships at that point . . . messed up.

Baggage claim at Logan [Airport]. Bags going around carousel. Karen's crying. She had a boyfriend in New York. I'm supposed to go home to my wife in Walpole. I started to cry too. So we said good-bye and Karen flew home to New York.

Karen Whitford: Brad flew down to New York the next day and then brought me up to Massachusetts. I stayed in a couple of hotels and then came back to New York when it didn't seem like things were working out. In August, Brad went into the hospital for minor surgery and while he was in, Lori cleaned out three bank accounts and split. After that, Brad and I moved into the house in Chestnut Hill that Joe and Elyssa had rented while their house was being redone after the fire.

Brad Whitford: I went to Walpole, picked up my clothes and the cars—if the band's doing well, Brad has a lot of cars—and settled

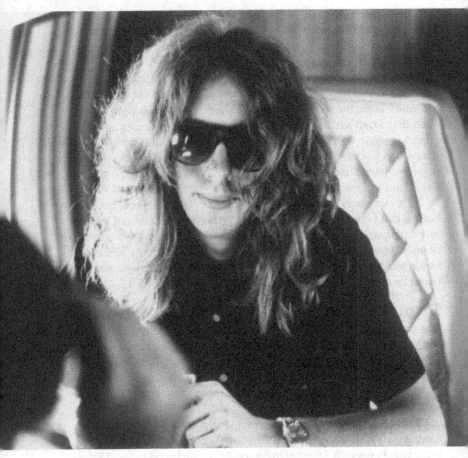

Brad Whitford
(PHOTO: RON POWNALL)

in with Karen. Lori cut her hair and moved to New York and I got the house. Karen and I got married in 1980 at the house in Walpole.

Aerosmith's sixth album, Live! Bootleg, was released that autumn, a concert album compiled from shows taped live in 1977–78 and the 1973 WBCN broadcast from the nightclub Paul's Mall in Boston. The double album in fake bootleg format (released in three separate editions with different band logos, rubber stamps, and color schemes) reached #13 in Billboard and was certified gold upon its official release in late November.

Steven Tyler: I came up with the idea of calling it *Live! Bootleg* because for years I'd seen people following us around selling unauthorized buttons, shirts, tapes—you name it—at our gigs. We'd gotten bootlegged so many times I felt we'd be bootlegging ourselves if we just put out an album of us playing live. Calling it a bootleg was supposed to be ironic.

Jack Douglas: *Live! Bootleg* came out and was totally misinterpreted. We didn't want a live-sounding album. We wanted something trashy, tinny, bootleggy. We wanted cassette-corder quality.

Columbia didn't get it, but they were afraid to tell us they wanted a remix. They went quietly crazy but kept it in the building because they were afraid of Aerosmith and David Krebs, who was capable of giving them massive amounts of grief. Anyway, Columbia thought that Aerosmith had run its course after *Draw the Line* bombed.

I thought *Live! Bootleg* was pretty good, but they didn't believe in it. If Columbia had said they couldn't deal with it, that it wasn't commercially acceptable, we could have given them what they wanted: *Aerosmith Comes Alive.* The tracks were great—clean, big, and solid. When it didn't sell, of course *then* they said it sounded like shit.

Joe Perry: I didn't want to do a live album at the time because there were so many perfect live albums coming out, all doctored and fixed and overdubbed. Big deal. Double live album—"standard of the industry." I felt like we had to avoid that and do a real live album like *Live at Leeds* or *Get Yer Ya-Ya's Out* or that old Kinks album. So I was trying to think of something that would justify a live album in my head.

Then we started finding these old tapes. The two Paul's Mall tracks, "I Ain't Got You" and "Mother Popcorn," are legitimate bootleg tapes. Someone taped it off the air on cassette. Everybody said, "Two-track? Too much hiss! We can't put that on the album." And we said, "What the fuck do you think they did ten years ago?" So we did a stereo mix for the album, and we wanted to put it on because that's what we sounded like long before anyone knew who we were.

ROLLING STONE
With the passage of time, even the truly monstrous becomes bearable, maybe even enjoyable in a perverse sort of way . . . sounds

like it was recorded inside a shoebox, using two tin cans and a couple yards of telephone wire . . . hoarse, spasmodic shrieks . . . the two guitars thrash around like a brontosaurus trying to get small animals off its back . . . (January 25, 1979)

5: Here's Glass in Your Eye

Laura Kaufman: Steven married Cyrinda on September 1, 1978. I went up to Sunapee for the wedding, which was on a mountaintop overlooking everything. It was the end of the summer and had a kind of wistful Labor Day feeling. It was casual dress, summertime, a much looser wedding than Joe's. There was a reception at Kingridge afterward and everyone had a great time. Cyrinda was five months pregnant.

Aerosmith's Bootleg tour began on September 27, 1978, at Memorial Auditorium in Buffalo and ran through December, touring behind the new live album and their hit single "Come Together." It was a tumultuous lurch around the country, ducking cherry bombs, beer bottles, Frisbees, hats, jackets, and scarves hurled onstage by the red-eyed Blue Army four nights a week, and feelings were running high. AC/DC, the Australian metal band managed by Leber-Krebs, opened most of the shows, along with Exile and Golden Earring in the later part of the tour.

Also on tour that autumn were the Eagles, Queen, Blondie, Bob Dylan, Jethro Tull, Alice Cooper, Neil Young, Van Morrison, Frank Zappa, Foreigner, Peter Gabriel, Genesis, and Hall and Oates. Led Zeppelin was finished as a touring band after Robert Plant's son died while the band was on the road the previous year. New bands Van Halen and Cheap Trick were beginning their careers. The Sex Pistols came to America and broke up on the road. Bassist Sid Vicious murdered his girlfriend and OD'd a few days later. Keith Moon, madcap drummer for the Who, died on September 7 of an overdose of a sedative he was taking to combat persistent alcoholism.

Aerosmith was in rough shape. The road crew was missing some familiar faces, including stage manager Joe Baptista, who took three weeks off to mourn a death in his family. (He was replaced by Ted Nugent's stage manager.) Friends of the band remarked that keyboardist Mark Radice looked like the only guy in Aerosmith who was going to live through the tour. Brad was in the middle of a divorce. Steven had a seizure after shooting up too much cocaine in his bathroom at Lake Sunapee. Joe Perry's injured hand still ached from the Philadelphia attack and had a horrible purple blotch right over the vein.

Henry Smith: You know why they were called the Toxic Twins? Because they'd take whatever drugs you put in front of them. And people were *always* putting drugs in front of them. I'd find Steven comatose in the dressing room twenty minutes before they were supposed to play to 30,000 kids. My job was to bring him around. I'd hold up two fingers. He'd insist there were four. The promoter's screaming outside the door, and I'm going, *Oh, God.*

When he came to, Steven started to complain: the monitor mix, missing lights, why can't we get anything right? You wanted to kill him. I'd carry him to the stage, piggyback, so it looked like it was a joke. Steven didn't want the fans to see that he literally couldn't walk. Then he'd get going on some cocaine and go on automatic pilot onstage and some of the shows were great. Unless he keeled over.

Cobo Hall, Detroit. Notre Dame Athletic Center. "Festival seating" was the order of the day, general admission, so the floors of the arena were packed thick with wriggling teenagers pressed up against Aerosmith's custom-designed steel mesh security fence with 120 decibels of power rolling out the front of the stage.

Toledo Sports Arena. Fort Wayne Coliseum, Thursday night, October 3, where zealous cops bust thirty fans for drinking beer, smoking cigarettes, and marijuana possession during Aerosmith's set. Steven's seamstress is arrested and manhandled for lighting a cigarette backstage. Steven stopped the show to complain about the police, referring to them as "scumbags" and "Gestapo." Aerosmith was then threatened with arrest on incitement to riot. Tyler publicly offered bail to anyone who was arrested. Twenty-eight fans accepted. Next day Aerosmith's tour accountant went to court and paid out $4,200 in bail and fines.

Riverfront Coliseum, Cincinnati. Two years later, eleven fans would be crushed to death in a "festival seating" melee during a Who concert. Aerosmith heard someone was shot at this show, but the stadium's management later denied it. Market Square Arena, Indianapolis. Wings Stadium, Kalamazoo. Pine Bluff Convention Center. St. Paul Civic Arena. Dane County Coliseum, Madison, Wisconsin.

Tom Hamilton: We were all staying at the Whitehall Hotel in Chicago and flying out to gigs by Learjet. I called it Heroin Hotel for obvious reasons.

Karen Whitford: The Whitehall in Chicago? Oh, God. We were based there for a month. Cyrinda had been staying in Sunapee but came out to be on the road.

One night we all went out to hear Karen Lawrence's band, and afterward we were in Joe and Elyssa's suite because Joe and Brad wanted to jam. And Joe's taping this jam on a cassette player that he borrowed from Steven.

A day or two later, the phone rang in our room at 7 A.M. It was Cyrinda, really angry, like I'd never heard. "Come down to the room right now. Right now!" I went to their suite—Joe and Steven had suites; Tom, Joey, and Brad got rooms—and there's Cyrinda, Steven, and the tape recorder he had loaned to Joe. Cyrinda says, "We want you to hear this." She turned on the tape.

ROCKY DONOHOE [AEROSMITH BODYGUARD]: "So I went in the room, and Steven's pants are down, and Karen Lawrence is there, and . . ."

ELYSSA: "HaHaHaHaHaHaHa!"

ROCKY: "Jeezus, he was practically glued to her in the bar the night before . . ."

And I'm wondering, *How did they get this tape?* Later Brad explained that Joe had borrowed the tape recorder and must have returned it with the tape of their jam still in it. We'd had this conversation, not knowing it was on the tape! The amazing thing was that Steven heard it and then deliberately played it for Cyrinda.

So Cyrinda stormed up to Elyssa's room. She's eight months pregnant, and she and Elyssa got into a fistfight. *Terrible.* Hotel security came up and pulled them apart. A very ugly scene, and things between Steven and Joe went immediately downhill, as you can imagine.

Terry Hamilton: That's what we heard: Elyssa tried to kick Cyrinda in the stomach after the tape incident. It really tore things apart. Cyrinda went back to Sunapee to have her baby and she was very worried. She'd call me and say she was scared that their baby wouldn't have a brain stem because of all the drugs.

Joey Kramer: The second half of the tour we were based in Boston, commuting to shows on a nine-seat Learjet. On November 21, we took off from Logan for the night's show in Syracuse, climbed to 10,000 feet. Steven was sitting in the last seat on the left side of the plane. I'm in front. Suddenly there's an explosion in the rear of the cabin and the plane is rocking and I'm thinking, *Now what'd he do?* We all turned white and felt our hearts begin to beat faster. Then it got really hot. Harold Buker comes back and checks things out and tells us we've blown an air pressure hose—first time he'd ever seen one go in thirty-five years in the air. Emergency landing time. Change planes. Golden Earring already offstage in Syracuse and they're waiting for us. But we never got to Syracuse that night. We did a make-up gig a few weeks later and one of the equipment trailers jackknifed on the New York Thruway.

Ray Tabano: On November 24, they played Madison Square Garden and were great, incredible. There was a big party afterward, everyone totally blotto. This was the night that Aerosmith and Ted Nugent were on *The Midnight Special* TV show and everyone watched.

Brad Whitford: On November 25, we finally went back to Philadelphia, the first time we'd played the Spectrum since the M-80 attack. [Near the hall, a large billboard read: WE'RE SORRY ABOUT LAST TIME, AEROSMITH. GLAD YOU'RE BACK!] We were really up for this show, one of the few times we did a sound check on that tour. Five songs into a sold-out show, someone threw a beer bottle from the balcony. It hit the stage dead center, right in front of the monitor, and exploded, sending shards of glass into Steven's face. I think some glass went right through his mouth. That's it. Backstage, Steven's holding a towel to his bloody face, and he wants to go back on! The vote was four-to-one against, and we were in the limos two minutes later. Fuck this. Police cars screaming up to the building to stop whatever riot was coming.

ROLLING STONE

Aerosmith is a dinosaur among bands, the last of a generation of rock 'n' rollers being edged out by more streamlined competition like Boston, Foreigner, and Fleetwood Mac.

What keeps Aerosmith rocking is their ability to relate to their loyal, largely male audience. Night after night, the band's success or failure hinges on something that's hard to package; they have to tap into a little of the teenage insanity that lures you to rock 'n' roll in the first place. (February 22, 1979)

GROOVES #5

Crude but real, Aerosmith will never be artsy-fartsy or simple-minded. Their message relates to the pains of growing up in a cold world, wanting everything, getting nothing. (Queen/Aerosmith issue, August 1978)

Card tricks on the Learjet. Rolling joints. Turbulence. "Air pocket!" Aerosmith plays for two hours in Boston Garden for the first time in two years. Five hundred guests assembled backstage while the Boston audience refused to let their band go. In Dallas, the band faces a furious bombardment of flying objects. Joe Perry wandered over to the guitar tech and said, "Maybe if I worked harder on my guitar playing, we'd attract a better class of people."

Joey Kramer's fingertips were bruised and swollen. The spaces between his thumbs and forefingers were black and blue.

Steven Tyler: It got really bad with Joe and Elyssa. When we'd start "Dream On," I'd be here, working with Tom and Brad and Joey, and Joe's over in his corner with Elyssa at the side of his amps—she's in all the pictures right *there*—and we'd start "Dream On" and he'd look at her and they'd laugh. At me. It really hurt bad. It may seem weird, but it was a huge issue. The band I had with this guy was . . . gone.

In December, Columbia released the studio version of "Chip Away the Stone" as a non-LP single. It got to #77 before the band left the road.

Tulsa, Oklahoma. Last show of the tour. Steven in satin jumpsuit and long leopardskin coat. Tom paces with his Music Man bass. Joey behind his white Ludwig drums, wearing a Zildjian T-shirt. Joe Perry wears his huge tiger's claw pendant and plays his new left-handed Stratocaster. Two other Strats are with him onstage, as well as an array of B. C. Rich and Dan Armstrong guitars and a '65 Telecaster. Brad deploys two B. C. Rich Eagles, a new Les Paul Custom, and a self-customized "Rich Bich" ten-string. Both guitarists use foot pedals to manipulate the "toybox" effects used all over the music. The hall is filled to capacity with boys in denim jackets with hand-lettered Aerosmith logos on the back, holding aloft lighters and flaming books of matches in the dark even before the band comes out.

Black curtain parts, spotlights blasting on and off. Steven wields his mike like a spear as Joe fires up "Toys in the Attic" and the whole building seems to launch off its pad like an Apollo mission.

There was a party after the show. Aerosmith and the crew rented the Presidential Suite plus thirty-five rooms at the local Holiday Inn. When the sun rose that morning, no one realized it would be one of the last parties the band would have for many years.

Terry Hamilton: Cyrinda's daughter, Mia Abagale Tallarico, was born right after that tour [December 22, 1978]. I remember after she was born Cyrinda called me, really excited. "Terry! She has ten fingers! Ten toes! She's beautiful. She's perfect!"

6: Right in the Nuts

Ray Tabano: By 1979, my time with Aerosmith was almost up. I'd been working at the Wherehouse since we built it, doing the fan club and shirt business. I edited the fan club newsletter, *Aero Knows*, for three years. Our motto: "You belong." We had 40,000 names on our mailing list and an average 8 percent bounce-back on buttons, patches, and shirts, which was a big deal back then. When the WBCN staff went on strike against the station's ownership in 1978, I'd print up a special edition Aerosmith shirt supporting the strike. That kind of thing. I also did stuff for Teddy [Nugent]. On the back of the newsletter, I'd run a fake Dewar's Profile ad roasting Krebs or Henry Smith.

I kept good records of our shirt sales and at the end of the *Bootleg* tour, I showed the band charts that said they were owed about $85,000 each. I asked for an exclusive contract to do the shirts, and Steven and Joe said OK. David Krebs called me the next day and said, "You're fired for going to the band behind our backs."

Krebs-Leber busted my balls good, made my life miserable, because they wanted me out. They gave me a $3,000 golden handshake and that was it. They told the band, "He stole from us." Not true. Nothing. Never. Not a dime. Anyway, that was when I left—and just in time too.

Steven Tyler: *Draw the Line* was a failure as, you know, "product." It came out and flopped after two incredibly successful albums. It was obvious that the creative relationship wasn't happening with Jack and we needed a new producer.

Tom Hamilton: Jack had left his wife and family for a new woman, which I remember really thinking was not too cool.

Steven Tyler: We'd spent time with Jack's wife and we liked her. I'd leave the Record Plant to write lyrics in an upstairs room in their home in New Jersey. She was a homebody, with thick glasses, a real mom, a wonderful person.

Tom Hamilton: Jack was a big wheel now, an important guy with money, success, and the sex appeal that goes with it. Life on the wild side, right? But that was Jack. He's a daredevil and was really into it. I was uncomfortable with it, like seeing someone I didn't know, because Jack was so into his family.

So we got this English guy, Gary Lyons, who had produced Foreigner. [Lyons had also worked with Humble Pie. An engineer as well as a producer, he had a production deal with Columbia.] He wore white boots. I called him Mr. Mug-ee, because he got mugged on the streets of New York two or three times during the record we did with him.

Steven Tyler: A living, walking victim. A personality that reeked of timidity. But I really liked his drum sound.

Tom Hamilton: Somebody threw a snake at Gary Lyons, and that snake was Aerosmith. We were raging along, man. Our creative processes were . . . pretty fucked up.

Jack Douglas: I think the label finally put a lot of pressure on them. It was: "Look at these sales numbers. Come up with another hit or there's gonna be trouble." David [Krebs] thought I no longer exercised control of the band, which was true. No one did.

Steven and Joe told me that Gary Lyons was coming in. Joe was especially adamant because he was so dissatisfied with the band. Joe said to me, "You aren't doing the next record." But it wasn't a real blow because I could see it falling apart. Joe had some tracks that could have saved Aerosmith. He had the next hit record they needed. But he held it back. He didn't give it to them because he was doing a solo album. And he was saying to me, "We're *both* outta here 'cause I'm getting out too."

What Joe didn't want to deal with anymore was pressure from his wife. But still I never thought that Joe could go off on his own. He had a drug problem, couldn't sing worth shit, couldn't hold a note to sing background even. But Elyssa could be pretty tough. She told him that he should have his own career and he wanted out.

Joe Perry: We started *Night in the Ruts* with Jack in the spring of 1979. I'm not sure why he wasn't involved later on, but he wasn't. We rehearsed a bunch of songs at the Wherehouse. Next thing we're down in New York to cut the tracks and Steven didn't have the vocals. It was hard for him, and this time he just couldn't come up with the lyrics. So the album got delayed. We were supposed to tour that summer and play with Led Zeppelin at Knebworth in England, but with no album it all got canceled.

There was other stuff going on at the same time. We had a very big, very rare financial meeting with Krebs. He says to me, "Well, Joe, actually you're in debt to the band for room service."

"Oh, yeah? How much do I owe?"

"$80,000."

He gave everybody a list. Each of us owed some money, but I owed $80,000. I got really pissed at this, because after the third album I was always questioning Krebs about how much we were making. Then I got Elyssa's cousin Cosmo, the only lawyer I knew, and had him look at the contracts when it came time to re-sign with Leber-Krebs. Cosmo met with them and they fuckin' steamrolled him.

I knew there was something wrong. We sold all these records, we couldn't play a place and not sell it out, we were making tons of money, it was the height of our career. "What is this $80,000 bullshit? What can I do about this?"

"Well, you could make a solo record. Get an advance and everything will be fine."

"OK, that's a good idea." That's how the seed was planted for a solo record. But at that point, I still had no intention of leaving the band.

Dr. J. Jones and the Interns resurfaced at the Main Act nightclub in Lynn, Mass., on March 27, to get ready for gigs in Omaha and Wichita after four months off the road. In April, Aerosmith headlined the two-day California World Music Festival at the L.A. Coliseum with Van Halen and Toto. The band flew to Florida, visited Walt Disney World, and headlined the Florida World Music Festival with Ted Nugent and Cheap Trick and one of David Krebs's beloved fireworks displays.

Backstage, Joe Perry was approached by Ralph Mormon, who had been the singer in the Boston band Daddy Warbux and was now working construction jobs. Mormon asked Joe, "Do you know anyone who's looking for a lead singer?" To Mormon's astonishment, Joe replied, "Yeah. Me."

Joe Perry: I had five things and I still like some of the stuff we did for *Night in the Ruts*. "Cheesecake" was done in one take with no overdubs, adapted from a Wherehouse track called "Let It Slide." I started the track playing a regular six-string, changed to a lap-steel, played bottleneck for the solo, and then back to the six-string, all live. Which is an indication of how weird things were, because even though the band was falling apart in every other way, we could still play really well together when we wanted to.

Most of the time, though, we just stopped giving a fuck. The Aerosmith album was in limbo from April on and at a certain point I had to wash my hands of it. I said, "It's your album. Do what you want with it. You've got my work. You can use it or erase it. I'm working on something else." My last session was on May 30, 1979. We cut a thirty-second jam labeled "Shithouse Shuffle" that I thought was pretty cool and filed it away for future use. *Maybe someone will be interested in it someday*, I thought.

Tom Hamilton: We worked on the album, but we couldn't finish it. It was supposed to come out in June and be called *Off Your Rocker*, but there were no lyrics. It was a big crisis. David Krebs took out three months to do the album and then booked gigs for that summer, months in advance, twenty-five huge festivals with Ted Nugent that we couldn't cancel out on without devastation. It was the worst frustration we'd ever faced, going out on the road before the album was finished. Krebs told us we had to, and everybody was freaked out, especially Joe

Perry. I remember coming down to New York one night, having long before finished my tracks, on one of my periodic in-the-loop visits. Someone said the lyrics still weren't finished and wouldn't be anytime soon. I got drunk on Jack Daniel's, came in the studio where they were working on overdubs, and made a scene. "Where are the vocals? I came down to hear some fuckin' vocals!" They just looked at me.

At the same time, we could see that Joe was working up his solo career in front of us. At one gig, someone said that Ralph Mormon was available. Joe says, "Oh? Really?" Next thing we knew, Joe had contacted him and was going forward with his solo record.

Joe Perry: There was all this fighting and bad energy going on. It was the long hot summer of '79. We're in New York, living in hotels, with no work getting done because we'd recorded all the tracks live in the studio and had no lead vocals. I was dissatisfied with Krebs, said, "Fuck this," and went back to Boston. Elyssa wanted me to quit the band. We consulted a music lawyer and he encouraged me to quit. And my ego was in the right place where I was willing to hear this. I was tired of all the fighting. Other stuff was going on. I was stopped for speeding and thrown in jail for an old warrant I'd already paid off.

One day around that time, I was flying to New York in Steven's plane with Zunk's father, Elyssa, and Rocky to do some tracks. I'd been up for a couple of days working on songs, hadn't eaten or slept. So we're on the runway, we got clearance, and just as he nailed the engines I had a convulsion right there—eyes back in head, stiffened up, passed out. The pilot aborted the takeoff and notified the tower, who sent out the state police in response. I woke up in the emergency room, where the doctors told me I was malnourished.

Then we had to go back out on the road before the album was done, because we needed money. We heard rumors that the album we were working on would never come out. Suddenly we were playing to 60,000 people again at JFK Stadium. It was pretty nuts. Then Elyssa and Terry Hamilton had a fight in Cleveland and it was all over after that. If we'd gone on vacation instead, it might have saved us.

7: Spilt Milk

On July 28, 1979, Aerosmith headlined the World Series of Rock at Cleveland Stadium with Ted Nugent and Thin Lizzy. The band's dressing room, as at most stadium shows, was a trailer, or mobile home, set up in the end zone.

Steven Tyler: This is where we started talking about our women, and it got way out of hand. It really lit the fuse. I remember saying to Joe in the trailer, "How could you let your old lady *do* that? How can you let her *be* like that?"

Tom Hamilton: Terry could be very blunt and really nail somebody, and I guess she said something to Elyssa, who threw a glass of milk at her. So there was this physical confrontation between them before we went on at Cleveland. It was loud. There was yelling, and we could hear it. No one got hurt, but it was also a reflection of the conflicts going on in the band.

There had been a pattern at the shows that summer where Steven would do something to piss Joe off, then Joe would cold-shoulder Steven onstage—it would be very obvious—Joe making a point of not singing his vocals and playing *real* loud, and Steven'd get even more pissed off and do or say something to Joe that would drive him even further away from the band.

By the end of this particular night, I remember Steven was over the top, he was so angry. We came offstage and went right into the trailer and we were freaked at Joe and started yelling at him. And then Joe's answer finally was "Well, maybe I should leave the band then." And Steven said, "Yeah, well, maybe you fuckin' should." And the rest of us stood there, basically agreeing with Steven. And then Joe stormed out.

Steven Tyler: That night—I remember it so well—Joe goes, "Maybe I should leave the band." I said, "Yeah, maybe you fuckin' should." Joe goes, "Oh, yeah?" and gets up. And I yell, "FUCK YOU

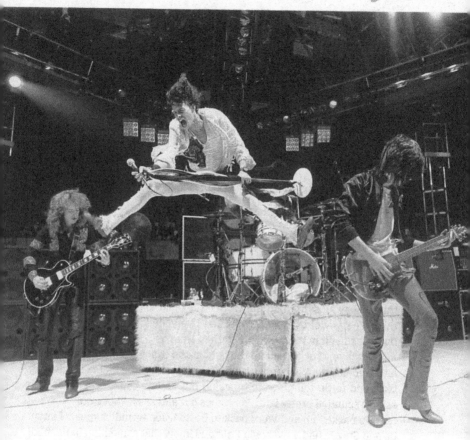

(PHOTO: RON POWNALL)

THEN! GET THE FUCK OUTTA HERE!!!" And he left. Aerosmith literally broke up over spilt milk.

I swore that night I'd never play onstage with Joe Perry again as long as I lived.

The drugs won.

Tom Hamilton: We very strongly agreed, after that Cleveland show, that Joe should leave. I was convinced that we had thrown him out of the band. I vividly remember stepping down out of that trailer onto the

ground. Joe had gone flying out, and I thought, *That's it. The band is over.*

The funny thing was we didn't talk about it. This became a dead baby in the closet, because we wanted to keep the old ladies out of it. Throwing *milk?* We didn't want this to get out, and it didn't for years.

Brad Whitford: I wouldn't even change in the dressing room because they were screaming and throwing shit. I thought, *These guys are nuts.* I'd just get my bag and go. Total insanity, and no part for me to play in it. Being in Aerosmith was like walking into a dogfight and both dogs bite you. Cleveland was just another show for me, hanging out with Bon Scott of AC/DC, drinking a beer and digging on the scene, trying to stay out of trouble.

Elyssa Perry: Something happened. Things were said. Terry and I didn't get along at all. I remember asking her something—sarcastic—and she might have thrown some ice at me. I had a glass of milk in my hand because I drank milk exclusively, and . . .

Then the guys started fighting. Tom said something, Joe said something. They all started fighting. Then they had to go onstage and it was the best show of the tour. Awesome! Everyone loved it. They were the best rock band in the world when they were on.

Offstage, they picked up the fight at the exact same spot that they'd left it when they went up the ramp. They went into the trailer, it's rocking back and forth, things were breaking but no one could hear what was said. It sounded pretty bad. Joe comes out and says, "Let's go."

We packed up and went back to Boston. Joe wouldn't speak. I knew he and Steven had a really big fight and knew that something happened, but he wouldn't speak to me for two weeks after that. It was always really stupid. Of course we were all insane. We were really young, made a lot of money, no kids. What do you do? Buy a home and party. That's what we did. And Joe doesn't like to talk to people. He'd say, "Tell so-and-so to do this," and I'd go tell them and suddenly I was like this bitch who wanted something done for myself. He did that a lot, and it was screwed up.

David Krebs: After the show in Cleveland, we all sat down, and instead of trying to hold it together, I agreed with Steven and said, "Let's break this up." She [Elyssa] was a big problem and I was a lot closer to Steven than I was to Joe Perry, and I think in retrospect I really underestimated Joe's musical importance. But there was this unspoken romantic implication—real or otherwise—of Elyssa and Joe versus Steven. This was from way back in Sunapee.

Rumors that Joe Perry had left Aerosmith began to circulate in the music business in August 1979, when the band's management canceled dates on a projected world tour that would have taken Aerosmith back to Europe and Japan late that year. Publicity outlets like Hit Parader and Circus continued to insist that Joe was still in the band. "We're doing the Aerosmith album right now," Joe was quoted in Hit Parader, "but I'm also about to make a deal to do my solo album. I've wanted to do one for a while and I've got some songs of my own I want to get out. Look, I feel strongly about Aerosmith because I put nine years of my life into it. It's my first love. It's a club I've been in for a long time and I don't want to quit it."

8: No Surprize

Tom Hamilton: There was a sense of relief after that day in Cleveland. When Joe was finally gone, I was strangely elated. Absolutely. I wouldn't have to spend my days playing games with Joe and Elyssa and Terry. I actually looked forward to going out and getting another guitar player and just continuing along without interruption. And Steven had that same feeling. At the same time, there was this undercurrent, because this *was* his partner. Brad Whitford was also less than thrilled about the situation.

Anyway, we were working at Media Sound in New York that summer, trying to finish the record that was supposed to be out in September. We had three tracks in the can: "Chiquita," "Reefer Head Woman," and "Remember," the Shangri-Las' song. We needed a guitar player to help us finish and go on the road. The first one we auditioned was Michael Schenker, this German rocker that Leber-Krebs managed.

Steven Tyler: He came to the studio, the way he walked in, it was like . . .

Tom Hamilton: It was like *Wolfen*. He was this blond guy in black leather regalia with penetrating laser eyes.

Steven Tyler: It was Raymond all over again. Personified. "Hello—I'm taking over. Before I join your band, I vant it clear I'm taking over right now. Here—my jacket—take and hang up."

Tom Hamilton: He was this boy genius that couldn't speak English too well. He had these classical-sounding guitar riffs, echo-reverb stuff, very European-sounding leads played on classical scales instead of blues scales. Gary Lyons insulted him and I think he ended up walking out.

Then we auditioned Derringer's guitarist, Danny Johnson, who'd been jamming with Brad in a trio called Axis in Los Angeles.

Brad Whitford: They said we were gonna audition guitar players. I asked, "Can we do this?" It didn't seem right to me, but—what were we gonna do? "So—let's try to put somebody in that spot." We saw some people and Danny Johnson was the best. If his hair was longer, he would've been the guy, because he played so good. But he'd just gotten a haircut and Steven didn't like it.

Steven Tyler: I think Jack Douglas knew Jimmy Crespo. He was twenty-three, from Brooklyn, had done some sessions, and came highly recommended. When I saw Jimmy, I thought, *That's it. He looks like Joe. He can really play.* He could *fingerpick!!* I went, *Wow*. He had his own technique, a classical background. He was in good soil for three years. We recorded *Night in the Ruts* mostly at Media Sound. Memories are a bit hazy: Billy Brigode burying money, dropping huge bundles of cash, lots of pot, Learjets. We got a room together: incredible heroin, duffel bags of cash, packets of twenties. I had to get cash advances from my manager to buy dope. We were supposed to be on $500 a week salary for the rest of the year.

One night: we lay out some lines of heroin and go out to eat in the diner around the corner from the studio—The Blue Jay—because we had guys who worked for us who'd look on the amps for lines we didn't do. They'd lick 'em and touch 'em. We came back an hour later and one of the tape ops was on the floor. He was turning blue and it looked like his heart had stopped. We almost had to call the ambulance but George Schak, who worked for us, finally brought him around.

Heroin. Shooting coke. Eating opium and it was just . . . I love that album—*Night in the Ruts*. It's like a fuckin' solar eclipse.

Tom Hamilton: One night we're in the St. Regis Hotel and Steven calls me and tells me to come down to his room. When I got there, he read me the lyrics to "No Surprize."

Steven Tyler: For two months, I'd been totally blocked, writing lyrics for this track we had done with Joe. "My name is nah nah nah, I come from Yonkers High, and I get drunk at night." One night I had such a revelation to write the story of the band, how Aerosmith got started:

> Nineteen seventy one
> We all heard the starter's gun
> New York was such a pity
> but at Max's Kansas City we won
> We all shot the shit at the bar
> With Johnnie O'Toole and his scar
> And then ol' Clive Davis said he's surely gonna make us a star
> "I'm gonna make you a star
> Just the way you are"
> But with all his style I could see in his eyes that we is going on trial
> It was no surprize . . .

It was like Helen Keller at the pump handle. I was so excited to be back on track. "Hey, guys! Listen to this!"

Tom Hamilton: We loved the lyrics because they were all true. Even the line about getting pot from the police came from an incident in Charleston, West Virginia, where the cops gave the band some pot they'd confiscated.

Anyway, Steven called me down to his room. He would have called Joe, but Joe was gone. The unfinished guitar parts on *Night in the Ruts* were played by Jimmy Crespo and Richie Supa.

Steven Tyler: Ever since I saw Mary Weiss in the bathroom in Cleveland when I was in the Chain Reaction I had this fantasy about the Shangri-Las and so I cut this song, "Remember (Walking in the Sand)." I harassed the singers—Beth Sussman and someone else—to whisper "Remember" with the little gasp at the end the way the Shangri-Las had done it. It took two hours to get that little gasp.

"Three Mile Smile" comes from the whole era of No Nukes and atomic energy paranoia. Three Mile Island had nearly melted down [March 1979] and everyone was freaked that year. That summer I was at the famous MUSE [Musicians United for Safe Energy] concert at Madison Square Garden, a complete blackout. I'm hanging backstage with David Crosby, Carly, Springsteen. I'm stoned. Supposed to sing the encore with Carly and all them, rewritten lyrics to some famous song, had lyrics written all over my arm. I'm out there singing away, two or three choruses, the place is standing up . . . I turn around and everybody's gone. I'm so high that I'm still out there at the mike, just me and the drummer. People are leaving the hall.

Tom Hamilton: People looked at us as a trashy, cheap band. Aerosmith was the stoned cousin who said something to embarrass you at the party.

Steven Tyler: "Bone to Bone (Coney Island Whitefish Boy)" is one of the tracks from before Joe left, along with "Chiquita," "Cheesecake," "Three Mile Smile," and "No Surprize." I had to explain to the press that a Coney Island whitefish is a used rubber. "Reefer Head Woman" was a 1940s blues record. I had the lyrics in a notebook that got stolen, and I had to call Dr. Demento from the Record Plant, where we finished the album, and the Doctor read the lyrics to me over the phone. "Think About It" was the Yardbirds' song. Joe Perry played on all these tracks and we left his leads on.

The album ended with "Mia," an Aerosmith ballad with Richie Supa and guitar tech Neil Thompson playing guitars. It was a lullaby I wrote on the piano for my daughter, but the tolling bell notes at the end of the song and the end of the album sounded more like the death knell of Aerosmith for people who knew what was going on.

On October 10, 1979, Leber-Krebs issued a press release:

Joe Perry and Aerosmith announced today in New York Perry's plans to depart the group to pursue a solo career. Perry's departure will officially commence upon completion of the new Aerosmith album, *Night in the Ruts*. Perry will remain on CBS and will continue to be managed by Leber-Krebs, the New York-based managers of Aerosmith. Perry plans a January release of his solo effort, the Joe Perry Project. His departure is described as amicable and his desire to explore a new musical direction has been cited as his reason for leaving the group.

Joe Perry: There was one of those moments around that time when I had the Aerosmith itinerary in one hand and my demo tapes in the other. It was a question of either playing the same songs again in the same fifty arenas or go out with my new band, not for the money but for the music again, for the sound, for the buzz of going back and playing the clubs and theaters.

I didn't feel great about leaving Aerosmith before the album was finished. At the time, I thought *Ruts* would be the last real Aerosmith album, and I told people I wasn't happy with the way it sounded because I hadn't been there for the mix.

Steven Tyler: If Joe had come to the studio instead of being home with his other band, he might have had more to say about the album. As it was, I had to bust my hump to get him down there to fuckin' do overdubs and put leads on. But he was pissed off. He was upset. He wouldn't come down. I tried my damndest. That's when our friendship broke up. I kept calling and calling. When I got through, he told me he wanted excitement, wanted to play clubs. I go, "Fuck you! Nobody in their *right mind* wants to go back and play clubs the rest of their lives after becoming a big band." We were playing to the biggest audiences at the time. "What the hell do you wanna go play in clubs again for?"

Joe Perry: I knew that Steven had mixed feelings because I did too. It was very hard. I thought that we'd had a lot of trouble dealing with each other for a while, but as I told people, it was always a love-hate relationship anyway. That's what gave it the power and the energy it had.

Joey Kramer: I wish someone had smacked us back then. But we were one of the biggest bands in the world. There was literally no one who could tell us anything.

Joe Perry: We were completely isolated, from our families, from anybody who was sane. No one had a clue, least of all management. The people around us fostered the isolation. We were wicked paranoid. At any moment, anyone in the band could get busted for holding drugs.

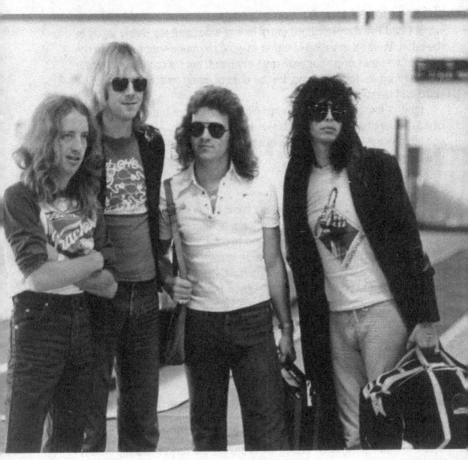

1979
(PHOTO: RON POWNALL)

We had a total outlaw mentality. We couldn't have anybody sane around us even if we wanted to; no sane person would stay up all night with us and then sleep all day. Anyone who got close to us was probably on the same trip we were.

It's amazing no one in the band ever died.

There were a lot of casualties. There are people out there who never completely recovered from trying to hang on to us around that time.

Night in the Ruts *was released in November 1979. It had cost over $1 million to make, most of it in wasted studio time when no one showed up. Joe Perry was on the album cover (the "Chip Away the Stone" miner photo) and played on five tracks. Jimmy Crespo and Richie Supa contributed guitar parts after Joe left the band. The (surprisingly strong) album, greeted in the press by a virulent tirade of critical abuse, made the Top 20 by the end of the year. Columbia released "Remember (Walking in the Sand)" as a single and promoted the album with the slogan "Aerosmith—Right Where It Hurts." That same month* Live! Bootleg *was awarded a platinum record.*

On November 16, 1979, the rip-roaring Joe Perry Project played its first gig, at Boston College. Steven Tyler appeared in the dressing room to say hello but left before the show began. Brad Whitford stayed for the show. On December 16, the Project sold out the Paradise on Commonwealth Avenue, got rave reviews from the local press, and the buzz was out: Joe Perry's new band was a monster.

Aerosmith's Night in the Ruts *arena tour was canceled. In early December 1979, at the band's Wherehouse in Waltham, where the Joe Perry Project was rehearsing, local kids spray-painted graffiti on the exterior wall by the door where the band parked their cars:*

GOOD LUCK JIMMY

COME BACK JOE!

Yo! Tyler! Hey! Where's Joe Fuckin' Perry??

8

Our story is basically
that we had it all
and then we pissed it away.

—Joe Perry

I snorted my airplane,
I snorted my Porsche,
I snorted my house,
It all went bye-bye.

—Steven Tyler

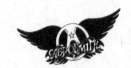

1: The Joe Perry
Project

Joe Perry: I was set up. It felt like that. It was: "Do a solo record, but don't break the band up." Leber-Krebs are going, "Yeah, let him do the solo record, let him fail, then we'll get him back."

There was a big Aerosmith tour planned after *Night in the Ruts* came out, and I realized they didn't give two shits if I had a solo thing I was supposed to do. Nothing mattered, they were going on tour, the same songs, the same bombed-out shows in the same stadiums. I thought, *I don't have any control over this anymore. I've gotta make a decision.* And I said, "Fuck 'em. I don't need them anymore. We're gonna fuckin' get on a bus and tour across the country, play theaters, and make a great record." I called some guys up and said, "Yeah, come join my band." I fired Krebs over the phone and was managing myself with this lawyer, Bob Casper. I was always on the phone with Leber-Krebs because they owed me money. As soon as I'd get an advance, I'd blow it and need another one.

It was a hard period in my life. There was a short time in there where I had no band, no recording contract, no management. It was just me and Elyssa alone in Boston. All I had was the idea to do some new music. I was psyched about doing my own thing, but a big part of me wanted to be in Aerosmith. A part of me was missing, and I just denied it.

But the seventies were over. I was almost thirty years old. Elyssa got pregnant by the end of the first Project tour.

The Joe Perry Project got put together over the summer of '79. Ralph Mormon was the singer. I remembered him from when Frank Connelly managed his outrageous band Daddy Warbux. He reminded me a lot of Paul Rodgers [from the English band Bad Company], always my favorite singer after Steven. Ralph was just great, but he drank a lot and was terrible on the road.

David Hull played bass and a lot of rhythm—really good. He came from a Connecticut band, the Dirty Angels. Before that, he'd played bass with Buddy Miles's band, which is how Steven knew him. Steven introduced me to David, who became my druggie bud. We roomed together, found girls to party with, copped dope. One of the first drummers we auditioned at the Wherehouse was Ronnie Stewart, who worked at E. U. Wurlitzer's music store in Boston. People told me he was the best drummer in Boston not involved in some other band. He was jazz-oriented but also played hot, funky rock and we hired him on the spot.

This band played all that summer and fall in my basement. Ronnie kept his day job. Our first gig was the Rathskeller—in reality, a cafeteria at Boston College—on November 17, 1979: I'm pacing nervously around a classroom upstairs, smoking two cigarettes at once. The set list was written on the blackboard. Steven Tyler came, said hello, and left before we played. People were kidding me: "Hey, you've played in arenas all over the world. What the fuck are you nervous about?" Little did they know.

The place was packed with kids hanging from the rafters and standing on tables. We played "Same Old Song and Dance," "Walk This Way," "Get the Lead Out." I sang on Jimi Hendrix's "Red House" and Elvis's "Heartbreak Hotel." We walked off and they started chanting, "We want Joe!" and "Two more!" We didn't know two more songs. The encore was "Life at a Glance," which I'd literally written the night before the gig. And that was it. The Joe Perry Project was off and running.

Brad Whitford: I went to Joe's first show at Boston College. People kept coming up to me and saying, "When are you guys getting back together?" I just told them, "When Steven and Joe bury the hatchets. Nothing I can even do."

Joe Perry: We rehearsed at the Wherehouse, which was like community property. I'd leave them [Aerosmith] notes on the blackboard, song lists, wiseguy stuff to provoke them. I tried to stay a little bit in touch. I'd stop by Tom's house on my motorcycle to say, "How ya doin'?" Brad brought over a copy of *Night in the Ruts* when it came out. I'd heard they'd gotten a couple of guitar players and I wished them the worst. I listened to it and was amazed that they'd left my parts on.

I had a new sense of freedom now, a focus on this new project. I was fucked up, but at least I had this band. I was full of fire that we were gonna have fun and make money, and from the start the fans didn't let me down. They came to the clubs and supported me and the band without an album, without anything except my name. We were rehearsing all week and doing clubs on the weekend, like every other band starting out. We used the clubs' PA systems and just tried to kick ass, create some excitement. I hadn't felt so turned on to playing in fuckin' *years*.

The Project did about ten gigs before I signed an album deal with Columbia. The label wasn't that eager because Aerosmith had been bringing albums in way late. But I went down and convinced them I was a walking, talking viability instead of the burn-out they thought I was. As soon as I knew I was doing a solo record, I called Jack Douglas. He said, "Fuck, yes!"

I was driven to write new stuff because I had a lot to get off my chest. I had something to prove. There was an element of risk.

I had always loved the punk thing. I was the one in the car playing the Sex Pistols. The rest of the band is going, "This *sucks*. Get this off." Those were the bands I liked: the Sex Pistols' energy, the pretentious Clash. The Police weren't punk, but their songs were short and punchy and I liked them. The economy of that sound was what I was after. Plus, I was writing lyrics about my life, leaving Aerosmith, taking on anxieties, and the songs reflected this maybe a little more than I was comfortable with. At the same time, I had these new tools, new possibilities.

Jack Douglas: I worked on Joe's first album at the Hit Factory [on West 48th Street in New York]. He played me the demos and I was pleasantly surprised by the tracks—*ferocious*. The title cut alone could have saved *Night in the Ruts*, but he had taken it with him. He held back some great songs, and he put together a really good band of his own.

I liked Ralph Mormon, who had a terrific voice, but Elyssa drew a line across the stage behind Joe and told the other band members: "Cross that line once, you're in trouble. Twice, by accident, OK. Three times and you're fired." Halfway through the first Project tour, Joe fired Ralph! He claimed he was watching the budget.

Joe Perry: We worked on the album for two months that winter, me and Elyssa living in Bob Casper's penthouse on Sutton Place, making the record with Jack. We cut the basic tracks in five days, finished the album in six weeks, and came in under budget. I'd preproduced, arranged everything at the Wherehouse, so we went in the studio and played the tracks live, no bullshit. It was like the first Aerosmith album—a soundtrack for the live shows. There was a lot of fun, dealers and friends in and out.

The songs came really fast. I wrote the riff on "Let the Music Do the Talking" when I was still in Aerosmith. It stuck to me like flypaper. The title of the song had to do with how sick I was of talking about Aerosmith. Let the music do the talking now. "Conflict of Interest" was about Krebs and my whole situation. "Rockin' Train" was the kind of funky, R&B-type song that I loved to do and could have done with Aerosmith. Ralph did the lyrics on that one. "Discount Dogs" was originally "Discount Drugs." "Break Song" was a jam we had. David Hull showed me the riff and I arranged it into one minute and fifty seconds of screaming guitar. "Shooting Star" and "Ready on the Firing Line" were just riffs that I liked. "The Mist Is Rising" was written at 4 A.M. at my house in Chestnut Hill. "Life at a Glance" was about my life, pure and simple. That was the record. I sang on four and a half songs, Ralph sang four and a half, and David Hull sang background vocals.

The album came out on Columbia in March 1980. The cover was a picture of nine suits sitting around a glass boardroom table. I'm standing up holding the master tape to the album. The reviewers were kind [*Creem:* "This album could boil Iran off the map."], but we didn't get much airplay. The fix was in and it didn't happen. [*Let the Music Do the Talking* got to #47, selling about a quarter of a million copies.] David Krebs has admitted burying the record on more than one occasion. Years later, Tim Collins heard from Bruce Lundvall that they made every effort to squash it in order to get me back in the band. It was fucked up.

There was another factor too. I was going after the feeling I got when I first heard the Sex Pistols. I'd been shut up in my basement, a frustrated New Waver. But by then the New Wave was already over. We [Aerosmith] had left this great gaping hole for the West Coast thing and for Van Halen. In 1979 Eddie Van Halen came out and started taking the lid off guitar playing again. Much later, Eddie told me that he'd started out on the suburban L.A. club circuit, playing Aerosmith songs.

I had to take the band on the road, so I rented this tour bus for the Project. This was my dream: Get on it and go. I'd never even been on a tour bus: bunk beds, lounge, bathroom, private compartment in the back, TV, VCR, the whole thing. This gleaming bus pulls up to my house, just as a friend of Jack's arrives with the most unbelievable heroin we'd ever seen. I figured I was gonna be away for six months, I didn't want to cop on the road, but I didn't want to be sick either. So I bought $6,000 worth.

I figured it would last.

I also went to a doctor in New York to get some Catapres, which took the edge off the heroin addiction. I got $1,000 worth of Darvon and Catapres from him. I got on the bus with the band and headed west.

2: Dark Night
of the Soul in
the Star Market

Joe Perry: We sold out almost every place we played.

Musically, they were some of the best moments of my career. I was playing real raw, very simply. I was using my left-handed Strat with a left-handed Telecaster neck and a midnight blue Travis Bean L-500 with dual pickups. I just went out every night and tried to blow them all away, real loud, real hard rock.

The only thing I really missed was Brad Whitford, my consummate string-bending comrade-in-arms. We had built up a certain chemistry that couldn't be replaced. I was shocked to realize that being the only guitar onstage meant I couldn't afford any off nights. Brad had backed me up, made me look good all those years.

I felt naked. I had to change my playing from long runs of notes to a more simultaneous lead/rhythm style.

I had wanted a change, and I got it.

The other thing was that Ralph Mormon was terrible on the road. He got shit-faced before shows until maybe the fourth show, when I smacked him around for fucking up. He wouldn't ride on the bus, so he'd follow us in a station wagon and would not get to the gig on time. He'd miss shows and disappear. If we made him ride in the bus, he'd fall asleep and piss in the bunk, which our driver took personally, creating a lot of tension.

The whole period is hazy. All I remember about San Francisco is that a friend of mine got me a lot of Dilaudids . . .

CREEM

Joe rises from the couch, strolls to the other side of the dressing room, plugs into an amp, and fingers a few warm-up riffs. A half hour later, he's attacking this same guitar on the small stage [of the Keystone in Berkeley, California], wrenching out howling leads and chugging rhythms . . .

Afterward, inside the Joe Perry Project tour bus parked in an alley behind the club, Perry cools out, changes clothes, and then emerges through a draped portal with his striking wife, Elyssa.

"Any future in it?" he asks as he settles into a cushy side chair. (Dave Zimmer, 1980)

Joe Perry: There was a lot of sniping back and forth. The press concentrated on me leaving Aerosmith. I said Aerosmith was ripping off its audience. I said I was embarrassed to get out there and play the same old shit because they wouldn't play new material that hadn't been recorded and put in front of an audience. I said they were afraid to take chances.

Tom Hamilton: The thing that Joe said that hurt the most was that Aerosmith wasn't ready for the eighties. It hurt so much because it was true.

Joe Perry: We finished the first Project tour in the late spring of '80. I was stretched to the limit with all the responsibility I'd taken on. The lows were really low, but the highs were higher too. The band was getting better every night, and when it was good it was like driving a Porsche with everything working right. We'd been playing clubs. The next tour would be a step up to theaters. I was talking about adding a second guitarist or a keyboard player to the Project to lighten the load on me a little.

One of the final gigs on that leg was in Texas, but we arrived there and they told us the gig got blown out, canceled. We found ourselves stuck in the Austin Travelodge with no money, no drugs except some speed and Catapres, and no credit cards to fly home on. I didn't have enough cash to get the bus back to New York. I was sick from abuse and the band started to fall apart. For a week, I gave them a little money and they spent their time getting drunk at Willie Nelson's club. Meanwhile in Boston, some heroin dealers had left a note on my Jeep parked in front of the house. It basically said: PAY UP OR WE'LL BREAK YOUR LEGS. My father-in-law found this under my windshield.

Elyssa finds out she's pregnant.

Stuck in Texas. I called Bob Casper, who came up with $10,000. It might have saved our lives.

The last club gig was at My Father's Place out on Long Island. I fired Ralph Mormon and replaced him with J. Mala [the singer for the New York club band Revolver] for the rest of the tour. He lasted for three gigs.

September 1980. John Bonham drank himself to death, which was the end of Led Zeppelin.

Two in the morning. I'm in the Star Market [supermarket] near my house in Chestnut Hill. Totally fucked up. A kid comes up to me and goes, " 'Scuse me, Mr. Perry, would you mind signing this?" My eyes swim into focus. He's holding somebody's album. The cover's red. I didn't know why he wanted me to sign it. I ask what it is and he goes, "Dude, it's your *new record!*"

Bastards! It was the first time I'd seen *Aerosmith's Greatest Hits*. Nobody even told me it was coming out. That's how out of the loop I was.

3: It Shook Everyone Up

Joe Perry: The Project played six nights a week on the road that fall [1980]. In October, we played in New York City for the first time, at the Palladium on 14th Street, which had been the Academy of Music when Aerosmith played there nine years earlier. It felt great—the show ended and the kids were on their chairs, chanting my name the way they used to chant Aerosmith's. The energy coming back from the fans was intense, really heavy. The economy was so bad that voters were about to get rid of Jimmy Carter and elect Ronald Reagan. Everyone was hurting financially, especially kids, who couldn't afford to see as many shows as they used to. So it meant a lot to me that they supported us.

In November, we started a six-week tour opening for Heart, which took us back around the country.

I was home in Boston one night in December when Jack Douglas called me. I was glad to hear from him, because he was originally going to produce the second Project album and it hadn't worked out, but I wasn't prepared for what he had to say.

Jack Douglas: I really got into heroin when I did *Let the Music Do the Talking* and for a while afterward I was isolating myself from the rest of the world. Then Yoko Ono called.

A year before, my wife and I had been having lunch in a restaurant in New York when she started to laugh at something happening behind my back. I turned around and there was John Lennon, making faces and goofing around, trying to get my attention. I hadn't really seen him since his "Lost Period" in L.A. in the early seventies, when I had been the getaway driver on the infamous Kotex-on-head drunken caper with Harry Nilsson.

He said, "Jack, I want to get back into it. I'm gonna make a record. Please call me." But I was busy and then was in California and didn't call him. I didn't want to bother the guy. He'd had a kid and was famous for taking care of him, obviously out of rock 'n' roll. I kept thinking: *One more call and I'll go.* But I put it off and didn't hear anything for a year.

At the time I was living with Rick Dufay, a guitar player I'd met when a girl on an airplane gave a friend of mine a tape of Rick to listen to. It was really good and I was gonna produce his band, but there were lawsuits flying everywhere and I was busy doing live Aerosmith stuff anyway. Rick and I became friends. One day he sees this voodoo charm around my neck and asked what it was. "Just something I got in Haiti," I told him. I was wearing it the night my son was conceived and had worn it ever since for good luck. "It isn't doing much good right now," I told him. Nothing was happening for me.

We were walking down Central Park West. When we got to 76th Street, Rick said, "That voodoo shit's run its course. Get rid of that thing." So I took it off and threw it over a wall into the churchyard. I'd been wearing the thing for years.

We went back to the house and ten minutes later Yoko Ono called and said, "John wants to talk to you about something very important." He was waiting for me at their house on the North Shore of Long Island, and she was sending her seaplane to pick me up at 29th Street and the East River. We flew to Glen Cove, landed right on the beach, pulled up to their gorgeous mansion. John wasn't there, but Yoko explained that John wanted to do an album. She handed me a thick envelope with John's writing on it: TO JACK DOUGLAS: FOR YOUR EYES AND EARS ONLY.

Yoko says, "I want to see that." "No, you can't," I said, beginning a series of major mind games with Yoko. Then John came back. "I want you to listen to these tapes, and I want it totally confidential. I don't know about any of this material, and I'm not sure I can do this. D'you understand, Jack? I want you to look over the material and if you like it, call me in Bermuda. Do the arrangements, hire the musicians, but keep it cool. I don't want anyone to know, not the press, not even the musicians."

I went back to New York and listened to John's tapes. All these great songs, and every song had a spoken, self-effacing narration: "OK, here's another song, but it's a piece of shit." It was the demo for "Watching the Wheels."

"Here's another piece of shit. It's called 'Woman.' I'll probably end up giving it to Richard Starkey."

I called him up and he said, "So, you think it sucks, right?" I said, "John, it's great. I'd love to do this with you!"

He said, "Then we'll go to the next step. I'm staying down here to write some more songs. I want an *eighties* record. Do what you have to do." So, beginning in August 1980, I booked the Hit Factory, did the charts, the arrangements, rehearsed the musicians, who didn't know what album they were working on. I sang the guide vocals. It sucked, but John didn't want the band to know who it was for until he started rehearsing with them.

There was a feeding frenzy that summer as word leaked out that John Lennon was looking for a record deal. Suddenly all the record executives were my best friends. It was a riot. I had a terrible reputation at Columbia because Aerosmith was always so late, but now they loved me. John kept the sessions closed, but Ahmet Ertegun wanted a shot and ended up getting bodily thrown out of the studio by John's six-foot-six bodyguard who didn't know anyone he wasn't supposed to know. "Omlet Hurtagain? Who the fuck are you?" The guy body-slammed Ahmet into an elevator and rode him down. "Nobody gets in. Boss's orders!"

Then John signed with Geffen Records. I didn't have to do anything to the songs except "Watching the Wheels." John said, "Could you make it more circular?" Other than that, we kept it pretty simple.

Then Yoko came up to me and said I couldn't say anything to John about what she was going to tell me. Yoko said, "John doesn't know it, but I am going to ask you to put a few of *my* songs on the album." I told her that she had to deal with it.

She had about fifty songs. We worked for another eight hours. I ended up having to do four albums with two artists who couldn't work with each other. I'd work with Yoko from eleven to seven and then with John from seven to whatever. We did *Double Fantasy*, which came out in October as John turned forty years old, and then went right into *Milk and Honey*. There was friction with Yoko, who resented me because I'd gotten her to sing on pitch. John couldn't deal with that stuff at all, and he'd put it totally in my hands.

The only time he ever participated on one of her sessions was the night he was killed—December 8, 1980. We were working on "Walking on Thin Ice." John wasn't supposed to be there. I'd worked with him that night, and he'd stayed around to help her out. Then they left.

Someone came to the studio and told me. I went right to the hospital, but John was gone. Then *I* was gone, into heroin for a long, long time.

Joe Perry: That was the night that Jack called me up in Boston. He'd just said good-bye to John a couple of hours before. It really shook me up. It shook everyone up.

4: I Shot
the Amplifier

Aerosmith went on the road in January 1980 with Jimmy Crespo on guitar, playing smaller cities in the Northeast. The tour opened in Binghamton, New York. David Krebs was on hand to monitor security arrangements; eleven kids had been trampled to death in a "festival seating" melee during a Who concert in Cincinnati the month before. The promoter had sixty uniformed police in the building, along with the usual security staff.

Backstage, Steven talking quietly with a reporter: "There are a lot of things Joe Perry's been saying in the press lately that just aren't true. If he keeps that shit up, we're gonna have to tell the truth about the whole thing and it ain't gonna be healthy. Let's just call it a mutual breakup. Joe . . . he's a very bitter man. Why did I go to see him? I wanted to see what was happening with my brother. I don't care what he or someone else thinks. I still love the guy . . . You know what? I still wish him the world. I hope to God he makes it with his band."

The other members of Aerosmith are nervous. The previous month in Port Chester, New York, on the last night of Jimmy Crespo's first bunch of shows with the band, Steven was hopelessly fucked up. He was forgetting lyrics and couldn't stand for more than a song or two before slumping against the drum riser. He finally fell over and was helped offstage but returned two minutes later with a little more energy. The band started the show again, but Steven couldn't remember the lyrics. He man-

aged to stay up until the very end, when he lost his balance and fell into the crowd.

Now Aerosmith goes on with a set of songs from Night in the Ruts. Steven performs in a bumblebee-striped jumpsuit with matching head-band. Jimmy Crespo sings along on "No Surprize" from a lyric sheet taped to the back of his stage monitor. Crespo is a fast, fluid player; Brad, Tom, and Joey are smoking away and the set goes well. The young wriggling fans throw their clothes at the band and go home happy. Afterward, Steven Tyler wondered to himself if he could do three more months of this without Joe Perry.

The next night Aerosmith played the sold-out Civic Center in Port-land, Maine. A few songs into the set Steven appeared to collapse onstage during "Reefer Head Woman." The band kept playing. He didn't get up. Brad went over and kneeled down next to Steven, whose foot was twitch-ing in spasms. Brad wondered: What do I do? Steven told Brad he couldn't get up. Joe Baptista and another roadie came out and carried Steven off-stage. The band stopped playing and the show was canceled. The pro-moter had to come out and explain. Sobered, the crowd left quietly. But Steven recovered in the dressing room, refused medical attention, made a phone call, and left. He slept it off at Tom Hamilton's house and the tour was postponed for a week.

Steven Tyler: I drank too much and realized I couldn't finish the show. I was so fuckin' drunk I couldn't even walk back to the drum riser. What was I gonna do? If I walked back to the dressing room, they'd say, "What the fuck is wrong with you? Go back out there!" If I passed out, there was nothing they could do. So in the middle of "Reefer Head Woman," I dropped down and faked passing out. I'm so good at it, I even shook my foot so it looked bad.

Bebe Buell: By then Liv and I were living in Portland, where I was getting my band [the Gargoyles] together.

When Aerosmith played in Portland, I'd always show up with pictures of Liv, and Steven and I would cry together. Then I saw him lying there, and I thought he was having a seizure onstage. I wanted to run to him, but I couldn't. It was horrible, to feel that helpless when someone you love is dying like that before your eyes.

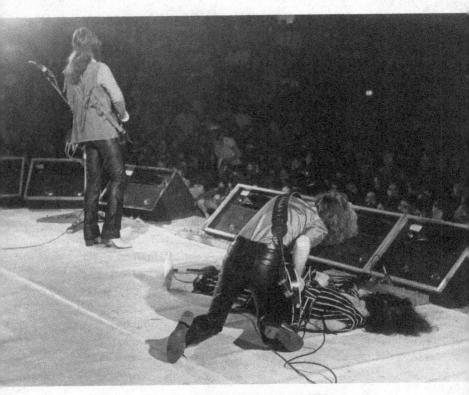

Portland, Maine, January 1980.
Jimmy Crespo plays on while Brad checks on Steven.
(PHOTO: RON POWNALL)

On January 11, 1980, Aerosmith sold out Maple Leaf Gardens in To-ronto. Jimmy Crespo started to hit his stride, playing with his head down, concentrating on improvising around Joe Perry's trademark licks. After the 20,000 kids gave Crespo a standing ovation, Steven charged the front of the stage and yelled, "Fills those fuckin' shoes pretty fuckin' good, don't he?" The crowd roared back in response. Two days later, the band played at Nassau Coliseum. Down in front, the kids started to yell for Joe Perry.

Steven Tyler: Jimmy Crespo was from Brooklyn. He'd been in a group called Flame and made a couple of records. Richie Supa recommended him. He was green, so I tortured him. "You think you can stand up in a stadium with 100,000 fuckin' people staring at you and not piss in your pants? Huh?" But he took it in his stride as much as he could. Jimmy Crespo was a kind of pure musician. He wasn't really in it for the money.

Tom Hamilton: I thought he was a brilliant musician and a very good writer. Steven wrote some good stuff with him, but I could see all along that what Steven wanted was to write with Joe.

Jimmy Crespo was a feather in the wind, sensitive, very fragile. He was allergic to everything on this planet, a guy that hid behind his music.

Steven Tyler: Which is called, "I'm hiding from something so big, and I can't let you know, so I'm just . . . gonna . . . ACHOOOO!!!"

He'd come and go, "I can't play tonight." I go, "Whassamatta you?" He goes, "I'm sick." "You don't look sick." "I'm sick, believe me, I'm sick." He'd never let me in on the downstairs of it. I'd go, "Whaddaya mean you're sick? You're fuckin' standing here talking to me. What's the matter with you?" "You don't understand. It's something deep. I got this problem." It was all tea, incense, a million drugs and remedies. But he could play his ass off, sho 'nuff!

Terry Hamilton: Everything changed when Joe left the band. Good-bye, limos. Now we drove ourselves. Good-bye, hotels. Hello, crummy dives like the Gorham in New York. The guys were barely making it.

Henry Smith: I left the band in 1980 because we were all in over our heads on drugs. I'd been their friend for all these years and now had to decide: Either I was going to be their friend or be codependent with them. It was tough. I had to leave to keep being their friend.

I was gonna get out of the music business, go to Woodstock and get into the building business. I did a *Beatlemania* tour for Krebs, and then Jack Douglas called and asked me to work for John Lennon. I met John and Yoko in a restaurant, and it was, "Yeah, come work for me." They were gonna play some shows when his record came out. Through them I met Roberta Flack, who had the apartment next to theirs in the Dakota. I was with Roberta in New Zealand when we heard Lennon had been killed.

Steven Tyler: One day in the fall of 1980, I was at Beck-with's on the lake. [ED. NOTE: Beckwith is not the family's real name.] They were a family that had a restaurant. Sue Beckwith was my secretary at the time, Bob Sr. was the cook, Bob Jr. was the son, Nancy was the seventeen-year-old daughter who worked for me and Cyrinda, taking care of Mia.

I'm at Beckwith's picking up Nancy to baby-sit Mia for us. I had a couple of drinks at the bar, a big vial of blow in my pocket, stayed about forty-five minutes. Shit-faced and drunk, I put Nancy on the back of my Yamaha trail bike. I'm on the gas tank, and I went around the opposite way to make the ride longer. I took a curve a little too fast, went to shift down, and because I was sitting on the gas tank my foot hit the ground instead of the shifter. The moccasin I was wearing disintegrated. We started to skid, lost control, the ground ripped off the shifter, the kick-stand, and most of my heel. Then we were down. Gravel in my mouth. Electric pain. There goes my foot. *Now what'd I do???*

Ever been in a motorcycle accident? Fun.

The whole back of my foot was off and flapping. I'm trying to walk around with my heel off!

Nancy cracked a tooth. Her family sued me.

I was in the hospital for two months, in a cast up to my eyeballs. Then there was the convalescence at home. Months went by. Years. 1981. 1982. When I got up again, I moved to New York to try to put Aerosmith back in business. I got an apartment in the West Seventies. I was still in a full leg cast and totally paranoid. I'd stumble about this apartment all night with a loaded .38 special tucked into the top of this cast. When the cast came off, I had this jagged Frankenstein scar on my heel and the doctors said to forget about touring, which was the kiss of death for *Night in the Ruts.*

On the weekends, I'd go to see the girls in my Cessna 310 Riley tur-boprop conversion, thing hauled ass, 200 miles per hour, unbelievable plane. Wish I still had it, but I snorted it up.

Back to New Hampshire to get drugs.

Typical family scene. I'm in the kitchen yelling at David Krebs on the phone. Cyrinda's in the living room listening to Led Zeppelin's "Black Dog" on these two giant Klipshorn speakers we had. My friend Rick Mas-tin's in the house.

I'm arguing with David, but I can't hear. "Hey! Will you turn it down?" I said, "Turn it down! TURN IT FUCKING DOWN!"

She turned it up.

I went over to the pit we had in the living room and turned it down and went back to the kitchen. Cyrinda came back in and turned it up. I just fuckin' grabbed my Walther PPK and went in and shot off a clip into the fucking amplifier. Five loud explosions.

It got very quiet.

I came back into the kitchen to continue my conversation and Rick's staring at me in disbelief. He swallowed hard before he could speak. "Steven, is she . . . dead?" He thought I'd shot Cyrinda. That's how bad things were.

I said, "Rick, man, take this gun and fucking throw it into the lake right now because I don't ever want to see it again."

This went on for a while. Eventually the band went back on the road. One night I got a call from Sue Beckwith, my secretary. "Steven, I went over to your house and found my son in bed with your wife."

And, being high and stoned, two mutually exclusive states of consciousness . . . I freaked out. I didn't know what to do. Maybe it wasn't true. Sue never got along with Cyrinda anyway and could have made this up. She said she went upstairs and saw fifteen-year-old Bob Jr. and my wife in bed together.

I didn't call Cyrinda for a couple of days. She came down to New York and we went over to Steve Marriott's apartment and just got into the worst fight. Really violent language at top volume. Stevie had to leave his own place because he was afraid. I confronted her about fucking my secretary's son and she denied it.

But it was one of the reasons I divorced her. It was just another good reason to hate out on her and leave.

So I went to New York and met this girl named Valerie. I was pissed off and angry. I hung out with Steve Marriott and told him my troubles. He said to get away, cool out somewhere for a week. So I got a lot of coke and split with Joe Baptista and this girl. Left New York and slowly made our way up to Boston, stopping on Cape Cod for a couple of days so I could cool out and fuck this girl six ways to Sunday. She was great, an incredible experience being with someone that loving and good . . . and that's when I moved down to New York and stayed there for the next three years.

Cyrinda stayed in New Hampshire. Soon friends were telling me she'd turned my house into a biker hangout.

5: Soldier of Fortune

Joe Perry: After Ralph Mormon, we listened to a hundred audition tapes and came up with Charlie Farren, who was in a local band called Balloon that had a single on the radio at the time. He was a good rhythm guitarist who could sing. We started rehearsing in my basement and came up with some songs: "Soldier of Fortune," "I've Got the Rock 'n' Rolls Again," and a bunch of others. I was so broke I was having difficulty keeping the band together and affording my lifestyle. I took every cent and spent it on drugs. I owed everyone money, including back taxes to the IRS. Nothing was coming in from Krebs, whose strategy was to starve me out to get me back in Aerosmith.

Around this time I replaced Bob Casper with Don Law, the veteran Boston promoter. Don had managed the Tea Party back in the old days and I had this notion in my head that he would be so thrilled to manage me he'd give me a big advance so I wouldn't lose my house.

Liv Taylor—also managed by Don—had to take me aside one night. "Uh, Joe, Don's a great guy and I know he'll do his best for you, but I don't think he's going to give you $100,000 just like that."

"Oh. Shit. Too bad."

In the spring [of 1981], the Project started working at my house on the new record. Then we moved over to the Wherehouse, where we developed songs by Charlie Farren ("East Coast, West Coast") and David Hull ("Dirty Little Things" and "Buzz Buzz"). We cut a version of Elvis's "Heartbreak Hotel," intended as a single. I took a shuffle I'd been working on and turned it into "South Station Blues." The record, originally titled *Soldier of Fortune*, was produced by Bruce Botnick, who had worked with the Doors as an engineer and had produced their last great album, *L.A. Woman*. We brought the Record Plant's truck back up to Boston, parked it on Washington Street in front of the Boston Opera House, and cut the album inside the elegant but decrepit old theater.

We mixed the album at the Record Plant in L.A. Columbia released the album as *I've Got the Rock 'n' Rolls Again* in the summer of 1981 and promptly buried it. Nobody ever even heard it except for the hardest of the hard-core fans.

To pay the bills, we went out on the road, playing with Heart, ZZ Top, and J. Geils, who had a hit record with "Centerfold."

One night that summer, I picked up the phone and Steven Tyler was on the other end of the line, the first time I'd talked to him in a year. I asked how the band was doing and he said they were working on an album and it was going pretty slow. I think the word "stranded" was used. We might have discussed writing some material together for the album, but nothing ever came of it except some rumors floated by interested parties that Aerosmith was getting back together.

But it wasn't. A couple of months later, Brad called and told me he'd left Aerosmith too.

Brad Whitford: Steven's motorcycle thing happened and everything just stopped. Nothing was going on and I was bored and very frustrated. We all were. Aerosmith was in chaos, with Steven in and out of drugs and rehab. Cyrinda was threatening to jump out of hotel room windows.

The year before (1980) I got together with my friend Derek St. Holmes, who I met when he was singing with Ted Nugent's band. Derek was in a similar situation to mine, between albums with Ted, and one afternoon we started to write songs in my house in Walpole.

Suddenly I felt better. So great to be working, doing things. We made some rough demos on a four-track, took them to David Krebs, and he got us a record deal with Columbia. He told me that Derek was a great singer but that Ted Nugent had egoed out and wanted to figure out a way to get rid of him. So we got together [with drummer Steve Pace and bassist Dave Hewitt], went down to Atlanta where Derek lived, and cut an album's worth of songs in about two weeks. We had days when we were writing six songs. Derek would come in late at night, do his vocals perfectly, and leave. It was so professional. This is how sane people make an album. It was a relief to realize I wasn't the cog in the wheel that didn't work. It wasn't a great album, but it was OK and we had high hopes. "If this album dies," Derek told the press, "keep all razor blades at a safe distance."

Whitford St. Holmes was released in the summer of '81 but didn't make the charts. We were competing against bands like Journey. We did a little bullshit tour—six seriously hungover guys in a station wagon driving from West Virginia to North Dakota—and that was it. Derek went back to work for Ted Nugent.

Walk This Way

In September (1981), we began to try to finish the next Aerosmith album, cutting some tracks at the Power Station in New York with Jimmy Crespo. Jimmy was a trained musician, a stickler for getting things precise. I found it hard to work with that attitude. Joe and I, we didn't have to say two words to each other about the guitar parts. It was a big part of the guitar magic that had sustained Aerosmith for ten years.

Meanwhile, Steven was well into one of his periods on heroin. Some nights they would basically wheel him into the studio and prop him up on a couch and hope something would happen. The insanity was driving me crazy.

I went back up to Boston and just started to enjoy the beautiful early summer weather for a few days before I had to go back to New York to work on the record. Whenever I thought about this, my shoulders would knot up and I'd be miserable. I knew I was gonna go down there and jerk off. Nothin' was gonna happen! I felt guilty, bitter. I'd never felt that way before.

I drove to the airport in Boston and was about to get on the Eastern shuttle to La Guardia when I felt something tear inside my head. I said to myself: *I can't do this anymore.*

I called David Krebs to tell him I was quitting the band. He was in a meeting and wouldn't take the call. So I called Mark Puma, who had been hired by David to handle the band. "Mark, it's Brad. Listen . . . I can't come down . . . I'm not coming . . . That's it . . . I can't even think about it . . . Tell the guys, OK? Sorry, man. Good-bye."

I couldn't bring myself to call the band. I was confused, distraught, wondering if I'd made the right decision. My shoulders told me that I had. I went home, opened a beer, and felt a lot better about the whole thing. This was in 1981, and I stayed out of Aerosmith for two and a half years. In '82, I worked with [singer] Rex Smith, one of David's clients. He was hosting the TV show *Solid Gold* and wanted to be a rock star. We made a record, but it never got released. In the fall of '82, I hooked back up with Joe Perry and played some occasional dates with the Project.

Joey Kramer: Joe Perry had originally asked me to play drums with him in the Project. I told him I would if he got David Hull to play bass, but then I changed my mind.

In 1981, Krebs told me I had to move to New York to help make this thing—getting Aerosmith back on track—work. So I rented a house in Westchester and Tom got an apartment in the city. Steven was at the

Gorham, but he was into some bad shit and the band started seriously not to happen. While we were waiting around, I started to put another band together that I wanted to call Renegade. It was me, Tom Hamilton, Jimmy Crespo, Bobby Mayo, and Marge Raymond, who'd been the singer in Jimmy Crespo's old band. We got together in SIR Studio in New York, snorting a *lot* of cocaine, and cut seven basic tracks for a project that never got finished. Krebs told us at one point that Renegade had a record deal, but first we had to finish the Aerosmith album. So Renegade got put on a back burner and nothing ever happened. What Renegade did do was trigger a revelation in Steven's mind that he should get his act together and come back to work.

6: Hard Place

Tom Hamilton: For two years, the album we were working on, *Rock in a Hard Place*, was always two months away. It was hard times. We sold our house and moved to a condo and everyone else cut back too. Joey and I were determined to hang in there with Steven, but Brad couldn't handle it.

Joey Kramer: One day Tom comes up to me and says, "Brad's not coming back." We just looked at each other.

Steven Tyler: They confronted me, and all I could do was yell at them. "OH, YEAH? WELL, WHY DON'T YOU FUCKIN' WRITE THE LYRICS THEN???" I didn't know what else to say because it was so hard and I was drowning in tears of frustration every day. At the end of the album, we covered Julie London's "Cry Me a River" because I ran out of lyrics.

Tom Hamilton: The truth is . . . we were raging. There were a lot of drugs around. This was when freebasing cocaine was in vogue, the pre-crack era, so you can imagine how nuts it was.

Joey Kramer: We ended up erasing the stuff that Brad did, and me, Tom, and Jimmy Crespo did all the tracks. I actually got to express myself a little, which hadn't happened before. I was writing songs, doing production work. Hey, it was almost like it was my own band. I did what I had to do to get the record out.

Tom Hamilton: By this time Jack Douglas was back on the project. The original producer, Tony Bongiovi [cousin of Jon Bon Jovi], either got fired or left. Things were insane and Jack came back to help us.

Jack Douglas: Steven and Jimmy wrote some good things together: "Jailbait," "Bitch's Brew," "Bolivian Ragamuffin," "The Jig Is Up." They had a couple of unfinished things—"Joanie's Butterfly," "Rock in a Hard Place"—that I was able to help them with. We worked in the winter and spring [of 1982] in New York and at Criteria Studios in Miami. All this time there was talk of them going on tour that fall to support the album, and they needed a guitar player to replace Brad. So I brought in Rick Dufay [Dufay released an album, *Tender Loving Abuse*, on Polydor in 1980], a true character, a kindred spirit. I thought he would mesh well with the band, so we flew him to Florida and he joined Aerosmith. I think he played on one track on the album, "Lightning Strikes," which Richie Supa wrote.

There were some interesting things on that album. We were doing stuff with Vocoders [on "Prelude," a spoken intro to "Joanie's Butterfly"] that hadn't been done before. We mixed the album so well that when it was released we started to get letters from kids: "We were smoking a joint and listening to 'Joanie's Butterfly' and we thought we heard something *behind our heads?* How do you do that?"

Steven Tyler: We needed another guy so we could go out on the road when the record came out. Rick Dufay was a friend of Jack's, a guitar player, a total asshole, and we loved him. Rick just so defined what a fuckin' asshole is. He would come up and spit in my face. He would do something brain-dead and just beg Jack to beat the shit out of him.

Tom Hamilton: Even *we* thought he was outrageous. He'd be an asshole just to say, "Look! You're not dead! I'm getting a reaction out of you!" He would attack you, start a wrestling match.

Steven Tyler: I'd get in fights with him. He'd knock me down and my elbows would smash on the cement floor of the studio. "YOU FUCKIN' ASSHOLE! LOOK HOW FUCKED UP MY ELBOWS ARE!"

Tom Hamilton: Rick would attack you mentally too. He'd assault you over something no decent person would even mention. The truth is—he was fucking great, an outrageous rock 'n' roller, a fuckin' riot! He could even play guitar—if he felt like it—if he wasn't too stoned.

Steven Tyler: Rick would try anything. He'd been in a mental institution, broke out of his cell, jumped out of a third floor window and survived. I used to make him explain this to me over and over. "How high were you? Weren't you afraid you were gonna kill yourself?"

"Yeah, but the birds were calling me."

Tom Hamilton: He was dedicated to living the absurdity of the rock 'n' roll life—just taking the piss out of everything.

Steven Tyler: I'm at the Gorham Hotel. The rooms were actually little apartments. All my stuff was stored at Private's, a nightclub on the East Side owned by Leber-Krebs. Other bands rehearsed there during the day and would pillage the stuff. It ain't easy, livin' like a Gypsy . . .

Down in the Village lived Footie, my favorite connection. You'd just go in, wait in line because Footie only liked one customer at a time, and he'd weigh you out a couple of T's of good, good New York dope. You'd get up to leave and there'd be a furtive knock on the door—the next customer—and you'd open the door and go, "Hey, Ronnie. What are *you* doing here?"

I went and copped from Footie one night and the next day they found him with a screwdriver sticking in his head. I was so scared because my fingerprints were all over the place. I was so paranoid I thought I'd be charged with Footie's murder.

A few nights later, trying to buy heroin on Eighth Avenue. There's a guy, he looks like a dealer. "Got any dope?" "Yeah, come with me." Down an alley, up the back staircase of a tenement, four flights of dark stairs. At the top he turns around and sticks a pistol in my mouth. *If this guy pulls the trigger,* I'm thinking, *my brains will be all over the ceiling.* "Gimme your money. Gimme those fuckin' rings too."

I hardly cared because heroin for me was life without anxiety. It's a floaty, godlike trip you're on and nothing matters. The reason people get strung out is because it makes you feel good. It doesn't matter if you're rich or poor, a genius or less than one—it's all the same. It'll take you down. If the height of human experience is the orgasm, heroin might be second-best.

In the beginning, it was a wonderful tool for me. You're so in the moment. It slows your life down and turns off the overintellectualizing part of your brain. But after a while, heroin starts to take away everything that it gave you. Soon all you care about is the drug and you'll drag yourself through hell to get it. Some people end up with no veins left and shooting up into their neck, their foot. It's killing you and you don't care because to the final beat of your heart, it still feels cool.

Around this time I knew I had to get off heroin. I went to a doctor and he gave me three weeks' worth of methadone so I could go to Florida and work and finish our album. We started out in a hotel, then moved into a house. One night I got so stoned on this methadone that I flushed the rest down the toilet so I wouldn't kill myself, and I spent the rest of the time jonesing, doing it cold turkey. I was so out of it that I passed out while sunbathing and woke up after nine hours in the Florida sun with severe burns and clumps of my hair falling out. If you ever see the video we did for "Lightning Strikes," don't look at my head too closely.

Then somebody new came into my life.

It was at the Record Plant, the new wing, back of Studio C by John Lennon's giant Mexican guitar in a glass display case. It was during one of my bottoms.

I'd been buying opium, an ounce at a time, black-pitch opium you roll in a ball and swallow and be fuckin' stoned for twelve hours, or opium powder, where you take a little speck and pack it in this half teaspoon, put it in some toilet paper, twist it and roll it up, take a glass of water, throw it against the back of your throat and swallow it quick. Ten minutes later, you're in Tibet.

I met Teresa back there. Teresa Barrick. Her twin sister Lisa was friends with this guy Brimstone [Gary Buermely], who was a professional dealer, also a bit of a bard and a sage about old music. [Brimstone ended up handcuffed and dead with his veins full of battery acid after someone gave him a hot shot in the backseat of a car in Michigan.] Brimstone was looking after us and getting us drugs while we made *Rock in a Hard Place*. One day Lisa invited Teresa to come to the studio.

"Nah."

"Steven Tyler's there. Remember him from Hawaii?"

"So what?"

"C'mon," Lisa told her sister. "I'll let you wear my silver shoes."

So Teresa came down with Lisa. Two beautiful blondes from Oklahoma, living the New York life in the eighties. My eyes popped out of my head on long stalks like an R. Crumb cartoon. I always had a thing for twins.

I started paying a whole lot of attention to Teresa. My God! I offered her my drugs. The sessions didn't finish until 9 A.M. I went over to say good night to her and we ended up making out for an hour. Everybody else went for breakfast and they came back and we were still making out.

It was dynamite, the very best, it was . . .

Love.

Teresa goes very deep with me.

I remember that day so well because there was a look in her eyes, a compassion, that I've never seen in another woman's eyes, nor have I ever experienced such a passion in any other relationship, not Bebe, not Cyrinda, nobody . . .

This is an amazing woman, I thought. *She's going to be my wife!!!*

Rock in a Hard Place was released by CBS in September 1982 and reached #32 during its short stay on the charts. It had cost $1.5 million to produce. The single, "Lightning Strikes," didn't make the charts, nor did its video version (Aerosmith as fifties street gang with slicked-back hair) get played on the new cable channel that was about to change the American music business: MTV.

Aerosmith went back out on the road for the first time in almost two years in the fall of 1982, playing big clubs and smaller arenas to support their album. It was the first tour of the Crespo/Dufay lineup and included Bobby Mayo, old Yonkers pal of Tallarico and Kramer, on keyboards. (Mayo had played with Peter Frampton and Foreigner. The Pat Travers Band opened many of the shows.) The set opened with "Back in the Saddle" and ran through "Big Ten Inch Record," "Sweet Emotion," "Walk This Way," "Reefer Head Woman," and two new songs, "Lightning Strikes" and "Jailbait," before climaxing with "Toys in the Attic" and "Train."

Every night kids in the audience would start to yell at the band: "Yo! Tyler! Hey! Where's Joe Fuckin' Perry??"

That fall they played second on the bill to Journey at the Tangerine Bowl in Miami. (The lineup was Bryan Adams opening, Sammy Hagar, Aerosmith, then Journey.) Journey singer Steve Perry visited Steven's dressing room to get his autograph and have Journey's tour photographer take their picture together, which left little wonder about who the real rock legend was at this show.

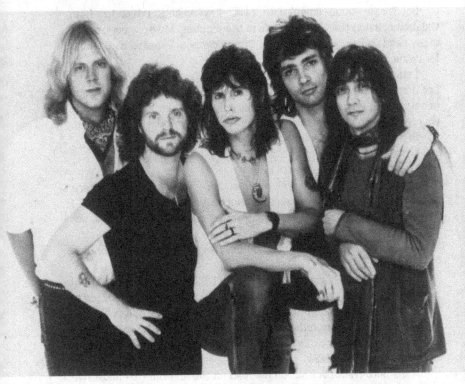

Tom Hamilton, Joey Kramer, Steven Tyler, Rick Dufay, Jimmy Crespo
(TYLER COLLECTION)

HIT PARADER

"Aerosmith has been completely revitalized over the past year," Steven Tyler explained as he sat in a New York hotel bar nursing a beer. "Some of our younger fans may view us as this mythical group that they've never had the chance to see, but we've never really been away . . ."

Tyler admitted feeling "very hurt" by Joe [Perry]'s desertion. Rumors have been circulating that Perry had been asked to contribute to Aerosmith's new album and that Tyler had practically begged him to rejoin. "Not so," says Steverino . . . "I know there are a lot of people out there who don't think Aerosmith is Aerosmith without Joe, and I understand that. But I'm just knocked out by the way this band looks and sounds right now. This group just looks *tit!*" (December 1982)

Steven Tyler: Jimmy Crespo was an artist. The Dufe drove him crazy because he purposely played fucked up to be like his idol Ronnie Wood. Rick *was* Ronnie Wood, standing there onstage with a cigarette dangling out of his mouth, copping that fuck-all attitude that Ronnie did so well.

Tom Hamilton: He did it really good though. He had this Fender guitar that didn't have enough of a cutaway, so he took a hatchet and chopped it out and just left it like that.

Joey Kramer: Dufay didn't give a shit because for him it was all an image thing. Rick would fix his hair onstage, his guitar just hanging there loose and ringing, while Jimmy's playing his fuckin' heart out. It drove Jimmy to drugs.

Steven Tyler: So many times I fired him, threw him outta the band. "You're fired! Get the fuck outta here!!"

Tom Hamilton: But he knew how to come back because in the end, Rick has a really big heart. He knew how to win you back.

Jack Douglas: Rick would not leave Steven alone because Steven was fucked up royally. He was dead onstage, lifeless, catatonic. One of the greatest, funniest movers in rock, but he wouldn't move. Rick didn't have a debilitating drug problem—maybe a few pills, some coke— and he wanted to literally kick some life into Steven, upstage him. They would chase each other around the stage. Steven couldn't believe it. It was like a rite of destruction. When Steven tried to fake a few steps, Rick would trip him.

The band tolerated it. Rick was doing it because he was a fan of Steven's. Joe and Brad were gone, and Tom was no extrovert. Jimmy Crespo wasn't confident enough to take a starring role. He was just trying to play Joe's leads and didn't know what else to do. He was scared shitless the rest of the time. Would he even have a job the next day?

Rock in a Hard Place: What an apropos title.

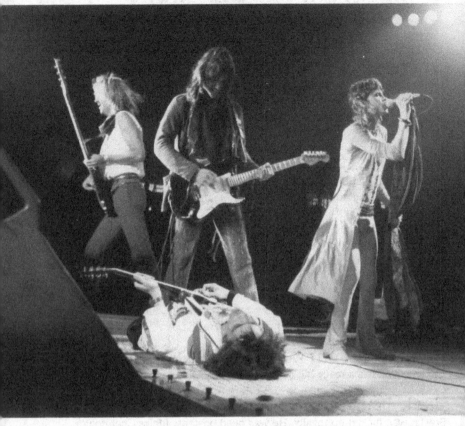

Rock in a Hard Place; Rick Dufay on his back
(PHOTO: RON POWNALL)

7: Are There Any More at Home Like You?

Teresa Tyler: My [identical] twin sister Lisa was going to Maui after we got out of high school in Tulsa [Oklahoma, in 1975], and I went along to keep an eye on her. So I was working at René's in

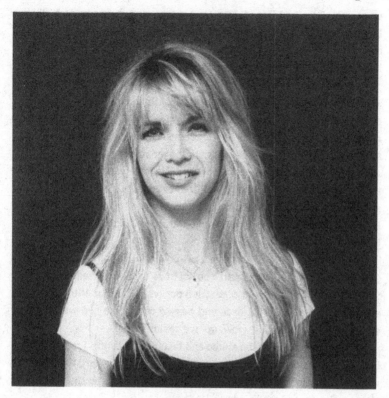

Teresa Tyler
(PHOTO: GEORGE CHIN)

Lahaina in 1976 when Steven Tyler came in with Diana and an entourage. I joined the party and went with them down to Nick's Fish Market, where Lisa worked, the only place to party in Lahaina. That was the first time I met him.

Maui then: small, safe, quiet, only a few older hotels, one condo. Too quiet, so we moved to Honolulu, my sister and me. I kept running into Steven—several times over the next few years—like something was trying to bring us together in some funny way. Then Lisa and I moved to New York City. One night I got invited to a benefit dinner at the Waldorf for the T. J. Martell Foundation, and Steven was there with Cyrinda.

Then Lisa met Brimstone and started hanging out with him at Steven's apartment. Brim had lots of drugs and was generous, but he was all over Lisa all the time. I guess Steven realized Brim was trying to make a move on her, so he said to Lisa, "Are there any more at home like you?" She laughed and told him she had an identical twin sister.

A week later—it was May 4, 1982—I went with Lisa to the studio where Aerosmith was recording after doing some of their record in Florida. We got there around 5 A.M., then Lisa left and I stayed with Brim. Steven finally came out to the waiting area as I was about to leave, but he asked me to stay and I did. (And we've been together ever since.)

I waited and Steven came out at noon. He took two hours to pick up his stuff, we kissed for two more hours in a doorway while waiting for a cab, and then I went with him to this apartment where he was living with Rick Dufay. Steven told me he was separated from Cyrinda, who was in St. Martin.

And we just . . . fell. We stayed in the apartment for a couple of days, getting high, talking. Steven had a box of tropical oils and creams from Florida that we played with, smelled, tried out on each other. We didn't have sex because we finally lay back and passed out on the bed with our feet still on the floor. When we woke up, we couldn't walk.

He had to go back to the studio and he put me in a taxi. I met him there later on and we just kissed for hours. I don't remember much about it. The whole week was so like a dream. We went back to the apartment, went to sleep, woke up, and made love.

Around this time both our leases were up. I packed up my apartment, then his. We stored our stuff in Private's and moved into the Milford Plaza on Eighth Avenue for a month. I remember Steven had this dream. He woke up and began singing as if he wrote it in his sleep. It turned into the song "Joanie's Butterfly." I started making him clothes, which is what I did. The first was a silk unicorn jacket. Then he went on the road and we moved to the Mayflower in the fall of '82.

Steven loved his wife, he loved his daughter. He has a very strong sense of family. I never once thought of stealing him away to be my man. But the two of them fought like cats and dogs and he didn't want to be around her— she was off living in another apartment. I'd encourage him to go see her, but he always came back to me. He didn't want to hurt her—Mia was only three—and he'd make me hide behind the refrigerator when Cyrinda came to see him at the Mayflower. It was humiliating and I was pissed off. At the time, Cyrinda was having an affair with one of the studio engineers [Godfrey Diamond], but I could tell he still loved her. It was hard for me, because now I loved him.

Steven could be really mean when he got high—yelling at me and stuff. But when he wasn't so high he'd be Steven Tallarico, and that was who I fell in love with, not this mean Tyler person—overwhelmed by drugs, ego, pressure, stress, all that.

When the tour was over, Steven went into rehab at the Hazelden Clinic. I went to see him and once he made me bring him one of those little bottles of booze from the airplane. He drank it and nearly died from the guilt.

Then we moved to the Gorham Hotel in New York. *Rock in a Hard Place* hadn't gone anywhere, the band wasn't happening, and it was quiet. David Krebs was giving Steven $20 a day and we wound up watching TV, going out to eat. We were a real couple and he was able to breathe for the first time. There was very little work, maybe a couple of videos. That was it.

I think of that period with a lot of fondness because he was a normal guy, not famous, no autographs, no hassles. He took me up to Sunapee to see his house and meet his parents. I can't describe how romantic the lake looked and felt as he paddled me around in his canoe—so peaceful and beautiful. Then Cyrinda went up and stayed for the next eight years.

At the Gorham one day [in 1983], Steven called Joe Perry and they spoke. Steven had never talked about Joe with me or about wanting to get the band together. As far as I knew, Steven really liked Jimmy Crespo. One night when we were in Cleveland, Lisa and I went to see Joe backstage after one of his gigs, and he was nasty to us. So at first I didn't think the chances were too great of them getting back together.

8: What Am I Getting Into?

Joe Perry: The Project worked again in the fall of '81. We had a road manager named Doc McGrath, who worked for Don Law, and Doc kept telling me about this guy named Tim Collins, a young booking agent in Boston. "Don Law isn't doing shit for you," he'd tell me. I was willing to try anything. I'd lost my record deal with Columbia and couldn't afford to keep my band. Every cent went to keep my house and my habit together.

Tim came to see us one night [in September 1981] at Charlie Farren's apartment in the Back Bay. I liked him, but Charlie Farren—then the Project's lead singer—didn't, so nothing happened. But the money thing was bad. I spent whatever I had on dope. The Internal Revenue Service was going to seize my house. Elyssa called Tim Collins in January 1982. We sat down and talked, did some blow. I liked him. He was young and we never discussed Aerosmith once. He didn't even know that much about Aerosmith. He just said he wanted to be my manager and thought we could make a good team.

I said, "Y'know, it's gonna be a fuckin' megillah here. It's already a nightmare. I've burned all my bridges. I'm a public drug addict. Everyone knows. It's the Toxic Twins and all that." Then I handed him six months' worth of unopened bills and said, "Tim, I hope you know what you're getting into." He said, "OK, let's start."

Tim Collins: I took this drawer full of mail back to my office and started opening seizure notices from the IRS, foreclosure demands from the bank that had loaned Joe the money for his house at 26 percent interest, some unsigned death threats, and about twenty-five grand in checks. Joe was broke and no money was coming in. His old management owned the publishing and had stopped paying royalties.

I sat back and thought, *What am I getting into?*

At that point, I'd been involved in the Boston music scene for about ten years. In high school in suburban Boston, I was an overweight, very entrepreneurial kid, working in the local clothing store and booking bands in school.

In 1976, I started working with a local manager, booking clubs, working with Boston acts: Jonathan Edwards, the Road Apples, Duke and the Drivers. I got turned on to cocaine and that whole world. We'd bring Derringer and Johnny Winter to Mr. C's Rock Palace in Lowell. I learned to deal with insane gangsters and Mafia nightclub guys. All part of the business. In 1979, I teamed up with a friend, Steve Barrasso. Our game plan was to start booking bands for cash flow and eventually become managers. My goal was simple: I wanted to be Brian Epstein.

When Doc McGrath introduced me to Joe, the meeting lasted about four minutes. Joe's hands were shaking so badly from alcohol that he couldn't hold his cup of coffee. He wouldn't look me in the eye. He spoke from behind an opaque curtain of long black hair over his face.

"You're a manager, huh?"

"Yeah, I manage Jonathan Edwards."

"Oh." That was it.

In November 1981, Joe and Elyssa came over to my office in the North End of Boston. He said nothing. She did all the talking. She told me that the second Project LP had gone down the tubes. "Joe should be a big star . . . Wrote all the Aerosmith songs, inspired by his love for me . . . Steven Tyler's the biggest asshole in the business . . . Krebs is destroying us." A whole paranoid, semidelusional rant.

A couple of months pass. January 1982. We had a Friday night ritual at our office. Lock the door, shut off the phones, have a few drinks and some blow with friends and clients. We're in the middle of this weekly party when the phone rings [not shut off that time]. A woman's voice: "Collins! Get your fat ass over here right now!" She hangs up without saying who it was. An hour later, it rings again. "Collins! WHERE THE FUCK ARE YOU?" It was Elyssa.

I drove over to their house in Chestnut Hill. Winter in Boston, extremely cold. Elyssa opens a peephole in the huge front door and growls, "Wait a minute." Half an hour goes by. I'm freezing to death. Door opens, Elyssa snaps, "Take off your goddamned boots and stay right there." Another half hour. The house is silent. Then Elyssa comes back downstairs, transformed, charming. "Tim! I'm really glad you came over. We really want to talk to you." I look up and Joe Perry's coming down this baronial staircase holding baby Adrian. *Oh, no,* I think. I'm big, 275 pounds, heavy beard, black leather jacket. *This kid's gonna hate me.* Instead Adrian starts pulling my beard and laughing. He grabs my glasses and makes happy noises. "Adrian is an excellent judge of character," Elyssa purrs. "You will manage Joe." She takes the baby and disappears.

We went upstairs to Joe's library. He sits behind a beautiful Victorian desk, his hands shaking, and tells me the whole story of why he left Aerosmith. I asked if he wanted to go back to the band and he said no. Joe said his life was all fucked up and he needed direction. We had a few drinks, did some blow, stayed up all night. In the morning, he said, "Tim, I want you to manage me."

Two weeks went by, and I left a hundred unreturned calls with his service. Finally I called the service. "Oh, they haven't picked up their messages for a year. We mail them once a month." It was preposterous. *How am I gonna get to him?* Finally he called and I went over again. That's when he gave me the drawer full of mail and I learned how broke he was.

I called Don Law, who told me to go fuck myself. So I told Joe he had to get the Project on the road so we could build a war chest. And I reached into my savings and started paying Joe's bills. That's when it became clear to me that I had met my first real hard-core drug addict. This guy didn't go an hour without putting something into his body. He was very manipulative. Joe got $20,000 out of me like *that*. I'd never been around the lifestyle before; Elyssa taking a limo to the supermarket, buying $500 worth of food, throwing it all out three days later. Their backyard raccoon weighed more than I did.

For the rest of that year [1982], we had the Project out on the road as much as we could. One of the first things we did with Joe was a benefit for gun control.

Joe Perry: The Project was a little weird. I couldn't pay the guys what their talents were worth, and David Hull was in the process of leaving. I was drinking, unhappy about so many things in my life.

The one good thing was that Brad Whitford started to work with me. We started doing three dates with him in the band and it turned into a month. It was like having a missing limb sutured back on. Just having him there, I felt like some of the old dynamic was back, and we wrote a song, "Wait for the Night."

Tim Collins: Back from the road, and Elyssa starts going crazy. We had Joe down in New York doing a photo shoot with some half-naked models for *Oui* [an offshoot of *Playboy* aimed at the college market]. She got wind of this and called me up, hysterical, and screamed that if Joe was photographed with any naked sluts she was going to throw Adrian off the balcony. She was threatening to hurt her son.

So I made a decision. Elyssa was irrational and out of control. Joe had a seizure while the Project was in North Carolina. He had to detox and get clear.

So I called Elyssa's mother and brought in their family doctor and got her committed to a locked psychiatric ward. Now we had to convince Joe. Sitting in my office, I asked Doc McGrath what was the worst thing we could do to shame Joe into cooperating with us.

"That's easy, boss. Tell his mother."

So I called Mary Perry. And we convinced Joe to go to a psychiatric hospital to dry out.

Joe Perry: Tim helped me to see I had to dry out. Couldn't sleep, pills, a quart of Jack Daniel's a day, and a gallon of beer to wash it down. They put me on the psychiatric floor, locked the door, and I went out of my mind. The addicts' unit. Full of kids. "Dude! Hey! Check it out! IT'S FUCKIN' JOE PERRY!!"

So I complained and they put me in a padded cell. After a few hours,

I checked out without medical approval. I went to Elyssa's mother's house on Beacon Street and she fed me soup. Elyssa had been put away too, against her will, and had talked her way out. The clinic had given me a bunch of Tuinals, so I had a little stash as soon as I was back on the street.

Tim Collins: So that was our first stab at a proactive approach. Later we detoxed Joe at Elyssa's mother's house with a doctor we were working with, but that didn't take either. We knew we had to get Joe clear, and we somehow knew that he could do it. Everyone could see that he needed to get away from Elyssa and that she needed it too. We talked about this and at some point known only to himself, he made the decision to leave her.

Joe Perry: I walked out the door in Newton and all of a sudden this fuckin' weight was lifted off my shoulders. I was free. I could go out and drive around if I wanted.

I thought, *What the fuck have I put myself through all these years?* Because within two days I was a new man. I hadn't even been *out* in years. It felt so great to just take off with my band and fuck off. That's when I finally got to do what most people think you do in a rock 'n' roll band: insane parties, a different girl every night. It was so unlike me, someone who'd always been in a stable relationship. I went nuts.

I did a lot of interviews and they all asked me about Aerosmith. I told them I wanted to be in a band and I want it to stand for something. I want it to stand for hard-edged rock 'n' roll. Not "punk" or "heavy metal," just American rock 'n' roll. That was my philosophy.

9: Get in the Van and *Go*

Joe Perry: I was living on the road for weeks at a time. When I came to Boston to visit my son, Tim would put me up in a rooming house. I was basically homeless. Elyssa didn't want me to have any contact with Adrian. Most of the time, I had to get a lawyer to see him. On his second birthday, she let me spend five minutes with him. If my support payments were two days late, she'd have me arrested. If I showed up at the house to get my guitars, she'd call the police. I was arrested again when I went over—I was flipping out, needed my instruments to make a living—and there was a restraining order against me I didn't even know about. Finally one time the cops let me get the guitars and go.

But some were missing because she'd sold them. Then I went into a jewelry store in Coolidge Corner, Brookline, and found some of my stuff there that she'd sold. Solid gold Aerosmith wings. My jewelry. Tim got calls from guys who'd just bought a guitar of mine for $1,000, who wanted to do us a favor by selling it back to us for $2,000. It was a hard time. There was no money. At one point, it looked like I was going to jail for nonsupport.

Mark Parenteau: I had known Joe Perry from when I was a deejay in Detroit.

Anyway, time passes and it's late '82 and I'm doing afternoons on WBCN and one night I'm at Spit [nightclub] on Lansdowne Street and I see and hear this black Porsche with a stabilizer on the back screaming down the street. The Porsche swerves up to the curb where I'm standing and stops with a lurch by a hydrant. Joe Perry gets out. Now, you never saw Joe Perry in Boston. Totally invisible. I kept waiting for the passenger door to open and it doesn't. *My God, he's alone.* "Joe! Hey, man, it's Mark. Mark Parenteau from BCN. What are you doing here?"

He told me he'd just had a fight with his wife. A bad fight. He needed a drink and didn't know where else to go. I asked if he wanted me to kind of look after him inside. "I'd appreciate that," he said. "Because it can get pretty weird." So I took him into Spit, and it *did* get pretty weird with people hitting on him. Then we went to Thumper the coke dealer's house in Brookline to buy some blow, then back to my bachelor pad at 15 The Fenway. It was near the station and was known as the Cotton Club because we had a lot of parties there. Joe passed out on my couch.

So we started hanging out. It was like Joe had surfaced after being underwater and not breathing for a couple of years.

Joe Perry: Mark kept telling me that we had to get Aerosmith back together, but I didn't really listen. I wanted to keep the Project going, but the only way I was holding the band together was by answering the phone and pleading for another week. The IRS had sealed my door, seized the property. Tim Collins said, "Listen, you gotta stay out on the road. I can get you the gigs. You gotta get out on the road and do it because it's the only way you're gonna get anywhere." So we went out in a van. I couldn't bring Elyssa, and that's when I really left, because I knew I was gonna die in that house if I didn't get out of that relationship. I remember being on the road and looking back and thinking, *maybe it's death for me back there.*

The last version of the Project was totally insane, and so was the year we spent together on the road doing the Project's MCA album [*Once a Rocker Always a Rocker*]. The new singer, Cowboy Mach Bell, was a rock 'n' roll guy who grew up in the next town over from me [Holliston, Massachusetts] and had a group called Thundertrain. He loved to rave and be in a band, so he replaced Charlie Farren. We auditioned Danny Hargrove and he replaced David Hull on bass. Joe Pet was the drummer. It was just for fun, a good-time band, no illusions about the group going straight to the top. They were young guys who didn't give a shit, like wild men, fuckin' pirates. Get in the van and *go.*

And I was free, single for the first time. I'd missed the whole "legendary" life of the rock star. We went out on the road and I went berserk for the first time in my life. Wine, women, and song. Exotic dancers. A Playboy Bunny. I'd never done this crazy stuff before. There was one Super Bowl Sunday in Cincinnati where we had the police at our hotel three times in one night. There was blood on the walls, which they didn't like. My road manager was rushed to the hospital. I had to talk to the cops and the hotel detectives and beg them not to throw us out in the cold. I learned that it's one thing when you get arrested in Boston and your lawyer can get you out in a couple of hours, but when you have to find a lawyer in another town, it's no fuckin' fun.

Tim Collins: The madness was only beginning. The band came back to Boston, where Doc McGrath showed up at my office with a gun, held me hostage, and tried to get me to sign papers naming him as Joe's co-manager—at gunpoint. We got him out of the office and fired him. We hired a guy named Jay Machin to take his place as road manager and the Project went back out on the road.

Two weeks go by. Then I get a call from Machin. More trouble. The band was driving from New Orleans to Florida in this beautiful air-conditioned van that we got them and had stopped for the night at a Holiday Inn family resort. Since Joe was wasted in the back of the van, they wrapped him in a blanket, carried him up to his room, and put him to bed. The band and their road sluts went swimming in the hotel pool, drunk out of their minds. These crazy roadies started to moon the tourist moms and dads, who supplied them with the horrified reaction they needed. Then this lunatic roadie got on the diving board, and people started to stampede out of there as he pissed in the pool. Mach Bell's parading around nude. Out of control. The police arrived, arrested Mach and the roadie, and threw the band out of the hotel.

Joe was comatose, so the roadies wrapped him back up in his sheet and carried him across the street—asleep—to another motel, where he wakes up, not realizing he'd been moved. Mach Bell calls me from jail: "Tim, what do I *do*?"

I freak out. *What the fuck am I doing with my life?*

I called Joe. He's schwacked, slurring his words, really out of it. "Tim, take it easy. What are you yelling about? Everything's fine. We're in the Holiday Inn."

"Joe, look at the phone."

"That's weird. It says Ramada Inn. How did I get here?" I hung up and called another road manager, Earthquake [Greg Mortin], who flew down, got them out of jail so they could finish their dates, and come home.

10: Horror
at the Centrum

Joe Perry: There were a few times when Steven and I would talk on the phone, run into each other, check in. Once the Project was in Canada and we heard that Aerosmith was playing twenty miles away. I was with my girlfriend Kirsten, who I'd met on the road and she ended up staying three months. I grabbed a bottle of Jack Daniel's and drove over to meet the guys, thinking how weird it was that I'd been out of Aerosmith almost four years. I went in the dressing room. There was Dufay, Crespo, all the guys. It was low-key. We drank a little, and I split.

I never saw Jimmy Crespo play. It was weird to think of those two other guitar players, but it wasn't strong enough to make me go back.

Tim Collins: I first met Steven Tyler when the Project was playing the Bottom Line in New York and Steven came to the show [September 1982]. I'm doing security in front of the dressing room. Steven comes up. "Can I go in?" "Sure." I turn sideways, but my belly is still in the way. "A few sit-ups will take care of that," Steven sneers. I go, "You're right, but what are you gonna do about your ugly face?" He snorted and went on in. I thought, *I've either gained his respect or just destroyed my career.* Later I introduced myself, gave Steven my phone number. A while afterward, he called me late at night from the Miami studio where they were working on *Rock in a Hard Place* and told me, "Joe should come back to the band." He accused me, blamed me for keeping Joe on the road with the Project. I told him, "It's not *me*, man. I'm on *your* side. I'd *love* to see Aerosmith back together." "Yeah, so would I." Then he hung up. I tried to keep tabs on Steven's whereabouts via this guy Brimstone. I usually knew where to reach Steven.

In the spring [of 1983], we were invited to Aerosmith's show at the new Worcester Centrum, a 14,000-seat arena forty miles west of Boston. Joe was living in my house with a girl he'd met in San Francisco, and we all went out together. Backstage, Steven grabbed Joe and disappeared into the dressing room. I tried to follow, but the huge bodyguard wouldn't let me in. I knew something was happening, so I went to get David Krebs, with whom I'd been having semicordial informal discussions about getting the band back together. I told Krebs, "Look, there may be problems. Joe's not doing heroin, but I don't know about your people." "Steven's clean," Krebs said. "We just had him in rehab." But when Krebs and I tried to get in, Floyd the bodyguard wouldn't let Krebs in either.

Joe told me later that they were snorting up some very pure heroin that Cyrinda had brought.

Showtime. The crowd is buzzing, yelling. The merchandise is selling. I felt like a shark tasting blood. It was my first encounter with Aerosmith—the anticipation, the almost religious power, the energy, the money. More than that: the rock 'n' roll history, the notoriety. It was such a force field. I'd never felt this huge energy so up close. *This is what it's all about,* I'm thinking. *This should happen.*

Then Steven passes out in front of 14,000 kids. They canceled the show and the rest of the band blamed Joe and me for bringing in heroin and sabotaging their big local homecoming.

Joe Perry: Steven and I got high in the dressing room. I stayed in—didn't want to see the band without me—and after ten minutes I hear the music stop. And then Tom and Joey came in and started accusing me.

Brad Whitford: I heard about the Centrum thing and thought, *If Joe and Steven are gonna sit down and work this out, I want to be there.* But as soon as Joe walked in, Steven was reunited with his heroin buddy, his mutually self-destructive relationship. Everybody assumed that Joe brought the dope and got Steven so high he collapsed. Man, it was scary, and I'd seen Steven hit the deck a couple of times. One night I thought he was dead. Another, I wanted to kill him myself. Anyway, they carried him back and all the wives were crying. It was very scary and sad. I left, sat in my car, thought about how broke I was, and still felt, *Whew, thank God I'm not part of that.*

Tom Hamilton: All the time we worked on *Rock in a Hard Place* we looked forward to getting the album out, going on the road, and picking up our huge success right where we'd left it. Then reality seeped in. Every show, kids at the stage door: "Where's Joe?" The album bombed, the gigs got smaller and smaller, everything deteriorated. Finally some of the club gigs didn't even sell out.

We knew we could count on the Worcester Centrum show. It was our hometown crowd, the heartland of Aeromania, at least a solid house. We were getting ready backstage when I heard Joe was there. I was excited because it would be the first time Joe saw the band since he left. We were supposed to go on at 9 P.M., but it didn't happen. Richie Guberti, our tour manager, came up and whispered that Joe had been in Steven's dressing room. David Krebs was there and I wondered if it had to do with Joe. David had been advocating a reconciliation between those two for a long time. I knew they weren't ready yet.

Steven popped out of his dressing room looking pretty buzzed. I myself was well prepped on Jack Daniel's. Joe looked distant. We made our way into the hall and went into the first song. The band and the audience were slamming! The crowd's energy flowed into us and we turned it into our own energy, really flowing. We cranked out three songs and started to gain momentum. But during the fourth song, Steven turned around and faced me, totally gray, and mouthed the words "I'm . . . fucked . . . up." Richie and another guy ran out and carried Steven off.

We ended up in a room just off the stage. The gig was trashed. I was livid. Joey was in the corner raging at Steven, who had partly recovered. Steven got up and lurched toward me. I think he was going to apologize, but I just shoved him away so hard I hurt my thumbs. I found Joe out in the hall, took him into a closet, and started yelling at him. He was stoned, disoriented, and kept insisting he hadn't given Steven anything. All I knew was that they were together and then this great gig went down the toilet.

As bad as that show was, it was an important step. It was now plain

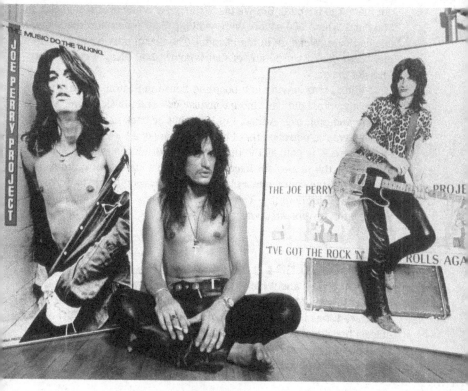

Joe Perry, 1983
(PHOTO: RON POWNALL)

and undeniable to everyone how much would have to get sorted out before Aerosmith was anywhere near ready to put itself back together again.

Joe Perry: [In early 1983] Tim booked the Project in Venezuela, where we spent two weeks snorting the indescribably fresh products of nearby Peru and eating delicious and cheap steaks. In Caracas, I met a hospitable girl named Adrianna who got a song named after her on *Once a Rocker*.

Back in the U.S.A., we're driving down south, cruising in our van. I'm watching this chain gang of prisoners working on the roadside when I had a convulsion. One of the roadies stuck his wallet in my mouth and got me to the hospital. But we made the gig at some overheated club in Maryland where 600 sailors were waiting. Two songs into the show, I crashed over. Woke up in the hospital. The doctor's trying to interview me. "Joe? Joe? Ever do any of that heroin?" Me: "No, of course not!" They let me go.

I think I was staying in a boarding house in Boston. I didn't have a home anymore. I did have more convulsions—and physical symptoms of anxiety and guilt over Adrian. But I couldn't go back to Elyssa. Our relationship was so poisoned that I had to stay away if I was gonna survive. I was a wreck, in pain all the time. I couldn't drink enough, because I no longer had the money for major dope. When I almost hit bottom, Tim grabbed me and sent me to a place called Westwood Lodge to dry out. It was a joke: dribble bibs, Thorazine, more drugs. When I got out two weeks later, my first stop was the liquor store.

Tim Collins: I started getting advice from some of the best doctors in Boston about how to stabilize Joe and wean him from his addiction. Cowboy Mach Bell, a swinging bachelor who knew all the girls, introduced Joe to a hairdresser named Glenda. Joe moved in with her and at least had a roof over his head. We got Joe a record deal with MCA, and that spring he made *Once a Rocker Always a Rocker* at Blue Jay Studio in Carlisle, Mass., Joe coproducing with Michael Golub.

Joe Perry: I liked that record. It sounded unproduced and was basically live. "Four Guns West" was what that band was all about. "Black Velvet Pants." "Bang a Gong" was the old T. Rex riff we used to warm up on. We played it at live shows and saw the kids really getting off on it. (They'd never heard of T. Rex.) "Women in Chains" came from a band in Nashville. I thought it was cool to do a pro-woman song after all the heavy metal misogyny that was around. I never liked that stuff. We put a disclaimer on the back of the record. "There are no synthesizers on this album."

Halfway through the record, MCA tried to drop me. They had a new president [Irving Azoff] and he just didn't want to know. In the end, they figured it would be cheaper to finish the record—and bury it—than to buy out my contract. I didn't really give a shit. I just wanted another record so I could tour. Then it came out late that year and bombed, which set the next episode in motion.

11: She Never Heard of Aerosmith

Joe Perry: Summer of '83. I'm living with Glenda the hairdresser, which is why I look the way I do on the cover of *Once a Rocker*, the third and last Project album. I thought it turned out pretty well—the album, not the cover. When it came time to do a video, we chose "Black Velvet Pants" and auditioned some people to be in the thing. That's how I met Billie Montgomery.

Tim Collins: We're auditioning in my office and in walks this beautiful blonde model. She came in, our hearts stopped for a second, and I saw her and Joe lock eyes. They flirted a little—she was seductive in a nice way—and I knew I had a big problem on my hands.

But we hired her and said we'd see her at the shoot in a few days. When she left, I said, "Joe, this girl is trouble. She's a married woman. You're in a good scene with Glenda and you're not even divorced from Elyssa yet. Be careful of your power. Please, just do me one favor here: Be careful."

He looked at me like I was insane. From that minute on, he wanted her every moment of every day. At the video shoot, Joe was all over her. Glenda took one look at this and went berserk. She went over, cursed Billie out, and punched her in the face. We had to pull them apart. Joe asked me to drive Glenda home and in the car I'm trying to soothe her. "Look, Glenda, don't worry. They're just flirting. C'mon, he's a rock star. It doesn't mean—"

"Shut up, you faggot," she blurted between sobs. "Don't you get it? HE'S GOING TO MARRY HER!!"

Glenda was right. Joe and Billie have been almost inseparable ever since. Billie's marriage was finished anyway. Joe moved in with her and her son, and she supported him and paid the rent during the long months that we fought to get the band back together.

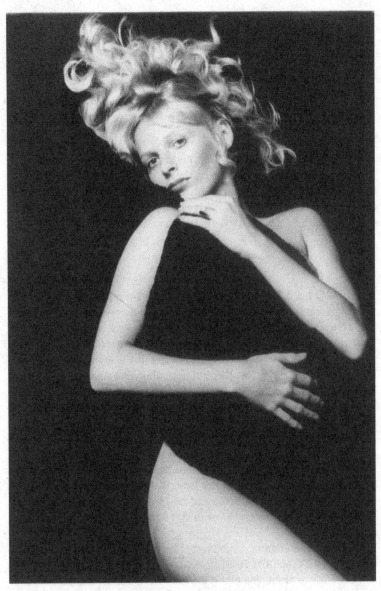

Billie Perry in her modeling days
(PERRY COLLECTION)

Yo! Tyler! Hey! Where's Joe Fuckin' Perry??

399

Billie Perry: The reason I didn't know about Aerosmith was because Willie—my husband at the time—always told me, "Beware of bands with logos."

Yes, I was married to someone else when I met Joe Perry, but I wasn't living with my husband. The marriage was pretty much over by then.

I was living with my son Aaron in an apartment on Broadway in Cambridge. I was working as a model to make ends meet when I did that video with Joe. Every few days I'd bake a batch of chocolate chip cookies for Aaron's snack when he got home from school. One day he came home and found Joe in our kitchen. Joe was sitting at the table with his back to us, his long black hair falling down his back. Aaron gives me an annoyed eleven-year-old's glance. "Hey, Mom," he whispered. "Who is this long-haired freaky-looking guy? And why is he eating my cookies?"

I was raised in Indiana, descended from old American stock, country people, hill people some of 'em, related to Davy Crockett on one side. My maiden name was Billie Paulette Montgomery.

I left home at fifteen to live with my older sister in Florida. My parents divorced and it really threw me off balance. In Florida, I met a college student from Boston, and we married and had Aaron when I was seventeen, which is how I got to Boston. Then I left my husband, moved to Cambridge, finished high school, and enrolled at the Mass. College of Art. In 1977, I met Willie "Loco" Alexander, a mainstay of the Boston rock 'n' roll scene, a true bohemian and an artist. We were involved in New Wave, kind of punk/Dada art, *Skunk Piss* magazine, the local art world. We got married and I started modeling after I made a head-sheet for myself out of color Xeroxes and sent them to an agency on Newbury Street. I started to get work and we moved to a rent-controlled apartment at 399 Broadway.

I was with Willie for six years until I got tired of living hand-to-mouth. I needed security and wanted more children. Willie was a true bohemian and wasn't interested in any of that. I didn't—and still don't—have the heart to change someone into something they're not meant to be.

When Willie moved out, I took a job selling advertising at WBOS, a local rock station that went to country programming not long after I got there. I kept taking modeling jobs, which is how I came to that audition for Joe Perry's video. I had a friend named Julia Bell, who is now married to Mach Bell, who I knew was in this band I'd never seen called the Project. He was also a friend of Willie's. Mach told Tim Collins about me. "Get her. She's stable, she's pretty, she's married to Willie."

It was a hot summer day. I'm in a white T-shirt, white culottes, white sneakers, like Keds. Tim was a really nice guy with gold records on the wall, very friendly, and then Joe walks in and my mind was just . . . freaking *blown*. He was in really tight faded jeans, sneakers, a faded T-shirt, really tan, *really* long hair.

This strange thing happened. I looked at him. It was like another part of me had walked into the room. That was the feeling I got. I stood up to shake his hand. And my heart and my soul said to him: *What took you so long to find me?*

It was like recovering a soul mate—a separated Platonic entity, so hard to explain without sounding corny—but it was like kindred spirits interweaving with each other down through the generations. It's hard to explain and it'll sound silly to most people, but that's how it felt—like a lost part of me, something very familiar.

We sat down. My head-sheet was on the table. Joe picked up his pictures and put them next to mine so the two faces were together. *Hmmm*, I thought. *Not a bad couple.*

Joe was living with someone. She was either a hairdresser or a stripper—or both. He was going through a divorce.

So they hired me. I worried about getting paid, because of the rumors I'd heard about Tim Collins' business practices. I went over to Strawberries Records on Memorial Drive and bought some Joe Perry Project records, and then I went up with Julia Bell to see them play at a state fair in New Hampshire. I saw how talented Joe was and thought he had a lot of potential. How come he hadn't made it?

I didn't know about Aerosmith. I knew about "Dream On," but not about the band. Or their logo.

Anyway, there was this real attraction to one another. We both knew something heavy was going on. And so I went to the video shoot [at the Strand Theater in Dorchester] and we did our thing. [The story line involved a girl putting on a pair of black velvet pants and going to see the Joe Perry Project, eventually ending up onstage playing sax with the band.] Again there was this electric magnetism between us and it freaked out Joe's girlfriend. At the break, I was walking down the hall and the next thing I knew this madwoman jumps on me and starts punching me. Tim Collins pulled her off and took her away. I thought I'd have a black eye, but I didn't. We finished filming and I went home.

When he found out that Willie and I weren't together, Joe started coming over. We'd talk and kind of became buddies. He was upset about his wife, his son, the marriage breaking apart. I was falling in love with him, but at the same time I didn't want another artist. This guy didn't even have a car. We drove around in my little Chevette. The first time he took me out to dinner, at a Mexican restaurant in Brookline, his credit card came back to the table cut in two. He said, "Billie, I'm $300,000 in debt."

I wanted a family, a house, a normal life. But I think Joe Perry cast a spell over me. It was like he seduced me when I wasn't looking.

At Christmas that year [1983], Elyssa invited him over. I told him, "Please, go spend time with your wife and son. See what kind of feelings you have."

The day after Christmas, my buzzer rang at three in the morning. It was Joe and his friend Michael Striar, both fucked up. I let them upstairs. Then Joe told Striar to go and he offered me a Quaalude. I said, "Joe, you don't have to give me a pill to go to bed with you." And so he stayed.

One night Joe took me to dinner in the North End. Under an outrageous full moon, he kissed me—so romantic. Driving home, near Logan Circle, the radio starts blasting "Back in the Saddle." Joe says, "That was my band." I said, "OK, cut the shit, you don't have to impress me. You got the girl!"

Joe Perry: All my life I'd always heard a lot of talk about people finding their soul mates. The moment I first saw Billie, I realized I'd finally found mine. It was literally incredible to me that she seemed to feel the same way. It was a pretty great feeling. It changed the way I lived my life and set up everything that happened for us later. A case of Fate smiling down on me once again—the only problem being that it seemed to make Tim Collins really jealous and a little bit nuts. I remember how he'd call me up and rail me for hours about how I shouldn't get involved with her. On some level he seemed to find it threatening and couldn't really relate to what was going on. The weird thing was, he didn't mind when I was fucking around with one-night-stands. Perhaps he knew that this was something special.

12: What Happened to My Band?

Tim Collins: By October [1983], we knew that *Once a Rocker* had bombed and that Joe's solo career was going down the tubes. Brad Whitford came and worked a bunch of shows with the Project, which contributed an amazing burst of energy, but it was getting harder to book them without any record company support. It was a low period.

We'd hang out at Mark Parenteau's house. We'd call up the local coke-heads in Boston and invite them to hang out with Joe Perry. We had a four-gram minimum to get into the party. We'd let them shmooze with Joe for an hour and then kick all the B-list people out, leaving us with thirty-five to forty grams of coke for free. After one of these parties, I did a lot of blow and got really depressed. Joe was passed out on the couch. It was three in the morning.

But Mark has all this energy and he starts in on me.

"You're fucking up, Tim. This band should be back together."

"Forget it. Joe *hates* Steven."

"No. He doesn't hate him. His *pride* is hurt. They just need to kiss and make up. It's like a love affair. You gotta make this your *mission*. You *have* to put Aerosmith back together. I mean, this is *insane*. They're one of the best bands that there ever was. You don't even *know* what you're dealing with. Here, look, listen to this."

He starts getting albums out of his collection and puts on "You See Me Crying." Then "Sweet Emotion," "Toys," "Walk This Way." Mark's one of the great FM deejays, and for the next two hours he programs a private Aerosmith radio show for me: live stuff, rare tracks, album classics. "Wait a minute, have you ever heard *this?*" He blasts "Back in the Saddle" until the walls begin to vibrate, all the time pontificating about the band's monumental stature, addictive charisma, utter coolness to the max, and hyping my brains out. "Greatest American Rock Band—*ever*. The American Rolling Stones—except they're *better* than the Stones. Steven is a better singer than Mick. Joe's a much better guitarist than Keith." He basically turned me on to who Aerosmith was that night.

"Tim, now you know. You gotta put this band together. It's your mission from God."

"But Joe and Steven still hate each other."

"Ah, that's just a *detail*. They're *brothers*. Don't you hate *your* brothers? They'll get over that crap."

So I went home, very upset, but feeling like I've had this strong experience listening to these Aerosmith songs. I didn't think putting Aerosmith together again was an option, because Joe said it wasn't. But Mark had lit a fire under me. I ended up staying up all night and into the morning, writing out a game plan on yellow legal paper until noon. At 2 P.M., I walked into my office and my partner, Steve Barrasso, is pissed off because I'd missed an important meeting about another of our clients. I said, "Steve, calm down. I've had a revelation. We're putting Aerosmith back together, come hell or high water." I gave him the rap—hit records, videos, stadiums, millionaires, biggest band in the world. He looks at me and says, "Tim, you've finally gone crazy." And he walked out.

That's how our partnership ended. I tried to convince him, but he said, "Get rid of Joe and we'll get back to our core business, do what we do best. We can't handle a big act. You can't handle it. Look at you, you're becoming a drug addict."

I said, "Maybe we'll co-manage them with David Krebs. But I'm gonna do it with or without you."

"David Krebs will fuck you in a second."

He was right, but my naïveté index was pretty high. Then other clients got wind of my plans. Jonathan Edwards, a great singer/songwriter, called up and said, "Tim, you have to make a choice. It's Joe Perry or me."

Joe hit bottom in Los Angeles, while he was playing some gigs at the Country Club on Reseda [in January 1984]. He'd played there before and done well; now he couldn't even sell out one gig. Up until then he'd still been resistant to anything I said about Aerosmith, but I knew I had to try again. We had severe IRS problems, child support problems that threatened to send Joe to jail. I'm draining my office to support my Aerosmith hobby that isn't going anywhere. All this time I'm trying to plant seeds in Joe's mind. Real manipulative stuff. We'd be driving around. "God, Joe, there's the Rose Bowl. Do you remember selling it out? Isn't it weird not to sell out the thousand-seat club you're playing tonight?"

It wasn't pretty, but I was getting desperate.

After the show, we went back to this apartment I'd rented while I was dealing with MCA. Joe didn't look happy. "Tim," he whispered, "throw everybody out. I'm bummed. We've gotta talk." And he opens up: the pain, the separation from his family, the fighting, the drugs. He just broke down. I'd never seen that before from Joe. No one had.

I gave him the rap about getting together with Steven. "Just try it," I begged. "All you have to do is pick up the phone. *This is your brother.*"

Joe picks up his head, brushes the hair out of his face, and looks me in the eye. "I want to do it," he said quietly. "I fuckin' wanna do it."

"That's incredible!"

"But I don't know how to reach him."

"I have his number. He's at the Gorham Hotel in New York. I talked to him."

Joe was surprised. *"You've been talking to Steven?"*

"Yeah, he calls me when he's looking for you." I dialed the number.

"What do I say?"

"Say anything. He's very emotional. You left his band, which means everything to him. Call him and put aside everything. Never mind what anyone did wrong or right. We'll fix it all later. Just do it."

Walk This Way

Joe Perry: Something occurred to me. *Elyssa isn't around anymore. What is it I have against Steven? What was it I had against Tom? And it dawned on me. I love the guys in the band. What happened to my band?*

Tim Collins: Joe called Steven and they stayed on the phone for two and a half hours and I'm thinking, *Oh, my God—my phone bill!*

Next day Joe Perry and I flew back east to find Steven and resurrect Aerosmith—or die trying.

The Battle
for Aerosmith

I don't want fans to think
we're clean, upstanding American
boys, but we are Americans,
and we do stand up.

—Joe Perry

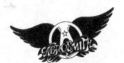

s Perry and Tyler undertook
the process of burying the hatchet, Aerosmith continued to play sporadically throughout 1983, including a string of Eastern dates in the spring and some California shows later in the year. Steven was in and out of several dry-out programs, which were unable to treat his problems.

It was a different music business from the one Aerosmith had fought its way into. MTV replaced FM radio as the preferred medium for showcasing bands. Prince and Madonna dominated dance music, with Van Halen and Def Leppard and U2 filling the hard rock gap left by Aerosmith's exile. On the horizon were the MTV bands—Bon Jovi, Duran Duran, Mötley Crüe, Ratt, and the beginnings of Guns N' Roses in L.A., playing "Mama Kin" in Sunset Strip rock clubs. The early rappers—Kurtis Blow, Grandmaster Flash—were starting to sell records. In Hollis, Queens, teenage deejays were cutting grooves out of old Aerosmith records for a new generation to rap over.

In California, a movie was in production based on a satirical cliché-driven rock band that looked a lot like Aerosmith. This Is Spinal Tap featured a desperate has-been band releasing a hack album with Stonehenge on the cover, which was a commercial bomb.

Sometime during that year, Aerosmith—Steven, Tom, and Joey—resigned with Leber-Krebs for another five albums.

In August, at an outdoor show in Anaheim, California, Steven stopped the band four songs into the set. He sat at the edge of the stage with his legs swinging and started telling jokes to the audience. The band tried to start again, but Steven waved them down, trying to finish his joke. Joey Kramer, writhing in agony on his drum riser, realized that it was Aerosmith itself that was the joke.

1: I'll Have the Welsh Rarebit

Steven Tyler: I started having these nightmares around this time. I arrive at the gig without any stage clothes, without any clothes at all, or the gear hadn't gotten there and we can't go on. Then I collapsed onstage a couple of times and there were the usual cancellations and inevitable bad press and speculation about the end of the band.

Then David Krebs and a psychiatrist, Dr. Lloyd Moglen, got me into rehab. I couldn't walk the streets of New York because I was wobbling so bad. I had to go get a big can of Foster's lager and chug it down, just to lose this feeling and get rid of the D.T.'s. They sent me first to Good Samaritan [Hospital]: This was my first bout with sobriety, two years before the rest of the band realized we were all in the same boat together.

Then I met an older woman who'd been to Hazelden [in Minnesota], and I went there next. Deathly sobering. Four nights of withdrawal, in solitary. Fifth night, they move me down to a shared room, four or five beds. I realize that I have absolutely no buzz going on inside me. I couldn't believe being straight. I hated it. I'd spin around like an autistic kid, just to get dizzy. Got on the phone, called David Krebs, screaming at the top of my lungs:

"They're trying to change me! They're altering my ego! I'm not gonna have the same personality! I don't even know who I am anymore! I'm terrified!"

He'd tell me, "We're going to give you *back* your personality."

Teresa would fly in for the weekend and bring me a nip-sized bottle from the plane. Then we'd go out on the grounds and do the horizontal bop.

I had a hard, hard time getting sober. I came out of Hazelden and David Krebs met me at the airport. He smoked a joint in the limo on the way into town. I stayed clean for a few seconds, then started using whatever I could get my hands on. I snorted my plane, my Porsche, my house. I'm broke, living in the Gorham Hotel with Teresa on the $20 a day that Krebs was doling out to me.

Joey Kramer: It was rough. There was no money. I was on the balls of my ass. Joe was off in one place, Brad in another, Steven's in the Gorham, and Tom and I are pulling our hair out, not knowing what was going on. I spent everything I had—Keogh plan, life insurance, Ferrari, houses, you name it, until, finally, *nothing*. I was living on advances.

Brad Whitford: No money, no income, all my savings going to alimony and mortgages. Karen's parents had to loan us money to buy a crib when our son Zack was born. I sold my Daytona. Sad to see it go. Sold my guitars—vintage Fender Broadcaster, old Strats, Les Pauls ('52, '55, two '58s, gold-top and a Sunburst, and a rare 1960 flame-top)—and it almost killed me. Guitars I let go for $6,500 are worth $75,000 today. Sold my house and we moved to a rental, and hoped somehow the band could get back together.

Tom Hamilton: We'd seen what was coming and sold our house in '81 and moved to a cheaper condo in Newton so we could survive the hard times. But every few months toward the end of 1983, I'd hear through a third party that Steven and Joe were talking on the phone. I'd get fuckin' scared, because I thought we'd just dive back into the same sicko situation we had before Joe left. It wasn't until 1984, when I knew Elyssa was gone, that I was comfortable with the idea of putting the band back together.

Tim Collins: When Joe and I got to New York, I called Steven at the Gorham. The phone rang ten times before Teresa picked it up. Steven got on and said to come over. We get to the Gorham and Joe calls up from the seedy lobby. He hangs up and says, "He only wants me to go up."

"Joe, you *can't* do heroin with him." (I'm the typical nervous co-dependent.)

"Don't worry. We've got work to do." An hour goes by. Agony. Finally Joe comes down and takes me back up to the apartment. Really funky. Bandannas over the lamps, burning incense, clothes everywhere, candles, a hippie opium den. Steven and Teresa are both totally suspicious of me, but I was prepared for it. Everyone knew that Aerosmith hated outsiders. Steven suggests we go have lunch, talk things over. It takes him five minutes to get ready because he's got four shoulder bags and satchels of stuff that he carried around with him.

We adjourn to Rouchaud's of London, an Olde English-style pub near the Gorham. Steven and Joe both order the Welsh rarebit and then Joe looks Steven right in the eye and starts talking.

Joe Perry: I told Steven, "Look, man, I've changed a lot, and things are different with me. It could be like it used to be. Let's get together and fuckin' try to put it all in the past. I feel like I'm nineteen years old again. I want my band back. C'mon—decks cleared, no baggage, do it right."

Tim Collins: Steven's eyes well up halfway through this. He tries to lean across the table and hug Joe, who was usually impassive, but even Joe's wiping his eyes a little. Steven's euphoric! He's talking headlining stadiums again, making millions, being a big band again, the I.R.S., ex-wives taking their money. We're all getting giddy. "Call Krebs," Steven tells us, "and we'll put all this together."

"Hold on," says Joe. "I'm not working with Krebs."

"What are you talking about? Who's gonna manage us?"

"Tim."

"HIM!!??"

"I want Tim to manage us."

"Leber-Krebs has the organization!"

"I won't work with Krebs again."

"No, no," I say. "Forget about Krebs and me. Just commit to doing it and worry about the music." They both go, "OK," and we all shake hands and the lunch is over. Joe goes home to Boston and I go to see David Krebs.

His office is a wreck. Dead plants, empty fishbowl, boxes piled everywhere. The receptionist is a rock 'n' roll slut from hell, David's secretary is rolling joints, and here's David sitting behind an overwhelmingly chaotic desk.

He was polite at first. He offered me one of his freshly rolled bombers and some blow, but I declined. I was scared and needed to be clear. I told him Joe was broke and David arrogantly admitted owing Joe $150,000.

After I left, Krebs freaked out and started putting out horrible rumors about me. This made Tom and Joey very resistant. Tom wouldn't even meet with me.

Next I went to see Brad at his house. He was still out on his own and came to occasional Project gigs to boost ticket sales. He's broke, but he tells me, "Tim, you don't know what you're doing. You're opening Pandora's box here." And he went on, but I wore him down and it ended with him saying: "OK, if you think you can put it together, I'll try it."

2: Svengali

Billie Perry: Joe was totally broke. He didn't have a car that worked. When he moved in, he wanted to pay half the rent. I said, "Don't bother until you can pay it all." I wanted him to go back to Aerosmith. Maybe we could get a house and have a kid and lead stable lives for a change. Seemed like a good job opportunity to me.

Teresa Tyler: The ice kind of broke around Valentine's Day. Joe and Billie came to see Aerosmith at the Orpheum in Boston [on February 11, 1984]. Brad came. Joe didn't stay for the show, but there wasn't animosity; he just didn't want to get up and play.

Brad Whitford: I went to the Orpheum and saw the band with Crespo and Dufay. It wasn't terrible, but after half an hour I thought, *I've seen enough.* Joe wasn't there, but he went to their hotel afterward.

Billie Perry: Steven called and said they were at the Parker House [Hotel in downtown Boston] and invited us for oysters and beer. Joe declined. I wanted to go because we had no money and I liked oysters. "Ah, I don't know if I want to see him," Joe says. "He can be such a jerk, y'know?" I said, "C'mon, you were in a band with him for such a long time. The worst that could happen would be free oysters." "OK, OK, we'll go." Besides, I wanted to see what Steven Tyler looked like.

He was holding court in the hotel bar with Joe Baptista, the road crew, and an entourage. It went OK, nothing special. Next day Joe didn't want to go to the show. We stayed home and watched *The Road Warrior* instead. We went back to the Parker House after the show—there was a wild party in someone's suite and everyone was really loaded. It was a pretty sleazy scene. Steven and Teresa were there, but they stayed in their room. After a while, we went up to see them. The place was set up like an apartment, with scarves draped over the lamps. I'd never seen anything like that before and thought it was really cool.

Teresa Tyler: Then Joe and Billie invited us up to Billie's apartment for the weekend. They picked us up at the airport in her tiny little white Chevette. It was a great snowy weekend. We barbecued, talked, made friends. Joe and Steven were like brothers who hadn't seen each other in a long time. There was no arguing. Billie and I kind of exchanged looks and hoped it would work out somehow. When we moved back to Boston, Billie took me under her wing, showed me around. She was great.

Billie Perry: They came and stayed at our house and hung out. I thought Steven was funny and that Teresa was down to earth and really pretty. I liked both of them, but Teresa and I hit it it off especially well because we had that mid-Westerner bond.

Tim Collins: The battle for Aerosmith began in February 1984, when Joe and Billie and Brad Whitford went to see Aerosmith's Valentine's Day gig at the Orpheum Theater in Boston. It was the first time all the guys had been together, and they agreed to meet later at Tom's house to talk about reforming the band. I thought my only role was going to be to look after Joe's affairs, because some of the guys didn't want to have anything to do with me, but Joe was adamant.

Joey Kramer: Joe was insisting on new management or he wouldn't come back. We didn't know what to make of Tim. After Krebs, I didn't even want a manager anymore. I was skeptical of Tim, but then I was skeptical of everything, including myself. I was mainly interested in where that day's drugs were coming from. I worked with Joe that spring after his drummer [Joe Pet] got fired, doing about ten Project gigs to help Joe fulfill commitments, so Aerosmith could get rolling.

Joe Perry: Tom's house. We said we'd put it all back together. Tim said he'd take care of business, and if the other guys accepted him as manager, it would happen. All I could do was show them what a great job he'd done for me. I told them I'd been followed around by this Krebs thing, how Krebs had been bad-mouthing me, and it had hurt my band and cost us good bookings. I told them how the pressure to rejoin Aerosmith had increased even as the band went downhill. But it wasn't gonna be that way. I told them, "I'm not gonna have Krebs manage me." I figured it was better to play clubs and give Krebs the finger. At least I was making my own music. I'd been down on the skids, on my own, in the streets and the boarding houses, and these guys hadn't. I'd made three good albums in the four years I'd been out of the band, and what did they have to show—*Rock in a Hard Place*. I was like, "Fuck, man. Let's get back to where we were because we got nothin' to lose."

Steven Tyler: When Tim Collins came along, Joe told me that Tim had taken him under his wing and had been a brother to him and was working his ass off day and night to help him get his life back. I was suspicious, because Tim had grandiose ideas. He'd say, "I'm going to turn you guys back into what you used to be." No one else came along and had the guts to say that to our faces. I still felt loyal to Krebs, but now I wasn't so sure. I had this lawyer named Rick Smith and Richie Supa telling me, "Look what they're doing to your publishing! They got 50 percent! You need to cut a new deal!"

But it was hard. Krebs had us working. I was trying to be loyal. So we postponed doing anything.

Brad Whitford: We all met at Tom's house, the whole band. Tom opened a six-pack of Budweiser and we decided we were gonna try to reform and we all clanked our beers together. Looking for a scapegoat—blame is always a big thing in our band—we settled on David Krebs.

I was psyched. I remember we talked about the fact that we didn't have a record company. "Yeah," someone said, "but we've got a huge fan base." I called my wife and said, "Karen, we're gonna do this."

Tim Collins: The guys couldn't decide about me. Elyssa blamed me for the breakup of her marriage—she told people she hadn't divorced Joe, she'd divorced me—and told Krebs that I was a pervert. It was pretty heavy. He told the guys in the band, "Tim is the Antichrist.

He's got Joe *under his spell*." The funny thing was we *did* have Joe repeatedly hypnotized by Dr. Howard Jonas in Boston, as part of our campaign to get him off drugs. But it all got twisted around and the band started calling me Svengali.

Meanwhile, Aerosmith is still on the road, playing clubs and small halls. [The band appeared with Crespo and Dufay at the 1,500-seat Ritz dance club in New York as late as April 1984. Krebs also had them in the studio, where they cut an instrumental by Jimmy Crespo called "Written in Stone," but Steven never finished the lyrics.] Krebs is still going to MIDEM and other industry conventions, wheeling and dealing, selling publishing rights, even as he knows he's about to lose control of the band. Rumors about Aerosmith getting together started to get around.

Then the cash flow stopped. My Aerosmith fixation had drained our agency dry, and Joe was going to jail for nonsupport. I borrowed $15,000 from a drug dealer friend and Mary Perry loaned Joe $25,000. It was a touch-and-go thing, but we paid everyone back.

HIT PARADER
Aside from the fact that a new generation of hard rock bands has emerged to usurp Aerosmith's premier position in the metal hierarchy, the band's increasingly unpredictable behavior has put their continued existence into question . . .

. . . Rumors continue to persist that Perry and Tyler will rejoin forces. While Perry dismisses the notion with a simple "We'll see," Tyler was more expressive. "I don't know if we'll ever work together again. He can be an arrogant motherfucker at times, but I guess I can be too. But I respect Joe more than anyone I know in this business." (April 1984)

Joe Perry: April 1984. Nothing much was happening except rumors, although I was even getting support from my own band, the Project, to get back with Aerosmith. Cowboy Mach Bell told me, "Go ahead, man. We don't wanna stand in your way." They were really good guys, who were probably more aware of what Aerosmith had meant to people than we were.

Then Tim got a call from Alice Cooper, who wanted me to help him write some songs for an album. I went out to Arizona to meet with him.

Steven Tyler: I called Tim one day trying to find out where Joe was. "Well, he's working with Alice Cooper." It was the first time I had the balls to call Joe Perry up with all this anger I had in me. "How can you fuckin' be working with Alice? YOU NEED TO BE HERE!!!"

Joe Perry: I told him, "If the other guys don't wanna come on board, I don't know what we're gonna do, but Leber and Krebs *aren't gonna be involved.*"

And Steven went along with it. A lot of ambivalence there, but then he usually makes the right decision out of all the wind and the fury.

Tim Collins: Tyler calls me: "Motherfucker! You're breaking my band up! Why do you have Joe writing with Alice Cooper? Asshole—who the fuck are you!?"

I said, "You're right. Fuck all this. If you were smart, you'd get on a plane today, move to Boston, and start rehearsing with Joe Perry. I'll get you Brad. Forget me and Krebs—we'll work it out. It's about music, man. Forget about the fucking lawyers. That's not how it started out in the Barn, back in New Hampshire."

He pondered this. I heard him say, "Wow," and we hung up. He went over to this club where all his stuff was packed in cardboard boxes and gathered it up and flew to Boston the next day on the Eastern shuttle. My friend Nick LaHage and I go to the airport to pick him up. He gets off the plane looking like the Queen of France. Huge sunglasses, leopardskin vest. Teresa looked beautiful and outrageous—garish lipstick, wild hair. Everyone's gaping. Their luggage was old cardboard, tied up with string. Refugees from New York.

I thought, *What am I doing?*

Steven was really cold to me. You could feel the rage dripping off him. We took him to the Howard Johnson's hotel in Cambridge. Joe and Billie kind of looked after them until we got them an apartment and a place to begin rehearsing.

Tom Hamilton: It was obvious what had to happen. Rick Dufay was even telling us we had to get back together with Joe. But I still feel kind of bad about Jimmy Crespo, just like I did when Pudge Scott had to leave. I feel weird that we never sat down with Jimmy and said, "Man, you did so fuckin' great, but we gotta put the band back together and someday we hope we can make it right for you."

Always meant to call him. Never did.

Joe Perry: Then David Krebs called Tim Collins and complained. Threats were issued, and soon the lawsuits would start flying like bats at sunset. For the next two years, it was war.

3: Large Penis Incorporated

Joe Perry: We wanted to go out on tour before we went back in the studio, to show that Aerosmith was back and actually playing better than ever, because we've always been a live band more than anything else.

A lot of kids had never seen the real Aerosmith live and in our prime. We were away for five years, a long time to a kid who's eighteen years old. We knew the best way to show them that we meant business was just to get out there and blow their ears off.

Tim Collins: One of the first guys I went to see when I was trying to get the band back together was Joe Baptista, Aerosmith's production manager, who literally did everything for them; a big, very gruff guy who put away a quart of Scotch and five packs of cigarettes every day. He was a battle-scarred veteran but a very cool, approachable guy. He drank at a bar up in Peabody on the North Shore, and I went to see him.

Joe Baptista says, "You wanna know the truth? Here it is. Steven Tyler is a fuckin' racehorse. A thoroughbred. High-strung. If you take care of him every day—brush him, feed him his grain, throw him a flake of hay, pick the shit out of his stall, *every day*, he'll run a great race for you. He's a fuckin' racehorse, Tim. You gotta take care of him.

"The other thing is just don't listen to anything he says because he's fuckin' nuts."

No matter how crazy things got, I always came back to the racehorse analogy. Joe Baptista came to work with us.

The plan was for a reunited Aerosmith to go on the road that summer. The Back in the Saddle tour. There was no new record for them to tour behind, no video, no support from their label. In fact, we discovered they didn't really have a label, since they were signed to Leber and Krebs, not CBS. We couldn't even get anyone at the record company to return our calls.

Brad Whitford: The band started rehearsing at the Glen Ellen Country Club in Millis, Mass., owned by Danny Striar, Michael's father. We went to this golf course, took over one of the club buildings, and just got ready to tour. The first rehearsal? Pretty rough. We couldn't remember some of the songs.

It was a little strange because we fired everybody. Anyone who had a connection to the old band was gone. Brian Rohan, who was helping us find a record company because CBS wouldn't talk to us, told us we had to break all the old ties.

Joe Perry: The first rehearsal? More than a little tense, y'know? I had to come back to the house and wash down about six Valiums the size of manhole covers with a six-pack of beer, just to calm down after rehearsal. Then everybody started getting things into perspective.

We're all in our thirties now. It's one thing to say, "All right men, let's go," and clink our beer bottles. It's another to show up at rehearsal, another to go onstage and see how the egos come together. Brad had played with the Project, so that was there. But me and Steven being on the same stage felt kind of weird. I wondered, *How much am I able to project myself in this? How much are these guys going to take from me?* It felt weird.

But we had to go out and play those songs again, instead of trying to write another album. I don't think we could've done it.

Tim Collins: I was trying to build up a war chest so we could get the band on tour and fight the legal battles we knew were coming with Leber-Krebs. Jack Boyle, big concert promoter [Cellar Door Productions], said, "Tell me your story," and wired me fifty grand before I could finish asking him for it. No papers, nothing. We hired a well-known San Francisco attorney, Brian Rohan, to help us make a record deal and he introduced us to booking agent Dan Weiner [of Monterey Peninsula Artists], who loaned us 50K. A promoter in the Midwest loaned us another fifty on the Aerosmith name alone. We got a good advance from a merchandiser for our T-shirts. We found there were people around who remembered how great this band once was and still had the faith that they could be great again.

People kept calling to warn us about what Leber-Krebs would do to us, but I didn't care. I was focused on getting the band together. We rented Steven an apartment on Beacon Hill. We rented another for Joey, who said he didn't want to come back from New York unless we bought them a house. First time I'm having a meeting with Steven and Joe at the Collins-Barrasso office in Allston—a tense meeting over some heavy issues—and Joey Kramer calls and insists he be put through. He was calling to complain that his couch was uncomfortable and that he was going back to New York if we didn't replace it right away. It wasn't the couch. He just wanted a reaction.

Tom Hamilton was resistant to everything because he didn't trust me. He was still hooked into Krebs, but I realized that he was the sanest one of them all. He hadn't lost his house or his cars. He was with the same girl he started with. I knew we could bring him around because he was a decent guy. And Brad was in it for the money, at least at the beginning. But as the rehearsals got really hot and they could smell the old magic coming back through the music, Brad got more into it.

But it was Joe and Steven's show. Everyone knew it.

They started out rehearsing their old material, songs like "Movin' Out," the first thing Joe and Steven wrote together. They got their old albums out and played them to remind themselves of what they liked. "Let the Music Do the Talking" finally became an Aerosmith song after Steven wrote some new lyrics to Joe's song. The energy was just incredible when they were on.

We had a meeting about getting a new record deal on a rainy Sunday afternoon that spring. The Celtics were hot, and we were at the Union Oyster House. This was the first meal the band had eaten together in five years. Joey Kramer brought his baby son Jesse. Everyone got stinking drunk and then went over to Mark Parenteau's house to hang out. Mark starts blasting old Aerosmith songs. He puts on "You See Me Crying" from *Toys in the Attic*. Steven says, "Hey! That's great! We should cover this. Who is it?"

Joe Perry says, "It's *us*, fuckhead."

"No way."

"Who the fuck do you think it is? It's that song you made us get a 109-piece orchestra for."

Steven hadn't recognized it. He'd never sung it in concert, so he'd forgotten it. That was one of the first times I realized how much work Steven needed. And this became a big theme: how fucked up Steven was and how he needed to get clear. It never dawned on us that *everybody* would have to get clear.

Aerosmith's Back in the Saddle tour started in May 1984. We let go of everyone who had worked for the band except for Joe Baptista, who ran the tour and who was the only person in the world who could get Steven Tyler onstage. There were a lot of jitters and nerves. The band still couldn't agree about me. I said, "OK, just call me the tour manager. We'll work it out later."

The band played more than seventy shows over the rest of 1984. They were taking a big risk, touring without an album, counting on their fans, who didn't let them down. Some of the nights were brilliant. Others were horrible.

I never wanted to be the guy that got drugs for Aerosmith, but in the beginning I was carrying a small pharmacy around with me in a metal Halliburton case. I was a traveling prescription drugstore. Then I hired an out-of-work promo guy whose job was to cop enough drugs to keep Steven alive. He'd steal boxes of records and sell them to get even more drugs, and eventually I had to fire him.

The first show of the tour was in Concord, New Hampshire. Steven calls that afternoon and does a number on me. "I'm not going onstage until you, personally, Tim Collins, and nobody else, get me two grams of blow." Usually the promoter took care of this, but Steven was adamant that I had to do this for him. He was serious. I call the coke dealer, who like all coke dealers cut his cocaine with Mannitol, the baby laxative. And I ask him, "Not that you would *ever dream* of cutting your blow, but could you possibly get me two grams of Mannitol? Yes, I know it's short notice, but here, we'll pay double. How many tickets do you need? I knew we could count on you, man."

I gave the Mannitol to Steven when the band convened at my office. He disappeared into the bathroom and snorted the whole thing. He started to fart in the limo on the way to the gig. Teresa goes, "*Steven!*" "Oh, sorry." Two songs into the show, Joe Perry walks over with a disgusted look on his face. "Jeezus, Steven's farting his brains out onstage!" Two songs later, Steven comes rushing off. "WHERE'S THE BATH-ROOM?"

Steven Tyler: We started doing press again, answering all the predictable questions. We tried to be honest. "Yes, I'd hated Joe's

guts, but time heals all wounds. Joe is nothing without me, and I'm nothing without him."

Joe Perry: I knew everybody's gonna ask if we got back together for the money, and I told them, "*Of course* we did. We always played straightforward to our audience. We were always *there*, way before MTV, and we're gonna be around for a long, long time, so everybody better get used to having us to kick around again."

Tim Collins: Then the war started. The Leber-Krebs lawyers began to ambush our tour, showing up backstage with court orders trying to attach our box office receipts. Technically they were still Aerosmith's managers. They'd been fired but still had a contractual hold over Steven, Tom, Joey, and the name of the band.

So we built all these dummy companies that would legally furnish the band's services on a per-concert basis. It was a guerrilla tactic—David against Goliath. We'd play a show in Cleveland and the constables would try to attach the Aerosmith Productions receipts. But they'd find that the promoter's contracts weren't with Aerosmith but with Big Belly Productions or LPI Productions (Large Penis Incorporated) or SPI Productions (Small Penis Incorporated) or LTA Productions (Large Tits Anonymous). A different company, every night, so they couldn't seize the money.

The promoters had to release the money to us, and that's how we survived the earliest battles with Krebs. I felt like a warlord presiding over an expensive team of lawyers. Finally Krebs gave up trying to take the money.

Mark Parenteau: They played out in Worcester and were having a problem because Steven had locked himself into his hotel room for three days and wouldn't come out. Tim was in despair and asked me to come out and try to get in the room with him.

The two of us finally got in. As our eyes adjusted to the dark, we realized it was like going into *The Exorcist*'s room: broken mirrors, beds upended, furniture smashed, curtains taped to the windows, filth everywhere. Someone had carved AEROSMITH WILL FUCK ANYTHING into an expensive tabletop. Steven took one look at Tim and said, "Gimme $100 right now."

Tim refused.

"You faggot! Gimme $100."

Tim looked at me. I mouthed the word "Belushi" to him. He wouldn't give Steven the money. Somehow they got him to the next gig.

Steven Tyler: A lot of this seems like total bullshit to me. First of all, when Tim asked me to move to Boston, he said, "I'll give you a gram of blow a day and turn you on to a doctor who'll give you whatever you want." That was our deal.

Two, the Mannitol story is great but totally fabricated. I used to cut my blow with Mannitol and would've been the first to say, "Hey, this is Mannitol" if I'd really snorted that much.

Three. I never called Tim Collins a faggot, although there were many occasions when I wanted to.

Tim Collins: July 1984. MTV had made stars of new bands like Mötley Crüe, Ratt, Quiet Riot, Twisted Sister. If you weren't on MTV, you were only marginally in the business, even if every show sold out, which ours did from the beginning. Aerosmith had never been on MTV [neither the "Lightning Strikes" nor "Black Velvet Pants" videos had made it into heavy rotation], there was no new video, and *MTV News* didn't mention the band getting back together or the tour.

One night I was in Chicago, on my way home after we had played there the night before, but had a premonition and detoured instead to the next stop, Springfield, Illinois, the heart of the heart of Aerosmith's Midwestern stronghold.

When I get there, they're already on, playing "Let the Music Do the Talking." Joe Baptista sees me and shakes his head and points to a wobbly Steven, weaving amid the colored spotlights onstage. He's schwacked on heroin. The band starts to fight. Steven stops singing. I give a roadie a gram of coke and tell him to give Steven a line. Steven takes the gram and snorts the whole thing.

Halfway through the next song, he keels over and falls into the audience. The show stops. Pandemonium, paramedics. People yelling. The cops are really pissed and the medics are yelling for a stretcher and someone says that Steven's dead. People are pushing around him. There is a scuffle or two.

"He better be dead," a state police captain standing next to me mutters, "because if he isn't, we're going to put him in fuckin' jail!"

The show was canceled. It was a big disgrace, because we'd been telling our extremely skeptical promoters all that was in the past. The police wanted to arrest Steven for drug possession, but we talked our way out of it and sent free *Greatest Hits* albums to everyone who'd been there.

News of this debacle was gleefully broadcast on MTV the next day, the only time the network mentioned Aerosmith that summer.

THE BOSTON GLOBE

The skeptics were debating right up until showtime. Would Steve Tyler be able to finish without passing out? What shape would Joe Perry be in? Would there still be the hard rock thunder of old, or would this be a long night with an over-the-hill band that didn't know when to quit?

But Aerosmith silenced them with a booming display that's dramatic proof they're still a major league band. It was a night of making amends . . . (Steve Morse, "Aerosmith in Concert with Orion the Hunter at the Worcester Centrum," August 6, 1984)

ROLLING STONE

"We paved the road, so to speak," [said Steven] Tyler. "So why not fucking get in our cars and drive down it again?"

"As far as I'm concerned, we're back for another ten years," said Perry, grinning. "As long as we don't kill each other, we'll be fine." (September 27, 1984)

4: Sue Us

Tim Collins: Steven pulled himself together, the band was raging, and the Back in the Saddle '84 tour kept up through the summer and early fall, a time of incredible pressure and transition for us. We stayed on the road and eventually paid all the money back to our investors.

All this time we're trying to get a record deal. This was one of the keys to the future. It was hard to focus because we had this huge legal fight going on to reclaim our independence, and it was total mayhem. Brian Rohan was bringing the cream of record company A&R guys to the shows, and as the music got hotter, there were some really interested people. All I knew was that I needed a guru, someone I could trust that would guide us through the whole process.

That's when John Kalodner [from Geffen Records] came into the picture. He even looked like a guru—piercing eyes, long straight hair, great bushy beard, impeccably tailored white suit. He didn't drink, didn't do drugs. He made successful records, didn't lie, and was interested in us. *This*, I thought, *could be our man*.

The reason I knew John didn't lie was because when I was trying to get Joe Perry a record deal, I sent a tape [of *Once a Rocker*] to John at Geffen and he called me up and said, in his characteristic nasal, deadpan voice: "I got your tape. It completely sucks. How could you even send out a piece-of-shit tape like this? I love Joe Perry, you've got a real artist here, but this tape just blows."

Everyone else had said, "Hey! Joe Perry! *Great* tape! No deal." So I knew I could trust this guy.

We had some offers. I told Brian Rohan I wanted to go with this guy Kalodner and Geffen Records, the Tiffany label of Warner Bros.

"Well, Geffen's a homo," Brian says. "Oh, right. You're a fuckin' homo too. Maybe you guys would get along. But Geffen's a scumbag. He'll fuck you for a nickel."

But I knew I could work with John. So one day that summer he flew into Boston. Brian and I picked him up at the airport and we took John to the band's rehearsal hall, an old theater someone had loaned us in Brockton, Mass. The boys were working out song arrangements, and afterward we went to lunch. John was upbeat, and I asked him what he thought.

"Well, they're all standing. They're walking and talking and taking on solid food. This is a good sign."

Then we took him to Cleveland to see them perform. This was two days after Steven collapsed onstage in Illinois. I was nervous about John seeing them so soon, but Brian Rohan was calling the shots around the record deal and he told me that John had a tight schedule and insisted on sticking to it. I crossed my fingers. We got there and I went to the dressing room to brief the band.

They were having a huge fight because Steven had been humping the other guys during the shows and they hated it. They were all shouting as I walked in and I thought, *Great, there goes the record deal.*

But they put on a killer show for John. "Let the Music Do the Talking," "Toys," "Walk This Way"—one blistering hit after another. Halfway through "Last Child," Steven went over to Brad while he was soloing and their heads collided. Steven's teeth connected with Brad's ear, and Brad was pissed.

Terrible fight after the show. Never saw Brad so angry. But then Rohan and John walk in, and the fight stops on a dime. Without missing a beat, Steven is Mr. Congeniality. "Hey, John! How ya doin'? Great to see you, man. Thanks for coming out . . ."

It was like in a movie. I shook my head in disbelief as they completely charmed him. Afterward, John sat down with us, looked me in the eye, and said, "I want to make this deal."

I was so relieved I could have cried.

*   *   *

There was one major problem. Steven, Tom, and Joey had reupped with CCC for five more albums six months before I met them. *Now they tell me.*

But I'm reading this self-help book, *Think and Grow Rich*. I convince myself that this is a minor obstacle and actually an opportunity for growth and try to stay focused on our vision of a free and independent Aerosmith. So we went ahead and made the deal with Geffen. The papers are readied in due course but remain unsigned until we can settle with CCC and CBS. Geffen had a distribution deal with CBS International, and they wouldn't sign off on our deal until CBS formally released Aerosmith to Geffen Records.

"How," I asked Brian Rohan, "do we get away from Leber-Krebs?" "Fucked if I know," he said. To make a long story short, we flew to New York and told our story to our regular lawyer, Marty Silfin. He says, "Gee, Tim, I don't know. You're in trouble." Then he went to Columbia and said, "Look, Aerosmith are drug addicts. They're with this Irish kid who doesn't know shit. Why don't you let 'em go for an override [a small percentage of the gross receipts]?"

Walter Yetnikoff agreed that he didn't need a bunch of aging heroin addicts on his label and let them go! We worked out a settlement that gave them $250,000 and an override.

But the war of nerves continued amid as much secrecy as possible. Everyone was under strict orders not to gossip; the slightest leak would kill the deal and send us back into court.

Geffen had told us they would sign our deal when CBS released us, but when push came to shove, they stalled. They were toying with us, playing games, trying to get us to settle with CCC. It didn't help that David Geffen hated Brian Rohan for punching him out one time over another matter.

I was swimming in the pool at the Meridien Hotel in New York when I got an idea. I called Brian Rohan and said, "Why don't we play these record companies off against each other like we used to do with club owners in Boston? It's gotta be the same mentality, just on a larger scale."

Rohan said, "OK, let's go see Clive Davis. He has an emotional stake in this. One, Clive originally signed Aerosmith and absolutely loved Steven. Two, Clive was once David Geffen's mentor."

"OK," I said, "that may be true, but Arista [Davis's record company] isn't right for Aerosmith."

"Where else are you gonna go?" Rohan asked.

Brian explained that when Clive had been president of Columbia Records, he had given David Geffen [the brilliant singer/songwriter] Laura Nyro to manage. But Geffen had signed her publishing as well, then sold it for $5 million. It was a famous story. Clive had been devastated because you just didn't do that to an artist. Now he and Geffen hated each other. "It'll be a big ego fight," Brian said. "It'll be a perfect revenge scenario for Clive if Arista steals Aerosmith from Geffen."

We went to see Clive Davis on a Friday, late in the year. Clive listened for about five minutes and said, "Done deal." He even upped Geffen's offer by half a million dollars to $1.5 million. Arista's legal department worked all weekend. The contracts were ready Sunday afternoon, and I called [Geffen Records president] Ed Rosenblatt and told him we had a problem. "Unless you guys get on a plane to New York, match this offer, and sign *right now*, we're going to sign with Arista Records at ten o'clock tomorrow morning."

Ed and John Kalodner flew to New York that night. Early next morning, there was a big meeting with all the lawyers. We reached an impasse, but Ed Rosenblatt and I finally sat down with yellow legal pads and closed the deal. Next day we flew to Boston and the band signed the contracts. The Geffen deal was done.

To David Krebs we said: "Sue us."

5: This Is Not Fixable

David Krebs: For the last tour I did with Aerosmith [in 1984], I hired a psychiatrist friend, Lloyd Moglen, to go out on the road with them. At the end of the tour, Lloyd called me and said, "David, this is not fixable."

I already knew that. "Let the Music Do the Talking" was a brilliant song, but you can't do away with Steven Tyler as a lead singer and end up with a band that measures up to Aerosmith. You can't replace Joe Perry with Jimmy Crespo, add into it whatever drug problems there were, and expect to come up with anything that made sense.

Tim Collins originally wanted to co-manage Aerosmith with me, bringing Joe Perry back into the group.

I spoke to Tom Hamilton, who told me that Tim's reputation was so unsavory in Boston that he didn't think we should do it. So I didn't. And the group is very lucky I let them go—because I would've killed them otherwise.

Tim was a new broom. They needed somebody who didn't understand the past to come in and say, "There it is, guys—*boom boom boom*."

I was too close to Steven to do what I should have done: spread the word that if you were a coke dealer and approached the band, you would have your neck broken. Literally.

I didn't want to be a shrink specializing in drug addiction. Tim was an addict, an eating addict and a coke addict. He had a problem like they did. I knew these guys had no cutoff point. They were going to kill themselves.

It's incumbent upon any new manager to discredit the old manager upon taking charge of the group. Tim Collins messed up my reputation by charging that we had stolen money from Aerosmith. Not true! So I said goodbye to Aerosmith and moved my family to California.

Steve Leber: [In 1984] I said to Steven Tyler, "I'm not giving you any more money. Our contract is over. You're out of here." If I'd continued feeding his habit, I'd have the band today.

We fought it out in court. [The lawsuits were settled in 1986.] We got an incremental piece of the catalogue—records and publishing, increased our stake in these, and gave them back their management and future albums.

We made a good deal, but so did they.

They [Aerosmith] got lucky that they met a Tim Collins who didn't have a wife and kids and could spend his life getting them off drugs.

Aerosmith had a lot of mystique when they started. They didn't know it, but I did. So did Krebs. I gave him 50 percent of my company because I knew he could break an Aerosmith. But he was socially immature, did drugs to get close to bands. David hurt our company [with his drug behavior].

Our big mistake was not to have all our acts on one label like Geffen or [Richard] Branson. CCC had Aerosmith on Columbia, AC/DC on Atlantic, Scorpions and Def Leppard on EMI. We could have been billionaires today.

But we did OK anyway. In 1994, twenty years after renegotiating Aerosmith's contract with CBS, we got back the master tapes. No one else—Streisand, *no one*—ever got this. Aerosmith was the biggest rock band in the world, and we owned the masters. Now CBS had to lease them back from us.

Tim Collins: End of the [Back in the Saddle] tour. Oakland Coliseum. Total chaos. Security finds Brian Rohan, the band's lawyer, selling laminated backstage passes for $50 apiece. We're filming the show and the video crew we've hired for twenty-five grand is stoned out of its mind. Meanwhile, Bill Graham, the promoter, is mesmerizing me with war stories—the Doors, the Dead, Janis, the Stones, Led Zeppelin. I'm like sitting at his feet.

They do the show and the kids love it, but the atmosphere backstage was poison. The video sucks. Rohan is denying everything. Bill Graham starts yelling at me again. Everything turns to shit.

Back to our hotel, the Hyatt at the airport. I was too depressed to go to the end-of-tour party up in Suite 1124. I ripped a hundred-dollar bill in two, gave half to the desk clerk, and told him he'd get the rest in the morning if no one finds me. "No problem, Mr. Collins."

I went to my room, took a Halcyon at midnight, and went to bed. Four in the morning, Steven Tyler starts banging on my door. He wants some blow. "How'd you find me?" "I made the guy a better deal!" I called the clerk and yelled at him. He goes, "But it was Steven Tyler from Aerosmith! He's famous! He was acting crazy!" I slammed the phone down. Steven had promised him another hundred in exchange for my room number.

Next morning. I'm really angry. *What am I doing with my life?* Upstairs in the party suite, I find fifteen naked bodies sleeping on the floor: boys, girls, like a bunch of porn stars after an orgy. Someone's shooting up in the bathroom. Time to leave. Then the roadies call because they can't get Steven out of his room. He and Teresa are asleep. It looked like we'd miss our flight home. I called the manager: "Excuse me, this is Mr. Collins with Vindaloo Music (the name of our holding company) and I've had thirty-four rooms here for the past three days. There's some asshole in Room 1124 who's impersonating my client Steven Tyler. That's right, an impostor. He's fake. I'd like him thrown out of the room immediately."

"Yes, sir, right away." They sent up six guys in suits. "But I *am* Steven Tyler." "Yeah, sure, buddy. Right." Twenty minutes later, Steven and Teresa and their bags are out on the front lawn. At the airport, Steven demands two seats in first-class. We all flew coach religiously back then, but I was too exhausted to fight and OK'd the seats with our tour accountant. Steven and Teresa passed out and slept the whole flight to Boston. I made the stews bring their dinner back to us in coach.

By the end of 1984, I was officially managing the band. They accepted me at last. The Saddle tour made money. We grossed $5 million at the box office, which translated to $2.5 to $3 million for the artists—gross. After expenses, it came to $1 million net, or about $200,000 apiece. There was a terrible row because Joey Kramer saw the $5 million gross figure in *Billboard* and demanded $1 million as his share.

It showed me that after more than ten years, these guys didn't know how their business worked. David Krebs had kept them in the dark, like children, and they stayed there willingly.

It turned out that Joey owed Krebs $2.5 million from advances paid during the time the band was in decline. The band absorbed this as a business debt. We held back 20 percent of Joey's income and then he used it to pay Krebs back.

On New Year's Eve [December 31, 1984], Aerosmith played the Orpheum Theater in Boston, played really well, lots of old songs like "Movin' Out," lots of old friends like Gary Cabozzi backstage, played so well that the tapes were later released by David Krebs [*Classics Live II*, 1987]. We all felt it was the end of one era and the beginning of another, because now we had to make our first record for Geffen and reestablish the band for a whole new generation—kids who watched MTV and had never even seen Aerosmith.

Teresa Tyler: After this tour, Steven just went crazy. We went to St. Martin for a month and he was mean to me, mean to everyone. He wanted to get off dope, but he just couldn't. Then we came back to Boston, checked into the Howard Johnson's in Cambridge. Two days after we got back, Tim and Joe put Steven in McClean Hospital, a psychiatric clinic [in Belmont, Mass.]. It was the only thing that could have happened for Steven because he was such an intense drug user, so deep into it, such a way of life. Everyone was scared about what would happen if Steven couldn't make it. Joe Perry called me up and told me he'd break my legs if I brought any drugs to Steven in the hospital.

The best thing about it was that there Steven met a guy named Bob Hearne, a therapist at McClean, the first person who ever got through to Steven about even the possibility of another way of life. But when Steven came out, the band and everyone around him was still getting blasted. He relapsed—started doing dope again—almost immediately.

6: They Don't Like Strangers

Joe Perry: I used to tell people that the reason we signed with Geffen was because we loved John Kalodner's beard.

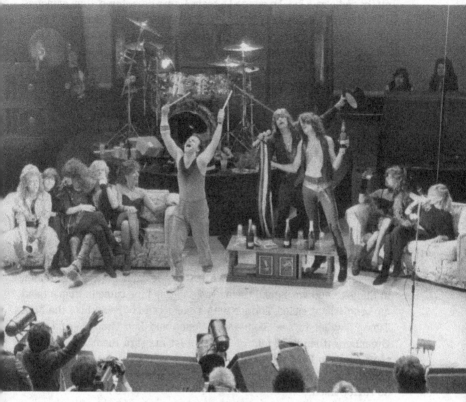

New Year's Eve, December 31, 1984
(PHOTO: RON POWNALL)

Steven Tyler: We took a hard look at the beard and how many musicians had already nested in it and found shelter, and we figured: "Why not us?"

Joey Kramer: Geffen believed in the band mainly because of John Kalodner. He's an important piece of the puzzle. John is pure A&R. He knows what the job is and takes care of business. We rubbed each other's feathers the wrong way when we first met, but we ironed things out, and he helped us to understand what our band was all about.

John Kalodner: I grew up in the suburbs of Philadelphia, listening to the Beatles and the Stones on the radio, picking hit singles off the radio as a kid. I managed a record store downtown, then managed a local band called the Wacks, which later became the Hooters. This is 1970. Then I built a rock club in Burlington, Vermont, that was like a prototype for the Bottom Line and the other rock clubs that came after it. Back in Philly in 1973–74, I started writing rock reviews and taking pictures for the two papers, first the *Bulletin* and then the *Inquirer*. I was the "populist" critic who liked commercial bands, whatever the kids liked.

In 1975, I started doing publicity for Atlantic Records in New York and gradually started listening to band tapes and going to industry functions, meeting people and learning the business. On the weekends, I'd go back to Philly and review concerts, which is how I came to be at the Spectrum the night that Aerosmith fans smashed through the doors of their sold-out show and then had a street riot outside afterward. There was a lot of damage, a big deal at the time. I thought Aerosmith was this mean, working-class, cretin band, but I could appreciate the fans' enthusiasm. It was a very exciting band.

In 1976, Atlantic's rock bands were huge: Led Zeppelin; the Stones; Emerson, Lake and Palmer; Yes. AC/DC's tape came in from Phil Carson in England and we signed them. One day this tape came in from a band on Long Island called Trigger with a song called "Feels Like the First Time." I went to see them—Mick Jones and Lou Gramm—and Jerry Greenberg [then president of Atlantic] let me sign them. We changed their name to Foreigner. Gary Lyons and John Sinclair produced, Mick Jones remixed the tapes, and by 1977 Foreigner was huge too. And I was an A&R person.

I moved to California, stayed at Atlantic until 1980, and then went to Geffen Records after David brought me out to his house and asked, "Do you wanna work for this new company?" I said yes, exercised the "key man" clause in my contract—because Jerry Greenberg had left—and got locked out of my office at Atlantic West Coast the same day.

At Geffen, I signed Sammy Hagar, then Asia, which came out of ELP, then Berlin, Madness, Wang Chung, Whitesnake, which had a big hit with *Slide It In* in 1984. While I was working with them, I got Joe Perry's tape and I called Tim Collins and said, "Look, Joe Perry's one of my favorite guitarists, but the singer sucks. The whole tape sucks, but you've got a great artist." And that was it.

After the first few years, David Geffen gave me and a few other executives a small interest in the company. It turned into a nice chunk of money a few years later when he sold the company to MCA.

In 1984, crazy Brian Rohan, a famous, flamboyant lawyer who'd made the deals for the Cars and Boston, called me. He said, "Aerosmith is getting together. Do you want to see them?" I said sure, even though David Geffen hated Rohan.

I flew to Boston on May 1, 1984. Tim Collins picked me up in a stretch limo with Rohan, who baited me about David Geffen all the way to the band rehearsal at some stinking old theater. That night I had dinner with them and the band at a Japanese steak joint in the Howard Johnson's where Rohan was staying. It didn't go well. They don't like strangers. I knew their music, but they knew nothing about me. To them, I was just some record company geek. It didn't matter that my albums—Foreigner, Asia—were selling in the millions. They were sullen, uncommunicative, made frequent runs to the bathroom to do blow.

But I was kind of innocent, and they weren't presented to me as five drug addicts. I went back to L.A. and told Ed Rosenblatt, the president of Geffen, that I wanted to make a deal with Aerosmith. "Follow it," he said.

I went to Cleveland, where Steven Tyler bit Brad Whitford on the head. Still not much rapport. Then in August, I went to see them play the Greek Theater in L.A. I think I was talking with Karen Whitford, Brad's wife, and she might have shown me her gun, because she liked to carry. So I pulled up the trouser leg of my white suit and showed her the .357 Magnum I was wearing in an ankle holster. "This is how I get around L.A.," I told her. I was showing off, but it worked. Soon as the band found out I was packing dynamite, they thought I was totally cool. It broke the ice with them because they loved guns.

I knew David Geffen believed in me when he made the Aerosmith deal with Brian Rohan, who he loathed. It was a big deal, front-loaded; they got a lot of money up front. I'm glad I didn't know how much, because I would have been scared.

We started to work on their first album for Geffen in early 1985. Aerosmith had never worked with an A&R person—someone who worked with the producer, brought in outside song writers, picked the songs, supervised the mixes if they weren't good. They didn't want to start now. Tim Collins asked me to get them a producer and I got Ted Templeman [from Warner Bros.], one of the biggest producers in the world. He was just coming off Van Halen's *1984* and was burning hot, this guy. What happened was they kept me at arm's length, Tim didn't yet understand the process, and we let Templeman make a lot of decisions and record and mix the album.

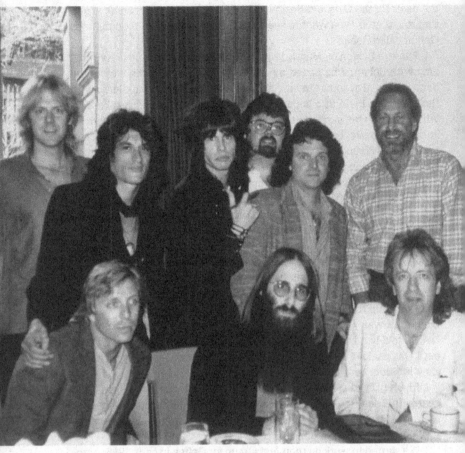

Aerosmith signs with Geffen Records, 1984. Tim Collins stands third from right, his partner, Steve Barrasso, sits at bottom left, next to A&R executive extraordinaire John Kalodner.
(GEFFEN RECORDS)

Joe Perry: Ted Templeman came to see us backstage and said, "You guys are a time machine. You lock into a groove like nobody. You've never been out on vinyl the way you should be."

Brad Whitford: He was one of my favorite producers, not for Van Halen but for Montrose. We rehearsed in a warehouse [the band's new rehearsal space in Somerville, Mass.] and I recorded the demos of new songs before taking them out to California to record.

Steven Tyler: We wrote all the songs for *Done with Mirrors* there in three or four weeks. Teddy flew in to see us three times. When we finally flew to California, we had seventeen songs. Getting it down to nine was the hardest part.

Joey Kramer: It was a chance to work with Ted Templeman at Fantasy Studios in Berkeley, but it turned into all drinking and drugging, which was allowed to get in the way. After the studio, it was back to our rooms in the hotel, doing coke and isolated from each other, like the old days and old ways. Amazing we even got through it.

Joe Perry: Ted was a hard-core West Coaster, and we were hard-core East Coasters. Sometimes we couldn't understand each other. And Ted had all these little tricks.

Steven Tyler: Ted used to tape over the red recording light so we wouldn't know it was on. We'd be playing along and say, "OK, let's put this one down." Ted would pop his head above the board—he'd been hiding under the board drinking carrot juice—and say, "We've already recorded it."

Tom Hamilton: We got there and Ted said, "We're going to run all these tunes down and get them on tape." I think we wound up using most of the takes from that first day of just slapping 'em down on tape.

Joey Kramer: It didn't work, which is why *Done with Mirrors* sounds to me like an incomplete record, without the finishing touches, the nuances, the personalities. Because we weren't all there.

Tim Collins: That fall [1985] we put Steven into rehab at McClean Hospital again. This is when, out of desperation, I started doing urine tests on Steven and Joe to know if they were sober. Steven cheated: He stored drug-free urine in condoms, which he taped to his thigh to use if I pulled a random drug test on him. Standing outside the stall while

Steven urinated, I didn't catch on until one of the lab reports came in and said the urine was a week old.

Steven Tyler: I'd saved it from the week before in the fridge. I didn't know anyone could tell.

Billie Perry: During that summer, Joe's mom was selling her house on Lake Sunapee. While I was helping clean the house, I found all these old magazines—*Circus, Creem*—with Joe and Steven on the covers. That's when I realized Aerosmith was *huge!* I finally realized how big they were then—and how small they were now.

That September we were in Hawaii with the band. We got word that Joe's divorce was final and we eloped. We got married on the side of a mountain with Tim and his friend Nick LaHage. We wore leis, they threw rice, and it was very sweet because at that time a big wedding was too expensive. Tim Collins gave us a wedding party on a beautiful catamaran, an incredible sunset sail that really meant a lot to us. Tim knew how broke we were, and it was a generous thing to do. It felt so romantic to have a proper celebration.

When we got back to Boston, we got married again by a justice of the peace in Cambridge [in January 1986] so the marriage would be legal in the eyes of the Massachusetts court. Tom and Terry Hamilton were our witnesses.

Joe Perry: I loved Billie so much that I didn't mind marrying her twice.

7: Rap This Way

Joe Perry: On *Done with Mirrors*, we tried to just be honest and play our music. We weren't focusing on what we do best. The songs had basic riffs that were really good but never got finished. I thought "My Fist Your Face" and "Shela" were pretty good. Two weeks before the record was supposed to be mastered, Steven was still in the hotel trying to write lyrics. We thought we worked best under pressure, but now I can't listen to the record.

Steven Tyler: It was just us, the stuff we put out. It's the twos and the fours, it's rock 'n' roll, and it was that particular slice and time. Joe Perry came up with the title, which meant magic. *Done with Mirrors*. To me, it was magic that we'd just gotten back together again.

Tim Collins: We gave John Kalodner the tapes. He took me out to lunch and said, "Tim, this record has no hits on it." I told him I thought it was the best the band could do at this point.

John Kalodner: They delivered the record. When I realized the only good song was "Let the Music Do the Talking"—an old Joe Perry song—I knew we were in trouble. Then Ted Templeman, [label executive] Jeff Ayeroff, and the band came up with the "done with mirrors" concept: Everything on the album was printed backward, so you couldn't read it without a mirror. *Done with Mirrors* came out [in November 1985], heavily promoted by Geffen, and only sold 400,000 records, way below expectations. Aerosmith went on tour and were mediocre. It was a tough period for me: Asia went down with alcohol problems, Sammy Hagar joined Van Halen, and Aerosmith bombed. Everything was wrong.

Steven Tyler: All anybody wanted to know about was video. I kept saying I wasn't into the whole video thing because Aerosmith is a *live* band, something that can't be captured any way but live. The beauty of a concert is the energy of the show, the event, *that night*. You gotta see it to believe it. You gotta be there. So the video we did of "Let the Music Do the Talking" [directed by Jerry Kramer, who did Michael Jackson's innovative videos] was about a kid who sneaks a Super-8 into our show. I liked it. It had that live feel. It didn't get on MTV, so we hardly officially existed.

Ted Nugent opened most of the shows on the Done with Mirrors *tour. It was 1986, the year of Bon Jovi, the Live Aid concerts, and the year former Doll David Johansen metamorphosed into a jaded saloon singer named Buster Poindexter. On March 8, Aerosmith and Nugent sold out the Spectrum in Philadelphia and played before 18,000 Bon Jovi clones, punk rockers, headbangers in Mötley Crüe headbands, and young Slayer fans escorted by their parents. Aerosmith opened with "Back in the Saddle" and alternated the hits with new songs— "Shela," "My Fist Your Face," "Gypsy Boots." (*Done with Mirrors was stuck at #70 and falling.*) When a hot version of the unfamiliar "Light-*

ning Strikes" failed to draw the same cheers as "Sweet Emotion," Steven told the crowd, "It's a new Aerosmith, folks." While he left the stage to fill his nose, Joe Perry would tear into a blistering "Red House." Ostensibly reformed and espousing sobriety in interviews, the band in fact was as stoned as ever. Still there were hints of a kinder, gentler Aerosmith when Steven would close the shows by telling the kids, "God bless you, and drive carefully!"

HIT PARADER

"Oh, yes. It's true," Joe Perry says. "I'm getting more pleasure now from playing onstage with the band than I've ever gotten before. It turns me on to look around and see the guys onstage with me."

"Oh?" Tyler laughed.

Perry considered. "Yes, my pants definitely get tighter when I'm onstage with Aerosmith." (April 1986)

Tim Collins: The band's fan loyalty never wavered, and the tour did well. The band was out on the road that spring when we were poleaxed by the unexpected release of *Classics Live!*: old concert tracks retouched by Jimmy Crespo and put out by David Krebs to cash in on whatever notoriety the band had.

I was in the midst of legal battles and generally struggling with the band and feeling sick about my codependent role. I was brutal to Steven at times, in order to protect him. I gave him coke to get him up for the show, gave him sleeping pills to calm him down. I had a great doctor coaching me and thought I knew everything I was doing. But I knew in my heart that time was running out. I had to find out how to teach Steven a new way to live.

This is when Rick Rubin called me. He said he had this black band called Run-D.M.C. and he wanted Steven and Joe to play on a rap version of "Walk This Way."

I go, "Um, Rick, what is rap?"

He explained the whole thing. Run-D.M.C. [Joseph "Run" Simmons, Darryl "DMC" McDaniels, and Jason "Jam Master Jay" Mizell] were from Hollis, Queens, and were an original rap band. For ten years, they'd been cutting "Walk This Way" 's funky drum pattern from one turntable to another while teenage MCs worked out their rhymes. These guys had learned to rap to "Walk This Way," which unknown to us had been a prime B-boy standard for years. [Run told *Rolling Stone*: "I made that record because I used to rap over it when I was twelve."]

Rick Rubin was this kid who had started a record company, Def Jam, in his dorm room at N.Y.U. and was now selling millions of rap records by L. L. Cool J, Run-D.M.C., and the Beastie Boys to white kids in the suburbs—our audience. Rick was just finishing an album with Run-D.M.C. called *Raising Hell* and he thought the two groups doing the song would be "a nice little kicker." He also said it would be a great crossover opportunity for both groups.

I called John Kalodner, who we relied on for advice on marketing decisions like this. He said, "I don't know if I want them singing with those fucking rappers. Let me look into it."

John called back an hour later. "I think this could be really cool. I think we should definitely do this."

Joe and Steven were lukewarm at first but went along for eight grand for a day in the studio. They flew up from Philadelphia, where they played the Spectrum without incident the night before. [The recording session took place on March 9, 1986, at Magic Ventures Studios in Manhattan.] We met the group's manager, Russell Simmons, and the rappers, who told us they thought the name of the group that did "Walk This Way" was Toys in the Attic.

Joe Perry: I didn't know what was gonna happen when I walked in to the studio. I thought they'd show us some ideas on how to rearrange the song, but all they had was a drum track. Rick Rubin says, "All you gotta do is play the song the way you play it." So I sat down—with my blond Schecter with the words PROTEST AND SURVIVE burned into the head—and played it.

Rick Rubin: Growing up, Aerosmith and AC/DC had been my favorite bands. I loved sitting in the studio that day with Joe Perry, having him do a solo, and being able to say, "I know you can play it better." I'd seen him hundreds of times, but I never knew how good a guitar player he was until he left Aerosmith, which seemed like such a balanced band that he didn't stick out. But when I went to see the Joe Perry Project, he was this great guitar player.

Steven Tyler: Run and D and Jay were huddled in a corner, really intent on something. I go, "Joe, what are they doing?" "Probably smoking crack," he says. Later we went over to the corner. They'd been eating lunch from McDonald's.

They wanted to work fast because they had a rented car overdue. Teresa took out her jeweled cigarette case and she and I disappeared into the bathroom before I cut my tracks. A camera crew from MTV distracted us for a while. Joe Perry's playing his ass off. Russell Simmons goes, "Yo! Run, go outside and get your lyrics down."

Run says, "I want it to be B-boy language."

"I keep on telling you," says Russell, "it already is."

"Hey, diddle-diddle with the tittie in the middle."

"No, no," I say, "it's 'Hey, diddle-diddle with the *kitty* in the middle.' Get some paper and I'll write it out."

"Yo, man, that's OK. We know it. We just gotta do one take, then we gotta leave so's we can return the car."

Two weeks after this session, Steven and Teresa, Joe and Billie, tour manager Bob Dowd, and Tim Collins arrived at the semiderelict Park Theater in a dangerous neighborhood in Union City, New Jersey, to shoot the video with Run-D.M.C. They spent several hours working with director Jon Small figuring out how to physically relate and connect with each other while they dismantled the wall in the set. There was a good buzz while they were filming, and they knew the video would be a big hit.

The video starts with the two bands in adjacent rehearsal halls. Aerosmith plays "Walk This Way" so loud it bothers Run-D.M.C. in the next room, who crank up their own verson with Jam Master Jay scratching away at top volume. The two groups break down the wall separating them, trying to get each other to turn down. When the wall crumbles, they realize the only wall separating rock from rap is racism. The clip ends with Joe and Steven, Run, and D performing together onstage—complete with Steven's trademark handspring and front flip—before a houseful of raving young fans.

Raising Hell was released in May 1986 on Profile Records, with "Walk This Way" the first single and video. It was a hit, going to #8 on the black singles chart, then crossing over to #4 on Billboard's Hot 100 after MTV started playing the video twice an hour.

It helped a lot. It made Aerosmith look hip for a change. It got Aerosmith on CHR—contemporary hit radio, the winning format of that era. It was very symbolic, the first rap/rock video, literally breaking down walls. It helped Run-D.M.C. too, since it was their big breakthrough and they sold millions of records. (According to Tim Collins, it took seven years for Profile to pay Aerosmith royalties from this record.)

It was also the first time this huge new audience (especially in Europe) saw Aerosmith on MTV, the medium they would use to relaunch themselves, but only after they took care of some extremely important business first.

8: New Souls

Joe Perry: This period was really hard. *Done with Mirrors* did badly, and we were frustrated because things weren't going our way. The drugs weren't working anymore, we were sick from them, and they were killing the spirit of what we wanted to do. So we focused out—the only way we knew how—and blamed everyone around us.

Tim Collins: The tour lurched through the summer [of 1986]. Everyone had relapsed on the road. *Done with Mirrors* was going down the tubes. I took John Kalodner to dinner at the Palm in L.A. and asked him what we could do to revive the record. "Forget it," he said. "Let it go. Let's go make a record *my* way—bring in some new blood, new writers. We can make a great record with this band."

Then I was called to the phone. It was our tour manager, Bob Dowd, with the band in Las Vegas. "Boss, you better get here right away. The boys are getting ready to fire you. They feel it's all your fault." I called Joe Perry from the kitchen of the restaurant. He told me they wanted to have a band meeting right away and hung up.

I caught the next plane to Vegas. Joe convened the meeting in his room, not mine, a significant change. Everyone was stoned. Steven wasn't there. And they started in on me. Templeman was a moron. Kalodner was a moron. Geffen were all morons. Steven was totally nuts.

I sat there and realized that now the drugs really had to go. Aerosmith was being killed from within. The shadow side of them was taking over and they were blaming everyone around them. If I didn't do something, I'd be fired.

John Kalodner: They were on tour and the shows were mediocre. I'm hanging around them more and starting to see that something is really wrong. There were some bad nights; the band seemed removed and abstracted. The record wasn't selling and Tim would either be too passive with the label or else he'd come in and scream at the president of the company. The whole band was pissed at Geffen, and finally they asked Ed Rosenblatt to come to Chicago for a meeting. He flew in, I met him at the hotel after the show, but the band never showed up. They stood us up, because there'd been another crisis at the gig.

Tim Collins stopped the tour.

In September, we had another meeting with Tim. He told us they had intervened on Steven, the whole band was cleaning up, he was buying out his partner, and that everything would change. We agreed to postpone the next Aerosmith record until things got straightened out.

Tim Collins: You've already heard the story of what happened after that last gig in Chicago. I went to New York, talked to some friends, started reading about Alcoholics Anonymous. I started working with Dr. Lou Cox and we got the band together and planned and carried out the intervention on Steven Tyler.

I said, "Joe, we're going to do this on Steven. You know it's our only hope of saving this. And the fact is you gotta clean up too or it won't work. I want you to go back into treatment."

He said he'd get off heroin. He said he would go right after the baby he and Billie were expecting was born. And after his son Tony was born in October of 1986, Joe went into Bournwood Hospital in Brookline. When he came out, he was clean. When we went to see Steven during family weekend at Chit Chat, where he was being treated, Joe was able to look Steven in the eye and say that, yes, he too was sober.

Joe Perry: It was very emotional. It was family weekend, and we were there as Steven's family. I just said to him, "Look, man, this is another chance for us. This makes it like a whole new band. Let's find a fuckin' garage and play some music, because when this is all over, we'll be new people. We're gonna be new *souls*."

Tim Collins: Steven came home from Chit Chat, got into AA, and really got going on it and started to work on himself. Gradually he became the leader of the band again, along with Joe. But he had a lot of bitterness about the intervention, most of it justified.

Later on, we called Steven "the Russian" when he started to rewrite history, giving interviews where he said that he got sober but the rest of us were all fucked up. But the other guys *were* still fucked up. Joe hadn't gone into rehab yet when Steven went away. Tom lived a seemingly normal life, but he was still a closet binger. Brad was drinking, Joey was using coke. But Steven was the most fucked up, and we felt that he was the key.

Brad Whitford: I was wrestling with this stuff. We all were.
I was an alcoholic, addicted to beer. I'd see a beer bottle and it would go, "Brad! Drink me!" I had no information about the disease of addiction until Lou Cox gave me a book called *I'll Quit Tomorrow*. I read three pages and put the book down and thought, *This is me. I'm this guy.* I started going to Alcoholics Anonymous meetings [in November 1986] in the town where we lived. There was no rehab or big intervention, nothing dramatic. I got into the program and it helped me stop.

Tim Collins: For the rest of 1986, we rested and worked on
getting ready to record the next Aerosmith record. Steven had this great little idea he was working on, called "Cruisin' for a Lady."

Steven Tyler: I just want to say one thing here. In my so-
briety, I learned to see that I had to give myself credit, because a lot of people won't. They'd tell me I was crazy, just like that. But if I didn't stop and pay homage to that guy inside me who's nuts and remind him— *You're not nuts. You're* unique—then I'd never get another song out. I'd never sit down and write that one song I don't think I've written yet.

OK, I think. *Let them pick on me. I've always had to pay the fiddler for being the insane man, but . . .* I still love it! *Because I get the best view. I get the house on top of the hill. It's all worth it.*

Bebe Buell: In December 1986, Todd Rundgren was playing
the Paradise Club in Boston. Liv and I were living in Portland [Maine], and we drove down to see "Daddy" play. It was nice. He had little things for her and we had a nice reunion.

Backstage, out of the corner of my eye, I saw Steven and Teresa come in to say hello, looking *much* better than usual. I couldn't believe how . . . *sober* they looked.

Steven's eyes shot to Liv, who was nine. She took one look at him and somehow just *knew*. She made an immediate attachment to this man. Todd had given her a Casio sampler, and for the rest of the time Steven

Walk This Way

taught her how to burp into it and then play it back. Then he taught her to play "Dream On."

It was a big turning point. Liv had never known him when he was getting high. There was a lot of whispering: "Should we tell her now?" But we didn't.

The $30 Million Sex Machine

Sex Machine

Aerosmith? I went to see them play in London. They've become born-again teetotalers. So there was this little question mark as to whether you can write it if you can't live it, but they were *great*. They were having a great time, and the humor was just so essential . . .

—Robert Plant

1: The Wall of Shame

Joe Perry: We stopped drinking. We stopped taking drugs. We started to work out and get back in shape until it seemed like we were in training for some competition—or a war. Lifting weights. Running. Working out. The physical stuff became an outlet for a lot of aggression we used to carry to the stage and turn on each other. I learned it could clear my head for what I do. It became more important to me for my mind to be . . . clear. You know what I mean?

Steven Tyler: I came out sober and stunned at the brightness of the world. I'm blinking at the light like a blind man whose sight has been restored. I'm wondering if I could still write an album.

And then, talking to the band, I told them: "Let's be friends and know right off the bat that as fucked up as I was when you first met me, I'm still that same guy. There's things I won't say now that I'd blurt out back then. I still think 'em. So don't fool yourself thinking I'm this new, wonderful, sober guy. Because when I walk out into the street, I don't have the same intentions—I'm not going to Ninth Avenue and cop a $20 bag of dope—but I still think the same way. I still have the same thoughts, repeat the same words, think about pussy and this one and that one.

"So don't fool yourself. I'm not wrong or bad for being the way I am. You don't like me? FUCK YOU!"

Joe Perry: We were about to make our first polished album. There was a lot of controversy about John Kalodner bringing people in to work with us and share credit on our songs. A lot.

We'd always worked our way, under the gun, boxed into terrible twenty-four-hour sessions. In spite of everything, the music always came out. *Permanent Vacation* was the first one where we laid the stuff down and then had a chance to sit back and look at it to see if it was any good.

Steven Tyler: [Late in 1986] I'm listening while Joe is playing a lick, like he always does, like he's probably doing in his room right now, and I'm going, "Hey, wait, what's that?" We start jamming on it, a great lick, and it inspired me. I'd just gotten a Korg, a wonderful [keyboard] instrument with a hundred presets, a songwriter's dream. Push a button—xylophones. Push—guitar feedback. Push—angels singing with violins. This jam the preset was on CLAVINET.

I wrote the chorus, based on this lick. Then I wrote the fuckin' bridge, the melody line—*wham*—there it was, in one afternoon.

When you got a good chorus, you wanna hang something good from it. It's better to end a chorus with something that ends in the "eee" sound, because it sings better and it pushes the chorus up through the roof, through the clouds. We had "Cruisin' for a ladeee," which lasted for a week. Then we got a sampler, watched a tape of some black comedian who was making fun of Mr. T, which led to a riff about cross-dressing.

Then one day we met Mötley Crüe, and they're all going, "Dude!" Dude this and Dude that, everything was Dude. "Dude (Looks Like a Lady)" came out of that session.

John Kalodner: In January 1987, I go to the band's rehearsal hall in Somerville in the dead of stinking Boston winter, during a horrible blizzard. They have a whole wall decorated with the bras and panties and stockings of girls who threw them onstage during the last tour. They play me what they've been rehearsing. Tyler had part of "Dude," but it wasn't together.

I returned two weeks later in another stinking blizzard and they'd made basically no progress. The songs were just a collection of rehearsal riffs, not really happening. I listened as politely as I could, made some notes, and thought, *I gotta get somebody to fix these songs.* I didn't know how they'd react to what I had to say next: "Look, here's what an A&R person does. I need to bring in some people to help you write songs."

I told them I wanted to bring in Desmond Child, who'd written "Livin' on a Prayer" and other songs on Bon Jovi's *Slippery When Wet*, which was a massive hit.

Steven Tyler: I told him if he knew someone I could write lyrics with and have as much fun as when I'm writing songs with Joe Perry, then *please* bring 'em in.

John Kalodner: In March, I started to bring people in. The first was Desmond. (My first call had been Jim Steinman, who was famous for Meat Loaf. He insisted he'd only work if Steven and Joe would come to his house in some bumfuck suburb somewhere. We had to pass.) Desmond agreed to do it and came up to Boston and helped finish the lyrics to "Dude" and a day or two later wrote "Angel" with Tyler, just like that. Desmond came in and took Tyler's idea, straightened it out, and made a song out of it. I heard the demo and I went, "Wow. Haven't heard *this* before. This is *happening*."

It was the beginning of the years of fighting that went on between me and them. They had never seen real A&R work. Jack Douglas had been one of them, hanging out and doing blow with them. I didn't work that way. I was just a record company douche bag to them, telling them what to do. And they were resistant. To this day, Tyler says that I ruined his career by making him write "Angel" with Desmond.

I'd pick my battles, and Tim backed me up. But it was always tense.

At least they were sober. At least you could now have a rational conversation with Steven Tyler.

While they were writing, I was talking to Ted Templeman. I'd been kept away from the *Done with Mirrors* sessions, and now I told him it had to be done my way. He didn't want to know, so I went over to his office and fired him to his face, out of respect for him and who he was—a senior vice president of Warner Bros. I was nervous about this, but I told him: "My ass is on the line here. You don't have to answer to David Geffen. I do."

Later that day, I called Bruce Fairbairn up in Vancouver and said, "You're on." We recorded *Permanent Vacation*, *Pump*, and most of *Get a Grip* at his studio, Little Mountain Sound, in Vancouver.

2: Don't Bore Us, Get to the Chorus

Tom Hamilton: I was the last one in the band to get sober. While we were making *Permanent Vacation*, I was still smoking a couple of bowls of pot every day. I'd get to the rehearsal, barbecued, and Steven would look me in the eyes and make me feel stupid and paranoid about being the only one of us still . . . out there. The other guys let me know they thought my priorities were wrong. Eventually I got sick of being paranoid and I quit.

It's hard not to hammer away at the fact that *Permanent Vacation* was the first record that Aerosmith ever did basically clean. Or that we all knew this album was do-or-die. Or that it was the first time we worked with Bruce Fairbairn, a very big, no-bullshit, in-focus, demanding producer who made sure the conditions were right to let the creativity happen.

I mean, this guy had the ability to make us play better than even we thought we could.

A lot of it was painful, because we gave up some control, big time. The days when Jack Douglas let us experiment were over. We made a decision that we wanted to come back, reestablish ourselves, and that ended up taking priority. That's how we made the album that saved our career.

John Kalodner: Bruce Fairbairn had been in a band called Prism. He produced some records for Geffen, most notably the last record by a young band called Black and Blue. He was very hot right then because he'd done Bon Jovi's *Slippery When Wet*.

In March [1987], Steven and Joe started to work with Desmond in Boston, writing "Dude," "Angel," and "Heart's Done Time." In April, they moved to Vancouver and started to work with Jim Vallance, a writer who was part of the Vancouver crew that worked with Fairbairn. [Vallance was best known for writing with Bryan Adams.] From then through June, they came up with most of the tracks: "Magic Touch," "Simoriah," and "Hangman Jury" [which incorporated the main lick from a Leadbelly-copyrighted gandy-dancers' chant, "Lining Track"]. They also had one called "Rag Time."

Tim Collins: John heard this and said, "What does 'Rag Time' mean? We gotta sell records this time. You gotta write about pussy!"

John Kalodner: I never heard the demo to this. I heard the track for the first time and said, "This is *killer*. But what the fuck is 'Rag Time'?" Steven gave me some bullshit about New Orleans, the old traditions, the roots of rock 'n' roll, the five-piece horn section Bruce was going to put on it. I said to him, "Kids won't give a fuck about 'Rag Time.' " So I called Holly Knight, who'd written for Pat Benatar and Heart.

Steven Tyler: I said, "Y'know, 'Rag Time'—rags, like my scarves." But he says, "No one will understand this." He got Holly Knight to come up and we brainstormed for three days in Vancouver. Nothing. Finally we're going through it again and Holly reads my lyrics—"I'm rippin' up a rag doll/Like throwing away an old toy"—and she says, "Hey! Call it 'Rag Doll.' Along with that, and changing a few other words, I gave her credit on the song.

Tim Collins: This was a big deal. John brought in Holly Knight, who changed one word and got a piece of the song. Later, when it was a big hit record, Tyler was enraged. He'd yell at me: "Who's to say that it wouldn't have been huge if it was 'Rag *Time*'?"

"We'll never know" was all I could tell him.

Meanwhile, they kept working. Steven and Joe wrote "Girl Keeps

Coming Apart." Steven had "St. John." He and Brad wrote "Permanent Vacation" and we used it as the album title.

John Kalodner: The songs really came to fruition when

Fairbairn worked with them. He put on sound effects [creaking porch swings, sirens, monkey love calls, jet planes, whales from the Vancouver Aquarium] that made it extremely atmospheric. Then Tyler put his stuff on and we were ready to go.

The last things we did were a couple of covers. First, the Beatles' "I'm Down," a real good rock 'n' roll song that had been a Beatle B-side. They love Beatles music and so do I. It was picked for strategic reasons, but then the album was so strong it turned out they didn't need it. [They also recorded Huey "Piano" Smith's "Rockin' Pneumonia and the Boogie Woogie Flu," released on the soundtrack to the film *Less Than Zero* in late 1987.]

David Geffen picked the first track [for single release]: "Dude (Looks Like a Lady)." They were going to use Jon Small to direct the video, but I picked Marty Callner and Geffen backed me up. That's where the whole Aerosmith video cycle began.

Tim Collins: Keith Garde [Aerosmith's marketing director],

and I met Marty to talk about the video. I asked to see his storyboard. He goes, "No storyboard, we're just gonna jazz." *Oh, no, here we go.* He wanted a lot of money, $150,000, to do it. I told him we were paying $50,000. John Kalodner took me to meet David Geffen, who convinced me that Marty Callner was a genius. So I caved. They filmed "Dude" in a concert setting at A&M's sound stage in Hollywood.

While the band was working in Vancouver, Columbia released Classics Live II as part of the settlement with David Krebs. Aerosmith had more input this time, and most of the cuts were taken from the reunited band's 1984 New Year's Eve show in Boston. But, as planned, it was completely overshadowed when Permanent Vacation was released [in August 1987].

MTV put the "Dude" video into heavy rotation and the album entered the Billboard chart in September and stayed on for the next seventy weeks. Reviews were great, acknowledging that Aerosmith had an album that both found their core audience and brought in a newer, younger pop-minded fan base. Almost immediately Aerosmith joined that select group of late-1980s superstars who commanded multiple hit singles from one album, continuous play on MTV, and multiplatinum status for every new record.

Within a year, Permanent Vacation *became Aerosmith's bestselling record ever.*

Joe Perry: So what happened was we burned out and hit the ground, then we came back. But it was a really hard thing, a scary time. The whole industry thrives on the new kids on the block, and we'd been around for a long time. It was a lot of work and never a sure thing.

When we started, I'd listen to "Walk This Way" and think, *What did I know then that I forgot when we were doing* Done with Mirrors? The answer was: *Don't bore us, get to the chorus.*

Working with the writers that John brought in was a refresher course in songwriting for me. Yes, we needed to sell records, but it was also important that a lot of the stuff held together as songs, like if I were to sit down with Steven and play acoustic guitar and him sing. That's a goal we still have in this band.

In 1987, a court in New Hampshire granted Steven and Cyrinda Tallarico a divorce. Cyrinda retained custody of their daughter, Mia, and was awarded substantial monthly support.

3: Appetite
for Redemption

Joey Kramer: My house burned in November [1986], just as we started to make *Permanent Vacation.* I lost the whole house and 90 percent of our belongings. It was a real blow, but I kept working, started to rebuild, went to Vancouver, and between May and June [1987] tried to get myself clean and sober. I went to meetings, went to therapy, started working out more—the whole thing.

On July 3, they intervened on me: the band, Tim Collins, Lou Cox, Keith Garde. (Tom wasn't there because he wasn't sober—yet. He was next.) They said I wouldn't do the tour unless I was clean. And I agreed with them. The only catch was that I couldn't go right then, because we were moving into our new house the next day. "I'll go *tomorrow*," I told them, which set off the alarms and there was a whole battle because they were ready to ship me out. In the end, I managed to convince Steven and he convinced Lou Cox that I would go.

I was away for a month, and it took.

Steven Tyler: It had been ten years since I'd been in Europe, and when I arrived I discovered we were like a new band to them because we'd never really been big there. Joe and I went in September to do a press tour, right after the album came out. We did interviews and talked about not taking drugs until we almost wanted to take them again. I told them I didn't want to say to kids, "Don't do drugs," because when I was a kid I tried to do exactly what adults told me not to. What I wanted to do was make a video for kids showing me having a seizure, turning blue, choking on my own tongue with a needle sticking in my arm. A video of me vomiting blood in the dressing room after the last encore. A video showing the reality of drug use.

I told them the truth, that I considered myself a walking, talking miracle. I hadn't touched a drug or drank in a year. I was walking on air. Like a blind guy that someone gave a pair of glasses to and suddenly he could see. Everything came into focus.

Tim Collins: Aerosmith went out on tour that fall—clean. We made sure that the wet bars were emptied of alcohol before any band member went to his room. The crew was told not to drink in front of the band. Even the opening bands—first Dokken, then White Lion—were ordered to keep drugs away from the band. We lost Joe Baptista because of this. He left, muttering, "We still got civil rights in this country." He was a valuable friend who'd taught Bob Dowd how to be a tour manager, but when it was time to get sober, he wouldn't go.

He died of a stroke a few years later.

The 160-show Permanent Vacation tour opened in Binghamton, New York, on October 16, 1987, and stayed in the Northeast and Canada through November. Working with new lighting and sound systems, the band deployed a set that included both Aerosmith warhorses and new hits like "Dude" and "Rag Doll." Steven's spectacular stage clothes were designed by Teresa and Lisa Barrick. The segment that seemed to get the biggest applause was when they sat down at the front of the stage to play "Hangman Jury" with National steel guitars and a harmonica. The kids sang along with "Oh, boy, don'tcha line the tracka-lacka" and knew every word of the song. A nightly audience favorite was also Joey Kra-mer's drum solo performed with electronically "sampled" drumsticks as Joey danced around the stage.

After Christmas, the tour resumed, with White Lion opening. (John Kalodner was showcasing the new metal bands at Geffen Records.) This second leg, starting January 16, 1988, in Seattle, moved through Califor-nia, the Southwest, Texas. Marty Callner and his video crew filmed con-cert sequences for the next video, "Angel" (the single reached #3 in the spring of 1988). They met the band in Louisiana around Mardi Gras in February, where the "Rag Doll" video was filmed in the French Quarter of New Orleans.

Tim Collins: We got great work from Marty, who is smart and funny and got on well with the band. But he arrived in New Orleans really fucked up on coke and pot. We staged a big Mardi Gras scene at 3 A.M. in the French Quarter and he forgot to bring the right lens for the camera, which is why everything looks so far away.

The second leg of the tour ended on May 22. Six days later, Steven Tyler married Teresa Barrick in Tulsa, Oklahoma, with Teresa's sister Lisa serving as maid of honor. Within a few weeks Teresa was pregnant. Their daughter, Chelsea Tallarico, was born in Boston in April 1989.

After a month off, the tour resumed in July and stayed on the road through October. Permanent Vacation was at the 3 million sales mark and climbing. Opening many of the shows that summer was the Los Angeles band Guns N' Roses, spiritual children of Aerosmith whose first record contained a proto-metal version of "Mama Kin." Gun N' Roses' current album, Appetite for Destruction, was at #2.

Tim Collins: John Kalodner said we needed a great opening act for the summer shows and suggested Guns N' Roses. I said, "We can't do this. We're sober. They're heroin users and drug addicts." But he in-sisted we find a way to handle this, so we came up with a plan. Guns would play, Aerosmith would arrive, then Guns would leave, all their drug scene contained in their room. At the beginning, it worked so well that the bands had no contact, but it gradually loosened up when the Gunners were respectful, and everyone got along great.

Steven Tyler: What got me was they were *us*. The bass player *is* Tom Hamilton. Slash *is* Joe Perry. Izzy *is* Brad, and the drummer is that close to Joey Kramer. Axl is the same as me, a visionary egomaniac. Sometimes I walked into their dressing room and it was like looking in the mirror.

I talked to them a little about drugs. Aerosmith was upset that the press was giving us a lot of shit about supposedly not letting them drink and smoke and do drugs. That offended us because we never presumed to tell anyone that. Before the first show, I got Izzy—who I once did drugs with—and Slash and maybe Duff to come to my dressing room. I told them where I came from with drugs and booze and just told them, "Look, if you got any blow, please keep it to yourself. Do it in your dressing room. If you do it in mine, I'm gonna have to leave my own dressing room."

But they were OK. They told us we were their idols. Billie and Teresa had tour shirts printed up with names of the rehabs we had gone through instead of tour dates, and we gave them to the guys in Guns. That was our statement.

The Aerosmith/Guns N' Roses juggernaut lurched through American major markets all summer. On August 16, they played for 65,000 at Giants Stadium in New Jersey. A week later, they did three sold-out shows at Great Woods, a new outdoor amphitheater in Mansfield, Mass., near the band members' homes in the suburbs of Boston.

Guns N' Roses played first, blasting out their hits "Welcome to the Jungle" and "Sweet Child O' Mine." Axl played in his EAT THE WORM *T-shirt, introduced the rhythm guitarist as "the king of beers," the drummer as "the biggest pothead I know," and paid nightly tribute to Aerosmith as the major influence on Guns N' Roses. This was echoed in Axl's mike-twirling and Slash's effort to look and play like Joe Perry. Their last number was Bob Dylan's "Knockin' on Heaven's Door."*

It would have been a tough act to follow for any band but Aerosmith. Bare-chested and incredibly strong from an almost religious regimen of weight lifting, Joe Perry ran the band with his raptor eyes. Steven Tyler, in scarves and diaphanous trousers, reached into the archives for songs like "No More No More" and "Same Old Song and Dance," new numbers from Vacation and the missile-launch dynamics of "Back in the Saddle" and "Train Kept A-Rollin'," which closed most of the shows.

Bebe Buell: Liv and I went to see Aerosmith at Great Woods in August 1988. She was eleven years old. We were the only ones allowed in Steven's dressing room, and Steven took her around and introduced her to everybody. She met her sister Mia for the first time.

This was when everything finally clicked for her. I noticed she looked at Mia *very* carefully. When Steven brought Liv to me so he could prepare for the show, she turned to me and asked, "Mom? Why does he cry every time he sees me?"

Halfway through the show, she's watching Steven onstage. She sees Mia in the wings. Liv turned to me and whispered: "Mom—that's my *father*, isn't it?"

I nodded, smiling and crying at the same time. It was such an electric moment.

After the show, I just said, "Steven—she knows." He gave me a long look, breathed a sigh, and said, "Holy shit."

The tour ended in Los Angeles. Aerosmith's road crew surprised Guns N' Roses by jumping around the stage in gorilla suits during "Welcome to the Jungle." Guns retaliated by joining Aerosmith for a long, loving jam on "Mama Kin."

While Steven was on the road, the Tallarico family sold their resort, Trow-Rico, in New Hampshire.

Steven Tyler: The family was up in arms. It was cut up into three pieces and they sold everything: tables, chairs, my rocking horse. All the silverware was sold in a box for 39¢. I'm still pissed off.

Tim Collins: By the end of the tour, Guns N' Roses were *huge*. They basically just exploded. We were all pissed that *Rolling Stone* showed up to do a story on Aerosmith, but Guns N' Roses ended up on the cover of the magazine. Suddenly the opening act was bigger than we were.

But we felt sorry for them. One, they were so fucked up it was ridiculous. Two, their stupid manager had negotiated a bad deal for them and never bothered to renegotiate it or even complain. Three, they were traveling like Gypsies, their old suitcases held together by twine and gaffers tape. At the end of the tour, we bought them all new Halliburton cases, which their manager took as an insult.

When the tour stories came out, I was quoted saying that Guns N' Roses was a lot like Aerosmith: They'd have to do $2.5 million worth of dope before they were ready to get help. This sent their manager into a psychotic rage. He came up and punched me at a restaurant on Melrose Avenue in L.A. a couple of weeks later, the moron.

He's not in the business anymore. David Geffen asked me to manage Guns and I thought about it for ten seconds and declined.

By October [1988], *Permanent Vacation* was up to 4 million. It got to #11 on the charts and did well in Europe and in Japan, a key element in our strategy to make Aerosmith a global band. "Rag Doll," the third single, got to #17, and the video was a huge hit on MTV.

Steven Tyler: OK—hit REWIND. One day I said to John Kalodner, "Wouldn't it be nice if I knew somebody I could write songs with?" He says, "I know some people." Yes, we used some other writers to help get us out of the hole. Yes, I did a whole lot of lame things: "Magic Touch," "Angel." I love soppy ballads, Beatles songs like "In My Life." Half of me loves them, the other half is whispering, *You fuckin' wimp. Don't put any more of that shit out!*

I learned how to operate in this system. When I tried to use Desmond [Child] as a song doctor, someone to fix a song after it's done, it didn't work for me. He put his two cents in and laid it over my song and it wasn't right for me. But when I used his skill and started to write *with* him, it became like a tapestry we worked on together. I showed him the chords to "Dream On" and we wrote "Angel" ten minutes later.

I realized what it boiled down to: how good Joe Perry looks when he's playing guitar onstage with Aerosmith, like a raging bull without a shirt on. When I look at Joe, I sometimes have to stop and think: *This is the guy I was shooting coke with a few years ago, and now look at us. We got sober!*

4: Let Out the Kid

Joe Perry: Two months after the tour ended, we wanted to get started again. We could feel something big was coming. On November 1 [1988], Steven and I started writing. We just went to work. The first day produced "Monkey on My Back," which started out as an Aerosmith folk song. We recorded it straight-ahead, the five of us playing live, and Steven redid the vocals later. It was about our adventures in body chemistry.

Tom Hamilton: We started to rehearse for the next album—the one we needed to make to get beyond the point we were at—at Rick

Tinory's studio in Cohasset, Mass., in December 1988. Winter was early that year; we kicked a lot of snow off our boots when we came into work every day. Bruce Fairbairn flew in and Steven played him the beginnings of "Love in an Elevator" and "Monkey on My Back." I had the intro riff for "Janie's Got a Gun," and Steven had the first part of the melody line. We worked in this tiny studio through February [1989], when we went back to Little Mountain [Sound Studio] in Vancouver to cut the album.

Steven Tyler: I'm forty years old now. The other guys are getting there. I sat at my Korg and talked to Joe and the guys a lot about kids who bought our records: what they listened to, what they wanted, what the younger bands were doing. Then it came to me that we didn't have to give a shit. All we had to do was look inside and let out the kid. "Let out the kid." It was a big theme for me when I was making that record.

As for the younger bands, we knew the only difference between us and them is that they're into jerking off and we're into fucking.

John Kalodner: It was the same stinking winter in Boston, the same bullshit all over again, except now they had a rehearsal place way out in the suburbs and it was really inconvenient. As soon as I walk in, the torture starts again about songwriting. First thing they tell me: "We're not gonna write with anyone on this album."

Tyler plays me the riff of what Hamilton has written, which became the intro to "Janie." He had the beginnings of "Elevator" and I thought, *This is great. This is Tyler at his best.* Meanwhile, all this is being video-taped by Tim Collins's employee David Robertson for a proposed documentary. He was told by Steven to shoot everything. (Later in Vancouver, when it got horrendous, they made him stop taping.)

The thing that stuck in my mind was Tom's "Janie" riff, but it was hard to get Tyler to work on it.

Steven Tyler: You can hear it in *Pump:* I went wild with women for a year there. When I was getting high, I didn't fuck around with women. Now I was angry I missed all the fruits that had been offered to me when all I wanted was a bag of dope with a little red crescent moon stamped on it and a closet to snort it up in. I thought that the gods owed me something. My attitude was: *Now that I'm sober, I deserve to get laid.*

One day before I got sober, I'm in a hot tub with a bunch of girls. Very mellow, intoxicatingly lubricious situation. We're in a fancy hotel. Maybe it was the Four Seasons. We decide to go upstairs and continue our discussions. We pile into the elevator. One of the girls is out of it and pushes all the buttons. We're wearing towels and bathrobes. I drop my hairbrush and kneel down and one of the girls opens her bathrobe. Just then the elevator door opens into the crowded lobby. That's where "Love in an Elevator" comes from.

We put it to this rhythm that Joe had while we were in Cohasset. We wrote it together and started jamming on a Buddy Miles type thing and I just got major wood. It was a bunch of pieces and we fused them together. Sometimes you do this with your pieces and it doesn't go together. This time it did. I came up with "Love in an Elevator." I said to Joe, "Dare I?"

"Why not? You wrote 'Dude (Looks Like a Lady),' didn't you? What the fuck?" So we did it.

Joe Perry: I had this interesting riff that needed a song around it. We wrote it at Tinory's while working on a jam. Bruce Fairbairn heard it and suggested we just open it up in the middle of the song, the first time we'd ever done a jam like that. So Brad played the whole thing and I played the whole thing on a '57 Strat. We took the best pieces and it sounded great. It was the thing we were most psyched about playing live.

Brad Whitford: When we get together, I listen closely to Joe. Joe Perry playing the guitar is like fuel for us. Flashes of lightning. Bolts of brilliance. A lot of songs begin that way.

Joe Perry: By April [1989], "Elevator" was coming together in Vancouver. We were jamming on "Monkey on My Back," working on "Deuces Are Wild" and "Don't Get Mad."

We had three weeks of preproduction in Vancouver before we actually recorded. I went down to Jim Vallance's house with the idea to write the first song on the album, just tear it up into something that sounded like a dinosaur eating cars. Y'know, let them know we're here when that double kick drum gets going. We came up with "Young Lust."

"F.I.N.E.*" was written by Steven and me, and we took the bridge from another song we were working on with Desmond Child and didn't use. We also wrote "What It Takes" with Desmond. It started out as a country and western type song that we ended up putting on electric guitars—a Leslie and Les Paul—to make it sound heavier.

Bruce Fairbairn was a taskmaster; he wasn't emotionally attached to songs we'd been living with for four months. He came in and cut and maimed. These songs—they're like your babies, y'know? It's like someone deciding if they're going to grow up or not.

Steven Tyler: An epiphany: In the old days I'd go to someone's house with a bag of blow and sit down and write, and I'd leave the next day with no songs and no idea where I'd been. Now, being sober as I was, I could go over to [songwriter] Jim Vallance's house [in suburban Vancouver] and leave a few hours later with a cassette of three or four new songs, and a new friend. It was always a moment for me. That's where "Deuces" and "The Other Side" come from.

Joey Kramer: "Janie's Got a Gun" is a song that means a lot to me. Steven hit upon a subject that most people were afraid to deal with and even unaware of—parental abuse and violence against their children.

Steven Tyler: That song is about a girl getting raped and pillaged by her father. It's about incest, something that happens to a lot of kids who don't even find out about it until they find themselves trying to work through some major fucking neurosis. It's a song about abuse in America.

Joe Perry: "Janie" was very close to the demo that Steven brought to the band. He wrote it on piano, and I adopted the part for the guitar, a Chet Atkins electric/acoustic plugged into an amp and cranked really loud.

John Kalodner: I heard the rough cut of "Janie" just after they recorded it [in May], and I knew it was a big hit, certainly one of Tyler's best moments as a songwriter. It was a work of art, a masterpiece, and so bizarre.

He went berserk when I told him it wouldn't get played on commercial radio with the word "rape" in it. He didn't want to take it out and there was a fight.

Steven Tyler: The real fight was over the line "put a bullet in his brain," which John wanted changed to "stand out in the pouring rain" because he was afraid they wouldn't play it on the radio. There was another one over "feeding that fuckin' monkey on my back." I screamed. "I can't take the 'fuck' out of it. Those words are in every kid's vocabulary and I use them to communicate with them. It's freedom of expression. Those words are the colors on my fuckin' palette." And later the program director at Z-100 in New York told me it was all bullshit anyway—they played songs with those kinds of lyrics.

Tom Hamilton: By June [1989], we're in a race to finish and the pressure is awful. Time to do our overdubs. I'd taken lessons between the albums, rediscovered John Paul Jones and James Jamerson [who played bass on many of the Motown songs], and had an inflamed tendon in one of my fingers from playing so much. My hand felt like it was on fire. Cortisone shots. I sit at the mixing console in the control room, ready to put in my bass part. The producers, engineers, and tape ops are looking at me. The other guys in the band are staring at me. *Oh, man.* There's an atmosphere of competition and criticism that keeps it electric. It can get vicious. *Who's fault is it?* It's never, "Let's get together and sort this out." It's "Let's hunt this down and shoot it." It's how we make the best records we can.

Joe Perry: Earlier, during preproduction, I was working by myself with Toby, our sound guy, and I couldn't think of anything. So I put "Rag Doll" on backward and tried to play along with it. I got the chord change and built "Don't Get Mad, Get Even" around it. I was after dynamics, fury. When this band gets together to make a record, you can't believe some of the shit that comes out.

One night we saw Keith Richards's band [the X-Pensive Winos] and they did the old Stones song "Connection," which got us thinking about how cool that song was, how cool the Kinks were, and about all the English rock songs we liked from the sixties; next day I started playing a riff, Steven's at the keyboard, and by the end of the afternoon, we had "My Girl."

Steven didn't like it, said he was afraid of it, said it seemed like a sellout because it sounded too pop. I told him it was heavy because it was trashy, a tribute to songs we used to like. To me, selling out was doing a power ballad.

For me, it wasn't about "letting out the kid." "Young Lust" wasn't about kids, it's about us at forty, having the same feelings we used to have, still listening to rock 'n' roll. I still have that side of me that loves Deep Purple and the Sex Pistols: "Highway Star," "Smoke on the Water." I still get goose bumps when I hear "Immigrant Song."

Tim Collins: There was a big power struggle at the end of the *Pump* sessions. Aerosmith had worked with John Kalodner on *Permanent Vacation*, and it had paid off. But now power shifted slightly because the band was at a creative peak and they were more reluctant to roll over and die for John and his team. There were some bad arguments over John's approving tracks.

John Kalodner: I realize that their record is their work of art, OK? But I want at least four songs on it that will make it a success and that kids will want to buy. That's what I do, and that's what makes it so hard if I don't hear it.

I thought "Don't Get Mad, Get Even" was going to be the lead track on the album, but then Tyler never got it right. "The Other Side" came late in the recording and was so good that it pushed "Deuces Are Wild" off the album.

Joe Perry: I didn't like a lot of the input we were getting from outside the band, but I accepted it. Did I like it as a musician and an artist? Maybe not. But were I that much of an artist, I'd be playing coffeehouses in Cambridge. Y'know? I'm an entertainer, playing rock 'n' roll, arena rock. In order to do that, you have to make compromises.

I wanted to call the album *F.I.N.E.** after the song we wrote with Desmond Child. [The title is an acronym for "Fucked Up, Insecure, Neurotic, Emotional."] Other titles considered were *Elevator*, *Monkey House*, and *Here's Looking Up Your Old Address*. I think Brad came up with *Pump*.

Brad Whitford: This actually came up at a band meeting after the *Permanent Vacation* tour. I was looking at the Aerosmith wings logo, and it reminded me of the old Flying A gas station sign, which led to a whole scenario of gasoline pumps and the humping old trucks we eventually put on the cover. Steven goes, "*Pump*—what the fuck does that mean?" I said, "I don't know. It just seems very . . . nineties."

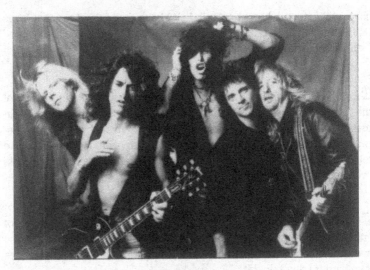

Pump, 1989
(GEFFEN RECORDS, PHOTO: NORMAN SEEFF)

John Kalodner: They played the WEA [Warner Elektra Atlantic] Convention that August, before the record came out, and they were just *spectacular*. They played an hour set, came out with "Love in an Elevator," and it was just smokin'.

Pump, *Aerosmith's tenth studio album, was released in September 1989, shipping platinum. The ten tracks were tied together with interludes of tribal chant, primitive instruments from the collection of Vancouver folklorist Randy Raine Reusch, and risqué playlets. An intense, brooding album that spilled over with suppressed rage,* Pump *got Aerosmith the best reviews of its career.* Rolling Stone *called it "a masterpiece of sexual innuendo and hellacious guitar."* Musician: *"Tyler's lyrics have taken on a new dimension as he's discovered more stuff to think about with a complete brain at his disposal."*

"Love in an Elevator" was released in August, before the album, along with a Marty Callner video filmed over three grueling days in Los Angeles. By October, the single was at #5 and the album was selling in the millions. The second single, "Janie's Got a Gun," came out in November and reached #4 in January 1990. The video, a dark mini-film by David Fincher [director of the science-fiction epic Alien 3], *quickly became one*

of the most requested in the history of MTV and ushered in an era of music video as high-gloss drama.

Aerosmith appeared on Saturday Night Live that winter, giving America a collective shudder with "Janie's Got a Gun." In addition, the band appeared on the popular "Wayne's World" skit as the object of intense adoration ("We are not worthy!") by Wayne (Mike Myers) and Garth (Dana Carvey). Tom Hamilton read some lines parodying Aerosmith as a group of closet existentialists, amid national hilarity. This appearance led to the sale of a couple of million more albums and eventually to the band's appearance in the movie Wayne's World 2 in 1993.

With the band on the road for the next eighteen months, "What It Takes" reached #9 in April 1990. "The Other Side" was #22 that summer. (The video portrayed Aerosmith as robots being taken out of boxes and assembled to perform onstage.) Pump stayed on the American charts for 110 weeks and sold 4 million copies in the first two years of release.

5: Bonzo's Grave

Steven Tyler: I'm getting tired of recovery stories. But I could now actually *hear* us getting sober on the albums. You could chart the whole story from the musical differences when we started, when we started using a little, when we were using, then when we first got sober, then *Pump*.

When we went back on the road, we were part of a network where any other bands who were going through anything similar to what Aerosmith went through could just call us up and talk, so we could pass on the message. You don't just go backstage and brag about your sobriety date and tell them they're assholes for using drugs. Maybe you talk about how hard it is, how beautiful it is that I didn't take a drink today, after twenty-five years. I told them it's like living in a cave with a boulder at the door and the boulder is dope. Get rid of the boulder, invite your friends in, and get out of yourself.

In October [1989], I went backstage to see the Rolling Stones [on the *Steel Wheels* tour]. I'd always regretted that the one chance I'd gotten to hang with Mick back in Malibu, I was so fucked up on Tuinals and blow that I couldn't hold a conversation.

This time it was nice. We were walking in the Stones' tent city behind Foxboro Stadium and Mick pulls me into his tent and we hugged. I said,

"Mick, you don't know what it means to be with you here, after all these years. Maybe I'll remember this one." I told him that I'd woken up that morning and gotten my daily report from the office and right next to Aerosmith at #2 were the Stones at #1.

Meanwhile, I'm thinking, *Watch yo' ass, mothafucka, 'cos next week we're gonna be #1.*

Aerosmith began touring in Germany that fall, augmented by Thom Gimbel (from the Boston band John Butcher Axis) on keyboards and saxophone. At London's Hammersmith Odeon on November 11, they started a blistering two-hour guitar clinic with "Rats in the Cellar" that segued into "Searching for Madge," a tribute to Aerosmith's deep roots in Peter Green's Fleetwood Mac. They mixed oldies with "Permanent Vacation" and the new material. Thom Gimbel played a massive keyboard fanfare to "Lightning Strikes."

Joey Kramer: Robert Plant came to see the band at the Hammersmith Odeon and we got to talking. Not trying to sound like the typical Led Zeppelin fan, I still found myself trying to express to him the irony I felt about my survival with regard to the cold fact that the guy—his friend—who had the most influence on what I'm doing today is now six feet under. I told Robert that I'd never met John Bonham, but I wish I could speak my piece and say some things to him.

Robert looked at me and rasped, "I'll tell you where his grave is, but you mustn't tell anyone else." Next day I hired a car and set out for the English Midlands; me, the driver, and Andy Gilman, who worked for me. Three hours later, we get to the top of this hill, just as Robert described it. The church was hundreds of years old; all the headstones were crooked, weatherbeaten. Robert had said, "Go around the right side of the church, open up this big gate, and go to the backyard."

It was a white marble headstone in an eight-foot square of grass, perfectly manicured. It looked out over a meadow. I was there for an hour in nasty weather. I said what I had to say and we drove back to London in the rain.

In December, the band began the first American leg of the tour, with Skid Row opening—an hour of frantic bad-attitude speed metal. In Springfield, Mass., singer Sebastian Bach got in the news when he threw a beer bottle back into the crowd and it brained a young girl. At the end of the month, they played three sold-out nights at Boston Garden, concentrating on recent songs. "Heart's Done Time" and "Magic Touch" from Permanent Vacation opened the shows, followed by "F.I.N.E.*," "Monkey on My Back," "Don't Get Mad," and "Janie." Joe Perry wielded his Chet Atkins guitar in fringed black leather pants. Joey Kramer played a revolving drum kit. They played on a set designed as a city rooftop, with skylights, antennas, smoking chimneys, and a sign that flashed BEAN-TOWN HOTEL. (The name of the hotel changed each night.) Steven was running up and down ramps, using every inch of the stage with tireless energy.

Joe and Brad stormed through "Red House" and then whipped out a few classics—"Dream On," "Sweet Emotion," "Seasons of Wither"—before overwhelming the audience with the heavy artillery: "Dude," "Rag Doll," "Elevator," and a climactic "Walk This Way."

The plane, Aeroforce One, was a Citation II formerly owned by Ferdinand Marcos, the Philippine dictator. Joe and Steven sat up front. The rhythm section, who called themselves the LI3 ("Less-Interesting Three"), read car magazines and chatted in the rear.

The second leg of the tour opened in April in Tampa, Florida, with "What It Takes" on the radio and the Black Crowes opening. Aerosmith was now starting off with "Young Lust," "F.I.N.E.*," "Monkey on My Back," and "Don't Get Mad," giving its audience an opening salvo from Pump. Favorite songs—"Sweet Emotion," "Mama Kin," "Back in the Saddle"—now came late in the show, which ended with "Love in an Elevator," scorching in its live version. The last encore was invariably "Walk This Way," pure rock 'n' roll that sent the 2 million fans who saw those 115 shows home with a time-tripping seventies/nineties buzz.

The American leg of the tour ended in July and the band went on vacation.

Joe Perry: One day I'm stopped for speeding on Cape Cod. I notice the trooper is spending an unusual amount of time with my license and registration. He comes back and says he'd got a warrant for my arrest on his computer. It turned out it was outstanding from a restraining order Elyssa had taken out on me in 1982. I was taken back to Newton handcuffed in the back of a state police car. It took all day to straighten it out, during which the born-again police chief tried to get me to accept Jesus Christ as my personal savior.

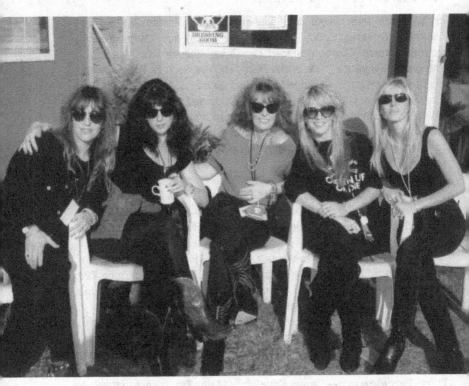

Castle Donnington, 1990. From left: Karen Whitford, Terry Hamilton, April Kramer, Teresa Tyler, Billie Perry
(PERRY COLLECTION)

Aerosmith spent the rest of the year in Europe and the Far East. On August 18, they headlined the giant Monsters of Rock metal fest at Castle Donnington in Leicestershire, England. Also on the bill were Whitesnake, Poison, and 80,000 English kids waving Union Jacks and Aerosmith T-shirts.

Brad Whitford: We're over in England and I'm onstage and I look over at my wife and there's Jimmy Page standing next to her. He's watching us play and I'm remembering when I saw him as a kid and I'm thinking, *This is ironic. I've traveled this circle now.* I come offstage and he comes up to me and says, "Brilliant! You were *brilliant.*"

I'm dreaming. Some people can take this stuff in their stride. I still have to pinch myself.

Then Page comes out to jam with us on "Train." As he hits the first notes, Steven looks at us and mouths the words, "I can't believe it!"

Two days later at the Marquee Club in London's Soho, Aerosmith played for an hour in front of 850 fans and guests. Joe Perry played slide guitar on "Monkey on My Back" and then ran the band through a set that mixed new songs with "Milk Cow Blues" and "Big Ten Inch Record" and climaxed with "Toys."

"We have a guest tonight," Steven Tyler announced. "The man who set us on the path: Jimmy Page!" Page came out, dressed in black, slinging a purple Les Paul. The crowd began to chant, "Jimmy! Jimmy!" Page smiled and nodded to Joe Perry. Steven Tyler yelled, "Mr. Kramer," the lights went out, then on again as the band went into "I Ain't Got You." Page got into it, prowling the stage, ripping off a fiery solo when called upon. They continued the Yardbirds tribute with "Think About It." Joe usually spoke to the audience before "Red House," but tonight he said he was speechless and just wanted to play some blues. He called Brad Whitford to solo first, played a couple of fluid bursts himself, then handed it over to Page, who was winding up to throw down—when his guitar went dead.

A fuse had blown in the old club. When they got power back, they finished the number, played Led Zeppelin's "Immigrant Song," and finished with "Train," Joe Perry broadcasting feedback into his amp, riding the electromagnetic flyway into the spiritual side of the song. The musicians stepped back when Steven started to swing his scarf-draped microphone around the Marquee's little stage.

Jimmy Page said good-bye, and Aerosmith came back and played "Young Lust," "Dream On," "Love in an Elevator," and "Walk This Way" for another half an hour.

John Kalodner: I thought they were maybe the greatest band in the world, as a band. In September 1990, I remember that they played "I'm Down" off-camera during a commercial at *The MTV Awards,* just to warm up for broadcasting "Dude (Looks Like a Lady)," and they were *incredible.* I thought, *Nobody else is this good right now.*

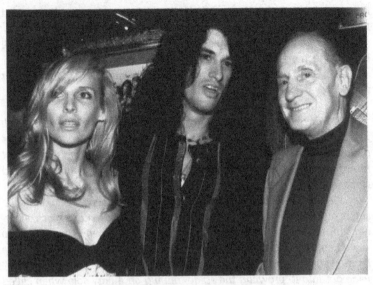

Billie and Joe Perry with Les Paul, 1990
(PERRY COLLECTION)

6: The $30 Million Sex Machine

Steven Tyler: I don't feel great about having to come out and say that it took me some time to get some sense of responsibility and learn what a man really is—someone that can be true to his wife and children. I learned this especially after my son Taj was born [in 1991]. Now I was watching my children grow up—an experience I never had before.

At the same time, something in me wanted to make up for all the years I spent in the bathroom, in the alleys, in the shadows—getting high. I didn't take care of my sexual desires, and when I started to get *really* sober I wanted to make up for lost time. Every life has a measure of sorrow, and sometimes this is what awakens us. My sobriety brought out a sexuality that lay dormant for so many years because of the drugs.

Rumors started to get out.

Everyone was mad at me. One day [in January 1991] Tim approached me and said, "I think you need to take a look at your sexuality, because all the signs point to you being a sex addict."

I go, "WHAT???"

He said he'd heard that I'd been showering with a couple of girls, *Penthouse* models, backstage after the shows. He said something about a girl backstage at a benefit we did for battered women at the Hard Rock in Las Vegas. He suggested I go away and look at this because I had a big problem, and did I want to bring any problems back to my family?

No. And it was all right because I wanted to go away and work on this. Psychologically speaking, I was grateful to be taking a look at this. There were other things bothering me as well. I was having problems talking to the other guys in the band and needed to figure out why. My therapist pointed out that we'd always been stoned when we were together and said a lot of cruel things to each other that were now backfiring on us in our sobriety. The other guys may not have worked on these issues, but here was a chance for me to go away and look at it.

So I went to Sierra Tucson. I check in for codependency issues, not sex addiction. When I got there, they asked me if I'd had any extramarital sex. When I said yes, they told me to take this class they called "Sex Addiction." Then they asked if anyone had died recently in my family, and I went off on them. "Yes! And I'm really pissed off because I was on the road and my Aunt Phyllis died, who taught me to sing in front of people and she was my inspiration and they told me *I didn't have time to go to the funeral* because of this fucking band."

They heard this and said, "OK—he's got another 'ism.' We'll get him to take the course on death and grieving."

So it wasn't just about sex addiction. But they put me in this class with these very damaged guys who wore their mother's underwear and masturbated near playgrounds. I knew I wasn't in the right place. I was someone these *Penthouse* girls were throwing themselves at. Then my roommate left early and two weeks later sold his story to one of the supermarket tabloids. He said I had to have three or four different women a week. It was bullshit, but that's how it got out.

ROLLING STONE

AEROSMITH INKS $30 MILLION DEAL

Aerosmith has signed a multialbum deal with Sony Music that appears to be one of the most lucrative ever negotiated by a rock 'n' roll band. Sources close to Aerosmith indicate that the group is guaranteed a minimum of $30 million, along with the exceptionally high royalty rate of nearly 25 percent. The deal puts Aerosmith in the company of Michael Jackson, Janet Jackson, and the Rolling Stones. (October 3, 1991)

Tim Collins: David Geffen was selling Geffen Records [to MCA]. Aerosmith still owed him three albums and was an important asset to him, so he wanted to re-sign the band for even more. "We'll extend your deal," he said.

"No bumps?" I ask. "No nothin'?"

"Ahh, give you another point."

It was almost an insult.

"Hey—go across the street and see what you're worth. You got an old band. A tired band. You know what? I don't even know if I *wanna* re-sign. I don't believe in you that much—you're lucky I even wanna re-sign."

So I called Michele Anthony. She's the daughter of Dee Anthony, who had managed Peter Frampton in the seventies. I'd met her when she was an attorney with a law firm we'd used and became friends with her through John Kalodner. Michele was now executive vice president of Sony Music, which had bought Columbia Records, Aerosmith's old label, the year before.

Michele goes, "What? Are you kidding? I'd sign them *in a second.*"

They offered us $25 million and some other stuff worth $5 million more.

I called Ed Rosenblatt at Geffen and said, "If you match 80 percent of Sony's offer, we'll stay." Ed called me the next day and said that Geffen didn't want to do the deal. A few days later, Geffen invited me to lunch, and we arranged to meet at Madre on Robertson. He offered me 60 percent of the Sony deal. I had to say no. Eventually the waiter handed me the bill, but I refused to pay. Geffen looked at me funny; it was well known that he *never* paid for lunch. I said, "David, you invited me."

"Well, ah, I don't have any credit cards."

"That's your problem, David." It was my symbolic standing up to him. We spoke on the phone a couple of days later, but he wouldn't budge. "Go make your fuckin' deal with Sony." *Slam.*

So we did, and it was announced in the press in September. It was pointed out that Aerosmith still owed Geffen albums and the band members would be almost fifty by the time their first album for Sony came out.

I knew if we could stay sober they'd be hotter than ever by then.

No regrets, ever. The only thing we missed about Geffen is the smallness and intimacy we had with them before Geffen sold the company and ended up making a billion when MCA was sold to Matsushita. After that, it was no longer an entrepreneur-driven company, and it lost some of its old feel.

Steven Tyler: I heard a lot about how I'm gonna be too old when we get to the Sony contract. The tone was: "What are you gonna have left, old fuck?" Inside I'm saying, *You ain't seen nothin' yet. I'm gonna get so much pleasure out of proving you wrong. I can climb a tree better than I could at sixteen, plus I know not to put all my weight on certain limbs. I figure I'm smarter and have more balls than I did back then. So watch out.*

While all this was going on, something special happened. For a long time, I wanted to acknowledge my fatherhood of Liv. Finally, for all the right reasons, I met her and her mother in New York, and we took blood tests to establish my paternity legally. When the results came back, we hugged for a long time and I offered Liv my name. "Use it," I told her. "Liv Tyler." I told her that Liv Tallarico was great too—I'm very proud of Tallarico—but that the name Tyler had power in our business, and Tallarico didn't.

That's how she became Liv Tyler, at the age of fourteen. A year later, she started working as a model, and today she's an actress. Maybe you've seen one of her films. She's *incredible!*

7: The Burr
Under the Saddle

Tom Hamilton: The Sony deal became this big thing hanging over us. It was exciting but also threatening. I thought it was also threatening to Tim, in terms of the magnitude of the deal he was making and how he felt about what he was representing.

After the tour, Steven got intervened on and went in for sex addiction—

which I was not part of. That was Tim's thing and I remember feeling really uncomfortable with it. I knew that once one person gets intervened on in this band, everyone winds up going through the same thing. Steven went, then Joey went, then our tour manager Bob Dowd had to go. Nobody was using or relapsing. It was Tim's fear of the always-impending relapse. "How can we head this off? This guy needs to go away to work on this, work on that." It made me feel weird. It was an unnatural, abnormal way to live.

Summer of 1991. Terry and I had just bought a house in Chestnut Hill, counting our chickens before they hatched. Working on the *Get a Grip* album for seven months. People started getting nervous: We had a bunch of material, but the lyrics weren't getting written, the songs weren't getting finished, we didn't have any hits yet. Kalodner was bringing this up to Tim in his blunt way, and I think Tim started to panic. His interpretation of the problems around the record was that this was the disease coming back in. The disease originally meant alcoholism and drug addiction. Now, in Tim's mind, it became any kind of dysfunctional behavior that interfered with the Plan. And there was a lot of it; this band has always had a lot of dysfunctional, fucked-up behavior. At one point, we wished that we had a manager who would be more involved in our personal lives to help solve these problems. But this was overkill.

We'd been working out at Longview [studio] that summer. I was talking to Bob Dowd, who was bitter because he'd just gotten back from Sierra Tucson. He said, "Hey, don't worry, pal. You're next." I knew he was probably right.

I was in this bookstore and found a little pamphlet called *Your Right to Say No*. I read it all the way through at my house on Cape Cod and spent three days obsessing. We were gonna have this big meeting at the Four Seasons [hotel in Boston] in a few days, and I was asking myself, *What am I gonna do? Are they gonna blow me out of the band if I don't go? How am I gonna say no and have it stick?* Because I knew it was coming.

Sure enough, we had this meeting, chairs in a circle. Tim had recruited Steven, Lou Cox, the band, maybe Dowd.

Tim's rap: "The disease is back. The new addiction is money. Something has to be done because we can't build a house on a weak foundation." Tim suggested that the three of us—Brad, Joe and myself—go to Sierra Tucson for a month, "for a recharge," he called it.

I just freaked out. Panic mode. I said, "No, I'm not gonna do it. I've got a house, a wife. I wanna control how I can reaffirm my contribution to the sobriety of the band. I want to negotiate this."

Joe Perry: We tried to explain why the timing of all this was really bad for some of us. Brad's wife, Karen, was about to give birth and, apart from the fact she wouldn't be able to travel out there for family week, Brad didn't want to risk missing the birth. Billie was also pregnant and didn't want to fly. But Tim said that he wouldn't manage a band that wasn't in recovery. We couldn't understand it. We were six years sober at that point. I didn't want to go, but equally, I didn't want to lose my band again.

Tom Hamilton: "No negotiations," they said. The therapeutic community went out of the room and had a meeting, came back in, and Tim said, "Look, this is the way it's gotta be. If you're not in recovery, I can't be your manager, and I won't sell Columbia a bill of goods."

He was playing a heavy card: "Either you do what I say or I'll blow off the Sony deal."

If it had just been me, the threat would've been that I'd be out of the band. But there were three of us. So he had to play a bigger card on that. We hadn't signed the Sony contracts yet, but they were being written up, and it was getting close.

Lou Cox said, "You have a choice. You don't have to go." This infuriated me because it was so easy for someone else to say. Enabling Tim's really compulsive, sick behavior. I mean, the record's not going well so we've gotta go away to a mental hospital for a month? I mean, give me a fuckin' break. People go to these places for a month because their lives are falling apart, they're killing themselves with drugs, or they're having a nervous breakdown. You have to really want to do it.

Meanwhile, Terry and I were going through arduous physical tests to see about having a kid, and we were moving into a new house. No leeway for that. Tim said I could stay two extra days with Terry after she had to have some surgery. And then I had to go. Because we had a record to do.

So we went to Sierra Tucson and hated it because we didn't belong there. We seethed with frustration for a whole month. I wrote Tim a letter, telling him how angry I was. I told him how completely wrong it was to invade other people's lives.

Joe Perry: The biggest rub of all was that while we were at Sierra Tucson, we were told by the therapists that we didn't really need to be there. That we could have done exactly the same thing as outpatients.

Tom Hamilton: The whole episode was a big foreshadowing of what would happen later. It was the burr under the saddle for the next five years.

After the third week, we had a full band meeting. Everyone was there. Even Fairbairn. I was vulnerable and getting ready to really get into the treatment. But this was essentially a business meeting in the middle of our supposed recovery process. Which said to us: *This isn't about recovery, is it? It's about control. It's about business and Tim's exaggerated fears about the business going down the shithole. Terror that things are gonna fall apart any minute unless you run around fixing it all the time.*

We were so bought-into our career, and we must have thought Tim was the only guy that would do it for us. Plus, we *wanted* to be in recovery. We didn't want to go back to where we were.

Joe Perry: When it was time to actually sign the Sony contract, our manager dealt us another shock. He had insisted we put all of our advance money from the new deal into escrow, in case things didn't work out. We'd agreed to this, because we were also worried about the pressure that this big a deal can bring and wanted some kind of fail-safe. But at the actual signing at the Sony offices, we're down to the wire, with all the top brass waiting for us outside, and Tim takes us aside and insists that he get all his commission on the money up front. What could we do? We thought we were all in this together, but we walked out of the Sony signing owing $1.2 million. We were the ones who felt like we'd been sold a bill of goods.

8: Angel of Mercy

Steven Tyler: Richie Supa used to be my heroin connection in New York City, but I hadn't seen him in years because he went to prison after getting busted by the DEA with two kilos of cocaine back in '84. He got fifteen-to-life under the Rockefeller drug laws, which got reduced to two-to-four after Clive Davis and people in the industry wrote letters to the judge. He got paroled, got busted again, and was shipped back to Sing Sing for another year. He got paroled while we were on the *Permanent Vacation* tour and came to see us backstage at Madison Square Garden.

Richie Supa:

I tried to bring Steven an ounce of coke, but when I gave it to him, he absolutely freaked. He was in recovery and he just freaked. I had no idea. He had that wherewithal, knew what he needed to do to save his ass. Then Aerosmith's security pulled me and Laura Kaufman out of a bathroom stall and escorted me from the building. They threw me out. It got into the trades and I became the Antichrist. To some people, I still am.

My parole officer sent me back to Rikers Island for nine months to finish my sentence. I got out of jail in October 1988 with $40 and a parole suit. The DEA had taken everything I owned. I went to Florida and walked into a Narcotics Anonymous meeting one night. I couldn't see life without drugs, but they were able to show me a better way to live.

I kept waiting for Steven to call me. But then I heard that he wouldn't call me until I was really sober. Some time went by, he finally called, and I was so fucking proud that I was able to say to him, "Steven! I got a *year!*" I sent him my one-year chip.

Steven Tyler:

Four years into his sobriety, I wanted to write with Richie again because I remembered what good stuff we got with "Chip Away the Stone." But Tim and Joe Perry kept us apart, Joe from jealousy and Tim from his overcautious, mother-hen controlling thing where he was afraid that Steven and Richie, the two worst drug addicts anyone had ever known, were gonna get back into dope together.

But Richie was sober and we did get together [in the summer of 1991]. When he came out of jail, he had nothing. The IRS had taken everything. I got him a keyboard and Joe gave him a guitar to help him jump-start his creative juices. One day he called me up to thank me. We got into war stories—the old days—and got so deep I could literally taste the coke in my mouth. My heart started pounding. We talked about what it feels like to shoot a load in your arm. Heroin is so hard to kick because you start to think about it and you get what's called "euphoric recall."

I said, "Richie, a lot of people were afraid of us getting together because they thought we'd start using again. And now—look at this. We're fuckin' *sober.* Isn't it wonderful? Isn't it *amazing?*"

And he says, "Yeah, I was at this meeting the other day and this black woman says, 'I kept the right ones out and let the wrong ones in.' "

I said automatically, "Had an angel of mercy to see me through all my sins."

That's how we wrote "Amazing" in four hours at my house in Boston, right at the beginning of the whole process that became *Get a Grip.*

John Kalodner: Aerosmith was a great rock 'n' roll band, had been at their peak with *Pump*, which sold 8 million records. When this Sony thing happened, the music industry thought Sony had overpaid and that it was unlikely Aerosmith could repeat their success.

I had been asked if Aerosmith was worth $30 million, and I was not prepared to advise David Geffen to do this. But we went ahead with the next album, and everyone was waiting for them to fail.

In early October, Aerosmith and a 57-piece orchestra taped a performance of "Dream On" for MTV's Tenth Anniversary Special, broadcast on ABC later that year. The venue was the Wang Center, formerly the Music Hall, on Boston's Tremont Street, across the way from the Charles Playhouse, where Aerosmith first rehearsed twenty years earlier.

It was the first time the band had been onstage in almost a year. The audience consisted of 4,000 radio contest winners. After a brief intro by the orchestra, a grand piano descended from the flies of the theater. Floating down with the instrument, playing the chords to "Dream On," was Steven Tyler, a formal tailcoat over his usual leather and leopard outfit. The kids ate it up and waved the miniature flashlights MTV handed out.

Then they did it six more times, until the director had what he needed. At midnight, Aerosmith launched into a six-song set for the fans. "Young Lust" was dedicated to embattled Supreme Court nominee Clarence Thomas. "Big Ten Inch Record" was dedicated to his accuser, Anita Hill. Somewhat rusty, the band aborted a couple of blues intros that Tyler was working on and went into "Last Child" instead, followed by "Walkin' the Dog," "Elevator," and "Walk This Way."

In November, Columbia released Pandora's Box, a three-CD set containing old early album tracks, live performances, and several rehearsal jams and other previously unreleased material. One of the most interesting cuts is "Circle Jerk," a Whitford/Hamilton/Kramer track from the Cenacle, which appears uncredited at the end of the third disc. Marty Callner made the brilliant "phone sex" video to accompany "Sweet Emotion," released as a single at this time.

John Kalodner: In the fall, Aerosmith went to Sierra Tucson as a group, with Bruce Fairbairn. When they came back, the band refused to record in Vancouver again. We settled on A&M Studios in Hollywood and the band settled in. I listened to the songs they were working on and didn't like them (except for "Crazy," which they'd written with Desmond

but didn't record because they thought it was too much like "Angel").
But I was worried about being too critical, too negative.

Steven Tyler: We had "Eat the Rich," "Get a Grip," "Fever," "Amazing," and "Crazy" and a few others. We fought all the time.
I took a long time with lyrics. Brad Whitford said, "Why don't you work
on the fucking lyrics and let us get on with this shit?" I said, "What are
you, a robot? You can hate out on me all you want, but you better work
it out because this is why we don't write together anymore."

I had a song called "Black Cherry," which I presented to the band.
Three days later, I'm confronted by Joe Perry, Tim Collins, and Lou Cox,
and they ripped a second asshole in me about sexuality, all because I was
reading fuck magazines in the studio and they were scared I was back-
sliding into sexual addiction. They made fun of the lyrics I was writing.
"Too juvenile. Too immature." They told me the line in "Fever" about
"the crack of her ass" was in bad taste.

I thought we were doing all right. I even said to Joe Perry, "Look,
we're on a roll. Let's write a bunch of new songs." This is when John
Kalodner said, "This album sucks. Stop now and write a new album or
I'm taking my name off the record."

I was so angered when this happened. Nobody threatens me like that.
Nobody. This was so pivotal, when he came in and said, "These songs
suck." When I saw Tim Collins sit there and let John say he's taking his
name off the record, I realized then that I'd lost an ally as a manager.

So there was a lot of turmoil and changes. I realized our therapist had
gotten too close to our manager when some of our group sessions—the
band sitting in a circle and talking—turned into business meetings. Tim
Collins with an agenda. I'd tried to say good-bye to Lou Cox during *Pump*
but had been accused of relapsing. Now I refused to go to meetings with
him and brought in [L.A. drug counselor] Bob Timmins to moderate the
band's sessions, a crucial way we do our business together.

John Kalodner: They worked all winter. In March of '92, I
listened to the finished tracks at A&M. I had a lot of trouble with the lyrics,
which were perverted, especially a song called "Black Cherry." They
were mean, very raw, with none of the humor you associate with Aerosmith.

I met with Tim and Fairbairn and said, "This isn't good enough. It's poorly produced and not happening. We've gotta stop, think this over, get some new people in and write some new songs." They went up to Vancouver to write for two weeks, and then I started bringing in people for them to write with: Lenny Kravitz worked on "Line Up." Jack Blades and Tommy Shaw [from Ted Nugent's band Damn Yankees] did "Shut Up and Dance." They gave Taylor Rhodes like *one day* and they wrote "Cryin'." I knew we were back on track when I heard this. I thought, *Jesus Christ, this is strong.* Mark Hudson (from the Hudson Brothers) came in and wrote "Livin' on the Edge." They fixed "Eat the Rich" with Jim Vallance. They were furious with me and it was just a terrible fuckin' scene. They just plain resented that I had some say over their music. They bad-mouthed me to the people I'd sent there, but I didn't care what they thought about me. My job wasn't to be their pal, it was to get the best record I can from them. I'm the listener standing there saying, "If you don't write this song, *I'm not gonna buy it.*"

Steven Tyler: We never bad-mouthed John. Whenever you meet someone and you have John Kalodner in common, you naturally spend the first half hour talking about what a colorful character he is.

Tim Collins: Look at the history of Aerosmith. Making an Aerosmith record is also about control: who has it, who's losing it, who's on top. John Kalodner had all the power during *Permanent Vacation*. During *Pump*, the power shifted and the band took more control. During the *Get a Grip* sessions, the band wanted to take back all the power and fire John Kalodner.

Steven Tyler was the ringleader. John had been brutal to him. He'd say, "This song's a piece of shit." Steven was connected to the song. He called a band meeting at the studio. Kalodner was in England doing an album with Jimmy Page, and they told me they wanted him fired. I said, "OK."

Steven said, "I want him fired *today*, you motherfucker."

But I didn't fire John. I couldn't. He was my friend and confidante and I had the same faith in his ears that Geffen did. I came back and basically told them, "If John goes, I go too." I threatened to resign, told Kalodner to temper his negativity and be more diplomatic, and we went back to work—in Vancouver at John's insistence, because that's where Bruce Fairbairn had to work.

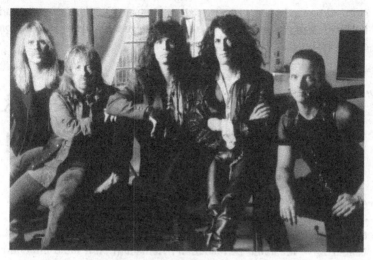

Get a Grip, 1993
(GEFFEN RECORDS, PHOTO: NORMAN SEEFF)

*Between October 1992 and January 1993, Steven and Joe wrote
"Livin' on the Edge" (about the Rodney King riots in L.A.), "Flesh" (with
Desmond Child), "Cryin'," "Gotta Love It," and "Shut Up and Dance." Joe
Perry wrote "Walk on Down" and "Boogie Man," a tribute to Peter Green
of the original Fleetwood Mac. Two other tracks, "Don't Stop" (written
with Jim Vallance) and "Can't Stop Messin' " (with Blades and Shaw),
were released as extra tracks on the CD single of "Livin' on the Edge,"
the first single from Get a Grip, released in April 1993 after the whole
album had been remixed by Atlanta producer Brendan O'Brien, who had
worked with the Black Crowes and achieved a band sound much admired
by Joe Perry.*

*Aerosmith held its breath when the album came out. The so-called
alternative music scene was ascendant; the grunge movement had come
roaring out of Seattle with a whiff of Chinese heroin and power chords.
Nirvana. Pearl Jam ruled. Whole chains of American FM rock stations
changed their formats overnight. It was a different world than the one
Aerosmith came up in. Could Get a Grip still cut it?*

*The second single, "Eat the Rich," almost killed the album. Then
"Crazy" and "Amazing" kicked in, big hit records. The videos, brain-*

stormed by the band and Marty Callner, featuring Alicia Silverstone and Liv Tyler, kept Aerosmith on TV, and within a year the band sold 8 million copies of Get a Grip all over the world.

9: Get the Fuck Offa the Phone!

Aerosmith began the 225-show Get a Grip *tour in Topeka, Kansas, on June 2, 1993. The speed metal band Megadeath opened a few shows until they were fired in Houston on June 17 after the band overheard 'Death Leader Dave Mustaine bad-mouthing Aerosmith on a radio interview. "Yeah, we think we oughta be headlining, but we don't mind because everyone knows this is Aerosmith's last hurrah."*

Steven Tyler: So we told this fuckin' guy, "Dave, we'd like to help you out. Which way did you come in?"

Jackyl and 4 Non Blondes opened the rest of the U.S. leg of the tour. As the house lights dimmed, the PA system blared the sublimely obscene rap song "You Suck" by the Yeastie Girls. The shows began with the band huddled around Joey Kramer's drums inside a kabuki curtain while Tyler's opening "Wake up, kids" rap from Get a Grip *played over the immense PA. The curtain dropped and the band ran to their places and launched into "Eat the Rich," usually followed by either "Toys" or "Train" or "Get a Grip."*

"Fever" was played third or fourth, followed by "Rag Doll," "Cryin'," "Flesh," and sometimes "Monkey on My Back" or "Walkin' the Dog" and "Draw the Line" (which included a brief segue into "Honky Tonk Women.") Variant set lists included "Mama Kin," "Shut Up and Dance," "Seasons of Wither," "Big Ten Inch Record" (featuring a hot Thom Gimbel saxophone solo), "Let the Music Do the Talking," "Rats in the Cellar," "Last Child," and "Amazing" after the single was released late in 1993. This part of the show ended with the laser lights and waterphone intro to "Janie's Got a Gun."

Then Joe Perry took over ("Ladies and gentlemen, singing his fuckin' ass off, Mr. Joe Fuckin' Perry!") and led the band into "Walk on Down," Peter Green's "Stop Messin' 'Round," and occasional forays into "Bright Light Fright" and "I'm a Man," played half Muddy Waters slow blues and half Yardbirds leaper flash.

Then Steven came back out and the band usually went into the show's climax: "Janie" (which came after Joe's set in the second year of the tour), "Elevator," "Sweet Emotion" with Tom Hamilton's solo introduction, and a blazing "Dude (Looks Like a Lady)" that sent the band offstage and left the rabid young crowds pleading for more. The first encores were "Dream On" and "Livin' on the Edge" (which Tyler spiced with bits of Jay and the Americans' "She Cried"). The second encore was "Walk This Way," Joey Kramer setting the beat, Steven yelling, "Get the fuck offa the phone!" before Joe hit his trademark guitar figure. This left entire stadiums, racetracks, festivals, fairgrounds, and sheds rocking on their foundations all over the world between June 1993 and December 1994.

In September 1993, Aerosmith appeared on the MTV acoustic program, Unplugged (taped in Ed Sullivan's old theater, where the Beatles had invaded America), and played an hour-long set that included "Hangman Jury," "Big Ten Inch Record," "Dream On," "Train," "Walkin' the Dog," and "Toys." While not a strictly acoustic performance, the set demonstrated Aerosmith's uncanny midtour tightness, as well as the impeccable touch of the rhythm section and the interplay between Brad Whitford and Joe Perry.

Providence, Rhode Island. September 13, 1993. Introducing "Rag Doll," Steven addresses the crowd: "All you need to get through life are the three M's—Music, Money, and 'MMMM, pussy!' " Big roar from the audience. Three songs later, introducing Joe's solo spot: "Ladies and gents, I was wrong about those three M's. It's really Music, Money, and Motherfuckin' Joe Perry!!"

The band played seventy shows in North America that summer and went to Europe in October 1993 to play twenty-nine more, appearing in Hungary, Finland, Austria, and Spain for the first time. In Brussels, on Halloween, their show was broadcast globally to an estimated radio audience of 150 million. On October 26, 1993, they played live on MTV Europe for the first time. In December 1993, the band did an in-store autograph session at Tower Records in London's Piccadilly Circus prior to that night's show at Wembley Arena. Outside a half-mile-long queue of black leather and long hair stretched down Regent Street. Steven Tyler dedicated that night's show to Frank Zappa, who had died the day before.

That morning at 2 A.M. Aerosmith played "Amazing" on a TV simulcast from London's Hard Rock Cafe on Park Lane to the Billboard (magazine) music awards in Los Angeles. Aerosmith had been voted as Best Rock Band. (They also won that category on the nationally televised People's Choice Awards earlier that year in the United States.)

That month (December 1993) the band played nine more North American shows. At every show, an assistant laid out Steven Tyler's stage gear on the drum riser: two towels; a cowbell; a drumstick; Kleenex; a harmonica belt containing instruments in the keys of E, F, G, A, B-flat, C, D, A-flat, and F-sharp; additional D and A harmonicas; a gris-gris shaker from Africa; a train whistle; a maracas cluster; a shakere gourd; and a pair of sunglasses.

On New Year's Eve, 1993, and New Year's Day, 1994, Aerosmith played two shows at Boston Garden, the band's last gigs at the old boxing arena, which was replaced the following year by a new arena built next door. At the New Year's Eve show, a roadie dressed as Father Time descended from the rafters on a wire, riding a Harley-Davidson. At midnight, the place went berserk and the band was joined by their families onstage for an emotional round of hugs and kisses.

Aerosmith played South America for the first time in January 1994—Brazil, Argentina, Chile, Mexico, and Puerto Rico. The tour opened in front of 70,000 Brazilian kids in Morumbi Stadium in São Paulo. In Argentina, security was lax at the airport and a big crowd of kids mobbed the band. Both boys and girls were passionately kissing Joe and Steven before they could get away. At the shows, the kids in the front rows started to "gob" the band—spitting on Steven as he prowled the edge of the stage. (The promoter told them it was a sign of great affection.) The second night in Buenos Aires, Aerosmith's new tour manager, Jimmy Eyers, solved the problem by turning the stage fans around, returning the flying gobs back at the spitters. Robert Plant's band was opening—and in some cases headlining.

Steven Tyler: Robert was interested in what we were doing. He called it "the Aerosmith miracle." He couldn't believe it. "Not even one drink?" He was one of many people that said to me something like, "If Tim Collins got you sober, maybe he could help me."

And I told Robert that God should get the credit, but it was my choice, not Tim Collins's choice. Hearing about Tim "owning" our getting sober never felt right to me.

February 1994. Steven Tyler chaired a packed meeting at the Fifth Avenue Presbyterian Church in New York.

"Hi, I'm Steven Tyler and I'm an alcoholic and drug addict from Boston."

"HI, STEVEN!"

"I'm really nervous to be here. My band is playing Madison Square Garden tonight. The show is sold out. I won't be nervous then, but I am now." Steven sat cross-legged on the dais and spoke for an hour about his sobriety and general relief at being alive. In response, people spoke of their strong feelings for Aerosmith, how they associated the music with the ups and down of their lives over the past twenty years.

That night the kids were nuts at Madison Square Garden. Dozens of bra-less, brazen New York teenagers leaned over the barriers to try to touch Steven. During "Walk This Way," young Italian girls from Brooklyn and Queens licked the tips of their fingers and held them out suggestively for Tyler to touch.

Two weeks later, Grammy Week in New York. A line of giant black limos outside the band's hotel on Central Park South. Three thousand kids outside Sam Goody's record store on 48th and Sixth, where the band is signing CDs (and bared breasts) inside. The band spends the afternoon at cavernous Radio City Music Hall blocking out TV shots for that night's awards ceremony, where they perform "Livin' on the Edge" (after a rambling Frank Sinatra is yanked off the air) and win two small golden gramophones. The next day Aerosmith appears on The Late Show with David Letterman and Joe Perry spends the rest of the week sitting in with the show's studio band. An undercurrent of the week was MTV's nervousness about broadcasting Aerosmith's video for "Crazy" with its intimations of teenage lesbian romance between Liv Tyler and Alicia Silverstone.

Joey Kramer was playing drums so hard he was literally smoking on his drum riser; steam rose off him like a cloud of gaseous mojo. His father was on his deathbed, and Joey was telling friends that he had suffered abuse and beatings as a child, that he had taken some of the energy that came from his father's often harsh discipline and channeled it toward what he wanted to do.

Joey Kramer: My father died in March 1994, which was very hard, but it meant so much for me that my brothers in the band were there for me in my time of grief and loss. They came to his funeral and stood there with me, a pivotal moment for both the band and for me.

Fathers and sons . . . one night around this time I'm talking to my own son, Jesse, eleven years old, hating sixth grade, just wanting to play drums. He didn't care about school because he was just at that age where he doesn't give a fuck. What he was saying was so familiar. I could hear myself talking years before. What could I tell him? "But, Jesse," I said, "it's *hard*. For everyone like me, there's a thousand guys whose bands didn't make it. Good musicians too. And having me for your father will more than likely work against you."

As for my father, we made our peace. I think getting sober broke the chain of abuse, and a few years later I was able to forgive him. Our slate was clean by the time he left, which was real important to me. After he died, my mother gave me the Purple Heart he had earned in combat during World War II.

10: Wild Sunflowers of Fire

May 1994. The band opened the House of Blues in Los Angeles (in which they were investors). There were hard feelings in the group because Tim Collins tried to intervene on Joe Perry to stop him from buying a $50,000 Neve soundboard for his home studio. Joe bought the Neve anyway. Afterward, Aerosmith flew to Japan for a month of shows. Commuting between provincial cities by bullet train, the band's equilibrium was upset when Brad Whitford flew home to visit his father, who was seriously ill and not expected to recover. (His rhythm guitar chores were handled by David Minehan, a Boston musician who had played with local band the Neighborhoods, whose 1990 record Brad had helped produce.)

Brad returned in time for Aerosmith's week of shows at the Tokyo Budokan. After an eighteen-hour flight, he went straight to the arena, strapped on one of the twenty guitars he was carrying on the road, and helped his band blast out "Eat the Rich" before the first audience of 10,000 kids they would entertain that week. The promoter, the legendary Mr. Udo, had offered Aerosmith another twenty nights at the Budokan, but prior commitments in Europe forced Tim to decline.

Later that week, Tim was walking outside the Budokan and wandered among the dozens of dealers peddling swag, unlicensed and unauthorized Aerosmith merchandise, to the throngs of kids coming out of the nearby subway station. Outside the famous martial arts arena, middle-aged Yakuza with missing fingers were scalping good seats for that night's show. When Tim politely complained to Mr. Udo, the gangsters vanished. The next night Mr. Udo threw a ten-course banquet for the band and the whole fifty-person crew—band, management, security, techs, sound and lighting engineers, carpenters, roadies—in a chic restaurant he owned in the Rappongi district. It was a gesture much appreciated by everyone.

Interviewers wanted to talk about Kurt Cobain, the Nirvana singer/songwriter and guitarist who'd shot himself a month earlier. Speaking for the band, Steven told the press that he was angry and blamed the suicide on Cobain's longtime heroin addiction.

The musicians had their families with them in Tokyo. They went shopping at the Oriental Bazaar, visited religious shrines in the country outside Tokyo, went to Disneyland with their kids. Joe Perry used the Japanese shows to try out recent material and fine-tune the set. He started playing the contemplative "Boogie Man" lick as a link between "Seasons of Wither" and "Shut Up." "Sweet Emotion," which ended the Japanese shows, developed into a jam that quoted the "Think About It" turnaround of the middle section of "Dazed and Confused" to pyrosonic effect. Noticing that this taste of Zeppelin sent the already hopped-up fans into paroxysms of hard rockdom, Joe kept it in the show's climax for the rest of the tour.

The band saw their families off and flew west to Frankfurt to begin a round of European festivals (with Soul Asylum and Therapy? opening) and Eastern European debuts in Prague, Budapest, and Warsaw. (The Boston band Extreme opened many of these shows.) While in Warsaw, Brad Whitford received news that his father had died and went home for the funeral. Aerosmith played the next two gigs—Ostrava in the Czech Republic and Halle in the former East Germany—as a somewhat low-key quartet.

The band was flying around Europe in a twelve-seat Canadian Challenger jet with a German crew supervised by tour manager Jimmy Eyers, who actually sat on the jump seat between the pilots, directing them through Swiss mountain passes and around thunderstorms over Sweden.

Walk This Way

Early in June, the band flew over the North Sea, landed at Leicester Airport at 3 A.M. and stayed at a health spa called Ragdale Hall for a few days. On June 4, they again headlined the Monsters of Rock fiesta at Donnington Park. Brad Whitford was back after missing two shows and the band felt it, playing an explosive set that finally detonated when Joe Perry hit the the signature lick to "Walk This Way."

THE TIMES OF LONDON

Tyler, a glamorous stick insect, brought the band out dancing through a two-hour set which took in all the best tunes of their career . . . "Shut Up and Dance," the latest single from the *Get a Grip* album, sped past with an acceleration to silence all critics. They saved "Walk This Way" for the last encore as the sunset grew to a distant purple glow. Tyler strutted and pouted until a giant fireworks display signaled the end. The shimmering brilliance belonged, however, to Aerosmith alone, a band who retain the power to astound. (June 7, 1994)

The band played in Europe through the middle of July. In June, they took a week off and settled into a ritzy hotel on the isle of Capri, where they recorded "Blind Man" and "Walk on the Water" for inclusion on Big Ones, a compilation of their Geffen-era hits released later in 1994. Their hotel asked the band to leave when the rich Italian clientele complained about the laundry hanging from Steven's balcony. Aerosmith stayed put until they were ready to go.

After a big festival near Milan and dates in Finland, Aerosmith flew to Israel for a gig at a public park in Tel Aviv. That morning the band drove to Jerusalem, visited the Wailing Wall, and walked the stations of the cross on the Via Dolorosa—backward. Steven played the Tel Aviv show on an injured foot and could barely walk unassisted by the end of the show.

A few weeks off. Joe Perry flying around Lake Sunapee on water skis. Then back on the road in August, the energy level high, a new James Brown vamp opening "Walk This Way," Aerosmith getting the best reviews of their career. The Rolling Stones were just starting their gigantic Voodoo Lounge tour, and critics who had long compared Steven Tyler unfavorably to Mick Jagger began to change their tune. Reviewing the band's Jones Beach Theater outdoor show late that month, the New York Times marked a significant milestone: "Mr. Tyler, even more now than the aging Mick Jagger, is the epitome of the hyperactive rock star." Sexual philosopher Camille Paglia, writing in the Boston Phoenix: "... Jagger has failed to keep pace with dance evolution. After Michael Jackson, Madonna, and Prince, he has ceased to convince as a mobile stage presence ... His true essence lives on in others today, notably Aerosmith's mercurial Steve Tyler, with his swooping, scarf-trailing dips and his slashing thrusts of his microphone stand." [August 26, 1994]

People finally realized, at the height of the Get a Grip tour, that Aerosmith were the uncrowned champions of rock 'n' roll. Steven Tyler responded to comparisons with Mick Jagger by telling interviewers that he was actually Jagger's bastard son.

They closed the show Saturday night at Woodstock '94, twenty-five years after Steven and Joey attended the original festival as citizens of Woodstock Nation. Steven brought along the original banner he'd stolen from the pills, hash, and pipe dealer along Groovy Way, as well as the duplicate he had made in 1970 and hung behind the group during early Aerosmith gigs. (When the band was getting along, the pipe-smoking demons faced each other; when Aerosmith was fighting, the demons had their backs to each other.)

It was a rainy day in August. The band flew to Poughkeepsie in the snug English jet they were using to tour, then drove to Red Hook on the eastern bank of the Hudson. A fast launch took them upriver to Saugerties, and they were escorted by van to the artists' compound behind the massive stage, where they could hear Crosby, Stills, and Nash entertaining half a million mud-caked music fans.

A crowd gathers around the band's dressing rooms. Autographs. Makeup. Interviews, photos, MTV, radio, sound bites. Shannon Hoon, lead singer of the popular grunge band Blind Melon, visited backstage as a client of Aerosmith counselor Bob Timmins.

Humid early evening. Catskill summer thunderstorms. Metallica takes the stage in a burst of pyro. Fists fly in Tim Collins's trailer when the promoter sucker-punches Jimmy Eyers during a dispute over merchandise. The promoter is forcibly ejected from the trailer.

While the stage is being set for Aerosmith, it starts to rain like a cow pissing on a flat rock. The band is supposed to play at midnight, but midnight comes and goes. At one-fifteen they launch into "Eat the Rich" and get their first look at the 350,000 mud people lit by the orange glow from the light towers. It pours during "Toys," "Fever, "F.I.N.E.*," and "Rag Doll." Working the unprotected lip of the stage, Steven is soon soaked. Then "Cryin'," "Crazy," "Monkey on My Back," "Mama Kin," and "Shut Up" as the crowd heaves and swells like a tidal river.

Two in the morning. Rain stops. Joe Perry takes over and telecasts "Stop Messin' 'Round" and "Walk on Down." Then on to the Final Four; the set list taped to the floor of the stage reads: JANIE, ELEVATOR, DUDE, SWEET E. When Aerosmith hits the Zeppelin lick at the end, the crowd responds with a mass convulsion and an inhuman roar as Aerosmith walks offstage.

John Lennon's "Come Together" is the first encore. A hundred thousand lighters flare during the opening chords of "Dream On." "Walk This Way" ends the show at three-thirty in the morning. Back at the deserted artists' compound, the band and their ladies are nearly blown away by the massive post-concert fireworks launched right over their heads. Up in the black sky, explosive novas of red light and wild sunflowers of fire. The tired musicians take in this brilliance and are astonished, illuminated at the magic of it all.

The boat ride back down the sleeping river just before dawn is like crossing to Avalon. A bright watch fire blazes on the dock. An hour later, Aerosmith rides the winds home, too tired to speak. It didn't seem real to them. Had they really closed the Saturday night show at Woodstock?

Dream on.

11: Quest for Fame

Steven Tyler: Split personality, right? I'm this rock 'n' roll person that got in a lot of trouble for being drug- and sexually oriented— and this other guy, who loves his family, loves his family structure and his quiet life in a small town in the country. After sixteen months on the road, I get unhappy. I gotta wake up in the morning, order breakfast, get in the car and drive for a half hour, get in an airplane, fly for an hour, get back in a car and drive for a half hour, spend five hours at the gig, get in a car and drive for a half hour, fly for an hour, get out of the plane, drive for a half hour, go to the hotel, and that is my day. That is my fucking day, day in, day out, and it doesn't stop. Yes, I also get to sign autographs and have lunch. I'm lucky if I can read [Camille Paglia's] *Sexual Personae* for fifteen minutes before I have to go to sleep.

I wanna change the channel, but I can't.

September 1994. Get a Grip has sold 12 million worldwide. The MTV Awards. "Cryin' " wins Best Video. Madonna presents Joe and Steven their statuettes and gives them each a big kiss. Now it's time for the speech.

"Hey, Joe," Tyler says with a lascivious leer, holding up two fingers for the camera. "Why does Madonna masturbate with these two fingers?"

The audience gasps. Madonna raises her eyebrows. Joe says, "Gee, Steven, I don't know."

"Because they're mine," Tyler rasps. Nervous laughter. Some boos. TV speeches are a big issue in the Aerosmith camp. Madonna walks over to the mike.

"Hey, excuse me," she says sarcastically, "but if I did it with your fingers, it wouldn't be masturbation."

This was unscripted. Curious, Tyler asks, "What would it be?"

"Sexual abuse!" Madonna snorts, thus winning the encounter. Backstage afterward, there were no hard feelings. Madonna gave Steven a big hug.

Before resuming the final leg of the Get a Grip tour, the band held a benefit for Senator Ted Kennedy's reelection campaign in Brad Whitford's backyard. It was the only overtly political gesture in the band's history. (In 1992, Aerosmith joined a national protest against restricted National Endowment for the Arts funding by donating $10,000 to a sexually graphic exhibition at the MIT art gallery, replacing a grant vetoed by the NEA's chairman.)

Aerosmith was everywhere that fall, especially in cyberspace and the new media. The band's marketing director, Keith Garde, got them on-line, interactive, downloaded, and video-gamed in virtual reality. In arcades around the world, Joe Perry's voice boomed, "They poisoned our food" as kids played the Aerosmith video game. The interactive computer game Quest for Fame featured a Virtual Guitar that players had to master as they traveled the band's road to success.

October 1994. The band is at the Four Seasons in Newport Beach, Cal-

ifornia, flying out of John Wayne/Orange County Airport to gigs around California and the Southwest. Steven and Brad do a meet-and-greet with fans and contest winners backstage at Desert Sky Blockbuster Amphitheater, a shed near Phoenix, Arizona. Snapshots. Embarrassed groans when cameras fail to flash. Autographs. Brad is patient and polite, Steven gracious but getting concerned as it draws near the precious hour he requires to prepare alone for that night's show. He signs a last autograph for a gawky kid of about fifteen, who stared intently at Tyler's clear eyes and youthful, smooth skin.

> KID: "How old are you?"
>
> TYLER: "Forty-six."
>
> KID: "No."
>
> TYLER: "Yeah."
>
> KID: "No way."
>
> TYLER: "Yeah."
>
> KID: "Really. That's . . . awesome."

Movie stars crowded backstage at the Glen Helen Pavilion near San Bernardino, California, on October 15, 1994, along with old friends and the band's families. Adrian Perry, Joe's bass-playing teenage son who lives with his mother Elyssa Perry in Los Angeles, was hanging out. (Elyssa tells old friends she still has an irresistible urge to pee when she hears "Dream On" on the radio because it was her bathroom song in the old days of the band.) Actress Pamela Anderson stood in the wings and watched the band lift off during "Let the Music Do the Talking," along with Jurassic Park stars Jeff Goldblum and Laura Dern. During the frenetic encores, girls in the front row bared their breasts to the band. It happened all the time.

Aerosmith returned to South America in November, selling out every show, brushing with tragedy when one fan was killed and twenty-five were trampled during a stampede caused by a tropical downpour outside a heavily promoted Aerosmith show in San Jose, Costa Rica.

December saw the long tour winding down as Aerosmith toured the upper Midwest and the Northeast. After 223 shows, everyone was burnt-out. At the Worcester Centrum on December 12, security emptied out the first row and Teresa Tyler, Billie Perry, April Kramer, Karen Whitford, and Terry Hamilton put on giant plastic bosoms and flashed their husbands.

Tim Collins: It's the last scheduled show of the tour, in an arena somewhere in New York. Outside the hall it looked like someone dropped a neutron bomb that killed all the people and left a desolate landscape of concrete buildings. Really ugly. Backstage was completely dead: no visitors, no buzz, no vibe. The crew's depressed, no one wants to go home, but it's over. Burt Goldstein and I went out into the crowd and couldn't find any pretty girls to stick in the front row.

Steven was by himself in his dressing room, waiting to go on. He looked downcast and I asked what was bothering him.

"I'm sad. What if this is our last show?"

"What do you mean?"

"What if it's all over? We may never do this again. Something could happen. Someone could die. This could be the last show we ever play. What are we doing this for? Money? This should be a gala event in Madison Square Garden."

I told him not to worry, that Aerosmith was a legend, a *living* legend. I told him there were years to come and worlds to conquer. "No worries, mate. It was a great tour," I told him. "Thank you." "You're welcome." We had a big hug.

Aerosmith went out and blew the doors off the place.

Steven Tyler: I was so pissed off I insisted on getting paid in cash. They gave me a huge bag of $20 bills. I took it home and it took me and Teresa a year to spend it.

12: Ain't That a Bitch?

Joe Perry: There's more. The two years between *Get a Grip* and *Nine Lives* were unlike any that had gone before. Just when you think you've got it down, all the rules change. Two more years in the Life. And we weren't the same people coming out of it that we were going into it.

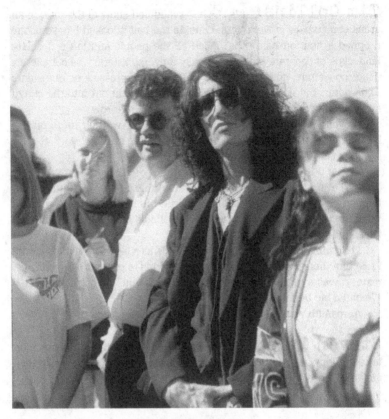

Tim Collins and Joe Perry
(PHOTO: JOHN GOODMAN)

Something that happens with a lot of bands is that they turn over their power to managers, record companies, outside forces. Things get really comfortable and they stop taking risks.

We can't live that way.

Over the years Tim Collins kept telling us, "You guys should take control."

But he wouldn't let us; he's a control freak, like most successful managers. And we were OK with concentrating on the music and the shows and letting him take care of business.

It got to be a problem for us. As soon as we started to make noise—

"What happens if we *don't* do that TV show because we're burnt and don't wanna fly 3,000 miles??"—we heard all this doom and gloom: "The band's gonna fall apart if you don't."

What happened for me is that the spirit of Aerosmith was always there, but a lot of the fun was taken out of it.

So we took back control.

I'm getting ahead of myself. Let's start in January 1995 . . .

One of the last legs of the *Get a Grip* tour was in South America, where we ran into Jimmy Page and Robert Plant, who were promoting their new record. Jimmy and I had lunch in Buenos Aires and he asked me to induct Led Zeppelin into the Rock and Roll Hall of Fame. I told him I'd do it if he showed me how to play "The Rain Song."

It was an honor to be asked, but actually going through with it—writing the speech, the dinner at the Waldorf, actually delivering the speech—was something else. Anytime I have to speak in public I really hate it, but this turned out pretty cool. I got Steven to help me, and he talked about crying the first time he heard Led Zeppelin play "Dazed and Confused" at the Boston Tea Party. Then he mentioned crying again an hour later when he saw Jimmy leave the dressing room with the girl Steven had been living with in New York up until that moment. I talked about how influential Zeppelin was, how much they meant to all of us who tried to follow them. Later Steven and I got onstage with Led Zeppelin, with Jason Bonham sitting in on drums, and jammed for half an hour: "Train Kept A-Rollin'," "For Your Love," "Reefer Head Woman," "Bring It On Home."

Spring 1995. After a few months off—too few as it turned out—we decided we had to get our new record out. We'd already delayed the Sony Machine because we extended the tour and everything got pushed back. The company was great and told us to take all the time we needed, but there were elements in our camp that thought we'd better get moving.

So Steven and I went into writing mode and a bunch of people came in to work with us in the studio we'd built in my basement: Glenn Ballard, who'd worked with Michael Jackson; Mark Hudson, who we wrote "Livin' on the Edge" with; Robert DeLeo from Stone Temple Pilots.

One of those weekends, my son Adrian was visiting from California, and we're in my basement working on a demo and Steven sees my son and says, "Hey, Adrian, grab your bass and see if you can learn this song."

Adrian nailed it in two minutes and ended up playing on the demo. Steven was impressed. So was I.

Sometimes Jesse Kramer sits in for his father when we're rehearsing at Joey's house. Chelsea Tallarico plays the drums too.

Summer 1995. After those sessions, Steven and I took our families to Florida, rented houses on the beach, went boar hunting, trying to take some time off. Meanwhile, our manager went into a deep depression, and it got so bad that we thought for a while we might lose him. It started when he scheduled a therapy session with our wives. We called this Black Monday. Tim was never a family man, and I think he found it difficult to relate to the close bond between Billie and me. Always searching for a label to try to explain our behavior, whatever it was, *he* decided that we were co-dependent and wanted everyone to confront us. But no one was interested. None of my partners or their wives wanted to get involved, because they knew that this was really about him and not about us.

It was a crisis for Aerosmith, because the whole thing felt wrong and sick. It was another burr under the band's saddle. Tim would call meetings and tell us that the band was breaking up. We'd look at each other. Was our reality that different from his? The band wasn't breaking up. That's not what our perception was. Then it started to get really nuts. Karen Whitford was pregnant that summer, and Terry Hamilton had a baby shower for her at their house on the Cape. The whole Aerosmith family was there. But Tim didn't show up. Instead he sent Bob Timmins to the party with a dire letter announcing the band was in relapse and was going to break up.

You almost had to laugh.

He'd tell us we were on dangerous ground, we were losing our spirit, our sobriety was in danger. But it wasn't true. We were working—*hard*. The band would sit around and I'd go, "Hey, look, Steven and I are writing the songs. There's a lot of stress, so we take some time off here and there. So what?"

All we heard from our manager was "Joey's acting out. Tom's acting out. Brad's acting out. Steven's acting out." It was Tim in a codependent seizure, not being able to control us.

We'd had trouble with him before. He'd threatened to squelch our record deal in 1991 if we didn't go into a rehab. To sit there and threaten people who are creating the energy and are five years sober was wrong. It felt like coercion. It felt like manipulation. It felt wrong to us.

It was bad that summer. Tim would go through these depressions and call and harangue me for an hour and a half. I'd sit and listen to it because he was my friend and our manager. We'd all been through a lot together.

October 1995. Usually we spent about five months doing the preproduction work for an album. Steven and I would write for a month or two and then start working with the band, playing together again. Usually we'd have one or two things we'd grab on to as the bones of new songs. But it didn't seem to go that way; as with most things artistic, you can't really plan on it.

Then we realized Aerosmith hadn't played together in a year. So we booked two nights in local Boston clubs as the G-Spots to give us a chance to play and rehearse some of the newer songs and just do what we're supposed to do—play music together.

We played two nights in November 1995, the first at the Middle East in Cambridge, the second at the Mama Kin Music Hall, our club in Boston. We opened both nights with "Make It," the first song on our first album, and ran through a lot of songs we needed to hear ourselves play again: "Bone to Bone," "Get the Lead Out," "Remember," "Reefer Head Woman," "Sick as a Dog," "S.O.S.," "Milk Cow Blues." We played "I'm a Man" and "Think About It." We premiered some new songs: "The Farm," "Trouble," "What Kind of Love Are You On?" The encore both nights was "Immigrant Song." It was cool to hear our band again, especially in these little clubs. The second night a bunch of bikers fought it out on Lansdowne Street outside Mama Kin, much like the old days.

All this time Steven and I were doing out-of-town writing jaunts, traveling the land as roving ambassadors of rock 'n' roll in search of the lost chord and the missing groove. We worked with Jimmy Jam and Terry Lewis in Minneapolis. We did a song called "Circle" with Taylor Rhodes in Nashville. In Los Angeles, we birthed "Taste of India" with Glenn Ballard as the midwife and wrote "Something's Gotta Give" with Marty Frederikson. By early 1996, we were ready to start thinking about getting a producer to work with us and begin cutting our new album.

John Kalodner, who had left Geffen Records to follow us to Sony, introduced us to Glenn Ballard early in the songwriting process. He'd been a staff producer with Quincy Jones and had just produced a new record by Alanis Morissette. I hadn't heard her record, but we really hit it off with Glenn during the early sessions. We started talking about having him produce us, because Bruce Fairbairn and Brendan O'Brien, who mixed *Get a Grip*, weren't available. Glenn Ballard had his shit together. He's a Southern gentleman with Mississippi blues roots for miles, and we thought with a little injection of Aerosmith rock 'n' roll we'd have a lethal combination. So we decided to go with Glenn and spent the winter and spring of 1996 working at the Marlin Hotel in South Beach. Richie Supa and Desmond Child live right around the corner, so we could write with them at the same time. Mark Hudson flew in from L.A. for some more madness, which resulted in "Fall Together" and "Kiss Your Past Goodbye."

South Beach. The whole Miami scene. We'd occasionally go out to a club and Steven would find himself draped with young models trying to have their pictures taken with him. Soon the town was full of people saying they were doing drugs with us. Sleeping with us. Rumors started to circulate like polluted air. We ignored them, but things got back to us that we didn't like. Sleazy rumors come with the territory in our business, and it's useless to deny them.

That was the undercurrent. We just worked every day on the songs, trying to build them, say something new, sprinkle a little magic on them by letting our muse dance naked with our subconscious.

Right around then, Tim Collins called me and said, "Joe, we have to let go of John Kalodner because his issues are clouding his judgment." That's a quote. Of course Tim told Steven something else and told other people other things. Tim said John wanted to use Glenn Ballard on another Sony project, and there were other problems as well. I didn't talk to John directly about it—one of my mistakes. So John Kalodner is benched, Bruce Fairbairn is busy, and we're writing at the Marlin for two months with Glenn. Then, as we were about to move to Criteria studio in Miami to begin tracking, Joey got sick—a delayed traumatic reaction to his dad passing away that we termed The Big Blue Funk—and didn't feel he could play on the record because he had to get his health back.

We sat down and looked at the situation. Our drummer was gone, our A&R man was gone, our manager was losing it, and we were working with an unfamiliar producer (who won a Grammy for Alanis's album in the middle of all of this). We just shook our heads. We felt like the Machine had taken control. We were given deadlines and spent a lot of money trying to make them. We pushed Sony to the wall. We wanted to get the record out. The time was right, and me and Steven had been sitting on some of these songs for nine months and the baby was overdue.

We sat there and said: "It sucks not having Joey, but what are we gonna do? Glenn said he had this other guy, we'll cut some tracks, and when Joey makes it back he can come in and play on the tracks later, at the end."

That's what we did. In April, we moved our families and everybody down to Miami and worked with Steve Ferrone on drums. He's like an English soul drummer, really professional, great sense of humor, nailed the arrangements right off. We did a lot of experimenting, did stuff digitally, flew it around. At first I thought this was great, because recording digitally happens a lot faster than working with analog systems. Then I started to notice the sound getting homogenized, doing it this way. Then we began hearing from other people that it didn't sound as rock as it could have. People said it didn't sound like Aerosmith.

That's cool, I thought. *Ferrone isn't a rock drummer. We're pushing the edges.*

One day Billie asked me why I wasn't listening to the tracks the way I usually did, always pumping them up, blowing the speakers out of the car. She was right. The excitement wasn't there. We started to hear feedback that the record wasn't turning anyone's crank. It wasn't the record they were expecting. So things got really frazzled. Steven was his usual out-there self, obsessed and passionate about the creative frenzy he gets into when working on a new record. Some good stuff was coming out, songs we were starting to really dig: "Pink," "Hole in My Soul." Joey was recovering in California and out of touch because Tim told us he was working on his own issues and not to call him. Meanwhile, the Miami rumor mill churned on, fueled by Steven's raucous birthday party in May at Bar None, a club in South Beach. Stallone was there, along with half the models in Miami, all of our wives, old friends like Jack Douglas and Henry Smith, and a couple of strippers.

At one point, Glenn left town early after an engineer told him that Steven had said he missed working with Bruce Fairbairn. So that had to be dealt with. Tim Collins called a business meeting. We'd just had the weekend off. Steven had taken his family to Disneyland, I'd taken mine to Fisher Island. Tim was in one of his depressions. The business meeting turned out to be: "You guys aren't in recovery. I'm hearing rumors. This is killing me. I can't manage a band that isn't in recovery."

A cloud of doom hung over the room. We were in shock. I'm saying, "Tim, what's the big problem? We're doing the best we possibly can without Joey. We're writing great songs and no one's had a drink or a drug in years. *What's your fucking problem?*"

But he's off on his trip. "The band's breaking up, it's over, it's blah blah blah." We spent hours going over this stuff with him. From then on, a lot of our so-called business meetings turned out to be confrontations, intervention-style character assassinations, and more bullshit interference in our domestic lives. We were dealing with a Sobriety Nazi.

By the time we left Miami, we were pretty blown out. We wrote "Ain't That a Bitch" at Desmond Child's studio as we were literally packing our gear to go home. We decided to take a couple of weeks off because we were supposed to go to L.A. and mix the record at Glenn's house, which looked to be a nightmare because the paper files for the tapes we'd made were twelve inches thick.

May 1996. Weird Times. Steven's in a creative hurricane and is torturing everyone and himself. Tim Collins stages a Spanish Inquisition meeting. He tells Joey and Tom that Steven wanted them out of the band, which turned out not to be true. He browbeats us into writing a confrontational letter to Steven. We told him we were angry with him for behaving badly toward the band, for being his prima donna self, for a thousand arrows he'd shot our way over the past few months. We told him we were waking up angry and going to bed angry, with very few moments of sunlight in the middle. The letter said we wanted him to take a look at that and do something about it.

There was controversy in the band about how to phrase this. When you confront someone about their behavior, you're supposed to put a consequence in there to make them stand up and listen. So, despite our better judgment, this letter ended up telling Steven that if he didn't change his ways, we didn't want to be in a band with him anymore.

Looking back, this wasn't called for, and if the situation ever arose again, I definitely wouldn't get sucked into it in the way I did. But Tim and his team of advisors convinced us it was our only course. And when the only tool you've got is a hammer, everything looks like a nail. The letter said that we didn't even want to hear from Steven until there was some resolution. No one really felt this way except for Tim and the therapists that he was paying to help him. And to this day, I'm really sorry that I signed it.

It was overkill. We were all upset. Tim is urgently telling us he has proof that Steven was acting out sexually, relapsing, taking drugs. Bob Timmins was telling us he couldn't intervene on Steven because there was no *real* proof to Tim's allegations. So there was nothing about drugs in this letter.

For the past three months, Steven had been telling me what he didn't like about Tim, and I admit I didn't believe him. I figured it was just more ranting and unhappiness. Tim had helped us out so much I just said we had to focus on the good part and leave the bad aside. But it was driving Steven crazy as much as anything else. Then Tim called Steven's wife and told her that Steven had slept with a couple of girls in Miami. Nothing was farther from the truth, but Tim had decided to believe the rumors. He thought that if he could get to Teresa and break her denial she might be able to shed some light on the drug situation and help bring Steven in.

Steven exploded and swore he'd never work with Tim Collins again. Then Steven got the letter and was basically put on ice for a pretty tough seven weeks. We had no communication with him. Tim ordered Glenn Ballard to keep Steven Tyler out of the studio until further notice.

So the band was separated. The process we had been working under for years had subverted itself. We could see clearly that something in Tim was trying to break up the band. *Of course* the band is going to break up if you feel it hard enough.

Be careful what you wish for.

July 1996. After weeks of silence, I got together with Tom Hamilton about what to do. Tom says, "It would be great if we could all go to some safe place and just fuckin' . . . *have it out.* Talk about it. Neutral ground, where we could tell each other what we're feeling. Just do it—whatever it takes to fix the band."

So we met with Tim and the therapists and said, "We want to get in a room with Steven." And everyone agreed. We got word to Steven and he said, "Yeah, I'll come."

Everyone was nervous. We'd heard that Steven had sworn he would never work with Tim again. Tim called me up and said, "Look, if it comes down to it, I'll step aside." I asked him if he really meant it, and he said it again: "I'll step aside if you want me to." It was one of those conversations you can play back to yourself like a tape recorder.

I just said, "Tim, I don't think it has to go that way." I wanted Tim in that room with us and Steven, but he said, "No, I'll wait while you guys figure it out. I'll be nearby, and whenever you want me to come in, I'll come in." The therapists we were working with supported him in this.

So the machinery was set up to meet at a place north of Malibu called Steps. We went through four anxious days waiting for this, calling each other up, offering support. Aerosmith was literally on the line. Everything was up in the air. I didn't think Steps was really a neutral space because it was run by Steve Chatoff, one of the therapists working with us on this stuff, who also had a relationship with Tim. But I got outvoted, so I just said that if I sensed anything funny going on, we were leaving.

We checked in, and the old feeling of enforced rehab sunk in. *Wait a minute—I'm not here for drugs.* "Fuck this," we said to each other, "I'm sober already. I don't want a rehab scene anymore." So we said, "We'll do the work here, but we're staying in a hotel." But they convinced us to stay there to stay focused, and besides it would be a good example for the thirty-day people who were there trying to get sober. So we decided it was cool. We complained about the coffee and they took us over to Starbucks so we could buy a couple of pounds and make our own.

Southern California in the summer. It was supposed to be hot, but instead it was cool right by the ocean. We all went out and bought sweaters. Tim was with us the first day, but then we didn't want him there. Steve Chatoff said, "Look, I want these guys to take their power back." And Tim was 100 percent supportive.

So we got to work and started comparing notes. "What? Tim said *that* about *me?* He told me the same thing about you." And we saw it unfolding, our recent isolation from each other, the triangulation, the divide-and-conquer mentality. There was a lot of anguish. At one point, Steven just came out and taunted us. "What *part* of you believed the stuff Tim was saying about me? What was in *you* that wanted to believe him?" Then he looks at me. "Joe, if you shot and killed my mother tomorrow, I'd still come and visit you in jail."

Soon we realized that Steven was pretty much on the mark about a lot of stuff. He turned it around. He puts his anger out on the table about stuff, and it frightens a lot of people, including us, because we didn't know if he was gonna run off, hurt himself, hurt us, whatever.

Maybe he had a good reason to be angry, and maybe it was OK to just let him do it.

We called it our Conflict Resolution Week. We voted on things. We reached a consensus about things. We put the band back together.

After a week of not hearing from us or Steve Chatoff, Tim Collins started going off the deep end. He'd had no news because it had been decided that it wasn't appropriate for anyone outside to know about what was going on inside. And our boundaries were starting to get stronger. For the first time, we stepped back and looked at how Tim had run things. We realized for the first time that the tactics that had worked for him ten years ago might not be working for us now. So finally we told him it was time to come in and do the work with us that he'd promised to do.

He wouldn't come in.

If he had, there's a chance he'd still be our manager. In spite of all the shit that went on, there's a chance. But when Tim started interfering with our family situations, he crossed a line that went beyond what we'd experienced before. I don't know if Steven could ever forgive Tim for that. I don't know if I could—or even trust him again. By doing that to Steven, he did it to me.

At least there would've been a chance for some kind of reconciliation if Tim had checked in, did the psychological testing, worked with us, found out where he was at. But he totally reneged on it.

In the middle of all this, we were called to a meeting with the people from our record company. We said, "Look, we're in the middle of a treatment program here. Can't this wait a week?"

"No. The Sony people are here and they want to meet with you and find out what's going on."

They thought we were up there for drugs. Tim didn't straighten that out for us. So we scheduled a meeting with Tim to discuss this before we met with our label, but he canceled it with fifteen minutes to go. We go, "OK, what the fuck is that about? You book a meeting and you don't show up?"

Next day. Big meeting at the Mandalay Beach Hotel in Anacapa. In walks John Kalodner, who I hadn't seen or spoken to in five months. And John is back on our case. He has mixes of our songs, and he told us point-blank, "Look, you gotta recut all the music because it doesn't sound like the Aerosmith that I know."

We're looking at each other. I said, "John, this is pretty heavy, because we spent five months working on these songs and now you want us to recut them?"

But, after being away from the project for a while, I listened to it and knew what they were hearing. Steven loved the stuff from Miami a lot, because he and Glenn had a real musical thing going on. We had all worked hard on it and thought it was pretty good. But we told Sony that we'd think about it and tell them our decision.

It was a big thing for us that John Kalodner was back on board. Glenn Ballard was out as producer, and we were kind of in shock about that. But I was ready to say, "OK, let's go and take a shot at something else."

Tim Collins sat quietly at this meeting and left right after. We went back to Malibu to talk it over. There was supposed to be another meeting with Tim that afternoon where we hoped we could persuade him to come into Steps with us. But he refused and left. An hour later we got him on his cell phone and asked him to meet us in an office on the Pacific Coast Highway. He said he'd be there.

It was our final request that he come in and work with us. We said, "Tim, it would really be a good idea if you checked in and went through with it. We're hurt that you didn't live up to the commitment you made to us. We went in here with the attitude that we have to settle this—and let the chips fall where they may. You were all gung-ho for it. You told us this was the best place to do it. What gives?"

He said, "I don't feel safe here. I'm not a member of the band. I shouldn't be doing this."

We're shaking our heads. This from the guy that sat in on every therapy meeting we'd had in the past twelve years? All of a sudden he's not part of the band and shouldn't be involved in this crucial moment? We're going, "What the fuck is this?"

We said, "OK." We didn't say, "You're fired." We didn't say, "You're not going to be our manager anymore." We just said, "We think you should do this. We think it would be a really good idea."

But he left, on his way to meet with Glenn Ballard in order to fire him.

We met with Glenn later. We had dinner with him. We said, "We're sorry about the way it's going, but we really gotta take it from here without you and see how it goes. The label thinks it could be better and we have to take a look at what they're talking about."

So we went home to New England. I took the weekend off and went up to Lake Sunapee. I spent a few summer days by the lake, thinking of ways to save it. Part of me wanted Tim to keep managing the band, but it looked like he was deliberately burning his bridges, making no effort at all to fix his thing with Steven.

Back in Boston, we took a suite at the Four Seasons and started having meetings. We brought in Wendy Laister, who had been working with us for three years, first as our publicist and then as associate manager, and our business manager, Burt Goldstein. We told them where we were at. We were silently appealing to them to work with us, but they told us they couldn't even think about it because it would be undercutting Tim.

They were honest with us, which made me trust them even more.

Next we had a meeting with Sony and told them what was going on. They told us they thought Tim had us locked down, told us they thought that Tim would take care of any problems. But they were very rational and told us they would support whatever decision we made. So Aerosmith went to the mattresses. We stayed in the Four Seasons, not talking to anyone. We decided Tim Collins wasn't going to manage us anymore. We called him and asked him to come to the hotel, because we didn't want to stretch this out and give anyone false hopes. It was clear to us that Tim didn't want to do it anymore, that he didn't want to learn a new way to do it.

There was a lot of emotion in the room that day. I said, "Tim, I really wish this could have gone another way. I wish I could say this in a more personal way, but this is how it's got to go. We've had a long relationship and I want to honor all the good things we've done together. But it's clear the time has come to take you up on your long-standing offer and ask you to step aside."

He said, "What does that mean?"

"It means we don't want you to be our manager anymore."

We went around the room. Everyone spoke and said basically the same thing. Everyone wanted to honor the twelve years we worked together. Everyone wanted to say many thanks, and it was time for us to move on. I thought it was honest, heartfelt, and warm. Even Steven tried to come from a loving place, which was probably the hardest thing he'd ever done, because his feelings were running pretty high. But he didn't rage out on Tim. The whole thing was very hard.

Tim thanked us and left, and that was it.

*   *   *

But within hours, Tim Collins was telling the press that the band was no longer sober. These stories appeared in *Newsweek* and *Rolling Stone* and did some damage.

It was a little tabloid scandal. Our fan mail went crazy. Steven bore the brunt of it. It really pissed me off to see my brother going through that kind of shit, especially since it wasn't true. It was sad because it didn't even serve Tim's personal interest, his own thing that he worked so hard to get. It hurt our ability to serve as a power of example. The rumors were utterly false.

Sobriety. We've gone out of our way not to preach to people, but to serve by doing what we do—in sobriety. It goes against the principles of most recovery programs to even say anything about anyone else, because when someone falls off the wagon it gives everybody license to say: "See? It doesn't work."

People always focus on someone who fucked up. They don't notice the hundred thousand staying quietly sober in the program. It's behind the philosophy of staying out of the press with this stuff. It's a program of attraction. People want to know, "What's he got that I haven't? How come he can do it if I can't? What's going on with him?"

If you want to hear the message, it's there to hear. That's the way we work, and we've worked really hard to stay that way. So when Tim started talking to the press, making these allegations, it hurt everything we tried so hard to build up. And then there were the looks my kids would get at school from other parents. That *really* hurt. People whose children played with ours had to be reassured that the rumors were false and that no one was using drugs.

We're just trying to stay true to what we do, and not react to it.

At first we wanted to manage ourselves. Then we remembered how the business really works. The manager runs it, gives the band just enough information so he can steer it. It's the old way. That's why so many bands break up—and why so many managers get fired. So, after a few days went by, in August we persuaded Wendy and Burt to stay on our management team in partnership with the band.

The bottom line is: We took Aerosmith back.

In the fall of 1996, we went back into the studio in New York to recut our new album, *Nine Lives*. John Kalodner found our new producer, Kevin

Shirley, a real tubey kind of guy: he hates digital, loves analog, the fastest man with a razor I've ever seen—cutting tape, throwing shit in, just great. He's into capturing the last 20 percent of air that separates the men from the boys, that live thing in the ether that makes you a 100 percent band. He has an old-fashioned method that reminds me a lot of Jack Douglas. When he plays a track back, Kevin wants to "see" the band playing it live.

Somehow we had gotten away from that in Miami, in part because of the process, in part because Joey wasn't there. Now our drummer was with us, and we went for live takes, live solos, live basics. It put the edge back in.

We're going on, and the main thing for Aerosmith is still to let the music do the talking, and that we're still rocking after all these mad, bad, and dangerous years.

Ain't that a bitch?

Epilogue:
Cats and Cobras

Yowling like veteran tomcats prowling their territory, Aerosmith released their twelfth studio album *Nine Lives* on March 18, 1997. Mixed with a searing guitar sound by producer Kevin Shirley, *Nine Lives* debuted at #1 in America and began to target itself into the hearts and minds of the band's huge audience. "Falling In Love (Is Hard on the Knees)" was the first single and video, followed in May by the talking ballad "Hole In My Soul."

Packaged in a bizarre and striking mélange of writhing cobras, hairless sphinx cats, and Hindu iconography, *Nine Lives* immediately drew fire from Hare Krishna devotees in California, who claimed the album's design was based on a painting in a book by His Grace A. C. Bhaktivedanta Swami Prabhupada. On the day the band's new label was shipping four million copies, a lawyer's letter informed Sony that Aerosmith's cover art defiled a famous image of Lord Krishna, depicting the Hindu god with a cat's head and sporting female cleavage. The band ended up licensing the original picture from the sect rather than scrap four million compact discs. Everyone was reminded of the furor over *Get a Grip*, when an animal rights group objected to the computer-generated image of a cow's udder pierced by a golden ring; but the Hare Krishna problem eventually turned nasty when Sony executives received death threats over the Internet. Some stores, under pressure from hypocritical protestors, started threatening to return the albums. So even though the band had paid handsomely to license the image, after a few weeks they decided to withdraw the existing album art and replace it with something less controversial.

After a big launch party at the Oscar Hammerstein Ballroom in New York in late March (where the band played a mini-set for fans, the media, record executives, and contest winners) and a two-song appearance on Saturday Night Live, Aerosmith moved into an empty arena in Hartford [Connecticut] for two weeks of production rehearsals for the forthcoming Nine Lives World Tour. Working with a mostly new road crew and a new production featuring the cats and cobras that adorn the album, Joe Perry and Brad Whitford began to develop the guitar parts that brought untested anthems like "Hole In My Soul" and "Taste of India" to life. Steven Tyler was playing the living shit out of his harmonica, testing the ramps and runways of Aerosmith's new stage. The rhythm section—Tom and Joey—settled into a groove early, and everyone around the band could see that Joey Kramer was out of his Blue Funk and playing with his usual kick-ass style, great time, and sense of focus.

As Nine Lives began to sell at a pace that out-performed Get A Grip four years earlier (by then Grip had sold more than twelve million copies), Aerosmith went out on the road in Europe in the spring. Starting at the NYNEX Arena in Newcastle, England, on May 13 and traveling around Europe by private jet, Aerosmith deployed a powerful show that mixed the hard-won new songs from Nine Lives with die-hard favorites from the band's 150-song catalog. In late May they played the two annual German outdoor Rock am Ring/Rock im Park festivals before going on through southern and central Europe. By early June Aerosmith was touring England in a series of shows that climaxed at London's Wembley Arena on two sold-out nights.

Backstage at Wembley, everything's under control. The band has their families with them, and the dining area is full of beautiful women and kids. In the long dressing room corridor, an MTV-Europe presenter with chains linking her nose ring to the piercings on her ear waits to interview Steven, while Jon Bon Jovi chats with Aerosmith business manager Burt Goldstein. Aerosmith's hospitality suite is awash with the full spectrum of English rockdom, from Phil May of the legendary Pretty Things to new bladerunners like Primal Scream and Korn. Reviews of that week's shows in Birmingham and Glasgow have been properly glowing, Nine Lives is selling well, and the band's manager, Wendy Laister, the first woman to manage a band of Aerosmith's stature, runs things in her cool and quiet way. There's a major buzz on when John Kalodner brings Jeff Beck back to greet the band on the first night, and another the next night when Jimmy Page turns up to say hello and see the show. As they warm up in the tuning room with guitars and drums, the musicians talk of the places they'd visited in London that week; how they still get a charge when their old heroes came around; and about the dark rumors of threatened lawsuits from former manager Tim Collins, whose longtime entanglements with Aerosmith remained unresolved.

In interviews they get the same questions over and over: how does a band with five disparate personalities stay together for 27 years? "Because we don't change the formula," answers Brad Whitford. "We don't put it in a bottle or a box. Aerosmith happens when the five of us get together and do what we do. We're still the biggest fans of the kind of music we play, so we just keep going to the show."

Steven Tyler's dressing room is hidden behind a scrim depicting cavorting Hindu gods. He tries on a new purple swallow-tailed stage suit, made by his wife Teresa, that got an ovation at Birmingham a few nights earlier. ("Tyler remains a remarkable performer," The Times observed in reviewing the Manchester show. "His tireless body lean and compact, his face simultaneously feminine and feral.") Steven is deep into the hour of preparation he requires before a show, so he's not saying much while getting ready to begin his vocal warmups with Russ Irwin, who's playing keyboards and singing harmonies on this leg of the tour.

Tour manager Jimmy Eyers announces five minutes to curtain, and the families file out to their seats. On the arena floor the fans are packed in near the stage, ready to mosh it up with the last of the great rock 'n' roll bands. A huge roar as the house goes dark and strobe lights trace patterns around the stage. Carnatic music from The Last Temptation of Christ casts a spiritual sonic aura as five huge Kabuki curtains painted with cats and cobras drop into place, enveloping the stage. Lit from within *while the crowd noise surges, the musicians can be seen taking their places in giant silhouette.*

An alley cat's growl, a blast of feedback, and the band launches into "Nine Lives" with its "Train Kept A 'Rollin' "energy and atomic rhythm. Then right into "Elevator," which gets a huge backwash from the audience in the chorus.

The show then kinetically settles into a dramatic pattern as new songs—"Falling In Love" and "Hole In My Soul"—alternate with "Monkey on My Back" and "Livin' on the Edge." Brad Whitford plays acoustic guitar on "Pink" while Steven blasts his harmonica into the big hall like Bob Dylan playing John Coltrane's sheets of sound. He slurs out the song's "And I think everything is going to be alright no matter what we do tonight" chorus like an Arab blues singer drenched in twentieth-century art song.

Then "Rag Doll" and into "Taste of India" as another set of curtains descend, depicting the elephant god Ganesh. Then "Janie," followed by the harmonica-driven explosion of "Something's Gotta Give" and "Toys" in all its mysterious fury. These are followed by "Dream On" and "Cryin.' " (The Daily Telegraph: "For 'Dream On' Tyler stretched his extensive vocal range to what seemed like breaking point, and then, without warning, shot up another octave. Dogs across London jumped feet into the air.")

Then, as Tyler steps to the front of the stage, shaker in hand, blasts of white lights are beamed at the audience; when they go down three immense cobras are revealed behind the band, electric eyes flashing red. They seem to shelter the musicians like the nagas of Hindu and Buddhist mythology, cobras that emerge from the earth to protect the great sages from the elements as they meditate. The giant swaying green snakes look on as Aerosmith goes into "Sweet Emotion" and "Mama Kin."

The encores: Joe Perry's showpiece "Falling Off," only available as a bonus track on the international editions of Nine Lives, but performed in Europe as an anthemic recall of the old Project. The show closed with a rapturous, hard-rocking "Dude" and a new reading of "Walk This Way" that restored the original rap song's 1975 tempo, and opened up the lyric so Steven's trademark rhymes could be appreciated.

This was basically the show in the spring of 1997 as Aerosmith renewed itself and took its protean energy around the planet. There was optimism and excitement in the atmosphere, and an "Under New Management" sign on the door.

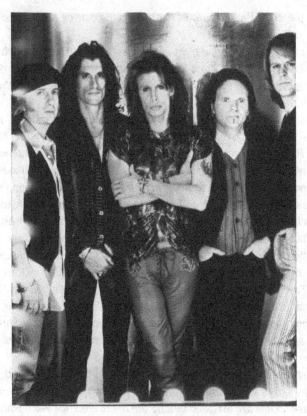

Nine Lives, 1997
(PHOTO: FRANK W. OCKENFELS 3)

It was in Alaska in the spring of 1998 that the whip came down. Aerosmith was jamming an explosive "Mama Kin" for an encore when Steven went into his mike-swinging dervish trance as the song crossed the finish line. When he lost his grip on a downward slash, the mike crashed into his knee like a battle-ax, ending the show and that part of the Nine Lives tour. Subsequent knee surgery postponed that summer's shows, and Steven had to perform the video of the new song "I Don't Want to Miss a Thing" in a leg cast. This plangent ballad, written by Hollywood tunesmith Diane Warren, was one of four Aerosmith numbers

on the soundtrack of the apocalyptic 1998 blockbuster movie Armaged-
don, which costarred Liv Tyler. That summer "I Don't Want to Miss a
Thing" became Aerosmith's first number one single, staying atop the Hot
Hundred for four straight weeks. The video then won the 1998 MTV
Award for Best Video from a Film.

In July, when the band was starting to think about going back on the
road, Joey Kramer's Ferrari exploded while being fueled near his home.
The drummer's third-degree burns kept Aerosmith off the road for a
while after that. The band's fans had to be content with their last album
release for Geffen Records, now absorbed into the Universal group of companies and only a dim shadow of its former self. A Little South of Sanity
was nevertheless a blistering two-CD set that supplied a composite live
show from the wild nineties, collecting tracks from both the Get a Grip
and Nine Lives tours, all mixed down by veteran 'Smith producer Jack
Douglas.

In 1999 the band took some time off to see to their families and write.
Changing direction in terms of business, Aerosmith signed on with talent
manager Howard Kaufman. The band was saddened to learn that their
great producer Bruce Fairbairn died at his home in Vancouver later that
year. They ended the twentieth century playing in Tokyo, a show televised live all over the world, and a harbinger of further heaviosity to come.

In 2000 Joe and Steven spent a lot of time in the basement studio under Joe's house on the south coast of Massachusetts, smoking cigars and
making song demos. When it was time to take them to New York to make
a record with some new producer, they decided instead to make Just Push
Play at home and produce it themselves. Joe upgraded the funky basement into a professional digital atelier, dubbed Boneyard Studio, and
bought the ancient colonial farmhouse next door and turned it into a mixing studio and lodge for the engineers. Gen X engineer/producer Marti
Frederiksen came in to collaborate, and the boys got to work.

September 2000: Joe Perry's fiftieth birthday party was held at Mount
Blue, the band-owned bistro south of Boston. It was a normal party, except for the Arkansas-quality barbecue and the band, Cheap Trick, flown
in to entertain a hundred enthralled guests on the restaurant's little stage.
(They'd originally been discovered by Jack Douglas in a Wisconsin bowling alley, and were a longtime Joe fave.) When Aerosmith got up to jam
afterward it was a cool moment. Slash, guitarist of the late Guns N' Roses,
presented Joe with the old guitar that Joe had used to make Toys in the

Attic and Rocks. Joe had lost the epochal ax in his divorce, and Slash had bought it later on the collector's market. Returning it was one of classic rock's great beaux gestes.

Meanwhile, Steven, Joe, and Marti Frederiksen had come up with "Jaded," a priceless riff distantly related to Led Zeppelin's "Dancing Days." It had a verse that slid down toward the chorus before slamming up against it like a blue wave. When the label guys heard it in New York, they almost soiled themselves. Management then brokered a deal between the band and Dodge for the car company to use another new track, "Just Push Play," to sell trucks. Right after that, Aerosmith won the Super Bowl in January 2001.

It was a rare triumph for an American band. Previous Super Bowl halftime shows had been soporific events, unable to compete even with the media circus's expensive commercials. But MTV programmed Super Bowl XXXV's halftime show as a rock concert that showcased Aerosmith performing with Britney Spears, *NSYNC, Mary J. Blige, and the rapper Nelly. The showstopping medley of "I Don't Want to Miss a Thing," "Jaded," and "Walk This Way" drew 87 million viewers, the highest ratings in the game's history. Steven Tyler found himself singing "Walk This Way" to the whole country.

"It was totally surreal, like a Salvador Dali painting," he said later. "Aerosmith, Super Bowl, Britney—fuhgeddaboudit. Up until then, I though NFL stood for Nice Fuckin' Lips."

A few months later Aerosmith was inducted into the Rock & Roll Hall of Fame, along with Queen, Steely Dan, Solomon Burke, and Michael Jackson, among others. Kid Rock did the honors. Aerosmith had first been eligible several years earlier, but had asked not to be nominated for fear of being categorized as an oldies group. With "Jaded" on the radio and Just Push Play about to be released, this was no longer a concern. Asked to describe the award show and subsequent all-star jam session, Liv Tyler told the press, "It was like the Oscars for fuckups."

After that, Aerosmith hit the road in 2001 to support their album. Joe and Brad and the families now traveled between shows in customized tour buses, carrying along tutors for their kids. The band played headbanging, hit-heavy sets backed by psychedelic video screens and explosive pyro effects, whose toxic smoke irritated Steven's throat and caused a series of cancellations later in the year. Back in the Boneyard, they came up with "Girls of Summer," another killer riff in the groove of "Janie's Got a Gun." This song hit the airwaves in the late spring of 2002 and anchored O, Yeah: Ultimate Aerosmith Hits, a two-CD set that compiles thirty years of the band's creative output.

At this writing, Aerosmith is on the road. They have sold more than a hundred million recordings. They've learned how to do it. They're still enjoying rock music's never-ending party without indulging in every risk available. Following Keith Richards's admonition to "make this music grow up," Aerosmith has somehow found an exceptionally cool way to live the rock myth into the terra incognita of middle age.

Steven Tyler: So now you know our story—at least most of it. It's been a fucking experience, I'll tell you that. Excessive? Okay, but . . . we lived through those excesses and found our way out. We went over the line and camped on the dark side, but we're still here to tell you about it. We rammed the iceberg but we never sank. We were real lucky. We shook hands with Blackbeard, but then we made it off the ship and reached dry land. The voyage still goes on, because it's too late to turn back now. Amen to that.

Authors' Notes

Work on this book began in London during a series of Aerosmith shows at Wembley Arena in November 1993. Interviews were conducted in hotel suites around the world during Aerosmith's year-long tour in 1994 and 1995, principally in Los Angeles, Tokyo, Frankfurt, Munich, Prague, Budapest, Warsaw, Leicestershire, many rural rock festival sites, Milan, Tel Aviv, and Boston. Work continued in Miami during 1996 and concluded in New York in 1997. *Walk This Way: The Autobiography of Aerosmith* was published late that year in New York, London, and Tokyo. The book appeared on the *New York Times* bestseller list.

The authors extend sincere thanks and praise to all who helped with this project:

Terry Hamilton, April Kramer, Billie Perry, Teresa Tyler, and Karen Whitford

Victor and Susan Tallarico, Mary Perry, and our families

Bebe Buell, Elyssa Perry, Ray Tabano, Henry Smith, Peter Agosta, Zunk Buker, Jack Douglas, Liz Derringer, Ron Pownall, Chris Smith, Patty Bourdon, David Scott, John Andrews, Robert Grasmere, and El Malhoit

Gary Cabozzi, Judy Nylon, George Paige, David Krebs, Steve Leber, Laura Kaufman, Maxanne Satori, James Isaacs, Jonnie Podell, Lou Cox, Marty Callner, Mr. Udo, George Chin, and Mark Parenteau

Richie Supa, Nightbob (Robert Czaykowski), Rabbit (Dick Hansen), Scott Sobel, Darren Winston, and David Beiber

John Kalodner

Tim Collins, Keith Garde, and everyone at Collins Management; Wendy Laister and the Magus Entertainment staff; Howard Kaufman, Trudy Green, and all at HK Management

John Bionelli, Mike Verge, Jackie Seaver, and the Vindaloo Music staff; Jimmy Ayres, Mike Henry, Andre Augustine, and the Aerosmith road crews

Lou Aronica, Jennifer Hershey, Mark Hurst, and Avon Books; Atticus Gannaway and the HarperCollins staff

JHA, Lily and India, and Chris Davis.

Special thanks to David Vigliano, the Big Buddha of Broadway, for doing what had to be done.

In memory of Stu Werbin, George Coleman, Bruce Fairbairn, Cyrinda Foxe-Tyler, and Jam Master Jay Mizell. "Whom the gods love, die young."

Boston, 2002

Selected
Bibliography

Adams, Mark. "Mud" [Reading Fest.], *Bedford Record* [UK], September 6, 1977.

Adler, B. *Tougher Than Leather*. New York: Signet, 1987.

Andrews, Rob. "Aerosmith: Caught In The Act," *Hit Parader*, July 1984.

Anon. "Rock Rites of Spring," *Circus Raves*, June 1975.

Anon. "Aerosmith—Masters of Metal," *Grooves #5 (Queen/Aerosmith issue)*, August 1978.

Anon. "Sgt. Pepper—The Stormy Story," *The Star*, August 8, 1978.

Anon. "Rock 'n' Roll News," *Creem*, December 1978.

Anon. "Aerosmith Bootleg Gold & Platinum," *Hit Parader*, May 1979.

Anon. "Aerosmith 80," *Hit Parader*, December 1979.

Anon. "Perry Quits Aerosmith," *Hit Parader Yearbook*, 1989.

Bartlett, John Henry. *The Story of Sunapee*. Washington: Byron S. Adams Press, 1941.

Bashe, Philip. "Solo Joe Perry parries pop music problems," *Circus*, August 31, 1981.

Bell, Oneida. "Different Drummer," *Circus*, November 25, 1976.

Bivona, Joe. "Aerosmith's Smart Axe Kids Perry & Whitford," *Circus Raves*, November 1975.

Bonutto, Dante. "Return of the Conquering Aero," *Kerrang!*, January 13, 1983.

Boyarski, Bill. "250,000 Pack Speedway for Rock Festival," *Los Angeles Times*, March 19, 1978.

Burns, Gary. "Bosstown," *Goldmine*, June 26, 1992.

Bustek, R. J. "Aerosmith Try To Stay Alive," *Rock*, August 1979.

Carson, Tom. *Live! Bootleg* (record review), *Rolling Stone*, January 25, 1979.

Charone, Barbara. "Can Tyler Out Jagger Jagger? Can Perry Out Wood Wood?" *Sounds* [UK], October 23, 1976.

Childers, Lee Black. "They Ain't So Tough: Aerosmith Unmasked," *Hit Parader*, December 1975.

Cohen, Scott. "Toys In The Attic Wonder When Their Kids Will Come Back Home," *Circus*, June 1975.

Cohen, Scott. "Steven Tyler," *Hit Parader*, October 1975.

Cohen, Scott. "Gaunt & Gifted: Joe Perry," *Circus*, October 10, 1976.

Coryat, Karl. "Tom Hamilton," *Bass Player*, March 1995.

Country Club Road Crew. "21 Rock & Roll Excuses," *Rock Scene*, June 1977.

Crespo, Charley. "Roots: Joe Perry," *Hit Parader*, September 1981.

Crespo, Charley. "Whitford/St. Holmes," *Hit Parader*, December 1981.

Crespo, Charley. "Tom Hamilton and Joey Kramer," *Hit Parader*, May 1983.

Crespo, Charley. "Aerosmith's Steven Tyler," *Hit Parader*, June 1983.

Cummings, Sue. "Burning The Kingdom," *Spin*, July 1986.

Demorest, Stephen. "Hot 'Rocks'," *Circus*, June 17, 1976.

Derringer, Liz and Chris Nicholson. "Aerosmith's Eros Myth," *Rock*, March 1977.

DeWitt, Dan. "Aerosmith" (record review), *Creem*, April 1973.

Doyle, Tom. "The Mellotron," *Q*, May 1995.

Duncan, Robert. "Aerosmith Beats The Clock," *Creem*, December 1978.

Epand, Len. "Boston's Aerosmith: Backstage Fighting Men," *Rolling Stone*, September 25, 1975.

Evans, Rick. "Aerosmith: To Be or Not To Be," *Hit Parader*, April 1984.

Everett, Todd. "Z.Z.Top/Aerosmith at L.A. Forum," *Rolling Stone*, July 31, 1975.

Fisher, Ben. "Tales From The Crypt," *Mojo*, February, 1996.

Flanagan, Bill. "The Best of Friends: Joe Perry and Aerosmith's love-hate affair," *Trouser Press*, February 1980.

Fricke, David. " 'Sgt. Pepper' on the Silver Screen," *Circus*, September 14, 1978.

Gabriel, Trip. "Cue The Flute," *New York Times*, 1994.

Gaines, Steven. "Aerosmith Maintain Mental Health," *Raves*, July 1975.

Gaines, Steven. "The Magical Mystery Tour Begins in Heartland," *Circus*, March 30, 1978.

Girard, Jim. "Aerosmith Do It Live," *Hit Parader*, April 1979.

Goldberg, Michael. "Aerosmith Inks $30 Million Deal," *Rolling Stone*, October 3, 1991.

Hall, Bob. "Darque Desires" in *Shadowman No. 19*, New York: Valiant Comics, 1993.

Hogan, Richard. "Joe Perry speaks out, blasts Aerosmith," *Circus*, May 27, 1980.

Howard, William. "Aerosmith, Mott the Hoople dazzle fans at Orpheum," *Boston Globe*, September 29, 1973.

Isaacs, James. "Aerosmith From Famine to Feast," *Boston Phoenix*, June 27, 1976.

Jackson, John. *Big Beat Heat*. New York: Schirmer, 1991.

Jerome, Jim. "For A Song" [Steven Tyler profile], *People*, August 9, 1976.

Johnson, Richard. "Aerosmith star's sky-high ways," *New York Post*, October 4, 1993.

Kagan, Shel. "Aerosmith Loses Joe Perry," *Circus*, March 4, 1980.

Katzeff, Paul. "Band In Limbo," Pictorial Living Coloroto Magazine, *Boston Herald Advertiser*, September 16, 1973.

Kenton, Gary. "Joe Perry Unleashed," *International Musician And Recording World*, May 1980.

Kirb. "Aerosmith" [club review], *Variety*, September 12, 1973.

Kirke, Mikael. "Joe Perry," *Oui*, July 1982.

Kritzler, Ed. "The Byrds Wing Their Way Out Of A Near Riot," *Yonkers Herald Statesman*, March 27, 1966.

Levinson, Alice. "Joe Perry's Rocky Road of Survival," *Rock World*, May 1984.

Levitt, Howard. "Aerosmith Conquers New York," *Record World*, September 15, 1973.

Levy, Annie. "Joe Perry In His Own Words," *Hit Parader*, May 1982.

Loder, Kurt. "Aerosmith Shot Down," *Circus Weekly*, January 2, 1979.

Loder, Kurt (ed.). "Rock Wrap-up '78," *Circus Weekly*, January 9, 1979.

Mascioni, Michael. "Joe Perry," *Hit Parader*, February 1984.

McCormack, Ed. "Aerosmith's Wrench Rock," *Rolling Stone*, August 26, 1976.

McLane, Daisann. "Aerosmith's train keeps a rollin'," *Rolling Stone*, February 22, 1979.

McLane, Daisann. "New Aerosmith LP due in September," *Rolling Stone*, August 23, 1979.

Mehler, Mark. "Aerosmith's Endless Bummer," *Circus Weekly*, December 5, 1978.

Morse, Steve. "A Night of Making Amends," *Boston Globe*, August 6, 1984.

Nussbaum, Beth. "Tyler and Perry Shine A Mirror on the Past,"*Rock Scene*, October 1986.

Nussbaum, Beth. "Aerosmith," *Concert Shots #7*, 1986.

Paglia, Camille. "The Stones," *Boston Phoenix*, August 26, 1994.

Papineau, Lou. "Aerosmith: The Eye of the Storm," *The Point*, April 1973.

Perry, Elyssa. "Aerosmith's Mudstock Tour," *Hit Parader*, March 1978.

Pollock, Bruce. "On Songwriting: Steven Tyler of Aerosmith," *Guitar*, April 1984.

Pond, Steve. "Boston's bad boys get back in the saddle," *Rolling Stone*, September 27, 1984.

Pownall, Ron. "At Home With Joe and Elyssa," *Rock Scene*, September 1977.

Putterford, Mark. *The Fall and Rise of Aerosmith*. London: Omnibus Press, 1991.

Rayl, Salley. "CalJam II Draws 250,000 Mellow Fans," *Circus*, May 11, 1978.

Raph, Riff. "Aerosmith's Steven Tyler Tells Some Raunchy Stories," *Rock*, June 1976.

Riva, Beppe. *Aerosmith: Testi Con Traduzione A Fronte*. Milan: Arcana Editrice, 1994.

Robins, Wayne. "Aerosmith: No Fear of Flying," *Creem*, September 1975.

Robbins, Ira. "Joe Perry Meets The Press," *Trouser Press*, November 1978.

Robinson, Lisa. "Tush, Tush Sweet Aerosmith," *Creem*, July 1975.

Robinson, Lisa. "On The Road with Elton and Aerosmith," *Hit Parader*, December 1975.

Robinson, Lisa. "Ray Davies Calls Us Harry Smith," *Hit Parader*, May 1976.

Robinson, Lisa. "Aerosmith Savor Success," *Hit Parader*, September 1976.

Robinson, Lisa. "Aerosmith: Train Kept A-Rollin'," *Creem*, December 1976.

Robinson, Lisa. "The Hit Parader Interview," *Hit Parader*, January 1978.

Robinson, Lisa. "Steven Tyler Says 'Everything's Fine,' " *Hit Parader*, July 1980.

Rosen, Steve. "Joe Perry," *Guitar Player*, March 1979.

Rosen, Steve. "Brad Whitford," *Guitar Player*, March 1979.

Rudnick, Bob. "Stage Antics Stall Aerosmith," *Circus*, September 15, 1977.

Rudnick, Bob. "Fan's Foolishness Injures Aerosmith," *Circus*, December 8, 1977.

Ruhlmann, William. "The Story of Aerosmith," *Goldmine*, June 26, 1992.

Santelli, Robert. "Joey Kramer," *Modern Drummer*, March 1984.

Santosuosso, Ernie. "Frank Connelly Had The Touch," *Boston Globe*, April 15, 1977.

Secher, Andy. "Aerosmith: Moment of Truth," *Hit Parader*, December 1982.

Secher, Andy. "Aerosmith back in the saddle," *Hit Parader*, December 1984.

Secher, Andy. "Done With Mirrors," *Hit Parader*, Feburary 1986.

Shaftoe, Robert. "Aero-myth." *Circus*, October 26, 1976.

Sherbin, Janet. "Social Council Works To Combat Apathy," *The [Boston University] Daily Free Press*, October 13, 1971.

Sippel, John. "Promoter's Suit Hits Aerosmith," *Billboard*, February 8, 1986.

Slash (Saul Hudson). "The Record That Changed My Life," *Q*, July 1995.

Smith, Giles. "The Beatles' Straight Man" [George Martin profile], *The New Yorker*, November 20, 1995.

Smith, Robert. "Aerosmith Lost No Ground," *Circus*, March 16, 1978.

Smoke, S. L. "Aerosmith Smashing," *Record World*, December 29, 1973.

Snow, Mat. "Hairspray and Hard Drugs," *Q*, January 1995.

Soocher, Stan. "A Bassman's Basics," *Circus*, October 1978.

Soocher, Stan. "Aerosmith Clears the Air," *Circus Weekly*, April 10, 1979.

Spina, James. "Aerosmith Back(tracking) In The Saddle," *Hit Parader*, August 1978.

Steinbach, Stella. "Fantastic Joe Perry Interview!" *Rock Stars*, May 1980.

Stigwood, R. "Aerosmith and the Boston Curse," *Phonograph Record*, April 1974.

Stix, John. "Joe Perry," *Guitar World*, September 1980.

Stix, John. "Aerosmith Out of the Ruts," *Guitar*, May 1986.

Stix, John. "Joe Perry/A Matter of Attitude," *Guitar*, October 1989.

Sundeen, Carl. "Rock Roundup in Texas," *Circus*, August 31, 1978.

Susman, Gary. "Dreaming On," *Boston Phoenix*, October 18, 1991.

Tabano, Raymond (ed.). *Aero Knows* [Aerosmith Fan Club newsletter]. Waltham, Mass.: Vols. 1–3, 1977–1979.

Tamarkin, Jeff. "Aerosmith: Getting their wings again," *Circus*, April 30, 1976.

Tannenbaum, Rob. "The US Interview: Steven Tyler," *US*, April 1993.

Train, Adrian. "Aerosmith Zooms Off to Stardom," *Circus Raves*, July 1974.

Verge, Mike (ed.). *Aerosmith Band Report* [in-house document compilation], 10 vols., December 1993–April 1997.

Welch, Chris. "Aero-dynamic," *Melody Maker* [UK], October 16, 1976.

Werbin, Stu. Album notes. *Aerosmith*, Columbia KC32005, 1973.

Wieder, Judy. "Street Fighting Men," *Hit Parader*, April 1986.

Wieder, Judy. "Another Shot of Aerosmith," *Creem Metal*, May 1986.

Wild, David. "Aerosmith," *Rolling Stone,* April 5, 1990.

Wild, David. Booklet notes. *Pandora's Box*, Columbia 46209, 1991.

Winston, Darren. "Aerosmith," *Penthouse*, July 1993.

Young, Charles M. "Rock & Roll Rehab," *Musician*, January 1990.

Young, Charles M. "The Thief of Kashmir," *Musician*, June 1990.

Zimmer, Dave. "Joe Perry Project Takes Off," *Creem*, August 1980.

Zimmerman, Deane. "Aerosmith News," *Hit Parader*, August 1980.

Zimmerman, Deane. "Joe Perry: The Thrill Is It," *Hit Parader*, September 1980.